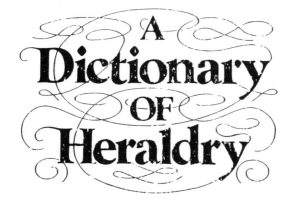

A Dictionary of Heraldry

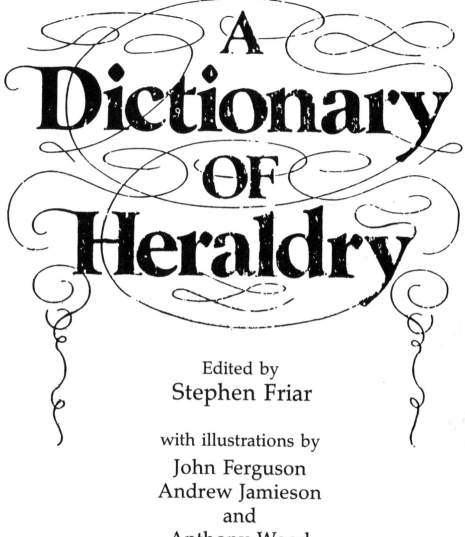

A Dictionary OF Heraldry

Edited by
Stephen Friar

with illustrations by
John Ferguson
Andrew Jamieson
and
Anthony Wood

Harmony Books/New York

Published in the United States by Harmony Books, a division of Crown Publishers, Inc., 225 Park Avenue South, New York, New York 10003 and represented in Canada by Canadian MANDA Group.

Originally published in Great Britain by Alphabooks Ltd, Sherborne, Dorset,
a subsidiary of A & C Black Plc, 35 Bedford Row, London WC1.

HARMONY and colophon are trademarks of Crown Publishers, Inc.

Manufactured in Great Britain.

Library of Congress Cataloging-in-Publication Data

A Dictionary of heraldry

　1. Heraldry—Dictionaries.　　I. Friar, Stephen
CR13.D53　　1987　　929.6'03'21　　87-8353

ISBN 0-517-56665-6
10 9 8 7 6 5 4 3 2 1
First Edition

List of Contributors

John Allen
Sedley Andrus LVO *Beaumont Herald Extraordinary*
John Brooke-Little CVO FSA FHS *Norroy and Ulster King of Arms*
Charles J. Burnett AMA FSA(Scot) AAIH *Dingwall Pursuivant of Arms*
John Campbell-Kease FRSA
Ben Chapman
D.H.B. Chesshyre FSA *Chester Herald of Arms*
John Coales FSA
William G. Crampton
Peter D. Esslemont
Peggy Foster
Peter Greenhill
Peter Gwynn-Jones *Lancaster Herald of Arms*
A.H. Hamilton-Hopkins Hon FHS
Kay W. Holmes
Cecil Humphery-Smith FSA FHG FSG FHS
Malcolm R. Innes of Edingight CVO WS *Lord Lyon King of Arms*
Dr David Johnson
Major Francis Jones CVO FSA *Wales Herald Extraordinary*
The Mac Carthy Mor
Michael G. Messer
Edward Paget-Tomlinson
Henry Paston-Bedingfeld *Rouge Croix Pursuivant of Arms*
Leslie G. Pierson Hon FHS
Prof Jonathan Riley-Smith FR Hist S
Stephen Slater
Peter Summers FSA FHS
Dr Conrad Swan CVO FSA *York Herald of Arms*
E.N. 'Pete' Taylor Hon FHS
John E. Titterton
Yvonne Weir
Simon Winter
Anthony Wood NDD FHS FRSA FSSI
Margaret Young

Artists:
Anthony Wood NDD FHS FRSA FSSI
John Ferguson ARCA FRSA
Andrew Jamieson HS DipAD(Hons)

Acknowledgements

I acknowledge with grateful thanks the assistance of the following people in the preparation of this book: The Bibliographer, The Royal Library, Windsor Castle; Sir Basil Blackwell; Miss E. Botker; Mr Thomas Brown; Mr Peter Brudgam; Sqn Ldr W.D. Brunger; Mr W. Burgess; The Chapter of the College of Arms; The Clerk of the Records, The House of Lords; Mr John Coales; Sir James Cobban; Lady Cooke; Henrik Degerman; Mrs Barbara Ferguson; Revd Michael Freeman; Mr J.H. Gaylor; Commander B.D. Gibson; Mr J. Grist; Mr Peter Hammond; Mr Michael H. Harrison; Mr Nicholas Hart; Miss L. Haugbyrd; Mr Jean O. Heineman; Mr Hugh Jaques; Mr Henk t'Jong; Dr Bernard Juby; Mr Arthur E. Linge; Mr L. Logan Russell; Mr Henry S. Lynn Jr.; Lord Lyon King of Arms; Mrs Caroline Morrison; Mr J.R. Newman; Mr David Peace; Mr Roger Peers; Mr K.S. Pundyke; Mr Sean O'Driscoll; Revd A. Pryse-Hawkins; Mrs C.G.W. Roads, Lyon Clerk and Keeper of the Records; Mrs Frances Robson; Miss Joan Robson; Mr George Squibb, Norfolk Herald Extraordinary; Mrs Nan Taylor; Mr T.W. Taylor; Lt Col H. Von Arnim; Mr H.R. Walden; Revd Canon D.C. Welander; Mr J. Howard Wright; Mr R.C. Yorke, Archivist at the College of Arms; the anonymous owner of the Grenville Diptych.

The entry entitled Wales, by Major Francis Jones, is reproduced by kind permission of the Heraldry Society. My especial thanks to John Campbell-Kease and John Ferguson, without whose friendship, enthusiasm and unselfish commitment this work would not have been possible. Finally, this book is for Kate, Thomas and Richard to whom I owe the greatest debt of all.

S.F.

Introduction

In the terminology of the computer age, this book is intended to be 'user-friendly'. It is compiled so that all readers, from the novice to the expert armorist, may enjoy immediate access to the subject of heraldry at whatever level and for whatever purpose they have in mind.

The appeal of heraldry is that it encompasses so many and such diverse areas of interest. Those who enjoy visiting churches, for example, will no doubt turn to the CHURCH entry and will there find, among various references, one to MONUMENTS. This, in turn, will lead them on to BRASSES, MONUMENTAL; EFFIGY; HATCHMENT and so on, until they eventually perceive a need to master the basics of BLAZON so that they may more accurately interpret the armorial devices with which they are confronted on their next visit to a church. There they may meet a family historian who, having turned to the GENEALOGY entry and realizing the importance of MARSHALLING in determining the relationships of his ancestors, has sought out the 'family' church in anticipation of discovering some new pieces of armorial evidence, aware also of the 'traps' that await the unsuspecting amateur.

This book is, effectively, two dictionaries in one. First there is the subject of Heraldry, defined as all matters relating to the duties and responsibilities of officers of arms; and the art of depicting armorial devices in paint, line, stone, glass, etc. Secondly, and fundamental to both aspects of heraldry, is Armory, which is concerned with the symbols and conventions relating to coats of arms and other devices, and it is the terminology of armory which forms the other subject of the dictionary.

The novice is recommended to approach the subject of armory through the section on blazon (together with the colour illustrations on pages 50 and 51). Blazon is far less complex than it may at first appear and used in conjunction with illustrations of arms, both in this book and elsewhere, it will soon become apparent that the language and conventions of armory are both simple and logical. Cross-references will lead the reader on to such matters as TINCTURES, ATTITUDES and ATTRIBUTES and various common charges such as ORDINARIES, SUB-ORDINARIES, CROSSES, CREST CORONETS, and so on.

Blazons in the text are given in italic throughout, though individual armorial terms are not. Cross-references are indicated by CAPITAL LETTERS and these are intended to refer the reader to relevant entries which will extend his understanding of a particular aspect of heraldry. Armorial terms are cross-referenced only where two-way referencing is considered helpful: attitudes and attributes, for example.

The dictionary contains a number of generic entries, such as KNIGHTHOOD AND

CHIVALRY, ORDERS OF; HEREDITARY OFFICES and OFFICER OF ARMS, which are intended to lead the reader to further entries on related subjects.

For the experienced armorist, the dictionary is intended primarily as an aide-memoire and is set out with this in mind, rather than in a strict dictionary format.

Addresses of organizations mentioned in entries will be found listed in a separate ADDRESSES entry.

Heraldry is such a broad subject that it has been possible only to touch on those peripheral matters which I call vernacular heraldry. I hope that the inclusion of such entries as MINIATURES, POSTCARDS, AIRLINE DEVICES and TRADE AND SERVICE MARKS will both encourage armorists to look beyond the confines of their discipline for further enjoyment and understanding, and lead those whose interests are at present concerned with these 'vernacular' subjects to greater appreciation of armory.

I am indebted to the many distinguished contributors who have so enthusiastically supported me in this venture and whose work may be identified by their initials at the end of an entry. All other texts are written by myself or compiled from contributors' material. Having written somewhat controversially at times, I feel obliged to point out that the views expressed in this book are not necessarily shared by all contributors.

Stephen Friar
Caundle Wake, Dorset
June 1987

A

Abaised An armorial charge depicted lower than its normal position.

Abatement This is the term given to certain armorial symbols or charges which in some countries were marks of dishonour, and in England, signs of bastardy. From time to time writers on armory have suggested that 'abatements' never existed. It is worth quoting Fox-Davies (*A Complete Guide to Heraldry*), who on the matter of STAINS says these tinctures were 'perhaps invented by the old heralds for the perpetration of their preposterous system of abatements which will be found set out in full in the old heraldry books, but which have yet to be found occurring in fact. The subject of abatements is one of those pleasant little insanities which have done so much to the detriment of heraldry.' The foregoing is not true of *all* such old books, for Porny's *Elements of Heraldry* (London 1795), whilst allowing that the author 'could not find a single instance of such dishonour in English coats of arms' nonetheless went on to describe 'divers figures said to be formerly added to Coat-armour of such as were to be punished and branded for cowardice, treason, etc., for which [earlier writers] give the name of abatements of honour.' In Boutell's *Heraldry* (London 1983) the editor, J.P. Brooke-Little, confirms that 'there is no such thing as a mark of dishonour in English heraldry.'

Such cannot be said, however, for all countries. Porny, in the work already cited, instances a volume *Science Heraldique*, by M. de la Colombiere, in which that author describes how the arms of one Jean d'Avensnes were abated for reviling his mother in the presence of King Louis IX, by having the lion on his shield 'disarmed', that is, shown henceforward without claws or tongue. A recent Scottish matriculation included a gusset sanguine as an abatement for adultery, though this is unique in Scottish armory. No Scottish heraldic author has so far even bothered to list abatement in indices. JC-K

See also BASTARDY *and* DEGRADATION, CEREMONIES OF

Abbreviations of the Classes of British and Commonwealth Orders

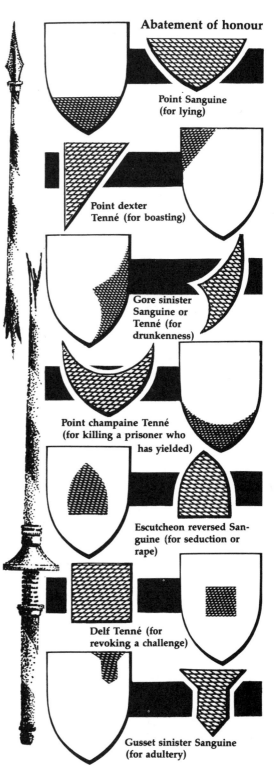

Abatement of honour

Point Sanguine (for lying)

Point dexter Tenné (for boasting)

Gore sinister Sanguine or Tenné (for drunkenness)

Point champaine Tenné (for killing a prisoner who has yielded)

Escutcheon reversed Sanguine (for seduction or rape)

Delf Tenné (for revoking a challenge)

Gusset sinister Sanguine (for adultery)

BARBADOS, ORDER OF Knight (of St Andrew): KA; Dame (of St Andrew): DA; Companion (of Honour of Barbados): CHB; Crown (of Merit, Gold): GCM; Crown (of Merit, Silver): SCM.

BARBADOS, SERVICE AWARD OF Holder of Star: BSS; Medallist: BSM.

BATH, ORDER OF Knight Grand Cross: GCB; Knight Commander: KCB; Companion: C.

BRITISH EMPIRE, ORDER OF Knight or Dame Grand Cross: GBE; Knight Commander: KBE; Dame Commander: DBE; Commander: CBE; Officer: OBE; Member: MBE; Holder of the British Empire Medal: BEM.

CANADA, ORDER OF Companion: CC; Officer: OC; Member: CM.

CANADA, ORDER OF MILITARY MERIT Commander: CMM; Officer: OMM; Member: MMM.

COMPANIONS OF HONOUR Companion: CH.

DISTINGUISHED SERVICE ORDER Companion: DSO.

GARTER, ORDER OF Knight: KG

IMPERIAL SERVICE ORDER Companion: ISO.

NEW ZEALAND, ORDER OF ONZ.

NEW ZEALAND, QUEEN'S SERVICE ORDER OF Companion: QSO.

ORDER OF MERIT Member: OM.

ROYAL VICTORIAN ORDER Knight or Dame Grand Cross: GCVO; Knight Commander: KCVO; Dame Commander: DCVO; Commander: CVO; Lieutenant: LVO; Member: MVO. (Members fourth and fifth class were originally entitled to the same distinguishing letters md MVO. For Members of the fourth class these were changed to SMVO, and later LVO, the class being renamed Lieutenant.)

ST JOHN OF JERUSALEM, ORDER OF Bailiff or Dame Grand Cross: GCStJ; Chaplain: CStJ (formerly ChapStJ); Knight of Justice and Grace: KStJ (formerly, when two classes, KJStJ and KGStJ): Dame of Justice and Grace: DStJ (formerly, when two classes, DJStJ and DGStJ); Commander (Brother or Sister): CStJ; Officer (Brother or Sister): OStJ; Serving Brother: SBStJ; Serving Sister: SSStJ.

ST MICHAEL AND ST GEORGE, ORDER OF Knight or Dame Grand Cross: GCMG; Knight Commander: KCMG; Dame Commander: DCMG; Companion: CMG.

THISTLE, ORDER OF Knight: KT.   JC-K

Abeyance A peerage falls into abeyance when more than one heir possesses an equal right of inheritance. A peerage may be brought out of abeyance when, by the death of the other claimants, only one remains and thus has the right to claim the peerage.

Abouté *see* **Attitude**

Académie Internationale d'Héraldique A prestigious body, founded in 1949 in Paris, to bring together experts in heraldry representing the various cultural areas of the world. Admission is by election, and the number of active academicians is limited to 75. There is no limit to the number of associate members. The general assembly usually meets once a year, and the headquarters are in Switzerland. The Académie's aim is to centralize heraldic studies on the basis of the largest possible international co-operation. Applications for admission are addressed to the Académie in writing, and must have the sponsorship of a member of the Council. The General Secretary is at present Baron Hervé Pinoteau, 4 bis, Boulevard de Glatigny, F-78000 Versailles, France.   SA

Accolade The ceremony of conferring knighthood, usually by a light blow on the shoulder or neck with the flat of a sword (Latin *collum* = neck).

Accollé Term used to describe one of the methods of marshalling. Two separate shields are placed side by side in order that a man may display insignia of a noble order, or arms of office. For example, a Knight of the Garter will display his arms encircled by the Garter, with his and his wife's arms impaled or in pretence in a separate shield alongside the first. For artistic balance the marital shield can be encircled with a wreath or garland. The same method is used for royal persons, but the arms of the person of higher rank are placed on the dexter side. For arms of office, such as a mayor, he or she bears their personal arms impaled by those of their office on one shield, and husband and wife arms on the second.   PF
See also MARSHALLING.

Accorné *see* **Attributes**

Achievement of Arms A pictorial representation of properly authorized armorial bearings. An achievement of arms may take the form of the conventional coat of arms, but not necessarily so. (Abbr. Achievement)

Acorned *see* **Attributes**

Addorsed *see* **Attitude**

Addresses

Heraldic Authorities

England and Wales
The College of Arms, Queen Victoria St, London EC4V 4BT
Scotland
Lord Lyon King of Arms and the Court of Lord Lyon, H.M. New Register House, Edinburgh EH1 3YT
Republic of Ireland
The Chief Herald of Ireland's Office (Genealogical Office), 2 Kildare St, Dublin

Heraldic and Genealogical Organizations

Australia

The Heraldry Council of Australia, P.O.Box B, Marden, SA 5070

The Heraldry Society (Australian Branch), 31 Crawford Rd, Lower Templestowe 3107, Victoria

The Heraldry Society of Australia, 3 Manor Grove, North Caulfield 3161, Victoria

South Australia Genealogy and Heraldry Society, P.O.Box 592, Adelaide, SA 5001

Heraldry and Genealogy Society of Canberra, P.O.Box 585, Canberra, ACT 2601

Austria

Heraldisch-Genealogishe Gesellschaft, Haarhof 4a, A1010 Wien 1

Belgium

Heraldique et Genealogique de Belgique (Office de), Musees Royaux d'Art et d'Histoire, Avenue des Nerviens 10, B-1040 Bruxelles

L'Office Genealogique et Héraldique de Belgique, Parc du Cinquantenaire 10, B-1040 Bruxelles

Canada

Heraldry Society of Canada (Société Héraldique du Canada), 612-810 Edgeworth Ave, Ottawa, Canada KB2 5L5

Denmark

Heraldica Scandinavica Societas, Sigmundsvej 8, DK-2880 Bagsvaerd

Dansk Genealogisk Institutt, Nørre Voldgade 80, 1358 København

Societas Heraldics Scandinavia, Azalaevej 26, DK-2500 Valby

Nordisk Flaggskrift, Solbakken, 3140 Alsgarde

England and Wales

The Heraldry Society, 44/45 Museum St, London WC1A 1LY (details of regional societies may be obtained from this address)

Institute of Heraldic and Genealogical Studies, Northgate, Canterbury, Kent CT1 1BA

Society of Genealogists, 14 Charterhouse Buildings, London EC1M 7BA

Finland

Heraldica Scandinavica, Injala Gård, SF-03400 Vichtis

Suomen Heraldinen Seura, Runeberginkatu 67 A 12, SF-00260 Helsinki

Finlands Nationalkommitte för Genealogi och Heraldik, Irjala Gård, SF-03400 Vichtis

Genealogiska Samfundet i Finland, Snellmannsgatan 9-11, 00170 Helsingfors

Heraldiske Sällskapet i Finland, Lønnrotsgatan 23 A, 00129 Helsingfors

France

De Héraldique et de Sigillographie Société Française, 60 Rue de Francs-Bourgeois, 75003 Paris

La Société du Grand Armorial de France, 179 Bvd Haussman, Paris

Federation des Sociétés de Genealogie, d'Héraldique et de Sigillographie, 64 Rue de Richelieu, 75002 Paris

Germany (West)

Der Herold, Archivstrasse 12-14, D-1000 Berlin 33

Genealogisch-Heraldische Gesellschaft, Postfach 2062, D-3400 Goettingen

Wappen Herold, Deutsche Heraldische Gesellschaft, Postfach 556, D-7000 Stuttgart 1

Iceland

Icelandic Heraldry Society, Bólstadarhlid 16, Reykjavic

International

Academe Internationale d'Héraldique, 4 bis Bvd d'Glatigny, F-78000 Versailles, France

Confederation Internationale de Genealogie et d'Héraldique, 24 Rue St Louis en L'Ile, 75004 Paris, France

International Congress of Genealogical and Heraldic Studies, Harmignies, Rue Martin Lindehens 57, B-1150 Bruxelles, Belgium

International Fellowship of Armorists (Heraldry International), Werastr. 105, D-7000 Stuttgart 1, West Germany

International Genealogical Institute, Church of Jesus Christ of Latter-Day Saints, 50 East Smith Temple St, Salt Lake City, Utah, USA

Ireland

The Heraldry Society of Ireland, Castle Matrix, Rathkeale, Co. Limerick

Italy

Araldico Collegio, 16 Via Santa Maria dell'Anima, Roma

Instituto Italiano di Genealogia e Araldica, Palazzo della Scimmia, 18 Via dei Portohesi, Roma

Luxembourg

Conseil Heraldique de Luxembourg, 25 Rue Bertholet

Japan

The Heraldry Society of Japan, 3-88-26 Higashi Toyonaka, Toyonaka, Osaka

Netherlands

Koninklijk Nederlands Genootschap voor Geslacht en Wapenkunde, 5 Bleijenburg, Den Haag

Central Bureau voor Genealogie, P.O.Box 11755, 2502 The Hague

New Zealand

The Heraldry Society of New Zealand, 60 Sayegh St, St Heliers, Auckland

The Commonwealth Heraldry Board, P.O.Box 23056, Papatoetoe, Auckland

The Heraldry Society (New Zealand Branch), P.O.Box 68-051, Newton, Auckland

Norway

Heraldisk Forening Norsk, Cappelan, Bygdøy Allé B, Oslo 2

Kunstindustrimuseet i Oslo, St Olavs Gate 1, 0165 Oslo 1

Middelalderforum, Universitetet i Oslo, Historisk Institutt, P.O.Box 1008-Blindern, N-0315 Oslo 3

Norsk Våpenring, P.O.Box 958-Oslo Sentrum, N-0104 Oslo 1

Norsk Slekthistorisk Forening, Ullernveien 2 B, 0280 Oslo 2

Universitetet i Oslo, Etnografisk Museum, Frederiksgate 2, 0164 Oslo 1

Universitetet i Oslo, Oldsaksamlingen, Frederiksgate 2/3, 0164 Oslo 1

Poland

Heraldic Records Archive, Warsawa, ul Dluga 7

Portugal

Instituto Heráldica de Portugés, Largo do Carmo, Lisboa 2

Scotland

The Heraldry Society of Scotland, 25 Craigentinny Cresc., Edinburgh EH7 6QA

The Scottish Genealogical Society, 21 Howard Place, Edinburgh

South Africa

The Heraldry Society of Southern Africa, P.O.Box 4039, Cape Town 8000

Addresses

Sweden

Heraldiska Sälskap, Vasta Sveriges Förtroligheten 4, S-41270 Göteborg

Svenska Heraldiska Föreningen, Sodra Vagen 12, S-41254, Göteborg

Svenska Nationalkommittén for Genealogi och Heraldik, Bernadottebiblioteket Kungl, Slottet, S-11130, Stockholm

Svenska Heraldiska Föreningen, P.O.Box 88, S-46700 Grästorp

Västra Sveriges Heraldiska Sälskap, Tanneskärsgatan 277, S-42160 Västra Frølunda

Switzerland

Heraldische Schweizerische Gesellschaft, Luzern, Lützel-masstrasse 4

United States of America

New England Historic Genealogical Society, 99-101 Newbury St., Boston, MA 02116

North American Institute of Heraldic and Flag Studies, North Pamet Rd, Box 88, Boston, Massachusetts 02666

American College of Heraldry, Drawer CG, University, Alabama 35486

The Augustan Society Inc., 1510 Cravens Ave, Torrance, CA 90501

Genealogical and Heraldic Institute of America, 111 Columbia Heights, Brooklyn, NY 11201

National Genealogical Society, 4527 17th St. North, Arlington, VA 22207-2363

Miscellaneous

(organizations are listed as they appear in the text)

Achievements Ltd, Northgate, Canterbury, Kent CT1 1BA

Antiquarian Booksellers' Association, 31 Gt Ormond St, London WC1

Army Museums Ogilby Trust, Aldershot, Hampshire GU11 2LR

American Society of Military Insignia Collectors (ASMEC), P.O.Box 5089, Tusculum College, Greenville, TN 37743, USA

Arms and Armour Society, 30 Alderney St, London SW1

Artworkers' Guild, 6 Queen Square, Bloomsbury, London WC1N 3AR

Association of Family History Societies of Wales, 2 Pen Lôn, Menai Bridge, Gwynedd LL59 5LW, North Wales

Association of Genealogists and Record Agents, 1 Woodside Close, Caterham, Surrey CR3 6AU

Association of Scottish Genealogists and Record Agents, 106 Brucefield Ave, Dunfermline, Fife, Scotland

Bodleian Library, Oxford OX1 3BG

Bookplate Society, 20a Delorme St, London W6 8DT

Borthwick Institute of Historical Research, York YO1 2PW

Bosworth Battlefield Visitors' Centre, Sutton Cheney, Market Bosworth, Leicestershire LE3 8RE

British Library, Great Russell St, London WC1B 3DG

British Model Soldier Society, 6 Anderson Close, Woodley, Romsey, Hampshire SO5 8UE

British Museum, London WC1B 3DG

British Records Association, Charterhouse Sq, London EC1M 6AU

British Records Society, University of Keele, Staffordshire ST5 5BG

British Toy Makers' Guild, 240 The Broadway, Wimbledon, London SW19

Burke's Peerage, Eden St, Kingston-upon-Thames, Surrey

Burrell Collection, Pollock Park, Glasgow G43 1AT, Scotland

Cambridge University Library, West Road, Cambridge CB3 9DR

Canterbury and York Society, 79 Whitewell Way, Cambridge CB3 7PW

Catholic Record Society, 114 Mount St, London WC2Y 6AH

Central Chancery of the Orders of Knighthood, St James's Palace, London SW1A 1BG

Chetham's Library, Long Millgate, Manchester M13 1SB

Chief Herald of Ireland's Office, 2 Kildare Street, Dublin, Republic of Ireland

Church Monuments Society, c/o Royal Armories, H.M. Tower of London, London EC3N 4AB

City of London Information Centre, St Paul's Churchyard, London EC4M 8BX

Company of Armigers:

    Australian Chapter, 5 Koonung St, North Balwyn 3104, Victoria

    Canadian Chapter, Box 1172; Station B, London, Ontario N6A 5K2

    English Chapter (pro tem), Eldersfield House, Bishop's Caundle, near Sherborne, Dorset DT9 5NG

Corporation of London Record Office, Guildhall, London EC2P 2EJ

Costume Society, c/o The Court Dress Collection, Kensington Palace, London W8 4PX

Court of Lord Lyon, H.M. New Register House, Edinburgh EH1 3YT, Scotland

Debrett's Peerage, 56 Walton Street, London W3

Duchy of Cornwall Office, 10 Buckingham Gate, London SW1E 6LA

Federation of Family History Societies, 17 Fox Lea Rd, Hayley Green, Halesowen, West Midlands B63 1DX

Fitzwilliam Museum, Trumpington St, Cambridge CB2 1RB

Flag Institute, 10 Vicarage Rd, Chester, Cheshire CH2 3HZ

Flag Research Center, 3 Edgehill Rd, Winchester, Massachusetts, USA

Friends of St George's Chapel, Curfew Tower, Windsor Castle, Berkshire SL4 1NJ

Genealogical Office, 2 Kildare St, Dublin, Republic of Ireland

Guild Church of St Benet, Pauls Wharf, Queen Victoria St, London EC4

Guildhall Library, Aldermanbury, London EC2P 2EJ

Guild of Glass Engravers, 19 Portland Place, London W1N 4BH

Guild of Master Craftsmen, 166 High St, Lewes, East Sussex BN7 1YE

Harleian Society, c/o The College of Arms, Queen Victoria St, London EC4V 4BT

Heirloom and Howard Ltd, 1 Hay Hill, Berkeley Sq., London W1X 7LF

Heraldry Today, 10 Beauchamp Place, London SW3

Heralds' Museum at the Tower of London, H.M. Tower of London, EC3N 4AB

Historical Association, 59a Kennington Rd, London SE11 4JH

House of Lords Record Office, Westminster, London SW1A 0PW

Huguenot Library, University College, London WC1E 6BT

Imperial Society of Knights Bachelor, 21 Old Buildings, Lincoln's Inn, London WC2A 3UJ

Institute of Heraldic and Genealogical Studies, Northgate, Canterbury, Kent CT1 1RB

International Association for Semiotic Studies, Den Haag, Netherlands

John Ryland's University Library, Deansgate, Manchester M3 3EH

Lambeth Palace Library, London SE1 7JU

List and Index Society, c/o Public Record Office, Chancery Lane, London WC2A 1LR

Lord Chamberlain's Office, St James's Palace, London SW1A 1BG

Lord Lyon King of Arms, H.M. New Register House, Edinburgh EH1 3YT

Manorial Society, 104 Kennington Rd, London SE11 6RE

Manor Lords, 470 London Rd, Slough, Berkshire

Mitchell Library, North Street, Glasgow G3 7DN, Scotland

Monumental Brass Society, c/o Society of Antiquaries, Burlington House, Piccadilly, London W1V 0HS

Museum of London, London Wall, London EC2Y 5HN

National Horse Brass Society, Orchard End, Farm Road, Sutton, Surrey

National Library of Scotland, George VI Bridge, Edinburgh EH1 1EW

National Library of Wales, Aberystwyth, Dyfed SY23 3BU

National Monuments Record, Fortress House, Savile Row, London W1X 1AB

National Monuments Record of Scotland, Melville St, Edinburgh EH3 7HF

National Monuments Record of Wales, Aberystwyth, Dyfed SY23 3BU

National Register of Archives, Quality Court, London WC2A 1HP

National Register of Archives in Scotland, Edinburgh EH1 3YY

Norris Library and Museum, St Ives, Huntingdon, Cambridgeshire PE17 4BX

Order of St John Library and Museum, St John's Gate, London EC1M 4DA

Orders and Medals Research Society, 123 Turnpike Link, Croydon CR0 5NU

Plantagenet Medieval Society, 1 Goodwood Green, Fernhill Heath, Worcester, Hereford and Worcester

Public Record Office, Chancery Lane, London WC2 1AH

Public Record Office, Kew, Richmond, Surrey TW9 4DU

Public Record Office, Portugal St, London WC2

Richard III Society, 65 Westpole Ave, Cockfosters, Barnet, Hertfordshire EN4 0AY

Royal Air Force Museum, Aerodrome Rd, Hendon, London NW9 5LL

Royal Commission for Historic Monuments, 23 Savile Row, London WX1 2HE

Royal Commission on Historical Manuscripts, Quality House, Quality Court, Chancery Lane, London WC2A 1HP

Royal Society of St George, 4 Wilton Mews, London SW1 8BD

St George's Chapel, The Aerary, Windsor Castle Berkshire SL4 1NJ

Scottish Record Office, Princes St, Edinburgh EH1 3YY

Societe Jersiaise (La), 9 Pier St, St Helier, Jersey, Channel Islands

Society for the Protection of Ancient Buildings, 37 Spital Sq., London E1 6DY

Society of Ancients, 6 Bullpond Lane, Dunstable, Bedfordshire LU6 3BJ

Society of Archer Antiquaries, 61 Lambert Rd, Bridlington, North Humberside YO16 5RD

Society of Antiquaries, Burlington House, Piccadilly, London W1V 0HS

Society of Genealogists, 14 Charterhouse Buildings, London EC1M 7BA

Society of Heraldic Arts, Eldersfield House, Bishop's Caundle, near Sherborne, Dorset DT9 5NG

Society of Master Glass Painters, c/o Artworkers' Guild

Society of Scribes and Illuminators, c/o British Craft Centre, London WC2H 9LD

Spalding Gentlemen's Society, The Museum, Broad St, Spalding, Lincolnshire

St John of Jerusalem, Orders of:

    Britain: St John's Gate, Clerkenwell, London EC1M 4DA

    Federal Republic of Germany: Johanniterstrasse 9, D-5300 Bonn 1

    Netherlands: 48 Lange Voorhout, Den Haag

    Sovereign Order: Palazzo di Malta, Casella Postale 674, 1-00100 Roma, Italy

    Sweden: Riddarhuset, S-10311 Stockholm 2

St Lazarus of Jerusalem, Order of, Chancery, 15 Wellington Park, Belfast, Northern Ireland

Trade Mark Registry, Stable House, 69/71 High Holborn, London WC1R

Ulster Historical Foundation, 66 Balmoral Ave, Belfast, Northern Ireland

University College of North Wales, Bangor, Gwynedd LL57 2DG

University of London Library, Senate House, Malet St, London WC1E 7HU

White Lion Society, Mrs Gillian Legg (Secretary), 18 Orchard St, Bristol BS1 5DX

William Salt Library, Eastgate St, Stafford, Staffordshire

Wrythe Heraldic Trust, c/o The Heraldry Society

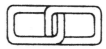

Adopted Children If legitimate issue, an adopted child may use his natural father's arms. Other adopted children are now entitled to use the arms of their adoptive parents providing a royal licence is obtained and the arms, when granted, are differenced by the addition of a charge comprising two interlaced links of chain. The English kings of arms are authorized to act for Canada in these matters.

Aesculapius *see* **Medical Heraldry** *and* **Serpent**

Affronty *see* **Attitude**

Agnus Dei *see* **Paschal Lamb**

Aiguilette *or* **Aiglet** Lacing points to fasten plate armour, especially at joints.

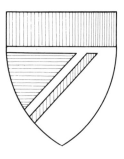

Ailettes Decorative shoulder guards, often bearing the wearer's arms.   PG

LEFT **British Airways arms.** ABOVE **Lion rampant and wings device on a civil aircraft tail.**

Airline Devices In the early days of ballooning and on the first powered aircraft, national ensigns were flown as a means of identification. Like the spinnaker of a sailing yacht, the fabric of air balloons and the wings of hang-gliders afford wonderful opportunities for armorial display not yet exploited by those who use them.

On aircraft, there are two principal means of identification: the roundels and fin flashes used by military aircraft, and the tail markings of civil aviation. Examples of the former are the familiar 'bull's-eye' roundels of Great Britain (red, white and blue), France (blue, white and red), Belgium (black, gold and red), Spain (red, gold and red), Greece (blue, white and blue) and Nigeria (green, white and green), and the armorial-type roundels of Canada (a red Maple leaf on white within a blue circle), Sweden (three gold crowns on blue within a gold circle) and Yugoslavia (a red star surmounting a white roundel edged in blue). Examples of flashes are the black fimbriated cross paty of the Federal Republic of Germany, the red star fimbriated gold of the USSR, and the quartered red and white square with a counter-coloured border of Poland.

Civil aviation is subject to constant change, and the devices depicted on the tailplanes, buildings, stationery, flags, etc., of a particular company reflect the volatile commercial fortunes of the industry and its desire always to improve its 'corporate image'. Many logotypes and livery schemes are in the best armorial traditions. In the 1920s and 1930s a number of carriers adopted formalized wing designs — the early PanAm device of a winged world, the Japanese rising sun between outspread wings, the winged 'O' of United Airlines, and the elegant 'speedbird' of Imperial Airways, for example. Many have retained symbols of flight: Aeroflot has a winged hammer

device, and Ghana Airways a winged black star. Others have adopted a variety of fabulous beasts, many in stylized form, such as the winged seahorse of Air France, the *mouflon* or winged goat of Cyprus, the green flying pachyderm of Nigeria, the flying kangaroo of Qantas, and the beautiful *tanchozuru* or sacred crane mon of Japanese Airlines. Other airlines have adapted their national symbols and colours for use as liveries: for example, Alitalia, El Al, Swissair, Kuwait Airways and Icelandair.

Conventional armory has not entirely disappeared from the roll of airline livery. In 1974 a new British Airways corporation was formed by the merger of eight companies, and a year later arms were granted: *Argent between a Chief and a Bendlet sinister couped Gules a Gyron issuing from the dexter point in sinister chief Azure.* For the crest *On a Wreath Argent and Gules a Sun irradiated proper from an Astral Crown Or* and for supporters *A Pegasus Argent crined unguled and winged Or gorged with an Astral Crown Azure holding in its mouth an Olive Sprig fructed proper* and *A Lion guardant winged Or similarly gorged.* The motto is 'To Fly, To Serve'. The design of the shield of arms is based on a segment of the Union Flag, and a representation of the full achievement now appears on the tailplanes of the corporation's fleet, together with the 'Union Flag' segment device.

Further reading

Mackintosh, I. *World Airline Colour Schemes Vol.11* (US airlines) Hounslow, 1977.

Tomkins, B. *World Airline Colour Schemes Vol.1* Hounslow, 1977.

Both volumes are of interest to the armorist, but neither may now be considered definitive. Indeed, the only means of obtaining up-to-date information is to write to the offices of the individual airline companies.   EPT

Aislé *see* **Attributes**

A la Cuisse *see* **Attributes**

Albania, Royal Arms of *Gules a double-headed Eagle Sable the shield ensigned by the Cap of Skanderbeg surmounted by a Goat's Head proper.*

Albany badge

Albany Herald of Arms A current Scottish herald of arms. Office first mentioned in a diplomatic mission from Scotland to England in 1401. The office was probably instituted on the creation of Robert Stewart, son of King Robert II, as Duke of Albany, 28 April 1398. Albany is an old name for that part of Scotland north of the River Forth.

The badge of office is *A Saltire Argent enfiling a Coronet of four Fleurs-de-lis Or ensigned of the Crown of Scotland proper.* CJB

Alcantara, Order of The first of the Spanish orders, formed in 1156, to fight against the Moors. It followed monastic rules, and bore a green Greek cross with Gothic letters. KH

Alderman Anciently, a nobleman of highest rank, a governor of an English shire or district, a high official. In English boroughs a civic dignitary next in rank to the mayor, elected by fellow councillors (now obsolete). A senior member of a guild or livery company.
See also LIVERY COMPANY, MEMBERSHIP OF

Alerion *or* **Allerion** An eagle displayed and dismembered, having neither beak nor legs. Almost unknown in British armory, but found in the arms of several European families.

Alisé *see* **Attributes**

Allusive Arms *or* **Armes Parlantes** Arms which allude to the name, title, office or property of an armiger. Examples of allusive arms are numerous in early heraldry and the practice is enjoying a revival in many late twentieth-century grants. The frequency of allusive arms in medieval heraldry suggests that many examples exist which have yet to be identified, the allusion being obscure to the twentieth-century mind. Well known early examples are those of De Ferres *Argent six Horseshoes* (ferrs) *Sable*, Wingfield *Argent on a*

Bend Gules cotised Sable three pairs of Wings conjoined in lure of the field and Tremain *Gules three dexter Arms conjoined and flexed in triangle Or hands clenched proper.* More recently, a pair of sarsen stones and lintel appear on a background of sky and grass in the arms of Sir Cecil Chubb, first Baronet of Stonehenge (created 1919 following his gift of Stonehenge to the nation in 1918): *Per fess Azure and Vert two Pales surmounted by a Chief Argent.* Recent grants include *a Cross Crosslet fitchy and a Key in saltire* in the arms of John Crosskey of Horsham (1979), *three Moor's Heads Sable* (Blackamoors) in the arms of John Blackmore of Yorkshire (1964), and a *per chevron Gules and Vert* field in the arms of Peter Greenhill of Bournemouth (1985).

Few coats of arms these days are designed purely for their aesthetic qualities. Charges are usually selected to refer covertly or indirectly to aspects of the armiger's life or character and may, therefore, be considered 'allusive'. An amusing example is the grant to Thomas Brown of Middlesbrough, a dentist whose arms *Gules a Pile reversed issuant from the base Argent a Chief dancetty of the last* represent the open mouth and teeth of one of his patients. However, whenever the term is met with it is generally intended to refer to arms which allude to an armiger's name or title.
See also CANTING ARMS

Almshouses Almshouses are houses endowed for the support and lodging of the poor. There is usually some form of commemorative plaque erected in a prominent position to record for posterity the benevolence of the patron or group of benefactors. Such plaques are often armorial, and bear the patron's arms or those of the principal benefactor, which may have been a guild or other fraternity.

Alphyn This curious creature, which does not appear very often in armory, is very much like an heraldic tyger but is stockier and has tufts of hair on its body, as well as a thick mane. It has a long thin tongue, long ears, and its tail is knotted in the middle. Sometimes

15

its forefeet are depicted like an eagle's claws, and sometimes they are cloven. Occasionally all four feet are claws like a lion's.

In English heraldry the alphyn was used as a badge of the Lords de la Warr, and it also appears on the guidon held by the knight in the Millefleur Tapestry at Montacute House, Somerset.   MY

Altar Tombs *see* **Tomb Chests**

Amphisbaena An armorial lizard.

Ancient (i) The standard (a livery flag).
(ii) The officer responsible for the maintenance of the standard.
(iii) Descriptive of the arms of a family who have subsequently been granted an additional or alternative coat.

Ancient Crown *or* **Ancient Coronet** *see* **Crest Coronet**

Ancient User A claim to bear arms based on constant use since 'time immemorial'. In common law this is deemed to be 1189, although in the Court of Chivalry it has been argued that the Norman Conquest (1066) should be regarded as the limit of legal memory. However, in the seventeenth century a claim with proof of a prescriptive use of arms from the beginning of the reign of Elizabeth I (1558) was considered to be sufficient.

Angel (i) Angels as armorial charges are not uncommon, though are generally to be found as crests or supporters, e.g. *Angel vested Argent mantled Azure winged crined and crowned Or* in the crest of the University of East Anglia.
(ii) For the Nine Orders of Angels *see* CHRISTIAN SYMBOLS.
(iii) An English coin known from the angel depicted in the design on its obverse. Introduced in 1465 to replace the noble. Worth about one-third of a pound sterling.
See also COINAGE

Angled *see* **Lines, Varied**

Animal Brands American cattle brands fall into three categories: letters and numbers, geometric symbols, and pictographs. A brand has to be read in a specific way, as does a blazon, from left to right, from top to bottom, and from outside to inside. For example, an inverted letter would be described as *crazy*, and if repeated would be *double, triple* or whatever. Geometric symbols speak for themselves, the bar, double bar, half circle, box, diamond, half diamond, etc. Pictographs are simple linear designs, such as an

arrow, key, anchor, stirrup or other familiar and easily recognizable objects. A bar between two letter Bs would read *B bar B*. An R inside a square would read *Boxed R*. An arrow with a bent shaft would read *Broken Arrow*, any letter, symbol or pictograph with two small curves protruding from the sides would be *Flying*, and two small projections from the base would be *Walking*.

American horses, too, were branded, usually on the hip, and studs in Europe branded their horses. The famous Lippizaner Stud used an L; the German Graditz Stud had two arrows saltirewise entwined with a serpent; the Fogaras Stud of Hungary used a crowned letter F.

In Middle Eastern countries, camels were branded by their owners, usually on the hip, neck or cheek, occasionally on the foreleg or buttocks. Camel brands usually consist of straight lines in varying arrangements and number; also circles and part curves.   BC
Further reading
Ford, G. *Texas Cattle Brands* Dallas, 1936.
Swanson, H.R. *Official State Brand Book of Nebraska* Lincoln, 1934.

Ankh

Ankh An Egyptian symbol for life. *See also* MEDICAL HERALDRY

Annelled *see* **Attributes**

Annulet A ring. In English armory the annulet is the cadency mark of the fifth son. Two annulets interlaced may be termed a *gimmel ring*, and a pattern of interlaced annulets is a *network of annulets interlaced*.

Annuletty Semy of annulets.

Annunziata, Order of the A Savoy order, formed *c.* 1362, which bore as its badge a medallion with a border of knots surrounding a picture of the Annunciation.   KH
Further reading
Prosser, R. *The Order of the Annunciation* 1984 (limited ed.).

Antelope The antelope of armory is depicted with the face of a (heraldic) tyger, tusks, serrated horns, an antelope's body, a lion's tail and tufts down its spine. In order to differentiate between the natural beast and the armorial version, the latter is usually blazoned as an heraldic antelope. Also blazoned as an argasill, though rarely so.

Antique Crown *see* **Crest Coronet**

Appaumé *see* **Attitude**

Apres A monster with the body of a bull and the tail of a bear.

Arbre de Batailles, L' *see* **Treatises**

Arch This word, meaning 'chief' or 'prime', has from early times been prefixed to such titles as bishop, butler, chamberlain, chanter, deacon, duchess and duke, as an indicator of pre-eminent rank.   JC-K

Arched *see* **Attitude**

Arched *or* **Enarched** *see* **Lines, Varied**

Archimandrite The superior or superintendent of a monastery.

Argasill An heraldic antelope.

Argent The armorial metal silver, usually represented by white. (Abbr. Ar.) *See also* TINCTURE

Argyll and The Isles, Baron of *see* **Baronage of Scotland**

Armed *see* **Attributes**

Armes Parlantes *see* **Allusive Arms**

Armet An innovative Italian helmet of the mid-fifteenth century, the lower parts of which were hinged so that it could be closed round the head, thus transferring the weight to the shoulders. The armet was considerably stronger and lighter than its predecessor, the bascinet, which had to be lifted over the head. Even so, the armet was not universally accepted in Britain.

Armiger One who bears arms by lawful authority.

Armigerous Bearing arms by lawful authority.

Armigers, The Company of Membership of the Company is available to those whose arms are registered at the College of Arms, London, or in the Public Register of All Arms and Bearings in Scotland. The aims of the Company are loyalty to the British Crown, to promote the degree of armiger, to record the arms of every created armiger throughout the British Commonwealth, and to establish a bond among armigerous families. *See* ADDRESSES.

Arming Doublet A padded under-jacket, worn as protection against staining and chafing.   PG

Arming Girdle *or* **Belt of Knighthood** The belt worn over a jupon, across the hips, of a knight or gentleman of coat armour.   PG

Armorial (i) Concerned with armory.
(ii) A manuscript or book concerned with armory.

Armorial Bearings The properly authorized devices appertaining to a particular armiger. These include the elements of a coat of arms (i.e. the shield of arms, helmet and coronet of rank, wreath, crest, mantling, supporters, insignia of honour and of office), personal and livery badges and, in those countries where such matters are subject to heraldic control, personal and livery flags and mottoes.
See also ACHIEVEMENT OF ARMS *and* COAT OF ARMS

Armorial Bearings, use of Many armigers possess an illogical reluctance to use their armorial bearings, believing that to do so is somehow pretentious. It cannot be wrong to use that which has been granted by lawful authority 'to be borne and used forever hereafter . . . according to the laws of Arms.' Only if borne without authority can arms be considered pretentious (*see* BOGUS HERALDRY), and armorial bearings should, therefore, be used 'wherever they can discreetly and tastefully ornament or identify'. (Brooke-Little)

It is most important to remember that the painting of armorial bearings in the margin of a patent or matriculation of arms is intended only to exemplify the arms as blazoned. How those arms are depicted thereafter is entirely a matter for individual taste and artistic interpretation. It is only the blazon that is unalterable. The following is, therefore, intended as a summary of current practice. It is not meant to be in any way proscriptive and certainly not definitive.

Personal arms

Stationery The choice of colours for paper and print should correspond with the armorial colours. Paper may, therefore, be white (argent) or cream (gold), and the ink black or a dark shade of red, blue or green. The shield of arms, unadorned and depicted as a simple line drawing about an inch (2½ cm) in height, is more

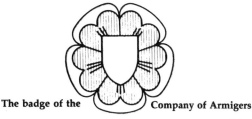

The badge of the Company of Armigers

appropriate than the full coat of arms which some may consider ostentatious. Alternatively, there is no reason why the badge may not be used, perhaps for informal correspondence. With the development of thermographic processes the tired old convention that stationery should always be embossed and never printed may finally be abandoned, and with it a good deal of expensive snobbery. The only criterion — as with all armorial artefacts — is that the workmanship and materials should do justice to the arms. Envelopes should conform to the same colour scheme as the notepaper, and could bear the shield of arms or crest and wreath (or crest-coronet) on the flap. (Printed envelopes can be expensive, and a possible alternative is the use of a small embossing press which, though initially expensive, may be used for a variety of other purposes. If this method is used, envelopes with a fairly narrow and straight-edged flap are recommended.) Cards, notelets and invitations should also conform to the colour scheme, but should not carry armorial devices. The use of full colour representations of armorial bearings on personal stationery is considered to be ostentatious.

Seals Official or legal documents may be sealed in wax or by embossing. For such documents it is essential that the shield of arms is used, this being peculiar to the armiger, as is his sign manual. Signet rings may still be used for sealing documents in the absence of a desk seal. These, too, should bear the shield of arms, though many are charged with the crest, which is strictly inappropriate. The colour of sealing wax may also correspond with the armorial colour. Embossed discs of adhesive coloured paper may be appended to minor documents in the form of seals. Again, these should bear the arms.

Flags In Scotland the use of armorial flags is strictly controlled. In England, however, an armiger may fly his personal banner of arms at any time. It is best reserved for family 'high days and holidays', and if he possesses a badge this may be flown on a livery flag at other times — a pennon being the most appropriate for daily use. The armiger should not be deterred by the cost of having a flag made; simple designs are not expensive, though multiple quarterings should be avoided! He may wish to make his own — a task which is by no means beyond the capabilities of an enthusiast. Most reputable flag-makers will be pleased to make up a plain or party-coloured basic flag of any size, roped and fitted with convenient Inglefield clips, at a very reasonable price. Ordinaries may then be cut from flag bunting (available in small quantities from many textile manufacturers), inserted into the original flag, and the charges painted in waterproof Polymer colour. Some armigers may even be fortunate enough to possess arms the field of which corresponds with one of the International

Code of Signals flags. These may also be obtained for a modest sum and the charges simply painted or appliquéd on to a ready-made field. (Several of the ICS flags are especially suitable for use as pennons.) Not all private houses will accommodate a flagstaff, and inexpensive, wall-mounted 'angle' poles are available from flag-makers. These may be removed when not in use and are not obtrusive. Flag sizes are measured in yards, the longer measurement being that of the fly. One yard of flag (fly length) should be allowed for every ten feet of staff (e.g. a 25 foot staff would take a 2½ yard flag). Banners are best if nearly square — proportions of three to two are probably the most effective for outdoor use, though much depends on the design of the arms. Flags for indoor use are usually embroidered — a task which is probably beyond the resources of the average enthusiast. Indoor banners are square and fringed. If suspended from a pole the flag should hang with the hoist uppermost. (*See also* FLAG)

Bookplates The bookplate serves to ornament and identify. Even the most vociferous opponent of armorial stationery will happily embellish his books with arms, badges, cyphers and rebuses, safe in the knowledge that they will be discovered only by chance, and that he cannot, therefore, be accused of ostentation! Here is an opportunity to be adventurous — to incorporate all the family's devices (armorial and otherwise) and to obtain the services of an heraldic artist whose greatest pleasure is to work uninhibited by the constraints of official patents and commemorative rolls. Bookplates may be of any reasonable size and it is best to commission a good-size drawing, which may be reduced by modern techniques to the required bookplate size, and later framed as a work of art in its own right. Regrettably, the prejudice against coloured bookplates remains. However, there is no reason why they may not be printed thermographically, either in the traditional black or a dark shade of red, blue or green. The words 'ex libris' are superfluous. Self-adhesive 'labels' are available, but care should be exercised to ensure that the quality of paper and printing is not sacrificed for the sake of convenience. (*See also* BOOKPLATES)

Decorative and domestic The various elements of armorial bearings may be incorporated in designs on china, glass, silverware, fabrics, etc., and in architectural features. However, some would consider the cost to be prohibitive and their use on single items, for commemorative purposes and as gifts, is a far better proposition. Items such as stone plaques, jewellery, glass panels, specialist book-bindings, pewter miniatures, gilded shields of arms, screens, cushions, rugs and wall hangings are naturally more expensive than mass-produced articles to which personal emblems are simply added during processing. However, many craftsman-made products may be obtained through organizations such as the Society of Heraldic Arts, and the guilds of craftsmen that are to be found in many English counties. It is, of course, important to ascertain a craftsman's qualifications as an *armorist* before commissioning work. New processes have resulted in the availability of numerous 'personalized' products at reasonable cost, and several of these lend themselves to armorial display and decoration. In most cases, a minimum of at least a dozen is required, and the badge therefore recommends itself as the most appropriate device for these purposes. Photographs and drawings of devices may now be reproduced in laminated form on such items as table mats, coasters, trays, etc., and even children's sweat shirts, sports bags and track suits, screen-printed with the badge, are available in reasonable quantities at an economic price. For those who wish to create their own 'stained glass' panel (or even a complete window), kits are available consisting of pots of transparent glass stain and rolls of self-adhesive strip lead which is easily applied to the glass once the stain is dried. All that is required is a competent drawing of the correct scale placed beneath the glass as a guide for the application of the coloured stain. The rest is a matter of practice.

Civic and corporate arms

The armorial badge, granted in conjunction with a coat of arms or obtained by means of a subsequent grant, is an invaluable device, particularly for the armigerous corporation. In armorial terms, the 'house' colours adopted by a corporate body are known as the livery colours, and it is with these that the badge is associated. The principal metal and colour of the shield of arms are known as the armorial colours, and in practice these may also be the livery colours.

Stationery It is entirely appropriate for the full coat of arms to be depicted on all stationery, either in full colour or as a line drawing in the armorial colour. However, an armigerous corporation may prefer to use its shield of arms (possibly within a circlet bearing the motto) or badge on circulars and pro-formas, reserving the full achievement for formal correspondence and official documents. Envelopes may be charged with the badge — either on the flap or at the top or bottom left on the front. Official invitations, compliment slips, etc., should be charged with the coat of arms.

Seals If possible, corporate seals should bear the full coat of arms and should be designed by an experienced heraldic artist. Should a smaller seal be required this should always contain the shield of arms.

Uniforms Employees and members of an armigerous corporation should wear uniforms, ties, etc., of the livery colours charged with the corporation's badge. Neither the arms nor any part of them should be used for this purpose. The governing bodies of armigerous schools and colleges should ensure that a badge is obtained and worn on uniforms of the school's colours. Non-armigerous state schools may be able to obtain the exclusive use of an armorial badge by means of an application made on their behalf by an armigerous local education authority. So, too, may organizations affiliated to an armigerous parent body, e.g. sporting clubs. Armigerous local authorities are also empowered to license the use of their own badge (subject to the tacit approval of the kings of arms) to organizations within their jurisdiction, e.g. sporting, social and cultural clubs and societies. If a local authority badge is licensed in this way, it should be used in conjunction with the organization's own colours on ties, sports kit, stationery, etc., and the licensing authority should therefore ensure that licences are granted on condition that the badge is used only in conjunction with a specified colour or colours.

Official pendants, etc. Pendants worn by heads of civic and corporate bodies should bear the full coat of arms, and if enamelled the ground-work should be one of the armorial colours. Pendants of other officers should bear the shield of arms, possibly within a circlet charged with the motto, on a similar ground. Chains of office may be composed of badges, cyphers and devices from the arms, and if a ribbon is used this should be of the armorial colours. (NB. A mayor's consort should wear a pendant charged with the badge.)

Flags Corporations may fly a banner of their arms (*not* an ensign banner) whenever they are in session, and certainly for special occasions. (If two flagstaffs are used, that to the sinister is the senior and should be used for the Union or national flag.) A livery flag may also be flown at any of the corporation's properties: this would normally be a guidon or standard, though the latter is not always a practicable proposition. The use of a small banner of arms on an official car, launch or aircraft should be reserved for the senior member of the corporate body, e.g. a lord mayor. Non-armigerous organizations who have obtained the use of a badge through an armigerous parent body should fly a guidon, the ground-work of which should be of their own livery colours, charged with the badge. In England, these livery flags are not prescribed by the College of Arms, though standards are often depicted in a patent to further exemplify a badge. In such cases it is important to ensure that the ground-work of the flag is composed of the house colours *actually used* by the corporation, and there are ample precedents to suggest that these do not have to be the conventional tinctures of armory. Any armiger who possesses a duly authorized badge may use it on an appropriate livery flag. However, in Scotland the use of armorial flags is strictly regulated, and armigers (both personal and corporate) who wish to fly a flag should first obtain the authority of Lord Lyon. (*See also* FLAG)

Property Corporate bodies should endeavour to incorporate their armorial or livery colours in direction and information on signs, and the colour scheme for exterior paintwork of their properties. The shield of arms rather than the full achievement is most effective on signs, particularly those on busy roads where immediate identification is necessary. Vehicles should be painted in the livery colours and if a device is depicted it should be the badge. On the majority of small items of property (e.g. car stickers, crockery, staff diaries, etc.) the badge should be used, the full achievement being reserved for official dinner services, official and civic plate, etc. Architectural features may incorporate the various elements of the arms, the badge being particularly suitable for repetitive designs, such as those in fabrics and carpets. Corporations should consider ways by which their armorial bearings may be afforded legal protection against commercial use, on souvenirs, for example.

Patent of arms The letters patent, being addressed 'to All and singular' should be in a public place: the council chamber or foyer of a county hall, for example, or in the entrance hall of a public company. (*See also* LETTERS PATENT for framing, etc.)

Non-armigerous bodies

Parish councils, local community groups and societies who may wish to use a device on stationery, etc., are recommended to investigate the history of their locality and adopt the badge of a prominent medieval lord of the manor, most of whom possessed armorial badges for their several estates. The use of a coat of arms for this purpose is not appropriate.

Armorial Board A canvas or wooden panel hanging on the wall of a church for the purpose of displaying armorial devices. There are three types:

Royal device A board on which the royal arms or other devices, such as the so-called 'Prince of Wales Feathers', are depicted. (*See also* ROYAL ARMS IN CHURCHES)
Hatchment A coat of arms depicted on a diamond-shaped funeral board, the background of which is painted in such a way as to indicate which of the marital partners is deceased. (*See* HATCHMENT)
Memorial board A board erected to the memory of an individual, bearing arms and inscription. (*See* MEMORIAL BOARD)

Of course, there are many armorial panels which fit

none of the above categories, and in some cases their original function is unclear. For example, at Sherborne Abbey, Dorset (in the muniment room) there is a rectangular wooden board bearing the impaled arms of the 3rd Earl of Bristol and his wife, and at Avington, Berkshire, a hexagonal panel bears the arms of Lord Howard de Walden. It is known that this was placed in the church by his wife during his lifetime and it cannot, therefore, be a memorial board. An even more unusual example is at Upper Dean, Bedfordshire. This is a black, diamond-shaped board with a coat of arms in the base and, in the centre, an inscription recording the donations to charity of one Joseph Neal (d. 1710).

Some churches contain conventional paintings on wood or canvas, and occasionally heraldry features in the subject matter. At Canterbury Cathedral, for example, there is a painted panel of the martyrdom of Thomas Becket in which his assassins are depicted in armorial jupons.   JET

Armorial Colours The dominant metal(s) and colour(s) of a shield or arms, generally referred to simply as 'the colours', but as such too easily confused with the livery colours.
See also COLOURS, THE *and* LIVERY COLOURS

Armorial de Gelre One of the most important heraldic documents descended to us from the Middle Ages. It was compiled between 1370 and 1395 by Claes Heijnen (or Heijnenszoon), Gelre Herald to John de Blois (sometime Duke of Guelders) and Beyeren Herald to Albert of Bavaria. (Manuscript 15652/56 preserved at the Bibliotheque Royale de Bruxelles contains 1762 achievements of arms of the leading armigerous families of Europe in the fourteenth century — 45 shields having been added for completeness in the mid-fifteenth century.) Folios 1 to 24 are divided into four sections, concerning: (a) the challenge of the Duke of Brabant by eighteen heads of State, January 1334; (b) the shields of fourteen lords killed at the battle of Staveren, April 1345; (c) an armorial chronicle of the Dukes of Brabant and of the Counts of Holland, mid-fourteenth century; (d) poetic praise of thirteen illustrious knights, celebrating their prowess. The fifth section, folios 26 to 122, is a feast of armorial compilation, culminating in an illustration of the herald himself.

Claes Heijnen was a consummate caricaturist of his day, and the exaggeration demonstrated in his craft serves to bring the illustrations to life for the reader. The work is outstanding amongst its contemporaries for the beautiful crests rendered on a thousand of the shields of arms, all in full colour. Fifty territories are represented, mainly arranged as fifteen shields per page. Apart from the European royal houses, there are some very interesting people featured. Jean le Bel, the

Crecy chronicler, is shown, and several 'foreigners' who fought for England include Bertrand, Lord de l'Esparre in Gascon particoat, and Sir Walter, Lord Manny, Hainaulter Knight of the Garter and the Queen's Champion. Unfamiliar are the dog crest of Daniel van Pesse, and the winged bear with barrel of Wilhelm von Quad. Sir Frank van Halle, the Brabanter Garter Knight, displays lion arms, pointing the lie to his wyvern stall plate. Famous gartered Englishmen include John Chandos, hero of Froissart, Thomas, great Lord Warwick and Sir James Audley, who, with four brave esquires, wrought havoc at Poitiers in 1356. A comic dragon head belching flame crests John Hawkewoode (alias Giovanni Acutus), remembered in Florence, adventurer ancestor of Shelley. Two hundred French coats include Oger, Vicomte d'Anglure, resplendent in bells and decoupages, and proud Marechal Clermont with the headstrong Arnoul d'Audrehem. Six portes-oriflamme recall the doomed Charny at Poitiers and Martel before Agincourt. Beneath a white bear is the greatest sword of his time, Eustace de Ribemont, who died at Poitiers, shrouded in the heraldic lilies of France.

Further reading
Adam-Even, P. *L'Armorial Universal du Heraut Gelre* Archives Heraldiques Suisses, 1971.

Armorial Dress, Female As medieval knights were identified by their armorial devices, so too were their ladies, though the application of armory in costume was essentially decorative, the full arms displayed on kirtle or mantle being reserved for ceremonial occasions, tournaments, etc. Badges and other devices were woven into fabrics and embroidered onto costumes and accessories, and were naturally a favourite subject for pendants, jewellery and personal artefacts. However, it is the heraldic mantle (cloak) and kirtle (gown or outer petticoat) which is most often depicted in medieval rolls and manuscripts and on tombs, either as brasses or effigies, and these garments invariably bear the marital arms.

One of the earliest examples of armorial costume is to be found in the effigy of Matilda, Countess of Salisbury (d. 1281) at Worcester Cathedral. Matilda was daughter and heiress of Walter de Clifford, and her cloak is powdered (on the right side) with small shields bearing her paternal arms *Chequy Or and Azure a Fess Gules*. A similar arrangement of small shields is to be found on the early brass of Margaret Lady Camoys at Trotton, Sussex, dated *c.* 1310. Between 1280 and 1330 it was usual for the arms to be borne on a mantle, the emblazoning reversed since it was intended to be viewed from the back. On monuments, the mantle is so arranged that the arms appear on the two front halves of the garment as it falls forward from the shoulders, those of the husband being on the dexter and the woman's paternal arms on the sinister.

Effigy of Elizabeth, Lady Marmion (left) and brass of Catherine, Lady Howard (right), engraved some eighty years after her death in 1465.

Thereafter, a close-fitting kirtle was worn beneath an equally close-fitting sleeveless cote-hardie, the female equivalent of the man's jupon, and this was often embroidered with the impaled arms. Good examples are the brass of Lady Foxley at Bray, Berkshire, in which the arms of Foxley *Gules two Bars Argent* impale her paternal arms of Brocas *Sable a Lion rampant Or*; and the charming effigy of Elizabeth, Lady Marmion at West Tanfield, Yorkshire, in which the Marmion arms *Vair a Fess Gules* impale those of St Quentin *Or three Chevrons Gules a Chief Vair*. Lady Marmion also wears a plain cloak, draped loosely about her shoulders and lightly secured by cords. Both are from the late fourteenth century. There are examples of arms on both gown and mantle: at St Mary's church, Warwick, the brass of the Countess of Warwick (d. 1406) shows her wearing a close-fitting kirtle emblazoned with her paternal arms *Gules seven voided Lozenges Or* (Ferrers) and a mantle of her husband's arms *Gules a Fess between six Cross-crosslets Or* (Beauchamp). It was the usual medieval practice to depict a husband's arms on the mantle in order to show 'dominion' over a woman's paternal coat which was borne on the kirtle. In the *Wrythe Garter Book*, Eleanor, daughter of Sir Thomas Holland, Earl of Kent, is shown chained to her husband Sir Thomas de Montacute, Earl of Salisbury KG, wearing a mantle of the quartered arms of Montacute and Monthermer over her right shoulder, and her paternal arms *England with a Bordure Argent* (Holland) on her left. Clearly, such garments were not merely part of a lady's wardrobe, and their use must have been subject to strict etiquette. However, it should also be remembered that armorial costume as depicted in such manuscripts is intended primarily as a vehicle for armorial display, and does not necessarily illustrate a contemporary fashion.

Occasionally we discover a case of fashion triumphing over armorial convention. On the brass of Lady Say (d. 1473) at Broxbourne, Hertfordshire, the mantle appears to be 'tierced in pale' (divided into three lengthways) with the paternal quarterings of Cheyne, Engayne and Pebenham side by side, instead of quartered: a far more attractive arrangement, though not strictly in accordance with the conventions of marshalling. Of course, it may not always have been possible for all the quarterings to be shown, and it is sometimes necessary to imagine 'missing' coats at the back of a mantle. An example is to be found in the small brass of Catherine, Lady Howard (d. 1465), at Stoke-by-Nayland, Suffolk. Catherine's paternal arms *Or three Pallets wavy Gules* (De Moleyns) are depicted on her left shoulder, but on her right only the Brotherton, Howard and Segrave quarterings of her husband's coat are shown, those of Warenne, Mowbray and Braose (presumably) being at the back.

Female heraldic display was evidently taken seriously, for at the time of the Dissolution the Royal Commissioners appointed by Henry VIII to destroy records relating to the papal institution and of any Catholic families who had caused him offence, wrote to the king concerning the Priory of Christchurch: 'In the church we found a monument . . . prepared by the late Mother of Reginald Pole for her burial, which we have caused to be defaced and all the arms and badges clearly to be deleted . . .'

Full heraldic costume continued to appear on monuments in the Tudor period: Lady Gascoigne, first wife of Sir William Gascoigne, and member of Cardinal Wolsey's household, is depicted in a brass (*c.* 1540) at Cardington, Bedfordshire, wearing a kirtle (now loose-fitting and without a waist) charged with her paternal arms of Winter, and an overmantle of her husband's arms quartering Gascoigne with Picot and Beauchamp of Bedford. However, it is unlikely that such costumes were used for practical purposes after the mid-sixteenth century, except for pageants and tournaments, and their application in monumental armory is seen to decline rapidly from this time. By the Elizabethan period, armorial devices (usually badges) were used in jewellery and occasionally in the decoration of costume, but the days of the ceremonial heraldic mantle were past. However, armorial dress was sometimes worn by ladies at festive occasions thereafter, at Jacobean tournaments and at the Eglington Tournament of 1839, for

example. The most recent manifestation of armorial costume was that worn by Miss Sarah Ferguson in Westminster Abbey in 1986, when she married the Duke of York. Shortly before her wedding, Miss Ferguson had been granted arms in her own right *Or issuant from a Mound in base a Thistle stalked and leaved and with three flowers alighting upon that in chief a Bumble Bee all proper*. The thistles and bees of her arms were incorporated into the design of her dress, train, veil and shoes, and into the needle-run lace worn by her bridesmaids.

A word of caution is necessary: it should be remembered that monumental brasses and effigies were often commissioned several years (sometimes decades) before or after the death of those they commemorate, and the style of costume depicted may not be contemporary with the date of interment.

Further reading

Anstruther, I. *The Knight and the Umbrella* The Eglington Tournament, 1963.

Ashelford, J. *The Visual History of Costume md the sixteenth century* London, 1984.

Cunnington, C.W. and P. *Handbook of English Costume in the Sixteenth Century* London, 1970.

— *Handbook of English Medieval Costume* London, 1973.

Franklin, C.A.H. *The Bearing of Coat Armour by Ladies* London, 1923.

Newton, S.M. *Fashion in the Age of the Black Prince* Woodbridge, 1980.

Scott, M. *The Visual History of Costume — the fourteenth and fifteenth centuries* London, 1984.

Armorial Equestre The *Armorial Equestre de la Toison d'Or et de l'Europe*, an early fifteenth-century manuscript at the Bibliothèque de l'Arsenal, Paris, contains a series of brilliantly coloured and animated paintings of the knights of the Golden Fleece, mounted and depicted with crests, tabards and caparisons gloriously emblazoned: the quintessence of heraldic vigour and vivacity (see colour page 101).

Further reading

Pinches, A. and A. Wood *A European Armorial Heraldry Today*, 1971.

Armorial Styles The depiction of early arms was very simple, both in content and treatment, and the execution of many early rolls of arms suggests that they were painted by the heralds themselves and were intended as records rather than finished pieces of art work.

The size and shape of the shield changed from the long, almost triangular style of the thirteenth century to the smaller, heater style of the fourteenth. Crests were not widely used before the fourteenth century and were rarely depicted in early armory. In fifteenth-century England a wide variety of shield shapes evolved, often gracefully cusped and fluted and *a bouché*, i.e. with a notch cut into the dexter chief to accommodate a lance. They were often shown 'couched', suspended at an angle which provided an asymmetrical and more interesting composition. By the middle of the century, body armour had become so efficient that it was no longer necessary for a knight to carry a shield for defence, and it came to be used purely as a vehicle for armorial display and was considerably reduced, both in size and in proportion to the helm and crest.

Mantling, either jagged or scalloped along its edges and tasseled, had such an affinity with prevailing civilian fashion in costume that the influence of one upon the other seems inescapable.

From the fourteenth century to the first quarter of the sixteenth, most two-dimensional heraldry was essentially coloured drawing rather than painting, executed with the same quill pens that wrote the accompanying text. The artistic unity in the manuscripts of artists such as John Rous (1411-91), a priest skilled both in heraldry and calligraphy, was lost by the end of the Middle Ages and is only now being regained.

Armorial style often reflected social change. By the early sixteenth century, many merchants and professional men had amassed considerable fortunes enabling them to live in a style hitherto enjoyed only by the nobility. The emergence of a merchant or middle class, and with it aspirations of gentility, resulted in a widespread adoption of bogus arms and the heralds' visitations which attempted to curb this abuse. The marshalling of arms now illustrated family relationships instead of feudal dependencies, and quarterings were acquired and displayed with enthusiasm. The notion of seize quartiers became popular and was, for a brief period, considered to represent incontrovertible proof of gentility. In order to accommodate such overcrowded quarterings shields had to be drawn in a much more rectangular shape, with rounded lower corners.

By the early sixteenth century, heraldry was increasingly being drawn and engraved on woodcuts and copper plates for reproduction by printing, and this too had an influence on subsequent style. Pattern books containing scrollwork based on classical acanthus leaf decoration used in architecture were readily available in workshops, and used extensively by artists and craftsmen in all media. The depiction of mantling changed from the comparatively simple styles favoured throughout the preceding century to much more elaborate ones based on the examples to be found in the pattern books.

From the early seventeenth century the helmet was used to denote rank both by its type and (later) by its position. Armory had not been used for military

'Coat of Arms of Death', by Albrecht Durer, 1503.

purposes for several generations, and this is evident from numerous contemporary grants, the helmets of which could never have been modelled or worn, and heraldic artists were faced with the problem of how to depict a crest which was blazoned as facing in one direction on top of a helmet which, for reasons of rank, was obliged to face another! Fortunately, this convention has been relaxed during the 1980s.

In the seventeenth and eighteenth centuries the growing importance of social class, and the corresponding requirement that nobility and gentility should be recognized armorially resulted in the proliferation of excessive rules and fanciful practices in armory, such as blazoning the arms of peers by

German renaissance achievement of arms

reference to the names of precious stones instead of the traditional tinctures. Many of the sillier practices were transitory, invented by heralds, several of whom had bought their offices and had little understanding of armory, intending simply to impress gullible clients.

Increasing emphasis was placed on the display of honours, decorations and the insignia of the orders of chivalry. In the eighteenth century there was, in the arts generally, a return to Greek and Roman classical styles. The once strong and beautiful tilting helm was replaced by one modelled on that of a Greek warrior, which after repeated modifications was ultimately transformed into a helmet that could only have been worn by Donald Duck!

Shields, once so simple and graceful, were replaced by cartouches borrowed from the sculptor and cartographer. Arms portrayed within the circlets of orders filled the available space, in some instances the shield being dispensed with entirely. The treatment of the whole achievement became realistic. Lions were depicted as beasts of nature, often lounging with studied indifference as supporters beside the shield. All this reflected what was happening in the fine art of the century.

Late eighteenth and nineteenth-century heraldry was, with few exceptions, so sterile as to possess little artistic merit. Much of it was beautifully executed and the element of craft was of a high order, but artistic qualities and an awareness of history were sadly lacking. The idea, still held by some today, that to produce good heraldic art did not require any artistic skill or specialist training was conceived. It was seen as something apart, divorced from the qualities of sound draughtsmanship, strong line and good design, colour and pattern, which are prerequisites in any other form of graphic art. Armorial tinctures were thought of necessity to be harsh and primary. At least one artists' supplier marketed a set of heraldic watercolours for the dilettante to colour in the line illustrations of heraldic books.

Manuals on the art of illumination and heraldic painting abounded, most of them, for some reason, written by architects. The instructions contained therein must inevitably have produced harsh and insensitive results.

In 1848 the Pre-Raphaelite Brotherhood was formed. Its objective was to emulate the ideas and values of medieval art and culture up to the time of the painter Raphael, and to reject the fussy, trivial and sentimental work of many contemporaries. The brotherhood lasted for only a few years but it had a profound effect on the Art and Craft Movement. Augustus Pugin was designing architecture, and much else beside, in the medieval manner. In 1880 Joseph Foster produced his *Baronetage and Peerage*, and whatever may be thought of him as an antiquarian he

made a significant choice in the artists he commissioned to illustrate it. The two principals were Anselm Baker, a Dominican monk living and working at Mount St Bernard's Abbey in Leicestershire, and John Forbes-Nixon, a well known heraldic artist of his day. They produced a series of woodcuts in strong contrast to the style of their contemporaries; achievements often asymmetrical in design and full of vitality, pattern and movement. It may be that they were, on occasion, rather too self-consciously quaint and that they abandoned too readily some of the artistically inconvenient armorial conventions. However, they brought back to English heraldic art a much-needed vitality and freshness.

John Forbes-Nixon's painting was rather less successful, but Dom. Anselm produced some strong, delicate paintings of arms, largely without outlines in an early medieval style, some of which are reproduced in G.W. Eve's *Decorative Heraldry*. They were two of the first artists to bring back another important quality into English heraldic art, that also achieved by the film cartoonist Walt Disney in the 1940s. He recognized the importance of encapsulating in his characters familiar and immediately recognizable human and animal characteristics. He endowed his creations with strong personalities. This is precisely what the good heraldic artist does, although not quite to the same extent. Medieval heraldic lions did not look like real ones, but contained the 'lion-ness' of the beast, the animal's essential characteristics as they were then perceived. Ideally, if there are three lions on a shield, each should have its own personality. Another interesting similarity is that the hands of cartoon characters generally have only three fingers, instead of four, in order to give more clarity and emphasis, and to simplify the drawing. Early heraldic lions had only three toes for the same reason. In the post-war years Robert Stewart Sherriffs (1908-61), drawing in *Punch*, produced weekly cartoons of current films and theatrical personalities. His drawings had a remarkable strength and economy of line. Some years ago his obituary revealed that he had trained when young at Edinburgh College of Art as an heraldic artist. Others who were similarly influenced were Sir William St John Hope, Revd E.E. Dorling, and George W. Eve.

The heraldry produced at the College of Arms evolved much more slowly. Until the 1930s all the important innovations in heraldic art were introduced by artists working independently. But early in this century Gerald Cobb went as a youth to work at the College. He was a gifted draughtsman with a strong sense of design and a natural affinity with all things heraldic. He was to become perhaps the most significant figure in contemporary English heraldic art, and his style, evolved over many years, has had a greater influence than any other. As is so often the case, change has been brought about by economic necessity. The acute shortage and high cost of gold and fine colours during the Second World War led Cobb to experiment with techniques which would make the available materials stretch as far as possible. From these came his distinctive way of drawing and painting mantling and motto scrolls, now part of the College style.

The work of the herald painters today has tended to integrate increasingly into a corporate style at once recognizable as that of the College of Arms, owing a great deal to Cobb's influence. It is becoming more difficult to identify the work of a particular artist, partly because when one evolves a pleasing way of treating a subject, others are quick to adopt it. The best of the College work is as good as any produced anywhere, but it allows of little personal expression or experimentation.

Most of the two-dimensional heraldry done professionally outside the College of Arms is produced by calligraphers. Many have been trained in the techniques and methods of illumination, and this enables them to seek the closest bond between the calligraphy and heraldry, with eight hundred years of artistic tradition behind them. Unfortunately some scribes are heraldically illiterate, and although their writing is of the highest order, their heraldry is not.

There are some graphic artists who have experimented with heraldry, employing contemporary graphics techniques and even using computer graphics in an attempt, as they see it, to update heraldic design. But heraldry has such a strong traditional imagery and simplicity of form, that to depart from it too far invariably becomes self-defeating.   AW

See also ART WORK AND MATERIALS; CALLIGRAPHY; ILLUMINATION; SOCIETY OF HERALDIC ARTS
Further reading
Child, H. *Heraldic Design* London, 1979.
Eve, George W. *Decorative Heraldry* London, 1897
— *Heraldry as Art* London, 1907.
Fox-Davies, A.C. *The Art of Heraldry* London, 1986.
St John Hope, W. *Stall Plates of the Knights of the Garter* London, 1901.
Von-Volborth, C.A. *The Art of Heraldry* Poole, 1987.

Armorist One who studies armory.

Armory (i) The function of devising, marshalling and regulating emblematic representations according to established conventions, practices and precedents, in order to create a unue and distinctive symbol by which authority, hereditary gentility or corporate pre-eminence may be recognized.
(ii) The study of (i).
(iii) A dictionary of armorial bearings listed alphabetically by surname.

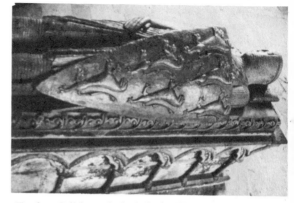

Tomb at Salisbury Cathedral of William Longespée, Earl of Salisbury, grandson of Geoffrey Plantagenet.

Armory, Origins of True armory is generally accepted as the hereditary use of an arrangement of charges or devices centred on a shield. The concept originated in the feudal society of the High Middle Ages in Western Europe.

Many forceful arguments and categorical statements defining the origin of armory have been offered; and yet the purpose for which it was intended remains obscure. Much favoured has been the argument that armory owes its existence to the need for identification in battle. The Bayeux Tapestry depicts Norman knights holding shields decorated with geometric designs or with dragon-like creatures. However, none of these formations has been shown to have become hereditary in any of the Norman families. By the First Crusade in 1096 such decoration may even have been replaced by a plain shield. The observant Princess Anna Comnena describes the shield borne by the Frankish knights as being 'extremely smooth and gleaming with a brilliant boss of molten brass'. There is no mention of anything on the surface of the shield suggestive of personal or hereditary devices. In 1127 King Henry I of England invested his son-in-law, Geoffrey Plantagenet, with a blue shield charged with gold lioncels. This same shield later appears on the tomb of Geoffrey's grandson, William Earl of Salisbury. It had thus acquired a significance that enabled it to become hereditary.

The investing of Geoffrey Plantagenet is generally regarded as the first known instance of recorded armory in Europe. Between 1135 and 1155 seals provide further evidence of shields bearing devices that were to become hereditary. It is therefore clear that the second quarter of the twelfth century was witness to the adoption of personal devices which acquired significance and characteristics seemingly different from anything that had existed previously. What then had brought about this change? The basic tactic of warfare, the mass cavalry charge, had remained unchanged. Certainly from the time of the Conquest there had been a growing complexity in armour; but even in 1066 recognition would have been difficult: this had necessitated William the Conqueror removing his helmet at the height of the Battle of Hastings to show that he was still alive. There is not much here to explain the sudden adoption of armory in the second quarter of the twelfth century. Even if such a need for identification had existed, the shield would have been an unsatisfactory choice to meet it.

The surface is essentially a two-dimensional object and can only be viewed from a limited angle. Furthermore, it was borne on the general level of the battlefield and rapidly acquired mud, scratches and battle filth. Much more effective would have been three-dimensional objects on top of poles, or even flags; flags flying high above the battlefield were and continued to be used for identification purposes and rallying points. Armory was eventually to find its way on to flags, but this was not applicable to the ordinary knight of the twelfth or thirteenth centuries, whose devices would seem to have had a different purpose. The difficulties in obtaining a clear view of and identifying a besmirched two-dimensional shield surface borne at body height in a medieval mêlée would have been further compounded by the nature of the charges used. An examination of early rolls of arms will show considerable similarity between designs as well as duplication of charges. The thirteenth-century Herald Roll, for example, consists of one hundred and ninety shields, of which no less than forty-three contain the lion. Again, this does not make for easy identification. Even if a would-be antagonist had gone to the lengths of apprising himself of his opponent's arms, it is likely that he would have been confronted with a difficult task of spotting those arms with any degree of certainty on the battlefield. If identification in battle was not a major factor in the origin of armory, another explanation must be sought.

The beginnings of armory in the twelfth century coincide exactly with the sudden explosive advance made by European civilisations, and known as the Twelfth Century Renaissance. he sheer exuberance of spirit and self-confidence inspired by this movement was manifested in a delight in visual decoration, which found an obvious outlet on the personal shields of individual knights. It is perhaps with this spirit rather than with military tactics that the real origin of armory should be sought.

Once decorated, shields became objects of personal pride. As such, there was a much greater element of the subjective, the wish to have a personal device, similar to a modern mascot, rather than any objective desire to provide a practical means of identification for others. Undoubtedly this was further stimulated by the tournament, where pomp and pageantry were again subjective rather than practical. It is this subjective element in armory which was to ease the transition from the Middle Ages to the Modern Era, and to prove armory's greatest strength with the advent of the Tudors. The sixteenth century was to witness an increasing number of grants of arms to new Tudor men quite unconnected with battlefield or tournament. That this could happen so readily suggests that the nature of armory had remained largely unchanged from its origins in the twelfth century.

Rodney Dennys, Arundel Herald of Arms Extraordinary, tends towards the same conclusion in his book *The Heraldic Imagination*, where he suggests that 'the elaborate and flamboyant crests worn by the jousters were, therefore, heraldic status symbols.' The subjective element manifest by tournament pageantry was therefore more important than practical reasons of identification. If this is true for three-dimensional crests set on the helm, it must almost certainly hold for flat two-dimensional shield surfaces.

The importance of pageantry and its association with the tournament excluded those who were unable to meet the expense, or who were of insufficient social standing. Lesser gentry did not obtain crests before the Tudor period, when the social value of the crest was allowed to depreciate.

The first shields of arms were essentially simple. Many knights adopted unadorned stripes or crosses, which may well have owed their origin to bands of metal or boiled leather which served to strengthen the wooden shield, and thus offered an obvious surface for paint. Others, not content with the abstract, chose specific objects, some of which had obvious desirable characteristics, such as the masculine and martial lion and eagle; others yielded a pun on surname or title.

More significant was the use of charges common to groups of families linked by blood or feudal tenure. It is possible that the use of such group emblems pre-dates armory. Beryl Platts has drawn attention to the Flemish element in the Norman Conquest, drawn from Flanders and its subsidiary *comptés*, severally ruled by descendants of Charlemagne. Her claim is that each bore emblems which originated with the Carolingian Empire, and 'were carried not on shields but on banners —and on seals, rings, tokens, coins, badges, and in some cases apparently on breastplates as well.' Her claim is both sweeping and intriguing. It is only unfortunate that her book *Origins of Heraldry*, though strongly inferential, is tantalizingly devoid of specific examples to support her argument. If it can indeed by substantiated, then a Carolingian element in armory must be accepted. Retained by Flanders and her allied counties, the practice of using emblems was then merged with the spirit of the Twelfth Century

Renaissance, transferred to the shield to rise to what is uncontroversially accepted as armory. Certainly, future research might be more rewarding if directed towards the Flemish rather than the Normans.

Like armory, the origin of the heralds is obscure. The early references to heralds are found in twelfth-century French poems, where they are usually mentioned in connection with tournaments. They were sent out to proclaim a tournament, they accompanied knights to that event and announced the jousters as they entered the lists. Perhaps the earliest known reference to a herald appears in *Le Chevalier de la Charrette*, an Arthurian romance written by Chrétien de Troyes between 1164 and 1172. The herald arrives on the scene running barefoot and clad only in his shirt, having pledged his clothes and shoes at the tavern. This suggestion of somewhat humble circumstances is further borne out by the heralds' association with minstrels, and there is evidence for considerable rivalry between the two callings. Both heralds and minstrels tended to be itinerant. However, with the development of the tournament, heralds were able to raise their status, and many became attached to specific households. By the end of the thirteenth century kings of heralds or kings of arms make their appearance. This development of specific rank and evidence for heralds co-ordinating their activities was leading the profession towards the ultimate formation of the College of Arms in 1484.   PG-J

Further reading
Dennys, R. *The Heraldic Imagination* London, 1975.
Platts, B. *Origins of Heraldry* London, 1980.
— *Scottish Hazard* 1985. The Flemish nobility and their impact on Scotland.

Armourers' Marks Like most craftsmen, armourers, swordsmiths and gunsmiths all took great pride in the pieces they produced, and many craftsmen marked their products with the aid of a metal punch at the finishing stage. Many choice pieces were thus identified, though a number of weapons, especially guns, bear no maker's mark at all. Many weapons were made and supplied to the small trader, who, in turn, would have his own name applied to the pieces.

The mark of the Armourers' Company is a crowned letter A, and the running wolf in all its various stylized forms is the mark found on weapons from Solingen, West Germany. Companies often had their marks stamped on weapons used by men in their service, the two prime examples being the VOAC monogram of the Dutch East India Company, and the heart-shaped stamp of the East India Company.   BC

Further reading
Gyngell, D.S.H. *Armourers' Marks* London, 1959.

Arms Specifically the shield of arms, but frequently used as an abbreviation for coat of arms.

Arms of Adoption The assumption of properly authorized arms by someone who has no entitlement to them by descent. This may only be achieved by obtaining a royal licence, as the result of a 'Name and Arms' clause in a will, for example.

Arms of Alliance Arms marshalled in one shield to demonstrate the alliance of families by marriage.

Arms of Assumption Arms assumed by the victor in medieval combat, when a vanquished opponent relinquished his arms either by death or in return for his life. Very rare. Not to be confused with 'assumed arms', which are arms borne without authority.

Arms of Community The arms of a corporate body, sometimes described as impersonal arms.

Arms of Concession Arms conceded as a reward or used in conjunction with existing arms as an augmentation by 'mere grace'. For example, Richard II's grant of the attributed arms of Edward the Confessor to Thomas Mowbray, Duke of Norfolk.

Arms of Descent Arms borne by hereditary right.

Arms of Dominion *or* **Arms of Sovereignty** Arms used by a sovereign in the territories over which he/ she has dominion. Arms of dominion are not personal devices, but are inseparable from the office and rank of sovereign. The familiar 'Royal Arms' used by the British monarchy are arms of dominion, Queen Elizabeth II's personal arms (which are never used) being those of her branch of the House of Saxony. Arms of dominion, whilst following the conventions of armory, are not subject to the Law of Arms, the sovereign determining what form they shall take and how they shall be used. Such are the complex relationships of the British Commonwealth that a new personal device was adopted by the Queen (in 1960) for use when the Royal Arms are considered 'inappropriate' (*See* QUEEN'S PERSONAL FLAG).

Arms of Expectation A term given to a nineteenth-century European practice, it being the custom for single women to divide their shield per pale, placing their paternal arms on the sinister side, leaving the dexter blank as a sign that they were resolved to marry. Lower (*The Curiosities of Heraldry*, 1845) suggests that maidens verging on the antique might consider advertising for a husband in this fashion, the odious appellation of 'old maid' giving way to the more courteous one of 'ladies of the half-blank shield'.   JC-K

Arms of Office

Arms of Office Arms borne in addition to personal arms by holders of certain offices, e.g. bishops, kings of arms. The English kings of arms have recently determined that any armiger who is the head of a body corporate may impale his personal arms with those of the corporation during his term of office. Arms so impaled may, therefore, be considered to be arms of office. Where an office is hereditary, so too are the arms associated with it. There are a number of interesting variations: Her Majesty The Queen Mother, for example, as Warden of the Cinque Ports, incorporates a narrow panel charged with the Royal Cypher in the hoist of the Warden's banner. *See also* INSIGNIA OF OFFICE

Arms of Pretension Arms borne to denote a claim to sovereignty, title, office or territory without actual possession of it. In 1337 Edward III of England laid claim to the throne of France and quartered the arms of France with those of England to emphasize his claim (France, the senior kingdom in the medieval hierarchy, being in the first and fourth quarters). It was not until 1801 that the gold fleurs-de-lis of France were removed from the royal arms of England!

Arms of Sovereignty *see* **Arms of Dominion**

Arms of Succession Defined by Boutell as 'arms taken on inheritance to certain estates, manors or dignities to which insignia appertain,' true arms of succession are rare, and are often confused with arms of office, some of which are hereditary. There are 'estates, manors or dignities' with which hereditary insignia are associated, but with the exception of certain feudal estates which are now vested in the Crown and which carry with them both arms and title, armorial bearings cannot normally be transferred with property unless there exists a corresponding right of armorial inheritance.

Arraché *see* **Attributes**

Arrayed *see* **Attributes**

Arriere-Garde The rearguard or reserve of a battle formation.

Art Heraldique, L' *see* **Treatises**

Arthur, King The real Arthur was probably a military leader in the post-Roman Britain of the fifth century who, for a time, resisted the Anglo-Saxon invaders. A sixth-century writer, Gildas, credits one Ambrosius Aurelianus with a series of victories over the Saxons, culminating in the battle of Mount Badon *c.* 490. The twelfth-century chronicle of Geoffrey of Monmouth, *History of the Kings of Britain* (*c.* 1138), is mostly pure fantasy, but it succeeded in raising an obscure and shadowy chieftain to the now familiar patriot-king of the Arthurian legends. The legend-cycle, the 'Matter of Britain', which is to be found principally in early medieval French verse and prose romances, especially those of Chretien de Troyes, was later retold in the anonymous *Sir Gawain and the Green Knight* (1360-70), Malory's *Morte d'Arthur* (1469 and later printed by Caxton) and Tennyson's *Morte d'Arthur* (1842).

The ideals of the Fellowship of the Knights of the Round Table are those of the chivalric code; the Quest for the Holy Grail by the perfect knight, Galahad, its highest achievement. It was the breakdown of the Code of Chivalry by infidelity, disloyalty and treachery which destroyed the Fellowship, and yet the mythical Arthur became the object of an international cult, and his Fellowship the model for the medieval orders of chivalry.

During Easter 1278, Edward I and his queen Eleanor were at Glastonbury, where a magnificent black marble tomb had been erected over the reputed remains of Arthur and Guinevere. Edward clearly recognized the political advantages of association with such an illustrious British king. 'Round Tables', festive pageants and tournaments, were held during his reign, and these were continued by his successors. Edward III had a circular house built at Windsor Castle to accommodate a round table, and at the conclusion of a great tournament held at Windsor in 1344 Edward took a solemn oath that in time he would follow in the footsteps of King Arthur and create a Round Table for his knights. In 1348 the Order of the Garter was founded. It consisted of twenty-six knights companion including the sovereign, and it cannot be by chance that the subsequent Tudor decoration of the Winchester Round Table depicts twenty-four sieges, or places, with the figure of the king occupying a further two. The Tudor kings were also to acknowledge the political significance of the 'Matter of Britain'. Henry VII, whose claim to the English throne included descent from Arthur through the Welsh princes, ordained that his son (also Arthur) should be born at Winchester; and Henry VIII entertained the Holy Roman Emperor, Charles V, in the Great Hall at Winchester Castle in 1522 beneath the Round Table which hung from the wall, as it does today. Following repairs to the table in 1516-17 it was decorated in anticipation of the Emperor's visit. The table, which is of oak and measures 18 feet (5 · 5 metres) in diameter, was painted with white and green segments which radiate from a Tudor Rose at the centre. These were the Tudor livery colours and badge. The table was already in position on the wall of the Great Hall in *c.* 1463, for the chronicler John Hardynge wrote: 'The rounde Table at Wynchester beganne and there it ended, and there it hangeth yet.' In 1976 a radiocarbon test on the plank of the table suggested that the felling date of the youngest tree used in its construction was *c.* 1255. A further test was carried out using a tree-ring dating technique, and this indicated that the table was made at some time between 1250 and 1280: during the reigns of Henry III and Edward I.

Further reading
Alcock, L. *Arthur's Britain* London, 1971.
Ashe, G. *The Quest for Arthur's Britain* London, 1972 (contains an excellent bibliography of reference material prior to 1968).
Barber, R. *The Arthurian Legends* London.
Geoffrey of Monmouth *The History of the Kings of Britain*, ed. L. Thorpe, Harmondsworth, 1966.
Loomis, R.S. 'Edward I: Arthurian Enthusiast' in *Speculum* xxviii, 1953.
See also ATTRIBUTED ARMS *and* GARTER, THE MOST NOBLE ORDER OF THE

Artwork and Materials Heraldic painting is based broadly on the practical experience of the artist illuminators of manuscripts for over a thousand years, although there are numerous personal variations. Firstly, the drawing is made, then it is traced down, the major outlines are put in, then the metals or their equivalents are applied, followed by the basic ground colours. These are then modelled up, any required detail added and lastly any lettering for mottoes or names.

It is essential to work cleanly rather than trusting to subsequent cleaning up. A drawing of the arms should be made with a fairly hard pencil (HB) on good quality cartridge paper. The complexity of the drawing will depend on the skill of the draughtsman or woman. From this drawing the tracing is made, with great care, for the better the tracing the better will be the finished result. Tracing paper should be of the best medium-weight quality and a hard (3H) pencil, kept sharp, used.

It is helpful to crease the tracing paper and position it so that the crease lies vertically down the middle of the drawing, where it should be taped while the tracing is made. When this is transferred to the working surface on which the painting is to be done, be it paper, board or vellum, one should go over every line of the design, on the *reverse* of the tracing, using a soft pencil. Never scribble or shade on the reverse, as this makes a mess on the finished drawing when transferred. The lines of the tracing can then be gone over on the right side with a hard pencil or stylus, and checked before lifting to make sure that the transfer is complete and nothing has been omitted.

The most suitable materials on which to paint are good quality cartridge paper, or what is sold in Britain as 'Fashion Board'. Calfskin vellum produces the most beautiful and permanent result, but is very expensive and difficult for the inexperienced to use. The main outlines can be put in first. Those that are geometrical, straight lines and parts of circles, in the outlines of shields for instance, can be made with draughtsman's pen and compass. The remainder must be done freehand with the finest quality sable brushes, size 0 or 00. Good brushes are expensive, but if looked after properly each will outlast several cheaper ones. They should never be allowed to dry full of paint.

Outlining is best done in a darkish brown, though it is by no means essential that the line should be the same colour or thickness throughout the painting. With careful painting afterwards, lines should only need minimal restoration before the work is complete. Pure black should never be used for any part of a painting.

When the main outlines are in place the metals are applied. If the working surface is fairly white, argent can either be left unpainted or a metallic silver watercolour used, but this can look heavy. Gold may be represented either by a suitable yellow or put in with a gold watercolour. This will, in time, tarnish to a dirty brown. Real gold, called by illuminators 'Shell gold', is by far the most beautiful and lasts indefinitely, but is very expensive and difficult to use well.

The ground colours of the remaining tinctures are next painted in, and when quite dry are modelled up as little as is absolutely necessary with two or three darker tones of the same colour. This must presuppose some knowledge of three-dimensional form and can never be really successful if slavishly copied from examples done by others, without understanding.

The best paints to use are gouache colours, which are basically the same as water colours but deliberately made opaque, so that in theory any one can be painted successfully over any other. In practice this is not always so, and it is advisable to work from light to dark. This ability is particularly useful when painting small detail so that, for instance, a sable field may be laid complete and, when quite dry, a white or silver lion painted in on top of it. This cannot be done with artists' watercolours.

Some of the best gouache colours are marketed in Britain under the trade name of Designers Colours, and are classified in three groups: A, B and C in decreasing order of permanence. Some of the colours in group C fade very quickly under prolonged exposure to daylight and should be avoided when possible. When several colours are mixed together they tend to lose their brilliance, so that excessive mixing should be avoided. Gouache colours should be mixed to the same consistency as thin cream. In a good heraldic painting, each part should be clearly and concisely stated. It is better to do something simple and well, rather than elaborate and poorly.

Recommended Designers' Colours

TINCTURE	BASE COLOUR	MODELLING COLOURS
Or	Brilliant Yellow	Burnt Sienna + Vandyke Brown
Argent	left unpainted	Zinc White + Dark Grey
Gules	Scarlet Lake	Alizarin Crimson + Havannah Lake
Azure	Cerulean Blue	Cobalt + Prussian Blue
Vert	Winsor Emerald	Cyprus Green + Prussian Blue
Sable	Dark Grey	Lamp Black or Zinc White
Purpure	Light Purple + Zinc White	Prussian Blue + Alizarin Crimson
Tenné	Orange Lake Light	Alizarin Crimson + Magenta
Sanguine	Alizarin Crimson	Havannah Lake
Murrey	Magenta + Zinc White	Alizarin Crimson
Outline	Burnt Sienna + Lamp Black	

The above colours are only a guide, and depend for their successful use on the skill of the artist.

Detail should only be put in if its omission detracts from the clarity of the arms. Ordinaries and charges should fill comfortably the available space without overcrowding. The shield in an achievement must have pride of place.

The helm should sit well on the shield but not be so prominent as to vie with the arms for attention. The crest should be large enough and drawn so as to sit firmly upon it, facing in the same direction when possible. The mantling should flow gracefully from the crown of the helm with well balanced areas of colour and fur or metal, and not curling about the crest so as to obscure it.

The whole achievement should form a well-balanced shape, complemented at the based by compartment or motto ribbon to make an integral whole. The lettering of names or mottoes looks best when written by those with some calligraphic skill. Most herald painters put them in with a fine brush, which does not look as well as pen and ink and takes much longer. For those without either skill or experience, instant rub-down letters are the best solution, if somewhat expensive.   AW

Further reading
Eve, G.W. *Heraldry as Art* London, 1907.
Mayer, R. *The Artist's Handbook* London, reprint 1975.
Metzig, W. *Heraldry for the Designer* New York, 1974.
See also ARMORIAL STYLES, CALLIGRAPHY, ILLUMINATION *and* HERALDIC ARTS, SOCIETY OF

Arundel Herald of Arms Extraordinary Arundel Herald was originally a private herald in the household of Thomas Fitzalan, Earl of Arundel. He is known to have served the Earl both in Portugal in 1413 and later in France, where he attended his dying master in October 1415. The title was revived in 1727 and the badge, assigned in 1958, is derived from that of the Fitzalan earls of the fourteenth century, and a supporter in the arms of the present Earl Marshal *A Horse courant Argent in its mouth a Sprig of Oak proper.*

Ascending *see* **Attitude**

Ashmolean Tract *see* **Treatises**

Ashmole Tract *see* **Treatises**

Aspilogia A word meaning 'armory/heraldry', coined by Sir Henry Spelman (1564?-1641) as the title to his Latin treatise on coats of arms. The *Dictionary of National Biography* and the *Revised Medieval Latin Word List* assign the appearance of the word to about 1595, perhaps earlier. Sir Anthony Wagner in *A Catalogue of Mediaeval Arms* (1950) argues that on etymological grounds a better form would have been 'Aspidologia', but retains Spelman's innovation on the basis of long tradition   JC-K

Assurgant *see* **Attitude**

Astral Crown *see* **Crest coronet**

At gaze *see* **Attitude**

At speed *see* **Attitude**

Arundel badge

Attainder Made after a judgement of death or outlawry on a capital charge, a declaration of attainder by act of parliament resulted in the absolute forfeiture of all civil rights and privileges. Frequently applied during the Middle Ages in association with charges of treason, when a declaration of attainder implied also a 'Corruption of Blood', whereby goods, lands, titles and armorial bearings of an attainted person could not be inherited by his heirs until the attainder had been revoked also by act of parliament. Lands, and any rights in them, reverted to a superior lord subject to the Crown's rights of forfeiture. During the Wars of the Roses, acts of attainder were regularly used by one side to liquidate the other. However, it is interesting to note that during the period 1453 to 1504, of 397 attainders no fewer than 256 were reversed. Attainder was ended as recently as 1870 by the Forfeiture Act.

Attired *see* **Attributes**

Attires *see* **Deer**

Attitude The posture or inclination of an armorial charge. Most charges, other than beasts, are depicted in an upright position except when borne on a bend or bend sinister. When another attitude is depicted, or when clarification is considered necessary, reference is made either to the geometry of the ordinaries (e.g. *a Lance palewise, two Keys saltirewise*) or to a variety of armorial terms, each of which has a specific meaning. If a charge emerges from the side of the shield or from an ordinary, its precise position and attitude should be given, e.g. *issuing from the dexter chief bendwise.*

Four-footed and chimerical creatures conform for the most part with the attitudes of the lion illustrated. Beasts are blazoned in the following order: (i) bodily attitude(s); (ii) position of head; (iii) inclination of tail. In the following example, the griffin's attitudes (segreant, reguardant and tail coward) precede its ATTRIBUTES (beaked, membered and tufted): *A Griffin segreant reguardant tail coward Sable beaked membered and tufted Or.*

abouté	end to end
addorsed	back to back
affronty	head and body facing observer
appaumé	hand or gauntlet open showing palm
arched	bent in the form of an arch
ascending	of a bird taking flight
assurgant	rising from, e.g. the sea
at gaze	of a stag standing with head facing observer
at speed	of a stag courant

aversant	clenched benediction, in a hand raised with first and second fingers erect
bicorporate	lions combatant sharing the same head
braced	interlaced
caboshed	an animal's head affronty and cut off with no part of the neck showing (not lions, leopards or panthers, to which the term 'face' applies)
chase, in full	of a hound in pursuit
clenched	a closed gauntlet
climant	a goat rampant
close	of a bird with the wings close to the body *or* a bascinet with the vizor closed
coiled	of a snake, head erect
combatant	two rampant beasts facing one another
contourné	reversed to face the sinister
conjoined	joined together (also cojoined)
couchant	(see figure of lion)
counter	prefix meaning opposite
counter passant	two passant beasts back to back
counter rampant	two rampant beasts back to back
courant	running at speed
course, in full	of a hound in pursuit
coward or *cowed*	the tail between the legs
debruised	overlaid
displayed	with wings expanded — 'spreadeagled'
distilling	shedding drops of
dormant	(see figure of lion)
elevated	pointing upwards
embowed	curved or bent
encircled	of a serpent when coiled
endorsed	back to back
enfile	passing through
enhanced	raised above normal position
ensigned	having a charge placed above, e.g. a crown
entoured	surrounded by
environed	encircled by
erect	upright (applied only to charges which are not normally so

	depicted, and to beasts such as the wyvern which have no hind legs)
extended	of a tail when held in a horizontal position
face	the head of a lion, panther, etc., when caboshed
flexed	bent or bowed
flotant	floating (of flags and ships)
forcene	a rearing horse with both hind hooves on the ground (also enraged)
glissant	of a snake when gliding
guardant	head turned to face the observer
hauriant	of a fish, head upwards
inverted	downwards, inverted
involved	encircled
issuant	emerging from behind or proceeding from
lodged	of a stag when couchant
lure, in	two wings joined, the tips upwards
naiant	swimming
naissant	emerging from the midst of
nowed	knotted
open	of a book
oppressed	overlaid
overt	open (of wings)
passant	(see figure of lion)
pendent	hanging from
perched	of a bird when standing on an object
piety, in its	of a pelican when wounding its breast with its beak and nourishing its young with blood
preying	devouring prey
pride, in its	of a peacock (or turkey) affronty with tail displayed
raised	of a portcullis, only the lower portion showing within the gateway
rampant	(see figure of lion)
reflexed	curved backwards
reguardant	a beast looking over its shoulder
respectant	of beasts facing each other
reversed	inverted

rising or *rousant*	of a bird about to take wing
salient	(see figure of lion)
segreant	of a griffin when rampant
sejant	(see figure of lion)
shut	of a book when closed
soaring	flying upwards
spancelled	fettered (of a horse)
springing	of a deer having both hind hooves on the ground, the forelegs raised and bent
statant	(see figure of lion)
stooping	of a bird of prey swooping on its quarry)
suppressed	overlaid
transfixed	pierced
transfluent	water flowing through or beneath
traversed	facing the sinister
trian aspect, in	position of head between guardant and profile
tricorporate	three beasts pallwise sharing the same head
trippant	a walking stag
trotting	of a horse
trussed	of wings when folded
trussing	of birds when devouring prey
uriant or *urinant*	of a fish when diving
veneration, in	kneeling as if in prayer
vigilance, in its	of a crane when standing on one leg and holding a stone in the other md should it fall asleep the stone will drop and awaken it!
vol, a	two wings joined, the tips upwards
volant	flying horizontally
vorant	devouring
vulning	wounding to produce blood

Attributed Arms Arms devised for someone who was incapable of bearing them. The heralds both of the medieval and post-medieval periods (the latter known as the 'Heraldry of the Decadence') shared with artists and writers of the time a sense that the characters of 'history' were somehow familiar contemporaries. Just as King Arthur, Charlemagne, Prester John and King David would be depicted in medieval costume and leading medieval lives, so too

Attitudes

statant

salient

dormant

sejant

rampant

passant

couchant

the heralds determined that, because all persons of consequence in their society were armigerous, so too were the characters of their religion and the heroes of legend and history.

Armorial bearings were devised and attributed not only to persons but also to concepts and abstractions. The *Scutum Fidei* or 'Arms of Faith' were devised to symbolize the Trinity, consisting of a diagrammatic representation of the triune nature of the Holy Trinity in silver on a red field, gules being the colour of rulers and princes (*see* CHRISTIAN SYMBOLS). The religious concepts of the Precious Blood, the Passion of Christ, and the Assumption of The Blessed Virgin Mary were provided with arms, as were the saints and martyrs, the apostles and disciples and the Old Testament prophets and kings. To the Blessed Virgin Mary were attributed several armorial devices, the most beautiful of which depicts a heart, winged in allusion to the angel of the Annunciation, pierced by a sword all on a blue shield to signify piety, recalling St Luke: 'Yea, a sword shall pierce through thy own soul also, that the thoughts of many hearts may be revealed.' However, of all the symbols associated with the Virgin it is the white lily which immediately springs to mind (another attributed coat of arms, again with a blue field, shows a gold vase containing three white lilies) and it is almost certainly in the beautiful curves of the Madonna Lily that the armorial fleur-de-lis has its origins. Early heralds were naturally reluctant to attribute arms to Christ or to represent his person armorially, the most glorious exception being the attributed arms of the enigmatic Prester John: *Azure upon a Passion Cross Gold the figure of Christ Crucified Argent*. However, the Instruments of the Passion were frequently depicted on shields and clearly these were considered to be personal emblems of Christ — the *Arma Christi* or *Scutum Salvationis* (Arms of Salvation). The *Boke of St Albans* tells us of 'that gentilman Jhesus . . . Kyng of the londe of Jude and of Jues, gentilman by his Modre Mary, prynce of Cote amure.' The hierarchical world of the Heavenly Host reflected the medieval obsession with rank and function, each of the nine Orders, descending from Seraphim through Cherubim, Thrones, Dominions, Virtues, Powers, Principalities and Archangels to Angels, possessing its particular attributes and performing specific functions. Many of the better known members were considered to be armigerous: the Archangel Michael, for example, bore *Argent a Cross Gules*.

Not to be outdone, Satan himself bore arms (as a former Seraphim he was assumed to be armigerous) and to him were attributed *Gules a Fess Gold between three Frogs proper*, a reference to the Book of Revelations in which St John tells us how he saw 'three unclean spirits like frogs come out of the mouth of the dragon . . . for they are the spirits of devils.' The heralds of the 'Decadence' were particularly

systematic, beginning with Adam (*Gules*) and Eve (*Argent*), the coats being combined with Eve's in pretence. Abel correctly quartered his paternal and maternal arms, though Cain, upon whom God 'set a mark', was required to difference his arms with engrailed and indented lines of partition. Joseph, whose multi-coloured coat should have been a 'gift' to the heralds, bore simply *Chequy Sable and Argent*. To King David was attributed a gold harp on a blue field. But we must not mock the medieval mind. The need for symbolism — particularly religious symbolism — was fundamental and an essential adjunct to the desperate search for salvation. Banners of the Trinity, Christ's Passion and the Blessed Virgin Mary accompanied the medieval army into battle, and many a warrior emblazoned the *inside* of his shield with religious emblems. Our churches provide abundant evidence in their glass and architectural decoration not only of medieval symbolism but also of the continued use of many of those devices today. Charges from the arms attributed to historical and legendary characters and to ancient kingdoms are much in evidence in the heraldry of civic and corporate bodies throughout Europe. For example, the three seaxes (notched swords) of the kingdoms of the East and Middle Saxons and the gold martlets (swallows) of the South Saxons may be found in numerous civic coats of arms throughout southeast England. To King Edward the Confessor, the heralds attributed five doves surrounding a gold cross (early devices depicted on his coinage) on a blue field. These arms later found their way into the heraldry of Westminster and the cross or doves into the arms of many other towns with which he is associated.

Examples of arms attributed to legendary characters are legion: to 'King' Arthur, the semi-mythical Romano-Briton, are attributed both *Azure three Crowns Gold* and *Vert a Cross Argent in the first quarter The Virgin holding the Christ Child Gold*. The Knights of the Round Table were armigerous, each accumulating a variety of coats of arms (the heralds being unable to agree on a definitive list). To Uther Pendragon were assigned the arms *Or two Dragons addorsed crowned Gules*, and to Merlin *Sable semy of Plates*. The list of such arms is endless, as is the variety of arms attributed to each character by successive generations of reverential heralds. Identification of attributed arms can be great sport — but beware! Occasional instances are known of medieval tombs on which attributed arms are emblazoned, usually those of the patron saint of the deceased. Marshalling is not to be recommended!

Attributes The properties and appendages associated with an armorial charge.

All charges have attributes (even the humble

roundel is round and flat!), and for the most part these are implicit in the terminology of armory, e.g. *a male Griffin* has no wings, a *Griffin* does. However, when variations occur or additions made they should be specified, e.g. a mullet is always depicted as having five points, a six-pointed mullet should be blazoned *a Mullet of six points*, therefore. The armorial vocabulary provides us with many terms to describe the properties and appendages of a charge. Some of these refer to its ATTITUDE, others describe such details as the tincture of beak, claws, tongue, etc., though there are certain conventions of BLAZON which render the inclusion of some of the more common attributes superfluous.

In the following example, the attitude (rampant) precedes the attributes, and the minor charge supported by the beast is blazoned separately. Notice also that repetition of the tincture Or is avoided by using the word Gold. *Issuant from an Ancient Crown Or a demi-Bull rampant polled Sable winged unguled tufted and having an Unicorn's Horn Gold and holding between the forelegs a Bristol Nail Argent* (Campbell-Kease, see colour page 250).

accorné	having horns or attires
acorned	bearing acorns
aislé	having wings
à la cuisse	at the thigh
alerion	without legs or beak
alisé	rounded
annelled	ringed, e.g. a bull
annuletty	terminating in rings
armed	having teeth, talons, horns or claws (beasts) *or* wearing armour (cap-à-pie = *fully armed)*
arraché	torn off
arrayed	richly apparelled
attired	having antlers
aulned	bearded (of corn)
banded	encircled with a band or ribbon
barbed	describing the head of an arrow *or* describing the sepals of a rose
barded	of a horse bridled, saddled and armoured
beaked	describing the beak of a bird or monster
belled	having a bell or bells attached
blasted	of a tree without leaves
blemished	broken
bound	describing the cover of a book
bridled	having a bridle
bristled	having bristles (e.g. boar)
burgeonee	of a fleur-de-lis with 'petals' about to open like buds
cabled	having a chain or rope attached
caparisoned	of a horse barded and covered by an armorial or ornamental cloth
chained	being possessed of a chain
clasped	describing the clasp of a book
coded	having a scrotum of a different tincture
collared	having a plain collar
combed	describing the crest of a cock
complement, in her	descriptive of the moon when full
corded	tied with a cord
crested	combed (a cock)
crined	describing hair or a mane
crowned	having a crown
couped	cut short by a straight horizontal line
couped close	cut short by a straight vertical line
cuffed	having cuffs
dechaussé	dismembered
defamed	having no tail
demi	only upper half depicted
dented	having teeth of a different colour
disarmed	without claws, beak, horns, etc.
dismembered	of a beast with head, paws and tail separated from body
doubled	having the lining turned up
double-headed	having two heads
edged	describing the surface formed by the closed pages of a book
embattled	having crenellations
embrued	spattered or dripping with blood
enflamed	flaming
enraged	having tongue and claws of a specific tincture
en soleil	surrounded by rays of the sun
equipped	fully armed
eradicated	uprooted

Attributes

erased	torn off in a horizontal plane leaving a ragged edge	*leathered*	describing the cover of a book
erased close	torn off in a vertical plane leaving a ragged edge	*leaved*	having leaves
		legged	describing legs, usually of a bird
eyed	having eyes of a specific colour	*lined*	having an inside lining *or* having cords or chains attached
feathered	describing an arrow		
figured	having a human face	*maned*	having a mane of a different colour
finned	having fins of a different colour		
fired	ignited	*masoned*	describing the cement of brickwork or other masonry
flamant	in flames		
flighted	describing an arrow	*membered*	describing the legs of a bird or griffin
fluted	of a pillar		
foliated	having leaves	*mutilé*	dismembered
fourché	forked, e.g. of a tail	*muzzled*	having a muzzle
fracted	broken	*nimbed*	encircled with a nimbus
fringed	having a fringe	*pierced*	perforated
fructed	bearing fruit	*pizzled*	having a penis of a different colour from the body
fumant	emitting smoke		
furnished	a horse caparisoned	*plenitude, in her*	descriptive of the moon when full
garnished	adorned, decorated		
gemmed	having or describing a precious stone	*plumed*	having a plume of feathers
		polled	having the horns removed
glory, in his	descriptive of the sun when depicted in full	*pommelled*	describing the pommel of a weapon
		purfled	decorated (of material)
gorged	encircled about the throat with, e.g. a crown	*queued*	tailed
		queue fourché	the tail of a beast divided at its mid point
gringoly	embellished with serpents' heads		
		quilled	describing the quill of an ostrich feather
guarded	having the lining turned up		
habited	clothed	*rayed*	having rays
hafted	describing the handles of tools and weapons	*rebated*	cut short
		replenished	filled
helmed	wearing a helmet	*ringed*	having a ring, e.g. that in a bull's nose
hilted	describing the handle and guard of a weapon		
		rompu	broken
hooded	of a hunting bird when hooded	*sans wings*	without wings: descriptive only of creatures who are normally possessed of wings
horned	describing horns		
imbrued	see *embrued*		
incensed	having flames issuing from mouth and ears	*sangliant*	blood-stained
		seeded	having seed vessels (of flowers)
inflamed	in flames	*sexed*	having genitals of a different colour from the body
irradiated	surrounded by rays of light		
jelloped	having wattles (of a cock)	*shafted*	of the shaft of a weapon *slipped* having a stalk (of a leaf, flower or twig)
jessant	emerging, springing forth		
jessed	having thongs attached		
langued	describing the tongue of a creature	*splendour, in his*	descriptive of the sun when depicted in full *spurred* having spurs (of a cock)

A well-attributed beast: *A Griffin passant queue fourché Sable armed and langued Azure membered beaked collared and chained Or the forepaw resting on a closed Book bound Gules clasped edged and irradiated Gold.*

steeled	being of steel
stringed	having a string or strings
studded	having studs
sur le tout	over all
tasselled	having tassels
towered	having towers
tufted	having tufts of hair on tail, limbs, etc. (of beasts)
unguled	describing the hooves of animals
vambraced	wearing armour (of an arm)
veiled	having a veil
vervelled	having thongs with rings attached (of hawks, etc.)
vested	clothed (usually of vestments)
viroled	having decorative bands
voided	of a charge, the centre of which is removed to reveal the field or another tincture
voluted	encircled
vulned	wounded
winged	having wings, descriptive only of creatures who would not normally be possessed of wings
wattled	of the wattles of a cock
wreathed	'wreathed about', encircled by, e.g. a garland

Augmentations of Honour Augmentations of honour are armorial 'additions' of great esteem, usually awarded by a sovereign to subjects deemed worthy of signal recognition. They are of two kinds; the first, now rare, being awarded by 'mere grace', the second being won by merit.

In the first category are such augmentations as those granted by Richard II (1377-99) to his kinsmen Surrey, Exeter and Norfolk, who were permitted to assume the attributed arms of St Edward the Confessor in addition to their own devices, and the three crowns of Ireland, borne within a silver border, to Robert de Vere as Lord of Ireland. In our own century the grant of supporters to Captain Mark Phillips, Princess Anne's husband, may be regarded as an exceptional augmentation.

In the second category there are many instances, again down to the present century, of augmentations granted as rewards for persons performing some outstanding act of valour or service. Such augmentations seem to have existed since the earliest days of armory. There is the story that in the year 1305 a member of the Dodge family was awarded the device of a woman's breast distilling drops of milk, allusive to the grantee's generosity in supplying the army of Edward I with provisions. However, the charge is probably a canting one, a 'dug' being a nipple. Another early 'augmentation' of doubtful provenance dates from 1356 when, after the battle of Poitiers, Sir John de Pelham was supposed to have been awarded two round buckles with thongs to commemorate his capture of the French king. It is true that the Pelham arms were quartered with the buckle device in the seventeenth century, but it is more likely that this was adopted as a personal badge following Poitiers and was not, therefore, a true augmentation. Pelham also adopted a badge of a caged bird, allusive to his capture of the French king. Clearly, many such 'augmentations' were acquired through family tradition and through the later adaptation of personal, commemorative badges into armorial devices.

An early augmentation of proven worth was that given to Piers Legh, who fought in the Black Prince's division at Crecy (1346), but whose family had to wait until the sixteenth century for the award to be promulgated. John Codderington, Henry V's banner-bearer 'in battaile, watch and ward', bore in his arms a red fess and three red lions on silver. In the following reign, his services were rewarded by an augmentation which deliberately broke the tincture convention: his fess was changed to *embattled counter embattled Sable fretty Gules*. Thomas Howard, the first earl of Surrey, the victor of Flodden Field (1513), was awarded an escutcheon charged with a demi-lion pierced in the mouth with an arrow within the double tressure flory counter flory of the Kingdom of Scotland. This, the 'Flodden Augmentation', is borne on the silver bend in the arms of the dukes of Norfolk to this day, commemorating Howard's victory and granted 'that it may be known to all that [victory] was achieved by the generalship, guidance and governance' of their illustrious ancestor. The arrow refers to the fact that King James IV of Scotland was discovered after the battle with his body pierced with arrows. Also in 1513, Sir John Clerk, who had captured the Duc de Longueville at the 'Battle of the Spurs', was granted as an augmentation a canton depicting on a blue field a silver demi-ram (the Duc's supporter, appropriately dissected) and two fleurs-de-lis with a silver baton sinister over all.

An interesting instance from the Elizabethan period is the gift (reputedly by the Queen's express command) of a complete coat of arms to Sir Francis Drake, who had been using the arms of another family of the same name, the Devonshire Drakes, who bore a red wyvern. A dispute between the two Drakes, which ended in Sir Bernard Drake, the lawful owner of the wyvern, boxing Sir Francis' ears, was resolved when Queen Elizabeth declared 'that he had earned better arms for himself, which he should bear by her special favour', and she thereupon granted him arms and crest to commemorate his famous voyage: *Sable a Fess wavy between two Estoils* (Pole Stars) and for a crest *a Ship being drawn round the Globe by the Hand of God issuant from Clouds*. However, Sir Francis had not finished with the unfortunate Sir Bernard, for, quite without authority, he added to his ship crest Sir Bernard's red wyvern, suspended from the rigging by its heels!

The English civil war of the seventeenth century occasioned devices of augmentation both from the hands of King Charles I and from his son. In 1645 Charles I empowered Garter King of Arms to award valiant royalists augmentations of honour. One notable grant was that to Dr Edward Lake who, for services to the king, was given a quartering of honour which included sixteen escutcheons, said to represent the sixteen wounds the doctor received at the battle of Naseby (1645). Other augmentations granted during the Stuart period included that to Major Carlis (later Carlos, in tribute to his sovereign). To commemorate his precarious refuge with the king in an oak tree after the battle of Worcester (1651), he was granted arms *Or on a Mount in base Vert an Oak Tree proper fructed Or surmounted by a Fess Gules charged with three Imperial Crowns of the third*. Colonel Newman, who also aided Charles II at Worcester, was granted an augmentation of *an Escutcheon Gules a Portcullis imperially crowned Or*, recalling Newman's service in enabling Charles to escape through the city gates after the battle. There are numerous other grants of augmentations of honour, made to supporters when 'the King enjoyed his own again', and these record his escapades and the bravado of those who served him, as well as any historical novel.

During the Stuart period, the family of Churchill received two augmentations of honour. The first was granted to Sir Winston Churchill for services to Charles I, and comprised *a Canton of St George*. The second, to his son John, Duke of Marlborough, following his victory at Blenheim, was *an Escutcheon of St George charged with another of France Modern to be borne in chief on his quartered arms*.

Two augmentations granted to members of notable Scottish families during the troubled seventeenth century relate to the keeping of that country's royal regalia during the civil war. The jewels were entrusted to the Keith family Earls Marischal of Scotland, and Sir John of that Name, 1st earl of Kintore, was granted an inescutcheon of *Gules a Sceptre and Sword in saltire in chief the Royal Crown within an orle of Thistles Or*. The second award was to George Ogilvy of Barras who, having played a part in saving the Crown Jewels, was created a baronet and assigned the arms *Argent a Lion passant guardant Gules holding in the dexter paw a Sword proper defending a Thistle ensigned with a Crown Or in the dexter chief point*.

Until the eighteenth century most augmentations were fairly restrained in design, but changes in fashion and the influence of 'new money' introduced what we may regard as vulgar practices in the design of armorial bearings, and augmentations were not excepted from this deterioration. Perhaps the worst (and best known) example is that of Horatio Nelson, who after the Battle of the Nile was allowed *A Chief undy* containing a landscape showing a palm tree, a disabled ship, and a battery in ruins. After Nelson's death a second augmentation was granted as *A Fess wavy Azure charged with the word Trafalgar Or*. These two additions almost obliterated the original arms *Or a Cross patonce sable*, and to modern eyes completely ruined them. The augmentation granted to Arthur Wellesley, Duke of Wellington, was more muted and comprised an inscutcheon of *the Union Badge of the United Kingdom*.

At this time many augmentations of honour incorporated objects from the wars both on land and sea. Those granted to Lord Gough for his victories in the Peninsular War and in India included a fortress, a French eagle, and the words 'China' and 'India'. The grant to General Ross, who won the Battle of Bladensburg during the war of 1812 and then took the city of Washington itself, was granted the augmentation of an arm holding the flag of the United States with a broken flagstaff. There were many more of a similarly ostentatious kind. Not all augmentations granted during this period were for deeds of valour or derring-do, nor indeed were they flamboyant. Just before the 1914-18 war Sir James Reid, a royal physician, was granted *on a Chief Gules a Lion passant guardant Or*, and two other doctors attendant on the royal family — Sir Frederick Treves and Sir Francis Laking — received augmentations bearing the lion of England.

Since that time very few augmentations of honour have been assigned; the City of Cardiff, on being declared the capital of Wales, was granted the Queen's royal badge for Wales suspended from the neck of each of its supporters, and in 1963 the former Governor-General of Canada, the Rt Hon. Vincent Massey, was given a blue canton charged with the crest of Canada. With the possible exception of the supporters granted to Captain Mark Phillips on his marriage to the Princess Anne, there have been no further grants of augmentation by grace or for merit. An interesting modern instance of what at first sight appears to be an augmentation of honour, but which in fact is not, concerns the armorial bearings of the island of Malta, which carry a representation of the George Cross in the dexter chief. This charge is an integral part of the arms assigned to Malta in 1964 when she achieved independence, replacing the arms borne by the island as a colony.

In Europe, augmentations (or similar marks of favour) have, from early times, been granted by appreciative rulers to loyal subjects. The following instances are typical:

France The use of devices taken from the royal arms was the normal favour. This is exemplified in the case of the family of Jeanne de Arc (given the surname du Lys by the French king) which was granted the addition of a fleur-de-lys, Jeanne herself receiving an augmentation of a sword. The addition of a 'roundel of France' (a blue circle carrying three gold fleurs-de-lys) was granted to Piero de Medici.

Belgium The Belgian kings (after 1831) have granted a number of augmentations in the form of a canton carrying the Belgian flag. A rather nice exception to this was to Francois Dhanis in 1894, who was permitted to assume, on a chief, the flag of the Congo where he had been an *inspecteur d'etat*.

Spain Augmentations in this country were frequently charges of an allegorical nature. The arms of two of the most distinguished Castilian families have picturesque additions which show representations of manacled Moorish sovereigns in allusion to the history of Spain. The arms of the Davila family bears the 'augmentation' of the French king chained to a bridge, illustrating the victory of Don Diego de Avila at the Battle of Pavia in 1528.

Portugal Various charges placed on a bordure appear in Portuguese augmentations. (In both Portugal and Spain the bordure is a symbol of strength.) A favourite device employed the use of escutcheons (*quintas*, or silver roundels) from the Portuguese royal arms placed within a distinctive bordure.

Norway and Sweden These Scandinavian countries were often at war with each other, and the augmentations granted to their armigerous families reflect the strife. One unusual example concerns the Spens, originally from Scotland, but who settled in Sweden in the seventeenth century. Sir James Spens, who helped to bring peace between Norway and his adopted country, was made a Swedish baron, and his arms were augmented with a canton showing the three crowns of Sweden.

Denmark Peter Wessel (later surnamed Tordenskjold when ennobled) was granted arms consisting entirely of augmentations. His crest, which bore a white eagle's leg holding a thunderbolt (*tordenskjold*) between two naval ensigns, alluded to the naval exploits of this famous commander.

Prussia The renowned field marshal Leberecht von Blücher was granted new armorial bearings in 1814 on being created Prince von Wahlstatt. Except for an inescutcheon and the crest the complete achievement consisted of augmentations: the eagle of Prussia, a field marshal's baton crossed saltirewise with a sword enfiled by a laurel wreath, and the Iron Cross.   SS

Further reading
Huxford, J.F. *Honour & Arms* London, 1985.
Scott-Giles, C.W. *The Romance of Heraldry* London, revised 1965.
Von Volborth, C.A. *Heraldry, Customs, Rules & Styles* Poole, 1981.

Aulned *see* **Attributes**

Australia, Order of This was instituted by the Queen upon the advice of her Australian ministers on 14 February, 1975. General division and military division in four categories: Knight or Dame, AK or AD; Companion, AC; Officer, AO; Member, AM. There is also a Medal of the Order, OAM.   CS

Austria, Armorial Practice From 1919 the laws of Austria forbade the official use of armorial achievements, although Decorations of Honour remain (*Ehrenzeichen für Verdienste um die Republik*). Even in the days of Empire there was no state body charged with recording arms, but armorial usage was rigidly controlled, and from about 1760 it was forbidden for families who were not of noble degree to display arms without specific royal permission. Armory followed the wide-spread European convention of depicting the shield, quartered and augmented where appropriate, with any supporters, on a manteau gathered at the upper extremities, 'tied' with cords, and topped by a crown (or hat) of the appropriate degree. Crested helms were depicted resting on the top of the shield (there were exceptions) and insignia were incorporated behind or surrounding the arms. Today there are many Austrians who continue to uphold the armorial and heraldic traditions of their country.

From 1950 an Austrian Roll of Arms (*Österreichishe Wappenrolle*) has been maintained by the Heraldisch-Genealogische Gesellschaft Adler (*see* ADDRESSES).
                    JC-K

Austria, Imperial Arms *A double-headed Eagle Sable armed and membered Gules the heads regally crowned holding in the dexter claw a Sword and Sceptre and in the sinister claw an Orb all proper charged on the breast with a Shield tierced palewise*: dexter *Or a Lion rampant Gules armed langued and crowned Azure* (Hapsburg): centre *Gules a Fess Argent* (Austria): sinister *Or on a Bend Gules three Ailerons Argent* (Lorraine). The shield surrounded by the Collar of the Golden Fleece.

On the wings and tail of the eagle are the shields for the kingdoms and provinces of the Empire: Hungary Ancient *Barry of eight Argent and Gules* impaling Hungary Modern *Gules on a Mount Vert an Open Crown Or issuant therefrom a Patriarchal Cross Argent*: Galicia *Azure a Bar Gules between in chief a Crow Sable and in base three Ancient Crowns Or*: Upper Austria *Per pale Or an Eagle displayed Sable dimidiating Gules two Pallets Argent* impaling Lower Austria *Azure five Eagles displayed Or armed Gules 2 2 and 1*: Salzburg *Per pale Or a Lion rampant Sable impaling Gules a Fess Argent*: Styria *Vert a Griffin segreant queue fourché Argent breathing Flames proper crowned Or*: Tyrol *Argent an Eagle displayed Gules crowned and having 'Klee Stengeln' on the wings Or*:

Bohemia *Gules a Lion rampant Argent double queued crowned Or*: Illyria *Azure an Antique Galley Or*: Siebenbürgen *Per Fess Azure and Or over all a Bar Gules issuant therefrom a demi-Eagle displayed Sable with in dexter chief a Sun in Splendour Or and in sinister chief a Crescent Argent in base seven Towers Gules 4 and 3*: Moravia *Azure an Eagle displayed chequy Gules and Argent Crowned Or* impaling Silesia *Or an Eagle displayed Sable crowned Or charged on the breast with a Crescent and Crosslet Argent*: Carinthia *Or three Lions passant contourné Sable* (Swabia) impaling Carniola *Argent an Eagle displayed Azure charged on the breast with a Crescent counter-compony Argent and Gules*. Above the two regally crowned heads of the Eagle the Imperial Crown of Austria.   KH
Further reading
Neubecker, O. *Heraldry, Sources, Symbols and Meaning* London, 1977.

Avant-Garde The front line in battle formation.   PG

Avenor Sometimes rendered 'avener', this was in feudal times the title of the chief officer of the stables, in charge of the animals' foodstuffs. As late as 1643 the Earl of Carnarvon was Hereditary Chief Avenor of the Crown.   JC-K

Aventille *or* **Avantail** The hood of a hauberk or the movable front lower edge of a helmet. (This term is also often used to describe a camail.)   PG

Aversant *see* **Attitude**

Azure The armorial tincture blue. Abbreviated Az, or preferably B, which cannot be confused with Ar (Argent).
See also TINCTURES

B

Bachelor A young knight who followed the banner of another, more senior, knight. The term may come from *bas-chevalier*. The phrase 'community of bachelors appears in the record of the October parliament of 1259. In the *Quo Warranto* rolls, the Lord (Prince) Edward, later Edward I, is described (in this sense of a young knight) as a bachelor. In the present century a knight bachelor is a simple knight, a member of no chivalric order.   JC-K

Kyng Edward
the iiij.

The Duc off Clarence — ...
A. 1000. Blake Bulle

The Duc of Gloucester — ...
A. 1000. Whytt Bore

The Duc off Norffolke — ...
A. 300. Whytt Lyon

The Duc of Suffolke — ...
A. 300. Lyon off Gold the Kew foregyled

The Duc off Bokyngham — ...
A. 200. the Stafford Knot...

Badge An armorial device, not part of the coat of arms, but in England available to an armigerous person or corporation for the purpose of identification. The armorial badge has acquired four distinct functions:

Personal Appropriate to an armiger for the adornment of clothing, jewellery, fabrics, furnishings and artefacts; for marking small personal possessions and for other decorative purposes, for example in stained glass and architectural features. Included in this category are badges bestowed by the Crown or nobility as a mark of personal favour, and those worn in place of coats of arms by knights who, for reasons of political or romantic deception, wished to remain anonymous in the tournament lists.

Livery (Household) Issued in conjunction with livery colours to retainers and armed retinues to be worn on uniforms and borne on livery flags.

Official Associated with specific household or corporate offices, including those of the Crown, government and judiciary.

Corporate Badges of members of corporate bodies (e.g. guilds and fraternities), orders of chivalry, etc.

In the fourteenth and fifteenth centuries, the household badge was more familiar to the medieval man in the street than were the armorial bearings of the nobility. Inns where local retainers congregated took the identity of their patron by painting his badge above the door. Allegiance to a faction or to a royal

Extract from a muster roll of Edward IV's French campaign in 1475.

house was often demonstrated in this way (many a white boar of Richard of Gloucester being changed hastily to the blue boar of de Vere following Bosworth Field!). Many such INN SIGNS are in evidence today, e.g. the ubiquitous white hart of Richard II, the swan of Bohun, the talbot of the Talbot earls of Shrewsbury, and the green dragon of the Herberts. Barnard's *Book of Badges*, a muster roll of Edward IV's expedition to France (1475), includes sketchy exemplifications of the magnates' livery badges in the margin: the black bull of Clarence, the white boar of Richard of Gloucester, the white lion of Norfolk, the Stafford knot of Buckingham, and numerous other household badges appear, alongside details of troops pledged to the wars, including that of Lord Hastings who commanded a contingent of forty lances and three-hundred archers, all wearing his black and gold bull's head device. However, in Fenn's *Book of badges*, compiled only five years earlier, Hastings' badge is listed as a mantyger, suggesting that the bull's head was a livery badge (it was also his crest) and the mantyger a personal one. Grants of badges were rare at this time, and there appears to have been little attempt at recording them until the early sixteenth century. Fox-Davies (*Heraldic Badges*) states: '... badges were personal, and though they were worn by retainers they were the property of the head of the family rather than (as the arms) the whole family. The likelihood is that cadets would render feudal service

41

The Yorkist falcon and fetterlock badge in the Royal Window, Canterbury Cathedral.

and wear the badge as retainers of the man whose standard they followed.'

The livery badge was generally associated with those medieval magnates who were capable of sustaining military levies of several hundred men. Power of this magnitude represented a constant threat to the peace of the realm, and successive English kings

attempted to suppress the private armies of the nobility by restricting the use of liveries and badges to household retainers (*see* LIVERY AND MAINTENANCE).

During the Middle Ages many badges were adopted as crests by the nobility and by the Tudor period the crest had become a symbol of particular distinction. It was inevitable, therefore, that armigers who were anxious to demonstrate their newly acquired gentility, but who did not possess a crest, should adopt their badges for this purpose. The practice was often legitimized by the heralds' visitations: the sledge badge of the Stourton family was recorded as a crest by a cadet of that house, for example.

Standards of the medieval and Tudor periods were often charged with more than one badge, the largest (that nearest the hoist) was the noble's principal device (often a beast badge) associated with his major estate, the others being those of subsidiary territories from which his retainers would also be drawn. Some nobles would require more than one standard for this purpose, and the soldier would wear the badge of the estate where he was retained. All would muster and march beneath the standard or follow the guidon into battle.

Badges of Office were highly prized and were often incorporated in livery collars and insignia as they are today. The badges of the present English and Scottish officers of arms afford excellent examples of this type of badge.

Although the use of badges was widespread in medieval Britain, their development in European countries seems to have been restricted to the higher echelons of the nobility and to the numerous orders of chivalry, e.g. the two fire buckets attached to a blazing branch, the badge of John Galeazzo, Duke of Milan; and the griffin, steel and flint insignia of the Order of the Golden Fleece, an order of knights based on feudal loyalty. French badges of the medieval period were essentially personal, and those of Italy (called *imprese*) were of the most abstruse kind. Many English badges were adopted for their hidden meaning, others were combinations of badges obtained through marriage and alliance. An example of the former type is the famous falcon and fetterlock badge of Richard Plantagenet, Duke of York. Political verses of the time suggest that this badge symbolized York's aspirations by showing the fetterlock (manacle) open so that the falcon was no longer confined, as Edmund of Langley had borne it. The badge of John de Vere, Earl of Oxford (a bottle with a blue cord) was a pun on his name: *de verre* being 'of glass'. The famous bear and ragged (raguly) staff badge of Richard Nevill, Earl of Warwick (the Kingmaker) is an example of the combined badges of two houses forming a single device, as is the well known Tudor Rose which symbolized the union of the houses of York and Lancaster by Henry VII's marriage with Elizabeth of York. The combined badges of Edward VI (the Tudor Rose and Sun in Splendour) have recently been granted in the arms of Sherborne, Dorset, where Sherborne School (King's School) was reconstituted by Edward in 1550. Badges were often dimidiated to illustrate alliance: that of Henry VIII, for example, which shows the dexter half of the Tudor Rose joined to the sinister half of the pomegranate badge of Grenada, during his marriage with Katherine of Aragon.

Following the period of heraldic decadence of the late Tudors, badges ceased to be used to any extent. Victorian armigers, denied both understanding of the function of badges and the encouragement of the heraldic authorities to register them, used crests on servants' buttons and liveries.

In 1906 the College of Arms began to grant badges, though the type of badge is not specified in the patent. Any English armiger to whom a badge is granted may have it depicted on a standard and, by inference, it must therefore be a livery badge. This practice is illogical for it assumes the existence of a 'following' which has need of a means of identification other than the personal arms of the armiger. Livery badges (and therefore standards) should be reserved for civic and corporate bodies, clubs, societies, schools, etc., who are able to demonstrate that such devices are necessary for use on the uniforms of members and employees. Other armigers should be granted personal badges which, by definition, should not be exemplified on standards.

Fox-Davies (*Heraldic Badges*) states 'In any matter of record the [livery] badge is almost invariably depicted on a background' and 'it may only be considered correct when the colour of the standard happens to be the right colour for the background of the badge.' Clearly, livery badges should be displayed on the livery colours, and yet the selection of colours for the fields of English standards appears to be entirely arbitrary. This, perhaps, further demonstrates the illogicality of assigning livery badges and standards to those who have no need of them.

Badges may be devolved to an heir, and may be licensed for use by subsidiary organizations within

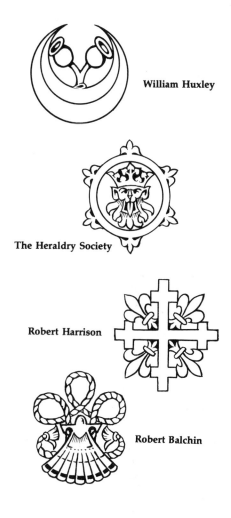

William Huxley

The Heraldry Society

Robert Harrison

Robert Balchin

Examples of twentieth century English armorial badges.

John Galeazzo, of the House of Visconti, Duke of Milan. Late 14th century *impresa*.

Clive Allen

43

the jurisdiction of an armigerous local authority. Such 'licensing' of livery badges is undertaken with the consent of the kings of arms, providing their rights are not abused.

But to what extent does the jurisdiction of the heraldic authorities apply to such devices? Anyone (whether armigerous or not) who wishes to adopt a device for his personal use is at liberty to do so, providing it has not been granted by letters patent as an armorial badge or is subject to copyright or trademark regulation. Indeed, there seems to be no reason why an armiger may not assume a device and use it in addition to his armorial bearings as did his medieval ancestors. The dilemma appears to be one of definition: how may a device be recognized as armorial other than by placing it on a shield?

In Scotland, armorial badges are strictly reserved for Chiefs of Clans and Families and members of the Baronage of Scotland. Lord Lyon exercises considerable authority in such matters, whilst the position of the English kings of arms remains obscure.

There are many medieval precedents for the display of personal badges in an achievement of arms. Thomas Mowbray, first Duke of Norfolk, incorporated his ostrich feather badge (a gift of Richard II) by placing one on either side of his shield. Badges have been depicted beside the crest or below the shield, and there are several instances of badges charged on the mantling, as in the Garter stall plate of Francis, Viscount Lovel, whose badge was a square padlock (see colour page 301). A modern example is that in the patent of arms of the Heraldry Society, in which the Society's badge is displayed on the mantling. Fox-Davies and Gayre (*Heraldic Standards and Other Ensigns*) suggest that in such cases the mantling should be of the livery colours associated with the badge.

See also ARMORIAL BEARINGS, USE OF; CYPHER; GUIDON; KNOT; LIVERY COLOURS; LIVERY AND MAINTENANCE; REBUS; STANDARD

Further reading
Fox-Davies, A.C. *Heraldic Badges* London, 1907. An alphabet of medieval badges and livery colours. The only book devoted to this subject and now not readily available.
Gayre, R. *Heraldic Standards and Other Ensigns* London, 1959. Includes an excellent chapter on 'The Household Badge'.

Badge Banner *see* **Livery Banner**

Bagwyn A monster similar to an heraldic antelope but with the tail of a horse and long curved horns.

Bailiff A manager of a district — be he the chief officer of a medieval hundred, a magistrate, a custodian of

important property, or a sheriff's deputy who executed writs.   JC-K

Baldric *or* **Baldrick** A shoulder belt, generally used to carry a weapon.   PG

Balista A firing machine for bombardment, using stones or darts, similar in function to a cross-bow but huge by comparison.   PG

Banded *see* **Attributes**

Banderolle

Banderolle (i) A small streamer attached to, for example, a crozier.
(ii) A fillet attached to the helm of a mounted knight to restrain the mantling. This consisted either of twisted silk cords or a ribbon which was sometimes decorated with armorial charges, and even the slogan. Frequently confused with the WREATH (also torse) which is similar in both appearance and function. However, there are examples of both banderolle *and* wreath depicted in the same achievement, which suggests that they were not synonymous: It is possible that the wreath was simply the mantling, rolled into a convenient fillet and tied at the back of the helmet, and that the banderolle was an additional means of holding it in place. Some armorists have suggested that the banderolle was the silk scarf (contoise or cointise) awarded to a knight as a mark of a lady's favour and carried throughout a tournament. Several banderolles appear in Scottish armory, where they are occasionally used instead of wreaths. They are of the principal tinctures of the arms, there being just three 'twists' in the affronty position, with the metal being the central one. From the side the ribbons appear to stream from each side of the helm, and have a very pleasing appearance.

Banner A square or oblong flag emblazoned with the arms and sometimes fringed with the livery or armorial colours. It was the principal personal flag, used throughout the Middle Ages by the nobility down to the knights banneret. During the 'Heraldry of the Decadence' specific proportions were laid down for the various ranks, following (apparently) medieval precedents, though it is highly unlikely that such regulations were ever observed. The banner was, and is, an indication of the presence of the armiger. Consequently, it was considered a great disgrace to lose one's banner in battle (unlike the standard, guidon, etc., which were not personal ensigns), and to raise one's banner in the field of battle was a clear indication of a noble's commitment. Unlike the livery flags, only one banner would be taken into battle, and this would accompany its owner wherever he went. Modern banners tend to be much too broad (the banners of the British royal family, for example), forcing the charges into all sorts of elongated contortions. Early banners were often longer in the hoist than in the fly, and those of the later Middle Ages were usually square. Fair-weather banners are now generally of the proportions three to two, while ceremonial banners for indoor use are square. In countries which are subject to the jurisdiction of the College of Arms, all armigers are permitted to display their arms in the form of a banner. In Scotland, Lord Lyon has laid down regulations for their use.

Another type of banner, used in medieval Europe though rarely in Britain, was a long, tapering flag similar in shape to an elongated pennon. It has been suggested in some reference books that such flags were STANDARDS; however, they were charged neither with liveries nor badges but with personal arms, and were, therefore, banners. In the Middle Ages the banner was also known as the lieutenant and was the responsibility of an officer of that name.
See also FLAG

Banneret (i) The rank of the nobility between knight bachelor and baron. Originally a chief feudal tenant (or lesser baron) as distinct from the knight bachelor.
(ii) The small banner of a knight banneret on which were depicted his personal arms.
See also FLAG

Banneroll *or* **Bannerole** (i) A small banner, often stiffened or supported along its upper edge, used at funerals to display the armorial bearings of families associated with the deceased.
(ii) During the 'Heraldry of the Decadence' the banner appropriate to a knight, esquire or gentleman, being three feet square.
See also FLAG

Bar *and* **Bars Gemel** *see* **Fess**

Barbados, Order of This was created by the Queen upon the advice of her Barbadian ministers by Letters Patent of 27 July, 1980. The Order comprises four classes: Knight or Dame of St Andrew, KA or DA;

Companion of Honour of Barbados, CHB; The Crown of Merit (gold or silver), GCM or SCM; The Barbados Service Award (star or medal), BSS or BSM. A Knight or Dame of St Andrew is entitled to the prefix Sir or Dame, as the case may be. A Companion of Honour is entitled to the description of The Honourable.   CS

Barbed *see* **Attributes**

Barbutte A salade helmet, often with a T-shaped opening at the front.   PG

Barded *see* **Attributes**

Barding A general term to describe both the armour and trappings of a horse. Early barding consisted of a heavy covering of mail with four 'skirts' to protect the animal's legs. Later horse armour consisted of a series of plates protecting the head and neck to which, at a later date, were added the peytral (covering the chest) and crupper (covering the hind quarters) of leather, wood or plate. Often used in armory as a synonym for CAPARISON.

Bargemaster The River Thames was once the main artery of the populous southeast of England. It provided a convenient and more reliable means of passage than the filthy and often dangerous streets of the metropolis, and barges of all sizes plied the river in the Middle Ages just as the familiar taxi cabs navigate the streets today. It was not by chance that the royal palaces, the Tower, Greenwich, Sheen, Windsor, Hampton Court and, of course, Westminster were sited at the river's edge.

Although the Royal State barge is no longer in regular use, the English sovereign continues to appoint one of her twenty-four Royal Watermen to be Queen's Bargemaster. From past occasions on which the Queen's Bargemaster and Royal Watermen personally conveyed the sovereign in water-borne procession remains the privilege of marching and riding in immediate attendance on the sovereign on state occasions, and the Watermen convey the royal crown in Queen Alexandra's coach from Buckingham Palace to the House of Lords for the State Opening of Parliament, just as their medieval predecessors carried the crown by water from the Tower to the Palace of Westminster. The uniform, of royal scarlet, is the skirted tunic of the Thames Watermen from whose ranks the Royal Watermen are selected. Each wears a dark blue cap, scarlet stockings, a white shirt and black shoes. On the chest and back they wear large, oval, silver badges of the royal crown above the EIIR cypher and conjoined shamrock, thistle and rose. The Queen's Bargemaster wears a tail-coat jacket with gold braid, his stockings are white and his badge is worn within a hexagonal gold-trimmed panel. The salary of a Royal Waterman is £3.50.

State barges were also maintained by several of the LIVERY COMPANIES OF THE CITY OF LONDON for use in mayoral processions, and the Fishmongers, the Vintners, the Dyers and the Guild of Watermen and Lightermen continue to appoint their own bargemasters, each with his distinctive livery. The Fishmongers' Company administers the longest and, possibly, the toughest sculling race in the world. The Doggett's Coat and Badge Race is rowed over a four-and-a-half mile course from the Old Swan at London Bridge to the White Swan at Chelsea, and commemorates the occasion, on 1 August 1715, when one Thomas Doggett, an Irish actor and comedian and an ardent royalist, placed a placard on London Bridge: 'This being the day of His Majesty's [George I] happy accession to the throne there will be given by Mr Doggett an Orange Colour Livery with a Badge representing Liberty to be rowed for by Six Watermen that are out of their time within the year past. They are to row from London Bridge to Chelsea. It will be continued annually on the same day forever.' The race is still held in July, and the coveted prize of the Coat (now red) and the silver Badge is presented in Fishmongers' Hall in November, when all former Doggetts form a guard of honour.   JA

Further reading
Cook, T.A. and G. Nickalls *Thomas Doggett, Deceased* London, 1908.

Baron The fifth and lowest rank in the British peerage. The word itself is of uncertain origin. It was introduced into England to identify the 'man' (that is to say, vassal) of a great lord, or of the Conqueror himself. Indeed, in the days following the Conquest all tenants-in-chief of the king, and below the rank of earl, were invariably called barons. From the thirteenth century onward, the title appears to have been reserved for those magnates summoned by writ to parliament, whilst at a later date barons were 'created' by letters patent.

The actual style of 'baron' was first introduced by Richard II in 1347, the next creation being in 1433, and various Acts of Parliament since have affected the creation of the rank: the most recent, the Life Peerage Act of 1958, enables the Crown to advance anyone to a peerage for life.

The robes of a baron are similar to those of a DUKE, with the exceptions that his coronation robe has two rows of ermine and his parliamentary robe of estate two guards of plain white fur. The coronet of a baron has six silver balls at equal distance around the rim. The armorial privileges of a baron are as those of a Duke, and the wife of a baron is styled Lady.   JC-K
See also BARONAGE OF SCOTLAND

Baronage of Scotland This is a feudal institution and is quite different from that of England. What in

England is a baron is, in Scotland, a Lord of Parliament. A Scottish baron is rather similar to an English lord of the manor with, in addition, nobiliary rights as accorded to certain European barons. A Scottish baron has various armorial prerogatives not unlike those of a peer, including a cap of maintenance, supporters, a barred helm garnished with gold, a robe or mantle, uniquely specified flags and, as befits the ancient institution, a Baron Court. A baron of Scotland is also permitted two pipers, each displaying an armorial pipe banner.

The style of the cap of maintenance varies according to whether the bearer is a Baron of the Kingdom (in possession of the barony or not), or a Baron of Argyll and the Isles (in possession or not). In the first case the cap is *Gules furred Ermine* and in the second *Azure furred Ermines*. The cap is depicted ensigning the shield of arms, beneath the helm and crest. The robe, or mantle, may be displayed draped (very much in the European fashion) behind the achievement of a baron actually in possession of a barony, and is described as *Gules doubled of Silk Argent fur edged of Miniver and Collar Ermine fastened on the right shoulder by five spherical Buttons Or.* The Scottish feudal baronial helm is of steel with one or three grilles (one being by far the more usual) garnished with gold. The helm is normally shown affronty. Supporters may be used by the heirs of baronies held before 1587, and possibly for baronies held between that date and 1627 (the point is not fully resolved). On the matter of flags, a Scottish baron may adorn the top of his staff with a cap of maintenance, and employ, as he sees fit, standards, guidons and pennons.   JC-K

Further reading
Agnew, C.H., Younger of Lochnaw 'The Baronage of Scotland' in *Coat of Arms* Vol.IX, No.72, October 1967.
Forrester, D.I.G. 'The Heraldry & Insignia of the Baronage of Scotland' in *Coat of Arms* Vol.V, No.126, Summer 1983.

Baron-Baillie *see* **Baron Court (Scotland)**

Baron Court (Scotland) As in England a lord of the manor had his local court, so in Scotland the holder of a feudal barony (*see* BARONAGE OF SCOTLAND) has, implicitly, a Baron Court. The president of such a court is a Baron-Baillie and the chief officer a Baron-Serjeant. The insignia of a Baron-Baillie is a flat cap of justice, environed by two guards of braid and usually in the livery colours of the baron concerned. A very few Baron-Baillies have gowns, badges and pendants relevant to the estate they serve. The symbols for a Baron-Serjeant are a white wand of peace one Scottish ell in length (3 feet, or just under a metre), and a horn.   JC-K

Baroness A baron's wife (usually called Lady), or a woman who holds a barony in her own right (usually called Baroness). The robe of a baroness is similar to that of a DUCHESS, with the exceptions that it is trimmed with two rows of ermine, the edging being two inches broad and the train one yard on the ground. The coronet of a baroness is also similar to that of a duchess, with the difference that it carries on the circlet six silver balls (representing pearls) not raised on points. The arms of a baroness in her own right are similar to those of a duchess, but surmounted by the coronet of her own degree. JC- K

Baronetcy This hereditary English rank was created by James I on 22 May 1611, with the objective of raising money to support troops in Ulster. The 'honour' cost the first recipients £1095, and they were allowed the prefix Sir and Lady (or Dame) with precedence above knights. On 28 May 1625 a baronetage of Scotland was established to provide funds for the colonization of Nova Scotia. Both creations lasted until 1707, when the ranks were replaced by the baronetage of Great Britain, which lasted until 31 December 1800. On 30 September 1619 the baronetage of Ireland was created, and this also lasted until 1800. On 1 January 1801 both the baronetage of Great Britain and that of Ireland were replaced by the baronetage of the United Kingdom, which continues to the present time.

Baronets are permitted to use a knight's helmet, affronty and open, in their armorial bearings, this convention dating from the time of the Restoration. It is, however, possible to find the occasional exception to the convention (the arms of Barry, 1899, show the vizor closed, for example), and a relaxation of the convention for aesthetic purposes has resulted in a number of recent exemplifications of arms in which the helmets both of baronets and knights have been depicted in positions more in keeping with their crests.

Baronets of England, Ireland, Great Britain and the United Kingdom have as their badge the 'bloody hand of Ulster' *Argent a sinister Hand couped at the wrist Gules*, and this is borne as an augmentation to their arms, either on an escutcheon or canton. In 1929 George V granted all baronets, other than those of Nova Scotia, a variation of this badge to be worn on the person or suspended beneath the shield of arms. The badge is contained within a blue border decorated with roses for baronets of England, shamrock for baronets of Ireland, roses and thistles for baronets of Great Britain, and roses, thistles and shamrock for baronets of the United Kingdom. This badge is ensigned with the Imperial Crown and is pendent from an orange-tawny ribbon with a dark blue edge, worn about the neck.

The Baronets of Scotland were originally authorized to augment their arms with a canton or escutcheon bearing the arms of the Province of Nova Scotia *Argent on a Saltire Azure an Escutcheon of the Royal Arms of Scotland*, together with the crest, supporters and motto. However, by a grant of Charles I they were assigned a badge comprising the shield of arms of Nova Scotia within a blue circlet edged and lettered in gold and inscribed with the motto 'Fax Mentis Honestae Gloria'. This is worn about the neck pendent from a tawny coloured ribbon or depicted below the shield in an achievement.

There seems to be no hard and fast rule regarding the granting of supporters to holders of baronetcies. Although the majority do not have supporters, it is possible to quote instances from all five creations where supporters are used: Dering (England) 1627, Johnston (Scotland) 1626, Cusack-Smith (Ireland) 1799, Dalrymple-Hay (Great Britain) 1728, Gordon-Cumming (United Kingdom) 1804, and numerous others. JC-K

Further reading
Cokayne, G.E. *Complete Baronetage* 1906 (reprinted 1982).

Baron of the Kingdom (Scotland) *see* **Baronage of Scotland**

Baron-Serjeant *see* **Baron Court (Scotland)**

Barrulet *see* **Fess**

Barry *and* **Barruly** *see* **Field, Varied**

Barry-Bendy *see* **Field, Varied**

Bascinet, Bacinet *or* **Basinet** Helmet for the upper head, usually joined by its lower edge to jaw and neck protection, and often with hinged vizor. A great bascinet incorporated jaw and neck protection, which were usually shaped plates riveted in position. PG

Base The lower portion of the shield. A charge depicted in this position is termed in base (*see* SHIELD, POINTS OF THE). In armory the base is considered to be inferior to the chief or upper portion.

Confusingly, armorists who insist that the CHIEF is an ordinary are equally insistent that the base is a partition. Logically there can be no *party per base* without a corresponding *party per chief* — and there is no such partition. Both are sub-ordinaries (as here defined); however, to the chief may be ascribed an additional function — that of augmentation — which endows it with a distinction not enjoyed by the humble base. Sometimes emblazoned as a champagne, and more commonly found in European armory than in British.

The **Bastard of Haubourdin** from the *Armorial Equestre de la Toison d'Or*. **Note the bendlet sinister 'debruising' the arms.**

Basilisk *see* **Cockatrice**

Bastardy If an illegitimate child can prove paternity, or if his natural father acknowledges paternity, he may petition for a royal warrant by which he may be granted the arms of his father charged with appropriate marks of distinction. The inheritance of honours is specifically excluded in current legislation relating to illegitimacy and inheritance, and it is unlikely that this will be amended in the foreseeable future. Such a change would also require the nature of arms to be redefined. Of course, there is nothing to prevent an illegitimate person from applying for arms in his own right.

Contrary to popular belief, it is not the bend sinister which signifies bastardy, but the particularly unattractive bordure wavy which has been in use since the eighteenth century and which replaced the bendlet sinister for this purpose. Occasionally other charges have been used, for example the maternal canton of Sir John de Warren, natural son of the Earl of Surrey, Sussex and Warrenne (1347). However, the armorist should not jump to conclusions and should always seek secondary evidence whenever illegitimacy appears to be indicated. Care should be exercised regarding the concept of bastardy itself: frequently such MARKS OF DISTINCTION are intended as an indication that the bearer is not in legitimate line of succession, not that he is personally illegitimate. In Scotland a variety of bordures is used in a complex system of cadency, the bordure compony being reserved to indicate illegitimacy. The baton sinister (erroneously called the 'bar' sinister by fiction writers) has been used, almost without exception, to denote the illegitimate offspring of the English royal family, though there have been notable variations, particularly during the Middle Ages when there were few established armorial conventions relating to bastardy. The Beauforts, for example, the illegitimate line of John of Gaunt and Katherine Swynford, adopted as their arms, on a shield per pale of the Lancastrian liveries, argent and azure, *a Bend charged with three Gold Lions and a Label Azure semy of Fleur-de-lis*. Following their legitimation in 1397 they used the famous *Bordure compony Argent and Azure* with the royal arms.

Although in England such marks of distinction are theoretically abatements of honour, in the Middle Ages to be in any way related to the Crown, or for that matter to the nobility, was considered a privilege worth advertising.

Further reading
Given-Wilson, C. and A. Curtels *The Royal Bastards of Medieval England* 1984.

Baston An alternative term for baton, a couped bendlet. *See also* BEND

Bataille The middle guard in battle formation, behind the avant-garde and before the arriere-garde.   PG

Bath, The Most Honourable Order of the This is the premier meritorious Order of the Crown. Established by George I on 18 May 1725, and modelled on a 'degree of knighthood, which hath been denominated the Knighthood of the Bath' by Henry IV in 1399, the designation 'of the Bath' acknowledged the ritual of purification undertaken by the knight-elect prior to receiving the accolade. In 1735 this degree of knighthood was restored as a 'regular military Order' of thirty-six Knights Companion, called the Most Honourable Military Order of the Bath. Henry VII's chapel in Westminster Abbey was appointed its chapel. In 1815 the Order was reorganized, with civil and military divisions. Further rearrangements followed in 1847, 1859, 1925 and 1972.

The Order now comprises: the Sovereign, the Great Master, 115 Knights (and Dames) Grand Cross (GCB), 328 Knights (and Dames) Commander (KCB), 1815 Companions (both ladies and gentlemen) (C), with six officers: Dean, Bath King of Arms, Secretary and Registrar, Genealogist, Gentleman Usher of the

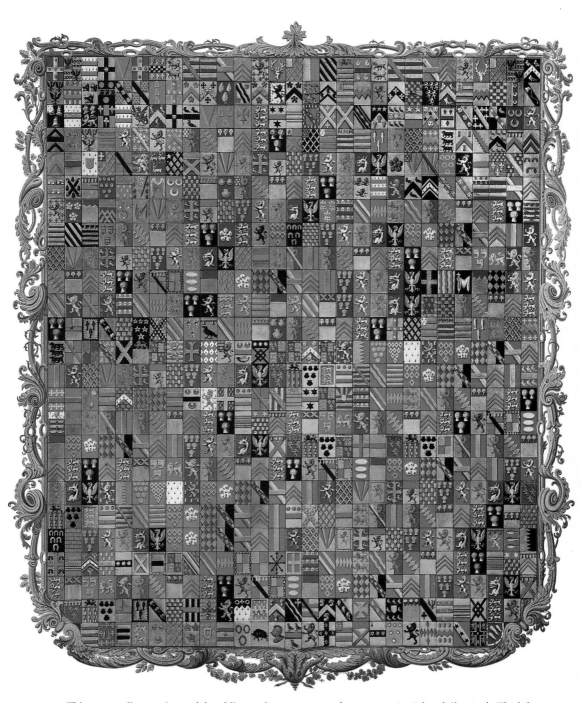

ABOVE This extraordinary piece of heraldic workmanship from the early nineteenth century was commissioned for Richard Plantagenet, Marquis of Chandos, son and heir of the first Duke of Buckingham and Chandos (ext.1889). The diptych shows 719 quarterings accumulated by the family of Temple-Nugent-Brydges-Chandos-Grenville, the only British family to have used a five-part surname. Each of the two panels measures 4 x 3 feet (1½ x 1 m). The left-hand panel (not illustrated) lists the quarterings, which include ten variations of the English royal arms, the arms of Spencer (the family of HRH The Princess of Wales), and the arms of many of the most prominent families of English history, such as De Clare, Valence, Mowbray, Mortimer and De Grey.

BLAZON

The Shield of Arms

**The
Armorial Bearings of
Stephen Friar**

Argent
(the field)

on a Saltire
(ordinary)

dovetailed
(variation of
line)

*per saltire and
quarterly*
(lines of partition)

*Azure and Sable
counterchanged*
(tinctures)

*a Lion's Face
crowned with an
Ancient Crown Or*
(charge borne on
the ordinary)

The Crest

Upon a Helm

*with a Wreath
Argent Azure and Sable*

*out of an
Ancient
Crown Or*

*a male Griffin
segreant Sable*

*armed beaked
and rayed Gold*

*langued and
holding a Key
ward downwards
and outwards
Gules*

*mantled Azure and Sable semy of Friar's
Knots Or doubled Argent tassels Gold*

51

ABOVE Banners, helms and crests of the senior Knights Grand Cross of the Most Honourable Order of the Bath above their stalls in King Henry VII's chapel, Westminster Abbey. When a Knight of the Order dies, his banner, helm and crest are taken down to be replaced by those of his successor. However, the knight's stall plate, emblazoned with his arms, remains affixed to the back of the stall as a permanent memorial.

RIGHT The stall plate of Dr of Dr Conrad Swan, CVO, York Herald of Arms, as Geneaologist of the Most Honourable Order of the Bath, whose duty it is to verify the armorial bearings of each new knight, and to supervise the making of his banner, crest and stall plate. Dr Swan is descended in the male line from Alexander Swięicki, of the *Herb Jastrzębiec*, Elector of King John-Casimir of Poland, 1648. The arms are here differenced by a compony bordure.

52

Scarlet Rod, and Deputy Secretary. To the unlimited honorary subdivision most non-royal heads of state and other distinguished persons, not subjects of the Crown, are admitted when they receive a high token of British recognition.

The insignia of the Order incorporates its arms *Azure three arched Imperial Crowns one and two Or*. That for the civil division follows the original insignia as worn between 1725 and 1815, the military division incorporating a Maltese Cross.

The mantle of the Knights and Dames Grand Cross is silk (murrey lined with white), a star of that grade being embroidered on the upper left side. The collar of the Order is worn over the mantle which, in turn, is worn over service uniform or civilian dress. The collar is composed of alternating gold imperial crowns and groups of rose, thistle and shamrock issuing from a gold sceptre, each linked with a gold knot enamelled in white. Pendent from the collar is the badge. That of the civil division is of gold and is composed of a rose, thistle and shamrock issuing from a sceptre between three imperial crowns one and two, the whole within a circlet bearing the motto 'Tria Juncta In Uno'. The badge of the military division is a gold Maltese Cross of eight points, enamelled in white edged gold, each point terminating in a small gold ball, and with a gold lion passant guardant in each of the four angles. At the centre is the sceptre and crowns device within a red circlet, edged and lettered in gold. This is encompassed by two branches of laurel issuant from an escroll azure bearing the words 'Ich Dien' in gold. The ribbon of the Order is murrey.

The Officers of the Order, excepting the Dean, wear similar mantles but with the colours reversed. On the upper right side are embroidered the arms of the Order. Each Officer wears the appropriate badge, with a triple row of gilt chains, suspended about his neck. The Dean wears, over his clerical vestments, the same robe as a Civil Grand Cross, and round his neck the badge of that rank suspended from a riband.

Installation in the Chapel takes place once every three or four years, coinciding with a service for the whole Order. The basic acts at an installation are essentially those laid down in the statute of 1725: Oath, Installation, Offering and Presentation of the Sword. The limited number of stalls available (34) means only the most senior Knights Grand Cross can be accommodated. Thus, when a stall becomes vacant through death, it passes to the next senior Grand Cross, Military or Civil. The Chapel of the Order contains a splendid display of armory which attests the past and present occupants of the stalls (see colour page 52). The banner above each stall identifies its current holder, and, at the apex of the canopy, is a knight's helm with the crest and mantling of the stall holder. A metal stall plate at the back of each stall includes a representation of the complete armorial

achievement of the occupant (see colour page 52). Some arms therein have supporters, a privilege for life of the Knights Grand Cross. The motto of the Order, 'Tria Juncta In Uno' (three joined in one — a reference to the kingdoms of England, Scotland and Ireland or France), surrounds the shield on a murrey ribband, from the lower edge of which hangs a representation of the badge. When a stall holder dies his banner and crest are taken down to make room for those of his successor, but his stall plate remains as a permanent memorial.

It is the duty of the Genealogist to verify the armorial bearings of each new stall holder, and to supervise the making of the banner, crest, mantling and stall plate for erection in and above the stall.

It may be noted that from 1725 until the early years after the Second World War the inscriptions on the plates were in French, since which time they have been mainly in English.   CS

Further reading
Risk, J.C. *The History of the Order of the Bath and its Insignia* 1972.

Baton *see* **Bend**

Battle Ensign An additional ensign flown by a ship in battle in case one is destroyed.

Bavaria, Royal Arms of Quarterly 1 *Sable a Lion rampant Or armed langued and crowned Gules* (Palatine of the Rhine) 2 *Per fess dancetty Gules and Argent* (Franconia) 3 *Bendy sinister of six Argent and Gules a Pale Or* (Burgau) 4 *Argent a Lion rampant Azure armed and langued Gules crowned Or* (Veldenz) over all an escutcheon *Paly bendy Argent and Azure* (Bavaria).

Bayeux Tapestry This is not a true tapestry but an enormously long piece of needlework comprising eight unequal sections of bleached linen, embroidered with coloured wool. It is 75 yards (69 metres) long and 20 inches (50 cm) wide, and is apparently incomplete, though no part of the narrative is actually missing. The eight colours in which the wool is dyed are terracotta, buff, blue-green, sage green, dark green, yellow, blue and dark blue. Several sections were repaired in the nineteenth century and some scenes (the death of Harold, for example) are therefore largely restorations.

The tapestry is in part historical and in part allegorical. The seventy consecutive scenes relate the events of the period 1064-66, including, of course, the battle of Hastings (14 October 1066). However, it is also intended as a clear warning of justice and retribution for those who, like Harold, choose to ignore a solemn oath.

It is likely that the tapestry was commissioned by

Semi-circular pennon at the battle of Hastings (from the Bayeux Tapestry).

Bishop Odo of Bayeaux, and that it was completed before 1082. Bishop Odo was rewarded for his part in the invasion of England with the Earldom of Kent. He was half brother to Duke William and features prominently in the tapestry. It is likely that it was made at Canterbury and was probably the work of a single designer and a team of embroiderers. Certainly there are influences in the design reminiscent of early Anglo-Saxon manuscript illumination, and the designer may have been English, even though the theme is chauvinistically Norman. Bishop Odo fell from favour in 1082 and returned to Bayeaux, apparently taking the tapestry with him. As a work of art it is without parallel.

The tapestry contains, among other things, 626 human figures, 190 horses, 541 other animals, 37 ships, 33 buildings, 243 shields and 27 flags. The shields are kite-shaped (233), round (9) or oval (1), though this last is probably a crude kite-shaped shield. The designs on the kite-shaped shields are interesting: 41 are studded, 20 have windmill sail-type crosses, 7 are charged with some form of beast, probably wyverns, 2 have crosses, one has a wavy bar across the top and 80 are plain or of one colour with a rim of a different tincture. Of the shields, 81 are

depicted from the back. Shields of the Norman period were made of wood covered with hide, and a rim of metal was fixed round the edge for added strength. The studs on some of the shields were originally added for extra protection, and lent themselves to embellishment with different colours. From these heavily studded shields may be traced the armorial escarbuncle, originally thought to be a device for strengthening the shield. The various 'windmill sails' which appear on a number of shields were probably painted decoration, the armorial gyronny from the French for whirligig. The wyvern shields are not necessarily those of the earls of Wessex (Harold succeeded his father as Earl of Wessex in 1053), for it is known that a number of European nobles used similar devices at the time.

Of the nine round shields, all of which are English, five are held by warriors and four are depicted in the border. These are typical Saxon round wooden shields with strengthening bars, rims and central boss.

A light lance is carried by many of the knights in the tapestry, and on 25 of these, just beneath the head, is attached a small square pennon with three or more pointed tails. These are decorated in various ways, which could be symbols of rank, and one solitary flag, of semi-circular shape, is possibly a representation of the Norse raven device. The banner which Pope Alexander II blessed and presented to William is thought to be represented in the tapestry, and at one time it was believed that this was the semi-circular flag described above. The first depiction occurs after the Normans have landed and are building fortifications at Hastings. Duke William is shown seated, holding a banner whilst listening to a gesticulating knight. The second depiction is at the point of the story when William shows his face to his followers to dispel rumours that he has been slain. Before him, Eustace of Boulogne holds aloft the banner.

The Wessex wyvern standard can be seen twice in the English camp just prior to the death of Harold. One lies on the ground and is trampled beneath the hooves of a knight's horse, and the other is held aloft by one of Harold's knights, perhaps a rallying call for one last effort to drive the Normans back.

Armorists are generally agreed that the devices depicted in flags and shields in the tapestry pre-date the first truly armorial use of such devices, by some seventy years. However, there is a growing body of opinion which suggests that flags were indeed used both for military purposes and to identify those in authority, not by the Normans but by their allies, many of whom accompanied William across the Channel. It is argued (see *Origins of Heraldry* by Beryl Platts, 1980) that in Flanders, for example, the substructural *comtés* each possessed distinctive devices which were used on coinage, customs stamps and seals as badges of office and wherever officialdom needed to identify itself. Further, that in conjunction with specific colours, these devices flew on pennants from the masts of ships, fluttered over frontier forts and above comital places, and in both war and peace were used to marshal the armed forces of the *comté*. Why then should not the torteaux of Boulogne, the mascles of Bethune, the vair of Guines, the silver and black tinctures of Alost, the wheatsheaves of St Pol, the escallops of Hesdin and the blue and gold chequers of Vermandois find their way into British armory via the Conquest? In the Bayeaux Tapestry, Harold's wyvern standard is precisely depicted. Why should other flags not also be identified? What of the pennon of the leading cavalryman in the scene following that in which William deploys his troops? Is it not the device of the counts of Boulogne? Perhaps we have become preoccupied with the notion that it is the shield which represents the rationale for the development of armory? Should we not do better to consider the role of the flag, which remains the only entirely satisfactory, functional means of armorial display? If so, the Bayeaux Tapestry may be of greater heraldic significance than is generally acknowledged. No doubt the controversy will continue.

See also ARMORY, ORIGINS OF

Further reading

Bernstein, D.J. *The Mystery of the Bayeaux Tapestry* London, 1986.

Gibbs-Smith, C.H. *The Bayeaux Tapestry* London, 1973.

Stenton, F. (Ed.) *The Bayeaux Tapestry* London, 1965.

Beacon A fire-bucket on a pole with a ladder.

Beaked *see* **Attributes**

Bear It is said that the bear produces her cubs without form, and that she shapes them by licking them with her tongue until they are perfect little bears. It is from this fable that the term 'to lick into shape' has arisen.

In the heavily wooded areas of some of the central European countries the bear was a familiar animal, and such was its power on the imagination of the people living there that it took the place of the lion, in their heraldry, for boldness, courage and majesty. As with the lion, the bear was represented much the same as the natural animal. The bear was also popular in civic heraldry and appeared on the shields of towns in countries such as Germany and Bavaria, sometimes (as in St Gallen, Switzerland) having the additional honour of a golden collar.

The bear appears quite frequently as a supporter of arms, and often has the collar and chain of the medieval tame bear. The badge of the earls of Warwick was a bear and ragged staff, the latter representing the tree trunk with which an early earl of Warwick was reputed to have killed a giant. MY

Bearings *see* **Armorial Bearings**

Beasts The vigorous medieval interpretation of beasts, birds, fish, reptiles and chimerical monsters is, for many, the very quintessence of heraldry.

The magnates of the Middle Ages often possessed one or more distinctive beasts as personal devices, culled from the pages of the bestiaries or from the shadowy traditions of ancestral crusaders. Many of these devices were incorporated into the shield of arms, but a far greater number were adopted as personal badges and were later translated into crests and supporters. The 'beast badge' remains a distinctive element in Scottish armory. Such beasts were essentially personal devices, ideally suited to decoration and illumination, and, in the form of jewelled pendants and collars, given as gifts to intimates and favoured retainers.

As long ago as 1237 a stone lion was set up on the gable of the King's Hall in Windsor Castle, and during the fifteenth and sixteenth centuries carved creatures of stone or wood embellished castles and manor houses on gateposts, parapets, balustrades and on the newels of staircases. Many beasts 'support' a shield or banner of arms or a secondary device, and it is likely that the armorial supporter of a coat of arms originated in these three-dimensional figures.

The use of beasts as emblems of authority pre-dates armory by many centuries: the Roman eagle, Norse raven and Wessex wyvern are but three well known examples. John of Marmoustier, in Touraine, related that Henry I, at the wedding of his daughter Matilda to Geoffrey of Anjou in 1128, placed about the neck of his fourteen-year-old son-in-law a shield painted with gold lions. From the reign of Richard I (1189-99) beasts became increasingly popular as royal devices, and by the fifteenth century the English kings had accumulated a variety of devices as the result of alliance or inheritance. Collectively these, with a number of later additions, are known as the Royal Beasts, of which there are three well-known series.

The King's Beasts at Hampton Court Palace Henry VIII's acquisition of Hampton Court resulted in refurbishing on a lavish scale, and an abundance of heraldic embellishment. Royal creatures, and those of his then queen, Anne Boleyn, were ubiquitous: there were sixteen on the coping stones of the gables of the Great Hall, sixteen on the battlements, and further beasts on the columns of the louvre and as ornaments throughout the grounds. It is likely that many of these held vanes, but there is no evidence to suggest how these were decorated. Anne Boleyn was executed in 1536 and was followed by Jane Seymour, whose arms and badges replaced those of her predecessor, Anne's leopards being altered to Jane's panthers by 'new makying of hedds and taylls' in the cause of economy. To commemorate this marriage, twelve beasts were erected on the parapet of the moat bridge. They consisted of two lions, two dragons, two unicorns, two panthers, a bull and a yale. These were demolished when the moat was filled in during the reign of William III, but fragments from the moat suggest that they held shields. In 1909 the bridge and the carvings were restored, though one greyhound and a unicorn were omitted from the new set. By 1950 these had become so badly eroded that they had to be replaced

with those which may be seen today. Facing the bridge they are, on the left:

1 The crowned lion of England holding a shield impaling the royal arms and the quarterings of Queen Jane: arms of augmentation (see below), the arms of Seymour, Beauchamp of Hache, Sturmy, MacWilliams and Coker (Jane was descended from heiresses of these families).
2 Jane's panther supporter, granted to her by King Henry, holding a shield of the Seymour arms.
3 The greyhound supporter of Henry VII (and sometimes Henry VIII) holding a shield of the arms of England. (The greyhound is here leashed, which is not correct.)
4 A yale, the Beaufort beast from Sir John Beaufort, Henry VII's grandfather, who adopted it on his creation as Earl of Kendal in succession to Henry VI's son John, Duke of Bedford, who was the first to use this strange creature. The yale holds a shield of the arms of augmentation granted by Henry VIII to his new wife. Such augmentations were granted to all those of his wives who were not of royal blood.
See HENRY VIII, ROYAL AUGMENTATIONS.
5 The Tudor dragon, indicative of the family's Welsh ancestry, supporting a shield charged with the portcullis badge of the Beauforts. (Henry VII ensigned the portcullis with a royal crown and this badge is still used at the Palace of Westminster.)

On the right-hand parapet:
1 The unicorn supporter granted to Jane Seymour, possibly as a symbol of purity and fertility, holding a shield charged with her six quarterings.
2 The Tudor dragon supporting a shield of France and England quarterly.
3 The lion of England, crowned with a coronet, holding a shield charged with Queen Jane's badge: a complex device based on the Tudor badge of a crowned hawthorn bush, allusive to the royal crown of Richard III, plucked from such a bush by Lord Stanley at Bosworth Field and placed on Henry Tudor's head.
4 The black bull of Clarence, the badge of Lionel Duke of Clarence, second son of Edward III, ancestor of the Yorkist kings, holding a shield charged with the badge of the Tudor Rose.
5 Queen Jane's panther supporter holding a shield impaling the royal arms with her own quartered coat.

The Queen's Beasts, at Kew Gardens These were devised to celebrate the coronation of Queen Elizabeth II in 1953, and were placed outside the entrance to Westminster Abbey. The coronation beasts were not coloured, except for their shields, and were cast in

Jane Seymour's panther: one of the King's beasts at Hampton Court Palace.

plaster. Later, a fine new set was carved in Portland stone and may now be seen in Kew Gardens:

1   The crowned lion of England holding the royal arms of Elizabeth II.

2   The griffin, from the signet of Edward III who sired the dynasties of York and Lancaster, holding a shield charged with the most recent royal badge, that of the House of Windsor: *The Round Tower of Windsor Castle on a Mount and with the Royal Banner flying above all between two Branches of Oak ensigned by the Royal Crown* on the present royal liveries of red and gold.

3   The silver falcon of the Plantagenets holding a shield charged with the falcon and fetterlock badge of the Yorkist kings on their liveries of blue and murrey.

4   The black bull of Clarence (see 4 above) supporting a shield of the royal arms as used between 1405 and 1603.

5   The white lion of Mortimer, through which family the Yorkists laid claim to the English throne, holding a shield of blue and murrey, emblazoned with another Yorkist badge, the white rose en soleil. The sun was the badge of Richard II, who named Mortimer heir to the throne.

6   The House of Lancaster is represented by the Beaufort yale supporting a shield of the Beaufort colours, blue and white, charged with a gold portcullis ensigned with the royal crown. As has previously been noted, the portcullis was a Beaufort badge and was adopted by the Tudors.

7   The greyhound of Richmond holding a shield of white and green, the Tudor livery colours, charged with a crowned Tudor Rose.

8   The red dragon of Wales holding the arms of the ancient princes of North Wales: *Quarterly Or and Gules four Lions passant guardant counterchanged.* In 1911 these arms, ensigned by his coronet, were assigned to the Prince of Wales to place over the royal arms as a central escutcheon, to symbolize the Principality.

9   The Stuarts are represented by the Scottish unicorn supporter holding the old royal arms of Scotland.

10   The white horse of Hanover was originally an emblem of Brunswick. Here it supports the royal arms which were used from the accession of George I in 1714 until the union with Ireland in 1801.

The Windsor Beasts at St George's Chapel, Windsor Above the clerestory parapet at St George's Chapel stand forty-two creatures, each 4 feet 6 inches (1 · 5 metres) in height, surmounting a pinnacle and supporting a pennon vane. Some twenty-four feet below them, a further thirty-four, holding shields, embellish the flying buttresses (24), western parapet (2), and niches of the transept wall (8). Beasts adorned the parapet and buttresses shortly after the chapel was completed in *c.* 1557, but when Sir Christopher Wren carried out his survey in 1682 they were found to be in a dangerous condition and were removed. Fortunately, his suggestion that they should be replaced with stone pineapples was not acted upon! The present beasts were carved by J. Armitage and erected in 1925, the gift of a London building contractor. There are seventy-six altogether, but only fourteen different creatures are represented:

1   The crowned lion of England supporting the English arms.

2   The Welsh dragon holding a shield charged with a portcullis and a Tudor Rose.

3   The Yorkist falcon supporting the arms of England.

4   The bull of Clarence holding a shield charged with the white rose en soleil.

5   A panther supporting the arms granted by Henry VI to his foundation at Eton in 1449 *Sable three Lilies Argent on a Chief per pale Azure and Gules on the dexter a Fleur-de-lis and on the sinister a Lion passant guardant Or.*

6   The Beaufort yale supporting the Beaufort arms

France and England Quarterly within a Bordure gobony Argent and Azure.

7   The lion of Mortimer holding that family's arms *Or three Bars Azure on a Chief Gold two Pallets between two Gyrons also Azure over all an Escutcheon Argent.*

8   The Richmond greyhound holding the arms of Neville *Gules a Saltire Argent.*

9   The white swan of Bohun, adopted by Henry IV in the right of his wife who was a daughter of one of the heiresses of Humphrey de Bohun, Earl of Hereford, holding the Bohun arms *Azure a Bend Argent cotised Or between six Lions rampant Gold.*

10   The white hart of Richard II holding a shield charged with the Plantagenet *planta genista* or broom-pod badge.

11   The silver antelope, another Bohun beast, gorged and chained bearing the arms of France Ancient and England quarterly. Like the Bohun swan, the antelope was also adopted by Henry IV as a royal badge.

12   The black dragon of the Earls of Ulster supporting the arms of de Burgh *Or a Cross Gules,* who held this earldom and from whom descended the Yorkist kings.

13   The unicorn of Edward III supporting a vane.

14   The hind of Edward V supporting a vane.

Further reading

Allen, A. and J. Griffiths *The Book of the Dragon* London, 1979.

Angel, M. *Beasts in Heraldry* 1974.

Begent, P. *A Noble Place Indeed: An Heraldic Tour of St George's Chapel, Windsor* Windsor, 1984.

Brooke-Little, J.P. *Royal Heraldry — Beasts and Badges of Britain* Derby, 1981.

Dennys, R. *The Heraldic Imagination* London, 1975.

Hathaway, N. *The Unicorn* Harmondsworth, 1982.

Nigg, J. *The Book of Gryphons* Cambridge/Watertown, 1982.

Pinches, J.H. and R.V. *The Royal Heraldry of England* London, 1974.

Stanford London, H. *The Queen's Beasts* London, 1954.

Vinycomb, J. *Fictitious and Symbolic Creatures in Art with Special Reference to their Use in British Heraldry* London, 1906.

White, T.H. *The Book of Beasts* London, 1954, translated from the Latin bestiary of the twelfth century.

Beaumont Herald of Arms Extraordinary Created in 1982, this office is named after the barony of Beaumont, a subsidiary title of the Earl Marshal, the Duke of Norfolk. The badge of office combines the cross potent of the Kings of Jerusalem from whom the Beaumonts are descended, with lion and fleurs-de-lis charges from the family arms *In front of a Cross Potent a Lion rampant within eight Fleurs-de-lis in orle Gold.*

Bee The universal symbol of industriousness, the bee is usually depicted in flight and viewed from above, blazoned volant.

Belgium, Armorial Practice The country of Belgium dates from the revolution of 1830, but the constituent provinces of Brabant, Flanders and Liege maintain many of their ancient traditions and institutions. Some of these, reflecting the history of the area, have Burgundian, Spanish, Austrian, French and Dutch elements.

In 1844 the first King of the Belgians (Prince Leopold of Saxe-Coburg) set up the *Conseil Heraldique* to verify titles of nobility and the rights to arms. Every Belgian is permitted to choose a coat of arms, but the use of emblems of nobility is strictly controlled for, as may be imagined (given the country's history), there are far more noble families, as a proportion of the population, than might otherwise obtain. The Heraldic Council keeps records of genealogies, nobility, letters patent and related documents, and its permission is required for the assumption of arms and nobiliary styles.

The design of arms follows normal European practices but, apart from the cap of a baron and the coronet of a feudal viscount, no other devices of *noblesse* exist.   JC-K

Belgium, Royal Arms of *Sable a Lion rampant Or armed and langued Gules.*

Belled *see* **Attributes**

Bend and **Bend Sinister** Ordinaries. A broad bend extending from dexter chief to sinister base (bend), or sinister chief to dexter base (bend sinister). Charges placed on a bend correspond with the direction of the bend unless otherwise specified, as do ermine spots and varied fields of compony, counter-compony and chequy.

The bend sinister is frequently referred to as a mark of illegitimacy, and although the bend itself was often used as an indication of differencing in early armory, it was the sinister versions of the bendlet (a diminutive of the bend), the even narrower riband and the baton (a couped bendlet, sometimes called a

Beaumont badge

baston) which were generally used for this purpose, particularly in the arms of royal bastards.

> Diminutives: bendlet and riband
> Parted field: per bend or per bend sinister
> Varied field: bendy or bendy sinister
> Disposition: in bend or in bend sinister
> Inclination: bendwise or bendwise sinister

See also ORDINARY

Bendlet The diminutive of the bend.

Bendy *and* **Bendy Sinister** *see* **Field, Varied**

Benediction *see* **Attitude**

Bestiaries To the writers of the medieval bestiaries the mythical birds and animals were probably as real as the natural ones, and the fantastic stories about real animals make them as mystical as the imaginary ones. Many of these creatures were imbued with medicinal and spiritual powers, and the readers of the books were advised to emulate the qualities of the saintly creatures and shun those of the evil ones. The purity of the unicorn was a shining example to be followed, whilst the snake, who put its tail in one ear to close it to the teaching of the church, and pressed the other to the ground to hear only earthly matters, was to be avoided. There are many references to the death and resurrection of Christ: in the three days that the lion's cubs remain dead after birth, until their father breathes life into them; the three days of sleep in which the panther indulges after eating; the three days of death between the killing and reviving of the pelican's babies. The different attributes of many of these creatures make them very suitable for special use in heraldry, and gives their presence there more meaning.   MY

Bevilled *see* **Lines, Varied**

Bevor *or* **Beavor** Fixed neck and jaw protection. Usually of plate armour.

Bezant, Besant, Besaunt *and rarely* **Talent** A gold disc, originally a gold coin from Byzantium.

Bezanty *or* **Bezanté** Semy of bezants.

Bibliography Books on specific subjects will be found at the conclusion of appropriate entries.

Early printed works

Printed books on armory began to appear soon after the Mainz-born Gutenberg contrived a platen press with movable type to produce his Bible and Psalter of 1456. *The Boke of St Albans* was reproduced by this method in 1486, and there followed a number of substantial works of which Gerard Leigh's *Accendence of Armorie* (1562) and John Ferne's *Blazon of Gentrie* (1586) are the most notable, the former published in a number of editions up to 1612. *A Display of Heraldrie* by John Guillim (1611) ran to six editions by 1724, when it was much augmented by its editor, James Coats. In 1780 another classic, *A Complete Body of Heraldry* by Joseph Edmondson, Mowbray Herald Extraordinary, was published in two fine folio volumes, the second of which contains an extensive alphabet of arms. It goes without saying that such books are rare and not usually within the resources of the average armorist. However, there are several late-eighteenth century works which are still to be found at reasonable prices and these represent an attractive investment for the enthusiast; M.A. Porny's little book *Elements of Heraldry* (1795), for example.

Victorian works

The Industrial Revolution of the nineteenth century created a new elite, anxious to acquire the trappings of gentility and with a voracious appetite for matters genealogical and armorial. This is reflected in the plethora of heraldic 'manuals' of the period, and a quite extraordinary level of genealogical activity exemplified by the works of the ubiquitous Sir Bernard Burke. Armorists became preoccupied with the minutia of their subject; 'research' was invariably mere compilation, uncritical and inaccurate. And yet the Victorian Age not only produced a number of reference works which today are considered to be indispensable, it also bred a group of armorists from whose scholarship our present perception of heraldry is largely derived. C.N. Elvin's *A Dictionary of Heraldry* (1889), A.H. Parker's *A Glossary of Terms used in British Heraldry* (1894), Sir Bernard Burke's *General Armory* (1842), J. Fairbairn's *Book of Crests of the Families of Great Britain and Ireland* (1859), and J.W. Papworth's *Ordinary of British Armorials* (1874) are currently available in facsimile or reprinted form, and, although the last three works are not entirely reliable they represent the nucleus of an armorist's reference collection.

Also recommended are the works of such scholars as Thomas Moule, whose *Bibliotheca Heraldica Magnae Britanniae* (essentially a bibliography of works on heraldry and associated subjects) was published in 1822; W. Berry who published his *Encyclopaedia Heraldica* in 1828; J.A. Montagu *A Guide to the Study of Heraldry* (1840); the Reverend Charles Boutell whose classic *The Manual of Heraldry* was first published in 1863 and thereafter continues in numerous editions as *Boutell's Heraldry*; and J.R. Planché, Somerset Herald, whose *The Pursuivant of Arms* appeared in its third edition in 1874. A fascinating book, recommended as a record of heraldic collections and related material in the late nineteenth century, is *A Manual for the Genealogist, Topographer and Antiquarian* by Richard Sims (of the British Museum), published in London in 1888.

A.C. Fox-Davies' seminal book *A Complete Guide to Heraldry* first appeared in 1909 and has since been revised in numerous editions. Although of the twentieth century, the *Complete Guide* has its roots in Victorian England, as has G.C. Rothery's *ABC of Heraldry*, published in 1915 and reprinted as the *Concise Encyclopedia of Heraldry* in 1985.

General List
Boutell, C. (revised J.P. Brooke-Little) *Boutell's Heraldry* London, 1863 (latest ed. 1983).
Brooke-Little, J.P. *An Heraldic Alphabet* London, 1973 (revised 1985).
Burke, Sir B. *The General Armory of England, Ireland, Scotland and Wales* Heraldry Today, 1842 to final edition 1884 (reprinted 1984). A flawed but essential reference work.
Burke's Family Index London. A comprehensive listing of the families which have appeared in the Burke's publications since 1826, and bibliography of all Burke's publications.
Debrett's Peerage and Baronetage London, 1985.
Dennys, R. *The Heraldic Imagination* London, 1975. — *Heraldry and the Heralds* London, 1982.
Elvin, C.N. *A Dictionary of Heraldry* Heraldry Today, 1889 (reprinted 1977). An invaluable illustrated dictionary of armorial charges.
Fairbairn, J. *Fairbairn's Book of Crests of the Families of Britain and Ireland* Baltimore, 1905 (reprinted 1983). An essential though not entirely reliable reference book, containing an ordinary of crests and list of mottoes.
Fox-Davies, A.C. (revised and annotated J.P. Brooke-Little) *A Complete Guide to Heraldry* London, 1909 (latest ed. 1985). — *The Art of Heraldry* London, 1904 (reprinted 1986). —*Armorial Families (A Directory of Gentlemen of Coat Armour)* London, 1902 (fourth ed.).
Franklyn, J. *Shield and Crest* London, 1960.
Gatfield, G. *Guide to Printed Books and Manuscripts relating to English and Foreign Heraldry and Genealogy* London, 1892 (reprinted 1966).
Gayre, Lt.Col. R. (Ed.) *The Armorial Who is Who* Edinburgh, 1979-80 (sixth ed.).
Lynch-Robinson, Sir C. and A.L. *Intelligible Heraldry* London, 1947.
MacKinnon, C. *The Observer's Book of Heraldry* London, 1986 (revised). An excellent and inexpensive pocket book.
Maclagan, M., C. Humphery-Smith and H.B. Pereira *The Colour of Heraldry* Heraldry Society, 1958.
Moncreiffe, I. and D. Pottinger *Simple Heraldry* London, 1953. This should be on every bookshelf!

Moule, T. *Bibliotheca Heraldica Magnae Britanniae* London, 1822 (reprinted 1966).
Neubecker, O. *Heraldry: Symbols, Sources and Meaning* London, 1976. — *A Guide to Heraldry* Maidenhead, 1979. Effectively a pocket version of his 1976 book.
Nisbet, A. *A System of Heraldry* Edinburgh, 1722/1816 (reprinted 1984).
Papworth, J.W. *Papworth's Ordinary of British Armorials* Bath, 1894 (reprinted 1977). An indispensable though not entirely reliable reference book.
Parker, A.H. *A Glossary of Terms used in British Heraldry* London, 1894 (reprinted 1970).
Pine, L.G. *International Heraldry* Newton Abbot, 1970. — *Teach Yourself Heraldry* London, 1971.
Rogers, Col. H.C.B. *The Pageant of Heraldry* London, 1957.
Rothery, G.C. *Concise Encyclopedia of Heraldry* London, 1915 (reprinted 1985).
St John Hope, W.H. *A Grammar of English Heraldry* London, 1913 (revised A.R. Wagner, 1953).
Scott-Giles, C.W. *The Romance of Heraldry* London, 1967 (revised). A fascinating introduction to heraldry through history.
Summers, P. *How to Read a Coat of Arms* Sherborne, 1986.
von Volborth, C.A. *Heraldry: Customs, Rules and Styles* Poole, 1981. — (Ed: D.H.B. Chesshyre) *Heraldry of the World* London, 1973.
Wagner, A. *Heraldry in England* London, 1946.
Woodward's Treatise on Heraldry Newton Abbot, 1892 (reprint 1969).

Bi-corporate *see* **Attitude**

Bill This pole-arm of the foot soldier bore a cutting head with stabber, piercer and gouger.

Billet A charge shaped like the rectangular face of a brick, and occasionally blazoned as a delve, as in the arms of John de Delves, one of Lord Audley's squires at Agincourt: *Argent a Chevron Gules fretty Or between three Delves Sable*. (The chevron was an augmentation of honour, granted by Lord Audley following the battle, Audley's arms being *Gules fretty Or*.)

Billetty *or* **Billeté** Semy of billets.

Blackamoor A negro.

Black Prince, The Edward Plantagenet, Prince of Wales (1330-76), 'The chief flower of chivalry of all the world' according to Froissart. He was a gallant soldier, victor of Crécy (1346), Poitiers (1356), and Najera (1367), and entirely ruthless as at Limoges (1370), when he exacted dreadful retribution on the population for their refusal to surrender. His effigy may be seen at Canterbury Cathedral on a tomb which is a masterpiece of medieval craftsmanship. His nickname is derived from his livery of black, which would have been worn by his retainers and soldiery and on which his famous ostrich feather device was depicted, repeated three times on his so-called 'shield for peace'.

Further reading

Barber, R. *The Life and Campaigns of the Black Prince* London, 1986.

Cole, H. *The Black Prince* London, 1976.

Emerson, B. *The Black Prince* London, 1976.

Black Rod A title, more properly the Gentleman Usher of the Black Rod, for an officer of both the House of Lords and the Order of the Garter. In the first capacity he participates in parliamentary ceremonial, and administers that part of the Palace of Westminster devoted to the Upper House. In the second capacity he has a role in the annual Garter ceremony and acts as 'doorkeeper' to the Chapter of the Order, as the medieval Latin root-word *ussarius* implies. The earliest reference to a Garter usher was in 1361, and to the duties as an officer in the House of Lords, around 1520. The Irish House of Lords also had a post of Black Rod (first mentioned in 1634) and, from its inception in 1783, the Gentleman Usher of the Black Rod to the Order of St Patrick was also the usher to the Irish Upper House. When the Irish parliament was abolished in 1800, appointments to the office of Black Rod to the Order continued, but when the last appointee died in 1933 he was not replaced.

The Upper Chambers of many Commonwealth countries have Black Rods as their disciplinary officers, the last one to be created being that for South Australia in 1953.   JC-K

Further reading

Bond, M. and D. Beamish *The Gentleman Usher of the Black Rod* HMSO, 1981 (second ed.).

Blasons des Batailles *see* **Treatises**

Blason des Couleurs, Le *see* **Treatises**

Blasted *see* **Attributes**

Blazon (i) A verbal or written description of armorial bearings.

(ii) To describe armorial bearings using generally acknowledged conventions and terminology.

Blazons are unpunctuated, except that the tinctures and charges begin with a capital letter. Adjectives (other than quantitative) follow the nouns they qualify, the tincture coming last: e.g. *three Griffins segreant reguardant Gules*. If a shield is impaled, the dexter coat is blazoned first. In a quartered shield the

quarterings are numbered, beginning with that in dexter chief (the paternal arms) and working across the shield and down, as with lines of print. If, as often happens, the last quartering is a repetition of the first, the blazon would commence *Quarterly 1st and 4th*, *Quarterly 1st and 8th* and so on, depending on the number of quarterings borne. When quarterings are themselves quartered they are described as *grandquarters*, each coat of which they are composed being a *sub-quarter*. In such cases the grandquarter is blazoned, sub-quarter by sub-quarter, before moving on to the next quartering. A shield containing several quarterings may also be surrounded by a bordure. This should always be blazoned last, together with any charges placed upon it. Crests, supporters and badges are blazoned as though they are charges on a shield. Armorial banners are blazoned in precisely the same way as shields of arms. Standards and other livery flags are blazoned from hoist to fly. The arms or national flag in the hoist is first mentioned — usually in the simple form *In the hoist the Arms* — followed by the field and the charges placed upon it, the motto bends and lettering, and lastly the fringe.

The ability to blazon accurately is an essential tool of the armorist. It enables him to record armorial devices quickly and accurately, to make effective use of ordinaries, armories, peerages, etc., and to communicate with other armorists. The objectives of blazon are brevity and precision. An accurate blazon is unambiguous and from it an achievement of arms which is correct in every detail may be painted (emblazoned). The conventions of blazon are well established but not inflexible, and current practice is nearer to the spirit of the medieval heralds than the prescriptive heraldic manuals of the last century, in which tautology was described as mortal sin, and clarity sacrificed for pedantry. All the well known heraldic books contain the technical minutiae of blazon, but it is recommended that the novice concentrate on perfecting his understanding of the basics before concerning himself with technicalities. Once the conventions are understood the terminology will come with practice and a few hours spent browsing through an illustrated peerage. See colour illustrations on pages 50/51 for typical blazons.

A number of conventions are worthy of note:

a.   The blazon of a parted or varied field always begins with the tincture of the partition or division in the 'senior' position, i.e. dexter chief.

b.   The position of a principal charge is assumed to be the centre of the shield, unless otherwise specified.

c.   The position of individual charges may be blazoned by reference to the parts and points of the shield, e.g. *in base, in dexter chief, in honour point*, etc.

d.   Where three similar charges are placed on a

shield it is assumed that two are in chief and one in base, unless otherwise specified.

e.   Where several dissimilar charges are depicted, each of apparently equal importance, that in dexter chief is blazoned first, followed by those in sinister chief, dexter base and sinister base.

f.   The disposition of a number of minor charges may be indicated by the use of numbers, e.g. *six Martlets three, two and one* —three in the top row, two in the centre row and one in the base of the shield.

g.   The disposition of minor charges may also be indicated by reference to the geometry of an ordinary, e.g. *five Oval Buckles in fess, four Eagles in cross, five Estoils in saltire*, etc.

h.   When no indication is given in the blazon as to the disposition of minor charges, they are so arranged as to accommodate the principal charge without being defaced, e.g. *a Lion rampant Argent between seven Cross-crosslets.*

i.   The attitude of a charge (i.e. the geometrical inclination) may be indicated by reference to the geometry of an ordinary, e.g. *a Sword bendwise, two Arrows chevronwise, two Tilting Spears saltirewise*, etc. (This is not necessary if a charge is obliged to follow the geometry of the ordinary on which it is placed, or if it is blazoned in such a way as to make its posture clear, e.g. *a Lion rampant* is always upright.)

j.   When a charge is surrounded by a number of minor charges it is said to be *between*. (Also *between* a pair of flaunches.)

k.   When a charge is encircled by minor charges it is said to be *within*. (Also *within* an Orle or Tressure.)

l.   When a specified number of charges is immediately followed by a similar number of other charges the words *as many* may be used, e.g. *Argent on a Chevron Gules between three Leopard's Faces Sable as many Castles Or* (de Sausmarez).

m.   Beasts are normally *armed and langued Gules* — that is, they have red claws and tongue (azure if the field or beast is itself red). The tincture of claws and tongue need be blazoned only if it differs from the convention.

n.   The crest should be blazoned *Upon a helm with a wreath* . . . or *within a wreath* . . . and **not** *on a wreath* . . . The tinctures are then specified, beginning with the dexter 'twist', the terms *of the colours* or (even worse) *of the liveries* being ambiguous.

o.   The mantling is blazoned, e.g. *Vert doubled Or* or *Gules and Sable doubled Argent*, the inner lining always being described last. *Party Gules and Sable doubled Argent* is also acceptable for mantlings of more than two tinctures.

p.   The position of supporters is said to be *on either side* for a matched pair, or *on the dexter/sinister side* if they are dissimilar, the dexter being blazoned first. A pair of supporters which differ only in their attributes may be blazoned, e.g. *on either side a Griffin segreant Sable that on the dexter side gorged with an Ancient Crown Or and that on the sinister side holding a Key erect Gules.*

q.   If a special compartment has been devised this should also be blazoned, beginning with *the whole upon a compartment of* . . . or *on a compartment composed of* . . .

The sequence of blazoning a coat of arms

The Shield

1   The Field
Parted: division of the shield by lines of partition
Varied: geometrically patterned shapes
Tincture: armorial metals, colours and furs
Semy charges: small charges scattered over the field

2a   The Ordinary
Identity
Lines, variations of
The Field (as above)

or

2b   The Principal Charge
Position (if necessary)
Identity
Attitude(s) and/or disposition
The Field of the charge (as above)
Attribute(s)

3   The Secondary Charges
As 2b above

4   Charges borne upon the Ordinary or Principal Charge
As 2b above

5   The Sub-ordinaries
As 2a above

6   Charges borne upon the Sub-odinaries
As 2b above

7   Any Ordinary or Charge borne over all
As 2 above (blazoned *over all*)

The Crest

1   The Coronet or Chapeau (Scotland) of rank (if appropriate)
2   The Helmet according to rank
3   The Wreath, Crest Coronet or Chapeau
4   The Crest (as for the Principal Charge above)
5   The Mantling

Supporters (if appropriate)
Blazoned as the Principal Charge above

The Motto
(In Scotland this follows the Crest)

Bleu-Céleste An uncommon armorial tincture of sky-blue colour, generally reserved for institutions or persons associated with aviation. A recent innovation in English armory. Abbreviated BlC. *See also* TINCTURES

Blemished *see* **Attributes**

Bluemantle Pursuivant of Arms in Ordinary This office is reputed to have been created by Henry V to serve the Order of the Garter, but there is no documentary evidence of this. There is, however, mention of an officer styled Blewmantle going to France in 1448. The first Bluemantle to be mentioned by name is found in a record *c.* 1484. The badge of office, probably derived from the original blue material of the Order of the Garter, is *a Blue Mantle lined Ermine cords and tassels Or*.

Blue Rod *see* **Gentleman Usher**

Boar The wild boar was much respected by huntsmen for its indomitable courage and fierceness, and has always been used widely in heraldry. It is worth noting that the boar's long, curving tusks are often called *tusses*, or *tushes*, and its curling tail, ending in a tuft, is referred to as a wreath. Probably the best known boar in heraldry is Richard III's white boar badge. His pursuivant of arms bore the title *Blanc Sanglier*.   MY

Silver Boar badge worn by the retainers of Richard, Duke of Gloucester, later King Richard III.

Bogus arms assumed by an English district council and abandoned in 1987 following censure by the College of Arms.

Bogus Heraldry Unauthorized armorial bearings assumed by individuals and corporations, and passed off as being exclusively and legitimately their own. It is perfectly acceptable for any person (whether armigerous or not) to display armorial bearings of corporate bodies with which he may be associated (e.g. colleges, professional associations etc.) providing such display is for decorative purposes only and does not imply personal entitlement to the arms, by using them on stationery, for example. However, to adopt a coat of arms to which one is not entitled is clearly unlawful and in bad taste. It is akin to adding honours and qualifications to one's name without entitlement.

An armiger may seek the protection of the Court of Chivalry if he discovers that his arms are being used unlawfully by another, but regrettably there seems to be little hope of redress for those who object to the use of bogus heraldry, even by corporate bodies, unless the kings of arms are moved to prosecute. The use of unauthorized arms constitutes not only an abuse of their Offices, but also an abuse of the Royal Prerogative. It is doubtful whether such action could be conducted through the Court of Chivalry, however. In response to a complaint in 1984 that a local authority was using unlawful armorial bearings, Garter King of Arms stated: 'I am by no means sure that a sufficient precedent exists among cases which have been heard in the Court of Chivalry in the past for the Court to be moved in the present matter.' Nevertheless, one must question the validity of legal documents issued under a corporate seal if the armorial bearings depicted on that seal are themselves unlawful! Fortunately for the Scots, matters armorial are subject to the strict (and enforceable) control of the Court of the Lord Lyon.

The status of an armiger is recognized by all heraldic authorities and armorial bearings used in a foreign country are not considered to be bogus, though it is normally necessary for an armiger to seek permission of the authorities to use them, and minor alterations may be required if they are found not to be unique in that particular heraldic jurisdiction.

Beware many of the well known armorial reference books! The experienced armorist will approach them with caution — even the works of the ubiquitous Burke are littered with bogus references! Beware, too, the registered trademark. Many appear to possess all the attributes of a coat of arms, but are entirely bogus.

See also BUCKET SHOP HERALDRY; HERALDIC OFFICES; SPURIOUS HERALDRY

Further reading

Squibb, G.D. *The Law of Arms in England* London, 1967.

The High Court of Chivalry Heraldry Society, London, 1955. A verbatim report of the most recent case, held in 1954 before the Court.

Boke of St Albans *see* Treatises

Bonacon A monster with the appearance of a bull, but with horns that curl inwards, a horse's tail and a short mane. The bonacon defends itself by firing its burning excrement at its enemies.

Bonnet *see* Electoral Cap

Bookplates Armorial bookplates originated in Germany, *c.* 1470, and in less than half a century other European countries were using them. About twenty German bookplates are known from the fifteenth century and in the sixteenth Durer and his followers designed and engraved many for patrons and friends. The artistry and quality of the majority of these plates have never been surpassed. However, in England no plates have been recorded for the fifteenth century and only three for the sixteenth, the earliest being the 1574 gift plate of Sir Nicholas Bacon to the Cambridge University Library. The other two are for Joseph Holand and Sir Thomas Tresame (a coat of twenty-five quarterings), both dated 1585. The Bacon plate was also used as an illustration in several editions of Gerard Legh's *Accendence of Armorie*. The armorial book stamp, the coat of arms impressed in blind or gilt on the leather or vellum bindings of the sixteenth and seventeenth centuries, was in Britain the precursor of and a handsome alternative to the armorial bookplate. Some early bookplates closely resemble the book stamps their owners used, for example the armorial gift plate of Rachel Bourchier, Dowager Countess of Bath, the earliest known bookplate for a lady (1670).

During the seventeenth century bookplates in Britain became more in evidence, and at least a hundred and fifty examples have been recorded, but they did not become really popular until the 1690s, this being effected by William Jackson, whose engraving shop was near the Inns of Court in London. He was responsible for most of the Oxford and Cambridge College bookplates, and over six hundred and thirty plates from Jackson's workshop are in the British Museum collection. Samuel Pepys used two armorial plates. Several armorials of the 1660s show the arms within a wreath, and this is referred to as the

Carolean style. In the latter part of the century, however, the Early Armorial style (fig. 1), characterized by the squarish straightsided shield and the full mantling, came into use.

The Jacobean style (fig. 2) appears from the beginning of the eighteenth century and became really popular around 1720. The bookplates in this distinctive form, with ornate floriated scrollwork surrounding the shield instead of mantling, and often further ornamented with brackets, escallop shells, cherub's heads, and fishscale, diaper or lattice patterning, allowed a wide scope for imagination and invention. The Chippendale style (fig. 3) which followed was characterized by asymmetry. The surround remains ornamental, but becomes even more intricate, sprays of flowers being an added attraction. However, later Chippendale plates are spoiled by an excess of ornament, which may include cherubs and dragons, shepherds and shepherdesses, flowers and fountains. The earliest examples date from around 1740, and they became so popular that they outnumber the plates of any other style until the plain armorial became the norm in the nineteenth century. During the period from about 1780 to 1810, the Chippendale style gave way to the spade shield plates, often with festoons or wreaths (fig. 4), chaste little designs, both symmetrical and elegant; they have a delicate charm, particularly suited to the period.

The use of only a crest as a bookplate first occurs in the eighteenth century, but became common in the nineteenth, an interesting example being the one used, without entitlement, by Charles Dickens. Dated plates occur from the seventeenth century and became common from 1700. The dates are normally to be relied upon, but one can occasionally be misled; for example the plate of Sir Francis Fust, dated 1662, is the date of the creation of the baronetcy, the plate being engraved at least sixty-six years later, since Francis did not succeed to the baronetcy until 1728. A uniquely British style of plate is the bookpile (fig. 5). It was first created by Pepys for Dr Charlett, and enjoyed modest popularity from 1699, surviving into recent times. It consists of a neatly symmetrical pile of books so arranged that they completely surround the shield. Many bookplates in the late eighteenth and early nineteenth century were pictorial, but some of these are also armorial, the shield hanging from an ornamental urn, leaning up against a tree, or otherwise artistically disposed. This treatment can be noted from time to time up to the present day.

During the nineteenth century bookplates became extensively used, but it should be borne in mind that on occasion the arms shown were either entirely bogus or used without any authority. They were often meticulously and skilfully engraved, and heraldically correct, but they lacked any artistic invention and imagination. However, in the last years of the century

1

2

3

4

there was a revival in the art of the bookplate, largely due to two highly talented artists and engravers, Charles W. Sherborn and George W. Eve; and they inspired others who also produced work of high quality.

Bookplates have by no means been used only by private individuals. Many belonged or belong to the books of corporate bodies, societies, libraries, colleges and schools. Among college plates, those of *c.* 1700 for Oxford and Cambridge from Jackson's engraving shop, already referred to, are noteworthy as a group. Among the numerous plates for schools and colleges, there are diverse but attractive nineteenth-century examples; and premium — or prize — bookplates are

DEUS MIHI PROVIDEBIT

George Goold

5

6

of especial interest. Many, including some of the earliest, are labels or allegoricals, but among the armorials the twenty different premiums used by Trinity College, Dublin, form an impressive series.

It was not until the reign of George III that the use of bookplates was generally adopted by the Sovereign and his family, but every monarch since then has used armorials. Before the reign of Edward VII, however, their bookplates are, with two exceptions, unimpressive. The two exceptions are the series of plates for the Royal Library at Windsor. It was Queen Victoria who adopted the use of bookplates in three different sizes for this library, and her reign was so long that two different series were used; the first, in red and black, engraved by Mary Byfield and C.A. Ferrier; the second, etched, by George W. Eve. The latter were so impressive that Edward VII used them also, with just the cypher changed; and Eve etched a further set of three armorials for the reign of George V. The Windsor bookplates used by George VI and modified for Elizabeth II were engraved by Stephen Gooden, and they are the finest royal bookplates ever used in England. Gooden's bookplates for the Queen (now Queen Elizabeth, the Queen Mother) and the Princesses Elizabeth and Margaret, are comparable in their majesty. Other members of the Royal Family have used armorials, though ladies have sometimes favoured a pictorial plate. There are probably upwards of a hundred bookplates of heralds and kings of arms, and they are of great interest and diversity. Some show the arms of the individual impaled with those of his office; others incorporate the tabard; and an example of especial interest is the plate used 1822-31 by Sir George Nayler, Garter King of Arms. This shows the armorials appropriate to his offices as Garter, as first King of Arms of the Hanoverian Guelphic Order, and as first King of Arms of the Order of St Michael and St George.

European continental bookplates are, of course, as fascinating and important as heraldic artefacts as British ones. Before 1600 they were used in Germany alone in hundreds; many German plates are of impressive size and sometimes elaborately ornamented. French bookplates have, on the whole, a greater delicacy of line. Books have been published on the bookplates of most continental countries, and the standard works published over half a century ago remain sufficient for students of heraldry, for in the intervening period pictorial bookplates predominate.

It should be borne in mind that most bookplates are modest and personal commissions. Their owners sometimes had as little sense of heraldic accuracy and nicety as their engravers, and incorrect blazons abound. As for the engravers, other than those who specialized in bookplates, these include some distinguished artists. Hollar engraved a plate for John Aubrey, and Hogarth's bookplate for the herald painter, John Holland, is large and impressive. Gribelin, Vertue, Strange and Bartolozzi also lent their talents to bookplate design, as in the medium of wood-engraving did Thomas Bewick and his pupils. Millais designed a charming little bookplate for Christopher Sykes, the canting arms denoting the patronymic: *Argent a Chevron Sable between three Sykes or Fountains*. Modern artists of note who have designed and also engraved bookplates include Eric Gill, Reynolds Stone (fig. 6) and Joan Hassall. Most of their engravings were labels or pictorials, but some armorials are included in the work of them all. No less important, and much more considerable numerically, have been the bookplates engraved through the centuries by trade engravers, of whom a few have made a speciality of this kind of work. There are now probably as many talented bookplate engravers as at any time since the first bookplate appeared. No longer, however, does the armorial hold sway, nor is there one style which distinguishes the period; each plate is designed by the artist to suit the owner's wishes.

The traditional method for bookplate making until the last half century was copper engraving, but etching was also used from the eighteenth century, and most consistently by George W. Eve between 1886 and 1914. Wood-engraved armorials of the seventeenth and eighteenth century are known, but they become more familiar in the nineteenth; the Jewitts and Le Keux, for instance, producing some marvellously meticulous engravings in the seal style. Aquatint and mezzotint were both very rarely used, but many mechanical processes were adopted in the last century and have remained. These include lithographic processes, line and half-tone blocks and collotype. There was also in Victorian times some recourse to coloured bookplates, armorial and pictorial. Bookplates printed in a single colour can be very effective, especially if different colours are used to suit individual books and endpapers, or to indicate a book's classification.

There is no doubt that a fine bookplate adds distinction to a book, apart from its usefulness as a form of indication of ownership. Incidentally, it is totally unnecessary to add the words 'Ex Libris' as is so frequently done; the name of the owner below is entirely adequate. Apart from their use as marks of identity and artistic adornment, bookplates can be most useful in the identification of arms, particularly of hatchments, and other anonymous coats such as on silver and porcelain; and they can be of assistance to genealogists and family historians.

There are many bookplate collections in libraries and museums, the largest being the Franks Collection at the British Museum, to which G.H. Viner added bookplates not already represented from his own collection; other assemblages of plates are there as well, and its international holdings are equally impressive. The National Library of Wales has the Sir Even Jones, Aneurin Williams, Elenor and Llangibby Castle Collections; the Henderson Smith Collection is in the National Library of Scotland; and the Turnbull Collection is at the Fitzwilliam Museum, Cambridge. Other fine provincial collections are the Liverpool Public Library Collection, the Wolseley Collection at Hove Public Library, and the John Johnson Collection at the Bodleian Library, Oxford. In London there is the Perez Collection at the National Book League, the Porteous Collection at the Heraldry Society, the Hall Crouch Collection at the Society of Antiquaries, and the Johnson and Cockburn Collections at Chelsea Public Library. The Royal College of Surgeons, like several other medical institutions, has a collection of the bookplates of doctors and surgeons. The collections noted above are not listed in order of importance, and are but a selection of the collections available for inspection in public institutions up and down the country.

Bookplate collecting, which became especially popular at the end of the nineteenth century, has recently enjoyed a revival. The Bookplate Society has over two hundred and fifty members in some twenty countries. It furthers the study of bookplates by its publications and talks, and holds a number of meetings each year in London, enabling exchange and sale of bookplates and opportunity to share the results of research (*see* ADDRESSES). PS

Further reading

Castle, Egerton *English Bookplates*, London, 1892. New and enlarged edition, London, 1893.

Fincham, Henry W. *Artists and Engravers of British and American Book Plates*, London, 1897.

Hamilton, Walter *Dated Book-plates*, London, 1895.

Hardy, W.J. *Book-plates*, London, 1893, second edition, 1897.

Howe, E.R.J. Gambier *Catalogue of British and American Book Plates bequeathed to the Trustees of the British Museum by Sir Augustus Wollaston Franks*, three volumes, London, British Museum, 1903-4.

Lee, Brian North *British Bookplates*, Newton Abbot, 1979.

Warren, the Hon. J. Leicester *A Guide to the Study of Bookplates*, London 1880, second edition (as Lord de Tabley, but published posthumously), Manchester, 1900.

The standard work on American bookplates is Charles Dexter Allen's book of that title, New York and London, 1894, second edition, London, 1895.

Leiningen-Westerberg's *German Bookplates*, 1891, and Walter Hamilton's *French Bookplates*, London, 1896 are helpful introductions to the bookplates of these countries.

Other works relating to British, American and continental bookplates will be found in George W.

Fuller's *A Bibliography of Bookplate Literature,* Spokane Public Library, 1926, republished Detroit, 1973. The Bookplate Society can give information about more recent publications.

Bordure In armory, a border abutting the edge of the shield. The bordure is a sub-ordinary but is invariably employed to indicate difference, distinction, etc. Indeed, in early armory, bordures were considered to be additions to the shield, depicted in relief and not subject to the tincture convention.

In impaled arms the bordure is truncated at the partition line. A bordure wavy has been a mark of bastardy in England since the late eighteenth century, and the bordure compony is employed in Scotland for the same purpose. The Scottish system of cadency uses a variety of bordures to indicate an armiger's independent position within a family. The bordure may be plain, parted, varied or charged, and its inner edge formed of any of the ornamental variations of line.

See also SUB-ORDINARY

Boreyne A similar monster to the bonacon, but with a barbed tongue, dorsal fin, the fore-legs of a lion and eagle's claws on the hind legs.

Bosses *see* **Ceilings**

Botrager Specifically the helmed lion depicted on the obverse of the *lion de deux gros,* a silver coin minted at Ghent (and later at Mechelen) by Louis de Male, Count of Flanders 1346-84. Other coins of the series also bore helmed lions, all with crests depicting a lion's head between two wings, that on the gold *lion* and *demi lion* being sejant and seated on a throne. The commercial influence of Flanders is reflected in the rapid adoption by neighbouring rulers of botrager-type devices, often on coinage of inferior metal and even in satirical form, such as the lions in the van Orije Missal (1366) which wear a bee hive and a flower pot! The term is sometimes applied generically to any helmed beast.

Bottle Seals From the middle of the seventeenth century, wealthy wine drinkers had their specially made bottles further embellished with a blob of glass attached to the bottle body. Into this blob of glass, in its molten stage, was impressed the customer's seal. This could comprise initials, arms, crest, other device or a combination of these, according to the whim of the customer, the finished effect being similar to a wax seal.

Tavern keepers also began to personalize their bottles in this manner. They usually had their own and their wives' initials surrounding a representation of their tavern sign, and often a date. The date would probably indicate when the wine was bottled, or when laid down in a cellar. By the year 1730, the sealing of tavern bottles had virtually ceased, though the tradition was carried on by private individuals for another hundred years, until the middle of the nineteenth century.

The Oxford colleges began using sealed bottles around the middle of the seventeenth century, and continued the practice until about 1730. The names of wine merchants began to appear on bottles from the late eighteenth century. A seal bearing a brand name is of a much later date, usually late nineteenth or early twentieth century. BC

Further reading
Morgan, R. *Sealed Bottles* London, 1971.
Ruggles-Brise, S. *Sealed Bottles* London, 1949.

Bouché *see* **Shield**

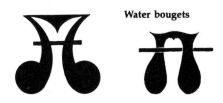

Water bougets

Bouget In armory a stylized representation of a yoke supporting two leather waterbags.

Late seventeenth-century bottle seal: the lozenges and dragon's wings of Daubeney. Wine purchased in casks was often bottled for the customer in his own bottles.

68

Bound *see* **Attributes**

Bow The shortbow of 3 or 4 feet (1 or 1½ m) in length was used until *c.* 1270, when the 6-foot (2 m) longbow, first developed in Wales, was adopted as the English national weapon. This had a pull of between 60 and 90 pounds, and fired a 3-foot arrow.

Braced Interlaced, especially used to describe interlaced chevronels.

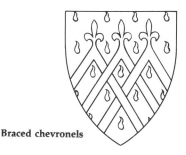

Braced chevronels

Brasses, Monumental A flat metal plate engraved with a figure and/or inscription and affixed as a memorial to the floor or wall of a church or to a tomb. There are some 7500 brasses in England, more than any other European country. Although termed brass, the material is more correctly a form of bronze, being a mixture of copper, zinc and a small amount of tin and lead. In the Middle Ages it was known as latten, and later *cuivre blanc* (white copper) or yellow metal. Those who worked on monumental brasses were known as 'marblers'.

Brasses are probably the best known of all MONUMENTS, and brass-rubbing with cobbler's heel ball on paper has become so popular that brass-rubbing centres have been established in many towns where reproduction brasses are available for rubbing, thereby preserving the originals from damage.

Brasses are a development of the INCISED SLAB memorial, and originated in the Low Countries in the thirteenth century. The earliest surviving figure brass is that of Bishop Yso von Wilpe (d. 1231) at Verden, West Germany. This depicts the bishop in his vestments holding a church in each hand and is surrounded by an inscription. By the beginning of the fourteenth century workshops had been established in England, and a distinctive style developed. English brasses consisted of separate pieces cut from a sheet of metal (imported from Europe) and placed in the slab after engraving. The indentation cut into the slab (which was usually of local stone or Purbeck marble) is called a matrix, and was made so that the surface of the brass was flush with that of the surrounding stonework. The matrix was flooded with black pitch which not only acted as an adhesive, but also prevented movement between the brass and stone and reduced corrosion. Later brasses were secured by brass rivets driven into lead plugs in the stone.

Flemish brasses of the fourteenth century were very large and elaborate and the figures were engraved on rectangular sheets of metal with the background between the figures decorated with diaper or other small figures, and the whole plate set within a slab. Some were exported to England, such as the brass of Abbot Thomas de la Mare at St Alban's, Hertfordshire, which measures 9 foot 3 inches by 4 foot 4 inches (2.8 x 1.5 metre). The majority of surviving English brasses came from workshops at Norwich, York and, particularly, London, and may be identified by comparing the different styles of design and manufacture. As with the EFFIGY, the brass of this period portrayed only a stylized representation of the deceased. Each workshop developed a series of standard patterns, from which a client would select the most appropriate and to which personal devices and inscriptions were added, and it is possible to identify the different 'schools' of engraving from the characteristics of a particular brass. There is evidence that in a considerable number of brasses the practice of letting coloured enamels into the concave surfaces was employed for heraldic decoration from the earliest period well into the sixteenth century.

Many of the earlier figures were life-size or slightly smaller, but demi-figures and miniature figures were also made. A brass at Chinnor, Oxfordshire (*c.* 1520) is only 7½ inches (19 cm) high. Figures may be accompanied by an inscription and secondary subjects such as the Trinity, and may be surrounded by a decorative canopy. That the complete brass consisted of several elements has meant that few surviving today are complete. The gaping matrix, whilst serving as a useful indication of the original composition, is particularly frustrating to the armorist.

The first English brasses are those of bishops or abbots, the earliest of which date from the 1280s. The earliest military brass, now only an indent, is at Aston Rowant, Oxfordshire, and is dated *c.* 1314. A series of military monuments, now dated between 1320 and 1330, illustrate well the early application of armorial devices to military equipment and are essentially functional. The brass of Sir John d'Abernon at Stoke d'Abernon, Surrey, which for many years has been regarded as the earliest English example, shows a knight bearing a shield on which there are traces of blue enamel (his arms were *Azure a Chevron Or*) and a pennon of his arms. This brass has now been re-dated to 1327. Three other splendid figures of 1320-30 are those of Sir Roger de Trumpington at Trumpington, Cambridgeshire, Sir William de Setvans at Chartham, Kent, and Sir Robert de Bures at Acton, Suffolk. In each case the arms are shown on a shield borne by the figure. On the Trumpington brass the arms are also

Brand of Henry Grene (d. 1467) at Lowick, Northamptonshire. The quartered arms (*Chequy Or and Argent a Bordure Gules* and *Argent a Cross engrailed Gules*) are on a garment which exemplifies the transition from jupon to tabard.

depicted on the ailettes and on the scabbard of the sword, and at Chartham the ailettes and surcoat of the Setvans brass are decorated with his punning arms of winnowing fans. With the revised dating of all four brasses, the earliest heraldic brass may be that of Margaret, Lady Camoys at Trotton, Sussex, dated *c.* 1310. Lady Margaret's dress originally had nine enamelled shields set into the brass, but regrettably all are now missing.

One of the most attractive armorial brasses is that of Sir Hugh Hastings in Elsing Church, Norfolk (1347). The brass, which is badly mutilated, depicts a maunch with a label for difference on the tunic and shield, and even on the pommel of the sword. The figure stands beneath the depiction of a canopy, on each column of which are four figures representing the friends and relatives of the deceased. Each figure also wears an

heraldic tunic. This is one of the last brasses to show a knight actually bearing a shield on his arm. From about 1360 the shield was placed within its own matrix and two or more shields were often depicted in this way.

Crests on helmets are numerous, particularly in the brasses of the fifteenth and sixteenth centuries. The helmet is usually placed beneath or near the head of the figure, so that it is seen in profile. Early examples are those of Sir John Harsyck (1384) at Southacre, Norfolk (a panache), and Sir William de Bryene (1395) at Seal Church, Kent (a hunting horn). Other good examples are the extraordinary eagle's head crest of Sir Nicholas Dagworth (1401) of Blickling, Norfolk, the demi-friar holding a scourge in the crest of the Stourton knight at Sawtry, Cambridgeshire (1404), and the immense bird with wings displayed in the crest of Henry Stathum at Morley, Derbyshire (1480).

The earliest types of outer garment shown on military brasses of the early fourteenth century were the long surcoat and the cyclas. These are usually charged with the arms, unlike the short, tight-fitting jupon of the camail period, so called from the introduction of the camail, a form of mail cape suspended from the bottom of the helmet *c.* 1360. For some unaccountable reason, the majority of brasses of this period do not depict the arms upon the jupon but on separate shields above or around the figure. This may simply have been a matter of fashion, or it may be that they were originally coloured in a medium of which no trace remains, though this seems unlikely. It is strange that contemporary workshops should have retained in their designs a garment which was ideally suited to armorial display, and yet the majority of clients should have chosen to ignore its potential. This fashion, if such it was, anticipated that of the following century, for between 1360 and 1460 only one tenth of figures of knights are shown wearing heraldic garments. From the beginning of the fifteenth century an increasing number of figures wear plate armour, uncovered and without embellishment, the heraldry of these brasses being confined to separate inset shields of arms and helms, crests and mantlings. This is undoubtedly a reflection of the contemporary fashion for exhibiting the magnificent (and extremely expensive) German plate armour in preference to covering it with some form of heraldic tunic. However, a significant number of late fifteenth century brasses show figures dressed in tabards (short loose-fitting garments with sleeves), and these are found well into the sixteenth century, the number and complexity of the quarterings depicted thereon increasing significantly in the Tudor period. Early examples may be seen at Great Snoring, Norfolk, where the brass of Sir Ralph Skelton (1423) was possibly enamelled, at Amberley in Sussex in the brass of John Wantele (1424), and at Childrey, Berkshire, in the brass of William Fynderne (1444), where the arms are in lead-like metal.

Possibly the finest heraldic brass of the period is that of the Earl of Essex and his wife (1483) at Little Easton, Essex. He is represented in his Garter robes, and the heads of both figures rest upon elaborate helmets with crests and mantlings, and their feet upon eagles.

There are numerous examples of armorial gowns and capes worn by women depicted in brasses throughout the medieval and Tudor periods. That of Joyce, Lady Tiptoft at Enfield, Middlesex (d. 1446, engraved 1470) is a fine example, as is that of Lady Katherine Howard (d. 1452, engraved 1535) at Stoke by Nayland, Suffolk. Two other notable female figures are those of Elizabeth, Countess of Oxford (1537) at Wivenhoe, Essex, and Elizabeth, wife of John Shelley (1526) at Clapham, Sussex, whose arms *Sable a Fess engrailed between three Whelk Shells Or* are clearly allusive. Women's garments were considered to be most appropriate vehicles for the display of quarterings, particularly during the sixteenth century. It was at this time also that many retrospective brasses were laid down, of both men and women, possibly to commemorate hereditary or marital connections with the 'old' nobility of the pre-Bosworth period.

Those who wish to trace the development of costume or armour through the study of monuments should be aware that many were not contemporary with the death of those they commemorate. Some were retrospective, others were prepared in anticipation of death, and the erection of others was delayed simply because executors were not reliable! The dating of brasses by reference to the style of armour or costume is similarly unreliable and may be demonstrated by further consideration of the famous Trumpington brass. For many years this was attributed to the first Roger de Trumpington, who died in 1289, the style of armour being used as evidence for this dating. However, it was later noted that the small shields on the sword scabbard and the representations of arms in the ailettes were charged with five-pointed labels, crudely incised as single lines and with the points unevenly spaced. These, it was concluded, were later additions and the question of dating was re-examined. It is now believed that the brass was prepared in anticipation of death by the son of Roger I, Sir Giles de Trumpington (d. 1332), and that it was appropriated, and the arms hastily amended, for the tomb of *his* son, Roger II, who predeceased his father *c.* 1326. The canting arms of de Trumpington are *Azure crusily two Trumpets palewise Or*, those of Roger II charged with *a Label Argent* in the roll of the battle of Boroughbridge (1322).

Insignia of office may also be found in monumental brasses. Several survive showing, for example, Canons of Windsor in their ceremonial dress of a cloak with a cross on the left shoulder, and brasses of yeomen of the guard may depict the distinctive rose and crown badge. There is a brass of John Borrell, Sergeant at Arms, at Broxbourne, Hertfordshire, in which he is seen carrying his mace of office.

Lancastrian collars of SS, Yorkist collars of suns and roses, and personal collars of badges and other devices are frequently encountered both in military and civilian brasses. The brass of Thomas, Lord Berkeley, at Wotton-under-Edge, Gloucestershire, shows him wearing a collar of mermaids, the family badge. Occasionally, badges may be found scattered within the overall design. The brass of Sir Thomas Beauchamp at St Mary's Church, Warwick, has the badge of the bear and ragged staff semy on his armour. At Wollaton, Nottinghamshire, the slab of Richard Willoughby (1471) has small brass whelk shells inset all over it, the whelk shell being the Willoughby badge. Viscount Beaumont, at Wivenhoe in Essex (1507) has his badge of an elephant bearing a castle, and armed men at his feet and repeated in the borders of the brass.

Garter brasses are also to be found, with the figure either robed or wearing the Garter on his left leg. The brass of Sir Thomas Boleyn (father of Anne Boleyn) at Hever, Kent, shows him in his full Garter robes. At Felbrigg, Norfolk, the brass of Sir Simon Felbrigg (1416) was engraved at his own direction and placed over the tomb of his first wife, Margaret, daughter of the Duke of Teschen. Sir Simon died in 1442 and was buried at Norwich: ample warning to the armorist that he should not always assume that a monument marks the place of interment. The brass depicts Sir Simon in full plate armour and wearing the Garter. On his shoulders are two white escutcheon plates, each charged with the red cross of the Order, and he holds the banner of Richard II, with the arms of the Confessor impaling France Ancient and England quarterly (he was banner-bearer to Richard II).

From about 1570 the heraldic figure declined in popularity and designs often comprised a central achievement, usually with a multi-quartered coat, surrounded by separate shields of arms. At Ilminster, Somerset, the brass of Nicholas and Dorothy Wadham, founders of Wadham College, Cambridge, has four shields and an achievement of fourteen quarterings.

In the sixteenth century, brass plates were used at the backs of WALL MONUMENTS. These plates were usually a single sheet engraved with figure(s), inscription and other decoration. Shields of arms were popular: the small wall monument of John Ashenhurst at Leek, Staffordshire, depicts four shields of his arms impaling the arms of each of his four wives.

From the mid-seventeenth century until the middle

of the nineteenth the monumental brass was unfashionable. At Taplow, Buckinghamshire, there are some small brasses of this period 'recovered from the crypt of the old Church'. The Gothic revival of the Victorian Age saw a return of the brass figure set into a slab. Also popular was the brass wall monument with an inscription in coloured Gothic lettering with the occasional shield or crest above.

The twentieth-century brass monument is of a much simpler design, usually an engraved crest or hatched or enamelled coat of arms on a simple and attractive wall plaque of metal. There are more elaborate memorials to the late Duke of Norfolk (Arundel) and Earl and Countess Mountbatten (Westminster Abbey).

For the Monumental Brass Society *see* ADDRESSES.

Further Reading
A List of Monumental Brasses in the British Isles Stephenson Mill, 1926; Appendix, London, 1938.
Bouquet, A.C. *Church Brasses* London, 1956.
Boutell, C. *The Monumental Brasses of England* London, 1849.
Cameron, H.K. *A List of Monumental Brasses on the Continent of Europe* London Monumental Brass Society, 1970.
Clayton, M. *Brass Rubbings* 1929 (reprint Victoria & Albert Museum, London, 1968).
— *Catalogue of Rubbings of Brasses and Incised Slabs* 1972.
Druitt, H. *A Manual of Costume as Illustrated on Monumental Brasses* London, 1906.
Haines, H. *A Manual of Monumental Brasses* Bath, 1861 (reprinted 1970).
Lewis, J.M. *Welsh Monumental Brasses* 1974.
Norris, M. *Monumental Brasses, The Craft* London, 1978.
Macklin, H.W. *Monumental Brasses* 1905 (revised J.P. Phillips, London, 1975).

Brethren of the Sword, Order of A small order formed in Livonia in 1202 to fight the pagans of Lithuania. It followed monastic rule, and bore red crossed swords as its badge. In 1237 it joined the Teutonic Knights, and became virtually absorbed into that larger order.   KH

Brewers' Devices The majority of British brewers' devices are pictographs or logotypes. Some may appear to have armorial origins but are entirely bogus, and others employ devices taken from the arms of their locality, that of the famous real-ale brewery Ruddles of Oakham being a horseshoe from the arms of the former county of Rutland, for example. A small number are genuinely armorial, however, the best known being the *Hind's Head erased Gules* on a silver and red wreath of the Whitbread Breweries, the crest

of the Whitbread family. The *Horse's Head couped Gules accoutred in Armour Argent bridled Or* of the Darley Brewery in Yorkshire was also the crest of that family, and the *demi-Tiger salient Vert in the dexter Paw a Cross-Crosslet fitchy Argent* crest of the Devenish family is now used as the device of the Cornish (formerly Dorset) brewery of that name. In Oxford, the *demi Lion rampant guardant holding in the dexter Paw a Sprig of three Roses Gules* is a familiar sight at Morrells pubs, and the Summerskill's Brewery of Plymouth uses as a device the *Hand holding a Leg in armour couped above the knee and Spurred proper* crest of the Bigsbury family after whom their best bitter is named. Of particular interest to members of the Heraldry Society, London, is the *Lion's Face crowned with an Ancient Crown* device of Herald, a traditional brewery of County Derry, Northern Ireland. The arms of the Society are charged with the same device.

Bridled *see* **Attributes**

Bristed *see* **Attributes**

Bristol Nails In medieval times trading was frequently conducted in the street. In Bristol a number of metal pedestals with flat tops were provided and, as they were used for counting money, to 'pay (cash) on the nail' passed into the language. Four such nails originally dating from *c.* 1600 were, in 1771, re-sited outside the Corn Exchange in Corn Street, Bristol. Bristol Nails have recently been granted by the College of Arms to a Bristolian whose father re-cast a damaged Nail in the 1930s. They appear as charges in his arms, crest and badge (see colour page 250).

Brisure *see* **Cadency**

British Empire, The Most Excellent Order of The Founded in 1917 by George V as a means of honouring British and Commonwealth subjects for conspicuous service at home and in the British Empire, the order is both the youngest and the largest of the British orders of chivalry, having in excess of 100,000 members, and is indeed the 'Order of Chivalry of the British Democracy' (a military division was created in 1918). From the outset it was intended that the new order should include people from all stations in life who had not previously been eligible for membership of other British orders. Various titles were suggested, including the Order of Mars (so called because the order was closely associated with the war effort), and the Order of St Lewis. Difficulties arose because of the large numbers of people who were apparently eligible for membership. Some even wrote to King George suggesting that they were worthy of the honour and that others were not, thereby ensuring their own disqualification! There are five classes: Knights and Dames Grand Cross, GBE; Knights and Dames Commander, KBE, DBE; Commanders, CBE; Officers, OBE; Members, MBE. There are also two British Empire medals, one being awarded for meritorious service and the other for gallantry. The latter has not been recommended since 1974, when a new award (the Queen's Gallantry Medal) was instituted for this purpose.

The ribbon of the order was originally purple with an additional red central stripe for the military division. However, in 1937 it was changed to rose pink with pearl grey edges, the ribbon for the military division having an additional central stripe of pearl grey.

The original badge consisted of a cross patonce ensigned by a Crown Imperial and bearing a central medallion of Britannia encircled by the motto of the order, 'For God And The Empire'. In 1937 the figure of Britannia was replaced by the crowned effigies of George V and Queen Mary. The reverse bears the cypher of George V. Both stars (those for Knights and Dames Grand Cross and for Knights and Dames Commander) consist of an eight-pointed, silver-chipped star bearing the medallion within a circlet of the order, the star for Knights and Dames Commander having shorter rays between the four principal points. Commanders wear the badge of the order on a neck ribbon, and Officers wear the badge in silver gilt on a chest ribbon or bow. The badge of Members is in silver and is similarly worn. The mantle of the order is rose-pink lined with pearl grey silk (before 1937 it was purple), and on the left side is a representation of the star of a Knight Grand Cross. The collar is of silver gilt and composed of six medallions of the royal arms and six of the royal and imperial cypher of George V, linked alternately by cables bearing the Imperial Crown between sea-lions with tridents. The badge is pendent from the central link.

The chapel of the order is in the crypt of St Paul's Cathedral in London. It was designed by Lord Mottistone and is entered through a wrought iron screen in which there are panels of grisaille glass decorated with representations of the services performed throughout the British Empire by members of the order, and depictions of the founders and royal members of the order. The panelling is carved with the star and badge, and in the chapel ambulatory is a series of stained glass windows designed by Brian Thompson. These include heraldic emblems of Britain and the Empire, the insignia of the order and the badges of office for, among others, the order's king of arms and the Gentleman Usher of the Purple Rod, whose office recalls the order's original livery. Banners of the royal members hang in the ambulatory.   SS

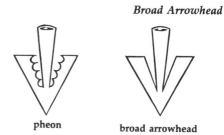

pheon   broad arrowhead

Broad Arrowhead (i) An armorial charge consisting of the iron head of the deadly fourteenth-century English broad-arrow. The term broad-arrow (*brodarewe*) implied a wood arrow, with barbed iron arrowhead, about one metre long. As early as 1486 the *Boke of St Albans* stated that 'feons be calde in armys brode arow hedys'. Generally, armorists apply the term PHEON to an arrowhead the inner edges of which are engrailed, the broad arrowhead having unserrated edges. Both pheon and broad arrowhead are borne with the point downwards, unless otherwise blazoned.

(ii) A sigillum, or mark, signifying the property of the British sovereign. In 1830 Marryat, in his novel *The King's Own*, wrote, 'The broad headed arrow was a mark assumed at the time of the Edwards (when it was considered the most powerful weapon of attack) as distinguishing the property of the King; and this mark has been continued down to the present day. Every article supplied to His Majesty's service from the arsenals and dockyards is thickly studded with this mark and to be found in possession of any property so marked is a capital offence, as it designates this property to the King's Own.' It is not true that the pheon mark derived from the *Or a Pheon Azure* arms of Henry Sidney (1641-1704), Earl of Romney and Master General of the Ordnance. Its use as a royal device clearly pre-dates that period. As late as the middle of the seventeenth century, the officers at the Tower of London still bore the names of their pre-firearm predecessors: *Balistarius* (Keeper of Cross-bows), *Attiliator Balistarum* (Keeper of Furniture for Cross-bows), *Bowyer* (Keeper of Bows), and *Fletcher* (Keeper of Arrows). At that time they were replaced by a Master General of Ordnance and seven officers who were responsible for applying the 'King's Mark' to military items. In 1685 Charles II commanded that the broad-arrow mark was to be used on buildings associated with the Tower, a decree which was later incorporated in a charter to the Tower by James II (1687). At this time the use of the broad arrowhead mark was ubiquitous: timber from the royal forests, destined for the naval shipyards, was so stamped as were numerous portable items 'for the better preventing of the Imbezzlement of His Majesties Stores of War' (Act of 1698). The mark first appeared on the 'course and Uniform apparel' of prisoners towards the end of the seventeenth century, though it was not until the end of the following century that the provision of uniform became a statutory requirement 'with certain obvious Marks of Badges affixed to the same . . . as well to humiliate the wearers as to facilitate Discovery in the case of escapes' (19 George III cap. LXX). As recently as 1922 this uniform was worn as a 'garb of shame' and sprinkled with broad-arrows which were probably cut-out facings sewn on by the prisoners themselves. At that time also, a broad-arrow diaper, printed in black and white, was the uniform of female prisoners. Officially the practice was discontinued in the 1920s.

Bucket Shop Heraldry The term is generally applied to coats of arms or 'parchment' scrolls which may be purchased by mail order or from certain trade shows or gift fairs. When a customer orders one of these he is purchasing a randomly selected coat of a given surname from such armorial reference books as those of Burke or Reitstap. The popularity of these 'personalized' products has rapidly accelerated in post-war years, and especially during the seventies and eighties with the ever increasingly popular pastime of family history research.

In the 1940s a northern company began producing good quality hand-painted wall plaques depicting British regimental, warship and squadron badges, insignia of schools, colleges, sporting clubs and societies, and civic arms to local councils. Family arms were also produced on a lesser scale. Over the years, many imitators appeared, and during the sixties small heraldic art workshops proliferated, producing mostly 'family arms' to cope with the huge demand from the American market and to satisfy the demands of the amateur genealogist, or those responding to the blatant 'snob-appeal' of the product. Off-the-peg family arms were also much easier for the small firm to produce than authentic commissions for work which required hand-carved dies from which the embossed pressings were taken. Ugly pressings were invariably produced, incorporating shield, helm, wreath, 'seaweed' mantling, and motto scrolls, the individual devices being hand-painted onto the blank pressings, often by artists who had no understanding of, or sensitivity for, heraldic art.

Such items are still available in a variety of materials and sizes. Some have the arms painted on wooden centrepieces, some on deeply embossed copper pressings and others on plastic. The so-called 'parchments' and 'certificates of authenticity' are usually supplied on varying grades of paper and may be painted by home-workers with little or no knowledge of good heraldic practice.

When a customer acquires one of these products he is, in fact, buying 'a coat of arms once recorded for a family of that surname' (as the manufacturers are always careful to point out). However, many believe quite wrongly that they are purchasing their own personal coat of arms. BC

See also BOGUS HERALDRY; HERALDIC OFFICES; SPURIOUS HERALDRY

Buckler A shield, usually circular but smaller than a target, used by mounted or foot archers.

Bulgaria, Royal Arms of *Gules a Lion rampant crowned Or armed and langued Vert.*

Bullicorn Club In 1953 J.P. Brooke-Little and Sir Colin Cole founded the Bullicorn Club — an heraldic dining club with a strictly limited membership. The Club's badge incorporates the red bull of Sir Colin's arms with the black unicorn's head from those of Brooke-Little, the whole beast fretted gold in honour of Sir George Bellew, and gorged with a viscount's coronet to commemorate Viscount Furness, as these gentlemen hosted the first dinners of the Club. (Sir Colin Cole and J.P. Brooke-Little are respectively Garter and Norroy and Ulster kings of arms.)

Bunting (i) Multi-coloured decorative material suspended from buildings, etc., at times of celebration. In the Middle Ages and the Tudor period, bunting would have been of the armorial colours of a magnate who, for example, sponsored a tournament. During Lancastrian coronations, the blue and white household liveries of Lancaster were specified for this purpose in the streets of London. Today, it is the national colours which are used *ad nauseam*, which is unfortunate when one considers the many alternatives available: civic and corporate livery colours, for example.
(ii) The material of which outdoor flags are made is also described as bunting.

Burgee (i) An armorial banner used at sea. Usually swallow-tailed but square or rectangular in the hoist.
(ii) The distinguishing flag of a yacht club.
(iii) A Royal Navy flag, rectangular in shape and swallow-tailed.
See also FLAG

Burgeonee *see* **Attributes**

Burgess Originally the citizen of a borough, the term 'burgess' came to apply to a member of parliament for a borough, a magistrate, or a member of the governing body of a town. In the State of Virginia a member of the legislature is called a burgess, and the body as a whole the House of Burgesses. JC-K

Bute Pursuivant of Arms A Scottish pursuivant of arms prior to 1867 (the office was first mentioned in 1488). The title is derived from the Island of Bute, which lies in the approaches of the Firth of Clyde. CJB

Buttons Armorial buttons are highly valued by armorists and yet collections may be established at no great expense, the majority of items in the 'button box' of antique dealers costing but a few pence. Military buttons are often the most expensive, as are the buttons of the former railway and steamship companies, these being collected by a wide range of enthusiasts other than armorists. The buttons of fire, police and other public services and of educational institutions and corporate bodies are also widely collected. For armorists, however, the livery badges of the 'old nobility' are the most satisfying to collect. Many of these bear either the full arms or (more often) the crest. Buttons of the livery companies, the royal household and of ancient offices make particularly rewarding collections, many still available in their original boxed sets. A recent revival in the manufacture of armorial buttons (together with associated items such as cuff-links and small lapel badges) reflects a parallel revival in grants of armorial badges which are more appropriate to this use than shield or crest.

Further reading

Squire, G. *Buttons: A Guide for Collectors* London, 1972.

— *Livery Buttons* London, 1976 (limited ed.).

'By Royal Appointment' *see* **Royal Warrant Holders**

C

Cabled *see* **Attributes**

Caboshed *see* **Attitude**

Cadency In armory, the methods whereby different male members of a particular family and its cadet branches may be identified.

During the Middle Ages marks of difference were also employed to indicate feudal tenure and even political allegiance, elements of one coat being transferred to another for this purpose. In England, since the end of the fifteenth century, cadency has been achieved by the use of small charges (brisures), each appropriate to a particular male member of a family.

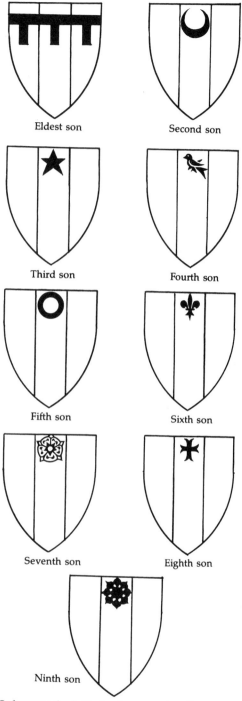

Eldest son

Second son

Third son

Fourth son

Fifth son

Sixth son

Seventh son

Eighth son

Ninth son

Cadency marks. In England, arms are hereditary to all legitimate descendants in the male line, and brisures may be dispensed with when quarterings are added, thereby making the arms distinctive from those of the senior branch.

First generation

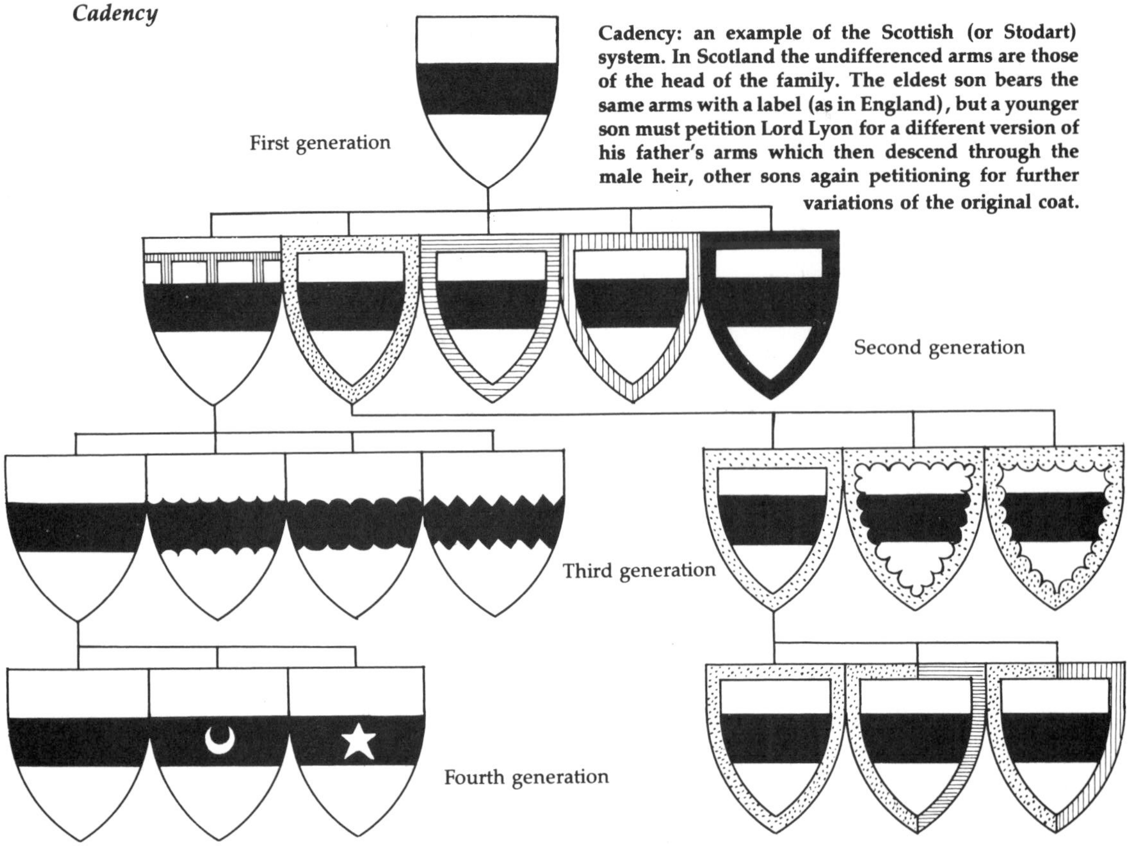

Cadency: an example of the Scottish (or Stodart) system. In Scotland the undifferenced arms are those of the head of the family. The eldest son bears the same arms with a label (as in England), but a younger son must petition Lord Lyon for a different version of his father's arms which then descend through the male heir, other sons again petitioning for further variations of the original coat.

Second generation

Third generation

Fourth generation

The label is borne across the top of the shield and is discarded on the death of the head of the family, the heir using the undifferenced arms. Other brisures are usually placed in fess point or nombril point, though this is not unalterable and may be varied for artistic purposes and to avoid ambiguity.

In succeeding generations these should, in theory, be charged with the appropriate cadency marks: for example, the second son of a second son would bear a crescent on a crescent, the fifth son of a third son would bear an annulet on a mullet, and so on. Such a system is clearly absurd and it is hardly surprising to find it more 'honour'd in the breach than the observance'! It has been observed that were differencing to be strictly applied today the heraldic authorities in England would enjoy greater control and pedigrees and records could be more easily maintained. There is clearly need of a new convention; one which is sufficiently flexible to provide greater control over the use of arms without becoming artistically intrusive.

In Scotland a system of bordures is used, each having different tinctures, partitions or sub charges. This is used by succeeding generations as a mark of difference which allows degree of kinship to the main stem of a family to be shown. Many armorists would

argue that even this system has its limitations, the ubiquitous bordure being a rather cumbrous charge and not conducive to imaginative artistic interpretation.

The principal tenet is the medieval one: 'one man one coat', and it is surely not beyond the heraldic imagination to devise a system whereby the paternal arms may be amended or augmented to indicate cadency without resorting to expedients which are contrary to good armorial practice?

In England women do not use cadency marks, for whilst arms may pass to a woman this occurs only in the absence of male heirs, and since in theory it is always possible that a man might produce a son, even an heiress presumptive may not place a label on her arms.

During the medieval period the label of three or five points was usually the mark of the eldest son, as it is today. However, no system of brisures was in common use and cadency was often indicated by, for example, a change of tinctures or minor charges, or by the addition of an ordinary or sub-ordinary. Care should be exercised when interpreting early arms, for similar methods were also used for MARSHALLING and MARKS OF DISTINCTION.   PF

Further reading Gayre, R. *Heraldic Cadency*, 1961.

Cadet The younger son of an armiger who is the progenitor of a subsidiary branch of a family.   CJB

Caduceus *see* **Medical Heraldry** *and* **Serpent**

Caerlaverock, The Siege of A famous siege of the Castle of Caerlaverock, near Dumfries in Scotland, by the forces of King Edward I in July 1300, noteworthy especially for the epic poem of that name, in which details of the banners and shields of more than one hundred nobles and knights are given. C.W. Scott-Giles' translation (somewhat condensed) into English verse is available from the Heraldry Society.

Calatrava, Order of A Spanish military order founded in 1158 to subjugate the Moors. It followed monastic rule, and bore a red Greek cross with Gothic letters.   KH

Calligraphy The word calligraphy comes from the Greek *kalos* and *graphos*, meaning beautiful writing. From the earliest times emblazoned armorial devices, in rolls of arms, manuscripts and elaborately decorated books of hours, were accompanied by a written text. The kind of writing used ranged from the formal book hands of the professional scribe to informal or cursive handwriting for business or personal use. 'Cursive', from the Latin *curro*, is the running characteristic in writing done at speed and usually accompanied by a slope to the right.

For the first years of armory's existence, book hands predominated. These were mostly varieties of Blackletter or 'Textur', the narrow angular hand which in later years was called 'Old English'. It formed a rich pattern on the page, although today people unaccustomed to it find it illegible. It was the staple book hand of every country in Europe (except Italy) and Scandinavia, and is still in use in German-speaking countries today. As literacy spread in Britain, so the cursive element in writing became more common during the fourteenth century.

The writing in the more important rolls of arms made between the thirteenth and fifteenth centuries varied from Blackletter written with differing degrees of skill to Court hands and a later, less formal version of Blackletter named Gothic Cursive, or Bastard Hand. But whichever hand was used, the scribe always seems to have had an acute awareness of the pattern and decorative quality of his writing.

Many heraldic documents such as the early grants of arms were written and illuminated superbly by professional artists. Some grants made in the sixteenth century were in the form of books. One such was a grant to Thomas Bell made by Sir Christopher Barker KB, Garter from 1534 to 1550. It is written in an early copperplate hand, with lively but clumsy illumination. Another in the form of a broadsheet, made to Charles Hewet in 1597, was written in a curious mixture of humanistic script and a poorly written late-fifteenth century vernacular hand.

The writing and decoration of manuscripts, and to a great extent the skills involved in their production, virtually ceased during the first half of the sixteenth century, except for legal, ecclesiastical and state documents. The adoption of the new humanist hand from Italy (e.g. Renaissance italic) affected all writing, both formal and informal, but the earlier Blackletter hands (with modifications) continued to be used for the most formal purposes.

In Italy one writing master, Francesco Moro, had the pages of his writing manual engraved on copper plates instead of being carved laboriously from blocks of wood. This gave better reproduction and a much longer run of prints. The engraving was done with a burin, a type of small triangular chisel which quickly began to influence the shape of the letters it made, to the extent that people began to cut their quill pens with long flexible points which enabled them to copy the new letters. This style developed into what became known as copperplate writing, used from the late sixteenth century onwards for most general purposes, with the addition of drawn formal Roman letters. It also became the basis of handwriting taught in schools.

In the eighteenth century another more ornate hand called the Engrossing Hand, with many variations, originating apparently in Germany, became popular with professional scribes and was used in conjunction with varieties of copperplate on contemporary patents of arms, deeds and indentures. All through the centuries, however, there has always been a wide variety of hands as diverse and individual

Blackletter

Gothic Cursive

Renaissance Italic

Engrossing Hand

Foundational Hand

in character as the scribes who wrote them. Copperplate is still used on occasion at the College of Arms, only reluctantly being abandoned for general purposes during the last twenty years.

In 1872 a young Scots medical student, Edward Johnston, became fascinated by medieval illuminated books and abandoned his medical studies to devote the rest of his life to the study of formal book hands and the design of manuscript books. He had a rare combination of abilities which led to his becoming the *force majeure* in lettering, and his teaching and calligraphy have had a profound and far reaching influence on the standard of lettering all over the world. He died in 1944.

Fairly early in his career. Johnston came to the conclusion that one hand, if it possessed the right qualities of balance, rhythm, proportion and legibility, based on a circular 'o' could serve as a sound basis for good formal writing. He evolved one over a period of years, modelled on what he considered to be the finest historical example, a Carolingian minuscule. Using this and classical Roman capitals, he arrived at a hand which he called Foundational, because he saw it as the foundation of all good book hands. It is in effect the grammar of calligraphy and it has had the influence he anticipated. The majority of contemporary formal hands have evolved from it, including a version commonly used on patents of arms.

Apart from copperplate, virtually all the writing done on heraldic documents is directly influenced by Johnston's teaching. Contemporary styles are more varied and generally of a higher quality than ever before. The principles of good manuscript design are much in evidence, and when work is produced by artists who are skilled both in heraldry and calligraphy, the results can indeed by formidable.   AW
See also ARMORIAL STYLES; ART WORK AND MATERIALS; ILLUMINATION. For the Society of Scribes and Illuminators *see* ADDRESSES.
Further reading
Fairbank, A. *A Book of Scripts* London, 1949. —and Wolpe *Renaissance Handwriting* London, 1960.
Johnston, E. *Writing and Illuminating and Lettering* 1980.
Knight, S. *Historical Scripts, a handbook for Calligraphers* 1984.
Lamb, C.M. (ed.) *The Calligrapher's Handbook* London, 1946.
Stribley, M. *The Calligraphy Source Book* London, 1986.
Whalley, J.I. *English Handwriting 1540 to 1853* HMSO, 1969.
Wright, C.E. *English Vernacular Hands* Oxford, 1960.

Caltrap *or* **Cheval-trap** Intended to maim horses in a cavalry charge. When strewn on the ground, metal

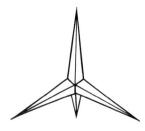

caltraps would always land with one of their four points upright.

Calygreyhound A rare monster with the head of a wild cat, tufted body and tail, claws on the fore-feet and bulbous horns.

Camail Defence for the neck and shoulders, usually made of chain mail or leather.   PG

Camelopard A variety of artistic interpretations will be found of this beast, which is essentially a giraffe. If it possesses two long horns curving backwards it is termed a camelopardel!

Canada, Orders of The Order of Canada was instituted by the Queen on the advice of her Canadian ministers on 1 July, 1967. It now comprises three grades: Companions, CC; Officers, OC; Members, CM.

The Order of Military Merit was established by the Queen on the advice of her ministers on 1 July, 1972, to recognize conspicuous merit and exceptional services by men and women of the Canadian Forces, both Regular and Reserve. There are three degrees: Commander, CMM; Officer, OMM; Member, MMM.   CS

Canadian Pale *see* **Pale**

Canal Devices The decoration of the boats and properties of the inland waterways in England stems from two quite distinct sources. The first was armorial in nature and came from the fact that canal and river navigation bodies were established by Act of Parliament, and hence required formal seals. Some of these were based on the arms of local towns. For example, the Aire and Calder service embraced, as their device, the arms of Leeds, Wakefield, the white rose of York and a sailing barge. Other organizations were less derivative; the Thames and Severn body sported a device showing the nymph, Sabrina, and Father Thames, for example. These quasi-armorial seals formed the basis of decoration on small articles like uniform buttons and cap badges, and also on more substantial properties such as bridges and buildings, where they were often cast as iron plaques or carved in stone. Today the 'three waves' logotype of the British Waterways Board can be seen in such places.

The second type of decorative device adopted in England was used for identification, sometimes painted on funnels, sometimes on hulls or the sides of cabins. These devices took various simple geometric forms, such as the red diamond used by the Pickford company, the black disc on the stem of Shropshire Union narrow-boats and two red discs on the Anderton boats employed in the pottery trade. House flags were sometimes flown carrying the symbol of the owner, and livery colours were painted on the masthead, funnels or other parts of vessels. In much the same way, following the Canal Boats Act of 1877, the local registration data now painted on British waterway craft is often embellished: a ship for Runcorn registration, a sheaf for Chester, a liver bird for Liverpool, and so on.

In England and on the continent of Europe the use of quasi-armorial signs was extended and developed in the nineteenth century, especially in those cases where the canal narrow-boats became family homes. Such canal craft became highly decorated with roses, castles, diamonds, scalloping, hearts, 'clubs' and other fancies. Various traditions developed, such as carving and gilding in Yorkshire, and geometric and foliated patterns and panels on the Leeds and Liverpool craft. In Germany, Rhine barges took to the lavish use of flags and immaculate paintwork. Swiss vessels had red gunwales and the white cross of that country painted on each side of the stem. To this day many European barges carry stars on their bows — perhaps a residual representation of the 'oculus', or eye, which, in classical times, enabled vessels to 'see' where they were going.   EP-T

Further reading

Frère-Cooke, G. et al *The Decorative Arts of the Mariner* London, 1966.

Hadley, D. *Waterways Heraldry* Waterways Museum, Stoke Bruerne, 1977.

Jones, B. *The Rose and the Castle* London, 1951. An important book covering a wide range of vernacular heraldry.

Lewery, A.J. *Narrow Boat Painting* Newton Abbot, 1974.

Canopy A roof-like projection over a tomb or memorial, usually of stone but also of wood or metal. A canopy is only one part of a MONUMENT. It may surmount a free-standing TOMB CHEST, a recessed tomb chest or a hanging WALL MONUMENT.

Canopies developed in the thirteenth century, principally over the tomb chests of bishops and archbishops, and may be a development of the structures placed over the shrines of saints. The overall design of the canopy followed contemporary architectural style and decoration. Interiors of

canopies were often painted with designs, and armorial badges and shields may have been included here, but the majority of painted decoration of the Middle Ages is lost to us today, and many canopies have also been destroyed or defaced.

One early heraldic example is the canopy of the Percy tomb at Beverley Minster, Yorkshire. On either side there is an ogee arch with Early English decoration. Each side has four shields carved with the arms of the Percy family and their close friends. It is thought, from the architectural style, to be the tomb of Eleanor Percy (d. 1328), but as it includes the Royal Arms *quarterly France Ancient and England* it must date from after 1340.

Canopies over recessed tombs in church walls were often simple affairs, although more elaborate ones with cupped and/or ogee arches were constructed. At Hereford Cathedral (*c.* 1300) a series of effigies was made for earlier bishops, and under each arch is a shield surmounted by a mitre. The recessed position of a tomb within a wall effectively provided spandrels on either side of the arch which could conveniently display shields, e.g. the tomb of Eleanor Bohun, again at Hereford. The later Perpendicular style provided a frieze along the top of the canopy which again accommodated shields.

In the late fifteenth century it became common practice to include badges, cyphers and heraldic beasts as decoration in addition to the shield. The free-standing tomb canopy in some cases was extended to form a chantry chapel (*see* CHANTRY). The Renaissance brought about a dramatic change to the canopy. The Gothic pillars and arches were replaced by Roman columns surmounted by classical pediments. This was during a period when families were eager to display all or, at least, the most significant of the heraldic quarterings to which they laid claim, and the canopy provided an excellent vehicle for such a display. There are various combinations to be found, but commonly a central achievement was flanked by two smaller ones above the pediment. Frequently displayed were the principal arms of the family, the quarterings they claimed, impalements of their spouse(s), and even arms of office. Supporters may appear on either side of the central shield or elsewhere, for example on either side of an obelisk. Arches provided spandrels for further shields, and the underside of the arch could be similarly decorated. Smaller shields in a frieze along the base of the pediment, or on the back plate of a wall monument, were used to display the marriage alliances of children and ancestors. The back plate could also be used to display badges and other devices. Where monuments were erected to the memory of two or more generations, the alliances of each generation would be shown.

Where such highly emblazoned canopies

surmounted tomb chests, the overall heraldic effect would be even greater as the chest itself would also bear arms, and might also be surrounded by iron work which included pennants. Two very fine examples of this combination are the tombs of Elizabeth Lady Hoby (d. 1609) at Bisham, Berkshire, which is set against a wall, and that of Bishop Montague (d. 1618) at Bath Abbey.

From the reign of Charles I there was an increasing tendency towards a purer classical treatment with less decoration. The achievement was usually accommodated in a segmental pediment, but the shield was gradually replaced by the cartouche. From the end of the seventeenth century, heraldry was to become a less important element of the design, and often its only place was in a cartouche or shield somewhere within the canopy. During the eighteenth century the canopy became an architectural feature, rather than a structure covering the whole base, and eventually was replaced by the wall monument. It was used again briefly in the nineteenth century as part of the Gothic revival. JET

Canting Arms A strict form of ALLUSIVE ARMS in which the entire design of a shield is devoted to a pictorial pun on the name of the armiger.

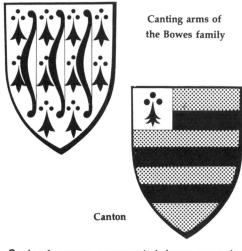

Canting arms of
the Bowes family

Canton

Canton In armory, a geometrical charge, square but smaller than a quarter, and depicted in dexter chief unless blazoned as a *sinister Canton*. The canton is a sub-ordinary but is invariably employed to indicate augmentation, differencing, etc., indeed in early armory every canton was theoretically a later addition to a coat. A canton of augmentation, etc., is assumed to be an addition to the shield, and may therefore debruise (deface) other charges and/or contravene the tincture convention. It may itself be surmounted only by a subsequent bordure of imbrication. The canton is subject to variations of field and line (though instances of the latter are rare), and may itself be charged. *See also* SUB-ORDINARY

Cap-à-Pie Fully armed.

Caparison (i) In armory, applied to a horse when fully equipped with bardings, trappings and caparison (see ii).
(ii) A favourite means of armorial display in the medieval and Tudor periods, particularly in tournaments and ceremonial processions. The body of the horse was covered in cloths richly embroidered or painted with armorial bearings. The rider's personal arms were often emblazoned on his shield, other quarterings decorating the caparison, usually without any pretence at marshalling. Fringes, reintrappings and other appendages were usually in the armorial or livery colours and charged with cyphers and badges. In battle, the abbreviated (and more practical) trapper was used.
See also BARDING.

Caparisoned *see* **Attributes**

Capitals Stone capitals at the tops of columns may be carved with many designs including geometrical patterns, grotesques and scenes. Heraldic ornamentation is rare, the thirteenth-century shields in the capitals of Cogenhoe Church, Northamptonshire, being exceptional. Usually it was the space above the capital, between the splays of the arches, which was better suited to armorial display, and shields (often held by figures such as angels) may be found in the arcades of several churches. At Cirencester, Gloucestershire, on the arcade wall above the capitals, angels bear shields charged with the arms or merchants' marks of benefactors who contributed to a rebuilding programme. JET

Cap of Dignity, Cap of Estate, Cap of Justice *and* **Cap of Maintenance** A ceremonial cap affixed to the helm in place of the wreath in a coat of arms or ensigning a robe of estate. In Scottish armory, depicted immediately above the shield in the arms of those of baronial rank. Boutell describes the ceremonial cap as 'an early symbol of high dignity'. However, Nisbet, writing in the early eighteenth century says, 'The Cap of State is frequently used in armories by the English, which they say is from, or in imitation of, the caps of the Roman generals, who having obtained a victory, and returning in triumph, had this cap of state carried before them, by their most worthy captive. It is now called a ducal cap. For the wearing of this cap had a beginning from the *dux* or duke, who was so called, a *ducendo* being leader in war, that is general of an army to emperors and kings, but is now given to others of inferior dignities and so cannot be an ensign of dignity, but given as a token of triumph and victory.'

Many consider caps of dignity, estate, justice and maintenance to be synonymous with each other and with the CHAPEAU. Certainly in British armory all take the *form* of the chapeau, however it seems unlikely that these terms should have survived independently of each other had not each been possessed of its own function. It may be that such caps were assigned as an indication of royal preferment to those who had given singular service to the Crown: to peers the Cap of Dignity, to holders of major offices of state the Cap of Estate, to those charged with the administration of justice the Cap of Justice, and to those whose service was of a more personal nature the Cap of Maintenance. It is also possible that a MANTLING of red doubled ermine possessed similar significance, and may have been adopted when a crest was not compatible with the chapeau, or a coronet was used instead. There were undoubtedly two types of chapeau: those which were indeed symbols of 'high dignity' and those which were simply integral to the crest and possessed no other significance. It seems likely that the latter type was widely adopted during the Tudor period when, inspired by the heralds' visitations, the lesser nobility and gentry acquired crests which had previously been denied them. Today, grants of ceremonial caps are rare and restricted to peers and Scottish feudal barons. In Europe, ceremonial caps continue in use in conjunction with MANTLES, though these tend to be the upright *toque* varieties.

In a peer's letters patent of creation, the ceremonial cap is described as 'a Cap of Honour', worn with 'a Coronet of Gold', and these are clearly the lineal descendants of the medieval chapeau and gold circlet.

Cardinal A member of the pope's council, or sacred college. These ecclesiastical princes comprise six cardinal bishops, fifty cardinal priests and fourteen cardinal deacons. When required, on the death of a pope, they elect a successor.   JC-K

Caretyne A rare beast, found in MS I.2 at the College of Arms as a badge of Sir Francis Bryan, Tudor courtier and diplomat. It has the body and horns of a bull, a head with snout, tusks and flames issuing from its mouth, one ear and cloven hooves. Its body is white and is covered with golden spots, and its attributes are also gold. The caretyne supporter in the arms of the Worshipful Company of Fuellers is similar and also has flames issuing from only one of its ears.

Carnation In armory, flesh-coloured.

Carrick Pursuivant of Arms A current Scottish pursuivant of arms. The title is derived from the Earl of Carrick, one of the titles borne by Robert the Bruce before his succession to the crown. Carrick is situated in the southwest of Scotland, and the first mention of the office is in 1364. The badge of office is *A Chevron Gules enfiling a Coronet of four Fleurs-de-lis and four Crosses paty proper.*   CJB

Cartulary *or* **Chartulary** (i) A collection of charters. (ii) A register of charters. (iii) A place where papers or records are kept.

Casque A close-fitting, open helmet, shaped to the head and often highly decorated.

Cat-a-mountain The wild cat, also blazoned musion.

Catherine Wheel A wheel of eight spokes, each ending in a curved spike.

Ceilings Many church roofs have been boarded or ceiled between the principal rafters to form ceilings, with bosses at the intersections. These bosses are often brightly coloured and gilded, and may incorporate heraldic motifs. The ceiling panels may also be carved, as at Shepton Mallet, Somerset, where a rounded 'wagon' roof contains three hundred and fifty carved panels with only one design duplicated. (Sometimes all the rafters of a wagon roof have been exposed during restoration. This is incorrect, for the spaces between the principal rafters should be plastered.) When the carved panels of a roof are coloured and gilded the result is superb, as at Cullompton in Devon. The most ornamental type of roof is the hammer-beam, found most frequently in the eastern counties of England. A hammer-beam is the projecting beam from which the main arch of the roof springs. In a double hammer-beam roof there are two tiers of such beams on each side. These projections often terminate in carved angels, sometimes in excess of one hundred in a single roof, and these often bear shields or other armorial devices. The base of the roof above the wall on either side forms a wall plate or cornice, and this too may be carved with angels, some of which hold shields. Aisle roofs are usually of simpler construction but, again, decoration often includes heraldic work. Corbels, on

which the wall posts of a roof are supported, are usually of stone and may be carved in the form of human heads, angels or monsters and should be coloured.

Arched roofs of stone are called vaults and these are usually found only in cathedrals, major churches and the smaller components of a simple parish church, such as the porch or tower. The shape of a vault follows the geometry of the arch. The simplest vault is, therefore, the barrel or tunnel which accompanies the semi-circular Norman arch. With the introduction of the pointed arch any span could be covered, and the construction and design of vaulting was revolutionized. A vault is constructed on temporary wooden structures (called cells) which fill the spaces between the stone ribs. The ribs are functional and spring from the wall to provide support for the roof. From the fourteenth century, however, the arrangement of ribs became extremely complex and included interlocking ribs which were purely decorative. These are known as lierne vaults. In the fifteenth century, fan vaulting was introduced. This is a purely English innovation and is undoubtedly the most beautiful of all vaults. All the ribs are of identical curve and spacing, and are carved from the stone slab instead of supporting it as previously. The finest fan vaults may be seen at King's College Chapel, Cambridge, Henry VII's Chapel in Westminster Abbey, and at Sherborne Abbey in Dorset. At Sherborne the enlarged keystones or bosses at the intersections of the ribs are beautifully carved and painted, and many are of armorial design: the cypher of Henry VII and his queen, Elizabeth of York, the Tudor Rose, shields of arms, dragons and other mythical beasts, and a rebus illustrative of the name of the great Abbot Ramsam showing a ram with the letters SAM. Altogether there are eight hundred of these painted and gilded bosses, some of those in the north transept weighing over half a ton. The great cloister at Canterbury Cathedral, remodelled *c.* 1400, contains over eight hundred shields of arms in its vaulted ceiling, and at St Alban's a series of fourteenth-century ceiling panels in the choir depicts the arms of Edward III, his family and alliances. These were discovered in the nineteenth century and, interestingly, the arms of England are shown in reverse, i.e. *Quarterly England and France Ancient.*

It should be remembered that, as with most other parts of the church, the medieval roof or vault would have been ablaze with the most brilliant colours and gilding. Although beyond the sight of man, the detail of carving and painting was always perfect, clearly executed for the greater glory of God. It is only with the modern camera or binoculars that we are privileged to have this beauty revealed to us in detail for the first time.

During the Tudor period, badges and armorial beasts were preferred as decorative motifs to personal

Heraldic bosses in the Presbytery vault of Winchester Cathedral: the royal arms, crowned thorn-bush device and HR monogram of Henry VII and the arms of the See of Winchester.

arms, the Tudor Rose and Beaufort portcullis being particularly popular. St George's Chapel, Windsor, is an excellent example of work of this period.

During the seventeenth century ceilings of moulded plasterwork were popular, and designs often included the heraldry of local nobles and benefactors — at Abbotsbury, Dorset, for example. From this period, heraldry figures infrequently in the classical church ceilings of the eighteenth and nineteenth centuries, nor (surprisingly) does it feature greatly in the Gothick revival of the Victorian age.

Much of the foregoing may also be applied to domestic ceilings. Early ceilings were made simply by placing boards to conceal the timbers installed as the floor of an upper chamber. They were often decorated and thus the plaster ceiling developed. An early example of a heraldic ceiling from the first half of the sixteenth century is that of the dining room at Haddon Hall, Derbyshire. It consists of several painted panels displaying badges and shields. Towards the end of the sixteenth century, the painted ceiling was replaced by the plastered motif, heraldic subjects being particularly popular at that time, e.g. the White Room at Broughton Castle, Oxfordshire (1599) and the Great Hall at Kellie Castle (1660).

During the eighteenth century domestic ceilings were decorated with classical designs and paintings, and heraldry did not feature again until the Victorian age, when once more ceilings were painted, e.g. the West Drawing Room at Oxburgh Hall, Norfolk, or constructed with Gothick wooden panelling with heraldic corbels and friezes.

In houses which incorporated former monastic buildings, surviving heraldic bosses may be found either in the vaulted ceilings of cloisters, crypts, etc., or scattered about the grounds for decorative purposes.   JET/SF

Celestial Crown *see* **Crest Coronet**

Centaur A creature from Greek mythology, the centaur has the body and legs of a horse with a man's trunk, arms and head. When depicted holding a bow and arrow it is termed a sagittary or sagittarius.

Ceramics Armorial ceramics is a rich field for the collector. It can also be a field for the rich collector! The modest end of many a market stall is weighed down with items of so-called 'Crested China' at prices within everybody's reach; on the other hand an English delft pill-slab bearing, in monochrome only, the arms of the Apothecaries Society realized £19,400 in a London sale room in the early 1980s.

Armorial delftware executed in blue, or sometimes polychrome, on a white ground has a very individual attractiveness. This is possibly because of the free-flowing, vigorous style of decoration, lacking in detail because of the absorbent nature of the tin-glazed body of the piece. Excavations in London have revealed many dishes made in this ware since the establishment of a pottery in the city in 1571, and the Museum of London holds numerous examples of this armorial domestic pottery from the seventeenth century. Chargers showing the arms of a City Livery Company are rarer but well documented and highly prized.

David Sanctuary Howard's monumental publication of 1974 provides an indispensable source of information for collectors of another much-admired body of ceramic material, Chinese Armorial Porcelain. Some four thousand services, giving a total of perhaps 800,000 pieces, were made in China between 1695 and 1820 for British families. They were exported from Canton at a rate of about one every six days for a century, until a prohibitive 150 per cent rate of tax, imposed to protect the growing English potteries, killed the trade in the early nineteenth century. The six-hundred-piece, richly decorated and heavily gilt Hannay service is the largest known of these. Made either for Alexander Hannay, Adjutant General in India, or for his brother Ramsay, a merchant trading between India and China, it came into the collection of the Winn family at Nostell Priory, Yorkshire, where it can now be seen, at a time when it had become acceptable, indeed fashionable, to possess antique items exhibiting arms other than one's own.

The naive and innocent exactitude with which the Chinese copyists transcribed their client's arms from drawings, engravings, bookplates or even seals into ceramic painting sometimes stimulates mild amusement today. But there is nothing that can diminish the admiration provoked by the richness of colouring, and the freedom and exuberance of decoration which is the characteristic of this much sought-after porcelain. There are collections in the Victoria and Albert Museum in London, the Ashmolean Museum in Oxford, and many National Trust properties in England. Like many other admired forms of applied art Chinese export porcelain had its cheap imitations, but such reproductions have now come to be collectable in their own right (see colour page 102.)

Reproductions were made by the Samson factory in Paris to make good missing or broken pieces of armorial services. These were distinguished from their models by having a distinctive letter S marked on the bottom of each piece, but this was so easily ground off by unscrupulous persons that it is rarely encountered today. The social interest of these pieces as well as the high standard of their craftsmanship makes the name Samson, now applied generically to many clever reproductions, greeted with almost as much respect as it was once treated with disdain.

The arms of the Duke of Norfolk are so often encountered on Samson porcelain that a very long run of a service, or incidental decorative pieces, must have originally been made for an uncritical popular market.

Wedgwood, Spode, Minton, Davenport and all the great English potteries which developed in the eighteenth century were able, once free from Chinese competition, to make finely decorated armorial porcelain for clients who commissioned it. These firms and their successors continue to do so to this day. The work is admired for the richness, discipline and precision of its armorial artwork.

In a different class are the transfer-printed pieces of armorially decorated Sunderland lustre-ware. Jugs and punch-bowls showing the arms of the Shipwrights Company must have been thought particularly saleable in a seaport, but the Cordwainers' arms and invented shields for masonic and agricultural fraternities show the market's receptiveness to heraldic subjects, even if there was no demand for armorial authenticity.

The royal arms or a portrait of Charles II, either in splendour or in the Boscobel Oak, were favourite decorations for Staffordshire slipware. Liquid, paste-like clay was either trailed or piped, like cake icing, on to the body of large dishes with diameters of up to 2 feet (60 cm). The effect was crude and peasant-like during the peak period of production between 1670 and 1690, but heraldic beasts were often featured on such ware.

Commemorative pottery of another era has a fervent and devoted band of enthusiastic collectors. The royal arms and various royal cyphers have been widely used on pottery mass-produced as souvenirs of various national occasions since the mid-nineteenth century. Happily the heraldic artwork produced by Anthony Wood for the Prince of Wales' wedding souvenirs, and by Musset for the Queen's Silver Jubilee in 1977, shows a quality of design which stands out by comparison with much of the inferior work that has been widely sold.

The violent swing of the pendulum of taste could not be more amply exemplified than by the world of popular heraldic porcelain. In 1883, Adolphus joined the china-manufacturing firm of his father, W.H. Goss, and hit on the idea of making miniatures of ancient artefacts that had been found in a particular area. They were hand-painted with the arms of their town of origin, and sold there through one selected retail shop. The collection of these souvenirs became enormously popular before the First World War, when railway travel and annual holidays came to have social importance. In an effort to decorate each new model with a shield the factories' enthusiasm outran discretion or heraldic propriety. But the ancient cities

and boroughs were well served: a contemporary catalogue of this ware lists 7000 different arms and decorations produced by the Goss factory alone, and there were many other manufacturers in this popular field. The craze lasted until about 1930, when bankruptcy ended the voluminous trading in Arcadian China by H.T. Robinson, who had bought-up Goss and many of the smaller producers. But the substantial outpourings of 'Crested China' during this period, and the ubiquity of its distribution, now enables a new generation of enthusiasts to be thematic in building up new collections.   JA

Further reading

Andrews, S. *Crested China, the History of Heraldic Souvenir Ware* Ascot, 1980.

Howard, D.S. *Chinese Armorial Porcelain* London, 1974.

Pugh, P.G.D. *Heraldic China Mementoes of the First World War* 1972.

Chained *see* **Attributes**

Champagne *or* **Champaine** (i) The base of a shield cut off by a horizontal line.
(ii) Concave.

Chancellor Literally a 'secretary'. Chancellors have been known in England since Edward the Confessor introduced the office of the King's Secretary. By stages the importance of the position grew, until the Chancellor of England (Lord Chancellor) became the highest judicial functionary, ranking in the order of precedence after the royal princes and the Archbishop of Canterbury. The chancellor is the keeper of the Great Seal and prolocutor of the House of Lords, as well as appointing all justices of the peace. The Lord Chancellor of England may depict two maces in saltire behind his shield of arms, and below it the purse containing the Great Seal.   JC-K

Chancery The court of the Lord Chancellor of England, the highest court of jurisdiction after the House of Lords. In the United States of America, a 'court of equity'.   JC-K

Chanfron *or* **Shanfron** (i) A plate covering the front

Arthur McAdam's
chanfron badge

of a horse's head, often with side plates, made of steel, boiled leather, papier-maché or brass.

(ii) As above, used as an armorial charge, e.g. the badge of Arthur McAdam of Manchester *A Chanfron Sable studded and garnished Or charged with a Nag's Head caboshed Argent.*

Chantry A private mass celebrated regularly for the repose of the soul of a testator and others nominated by him in his will.

It was the conviction that a regular offering of the eucharist was the most effective means of redemption that encouraged medieval man to make financial provision in his will for a chantry or chantries. This was particularly so during the fourteenth and fifteenth centuries, when the liturgy of the Catholic Church increasingly emphasized the importance of the mass. Some chantries were endowed during the lifetime of the founder, and the mass priest would be obliged to celebrate masses for his well-being on earth and for his soul after death. Chantries were also endowed by guilds and fraternities for the benefit of their members.

Chantries were, in fact, a very cheap form of endowment and even the most humble testator could arrange for one or two masses to be said for his soul. However, it was those with the largest purses and the heaviest consciences who were responsible for the erection of the magnificent chantry chapels of the late Middle Ages. The essential difference between an ornate, canopied MONUMENT and a chantry chapel is the presence in the latter of an altar at which masses were celebrated. Cardinal Beaufort (d. 1447) provided for three thousand masses to be said at the altar of his magnificent chapel at Winchester Cathedral. Such chapels are generally found bridging the piers of the chancel arcade or adjacent to the presbytery. Others were additional chapels, built on to the main structure of the church, such as those at Ely Cathedral and the glorious Beauchamp Chapel at St Mary's Church, Warwick. Henry VII's chapel at Westminster Abbey is, of course, a chantry chapel. At several churches an additional aisle was constructed to accommodate chantry chapels, for example those at Devizes in Wiltshire and Tiverton in Devon.

It is significant that the chantry chapel of the high Middle Ages should coincide with the flowering of the perpendicular style of architecture in England. Heraldic embellishment is often sumptuous and will invariably include badges and other devices, cyphers and rebuses as well as arms and crest incorporated into mouldings, bosses and panels.

Chantries came to an end in the sixteenth century, following the dissolution of the monasteries, and in 1547 an act was passed dissolving all chantry foundations. By this, chantry property was transferred to the Crown to be used for the relief of the poor and the endowment of grammar schools.

Further reading
Cook, G.H. *Medieval Chantries and Chantry Chapels* London, 1968.

Chapé Parted per chevron enhanced.

Chapeau

Chapeau (i) A ceremonial cap affixed to the helm in a coat of arms in place of the wreath. This may be a cap of Dignity, Estate, Justice or Maintenance, and therefore indicative of rank or preferment, or it may be integral to the crest itself, in which case it has no further function or significance.

(ii) A similar cap used as an armorial charge.

Armorial interpretation of the chapeau varies in detail throughout European heraldry, but the most common type is that which has been depicted in British armory since the Middle Ages. This is a velvet cap, the fur lining of which is turned up to form a brim ending in two 'tails' at the back. The cap is now assumed to be red unless otherwise stated in the blazon. However, medieval chapeaux were of a variety of colours and linings, and were sometimes charged with armorial devices.

Although it is likely that medieval chapeaux were intended to indicate rank or preferment, later ones were not and should be considered as integral to the crest unless there is evidence to the contrary. Chapeaux are rarely granted in modern times, caps of Dignity, etc., being available only to peers and Scottish feudal barons (*see* BARONAGE OF SCOTLAND).

Instances of chapeaux granted as charges in shields of arms are rare, that of Sefton *Or three Chapeaux Vert turned up Ermine* being one example of only a dozen or so.

See also CAP OF DIGNITY, etc.

Chapel de Fer An iron hat sometimes known as a kettle hat, with crown and brim, favoured from the twelfth to the fifteenth century.   PG

Chaplet *see* **Garland**

Charge (i) A single pictorial representation or geometrical shape depicted in relief and used for armorial purposes.

(ii) Something is 'charged' when it has a charge placed upon it.

Two of the most comprehensive glossaries of

charges are *A Dictionary of Heraldry* by C.N. Elvin (1889) reprinted in 1969, and *A Glossary of Terms Used in Heraldry* by James Parker (1894) reprinted in 1970. *An Heraldic Alphabet* by J.P. Brooke-Little, Norroy and Ulster King of Arms, published in 1985 is an excellent handbook of armorial terms.

Chase, in full *see* **Attitude**

Chatelain The governor or constable of a castle. Sometimes rendered as 'casteller'.

Chatloup A monster with a wolf's body, cat's face and goat's horns. If blazoned proper it is depicted as white with brown spots.

Chequy *or* **Checky** *see* **Field, Varied**

Chess Rook A stylized chess-piece having a bifurcated top.

Chess rook
RIGHT Chester badge

Chester Herald of Arms in Ordinary The office of Chester Herald dates from the fourteenth century, and it is reputed that the holder was herald to Edward, Prince of Wales, the Black Prince. In the reign of King Richard II the officer was attached to the Principality of Chester, which was a perquisite of the then Prince of Wales. In the reign of King Henry VIII the title lapsed for a time but, since 1525, the office of Chester has been one of unbroken succession, as a herald in ordinary.

The badge of the office is taken from the arms of the Earl of Chester — a gold garb, royally crowned.   JC-K

Chest Tombs *see* **Tomb Chests**

Chevalier Strictly 'a horseman'. The term was used to describe a knight, chivalrous man, or a gallant. It was (and is) also applied to members of certain orders of chivalry, especially in France.   JC-K

Chevron *and* **Chevron Reversed** The chevron is an ORDINARY consisting of an inverted V issuing from the base of the shield (Fr. *chevron* = a rafter). The chevron reversed is also an ordinary, of similar shape but reversed and issuing from chief. Both correspond with the geometry of the two diagonal lines of partition, though their precise position on the field, and the angle formed by the two 'limbs', are dependent both upon the shape of the shield and the nature and disposition of minor charges. The chevron reversed is rare, and not particularly attractive. Charges on a chevron are depicted in an upright position unless otherwise specified. Most reference books state that two chevrons may be borne on the same shield, three or more being diminutives termed chevronels. Clearly this practice was perfectly acceptable in the early, uncluttered days of armory, but in these more complex times it can be ambiguous and the diminutive should be used to denote more than one. The chevronel may be interlaced or braced, usually in twos or threes, and there are rare examples of a chevronel and chevronel reversed interlaced. The chevron, depicted between three minor charges, is by far the most common armorial combination in Britain: Papworth devotes one-sixth of his *Ordinary* to chevron variations. It is also popular in France, but comparatively rare in Germany. A chevron quarterly is depicted as *party per chevron and per pale.*

> Diminutive: chevronel or chevronel reversed
> Parted field: per chevron or per chevron reversed
> Varied field: chevronny or chevronny reversed
> Disposition: in chevron or in chevron reversed
> Inclination: chevronwise or chevronwise reversed

Chevronel Diminutive of CHEVRON.

Chevronny *see* **Field, Varied**

Chief In armory, a broad horizontal band covering (or added to) the uppermost portion of the shield. Universally designated as an ordinary but here defined as a sub-ordinary (*see* ORDINARY) and frequently employed for the purpose of augmentation, etc.

The chief is probably the most enigmatic and controversial of armorial charges. Indeed, some armorists argue that because there are so many instances of chiefs which apparently contravene the tincture convention it cannot be a charge and is, therefore, a partition. Instances of 'per chief' are to be found, notably in Papworth's *Ordinary of Arms*. One suspects, however, that many of these were contrived simply to comply with the system of the ordinary (Papworth uses the term in relation to 'per chief' fields charged over all).

One explanation for this apparent contradiction may be found in the development of early armorial figures. It is significant that the chief is never depicted in the same shield as a fess, and it may be that it evolved through an upward movement of the per fess partition. In early armory there appears to have been considerable latitude in the depiction of simple geometrical figures, and it may be that, in coats of some antiquity, a chief which contravenes the tincture convention does so as the result of early artistic licence in the treatment of the per fess partition. In such cases the chief should not be depicted in relief, and could be blazoned *per fess enhanced*.

Other chiefs which contravene the convention may do so because 'the chief especially lent itself to the purposes of honourable augmentation and is so constantly found employed' (A.C. Fox-Davies). As such it is, in effect, an *addition* to an original coat (in the manner of the bordure) and therefore not subject to the convention. This may also explain why a chief is never debruised or surmounted by an ordinary (unless subsequently added for augmentation, etc.). Both the chief of augmentation and that which is simply a straight-forward armorial charge should be depicted in relief, the latter always conforming with the tincture convention.

The chief is neither couped nor cotised, and the diminutive 'comble' is not used in British armory. A charge blazoned *in chief* is depicted in the upper portion of the shield (*see* SHIELD, POINTS OF THE). In French armory combinations of the ordinaries and chief are blazoned *chef-pal*, *chef-barre*, etc, The chief may be plain, parted, varied or charged and its lower edge formed of any of the ornamental variations of line.

See also SUB-ORDINARY

Chieftain The head of a clan sub-group.

Chimerical Descriptive of mythical and armorial creatures compounded of incongruous elements.

Chi-Rho *see* **Christian Symbols**

Chivalry This meant both the code of courage and courtesy which were the ideals of knighthood, and the system of knighthood itself. From the same linguistic root come both chivalry and cavalry, indications that knighthood was the prerogative of the mounted warrior. Technical advances which made the armoured horseman so effective in battle were the introduction of the stirrup and the development of the saddle-bow, which greatly enhanced both his stability and manoeuvrability. The cost of maintaining a horse and equipment was considerable, and membership of such an elite presupposed a man of some position and wealth, normally in the form of a holding of land.

This exclusive class of knighthood adopted a code of conduct which aspired to the highest ideals. The fact that few could reach these ideals, and none could achieve the perfection of Galahad or Percival, did not lessen the value of the code, which men of goodwill in all ages could come to respect. Since chivalry grew up

in Christendom — western Europe — it was natural that the Church and chivalry should exert strong influence upon each other.   KH

See also CHIVALRY, CODE OF

Further reading
Barber, R. *The Knight and Chivalry* London, 1970. An excellent bibliography.
Evans, J. (Ed.) *The Flowering of the Middle Ages* London, 1966.
Foss, M. *Chivalry* London, 1975.
Keen, M. *Chivalry* Yale, 1984.
Rudorff, R. *The Knights and Their World* London, 1974.
Turnbull, S.R. *The Book of the Medieval Knight* London, 1985.
Uden, G. *A Dictionary of Chivalry* London, 1968.

Chivalry, Code of This may be summarized under three main aspects:
1. Belief in the Church, and its defence, especially against the heathen, this latter finding its main expression in the Crusades.
2. Courage, and loyalty towards companions, feudal lord and monarch.
3. Respect, pity and generosity for, and in defence of, the weak, the poor and women.

To these were added the notion of romantic love, which was the inspiration of much of the literature of chivalry. France had Roland, England had Arthur, Spain had El Cid, Germany had the Minnesänger, but it was in Provence that romantic chivalry reached its zenith.   KH

Chivalry, Court of No one denies that in the formative years of heraldry, namely the end of the twelfth and the beginning of the thirteenth centuries, coats of arms were assumed, probably with the help and advice of the heralds, by the knightly and noble class. That such a system, if such it can be called, left much to be desired, is evidenced by the establishment of the Court of the Constable and Marshal, sometimes called the Court of Chivalry (and more recently also the Court of the Earl Marshal), in the first half of the fourteenth century.

The judges in the court were the Constable and Marshal of England, and the court had jurisdiction in causes armorial. After the execution in 1521 of Edward Stafford, Duke of Buckingham and Lord High Constable, the office of Constable became vacant and no new creations were made, save only for the day of a coronation. From that time to the present day the Marshal, now called the Earl Marshal, sits alone, although usually appointing a Surrogate or Assessor to act for him.

The law administered by the court is not the

Common Law of England, as practised in the King's Bench and other Common Law courts, but the Civil Law, that is the *Corpus Juris Civilis* of the Roman Emperor Justinian, as was practised in the Court of Admiralty and in the ecclesiastical courts. It may seem absurd that legal canons laid down in the sixth century should apply to a court which had jurisdiction over a system of personal and corporate identity unknown to the Romans, but it must be understood that it is only the procedure of the court which is governed by the Civil Law. The law it administers is accepted as the law of England.

There are few reports of early cases before the Court of Chivalry, but the most noted cases are Carminow v Scrope, Scrope v Grosvenor, Lovell v Morley, and Grey v Hastings. These make it abundantly clear that a right to arms is only established by descent from one who has borne arms from time immemorial or by grant from a lawful authority, such as the sovereign, or a king of arms acting with the authority of the sovereign. 'Time immemorial' is a legal phrase which in the Common Law is taken to be the year 1189, but in the Court of Chivalry it meant 1066.

Records of the proceedings of the Court are sparse until the late seventeenth century, when the Court, after a lapse of some years, was revived and records were kept. The King's Advocate in the Court (the equivalent of the Attorney General), who prosecuted offenders, set out articles detailing the offences alleged to have been committed, and cited case law which hitherto had been virtually unknown in the Court. The Court enjoyed a period of frenetic activity from 1687 until 1737, during which time Dr William Oldys and other zealous doctors of Civil Law were the King's or Queen's Advocates.

After 1737 the Court did not sit until a test case was brought in 1954: the Lord Mayor, Aldermen and Citizens of Manchester v Manchester Palace of Varieties Ltd. The plaintiffs alleged that the defendants had used the arms of the Corporation on their Common Seal and on the proscenium of their theatre. It was established that the Court, despite a hiatus of over two hundred years in its sitting, still existed, could hear and determine causes armorial and could inflict penalties. The plaintiffs won the case and the judgement delivered by Lord Chief Justice Goddard, acting as Lieutenant, Surrogate and Assessor to the Earl Marshal, made three important points, two regarding the law of arms and the other recommending future procedure.

In the sentence porrected by the plaintiffs (i.e. the judgement they sought) they prayed *inter alia* that the defendants should not display representations of their arms 'without the leave and licence' of the plaintiffs. The Surrogate, both Counsel consenting, deleted that particular phrase as it suggested that an armiger might have the right to authorize and permit another to use his arms. The Surrogate explained that if this phrase were included it would infringe the rights of the officers of arms, who alone can make grants of arms, and might deprive them of revenue.

The Surrogate also drew a distinction between bearing and using arms as a personal hereditament, and displaying them, as on armorial souvenirs. Display in such circumstances, he contended, would not be a ground for intervention by the Court.

As to the future of the Court, the Surrogate suggested that should there be any considerable desire to institute proceedings ... it be put upon a statutory basis, defining its jurisdiction and the sanctions it can impose. The 'considerable desire' has not been evidenced, but abuses of arms occur and it could be that cases will be brought before the Court now that it is known to exist and to have jurisdiction.

In the Commonwealth, although the Earl Marshal enjoys an Imperial jurisdiction, no cause of arms in a Commonwealth country has been brought before the Court of Chivalry, and it is only fair to predict that it never will. It is up to the individual Commonwealth countries to institute legal protection for arms by statute, if so desired.   JB-L

Further reading
A Verbatim Report of the Case in The High Court of Chivalry of the Lord Mayor, Aldermen and Citizens of Manchester versus the Manchester Palace of Varieties Limited on Tuesday 21 December 1954 Heraldry Society, 1955.
Squibb, G.D.*The High Court of Chivalry* Heraldry Society, 1959.
— *Heraldic Cases in the Court of Chivalry 1623-1732* Heraldry Society, 1979.

Chough Usually blazoned as a Cornish chough, this once common bird is a member of the crow family and is black with red legs and bill.

A chough, badge of St Edmund Hall, Oxford, woven into a college tie.

Christ, Order of (Ordem Militar de Christo) A branch of the Knights Templar which, after the abolition of the main order in 1318, was re-established in Portugal under its original name. The order was secularized in 1789, reorganized in 1918, and on 24 November 1963 reconstituted. It has five classes: Grand Cross, Grand Officer, Commander, Officer and Knight. The badge is a red enamelled Latin Cross in gold with a white enamelled Latin Cross at the centre. The star of the order has eight points with faceted rays. The riband is plain green.   JC-K

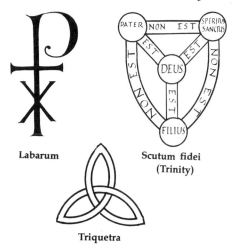

Labarum   Scutum fidei
                              (Trinity)

Triquetra

Christian Symbols

Monogram Two or more letters interwoven to form a symbol, e.g. the *Labarum* consisting of the letters *chi* and *rho*, which begin the Greek word for Christ, and IHS, the first three letters for Jesus. MR for *Maria Regina* was a favourite medieval combination, as was the crowned M and the letters of MARIA. *Alpha* and *Omega*, the first and last letters of the Greek alphabet, signify that Christ is both the beginning and the end.

God and the Trinity To represent God in pictorial form was considered blasphemous, so various symbols developed, the best known of which are: (a) the ray of light; (b) the Father supporting the crucifix; (c) a hand encompassed by a nimbus; (d) three crowned figures, usually medieval in origin; (e) a Trinity; (f) three interlaced fishes.

Geometrical symbolism To the medieval mind every number had a mystic significance and was easily translated into a geometrical shape. The equilateral triangle represents the Trinity; two interwoven triangles form the six-pointed star of David, or Creator's Star, each point representing a day of creation. The Triquetra is an ancient symbol whose three equal arcs express the Trinity, its continuous form representing eternity. (The Triquetra is frequently found in Celtic crosses and may be constructed from interlaced circles or three continuous arcs.) Baptismal fonts are often octagonal, the number eight representing resurrection and new life.

The Cross The universal Christian symbol, though the cross itself pre-dates Christianity (*see* CROSS). In churches its most common forms are: (a) the *Christus Rex* showing Christ on the Cross, crowned and robed; (b) the Rood, a large crucifix suspended or fixed beneath the chancel arch together with the figures of the Virgin Mary and John; (c) the Latin or Passion Cross, which has an elongated upright; (d) the Greek Cross, which has arms of equal length (five of these together represent the Wounds of Christ and may be found carved on the altar front); (e) the Cavalry Cross, which is a Latin Cross mounted on three steps, symbolizing Faith (the uppermost), Hope and Charity; (f) the Celtic or Iona Cross, in which the circle symbolizes Eternity.

The Passion The instruments of the Passion include: The Title (INRI), The Crown of Thorns and Nails, The Dice, The Seamless Robe, The Scourges, The Cross and Sheet (that used to lower the body following crucifixion), The Ladder and Sponge (usually depicted saltirewise, the sponge affixed to the end of a reed), The Lantern (used during the arrest in Gethsemane), The Five Wounds, The Cockerel of Peter's Denial, The Thirty Pieces of Silver, and The Hammer and Pincers.

Colours (used in vestments, etc., to mark the liturgical seasons)
White: Christmas, Easter, Corpus Christi, the Feast of St Mary and feasts of saints who were not martyrs.
Red: Pentecost (Whit Sunday), Palm Sunday, Holy Cross Day and feasts of saints who were martyrs.
Green: the period following Trinity and Epiphany.
Purple: Advent and Lent (in some churches unbleached linen is used during Lent to represent penitence).
Black: funerals and requiems.
Yellow is considered to be the colour of jealousy and treason, and attributed to Judas for this reason. Blue is associated with the Virgin Mary.

The Angels During the Middle Ages nine orders of angels were identified: Seraphim, Cherubim, Thrones, Dominions, Virtues, Powers, Principalities, Archangels and Angels. Seraphim and Cherubim often have six wings which may be strewn with eyes. Thrones are represented as scarlet wheels with wings and sometimes with eyes, and all three principal orders may also be depicted as warriors or judges. Angels usually have a pair of wings and nimbus, and they may hold scrolls, instruments of the Passion or musical instruments.

Agnus Dei

Symbols and Attributes The lamb is a well-known symbol for Christ, the *Agnus Dei* (Lamb of God) carries a banner of victory and has a halo charged with a cross above its head. A dove is frequently found on baptism fonts, where it represents the descent of the Holy Spirit at baptism. Seven doves represent the Seven Gifts of the Holy Spirit. The Tree of Jesse is usually found in stained glass and is intended to depict Christ's ancestry from Jesse, the father of King David. The evangelists are represented by a winged man (Matthew), a winged lion (Mark), a winged ox (Luke) and an eagle (John). Each has a nimbus about its head and sometimes carries a script. The fish was used by early Christians as a secret sign, the letters of the Greek word for 'fish' being the initial letters of the Greek 'Jesus Christ, Son of God, Saviour'. Martyrs usually hold a palm, hermits a T-shaped staff and rosary, pilgrims wear a hat with a shell and carry a staff and wallet, founders usually hold models of the buildings they founded, bishops or abbots hold a crozier or pastoral staff, and popes wear the triple tiara, cope and pallium and carry a triple cross. John the Baptist is usually depicted as wearing a hair coat and carrying a staff and lamb.

Christian Symbols

anchor	Clement
anvil	Adrian
apple	the fall of man
arrow (piercing breast or hand)	Giles
arrow(s) (enfiling crown)	Edmund
arrow(s) (piercing body)	Sebastian (bound)
axe	Matthias
balls (3)	Nicholas
banner (red cross)	Ursula
basket of fruit or flowers	Dorothea
basket of loaves	Philip
bedstead	Faith

beehive	Ambrose
beggar (feet washed by)	Edith of Wilton
beggar or cripple	Martin (offering cloak)
bell	Anthony
birds	Francis of Assisi
boat	Jude
bones	Ambrose
book and crook	Chad
bottle	James the Great
box of alabaster	Mary of Magdela
breasts (on a plate)	Agatha
builders square	Thomas
bundle of rods	Faith
calves	King Walstan (holds scythe)
candle and devil	Genevieve
cauldron of oil	Vitus
chains (held by)	Leonard
chalice (containing dragon)	John the Apostle
child crucified	William of Norwich
children (2 carried by)	Eustace
children (3 in a tub)	Nicholas
cloak (half)	Martin
cock	Peter and Vitus
comb (iron)	Blaise
cow	Bridget
cross (red on white)	George
cross (saltire)	Andrew
cross (inverted)	Peter
cross — T (carried)	Anthony
cross — T	Philip
devil (with bellows)	Genevieve
devil (underfoot)	Michael
distaff	Eve's expulsion
dog (with wounded leg)	Roch
dogs (torches in mouths)	Dominic
doorpost and lintel	Passover
dove	Pope Gregory
dove (on sceptre)	King Edmund
dove (on shoulder)	David of Wales
doves (in cage)	Joseph
dragon	George, Archangel Michael and Martha, Satan and sin
dragon and cross	Margaret of Antioch
dragon (led by chain)	Juliana
dragon under foot	victory over evil
eyes (in dish)	Lucy
fleur-de-lis	Virgin Mary
gridiron	Laurence
halberd	Jude
head (crowned)	Cuthbert or Dennis
head (man's at feet of)	Catherine of Alexandra
head (carried before altar)	Winifred
heart (flaming/transfixed by sword)	Augustine or Mary

hermit	Anthony
hog	Anthony
hook (iron)	Faith or Vincent
horseshoe	Eloy
idols (broken)	Wilfred
keys	Peter
knife (and skin)	Bartholomew
lamb	Agnes, Francis and John Baptist
Lamb (Paschal)	Passover
lash and bricks	Israel's captivity
lily	Virgin Mary and Joseph
lion	Adrian or Jerome
lion and raven	Vincent
loaves and fishes	disciples
manacles	Leonard
money bag	Matthew
mule (kneeling)	Anthony of Padua
musical instruments	Cecilia
olive branch	Agnes
organ (portable)	Cecilia
otter	Cuthbert
palm	Agnes
pagans (being baptized)	Wilfred
partridge	Jerome
pelican	Sacrifice of the Cross
pen, ink and scroll	Mark or Matthew
phoenix	resurrection
pincers	Agatha or Dunstan
pincers and tooth	Apollonia
pomegranate	resurrection and unity
pot and ladle	Martha
roses (crown of)	Cecilia, Dorothy and Teresa
saw	Simon
scallop shell	James the Great
scourge	Ambrose
scroll	the Five Books of Moses
serpent	Satan
shears	Agatha
sheep	Genevieve
sieve (broken)	Benedict
staff	James the Great
stag	Adrian, Eustace or Hubert
stone(s)	Stephen
swan (and flowers)	Hugh of Lincoln
sword	Paul or Barbara
sword (flaming)	Adam's expulsion
sword (through breast)	Euphemia
sword (through neck)	Lucy
tower	Barbara
tree (beneath foot of)	Boniface
tree (sleeping beneath)	Etheldreda
Unicorn	Virgin Mary
weighing souls	Michael
wheel (spiked)	Catherine

windlass	Erasmus
wolf (guarding his head)	King Edmund
wounded forehead	Bridget of Sweden
Wounds of Christ	Francis of Assisi

Further reading
Child, H. and D. Colles *Christian Symbols Ancient and Modern* London, 1979.
Ellwood Post, W. *Saints Signs and Symbols* London, 1964.
Whittemore, C.E. *Symbols of the Church* London, 1959.

Churches Churches collectively provide one of the greatest sources of heraldry available to the armorist. Inside are to be found examples of heraldry from the thirteenth century to the present day, crafted in a wide variety of media, such as stone, glass, wood, brass, canvas and textiles.

Such heraldic wealth derives from the special relationship of a parish church with the local nobility and gentry, and from the benevolence of medieval guilds and fraternities. The manor house and church often occupied adjacent sites, with the lord having a right to present the incumbent. The building and the furbishing of churches required considerable financial resources, and those people with the necessary wealth and motivation were invariably of the armigerous classes. Armorial devices displayed in the fabric, furnishings and MONUMENTS of a church would be recognized by the entire community, even the illiterate. Heraldry was originally associated with the medieval knightly and baronial classes, and later the wealthy merchant class which aspired to join the former by acquiring not only suitable houses and land, but also arms. It is the possession of both wealth and hereditary armorial devices which, over a period of seven hundred years, has produced the extraordinary quantity of heraldry to be found in churches today.

That which has survived is but a small proportion of that which was created. Much heraldry has been destroyed either through deliberate defacement, through neglect or to make way for new construction. The extent of this loss may be established by comparing what is extant at a particular church with that detailed in the heralds' visitations and the records of local antiquarians.

The heraldry found in churches may have been placed there by an individual during his lifetime or, as in the particular case of monuments, financed by a bequest or by a deceased's family. Thomas Mussenden of Healing, Lincolnshire, in his will dated 1402, left one hundred shillings 'to make a window of glass over the high altar of the church of Helyng aforesaid with my arms in the said window.' Wills may also include instructions concerning armorial display on monuments. In the 1524 will of John, 2nd Baron Marny of Layer Marny, Essex, there are instructions regarding the construction of his tomb which include that 'the vault above and the arms about the tomb' should be embellished 'according to the direction of the herald' and 'upon it [the tomb] an image of myself . . . portrayed in coat armour with my helmet and crest at the head and a white leopard at the feet' (N.H. Nicholas *Testamenta Vetusta* London, 1826).

The erection of armorial devices in churches in the present century is still subject to the approval of the heraldic authorities. It is unlikely that they would permit ostentation on the scale of a tomb at Easton Maudit, Northamptonshire, which contains no fewer than one hundred quarterings!

Church exteriors

There are many materials from which the exterior structure of a church may be built, ranging from sandstone and limestone to flint or brick. Often there is a combination of materials, either by design or because different parts of the church were built at different times. The choice was usually restricted to locally available material, and materials were imported only where the builder (often the local lord or religious establishment) was wealthy, e.g. at Malvern Priory, which is built of Cotswold limestone.

Irrespective of period or materials armorial decoration is limited, but sometimes striking. At Woodbridge in Suffolk the church exterior is decorated with shields and other devices in flint flushwork. Designs in brickwork are not unknown, but more common are stone-carved arms set in the walls. These may be within the over-all decoration of the porch, as at Pulham St Mary, Norfolk, or set alone as at Purley-on-Thames, Berkshire. Such work often records the financing of some building or rebuilding works and may be dated. Beasts and badges are also to be found, especially in larger churches and cathedrals.

Gargoyles, the carved stone water-spouts projecting from towers and the upper parts of walls, often depict fantastic monsters and figures in every possible attitude. Regrettably, very few are genuinely armorial in character, unlike their counterparts on domestic buildings. JET

See also ARMORIAL BOARD; CEILINGS; FLOOR TILES; FONTS; GLASS; MASONS' MARKS; PULPITS; ROYAL ARMS IN CHURCHES; SCREENS; TEXTILES; WALL PAINTING; WINDOW MARKS; WOOD CARVING

Further reading

Dirsztay, P. *Church Furnishings* London, 1978. An excellent, inexpensive guide to all aspects of church furnishings, decorations, symbols, monuments, etc. Includes comprehensive bibliography.

Church of England, Clergy of Clergymen of the Church of England are permitted to use their personal arms. Archbishops and diocesan bishops may impale these (to the sinister) with the arms of their see. Clergy of non-episcopal degree may also use their helmet, crest and motto (unlike the clergy of the Roman Catholic Church) or, if they wish, one of the ECCLESIASTICAL HATS prescribed by Earl Marshal's warrant in 1976. Archbishops and bishops ensign their arms with a mitre and may place behind the shield a crozier palewise or bendwise, or a pair of croziers saltirewise. Some archbishops prefer to use a single cross instead of the crozier. In order that future generations should not be denied the use of a crest, newly armigerous archbishops and bishops may be granted helm, wreath, crest and mantling. These are exemplified in the body of the patent but not depicted with the arms in the margin where the mitre is used. For more than seven centuries (until 1836) the County of Durham lay within the palatinate jurisdiction of the bishops of Durham. This is reflected in the ducal coronet enfiled by the mitre and the sword and crozier saltirewise behind the shield. Interestingly, the two principal armorial devices favoured by the Church of England — the mitre (symbol of episcopal dignity) and the crozier (episcopal jurisdiction) — are currently out of favour with the Catholic Church. All ecclesiastical hats used in the Church of England are black.

Members of the Ecclesiastical Household of the British Sovereign may use an appropriate ecclesiastical hat charged in the centre with a Tudor Rose. Ordained clergymen within the Anglican Communion do not receive the accolade of knighthood, but may place letters signifying an order of knighthood after their name. Clergy may succeed to a title or possess a courtesy title or style, the ecclesiastical style always preceding the temporal. The Archbishops of Canterbury and York (Primate of all England and Metropolitan, and Primate of England and Metropolitan respectively) are Privy Councillors and are therefore addressed as 'The Most Reverend and Right Honourable . . .' and have seats in the House of Lords. Both archbishops take precedence over dukes. On retirement they assume the status of bishops, Canterbury usually receiving a peerage. The Bishop of London is always a Privy Councillor and is addressed as 'Right Reverend and Right Honourable . . .' The bishops of London, Durham and Winchester precede all other bishops and have seats in the House of Lords. Until 1841 all other diocesan bishops (except the Bishop of Sodor and Man) also had seats, but since then only twenty-one sit in the Lords, vacancies being filled by the senior diocesan bishop without a seat. In each diocese one or more suffragan bishops may be appointed by the diocesan bishop. These are styled by

TITLE	ARMS	ENSIGNED BY	OTHER INSIGNIA
Archbishop	see impaling personal	mitre	crozier palewise or bendwise, or croziers saltirewise (sometimes a single cross)
Diocesan Bishop	see impaling personal	mitre	crozier palewise or bendwise, or croziers saltirewise
Bishop of Durham	see impaling personal	mitre within ducal coronet	sword and crozier saltirewise
Suffragan Bishop	personal	mitre	crozier palewise or bendwise, or croziers saltirewise
Dean	personal	personal crest or hat with 3 red tassels each side, cords purple	none
Archdeacon	personal	personal crest or hat with 3 purple tassels each side, cords purple	none
Canon	personal	personal crest or hat with 3 red tassels each side, cords black	none
Prebendary	personal	personal crest or hat with 3 red tassels each side, cords black	none
Rector or Vicar	personal	personal crest or hat with one black tassel each side, cords black and white	none
Deacon	personal	personal crest or hat without tassels or cord	none
Doctor of Divinity	according to degree, but cords of ecclesiastical hat are interlaced with a scarlet thread		

the name of a town in the diocese. They do not sit in the House of Lords and are not styled 'Lord Bishop', though the prefix may be given as a matter of courtesy. All Anglican bishops take precedence above barons but below viscounts. A dean is the incumbent of a cathedral or collegiate church, a provost being the incumbent of a cathedral which has been created out of a parish church. An archdeacon is a senior clergyman having administrative authority delegated to him by a bishop and a territorial designation, being that of his archdeaconry. A canon is either residentiary with cathedral duties, or honorary, so designated as a reward for honourable service in the diocese. (A minor canon is a clergyman attached to a cathedral or collegiate church to assist in services and is not a canon.) In certain cathedrals prebendal stalls are reserved for prebendaries. In the Middle Ages the endowment of most non-monastic cathedrals was divided into prebends, each intended to support a single member of a chapter. Holders of prebends became known as prebendaries and in some English cathedrals the territorial titles have been retained, but not their incomes. A vicar is now appointed to all new livings, the designation 'rector' being applied to an incumbent who was formerly in receipt of greater and lesser tithes, a vicar receiving the lesser tithes only. Tithes were virtually abolished in 1936.

See also SIGNATURES, ARCHBISHOPS AND BISHOPS

Further reading
Barraclough, G. *The Christian World* London, 1981.
Hinnels, J.R. *Dictionary of Religions* London, 1984.
Livingstone, E.A. (Ed.) *The Concise Oxford Dictionary of the Christian Church* Oxford, 1983.
Montague-Smith, P. *Correct Form* London, 1976. For correct forms of address, etc.

Church of Scotland The General Assembly of the Church of Scotland bears *Azure A Saltire Argent surmounted of a Burning Bush Vert enflamed proper and enhallowed of the Divine Effulgence Or its stem proper and issuing from a Mount in Base Vert* (recorded in the Lyon Register 1959). This device may be used *within a Vesica environed of a vesical border Or with the words 'Nec Tamen Consumebatur' in letters Sable alternately with three Crosses fitchy Sable.* As such it may be flown as the banner of the General Assembly and, in 1960, the arms were incorporated in two devices for use by the Right Reverend the Moderator of the Church of Scotland. The 'Great Emblem' is the above shield of arms with the addition of a *Chief enarched Sable* and, palewise behind the shield, the Moderator's staff — the Cuigrich. This has a black shaft and the crook is decorated with purple stones and a blue saltire motif. The arms are ensigned by a black ECCLESIASTICAL HAT with ten blue tassels pendent from each side. The 'Ordinary Emblem' is the same shield (with the enarched chief) but around it is placed an *Annulet Or stoned Purpure* (the Ring of Investiture), and above a black Geneva Bonnet Sable with blue cords and single tassels.

Armorial bearings have been recorded for a provincial synod, with a clerical hat 'of the type associated with the eminent reformer John Knox' coloured black, and with six green tassels on each side suspended from blue cords. Many kirk sessions have been granted arms but as such are not given ecclesiastical hats, though the minister may use these arms in conjunction with a hat appropriate to his own ecclesiastical degree. The ecclesiastical hat assigned to a minister of the Church of Scotland is black with a single black tassel on either side. The hats of Chaplains of the Queen have scarlet cords and three tassels on either side, and those of the Chaplain to the Palace of Holyroodhouse and Edinburgh Castle have a scarlet cord and one purple tassel on either side.

Further reading
Innes of Learney, T. *Scottish Heraldry* London, revised 1977.

Churchyard Monuments Heraldic MONUMENTS in churchyards are rare and those that exist are invariably overlooked by the visitor. Many churchyards contain eighteenth- and nineteenth-century chest tombs which warrant investigation. Some may be surmounted by an incised slab with the arms displayed on a roundel, similar to those more usually found set into the floor inside the church. However, their open position makes them vulnerable to weathering and it is often difficult to identify the devices carved thereon without reference to other memorials to the same family inside the church. The sides and ends of chest tombs may also have been used for armorial display.

In the late nineteenth and twentieth centuries arms may be found on the simple headstone or monument. More unusual is an example at Morwenstow, Cornwall, where a small brass casting is rivetted to the gravestone. Monuments of a more elaborate construction may incorporate armorial decoration. JET

Further reading
Burgess, F. *English Churchyard Memorials* London, 1979.

Cid, El Rodrigo Diaz de Bivar (1040-99). *Cid Campeador* (Lord Champion) of Sancho II of Castile and his successor, Alfonso VI. Exiled in 1081 for suspected treachery, he became a soldier of fortune and fought for the Moorish kings of Saragossa. From 1089 to 1094 he employed war and intrigue for personal gain, taking Valencia and Murcia. Despite this, he was to become a national hero and around his name was gathered an immense body of legend and tradition, so that it is difficult to identify truth and fiction. The term *cid* is derived from the Arabic *sayyid*, meaning lord. El Cid was eventually defeated by the Moors in 1099.

Cigarette Cards Cigarette cards bearing armorial subjects can be classified in four categories: truly armorial, devices, flags, and other insignia.

The truly armorial cards range from excellent sets of *County Seats and Arms* by John Player and Sons, *Clan Tartans* by Stephen Mitchell and Sons, and other companies, *School Arms* and *Arms of the Oxford and Cambridge Colleges* by W.D. & H.O. Wills Ltd. Both Player and Wills produced excellent sets of cards depicting civic armory. The popular series *Borough Arms*, and *Arms of the British Empire*, are outstanding. The former by R.J. Dexter depicts the full coats of arms of English boroughs in blind embossing on white card, on pale blue backgrounds. Cards depicting armory are uncommon, but three excellent sets were produced: *Heraldry Series* by Taddy & Co. in 1911; a set of larger cards by Wills, *Heraldic Signs and Their Origins*, issued in 1925; and silk cards entitled *Heraldic Series*, which were produced between 1910 and 1925 by Godfrey Phillips Ltd.

Religious examples are represented by Arms of the English Sees by Godfrey Phillips, and *Arms of the Bishoprics* by Wills. The latter company also issued a fine set of *Arms of the Companies* in 1923.

Many sets of cards bearing devices can be found, ranging from regimental, naval, air force, sporting and schools' badges, to car radiator and boy scout emblems. By far the most numerous are of a military flavour. Gallaher Ltd produced one of the finest sets of *Army Badges* in 1939. Many silk badges were woven on to cards during the early part of the First World War, many series being issued by B. Muratti, Sons & Co.,

Singleton Cole, Player and Godfrey Phillips. A comparatively modern series entitled *Army Badges Past and Present* was produced in 1961 by Mills, and John Player issued two fine sets of cards (one of 50, the other 100) depicting *Army Corps and Divisional Signs.* Cards showing *Regimental Colours and Standards* were issued by Gallaher Ltd, and *Drum Banners and Cap Badges* by Player.

Only one set of *RAF Badges* has been produced, by Player in 1937, though a set of *Aeroplane Markings* depicting the insignia of the world's air forces was issued by Lambert & Butler in the same year.

The Royal Navy is well represented, as are its counterparts in the Merchant Navy. A fine series of *Ships Badges* was produced in 1925 by Wills, and a series of *Battleship Crests* had been issued by R. & J. Hill Ltd as early as 1900. Two very interesting series of *Naval Dress and Badges* were produced by Wills, and by Franklyn Davey & Co.; Hignett Bros & Co. issued a fine set of *Ships Flags and Cap Badges.* Very colourful and unusual sets depicting *Flags and Funnels of Leading Steamship Lines* have been produced by W.A. & A.C. Churchman, W.T. Davies & Sons, and Ogdens Ltd.

An interesting and colourful series entitled *Civic Insignia and Plate* was issued by Churchman in 1926. A set of *Decorations and Medals* by R. & J. Hill Ltd and a fine series of silk cards depicting *Orders of Chivalry,* 1925, by Murray, Sons & Co. typify the type of armorial cigarette cards which are still available to the collector.   BC

Further reading
Catalogues issued by various dealers.

Cinquefoil An armorial charge consisting of a figure with five radiating stylized petals or leaves.

Circlet *see* **Crest Coronet**

Civic Dress and Insignia of Office The wearing of special, distinctive dress by civic dignitaries has a long and well documented history in many countries.

In England such apparel of office has certainly been in use since the fifteenth century, as witness various city charters dating from that time, and it would appear that a great deal of money was expended on such finery. Indeed, royal charters sometimes contained clauses exempting 'mayors, sheriffs, aldermen and recorders' from penalties for wearing 'excessive apparel'.

Documents show that in the late fifteenth century the senior officials of the City of London wore scarlet robes for festivals and other great occasions, reserving their velvet costumes for lesser affairs. At about the same time the *Kalendar of the Lord Mayor of Bristol* notes that the ceremonial habit of that worthy was a 'scarlet cloke, furred . . . with a lyte hode, or tepet of black felt.' By the sixteenth century it had also become the custom in other large and wealthy towns for the mayor to don scarlet trimmed with fur, his senior officers wearing black or purple. Not long after this the wives of civic leaders also adopted quasi-official finery. In Shrewsbury in 1558 bailiffs, former bailiffs and their wives were directed by the Council to wear red gowns on special occasions known as 'scarlet days'. In Winchester from 1580 mayors were required to provide their wives with gowns of scarlet, whilst in nearby Salisbury the mayor could, about this time, be fined £20 if he did not outfit his wife with a suitable robe.

Mayoral chains — one or more rows of plain links — appeared in the sixteenth century, although there is reason to believe that to begin with these ornaments did not have the ritual significance they later gained, being merely augmentations to the robes of their wealthy wearers. In 1545 Sir John Allen bequeathed to the Lord Mayor of the City of London his 'knightly collar of SS'. Until the seventeenth century only three instances of truly mayoral chains (or collars) are known. That of Kingston-upon-Hull dates from around 1564, of York 1612, and of Guildford 1623.

For the most part (but there are exceptions) modern local governments in England have retained evolved styles of the traditional form of dress for their senior officials. The mayoral robe is usually, although not always, of scarlet cloth with broad facings and sleeves trimmed with fur and black velvet; a black cocked (or tricorn) hat with gold loop and button, lace jabot and white gloves completing the ensemble. The robes of councillors are usually simpler versions of those just described. For ordinary, non-ceremonial functions, mayors and their consorts normally wear silver-gilt chains of office with pendent badges of their municipality. On ceremonial occasions town clerks, and holders of the recently created office of chief executive also wear formal costumes. The former's robe is often of black silk trimmed with black velvet, braid and woven silk tassels. Also worn are a wig (sometimes full-bottomed), winged collar and starched linen hanging neckbands. The robe worn by the chief executive is of scarlet cloth faced and trimmed with black velvet.

One final modern ceremonial civic uniform may also be mentioned: that of the 'honorary alderman' —a

rank recently introduced in some boroughs to reward councillors of long and valued service who now can never aspire to the ancient aldermanic rank abolished by the local government changes in the 1970s. Such 'honorary' dignitaries are usually dressed in purple and black robes, with enamelled badges suspended around the neck or fastened to the robe.   SS
Further reading
Smith, H. and K. Sheard *Academic Dress and Insignia of the World* 3 vols, 1970.

Clan A social group officially recognized by the Lord Lyon consisting of an aggregate of distinct families actually descended from, or accepting themselves as descendants of, a common ancestor. The clan chief is the officially recognized head of a group of people forming 'an honourable community', often of the same surname or of related groups. The crest badge of a clan chief is his crest contained within a belt and buckle upon which appears his motto. Members of a clan are permitted to wear this device to demonstrate loyalty to the chief.   CJB

Clarenceux badge

Clarenceux King of Arms This is the senior of the two provincial kings and his jurisdiction is that part of England south of the River Trent. With certainty the office existed in 1420, and there is a fair degree of probability that there was a *Claroncell rex heraldus armorum* in 1334. There are some early references to the southern part of England being termed Surroy, but there is no firm evidence that there was ever a king of arms so called. The title of Clarenceux is supposed to derive either from the Honor (the estates of dominion) of the Clare earls of Gloucester, or from the dukedom of Clarence (1362). With minor variations the arms of Clarenceux have, from the late fifteenth century, been *Argent a Cross Gules on a Chief Gules a Lion passant guardant crowned with an open Crown Or.*   JC-K

Clarion *see* **Musical Heraldry**

Clasped *see* **Attributes**

Claymore A Scottish two-handed broadsword, long and heavy with a straight grip. Also the name applied to the Venetian *schiavona* with an ornate basket hilt.   PG

Clay Pipe Marks From the Elizabethan period, when tobacco was first introduced into England, the bowls of pipes have often been embellished with armorial devices. The earliest pipes were of metal which proved most unsatisfactory, but later clay pipes, with long, narrow stems and small bowls, were frequently decorated with Tudor Roses, fleurs-de-lis, crowned roses, trefoils, buglehorns and a host of other familiar devices. Several elaborate styles of pipe were exported from Holland during the nineteenth century, and these were often embossed with coats of arms on the side of the bowl, those of Dutch towns and cities being particularly popular. The larger pipe bowls of the twentieth century are often carved or moulded but few of these portray armorial devices.   BC

Clenched *see* **Attitude**

Climant *see* **Attitude**

Close *see* **Attitude**

Clover Leaf *see* **Lines, Varied**

Coat Armour (i) A surcoat.
(ii) The armorial devices borne on a surcoat or jupon.
(iii) A 'Gentleman of Coat Armour' is an armiger.

Coat of Arms (Abbr. Arms) Correctly this term should be applied only to the shield of arms, the design of which was often repeated on the surcoat or jupon of the medieval armiger. However, it is now invariably used to mean the conventional representation in pictorial form of the principal armorial bearings to which an armiger is entitled, the shield of arms being the essential and central element.
See also ACHIEVEMENT OF ARMS: ARMORIAL BEARINGS

Cock The farmyard fowl, other types are specified.

Cockade (i) A raised 'comb' on helmets and ceremonial hats worn by members of military and civilian uniformed services. Clearly this type of cockade has its origins in the headgear of the barbarians and the fan-shaped helmets of the Roman legionary, and may be traced through the early cockscomb crests and panaches of the Middle Ages to the stylized helmets of recent centuries.
(ii) A rosette or similar ornament worn on the hat as a badge. This cockade is of particular interest to

armorists for it is, in effect, a direct descendant of armorial wreaths and mantlings, though more recently to be found in the buttons and knots of ribbons which tied up the flaps of three-cornered and 'cocked' hats in the eighteenth century.

The cockade was particularly popular in France prior to and during the Revolution when, affixed to a livery cap, it served as a badge. Under Louis XVI the partisans assumed a black cockade in contrast to the white worn by royal servants and troops. The Bastille was stormed by citizens wearing cockades of green leaves. In 1789 the National Assembly determined that only the tricolour cockade should be worn, though this developed into several quite complex forms. In secret the royalists continued to favour the white cockade in contradistinction to the revolutionary red of the Terror. Under the Consulate and the Empire the blue, white and red cockade was used, though a Napoleonic violet cockade was fashionable for a time. Under Louis XVIII and Charles X the white cockade again became the official badge, to be replaced once more by the tricolour under Louis Philippe, Napoleon III and the Third Republic.

In England the Jacobites adopted a white cockade on the expulsion of the Stuarts as a contrast to the orange ones of Nassau and the black of Hanover.

Although not regulated by the heraldic authorities, etiquette has recognized the cockade as a badge of service. In many countries it remains part of the uniform of both military and civilian services. In England it is almost always black, the knot of ribbons at the centre of the rosette correctly being of the livery colours. The coloured cockade is reserved for members of embassies and consulates as a diplomatic badge, though it is rarely used. On the continent of Europe the cockade is worn at the front of the hat. In Britain it is worn at the side of 'cocked' hats by those holding office under the Crown, and occasionally at the front of caps worn by domestic employees such as chauffeurs.

Further reading
Rothery, G.C. *Concise Encyclopedia of Heraldry* London, 1915 (reprinted 1985).

Cockatrice *and* **Basilisk** The magnificent lion is the king of the beasts, the equally magnificent eagle is the king of the birds, but the king of the serpents is the small and evil cockatrice.

This legendary monster, hatched on a dunghill from a cock's egg by a serpent, is so venomous that its look or breath is said to be deadly poison. With its cock's crested head, dangling wattles, glittering, death-dealing eye, barbed tongue and serpent's tail, it is truly a fearsome object to behold. Even serpents will flee from it to escape death, and all other creatures are easily overpowered and killed by it, even from a distance, all except the weasel, who will pursue it even to its den and kill it.

It is said that a cockatrice will observe a lark singing high in the sky, and will creep along until it is just beneath the bird, when it will breathe out its poison into the air and the lark will fall dead into its mouth.

A cockatrice which achieves the age of nine years will lay an egg on a dungheap, and a toad will come to hatch it, to produce, not another cockatrice, but a basilisk. In every way as evil as its parent, the basilisk has the added terror of a dragon's head at the end of its tail, and is sometimes known as the amphisian cockatrice because of its similarity to the amphiptre, a serpent with a head at each end of its body. So dreadful is the appearance of the basilisk that if a mirror is held up, so that it must look at itself instead of its victim; it will instantly burst asunder with horror and fear.

Cockatrice and basilisk derive from one origin, although later fables have separated them into two creatures. In spite of their unpleasant natures they are well represented in armory, several families using them as supporters and crests. Perhaps it was thought that ill-wishers would be repulsed by these venomous creatures.   MY

Coded *see* **Attributes**

Cognizance Any device used for the purpose of identification. In heraldry, generally taken to mean a badge.

Coheir *and* **Coheiress** *see* **Heir Apparent** *and* **Heiress**

Coif of Mail A mail hood covering top, side and back of head and neck.   PG

Coiled *see* **Attributes**

Coinage In Britain it was the Saxon kings who first achieved the creation of a sound and stable system of coinage, based on a metallic standard. As trade developed in the seventh and eighth centuries, so the need was perceived for an acceptable medium of

Coin of Edward the Confessor (*c.* 1005-66). The design of a cross between four doves was later adopted by the medieval heralds when atttributing arms to the Saxon kings of England.

exchange, and both gold and silver coins were struck for this purpose. After the last quarter of the seventh century, however, until the thirteenth century, the only denomination of coinage was the silver penny. Throughout this intervening period of six hundred years there developed a strong measure of central control over the design and supply of coin, and this is reflected in the devices adopted to signify royal authority. Prior to the Conquest, some coins bore quasi-armorial symbols such as the strange cross of Offa, King of Mercia during the eighth century, the raven device of the Dane, Olaf Quaran, and the cross parted and fretted between four doves of Edward the Confessor, upon which his attributed arms were later based. During his reign, and that of William I, coins were struck at sixty or seventy mints, most of them in central or southern England. However, the dies upon which coins were struck could be issued from only a limited number of workshops, and the king's monopoly over the supply of dies enabled him to control the economy. Dies were frequently changed, and the coins cut by hand, flattened and fashioned by use of a hammer and anvil. No standard weight was set for coins until the reign of James I, but it was essential that the correct number should be produced from each pound of metal.

During the reigns of the first two Norman kings thirteen different types of coin were minted, all of them inscribed WILLEM. After the accession of Henry II, dies were changed less frequently and in 1180 the first so-called short cross coins were issued, all of which were inscribed ENRICUS even though they circulated during the reigns of Henry II, Richard I, John and the early years of Henry III. By 1247, clipping had become a serious problem and a new coin, the long cross, was issued. This cross, on the reverse, continued to the edge of the coin and any penny on which the four ends of the cross were not visible was not considered legal tender. In 1279, Edward I introduced further denominations: the groat and the farthing. The obverse of the penny continued

to bear the long cross, but with three pellets in each of the angles. As the pace of European trade quickened, so the demand for coinage of higher value, more appropriate to international trade, grew, and in 1252 the City of Florence minted a golden florin — the first Western European gold coin since the Dark Ages. Consequently, Henry III introduced a gold penny in 1257. This exchanged for twenty silver pennies, though its inferior quality reduced its value to twenty-four silver pence and it was finally withdrawn in 1270.

Since the time of Edward III authoritative examples of the royal arms and other armorial devices have appeared on both sides of the English coinage. The first coin to incorporate a truly armorial design was the gold issue of 1344. The obverse design of the florin or double leopard shows the king enthroned beneath a canopy flanked by two leopards upon a fleuretty field. The half florin or leopard (the early heralds considered a lion passant to be behaving in the manner of a leopard) shows a crowned leopard. Draped about the leopard's shoulders in the fashion of a cloak was a banner bearing the quartered arms of France and England. The reverse showed a cross within a quatrefoil and in the angles of the quatrefoil a leopard. The quarter florin or helm depicted upon a fleuretty field a helmet with chapeau and crest of a statant crowned lion. The leopard was superseded in 1344 by the gold noble. This coin bore, for the first time in the English series, a shield of arms showing the quartered arms of Edward III. This shield continued to appear exclusively on the gold coinage — the noble, the ryal and the angel, in conjunction with a ship. The shield was sometimes held by the king (on the noble and royal) or hung on the side of the ship (on the angel and half angel). Armorial symbols made their first appearance on the ship's rudder during the reign of Richard II.

During the reign of Edward IV personal and ecclesiastical devices (the Bourchier Knot and the pallium) appear for the first time, on coins minted at the metropolitan furnaces at Canterbury — a graceful gesture to the archbishop who had been such a staunch supporter of his king.

The Tudors introduced some new denominations of coinage and there was a change from the late medieval to Tudor-Renaissance style. On the obverse of the 1489 sovereign, Henry VII is shown seated on a low throne set against a backcloth of fleurs-de-lis, the reverse has a large Tudor Rose surmounted by a shield of the royal arms. The type III sovereigns show the king on a very ornamental high-backed throne, with greyhound and dragon on side pillars. Some coins had a portcullis at the king's feet. The royal arms now appeared on the silver coins. The obverse of the 1489 penny was redesigned to show the king enthroned holding orb and sceptre, and a long cross quartered the royal arms on the reverse; the testoons had a similar reverse design. The posthumous coinage of Henry VIII incorporated a crown over the shield with supporters of lion and dragon.

Four new denominations were added to the coinage during the reign of Edward VI; the silver crown, halfcrown, sixpence and threepence, all with similar reverse to the silver coins of previous Tudors. The reverse design of the angel with ship and shield continued during Mary's reign, but the silver coins of Philip and Mary showed facing busts on the obverse, with England impaled by Spain on an oval shield on the reverse. Elizabeth I coins reverted to the former quarterings of fleurs-de-lis and lions. With the accession of James VI of Scotland to the English throne, the royal arms and titles were altered on the coinage, and the Scottish lion and the Irish harp now appeared. During the Civil War coins were struck at a number of towns to supply areas of the country under Royalist control. At the mint of Coombe Martin a halfcrown was struck in 1645 with crowned shield encircled by the Garter and motto *Honi Soit Qui Mal Y Pense*, with supporters of lion and unicorn.

The coins struck during the Commonwealth had legends wholly in English (the first and last occasions that English coins have borne an English inscription), and in the Puritan manner were bare of all decoration. The larger coins bore the motto 'God With Us' on the reverse with the conjoined shields of St George and Ireland. The halfpenny had the cross of St George on the obverse and the Irish harp on the reverse. This was the first and only time that a coat of arms appeared on an English copper coin. With the introduction of milled coinage in 1662, from which date the British modern coinage may be said to commence, the royal arms were shown on four separate shields in cruciform with the Garter Star in the centre. This design was used intermittently until the cupro-nickel crown of 1953. The shield on the crown and halfcrown of George IV was surmounted by a barred helm affronty with royal crown and mantling. The motto *Dieu et Mon Droit* was on a scroll below the shield.

Various designs from the previous reigns were reintroduced on the 'Jubilee' coinage of Victoria; the florin and double florin had four crowned shields between four sceptres, surmounted by crosses formy, harp and thistle, with a centre piece of the Garter Star. The shield of the sovereign of the 'young head' series was ensigned by a royal crown, the whole within a wreath of laurel. The same design was used on the crown piece. The beautiful 'Gothic crown' of 1847 incorporated the badges of England, Scotland and Ireland — the rose, thistle and shamrock respectively — between the cruciform shield. On the halfcrown of the 'veiled head' series the shield was spade-shaped ensigned by the royal crown and encircled with the collar of the Garter. A similar design was used in the first silver coins of George V; his second issue of debased silver showed the royal arms on a shield a bouché. The florin showed four shields in cruciform with four sceptres in saltire each ensigned by royal crowns. The shilling had a lion statant upon a royal crown. The threepence and sixpence had oak leaves and acorns — three and six respectively. The crown coin of 1927 has a crown within a wreath of shamrocks, thistles and roses. This design was used from 1927 to 1936 except for 1935, when a special 'Silver Jubilee' crown was struck. The very modernistic rendering of St George and the Dragon was greeted with rather mixed feelings.

During the reign of George VI two different shillings were issued, that for Scotland having a lion sejant affronty on an imperial crown, holding in the dexter paw a sword and in the sinister paw a sceptre; to the dexter was a shield bearing the device of St Andrew, and to the sinister the thistle badge. The English shilling had a lion statant guardant on the crown. On the English coin the crown was of familiar type with the arches rising from behind the crosses formy, while the Scottish crown had the arches springing from behind the fleurs-de-lis, a detail which bore a slight resemblance to the Crown of Scotland preserved at Edinburgh Castle. The Scottish shilling was issued as a compliment to Elizabeth, Queen of George VI. The silver threepence had a shield bearing the cross of St George, whilst the dodecagonal coin of 1937 had a thrift plant motif. The 1937 crown, designed by George Kruger Gray, is a fine example of mid twentieth century heraldic work. The shillings of Elizabeth II were redesigned by William Gardner. The English coin had the three leopards of England, and that for Scotland the rampant lion within a double tressure flory counter flory. The crown had four shields in cruciform between the badges of England, Scotland, Ireland and Wales — rose, thistle, shamrock and leek. This was the first appearance in the coinage of the leek as the emblem for Wales. The halfcrown had the royal arms ensigned by the royal crown, the florin a double rose within a circlet of rose, thistle, shamrock and leek. The threepenny piece of nickel-based alloy had a chained portcullis, perhaps with the idea of linking the second Elizabeth with the first, in whose reign the portcullis was used as a badge.

With the inception of decimal currency in 1967, the royal arms disappeared from the English coinage in favour of more simple armorial designs, but reappeared in the pound series introduced in 1984.

LGP/SF

Further reading

Brooke, G.C. *English Coins* London, 1950.

Seaby, H.A. Ltd *Standard Catalogue of British Coins* for illustrations of English and British coins.

— *The Story of British Coinage* London, 1985.

Cointise, Contoise *see* **Banderolle** *and* **Wreath**

Collar (i) During the fourteenth and fifteenth centuries collars composed of armorial devices were worn as an indication of adherence to a royal or noble house, or to a political cause. They were, in effect, a superior form of livery badge, and some were later adopted as insignia of office. Henry VI adopted the famous Collar of SS, the origins of which remain obscure, as a Lancastrian device. The corresponding Yorkist collars were composed of alternate suns and white roses with a white lion pendant, and (under Richard III) white roses en soleil with a white boar pendant. The Tudors adopted a variation of the Lancastrian collar, indicative of their descent, and added portcullises (from the Beauforts) which alternated with pairs of esses, and pendants of the Tudor Rose or portcullis. Many of the nobility had their own collars, that of Thomas, fourth Baron Berkeley, being composed of mermaids. In the Middle Ages such collars were not insignia, though their use was regulated: the SS collar was reserved for knights by Henry VIII, for example.

(ii) The collars of orders of chivalry may be depicted encircling the arms of certain degrees of knight, as may the collar of SS encircle the arms of those who are entitled to wear it.

(iii) In blazon, a collar is a plain circlet unless otherwise specified.

Collared *see* **Attributes**

A Yorkist collar of suns and roses on the effigy of Sir Henry Pierrepoint.

Effigy of Sir John Cheyney wearing a collar of SS, at Salisbury Cathedral.

Collar of SS Of obscure origin, this royal collar composed of or studded with esses is thought to have been worn by knights and esquires prior to its adoption as a Lancastrian device by Henry IV, who also used a badge of two linked esses. This appears on the effigy of his queen in Canterbury Cathedral, and is thought by many to represent the initial S of his motto 'Souverayne'. This collar sometimes had the De Bohun swan as a pendant. Henry VI also used the device, alternating the SS with portcullises and with a Tudor Rose or portcullis as a pendant. Henry VIII restricted the collar to knights. It is still worn by kings of arms (in silver gilt), and heralds and serjeants at arms (silver). The Lord Mayor of London and Lord Chief Justice also wear forms of this device.   KH

RIGHT **Charles VII, King of France (1422-61), from the early fifteenth-century manuscript** *Armorial Equestre de la Toison d'Or et de l'Europe* **at the Bibliotheque de l'Arsenal in Paris, generally known simply as the** *Toison d'Or.* **The manuscript contains a series of brilliantly coloured and animated paintings of 34 of the 37 knights promoted to the Order of the Golden Fleece during the period 1430-40, together with a further 26 uncoloured drawings of knights from the period 1440-61 and an armorial of the principal peers of France and those who undertook duties at coronations of the Electors of the Holy Roman Empire. In this last group are the figures of 4 kings, 4 dukes and 2 counts (together with their retainers' shields of arms) and 10 war-like bishops.**

Collar of St Agatha of Paterno, Military Order of
The Order was founded by the Aragonese sovereigns of the Kingdom of Majorca in about 1200 for the purpose of subduing Arab pirates then troubling the Mediterranean. The Order was formally revived in 1851 after a period of desuetude, and publicly recognized by the King of the Two Sicilies in 1860. The statutes of the Order were most recently revised in June 1971.   JA

Collections No attempt is made in the following to provide details of collections of heraldic or related material outside the British Isles. Without doubt, museums, learned institutions, public archives, and private individuals throughout the civilized world have such things in many forms, and access to some of them can be obtained by the dedicated traveller, correspondent and assiduous student. What now follows is a list of British collections whose custodians or owners have published relevant information (*see* ADDRESSES). It cannot be complete, for some collections are very private, and there is nothing wrong with that. A very useful reference directory is *British Archives* (1983).

Army Museums Ogilby Trust One thousand box files in regimental sequence dealing with dress of British, Empire and Commonwealth forces. Has excellent collection of regimental histories.

Bodleian Library Department of Western Manuscripts. Vast collection of deeds and rolls, local history collections, family and ecclesiastical records.

Borthwick Institute of Historical Research Diocesan records, papers of archbishops and others from the thirteenth century to present. Halifax (Wood family) archives.

British Library Department of Manuscripts. Foundation collections (Sloane, Cotton, Harley), plus material added since 1753. Large collection of seals. See Nickson, M.A.E. *The British Library, Guide to the Catalogues and Indexes, Rough Register of Acquisitions.*

The Burrell Collection Much heraldic painted glass.

Cambridge University Library Some family and estate archives.

Chetham's Library Early English manuscripts.

College of Arms The official records include visitations, grants of arms, pedigrees, etc. Semi-official and unofficial records include rolls of arms, armorials, ordinaries, work books and papers relating to the orders of chivalry. There are some fifty collections of individual heralds and others, and miscellaneous family papers, together with bookplate and seal collections. There is material from well before 1484 when the College was founded. See Wagner, A.R. *The Records and Collections of the College of Arms* (1952), and Jones, F. *Report on the Welsh Manuscripts contained in the Muniments of the College of Arms.*

Corporation of London Records Office Official archives of the corporation from the eleventh to the twentieth centuries. See Jones, P.E. and R. Smith *Guide to the Records at Guildhall* (1951).

Duchy of Cornwall Office All records of the Duchy. See *On the Historical Documents in the Duchy of Cornwall Office* (1930).

Fitzwilliam Museum Extensive collection of coins, medals and illuminated manuscripts.

Genealogical Office (Office of Arms) Dublin The Chief Herald of Ireland's office incorporates the State Heraldic Museum.

Guildhall Library Manuscripts Department. In effect the county records of the City of London, with the exception of the Corporation of London. See *Guide to the London Collections* (1978), and *Guide to Genealogical Sources.*

The Heralds' Museum at the Tower of London includes material and artefacts from the College of Arms and elsewhere.

House of Lords Record Office Records dating from 1497, including peerage claims from 1597. See *Reports of Historical Manuscripts Commission* (1-14) dealing with 1498 to 1693, *Manuscripts of House of Lords 1693-1718* 12 volumes, *Annual Reports of House of Lords Record Office 1950-1981*, and *Guide to the Records of Parliament* (1971).

Huguenot Library Collection of Huguenot pedigrees and other genealogical material.

Institute of Heraldic and Genealogical Studies Many thousands of unpublished manuscripts on family histories. Manorial papers from thirteenth to twentieth centuries, records of armorial bearings in all the Sussex churches and Canterbury Cathedral. Large indexes of British and European arms, transcripts of rolls of arms and heraldic treatises with related notes. A number of heralds' original notebooks, painted and blazoned armorials, bound manuscript books of nineteenth-century working papers on genealogical and heraldic practice.

Lambeth Palace Library Small amount of heraldic material from thirteenth century to present day. See *The Resources and Facilities of Lambeth Palace Library* (1981).

La Societe Jersiaise Large manuscript collection.

The Mitchell Library Rare Books and Manuscripts Department. Special collections, family and regimental history, estate and family papers.

Museum of London Major document collections with some heraldic content, from fifteenth century onwards.

National Library of Scotland Department of Manuscripts. Manuscript material relating to the history of Scotland and Scots throughout the world. In recent years emphasis has been placed on family papers.

National Library of Wales Department of Manuscripts and Records. Many large archives of Welsh estates and families, in addition to what one would expect of a great national library.

National Monuments Record Two million photographs, drawings and reports of historic buildings and sites. Contains many thousands of records of armorial bearings in stone, glass, wood and other media.

National Monuments Record of Scotland Vast collection of photographs, drawings and reports on historic buildings and sites. Contains many records of armorial bearings in stone, glass, wood and other media.

National Monuments Record of Wales Comparable with those of England and Scotland.

National Register of Archives Royal Commission on Historical Manuscripts. Collecting point for information about manuscript sources. Holds catalogues and indexes to papers and records in the United Kingdom.

National Register of Archives — Scotland Counterpart of NRA in London.

Norris Library and Museum Large manuscript collection, including papers relating to the Victoria County History of Huntingdonshire.

Order of St John Library and Museum Manuscript records of English estates in England, France, Malta and Rhodes from 1140 onwards. Collection of prints and drawings, together with crusader and OSJ coin collections.

Public Record Office Houses all government archives selected for permanent preservation. Distributes, through the List and Index Society, copies of all PRO lists and other public archives to subscribing members.

John Rylands Library Charter rooms with extensive collection of genealogical papers, family documents and deeds over the period of the twelfth to twentieth centuries.

St George's Chapel, Windsor Castle Deeds and Documents from 1140 onwards. Some records of the Order of the Garter, and papers of members of the College of St George. See Dalton, J.N. *The Inventories of St George's Chapel* (1957).

William Salt Library Major manuscript and non-MS material, including transcripts of Staffordshire material in the College of Arms library, and two books of Staffordshire heraldry.

Scottish Record Office Originated in the office of Clerk of the Rolls (thirteenth century). The repository for the public records of Scotland.

Society of Antiquaries Library and manuscript collection dating from 1100. Has a collection of more than 10,000 casts of seals, armorial bookplates and brass rubbings.

Society of Genealogists Large library and document collection. There is a 'Great Index' containing over three million references extracted from parish registers, memorial inscriptions, will indexes, Chancery suits and other records.

Spalding Gentlemen's Society Medieval illuminated manuscripts and charters. It is interesting to note that, with the exception of the Ashmolean Museum in Oxford, the museum of this society is the oldest in England.

Ulster Historical Foundation Genealogical material and specialist publications on genealogy and history.

University College of North Wales Department of Manuscripts. Half a million items including many family and estate papers.

University of London Library Small amount of heraldic material, but it houses the University's collection of detached seals, proofs and casts.   JC-K

The College of Arms The term College of Arms is today applied, sometimes without discrimination, to two quite separate things. The first is the Corporation of the OFFICERS OF ARMS, comprising the kings, heralds, and pursuivants of arms, which forms part of the Royal Household, and which, under the chairmanship of Garter King of Arms, has authority concerning all matters heraldic in England, Wales and Northern Ireland. The second is the splendid building in Queen Victoria Street in London, in which the heralds have their apartments and which houses the records of the College and the Court of the Earl Marshal of England.

Arms of the College of Arms

The posts of heralds of arms had been known in England since the twelfth century, and there is good reason to believe that by 1285 there were two kings of arms, with territorial jurisdiction, north and south, corresponding to the ancient division of the king's demesne, and the authority of his escheators.

The functions of the kings, heralds and pursuivants (originally apprentice heralds) of the Crown grew in importance, and by the time of the appointment of the first Garter in 1415 (with, from 1417, *ex officio* seniority over the other officers), it was becoming apparent that it was desirable that the officers should have a charter of incorporation, and a place of common residence from which to exercise their functions. However, the 'office of arms' (as the officers were collectively termed) continued as an unincorporated body for some time, and it was not until 2 March 1484 that King Richard III founded the College of Arms by letters patent constituting them a body corporate. At the same time the king granted them a house named Coldharbour in the parish of All Hallows the Less in the City of London (on the site of Mondial House in Upper Thames Street) with perpetual succession to hold the property to the use of the twelve principal officers of arms. (This document is now in the British Museum, MS. Cotton, Faustina E 1.2.) Unfortunately, the king was killed at the battle of Bosworth on 22 August 1485, and King Henry VII cancelled, by means of the Act of Resumption, all grants made by King Richard. This included Coldharbour, which was given to the new king's mother, Margaret, Countess of Richmond. Thus the officers of arms were again without a home.

John Wrythe, the then Garter, took charge of the rolls and books, preserving them on his own premises and, around 1504, they appear to have passed into the hands of various crown officers of arms who were located in the chapter house of the Black Friars. On 18 July 1555, premises known as Derby House were granted by letters patent to the heralds by Philip and Mary (King and Queen of England, France, Naples, Jerusalem and Ireland, etc.) and the reconstituted body of 'The Corporation of Kings, Heralds, and Pursuivants of Arms' (or 'The Kings, Heralds and Pursuivants of the Corporation of the Office of Arms, London', as they were also termed) gained full occupancy in 1565.

For the next hundred years the Corporation was safely housed, but in 1666 Derby House was destroyed in the Great Fire of London. Its books, records and collections were saved, but it was not until new letters patent were obtained from King Charles II in December 1671 that the heralds were able to effect 'fitte meanes' to receive subscriptions at the 'voluntary benevolence' of the nobility and the gentry to build a new college.

In due time a new building was erected. A licence in mortmain in 1819 allowed a house next to the main building to be purchased and in 1820 King George IV issued a royal warrant permitting the collection of additional fees to help defray the cost. Subsequent rebuilding, including the construction of Queen Victoria Street *c.* 1870, modified the structure of the College premises to their present form — three wings (or ranges) to the west, north and east of what was, before the mid-nineteenth century, the College quadrangle.

The College is owned and governed by a Chapter comprising the three kings, six heralds and four pursuivants of arms in ordinary. Garter King of Arms presides over the monthly meetings of the Chapter, and senior officers act as Registrar (with responsibility for maintaining the records of the College and whose signature is appended on the reverse of every patent), Treasurer, and Librarian (who is also responsible for the College's conservation department). The Earl Marshal has jurisdiction over the officers of arms, who are members of the Royal Household and receive a (modest) salary from the Crown. However, he enjoys only 'visitorial powers' (Brooke-Little) and is not a member of the body corporate of the College. The official records of the College are kept in the Records Room, but are not available for public inspection. From 10.00 a.m. to 4.00 p.m., Monday to Friday, an Officer in Waiting is on duty to receive enquiries and to give advice. The officers of arms also have private practices as heraldic, genealogical and ceremonial consultants, though their principal responsibilities remain those of ceremonial officers to the Crown, arranging state ceremonies under the direction of the Earl Marshal and custodians of the official armorial and genealogical records. Only the kings of arms actually grant armorial bearings by warrant of the Earl Marshal, the other officers acting on behalf of clients in these matters in an advisory capacity.

The arms of the College are *Argent a Cross Gules between four Doves the dexter wing of each expanded and inverted Azure*. Crest: *Out of a Ducal Coronet Or a Dove rising Azure*. Supporters: *On either side a Lion rampant guardant Argent ducally gorged Or*. Motto: 'Diligent And Secret'. JC-K

Further reading
Chesshyre, H. and A. Ailes *Heralds of Today* London, 1986. A biographical list of the officers of the College of Arms 1963-86.
Dennys, R. *Heraldry and the Heralds* London, 1982.
Milton, R. *Heralds and History* 1978.
Noble, M. *A History of the College of Arms* London, 1805.
Squibb, G.D. *Munimenta Heraldica 1484 to 1984* Harleian Society, 1985. Anthology of the texts of royal letters patent to the College of Arms since 1485.
Wagner, A. *The Records and Collections of the College of Arms* 1952.
— *Heralds and Heraldry in the Middle Ages* second ed. 1956.
— *Heralds of England* London, 1967 (reissued 1985). A truly magnificent book.

College of Arms Foundation, The This is an American foundation, established in 1984 with the principal purpose of passing to the College of Arms Trust tax-deductable donations from American sources. It is approved by the United States Inland Revenue Service. Enquiries should be addressed to the College of Arms (*see* ADDRESSES). JB-L

College of Heralds *see* **College of Arms**

Colours, The (i) The principal METAL and COLOUR of a shield of arms, and those first mentioned in a blazon. (If a fur, the dominant metal or colour is used, e.g. ermine = argent.) Frequently and erroneously described as the livery colours, e.g. 'on a wreath of the

liveries'. To avoid confusion they are referred to as armorial colours throughout this book.
See also LIVERY COLOURS
(ii) For colours used in armory *see* TINCTURES and individual entries.
(iii) A military flag dating from the Elizabethan period when large square livery flags were in general use. These were of a plain colour or barry, and sometimes had the Cross of St George displayed on a canton. These were really ensigns and an attempt at classification and regulation was made as early as 1600, when flags of barry, barry wavy and lozengy of two or three tinctures were recorded for the Armed and Trained Companies of London. Most of them were charged with a Cross of St George on a canton, at the centre or over all. (Another flag, the cornet, was at this time carried by heavy cavalry units. This too was square.) During the seventeenth century, as a regimental flag system developed, so too did regulations regarding military (though not cavalry) flags. After the Restoration regimental designs were universally adopted, though the cavalry still had no fixed system like that of the infantry, their flags being charged with personal devices from the heraldry of their colonels, and cyphers if the regiment had a colonel of the royal family. A warrant of 1751 prohibited the use of personal arms, crests or livery colours on military flags. It is at this time that we witness the divergence of nomenclature which is so evident today, there being entirely different military and heraldic flags of the same name. Subsequent legislation and regulation has removed military 'heraldry' so far from the simplicity, beauty and dignity of its medieval origins that the armorist is likely to discover more pain than pleasure in the subject. Fortunately, the Royal Navy and Royal Air Force have contrived to manage their armorial affairs in a far more attractive and well-ordered fashion!
(iv) A naval ensign.

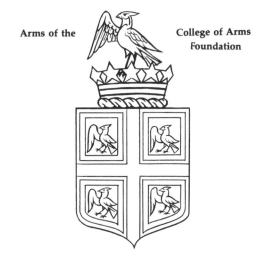

Arms of the College of Arms Foundation

Columbus, Knights of Founded in 1882 by the Revd M.J. McGiveny in New Haven, Connecticut, USA, as a Catholic layman's organization, within fifty years its membership touched half a million persons. The 'order' operates mainly in the Americas and is recognized for its great religious and civic usefulness. The 'Columbian Squires' branch was established in 1928, as an organization of Catholic youth.   JC-K

Combatant *see* **Attitude**

Combed *see* **Attributes**

Commissioner In the fifteenth century, a man appointed by Crown or government to carry out a specific task, or to act for the supreme authority in a district. In Scotland the Lord High Commissioner represents the Crown at the General Assembly of the Church.   JC-K

Commonwealth, The (1649-60) Following the execution of Charles I and the proclamation of a commonwealth, the royal arms were in many places removed or defaced. However, the devices by which they were replaced provide an interesting insight into the motivation of the republican government, and particularly of the Protector, Oliver Cromwell.

The Great Seal of 1655 is a curious blend of the devices of sovereignty and of the new Commonwealth. The arms are *Quarterly 1 and 4 the Cross of St George for England, 2 the Cross of St Andrew for Scotland and 3 the Harp of Ireland* with, significantly, the Protector's personal arms *Sable a Lion rampant Argent* over all on an inescutcheon. (Cromwell had inherited these arms through his paternal grandfather, Sir Richard Williams, alias Cromwell, who had taken the latter name from his mother, a sister of Henry VIII's minister, whilst retaining the Williams arms.) Over this shield is set the affronty six-barred gold helm of the sovereign, surmounted by the royal crown and lion crest, and on either side are the Tudor supporters of a golden crowned lion and the red dragon. The retention of these royal symbols is quite extraordinary, as is the use of the royal crown on coinage of the period. It has been suggested that although Cromwell had refused the Crown of England for himself, he recognized the transitory nature of the Republic and regarded himself as holding the monarchy in trust. The motto which accompanied these arms was 'Pax Quaeritur Bello' — 'If you seek peace, prepare for war'. According to Sir Bernard Burke, when Cromwell's coffin was opened it was found to contain a copper plate engraved with the royal arms of England impaling those of Cromwell.

Companion of Honour (Abbr. CH) Properly a Member of the Order of the Companions of Honour.

The Order was initiated by King George V on 4 June 1917, and is limited to 65 members of both sexes. The gold badge is oval, enclosing an oblong plaque on which is an oak tree bearing a shield of the royal arms. To the dexter is a knight in armour on horseback. The blue border of the badge bears in gold letters the motto 'In Action Faithful And In Honour Clear'. The riband is crimson edged with gold. The Order confers no precedence, but ranks next after the GBE (Knight or Dame Grand Cross of the British Empire).   SA

Compartment In a coat of arms the base on which the SUPPORTERS rest. Considered to be part of the armorial bearings only when specified and exemplified in the patent granting supporters. As such the compartment would be unalterable in form and subject to the same conditions of inheritance as supporters, which would be considered incomplete without it. Many of these compartments are semy of armorial devices, or are of a specific design relevant only to the arms they accompany. It may be assumed, therefore, that other compartments are of a temporary nature to be adopted or rejected at will.

By far the most common representation is the grassy hillock upon which may be depicted appropriate flora — the thrift plant associated with financial institutions, for example. Popular in the recent past was the 'gas bracket' — floral scrollwork upon which supporters perched precariously. Natural features and architectural structures have been adopted as compartments, appropriate to the corporations whose arms they embellish, such as the depiction of Telford's Iron Bridge in the arms of the Worshipful Company of Engineers (see colour page 249). Craggy mountain tops accompany the arms of the former Welsh county of Merioneth — both in compartment and crest; *a Fillet wavy per fess wavy Argent and Azure* represents the Thames in the compartment of the Royal Borough of Kingston-upon-Thames, and the two farm labourer supporters of the Company of Farmers stand, sickles at the ready, on the furrows of a ploughed field. The compartment of the Police Federation, comprising *a grassy Mound traversed on either side by a Path of Paving Stones proper*, is a clear reference to the police officer 'pounding his beat', and the dimidiated *Grassy Mound proper* and *barry wavy Azure and Argent* compartment of British Airways represents the continents and oceans over which BA passengers are transported. Current practice is to grant supporters without a corresponding compartment unless there is a clear rationale for its inclusion. It is then specified in the patent.

Complement, in her *see* **Attributes**

Compony *or* **Gobony** *see* **Field, Varied**

Compounded Arms A system of combining charges from two or more coats of arms to form a new and distinct coat. The system has been used to show elements of arms from the female side of a family, or for feudal and other associations. PF

See also MARSHALLING

Compound Quarterings The process of further dividing a quartered shield of arms into sub-quarters. *See also* QUARTERING

Computers Graphic artists are beginning to investigate computer-based techniques, but only the most powerful hardware has the command structure, line resolution capability and comprehensive palette to make the attempt worthwhile. In addition, the limitations of equipment to translate computer image into hard copy make it difficult to see how imaginative, vigorous heraldry will ever be produced other than by the skilled artist using conventional materials.

Indexing, sorting, storing and retrieving information by means of data-based computer systems have an undoubted future, however, and it can only be a matter of time before works such as Burke's *General Armory*, Papworth's *Ordinary of Arms* and Fairbairn's *Book of Crests* will be available on disc.

Comte *see* **Count**

Coney The common rabbit.

Confirmation of Arms A document issued by an heraldic authority confirming a right to armorial bearings established on the provision of acceptable genealogical proof of male descent from an armigerous ancestor.

Conjoined *see* **Attitude**

Conservation (i) There can be few armorists who have not entered an ancient church and cringed at the dilapidation of memorials, tombs, glass, hatchments and painted stonework. Before rushing to the incumbent to volunteer, pause for thought! Competent in matters armorial you may be — an expert in the conservation of ancient fabric you almost certainly are not. In England it is unlawful for any person to authorize or undertake such restoration work without obtaining a faculty through a diocesan chancellor and the advisory committee responsible for the care of churches. If the incumbent fails to observe the correct procedure he (and you) may face prosecution and a hefty fine. So, seek advice as well as offering it. Combine your expertise in armory with the specialist skills of a qualified restorer. Your enthusiasm may result in the restoration of fading armorial gems for the enjoyment of future generations, but amateur attempts at conservation may do more harm than good.

(ii) The Conservation Department of the College of Arms undertakes archival conservation, restoration of paper, parchment, vellum and fine bindings (and new bindings), restoration of prints and drawings (not photographs), the conservation of non-metallic seals, box and case making and facsimile repair. They will also advise on environmental conditions, fungus and insect infestation, fire and flood damage, etc. Enquiries to the College of Arms (*see* ADDRESSES).

Conservator Although a general word, this term was often used as a short form of Conservator of the Peace and, in the Middle Ages, could refer to the king, lord chancellor and the justices of the king's bench. JC-K

Consolation Peerages A term used in the nineteenth century to describe peerages conferred on members of parliament or candidates defeated at the polls, or on ex-ministers not given office when their party was returned to power. The practice of ennobling such gentlemen has continued in the twentieth century, but the descriptive term seems not now to be used. JC-K

Constable The Constable of England (from the reign of Stephen *Lord Chief Constable*) was, until the sixteenth century, the seventh of the great offices of state. Originally the constable was the quartermaster of the armies and master of the horse, and later (with the Earl Marshal) the president of the Court of Chivalry. When the Constable, Edward (Stafford), Duke of Buckingham was executed in 1521 the office remained vacant thereafter except for temporary appointments for special occasions, such as coronations.

The office had its equivalents in the kingdoms of France (until 1627), Gothic Spain and Naples.

In Ireland in the twelfth and fourteenth centuries the families of Lacy and Verdun provided hereditary constables, whilst in Scotland the Hays, earls of Errol, have from the fourteenth century provided that officer.

In the United States the civic title of High Constable was used by Philadelphia and New York, in the latter case until as late as 1830. To this day some American towns retain the title for the Chief of Police.

The Lord High Constables of England and Scotland are entitled to place behind their shields the batons of their offices saltirewise, those of Scotland being silver tipped in gold. JC-K

Constantine St George of Naples, Sacred Military Order of The foundation of this order has been attributed to the Emperor Constantine the Great in the fourth century. Were this true it would be the oldest extant order of chivalry in the world. The story seems to have arisen because the Chi-Rho symbol adopted by the order was the celestial sign supposed to have been seen by the emperor, and which he figured on his labarum or standard. In addition, there are some sixth-century mosaics which depict the Emperor Justinian being escorted by soldiers whose shields bear the device. The Chi-Rho was, in fact, a widely used Christian symbol, and it is far more likely that the order was founded *c.* 1190 by the Emperor Isaac Angelas Comnenus of Byzantium, who also used the Chi-Rho on his coins.

The order continued in Italy after the Empire was overrun by the Turks, where at the court of Parma a descendant of the emperor sold the grand mastership in 1699 to Duke Francis I. The title was confirmed by popes Innocent XV and Clement XI, and the order became highly respected throughout Europe. When the ducal house of Parma became extinct the grand mastership passed by right of primogeniture to the royal house of Bourbon of the Two Sicilies.

In the 1960s a dispute arose between the two princes of the dynasty as to where the grand mastership should lie. The Duke of Calabria claimed the office by right of primogeniture, whilst the Duke of Castro sought it as head of the royal house of the Two Sicilies. The first-named nobleman has a substantial claim and is recognized as the head of the royal house of the Two Sicilies and grand master of the order by King Juan Carlos of Spain, a regnant Bourbon. On the other hand, the second-named grandee also claims to be the head of the dynasty, and points to the recognition given to the work of the order by the president of Italy. The dispute remains unresolved in 1987.   JC-K

Consul A word used by medieval Latin writers as equivalent to *comes*, meaning count or earl. A consul was originally an elected supreme magistrate in the Roman Republic, and later one of the chief magistrates of the French Republic of 1799-1804. (Also, at the present time, a title for an agent commissioned by one state to reside in another and to represent it.)   JC-K

Contoise, Cointise *see* **Banderolle** *and* **Wreath**

Contourné *see* **Attribute**

Convenience, Flag of A national ensign flown as an indication of a ship's country of registration rather than its country of origin.

Convention An accepted practice of armory.

In early armory, shields of arms were simple and uncluttered. Such terms as ordinary, sub-ordinary,

diminutive, etc., were unnecessary, and charges could safely be borne in any reasonable number and disposition. The only apparent convention of the time was the TINCTURE CONVENTION, and this remains the only inviolable 'rule' (exceptions being deliberate and intended to draw attention to the transgression, as augmentations of honour, for example). However, as the number of armigers increased so the conventions and terminology of armory became more complex in response both to the need to provide a means of differencing arms within a particular family and its cadet branches, and to the essential requirement that all arms should be unique. The majority of conventions remain eminently sensible and have survived the test of time. However, many of those which originated during the Heraldry of the Decadence were both bizarre and superfluous, and fortunately have not survived.

Most conventions are concerned with BLAZON and may be compared with the syntax and grammar of a foreign language. Unfortunately, a number of terms have survived which possess only a vague definition (e.g. ordinary, sub-ordinary), and yet are widely used. If the language and conventions of blazon are to keep pace with the development of armory in the present century, it is essential that such terms should be accurately defined and their functions clarified.

Corbie A raven.

Cordelière A knotted gold or silver cord encircling the arms of a widow. In Scottish armory a widow whose paternal family is not armigerous may bear her late husband's arms in a lozenge within a cordelière. These are also occasionally found in hatchments.

Corded *see* **Attributes**

Cornet (i) A seventeenth-century square cavalry flag.
(ii) A naval signal flag, swallow-tailed at the fly (obsolete).

Coronation, Symbols of Throughout the history of Christendom, monarchs have undertaken the rites of coronation in order to legitimize their sovereignty before God and their people. The English rite of the ninth century was based on that used for the coronation of popes. This was replaced in 973 by a rite more closely associated with that used in the imperial coronations of Europe, and in 1603 it was translated from Latin into English. The English rite is in three parts: the promises made by the sovereign and his acclamation by the people; the consecration and anointing of the sovereign; and the vesting, coronation and enthronement, followed by the homage and the sovereign's communion. Many of the insignia and garments used in the coronation are of great antiquity and possess symbolic properties:

Ampulla A vessel of gold of fourteenth-century date, renovated by Sir Robert Vyner, Goldsmith to King Charles II. It contains the holy oil for the anointing of the sovereign, and is in the form of an eagle with wings outstretched.

Colobium Sindonis An alb or undergarment made of sindon, a kind of fine thin linen or cambric. The first of the priestly garments with which the sovereign is invested immediately after the anointing.

Supertunica or *Close Pall* A priestly garment known as a dalmatic, made of cloth of gold and closely fitting, with which the sovereign is invested after being arrayed with the Colobium Sindonis. It denotes the sovereign's supremacy over the Church and guardianship of her rights.

Golden Spurs of Chivalry The insignia of knighthood. The straps are of crimson velvet, gold embroidered. Either the sovereign's heels are touched with the spurs, or, in the case of a female sovereign, they are presented to her and she touches them in token of acceptance.

Sword The jewelled Sword of State was made for King George IV's coronation at a cost of £6000. It is given to the sovereign, who offers it at the altar. Then it is redeemed and carried naked before the sovereign during the remainder of the coronation service.

Robe Royal or *Pall* The Pallium Regale, with four corners, is fastened beneath the chin and worn like a cape. It is made of cloth of gold, and symbolizes the world being under the sovereignty of God.

Orb A golden sphere surmounted by a cross, symbolizing that the whole world is subject to the authority of Christ.

Ring The ring 'wherein is set a sapphire and upon it a ruby cross' is placed on the fourth finger of the sovereign's right hand at the coronation, where it is called 'the Ring of kingly dignity and the seal of Catholic Faith'.

Sceptre with the Cross Made in 1661, but further embellished in 1911 when the largest portion of the Cullinan diamond, the 'Star of Africa', was inserted beneath the orb of amethyst at the head. The Sceptre is the symbol of kingly power and justice.

Rod with the Dove At the head is a golden orb surmounted by a cross on which is a dove with outstretched wings symbolizing the Holy Spirit. The Rod represents equity and mercy.

Saint Edward's Crown Made in 1661 of gold set with precious stones. The crown's two arches symbolic of independent sovereignty are surmounted by an orb, thereon a cross denoting that earthly sovereignty is under the dominion of Christ.

Imperial State Crown Made in 1838 by the jewellers Rundell & Bridge. Contains a sapphire thought to have been taken from Edward the Confessor's ring; the Black Prince's ruby; four pearls, probably earrings of Queen Elizabeth I; and the second largest portion of the Cullinan diamond.   SA/SF

Coronet (i) A ceremonial cap, usually of velvet lined ermine, enfiling an ornamental circlet of gold, the design of which is indicative of a particular rank or office. Coronets of rank and office are worn by peers and certain officers of the Crown at state occasions, together with other robes and insignia appropriate to rank or degree. Coronets of rank are depicted in representational form in the armorial bearings of peers, coronets of office being used in lieu of a crest in the arms of office of the English kings of arms. (*See* CORONET OF OFFICE, CORONET OF RANK *and peers under individual entries*)

(ii) Ornamental circlets of various forms depicted in a coat of arms in place of, or in addition to, the wreath. Although certain types of crest coronet are reserved for specific purposes they are not indicative of rank and should, therefore, be considered as integral to the crest. Many crest coronets are erroneously described as crowns. (*See* CREST CORONET)

(iii) As (ii) above, but used as armorial charges in a shield of arms.

Coronet of Office A ceremonial cap of velvet lined ermine enfiling a circlet and used for ceremonial purposes by senior officers of the Crown. In practice the only coronet of office currently used in Britain is that of the kings of arms, which is a red velvet cap lined ermine within a silver-gilt circlet of sixteen acanthus leaves, alternating in height, the rim inscribed with the words *Miserere mei Deus secundum magnum misericordiam tuam*. Nine leaves and the first three words are shown where the coronet is depicted in representational form. Known as the crown of a king of arms, it is worn only at coronations. However, it may be used in place of the crest in the arms of office of a king of arms, and is occasionally depicted above the shield with the king of arms' personal helm and crest issuing from it, as in the devisal of arms illustrated on page 126.

Coronet of Rank A ceremonial cap of velvet lined ermine enfiling a gold circlet, the design of which is indicative of a particular rank within the peerage. In Britain such caps are of red velvet with a gold tassel at the crown, and are probably a development of the CAP OF DIGNITY used in conjunction with circlets of varying designs, examples of which may be found in illustrations of the medieval period. In the fourteenth century, coronets as insignia of the higher nobility were restricted to dukes and marquesses and, after 1444, to earls. At this time they do not appear to conform to any particular pattern. Coronets were

Coronets of Rank

Duke

Marquess

Earl

Viscount

Baron

granted to viscounts by James I and to barons by Charles II in 1661. Coronets of rank are worn at state occasions by peers, and are depicted in representational form in their armorial bearings immediately above the shield of arms.

See also peers under individual headings

Corporate and Civic Armory From the late twelfth century officials of boroughs and other towns made use of seals carrying devices. Initially, these were rarely depicted on shields and were simply religious or other emblems of local significance, or seigniorial devices indicative of feudal ownership or benefaction, contained within an inscribed border. With the gradual development of corporate authority in the Middle Ages came a natural desire to assert corporate identity in a form which could be equated with that of the feudal magnate, and by the fourteenth century many towns had adopted the devices of their seals as coats of arms, simply by depicting them in colour on a shield, and sometimes rearranging charges to conform with armorial conventions. In the sixteenth and seventeenth centuries several took advantage of the heralds' visitations to record their previously unauthorized arms, and by 1700 ninety English towns and cities had acquired armorial bearings, either by prescriptive right or by grant. Of these, twenty-seven were composed of royal or seigniorial devices,

eighteen bore religious emblems (usually those of patron saints), eighteen included castles, and seventeen ships or other maritime references. It is apparent, therefore, that the majority of these early civic arms derived, in part at least, from the devices used on even earlier seals. Other towns retained their original emblems, many of which are still used today; for example, the triple-towered castle charged with the royal arms (*Quarterly France Ancient and England*) of Dorchester in Dorset, which although clearly derived from the town's medieval seal, is *not* a coat of arms.

The use of unauthorized coats of arms burgeoned in the nineteenth century when civic pride and corporate rivalry marched hand in hand with vulgarity and ostentation. An example is the town of Crewe which, before the coming of the London, Midland and Scottish Railway, consisted of a single farmhouse in 1841. The new town assumed arms which almost defy blazon. The shield was quarterly and contained a canal boat, a stage coach, a packhorse and a pillion or saddle in each of the quarters. Its crest was a locomotive and tender. None of these charges was retained when the Borough of Crewe obtained arms in 1955: *Ermine a Wheel Or on a Chief wavy Azure a Maunch between two Garbs Gold*, and for the crest *A demi-Lion Argent holding between the claws a Cog Wheel Or*. These 'official' arms are typical of civic grants of the period, in that they are generally more complex and contain a greater number of different charges

The arms of Sherborne Town Council

than personal arms. These are intended to represent historical as well as contemporary features of a particular civic authority, and there is often an understandable desire on the part of local dignitaries to include far too much information, thereby detracting from the aesthetic quality of the arms. This was particularly true when several authorities were combined, as during local government reorganization of 1974, though for the most part the kings of arms avoided conglomerations of existing devices and granted entirely new and fairly simple coats.

The use of supporters is reserved for civic authorities of particular eminence and distinction, though the precise criteria are not clear. The town council of Sherborne, Dorset, for example, enjoys only parish council status and yet in 1986 was granted arms which include supporters because of its pre-eminence in the annals of English history. These arms provide an example of how a considerable amount of local information may be incorporated into a simple and attractive design: *Azure a Cross triparted and fretted Argent between four double Roses Gules on Argent en soleil barbed and seeded Gold*, and for the crest *Within a Wreath Argent and Azure out of an Ancient Crown Or a double headed and twin-tailed Wyvern displayed Argent armed and langued Gules*. Supporters: *On either side a Griffin segreant reguardant the aquiline parts Argent beaked and gorged with an Ancient Crown Or the leonine parts also Or armed and langued Gules*. The shield contains references to the town's benefactors: the blue field from the arms of the Digby family, lords of the manor of Sherborne, the silver cross from the arms of Sherborne Abbey triparted and fretted to symbolize the town's ancient weaving industry, and the combined Tudor Rose and sunburst badges of Edward VI who reconstituted Sherborne School (King's School) in 1550. The colours of silver and blue

are those of Bishop le Poore, who in 1228 granted a charter to the town, and were also the colours of the former urban district council. The crest is the Wessex wyvern, a reference to the town's Saxon origins. It is double headed because of Sherborne's location on the borders of two counties (Dorset and Somerset), both originally part of the ancient kingdom of Wessex in which St Aldhelm established his cathedral at Sherborne in 705. The ancient crowns are those of the two Saxon kings, Ethelbert and Ethelbald, who are buried in the Abbey, and the third is that of Aldhelm who was himself a member of the Wessex royal family. The griffin supporters, legendary guardians of treasure, symbolize the town's pre-eminence as a centre of learning and its vigilance in conserving its heritage, the reguardant attitude of the beasts emphasizing their watchfulness and their respect for the past. Griffins are half eagle and half lion, and here the silver eagles are from the arms of Roger de Caen, builder of Sherborne Old Castle and, as Bishop of Sarum, chiefly responsible for the construction of the Norman abbey at Sherborne. The gold lions represent the town's royal associations and are reminiscent of the lions in the arms of Dorset County Council. The motto is taken from the Sherborne Missal, a magnificent medieval manuscript, now in the possession of the Duke of Northumberland. The town was also granted a badge *A Crozier Or enfiling a Tower with a portal Argent* and this is used by organizations within the jurisdiction of the town council.

Regrettably, local authorities are these days subject to constant political change, and this is reflected in the attitudes of many politicians to the use of armorial bearings. In many instances arms are dismissed as 'irrelevant' or even 'élitist', and are replaced by logotypes and slogans. Of course, there is no obligation on a local authority to obtain arms. However, the adoption of other, non-armorial devices will not enjoy the status of 'tokens of honour' derived from the crown, though even logotypes are preferable to the assumption of bogus armorial bearings, the use of which may be compared with the practice of adding initials to one's name, indicative of honours or qualifications to which one is not entitled. In Scotland, Lord Lyon exercises absolute authority over the use of armorial bearings by corporations, and such abuses are virtually unknown. In both countries arms are granted to bodies corporate, and are therefore of equal status as arms granted to an individual below the rank of knight. This is reflected in the use of the esquire's helmet in English corporate grants, and the sallet in those of Scotland. Technically, therefore, there is no such thing as 'county arms' or 'city arms', for they are possessed by the body corporate on whose seals they are engraved.

Corporate arms, other than those to civic authorities, include those of schools, colleges and universities, public utilities, nationalized industries, public or limited liability companies, professional associations, eminent learned and academic societies, and so on. The criteria for grants of arms to such bodies seem to be stability and permanence. Many of these arms date from the earliest heraldic period, for example those of Oxford University, which in their 'modern' form are from the fifteenth century but are derived from the attributed arms of Edmund the Martyr, the ninth-century king of East Anglia, *Azure three open Crowns two and one Or*. Other early institutions adopted the arms of their founders: St John's College (Sir Thomas White), and Exeter College (Walter de Stapledon), are but two examples. Many recent grants of arms to corporate bodies have been in the very best traditions of medieval armory: simple, symbolic and essentially memorable. The arms of British Airways are extraordinarily ingenious and incorporate a segment of the Union Flag as depicted on the tail-planes of their aircraft. The Milk Marketing Board bears *Vert issuant from the sinister base three Piles wavy bendwise conjoined at the dexter chief point Argent* in graphic representation of streams of milk, and the arms of the United Kingdom Atomic Energy Authority represent an atomic reactor *Sable semy of Plates a Pile barry dancetty Or and Gules*.

Further reading

Briggs, G. *Civic and Corporate Heraldry* Heraldry Today, 1971.

Fox-Davies, A.C. *The Book of Public Arms* London, 1915.

Humphery-Smith, C.R. (Ed.) *The Cambridge Armorial* Canterbury, 1985.

Louda, J. *European Civic Coats of Arms* 1966.

Patton, D.L.H. *Arms of the County Councils of Scotland* 1977.

Scott-Giles, W.C. *Civic Heraldry of England and Wales* London (revised 1953).

Urquhart, R.M. *Scottish Burgh and County Heraldry* 1973.

— *Scottish Civic Heraldry* 1979.

Corruption of Blood *see* **Attainder**

Cotises Originally diminutives of the bend, depicted one on either side and parallel to it. Any ordinary may now be cotised (the pale is said to be endorsed). When two cotises are shown on either side of the ordinary it is double cotised. Treble cotised is also possible in theory, but is rarely used.

Cottells' Book *see* **Treatises**

Couchant *see* **Attitude**

Couché *see* **Shield**

The arms of Kent County Council

Count, Compte *or* **Comte** Strictly speaking, the root word *comitem* means 'a companion', but the term gradually became a foreign title of nobility equivalent to the rank of earl. The French rendering is *comte*, and the Italian is *conte*. In the sixteenth and seventeenth centuries the word 'county' was sometimes used to describe such noblemen.   JC-K

Counter A common prefix used in blazon to mean opposite or reverse, e.g. *counter-embattled* indicates that an ordinary is embattled on both sides, *counter-rampant* that a beast is depicted rampant to the sinister.

Counterchange *or* **Counter-colour** One of the most attractive (and most popular) conventions in armory whereby a shield may be divided by any of the lines of partition, and the metals and colours, both of the field and of any charges placed thereon, reversed on either side of the line; e.g. *Per fess Sable and Or a Lion rampant counterchanged gorged with an Eastern Coronet Gules and holding in the forepaws a Harp Or* (Harper of Western Australia).

A chevron cotised   Counterchanged arms

Counter Compony *see* **Field, Varied**

Counter Passant *see* **Attitude**

Counter Potent *see* **Fur**

Counter Rampant *see* **Attitude**

Counter Vair *or* **Contre Vair** *see* **Fur**

Countess The wife of an earl, or a lady who holds an earldom in her own right.

The robe of a countess is similar to that of a DUCHESS except that it is trimmed with three rows of ermine, the edging being 3 inches (7.5 cm) broad and the train being 1½ yards (1.4 m) on the ground. The coronet of a countess is likewise similar to that worn by a duchess, except that it carries eight silver balls (representing pearls) raised on points and interspersed with small strawberry leaves. The arms of a countess holding an earldom in her own right are similar to those of a duchess but surmounted by the coronet of her own degree.   JC-K

Count Palatine In the later Roman Empire this person was a count (*comes*) attached to the imperial family, with supreme authority in certain matters.   JC-K

Couped Cut off. An ordinary is said to be couped when it is terminated before reaching the edge of the shield.

Couped Close *see* **Attributes**

Couple Close *see* **Chevron**

Courant *see* **Attitude**

Course, in full *see* **Attitude**

Court Baron An English manorial court of the Middle Ages. The term means 'the Baron's Court' (*curia baronis, la court de seigneur*). The court administered the authority of the LORD OF THE MANOR over his tenants and land. The chief business of the court was to ensure the upholding of the 'custom of the manor' — admitting new tenants, collecting the entry fees (fines) due on those occasions, enforcing the payment of rents, heriots and so on. The steward of the manor was usually the presiding officer. Records were kept in the form of court rolls. A number of courts baron still meet for purely formal purposes.   JC-K

See also COURT LEET; BARON COURT (SCOTLAND)

Courtesy Although in the strictest sense this word (which occurs in several forms) means manners appropriate to a court, it has a number of applications

touching on things granted by favour and not by right. Good examples are the COURTESY TITLES accorded to offspring of senior members of the peerage. The word 'curtsey', once applied to the display of courtesy by gesture, is now used only to identify the female equivalent of the bow. Before 1925 'curtsey' was the name given to the interest a husband was permitted in land held by his wife for her lifetime.   JC-K

Courtesy Ensign The merchant ensign of a country being visited by a ship of different nationality, usually flown at the fore or yard-arm.

Courtesy Title Styles conceded by courtesy of the sovereign to the children of peers. Sons of dukes and marquesses use the style 'lord'. Their daughters and those of an earl use the style 'lady' before their names. The sons of earls and the sons and daughters of viscounts and barons use 'honourable'. The eldest son of a duke, marquess or earl takes his father's second title but is not thereby a peer.

Courtier A general term meaning one who, by office or personal standing, attends or frequents the court of a monarch.   JC-K

Court Leet An English manorial court of the Middle Ages which, around the early fourteenth century, seems to have grown out of, and separated from the COURT BARON. It was concerned with petty crime and other offences in the manor, including overgrazing the common land, dealing with stray animals, tenants who did not help to maintain the manorial roads, and so on. It was presided over by the steward to the LORD OF THE MANOR, who acted as judge. Many manorial court rolls survive and are of great value to historians of all classes. The Courts Leet have never become officially extinct, and some still survive to execute pieces of purely formal business.   JC-K
See also BARON COURT (SCOTLAND)

Court Martial A court for the trial of offences by members of the armed services. In England the courts martial system (dating in its modern form from an Act of 1689) inherited some of the jurisdiction of the COURT OF CHIVALRY — the *curia militaris*.   JC-K

Couter, Coute *or* **Cop** Elbow guard, usually of plate.

Coward *see* **Attitude**

Creatures *see* **Beasts** *and individual entries under name of beast.*

Crescent An armorial charge, consisting of a half-moon with the 'horns' pointing upwards. The cadency mark of a second son. If the horns point to the dexter it is said to be an *increscent*, if to the sinister a *decrescent*.

Cresset A fire basket, usually depicted at the top of a pole.

Crest A three-dimensional device mounted on the helmet and so depicted in a coat of arms, together with the WREATH (or CREST CORONET) and MANTLING, both of which are now considered to be components of the crest in British armory. Crests are only granted in conjunction with arms or to a person who has inherited arms but no crest. Women are not granted crests, neither may they inherit them. Corporate bodies may be granted crests, though some armorists take the view that a crest is a personal device and therefore not appropriate to a corporation.

A crest should never be depicted without its accessories, though in practice the crest and wreath are frequently employed when a full achievement is considered inappropriate. This is more correctly the role of the armorial BADGE. During the eighteenth and nineteenth centuries, when badges were not available to armigers, crests and wreaths were used on livery buttons of retainers, for example.

For the origins of the crest one must consider the armorial practices of central and eastern Europe, where either the entire shield of arms or charges and tinctures from it were often displayed in crests: on panaches, wings, between pairs of horns and, indeed, in three-dimensional form. Although not universal, this practice of repeating charges and tinctures in shield and crest is a characteristic of, for example, German armory, but the exception in Britain — as a glance at Burke's *Peerage* will confirm. However, there can be little doubt that the 'crests' of twelfth and thirteenth century, in Britain as in Europe, were simply additional flat surfaces on which devices from the arms were repeated. A well known fourteenth-century illustration in the Luttrell Psalter (British Museum) shows armorial display in the grand manner: Sir Geoffrey Luttrell's arms (*Azure a Bend between six Martlets Argent*) are visible on his shield, pennon, ailettes, horse trapper, saddle, his horse's chanfron and fan 'crest', and on his own 'crest' — all-told he carried the Luttrell arms seventeen times! The early cock's comb (*crista*) or metal fan-shaped plate, usually scalloped at the upper edge, which rose from the crown of the helmet, was ideally suited to such display, though at first it may have been a purely decorative embellishment being an extension of the helmet's 'spine'. That it was intended to afford additional protection in battle, as has been suggested, seems a somewhat dubious proposition as it increased the target area significantly and, although of no great weight, must have impaired stability at

The finely proportioned achievement of the Worshipful Company of Fletchers.

speed. It is likely that charges from the shield were adapted to fill the space provided by the fan: for example, the rampant lions in the arms of Percy and Talbot were translated into passant and statant lions, at first painted on fans and later modelled as elaborate tournament crests. It is also reasonable to assume that early crests were visible only in profile, either as paintings on a fan or as fans cut to the shape of the device.

The built-up 'spine' of Greek and Roman attic helmets (survivals of which may be seen today in the helmets of the uniformed civilian services and some ceremonial military helmets) were undoubtedly intended to add strength to the vulnerable area at the back of the head. However, these too were extended or embellished for purely decorative purposes or to signify rank, and from them came the medieval panache, plume or bush of feathers, often depicted in the colours of the arms they accompanied.

Why, then, should there be so few surviving examples in British armory of devices from the shield of arms being employed as crests? There may be two reasons for this. During the Middle Ages crests were considered to be the perquisite of the knightly class, those who possessed both the rank and the resources which enabled them to participate in tournaments where crests were used (it is most unlikely that the later type of modelled tournament crest was ever used in battle, where it would have been a most unwelcome encumbrance). At that time, crests were hereditary and could be transmitted through heiresses, but they could not be marshalled for display in the manner of inherited quarterings of arms and there are many instances if inherited crests being adopted in preference to paternal ones, possibly as an indication of the transfer of territorial rights, whilst the paternal shield of arms was retained. Secondly, a characteristic of medieval English armory was the widespread use of personal and livery badges which often differed from the devices found in an armiger's shield of arms. Many of these were later adopted as crests, particularly after the sixteenth century, when crests became available to all and sundry, irrespective of rank, encouraged by the heralds' visitations and a rapid decline into armorial decadence. In the thirteenth century German crests were accorded equal or even greater value than the shield of arms, the *oberwappen* (helm and crest) being a common feature on seals of the period. It was undoubtedly the case that the right to bear a crest was considered to be a privilege and honour over and above the right to bear arms, and it is hardly surprising, therefore, that the post-Tudor armiger should wish to acquire one, the family badge being a logical choice.

The ceremonial and tournament crests of the high Middle Ages were made of light materials: paste board, cloth or boiled leather over a wooden or wire framework or basketwork. These were fastened to the helmet by means of laces or rivets, the unsightly join being concealed by a wreath or coronet or by the material of the crest itself, the lower edge of which formed the mantling, often in the form of a beast's fur or feathers. In the Tudor period crests retained their simplicity, but the insistence of later English heralds that the crest, like the shield of arms, should be unique, resulted in grants of the most incredible complexity, few of which could ever have been affixed to a helm, e.g. *A Ship in distress on a Rock proper* (Pellew). Conversely, the simplicity of many Scottish crests is attractive, but confusing when grants of identical crests have been made or confirmed to entirely unrelated families.

Present-day practice insists that crests should be of three dimensions. This, of course, is in keeping with the current 'medieval' philosophy of the heraldic authorities, who have also relaxed the rules relating to the position of the helmet, thereby avoiding some of the more ridiculous contortions required of crests in the past. However, this welcome return to medieval simplicity has inevitably restricted the number of devices available, stimulating the herald's ingenuity in the search for means of 'differencing' familiar beasts and devices.

During the Middle Ages crests were transmitted in the manner of arms, and, as has been noted, inherited crests were often adopted to symbolize a significant shift in a family's foundation. However, by the Restoration the transmission of crests through heiresses had been abandoned.

In Scotland crests are permitted greater flexibility and may be altered or substituted on matriculation. When encircled by a strap and buckle they may be used as livery badges, and in both English and Scottish armory crests are often depicted on standards together with livery badges — an unsatisfactory and illogical practice.

The use of the crest in French armory declined rapidly in the post-medieval period, in Spain and Portugal examples of crests are rare and in Italy exceptional.

English crests are theoretically subject to marks of cadency, though with the exception of those exemplified in patents under royal licence, the requirement has never been enforced. The use of multiple crests in achievements of arms was common in German armory where the crest had a distinctive territorial implication (see colour page 336). When two or more crests are depicted in an achievement, that to the dexter is always the principal crest and those in the centre precede those on the outside. Thus two crests would be (in order) 1-2, three crests 2-1-3, four crests 3-1-2-4, and so on.

During the eighteenth century several crests were granted as augmentations of honour, and the armorist should be alert to this possibility when attempting identification of an achievement which includes more than one crest.

Crest Coronet Not to be confused with CORONETS OF RANK, crest coronets are ornamental circlets depicted in a coat of arms in place of, or in addition to, the wreath. They should be considered as integral to the crest, therefore, though certain types of crest coronet are reserved for specific purposes. Disconcertingly, nearly all crest coronets are termed 'crowns' but may also be found blazoned 'coronet'. Most are also employed as armorial charges. The most common types are:

Ancient Crown A circlet of trefoil-like projections or fleurs-de-lis set upon a plain rim. These are generally granted to armigers with antiquarian interests or corporate bodies with royal or ancient associations. The Ancient Crown has become particularly popular with armorists since it was first granted to the Heraldry Society in 1957. In Scotland, the term Ancient Crown is applied to that type of coronet known in England as an Eastern Crown (see below).

Mural Crown A crown in the form of an embattled wall, normally with three visible battlements unless otherwise specified. Widely used in civic heraldry and in the arms of distinguished soldiers, where such a crown *may* be an augmentation of the crest. The Mural Crown is also employed in the arms of some English county councils in lieu of a crest.

Crest Coronets

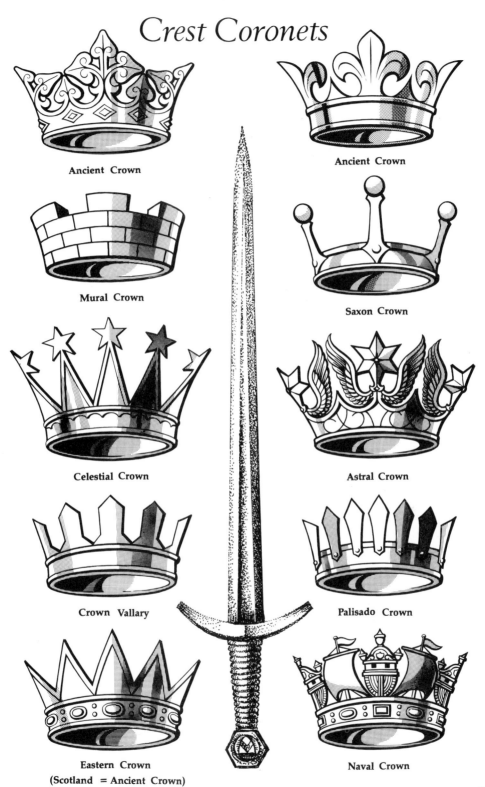

Ancient Crown

Ancient Crown

Mural Crown

Saxon Crown

Celestial Crown

Astral Crown

Crown Vallary

Palisado Crown

Eastern Crown
(Scotland = Ancient Crown)

Naval Crown

Saxon Crown A simple circlet with four tapering uprights (three visible), each surmounted by a ball. The most common pre-Conquest crown depicted on coinage and as such popular in the civic heraldry of English corporations having Saxon associations.

Celestial Crown Similar to the Eastern Crown (below) but having a star at the point of each ray.

Astral Crown Four pairs of wings (one pair and two halves visible), each enclosing a mullet and all set on a plain rim. Assigned to distinguished members of the Royal Air Force, eminent aviators and institutions associated with aviation.

Crown Vallary From the Latin *vallare*, to fortify, the Crown Vallary is probably a corruption of the Palisado Crown (see below). Its defensive characteristics have commended it to the forces of law and order, and it appears in the arms of several police authorities. It has five visible projections.

Palisado Crown Similar in appearance to the Crown Vallary but with seven projections clearly riveted to the rim. The origin of the Crown Palisado is the defensive palisade and it is to be found in the heraldry of, for example, towns with Roman associations or those constructed within ancient fortifications.

Eastern Crown In Scotland this is known as the Ancient Crown. A crown of eight tall points (five visible) set on a plain rim. Associated with distinguished service in the Near or Far East. Also known as the Antique Crown.

Naval Crown Depicted as ships' sterns and sails set alternately on a plain rim and reserved for distinguished sailors and towns with naval associations. Badges of Royal Navy ships are ensigned with Naval Crowns.

Circlets Plain circlets or circlets set about with roses, garbs, acorns, etc., are now out of favour with the English kings of arms, though occasional variations are to be found, such as the *Circlet Sable edged and ermined Or* granted in lieu of a crest wreath to Stephen Slater of Wiltshire in 1985.

Ducal Coronet see separate entry.

Coronet of Thistles Introduced into Scotland after the reorganization of local government in 1973, there are two versions: that for regional councils consists of a circlet *richly chased from which are issuant four Thistles leaved Or* (one and two halves visible), and that for district councils is a similar circlet *from which are issuant eight Thistle Heads Or* (three and two halves visible).

Coronet of Dolphins Also introduced following local government reorganization, this coronet is used by island area councils. It consists of *a Circlet richly chased from which are issuant four Dolphins two and two respectant naiant embowed Or* (two visible).

Coronet of Pine Cones and Thistle Leaves Also introduced after 1973 to distinguish a community council, this is *a Circlet richly chased from which are issuant four Thistle leaves* (one and two halves visible) *and four Pine Cones Or* (two visible).

Prior to local government reorganization in 1973 the Scottish counties and burghs used distinctive coronets. That for a county consisted of alternate pointed projections (5 visible) and garbs (4 visible). The burghal coronet was similar in appearance to the Mural Crown (see above), but had five visible projections and was coloured according to the type of burgh: a royal burgh had a *coronet proper* (i.e. grey) *masoned sable*, a police burgh had a *coronet azure masoned argent* and that of a burgh of barony was *gules masoned argent*.

Crested *see* **Attributes** *and* **Lines, Varied**

Cri de Guerre A war cry. It is likely that many (shorter) mottoes originated as war cries, hence their appearance on livery flags which were used as mustering points before and during a battle, and their association (especially in Scotland) with livery badges. A war cry was employed as a means of rallying support in the press of battle, and only occasionally as a blood-curdling adjunct to a cavalry charge (the popular interpretation). For this reason a war cry had to be short and distinctive, the Scottish 'I Dar' (Dalzell) and 'Grip Fast' (Leslie) being good examples. In Scottish patents of arms the motto or cri de guerre is specified and is, therefore, unalterable. In English patents it is not.
See also MOTTO

Crined *see* **Attributes**

Cross (i) An ordinary composed of a broad, central vertical band intersecting a similar horizontal one, the four limbs extending to the edges of the shield. Often termed a *cross passant* in ancient armory, it is subject to all the variations of field and line, and charges placed upon it are depicted in the upright position unless otherwise specified.

Diminutives: fillet cross
Parted field: quarterly
Varied field: none
Disposition: in cross
Inclination: crosswise

See also ORDINARY
(ii) An armorial charge with numerous variations of form. The preponderance of crosses in armory

Scottish Civic Coronets

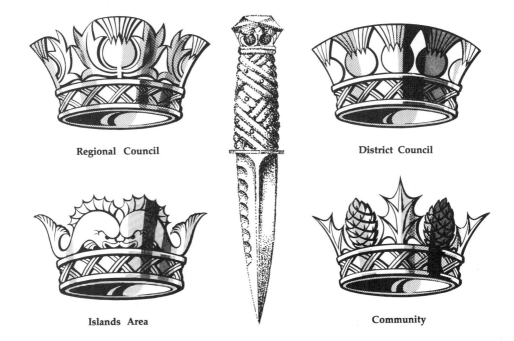

Regional Council

District Council

Islands Area

Community

Scottish county councils and burghs were entitled to use distinctive crest coronets. Between 1849 and 1903 fifteen royal, parliamentary and police burghs recorded arms which included burghal coronets (a form of mural coronet) though it was not until 1912 that the device was officially introduced by Lord Lyon Balfour-Paul, much to the annoyance of his English con-temporary, A.C. Fox-Davies, who only three years earlier had stated (*A Complete Guide to Heraldry*) '... the practice is not permissible in British armory.' The crest coronet used by counties was vert with gold garbs set on the rim. With the creation of new administrative areas in 1975 these coronets were abandoned and those illustrated above were introduced.

County

Burghal

accurately reflects the influence of the crusades and medieval man's preoccupation with his religion. According to various sources there are three, four or even five hundred different crosses employed in armory, though of these only twenty or so are in regular use. (Jonkheer Graafland discovered over one hundred forms *in use* throughout European armory.) The symbolism of the cross is older than armory, and the cross itself pre-dates Christianity. T. Rylance (*Coat of Arms* Vol. 5, No. 127) suggests that there are two types of cross: the *accidental* variety which was in existence before the development of armory as a means of strengthening the shield, and the *intentional* crosses, borne deliberately to represent the Christian symbol. There can be little doubt that the earliest forms of armorial cross were of the simplest kind and

119

**Relief carving of
King Aethelbald.**

that the proliferation of variants resulted either through casual embellishment or the enthusiasm of later heralds for defining forms which had been arrived at by accident or artistic licence. It must be recognized that medieval heralds frequently substituted terms which may now be applied with precision.

When the lower limb of any cross tapers to a point it is blazoned *fitchy*. The term *fitchy at the foot* is used to describe a cross when the point is depicted as an appendage to the lower limb. When the limbs of a cross project from a squared centre it is said to be *quadrate*. The fillet cross is a diminutive of the ordinary and is most often used to unite a quarterly coat into an indivisible one (*see* IMPARTIBLE ARMS).

Cross-crosslet An armorial charge. A plain cross with each of its four limbs also terminating in a cross. A cross-crosslet fitched has its three upper limbs terminating in crosses, but the lower limb is pointed. A field semy of cross-crosslets is termed crusily. Crusily fitchy is semy of cross-crosslets fitched.

Cross of Liberty, Order of (Finland) Founded on 18 August 1944 the order has ten classes ranging from Grand Cross to Medal of Merit, Second Class. There are a number of special decorations associated with the order. These start with the Cross of Mannerheim, First Class and end with the Medal of Mourning.   JC-K

Crown (i) An ornamental circlet of gold and gems worn about the head and depicted in representational form as a symbol of majesty and sovereignty.

The simple fillet, tied round the head of primitive man to restrain the hair, was adopted in a variety of forms as a symbol of authority in the ancient civilizations of Europe and the East, and remains as such today in the armorial crest wreath. In Rome, the royal diadem was originally a white ribbon; and wreaths of gold leaves and laurel were prizes accorded to triumphant generals and distinguished

citizens. In Britain, the torse or WREATH was worn by rulers of the ancient kingdoms and a sculpture, discovered at Repton in Derbyshire in 1979, depicts Aethelbald, King of Mercia (d. 757), wearing just such a wreath of twisted material. In central Europe, crowns of great complexity and beauty were depicted on coinage and artefacts. During the Middle Ages in Western Europe, the circlet continued in use as a symbol of authority among the nobility, whilst the true crown became enclosed and arched, and remained the prerogative of the monarch. In armory both the crown and the CORONET (the 'open' crown) are used in conjunction with caps of dignity. In the medieval period these invariably took the form of the CHAPEAU. However, the gradual introduction of the arched crown in the arms of the late medieval and Tudor kings was accompanied by the use of a more appropriate rounded cap of red velvet lined ermine, essentially that which continues in use today.

For the development of the crown of Great Britain see *A Complete Guide to Heraldry* by A.C. Fox-Davies. (ii) Several so-called crowns are depicted as armorial charges, both in shields of arms and in crests. CREST CORONETS are used in place of, or in addition to, the wreath and as such should be considered as integral to the crest.

Crowned *see* **Attributes**

Crown Herald An officer of arms whose salary is paid by the Crown.

Crown of India, Imperial Order of This Order was reserved exclusively for ladies and ranked with the Order of the Indian Empire. It is not now bestowed, following the granting of Indian independence in 1947.   JC-K

Crown Prince The heir apparent to a sovereign, especially German.

Crown Vallary *see* **Crest Coronet**

Crupper The armour for the hind quarters of a horse, either of leather, mail or plate.

Crusades The Wars of the Cross, to free the Holy Land from the Saracens, began with high hopes and ideals. They occupied much of the best of Western Christendom's military, religious and chivalric fervour for three centuries. Yet they achieved virtually nothing, largely because of lack of organization arising from jealousies among the leaders, and failure to understand the terrain, the climate, and the need for hygiene.

First Crusade (1096-99) inspired by Peter the Hermit and Pope Urban II, began with great enthusiasm and

The Cross

1 Moline
2 Cross-crosslet fitchy
3 Saxon
4 Recercely
5 Celtic
6 Formy or paty
7 Tau (St Anthony's)
8 Potent
9 Fylfot or cramponned
10 Bottony
11 Patonce
12 Flory
13 Formy fitchy
14 Fourché
15 Potent quadrate
16 Formy fitchy at the foot
17 Maltese
18 Celtic
19 Cross-crosslet
20 Fleuretty
21 Patriarchal

no planning. The first arrivals, little better than a rabble, were almost annihilated by disease and the Turks. The second phase, led by experienced Norman warriors, among them Bohemond of Sicily, Godfrey of Bouillon, and Robert of Normandy, son of the Conqueror, captured Jerusalem in 1099. The glory and bravery of this early success was immediately sullied by the most appalling massacre of the inhabitants of the Holy City. Godfrey became Guardian of the Holy Sepulchre, refusing the title of king in the city where Christ wore a crown of thorns. His successors were less modest and called themselves Kings of Jerusalem. Their followers set up feudal estates from their conquests.

Second Crusade (1146-49) led by Louis VII of France and the Emperor Conrad III, was costly in lives, suffering and disillusion, achieving nothing. In 1187, after Saladin's great victory at Hattin, Jerusalem fell again into the hands of the Turks.

Third Crusade (1189-92) With Philip II of France, the Emperor Frederick Barbarossa and Richard I of England as leaders, this appeared to have the power to defeat Saladin. It failed through jealousy and lack of cohesion among the leaders. Barbarossa, after initial success in Asia Minor, was drowned and his army disintegrated. Richard of England showed great valour, and cruelty, in battle, but alienated the other leaders, who departed. Saladin, undefeated, agreed to a truce with Richard, who saw, but did not enter, the Holy City.

Fourth Crusade (1202-04) Religious fervour was already waning, and the Venetians were able to divert the Crusaders' attack against Christian Constantinople.

Fifth Crusade (1218-21) Although aimed against Egypt, this had some success, such that the Egyptians offered to hand over Jerusalem if the Crusaders would withdraw, but the leaders refused to negotiate with the infidel.

Sixth Crusade (1228-29) Ironically, this was led by the Emperor Frederick II while under ban of excommunication. He was able to negotiate the return of Jerusalem, which remained in Christian hands for fifteen years.

Seventh Crusade (1245-69) The last Crusade of note was led by Louis IX (St Louis) of France, against Egypt. After some early success, disease and the climate brought about defeat and the capture of the king. Released after payment of a huge ransom, Louis went on to Palestine for three more years until the death of his mother and the Regent compelled his return to France. He led another expedition to Tunis, where he died of fever. As his successor was negotiating a truce, Prince Edward, later Edward I of England, arrived. Disappointed, Edward went on to the Holy Land.

The last king of England to express a serious desire to go on Crusade was Henry IV, but he did not achieve his aim. KH

See also KNIGHTHOOD AND CHIVALRY, ORDERS OF
Further reading
Runciman, Sir Stephen *A History of the Crusades* West Drayton, 1965 (reprint 1985)
Billings, M. *The Cross and the Crescent* London, 1987.

Crusily, Crusilly, Crusilé, Crucily *or* **Crusuly** A field semy of cross-crosslets.

Crusily Fitchy A field semy of cross-crosslets fitched.

Cuffed *see* **Attributes**

Cuirass A breastplate and backplate of leather, bronze or steel.

Cuisse Protection for the upper leg of plates, plate or studded leather.

Cyclas A surcoat cut short at the front and long at the back.

Cypher A monogram, sometimes ensigned with a coronet of rank and used as a personal or household device. Cyphers were particularly popular during the eighteenth and nineteenth centuries when the use of armorial badges was in decline, and the new rich of the Industrial Revolution felt a need for some means of personal identity. The cyphers of this period were often ensigned with a crest (frequently bogus) and were used both as personal devices on stationery,

Cyphers on a caparison

glass, silver, etc., and in place of livery badges on servants' buttons, coach-panels, etc. The reintroduction of grants of badges by the College of Arms in 1906 was instrumental in stemming the tide to some extent, but the use of cyphers is still widespread, particularly in departments of government and state. Cyphers are not generally subject to heraldic authority, though those of the English royal family are usually recorded at the College of Arms.

Czechoslovakia, Armorial Practice Today the Czechoslovak Socialist Republic exists within the Communist bloc of eastern European nations, having been formed in 1918 from mainly Slavic ethnic groups of the ancient kingdom of Bohemia after the wars of liberation in the Balkans.

There are within the country Magyar, Ukranian, Ruthene, German-Austrian and other elements, as well as the two major groups, the Czechs and the Slovenes. In consequence its heraldic history reflects a number of influences.

Before 1621 armorial bearings were registered at the royal court of Bohemia in Prague (the capital of that country, later to become the capital of Czechoslovakia), but afterwards, when Bohemia was swept into the Austrian empire, they were recorded in Vienna. This practice continued until 1918.

The design of Bohemian arms followed central European conventions (*see* AUSTRIA, ARMORIAL PRACTICE). At the time of writing, the traditions of armory play a negligible part in Czechoslovak life, but the archives of the National Museum have much to offer the student and enthusiast.   JC-K

Cyphers

The Duke and Duchess of Windsor

Albrecht Durer

Philharmonia Orchestra

Edward VII

Norroy and Ulster King of Arms

Wilson Metcalf

George V (postage stamp watermark *c.* 1929)

D

Dame A title given to women who are admitted to orders of chivalry at the level of knights of any degree. In earlier centuries the word was used as comparable with 'lord' when the woman concerned was the head of a noble household. In the sixteenth century the title was also used when referring to the wife of a knight, squire, citizen or yeoman. The title may also be used by a professed nun.   JC-K

Dance A fess dancetty.

Dancetty *see* **Lines, Varied**

Dannebrog, Order of the A Danish Order, formed in 1671, but with traditions dating back to 1219. The badge is a Latin cross formy, white enamelled with red

edges, with gold royal crowns between the arms, and surmounted by a crown, the letter R and the initials of the monarch. On the cross are the cypher of Christian V, and the motto of the Order.   KH

Dauphin From 1349 to 1830 the title of the eldest son of the king of France. Said to derive from the proper name *Delphinus*, of the lords of Viennois, their province being called Dauphine. In 1349 the province was ceded to Philip of Valois, on the condition that the title be borne always by the eldest son of the monarch, together with the arms *Or a Dolphin Azure* (sometimes *finned and tailed Gules*). The arms of Dauphin de Viennois were first borne by the heir to the French throne, Charles, first son of King Jean II. Jean was descended of the House of Valois and his son quartered Valois (*France Ancient within a Bordure Gules*) with Dauphin.

In 1349 Charles also became Prince of Normandy and at the battle of Poitiers (1356) fought under Normandy's banner. The heirs to the French throne after 1364 bore the arms of France (modern) without the bordure, quarterly with Dauphin.   PG

David, Shield of *and* **Star of** Two interlaced triangles forming a six-pointed star.

'de', in titles The use of this element in titles is fairly modern and, according to Cokayne, 'was presumably adopted to give an air of antiquity to new creations. The practice was based on ignorance of the nomenclature of the Middle Ages, and has defeated its object, for the prefix *de* in a title is almost always a sign that the dignity, if not the man, is new.'

The subject is discussed at length in Volume VI, of *The Complete Peerage*, by G.E. Cokayne.   JC-K

Debruised An ordinary or sub-ordinary when placed upon a shield of arms so that it overlays existing charges. Debruisement is usually indicative of differencing, distinction, etc. The terms 'suppressed' and 'oppressed' may also be encountered, synonymous with debruised but virtually obsolete.

When a charge is laid over another as part of the original armorial design, the term 'surmounted' is used.

Decadence, The *see* **Heraldry of the Decadence**

Dechaussé *see* **Attributes**

Decrescent A crescent with the 'horns' facing the sinister.

Deer The stag or red deer, unless it is otherwise blazoned, e.g. buck, hart, hind, etc. Deer possess special attitudes and atttributes, its antlers are 'attires' and its horns 'tines', for example.

Defamed *see* **Attributes**

Degradation, Ceremonies of The word 'degrade' means 'to bring into dishonour or contempt', thus in this context its derivative 'degradation' means publicly to proclaim or demonstrate the dishonour of an individual. Many authors have written fancifully and at length on the subject of the 'ceremonies of degradation' visited on disgraced members of the knightly class, but the truth is that (in England, at any rate) recorded cases of the formal degradation of a knight are very few. Up to the year 1621 only three instances appear in the records of the College of Arms. In this century Sir Roger Casement was

deprived of his knighthood in 1916, and Sir Anthony Blunt in the late 1970s, although on neither occasion was there a 'ceremony' attaching to their degradation. To learn of one such event we must go back to the seventeenth century, when, in 1621, Sir Francis Michell was, on proven charges of corruption, proclaimed 'no knight but an arrant knave'. At a ceremony at Westminster Hall he had his spurs hacked from his heels, his sword belt cut and his sword broken over his head by the heralds. The last case of degradation was that of the Duke of Ormond in 1715. Beyond this example, based on records contemporary with the events discussed, there exist the 'traditional' accounts of degradation ceremonies visited upon knights who had fallen from the highest practice of the ideals of chivalry. What follows is drawn from such medieval traditional accounts. Its historical accuracy is very doubtful, but it is worth recording as a piece of heraldic lore.

It has been averred that on being found guilty of treason or some crime of equal gravity a knight, before being lead away for execution, would have his insignia removed from the chapel of his order by the heralds. The miscreant would then be roughly stripped of his armour, and his shield broken in front of him. As each piece was removed an officer of arms would declaim why the particular piece was itself a symbol of knightly virtue and therefore was not fitted to be worn by a traitor. The final act of degradation was for the disgraced knight to have his spurs and sword broken upon him, his surcoat torn away and replaced by a paper version bearing his arms reversed.

The Scottish officers of arms have supervised the burning of reversed shields (by the Public Hangman at Edinburgh Mercat Cross) of armigers found to have committed treason. *See also* ABATEMENT   SS

Delf *see* **Abatement**

Delve *see* **Billet**

Demi *see* **Attributes**

Denmark, Armorial Practice Denmark has an armorial tradition dating from the mid-twelfth century. However, it was during the early fifteenth century, and the reign of King Eric of Pomerania (whose queen, Philippa, was a grand-daughter of John of Gaunt) that armory was first subjected to regulation, though there had been an organization of kings of arms, heralds and pursuivants since the beginning of the previous century. These offices did not survive the ending of the Kalmar Union at the beginning of the sixteenth century, though the term 'herald' was retained for certain officers of the court for a further three hundred years.

Following the inception of the Absolute Monarchy in 1660 the arms of the nobility were augmented with coronets to indicate rank, and it became possible to marshal several coats into hereditary arms whereas, prior to that date, it was customary to quarter only the arms of the four grandparents. With the exception of the coronet, there has never been any distinction made between the arms of the nobility and those of other armigers.

In Denmark today, armory is respected and continues to develop. There is no official body of heralds but the Heraldic Council of the Danish State deals with civic and corporate arms, the orders of chivalry and armorial matters pertaining to them. The arms of the knights of the great Danish orders of the Elephant and Dannebrog may be seen at the chapel of the orders in Frederiksborg Castle. JC-K

Denmark, Military Insignia Since the end of World War II the Danish military authorities have worked with the state heraldic authorities to produce a variety of original and attractive unit arms and insignia. Actual shields bearing arms are mainly used by Danish naval and airforce units, bases, ships and squadrons. In the Danish Air Force the arms are ensigned by the Royal Crown and are borne within scrolls carrying unit mottoes and unit designations. Indication of RDAF status is further shown by the arms being placed within a pair of outspread wings. Royal Danish Navy units and ships superimpose their arms on an anchor palewise ensigned by the Royal Danish Crown. Naval bases and stations bear their arms on an oval shield with a chief charged with a canon barrel fesswise. Naval command districts for the Faroe Islands and Greenland each bear arms on a heater-shaped shield, the chief of which is charged with three torteaux, and in base the white ram of the Faroe Islands or the polar bear of Greenland. Many Danish army units wear collar and beret badges charged with devices taken from regional arms. In recent years army brigades and regions have been

allocated badges with rather striking armorial-type designs. The drawing illustrates the badge of Army Region IV. In recent years cloth arm badges have also been issued to army units and these usually depict the collar badge on a shield of the unit colours. All Danish Army Home Guard regions have collar badges consisting of the regional arms in metal. Danish army officers wear cap badges charged with the lesser arms of Denmark, which date from the thirteenth century. The national cockade of red and white is worn by all ranks on certain forms of headgear, whilst the Royal Lifeguard bearskin caps bear a metal badge depicting the great arms of the Kingdom of Denmark. SS

Denmark, Royal Arms of *A cross paty throughout Argent fimbriated Gules* (Dannebrog) *between 1 and 4 Or semy of Hearts Gules three Lions passant Azure crowned Or* (Denmark) *2 Or two Lions passant Azure* (Schleswig) *3 Per fess in chief Azure three Crowns Or* (Sweden) *in base per pale dexter Azure a Ram Argent* (Faroes) *sinister Azure a Polar Bear sejant Argent* (Greenland) *over all an escutcheon Or two Bars Gules* (Oldenburg).

Dented *see* **Attributes**

Deputy Earl Marshal The Earl Marshal's deputy may place a gold baton tipped with black bendwise behind his shield.

Destrier The war horse: usually of great size, strength and stamina.

Device An emblematic representation.

Devisal of Arms By Warrant of the Earl Marshal, dated 25 July 1960, the kings of arms were empowered to devise, that is to design and record, arms for towns in the United States of America. By another Warrant dated 2 October 1961, the kings of arms were further authorized to devise arms for bodies corporate in the Republic of South Africa (South Africa became an independent republic and seceded from the Commonwealth on 31 May 1961). Then by another Warrant dated 1 February 1962 the permission to devise arms in the United States was extended to include corporate bodies other than towns. Before a devisal is made in the United States, the consent and approval of the Governor of the State in which the devisal is to be made is always obtained.

Such devisals are made on the same terms as grants of arms. Like all other new coats they must be unique, and after they have been devised they are recorded and thereafter are never again devised nor granted.

The document by which arms are devised is similar in appearance to an ordinary grant, but the wording is, of course, quite different. The arms of the sovereign,

Devisal of Arms to the Cathedral Church of the Advent, Birmingham, Alabama, USA (1985). The arms are gold and purple, the liturgical colour for the Advent season, and incorporate further symbols of Advent in the Tau Cross, candles and motto, which is from the Lord's Prayer — 'Thy Kingdom Come'. At the head of the patent are the arms of office of the kings of arms with their personal crests and coronets of office. This is the first time that the arms of the kings of arms have been so depicted; normally just the shields and coronets are shown. The devisal also includes a badge which is exemplified on a standard.

the Earl Marshal and the College of Arms do not appear at the head of the patent, but they may be replaced by either the arms or just the crowns of the kings of arms. The wording simply states that the kings of arms, having been requested by a certain body corporate in a certain State to devise its arms, and the Governor of the said State having signified his approval, they are pleased to devise certain arms, which are then blazoned in the usual way. The arms are painted in the margin and the document is signed and sealed by all three kings of arms.   JB-L

Dexter The left-hand side of the shield when viewed from the front. In armory, the dexter is considered to be superior to the sinister, or right-hand side.
See also SHIELD, POINTS OF THE

Dextrochère

Dextrochère An armorial charge, similar in appearance to the maunch, but with a human hand extended therefrom, often clasping a further device. Literally, a 'beloved's right'. In French armory, the dextrochère is normally assumed to be ermine unless otherwise blazoned, e.g. *vested Gules*.

Diaper A method of decorating plain surfaces on a shield of arms by covering them with patterns, usually in shades of the same colour. When applied in too heavy a fashion diaper may have the appearance of a charged or varied field, and caution should be exercised in interpretation. In European armory, the term diaper may also imply a field similar in type to papelloné or plumeté, though these are strictly types of fur whereas diaper is not. The arms of Alwand, for example, include a field *Argent diapered Or*. The term may also be applied to the artistic embellishment of plain surfaces *surrounding* armorial bearings, e.g. on seals, tiles, glass, etc. In such instances armorial devices may be repeated to form the pattern, or allusive figures such as the ferns (fougère) in the seal of William of Filgeriis (1200).

Difference, for In blazon, a term used to imply that an addition or amendment has been made to indicate cadency (i.e. blood relationship of male members of a family).

Difference, Mark of A charge added to a coat of arms to indicate cadency. Charges borne to indicate an

Cornwall dimidiating De Clare

absence of blood relationship are termed marks of distinction.

Dimidiation An old method of impalement in which the dexter half of one coat was joined to the sinister half of the other, often with quite extraordinary artistic results! Examples of this early practice are still to be seen in the arms of the Cinque Ports. Although the method of dimidiation enjoyed but 'a short and merry life' (Brooke-Little), vestiges of the system may still be found in the treatment of the bordure, orle, tressure and charges in orle, all of which are dimidiated at the palar line in impaled arms.
See also MARSHALLING

Diminutive A narrow version of an ordinary. Diminutives are rarely borne singly and are not usually of sufficient width to bear charges. Whilst the need to differentiate between ordinaries and their

Diaper used as decoration on a pile argent in the arms of John Allen.

127

diminutives remains, the practice of bestowing diminutives on charges other than geometrical ones seems absurd (e.g. lioncels for small lions) and is now seldom used by the kings of arms.
See also CONVENTION

Dingwall Pursuivant of Arms A current Scottish pursuivant of arms, first mentioned in 1460. The burgh of Dingwall lies north of Inverness and was the northern capital of the Lord of the Isles.

The badge of office is *A Sun in Splendour Or charged of a Plate thereon a Mullet Or enfiling in chief a Coronet of four Fleurs-de-lis and four Crosses paty proper.*   CJB

Diptych (i) A folding pair of pictures or tablets containing genealogical and armorial information. (ii) a double-folding writing tablet.
See also TRIPTYCH

Dirk The dagger of the Scottish Highlander and the short-sword of a midshipman.

Disarmed *see* **Attributes**

Dismembered *see* **Attributes**

Displayed *see* **Attitude**

Disposition The arrangement of armorial charges on a field. For the conventions relating to the disposition of charges *see* BLAZON.

Distilling *see* **Attitude**

Distinction, for In blazon, a term used to imply that an addition or amendment has been made to indicate an absence of blood relationship (e.g. adoption, bastardy, or in arms granted by royal licence).

Distinction, Marks of A charge added to a coat of arms to indicate bastardy, adoption or arms granted by virtue of royal licence. Similar charges, borne to indicate cadency (i.e. blood relationship) are called marks of difference.
See also ADOPTED CHILDREN

Distinguished Service Order (Abbr. DSO) Founded in 1886 by Queen Victoria as an order of military merit to recognize the special services of officers in the armed forces.   JC-K

Distinguishing Flag A flag used to denote the presence of one holding office, command, rank or authority.

Distress, Flag of A nautical flag turned upside-down as an indication that a ship is in distress.

Division One segment of a varied field. Frequently used in armory as a synonym for PARTITION.

Divorce A divorced woman bears her paternal arms on a lozenge charged with a mascle which is removed in the event of her remarrying. *See also* MARSHALLING *and* WOMEN BEARING ARMS

Doggett's Coat and Badge *see* **Bargemaster**

Doloire A trowel-shaped battle pole-axe, spatulated at the base and pointed at the tip.

Dolphin The most common heraldic aquatic creature, always depicted embowed and with pronounced beak, fins and tongue. It is assumed to be naiant unless otherwise blazoned.

Domestic Buildings The extraordinary range of domestic buildings in which heraldry has been used for the purposes of decoration and identification extends from the medieval fortress and the ostentatious palace of the eighteenth century to the moated manor house and fashionable urban crescent. Some may be of a single architectural style, others incorporate features of many periods. Many have developed as the result of changing political circumstances.

Heraldry prior to the sixteenth century was but one important element of daily life. Armorial devices displayed on flags and incorporated into the fabric and furnishings of a lord's residence were as familiar in the community as were the badges and liveries of his retainers. The preoccupation of the medieval mind with religion is reflected in the abundance of churches of this period, and in the extraordinary expenditure lavished on them by the nobility in order to secure salvation.

However, the Dissolution of the Monasteries during the sixteenth century was to have a significant effect on the application of heraldry. Firstly, the sale of monastic buildings and lands encouraged a new class of property-owning gentlemen, eager to emulate the nobility and, often, to join its ranks. Such men inevitably became armigerous. Secondly, the

Pargeting on a house at Clare, Suffolk, includes the arms of the family of Clare: *Or three Chevronels Gules.*

Reformation and the desecration of church interiors, combined with legislation which encouraged ecclesiastical austerity, resulted in the diversion of expenditure from the church to the home. This is reflected in the magnificent armorial window glass, fabrics, furnishings and architectural features of the period. Armorial decoration was generally consistent with the artistic and architectural fashions of a particular period, and was at its height during the sixteenth and early seventeenth centuries, and again during the Gothic Revival.

On many estates armorial devices were incorporated into the stonework of tied cottages, village SCHOOLS, ALMSHOUSES and other buildings, and may be found today in many village INN SIGNS. The cottages of the Digby Estate in Dorset may still be distinguished by their uniform paintwork and enamelled door plates, bearing the family crest of an ostrich together with an estate number.

See also CEILINGS; ENTRANCE PORCHES; FIREPLACES; GLASS; LODGE GATES; METALWORK; SCREENS; STAIRCASES; TEXTILES

Dormant *see* **Attitude**

Doubled Lined with. Usually applied to the inner lining of mantling, mantles and chapeaux, the terms 'lined' and 'turned' being synonymous.

Double-headed *see* **Attributes**

Double Tressure *see* **Orle**

Dove, Order of the *or* **Order of the Holy Ghost** A Castilian order of the late 1300s; the badge a silver dove surrounded by gold rays.　　　　KH

Dovetailed *see* **Lines, Varied**

Dragon *see* **Wyvern and Dragon**

Dragon, Order of the A Hungarian order formed *c.* 1400. The badge was a golden dragon, stained with blood and biting its own tail, surmounted by a red flaming cross.　　　　KH

Drois d'Armes, Les *see* **Treatises**

Ducal Coronet (i) Originally any coronet used in lieu of a wreath in a crest, the modern ducal coronet is depicted as having four strawberry leaves (three visible) set on a rim, the jewels of which are shown but not coloured. Early coronets were often more ornate, with no prescribed form and of any tincture. Today, the ducal coronet is assumed to be gold unless otherwise blazoned. The ducal coronet's designation is misleading, for it is neither the coronet of a duke nor does it resemble one. An alternative term, CREST CORONET, is equally ambiguous, for this term may be applied to a variety of coronets and circlets which may be used in conjunction with the crest. The inclusion of such a coronet in a crest does not imply rank, neither is it an indication of illustrious ancestry, as some would have us believe. The ducal coronet should be considered as integral to the crest even when it replaces the wreath, indeed the majority of medieval crest coronets were borne without wreaths and the variety of colours employed clearly indicates that they were not associated with rank, but with the crest. It is incorrect to depict a cap within a ducal or other crest coronet, as one would with a coronet of rank or of office. Few ducal coronets have been granted in the recent past.

(ii) A similar coronet as an armorial charge in a shield of arms.

(iii) When a creature is blazoned crowned or gorged with a coronet, the ducal coronet is depicted unless otherwise stated. It is also assumed that the coronet is gold unless a different colour is specified. The terms 'ducally crowned' and 'ducally gorged' are sometimes encountered and have the same application.

Ducally Crowned *or* **Gorged** *see* **Ducal Coronet**

Duchess The wife of a duke, or a lady who holds a dukedom in her own right.

The robe of a duchess is of crimson velvet, the cape being trimmed with pure miniver and decorated with four rows of ermine, the edging 5 inches (13 cm) broad, the train 2 yards (metres) on the ground. The cap of the coronet is of crimson velvet, turned up with ermine, and with a gold tassel on the top. The coronet is composed, on the circle, of eight strawberry leaves, all of equal height above the rim.

The duchess in her own right bears her arms on a lozenge, surmounted by the coronet of her degree and flanked by supporters.   JC-K

Duke The most senior rank in the peerage of Britain. The word 'duke' is derived from the Latin *dux*, meaning 'leader'. The rank was introduced in England in 1337, when Edward the Black Prince was made Duke of Cornwall, although the style had been known before that date, the Conqueror being referred to, for example, as *Ducis Normannorum et Regis Anglorum*.

The first English non-royal dukedom was that granted to Henry, Earl of Lancaster, Derby, Lincoln and Leicester, who was created Duke of Lancaster in 1351. In Scotland the title of duke was bestowed in 1398 by Robert III on his eldest son, David, who became Duke of Rothesay, and on his brother, who became Duke of Albany.

The robes of a duke date from the earliest times of that rank, but their date of introduction is not known with certainty. The colour seems at first to have been scarlet or crimson, varying to purple. They consisted of a long gown, or surcoat, with a girdle, a mantle lined with ermine, a hood and tippet adorned with four rows of ermine. Today, a duke's robes are of two kinds, coronation and estate. The coronation robe is of crimson velvet, edged with miniver, the cape being furred with miniver, and embellished with four bars of ermine. The robe is worn over full court dress, uniform or regimentals. The coronet of a duke is of silver gilt, the cap being of crimson velvet turned up with ermine, and with a gold tassel on the top. No jewels or precious stones are set or used on the coronet, which is enhanced with, on the circle, eight gilt strawberry leaves. The parliamentary robe of estate of a duke is of fine scarlet cloth lined with taffeta. It is trimmed with four guards (or bands) of ermine at equal distances, with gold lace above, and is tied up at the left shoulder by a white ribbon.

The duke (in common with other peers) has certain armorial privileges: he employs a silver helm with gold bars facing the dexter, his coronet of rank ensigns his arms, and he normally has supporters. The wife of a duke is known as a duchess.   JC-K

E

Eagle The eagle has dominion over all the birds and its majestic soaring has given it an exalted place in many civilizations. Both the Greeks and the Romans associated it with their gods, and in the Christian religion it has become the emblem of St John. As the standard of the Roman legions it led the way into all parts of the Empire. When in the year 800 AD Charlemagne was crowned Emperor of the Holy Roman Empire, the eagle was the obvious symbol to show on his shield, and later it was established as the heraldic device of the Holy Roman emperors, but became double-headed. The fierceness of the eagle, with its sharp beak and long outstretched talons, made it a popular heraldic emblem, and was much in use, particularly in Germany and Austria.

'When the eagle grows old and his wings become heavy and his eyes become darkened with a mist, then he goes in search of a fountain, and, over against it, he flies up to the height of heaven, even into the circle of the sun, and there he singes his wings and at the same time evaporates the fog of his eyes in a ray of the sun. Then at length taking a header down into the fountain, he dips himself three times in it, and instantly he is renewed with a great vigour of plumage and splendour of vision' (from the twelfth-century *The Book of Beasts*, trans. T.H. White, London 1954). Erasmus, the Dutch renaissance scholar, does not share this romantic view of the eagle: 'Of all the birds the eagle alone has seemed to wise men the type of royalty, a bird neither beautiful nor musical nor good for food, but murderous, greedy, hateful to all, the curse of all, and with its great powers of doing harm only surpassed by its desire to do it.'   MY

Eaglet A small eagle. This term was used when more than one eagle was depicted in a shield of arms. Like the similarly quaint lioncel, the term is no longer used.

Earl The third rank in the British peerage (corresponding with the Latin *comes*, and the French *comte*). The title 'earl' (which is quite different from the Saxon *ealdorman*) came originally from Scandinavia, and appeared in England in the time of Canute as an English form of *jarl*. It is thus the oldest title and rank of English nobles, and was the highest until 1337, when the Black Prince was made a duke. The earliest known charter creating an hereditary earl is that by which King Stephen bestowed the earldom of Essex on Geoffrey de Mandeville *c.* 1140.

The robes of an earl are similar to those of a DUKE, with the exceptions that his coronation robe has three rows of ermine, and his parliamentary robe of estate has three guards of ermine. The coronet of an earl has, on the circle, eight silver balls raised on points, with gold strawberry leaves between the points. The armorial privileges of an earl are as those of a duke. The wife of an earl is known as a countess.   JC-K

Earl Marischal of Scotland The insignia of office were two batons gules semy of thistles and tipped with a gold Imperial Crown saltirewise behind the arms. The office is no longer extant.

Earl Marshal and Hereditary Marshal of England One of the great Officers of State responsible for the organization of state ceremonies (though not 'royal' occasions, e.g. weddings), hereditary judge in the Court of Chivalry and ultimately responsible to the sovereign for all matters relating to heraldry, honour, precedence, etc. The Earl Marshal has jurisdiction over the officers of arms, but is not a member of the body corporate of the College of Arms.

Before 1386 the office was known simply as Marshal, and was originally the title of an officer whose duties included supervision of the royal stables. In 1385 the office, which by that time had assumed considerably greater significance, was granted to Thomas Mowbray, Earl of Nottingham, who a year later was given the title of Earl Marshal.

In the Middle Ages the Marshal was, with the Lord High Constable, the first in military rank beneath the sovereign, and it was his responsibility to marshal the various contingents of troops and retainers in battle, a task which would require familiarity with the devices borne on the flags and uniforms of an assembled host. No doubt he was assisted by attendant heralds whose business it was to be conversant with such matters. The Marshal was also responsible for the organization of state ceremonies, and, with the Constable, presided over the Court of Chivalry 'either at Westminster in the Painted Chamber ... or in his own house, where in the great hall he hath a large table or stage, four square, built with rails thereabout, and benches therein, and an half pace raised above the same; there the Earl sitteth in the midst thereof ...'

The office was anciently granted by the sovereign at pleasure, sometimes for life, sometimes *durante bene*

placito, and (more than once) as an hereditary office, though it was not until 1672 that Charles II finally annexed it to the Dukedom of Norfolk, with which it had long been associated through both the Mowbray and (from 1483) Howard families.

It is interesting to note that from 1673 to 1824, several earls marshal were, by virtue of being Roman Catholics, forced to appoint Protestant deputies to supervize the officers of arms. From the latter date, acts of parliament rendered this and other limitations obsolete.

The Earl Marshal appends the letters EM to his signature, and displays behind his shield two gold batons saltirewise, the ends enamelled black with the royal arms at the top, and those of the Earl Marshal at the lower end. These batons represent the *virga* or marshal's rod, a symbol of office dating from the Norman period.

Earl Marshal's Lieutenant, Assessor and Surrogate in his High Court of Chivalry or Court Military The Earl Marshal's warrant of appointment to the above office lays down in considerable detail what the duties are. They can be summarized as follows: to issue citations and attachments, to receive bonds and obligations, to admit libels and articles, to control witnesses and to publish their evidence and depositions, to assign times for the hearing of sentences, to give definitive sentences in writing and to order the execution thereof, to tax all costs, to make interlocutory decrees having the force of definitive sentences, to continue and prorogue the Court to convenient days and places, to summon all parties concerned and generally on the Earl Marshal's behalf to do all things needful for the expedition of the business of the Court, as well by Law as by Custom, in the way that any previous Lieutenant, Assessor or Surrogate did or might or ought to have done.   SA

Eastern Crown *see* **Crest Coronet**

Ecclesiastical Hat A domed hat with a wide brim from which depend cords and tassels, the cords being affixed by visible knots on the upper surface of the brim. (The degree of floppiness of the brim seems to increase from high to low church, though this is most assuredly an illusion!) Such hats ensign the arms of clergy in the Roman Catholic Church, the Church of England (of non-episcopal degree) and the Church of

Scotland; the colour of the hat, cord and tassels signifying degree, as does the number of tassels. Clergymen in the Church of England may choose either to use helm, crest and motto with their shield, or to ensign their arms with an appropriate ecclesiastical hat, the design of which was regularized by Earl Marshal's Warrant in 1967.

See also CHURCH OF ENGLAND, CLERGY OF; CHURCH OF SCOTLAND; ROMAN CATHOLIC CHURCH, CLERGY OF

Edged *see* **Attributes**

Edinburgh Castle, Governor of First appointment made in 1107 and thereafter there was a series of seventy-five governors until 1860. The office was re-established in 1936 and held by the General Officer commanding the forces in Scotland. From 1936 to 1986 there have been nineteen holders of the office.   CJB

Edinburgh, Duke of A United Kingdom peerage title granted to HRH Prince Philip, consort of the sovereign, in 1947. The title was first created for the second son of Queen Victoria, Prince Alfred Ernest Albert, on 24 May 1866.   CJB

Effigy Effigies of the deceased have appeared on church MONUMENTS since the twelfth century. Early examples were of bishops, abbots and other ecclesiastics. They were carved in low relief and although the figure was horizontal, the deceased was depicted as if standing. During the thirteenth century effigies were portrayed in a recumbent position, and lay figures were represented. Among the earliest laymen were William Longespee, Earl of Salisbury (d. 1226) at Salisbury Cathedral, and King John (d. 1216) at Worcester Cathedral (monument made *c.* 1230). The effigy was now a true three-dimensional representation. However, two-dimensional figures continued in the form of INCISED SLABS and monumental BRASSES.

Through the thirteenth century the majority of monuments were carved in stone, but wood was also used. Gilt bronze effigies were fashioned for members of the English royal family, the first being for Henry III (d. 1272) at Westminster Abbey, and very wealthy barons, e.g. Richard Beauchamp at St Mary's Warwick.

Medieval effigies of knights provide invaluable evidence of the development of armour and dress. It was the custom to wear a garment over the armour, and it was on this, whether surcoat, cyclas or jupon, that the arms were carved or painted. Until the middle of the fourteenth century the effigy of a knight usually bore a shield. After this date the shield was separated from the effigy and displayed only on the tomb-chest or canopy. The carving of arms on the shield and tunic

may still be visible, depending upon the depth of carving and the effects of erosion and defacement. Many effigies were painted, and a good example is that of Sir John Beauchamp at Worcester Cathedral *Gules a Fess between six Martlets Or*, the differenced arms for this branch of the family. However, surviving contemporary medieval paintwork is regrettably limited to a few fragments.

Whilst in general the tunic was used to give a single over all display of the arms, two other practices are found which relate to the late thirteenth and early fourteenth centuries. The surcoat on the effigy of William Valence (d. 1296) in Westminster Abbey was decorated with small enamelled shields, although only two now survive. The effigy of Matilda de Clifford (d. 1281) in Worcester Cathedral was similarly treated. The use of a number of small shields as decoration to clothing can also be found in ecclesiastical vestments, e.g. those of an unknown mass priest at Beverley Minster, Yorkshire. A further device was to depict an effigy covered by a shroud with a shield resting upon it, e.g. Bayous at Careby, Lincolnshire. The use of heraldically decorated effigies continued into the fifteenth century and included the heraldic treatment of wives' clothing and the display of quarterings. The jupon was replaced by the tabard, which was usually emblazoned with the arms on both sleeves as well as the body. However, during this period, figures were first represented in their plate armour, which was neither decorated nor concealed by an armorial tunic, and this became normal practice from the late sixteenth century.

The shield and garments of an effigy were not the only vehicles for heraldic decoration. Recumbent effigies, both male and female, frequently have their heads resting on cushions which may be supported by angels or other figures. These cushions were decorated with painting, engraving or diaper, and armorial devices were often used for this purpose. The cushion beneath the head of Eleanor of Castile, Queen of Edward I, is a patchwork of lions and castles.

From the fourteenth century the knight's head normally rested on the helm, which was frequently surmounted by the crest wreath and mantling. Also, most effigies had their feet resting on beasts. The use

---

Alabaster effigies of Nicholas Fitzherbert (d. 1473) and, in the foreground, his son Ralph (d. 1483) with his wife Elizabeth. The Fitzherbert family can trace uninterrupted male descent from the Norman Conquest and have held lands at Norbury, Northamptonshire, from the reign of Henry I (1125). Ralph Fitzherbert wears a collar of Yorkist suns and roses with a pendant of Richard III's white boar. This is believed to be the only collar of its type extant in England.

of a lion for a man and a dog for a woman is probably symbolic rather than heraldic, although a large number of families used the lion as an armorial device. The use of other animals is almost certainly of significance. For example, at Puddletown, Dorset, effigies of the Martin family of Athelhampton rest their feet on an ape, which was the family crest.

The sword belt (baldric), scabbard and pommel were usually decorated with flowers, quatre-foils, etc., but occasionally an armorial charge or badge would be used. Some effigies also included the insignia of chivalric orders or of office. The most common is the collar. In the first half of the fifteenth century the SS collar of the House of Lancaster appears on many figures, and again during the early Tudor period, often with the portcullis badge pendant. The collar of suns and roses for the House of York is found in the latter half of the fifteenth century.

Regrettably few monuments are complete today, but by reference to other monuments and to the notes of county antiquarians one may visualize the effigy in its former glory. It should be remembered that, like brasses, effigies were generally stylized representations of the deceased, actual portraits being rare prior to the Restoration period.   JET
See also HEARSE

Elector A prince of Germany, formerly entitled to take part in the election of the Holy Roman Emperor. In the United States the word is used to describe a person chosen by the individual states to elect the President and Vice President. In Great Britain and Ireland the term describes one who has the parliamentary vote.   JC-K

Electoral Cap *or* **Electoral Bonnet** A tall crimson cap on a circlet turned up ermine. Borne by all the Electoral Princes of Germany. In the case of Hanover it was converted to a crown when the Electorate became a Kingdom.

Elephant, Order of the A Danish order formed in 1462. Its badge is a gold and white elephant, with a black mahout, on its side a Greek cross, and on its back a red tower.   KH

Elevated *see* **Attitudes**

Embattled *see* **Lines, Varied**

Embattled Grady *see* **Lines, Varied**

Emblazon To depict armorial bearings in colour.

Emblem A pictorial representation associated with a specific person, organization or cause.

Embowed *see* **Attitude**

Embrued *see* **Attitude**

Key to armorial flags RIGHT

1 Standard of King Richard II (d. 1400) charged with his badges, a white hart and sun-in-splendour on liveries of white and green.
2 Pennoncelle of the Knights Templar.
3 Banner of the arms of Frankenstein.
4 Weather-vane of the arms of Scrope.
5 Banneret of the arms of Veberlinger
6 Ensign banner of Edward Stafford, Duke of Buckingham (d. 1521), depicting his achievement of arms on a field of his livery colours, gules and sable.
7 Gonfannon of the Vatican, charged with the arms and with 'tails' of the Papal livery colours, or and argent.
8 Livery pennon ('Pavon' type) of John Mowbray, Duke of Norfolk (d. 1476): his white lion badge on liveries of 'blewe and tawny, bothe darke colors'.
9 Livery pennoncelle of Henry Percy, Earl of North-umberland (d. 1527): his badge of a silver crescent on liveries of russet, yellow and tawny.
10 Guidon of King Richard III (d. 1485): his silver boar on the Yorkist liveries of blue and murrey.
11 Personal Pennon of von Singenburg.
12 Trumpet banner of the arms of Rogalla von Bieberstein.
13 Livery banner of Thomas Grey, Marquess of Dorset (d. 1501): his badge of a unicorn ermine on liveries of white and pink.
14 National ensign of St George of England.

Nautical flags of Lord William de Hastings (d. 1483)
15 Streamer of his liveries, purpure and azure, charged with his badge, *A Bull's Head erased Sable ducally gorged and armed Or.*
16 Pennant with the Hastings arms, *Argent a Maunch Sable*, in the hoist and the liveries in the fly.
17 Sail charged with the Hastings arms.
18 Livery pennant of the badge on the livery colours.

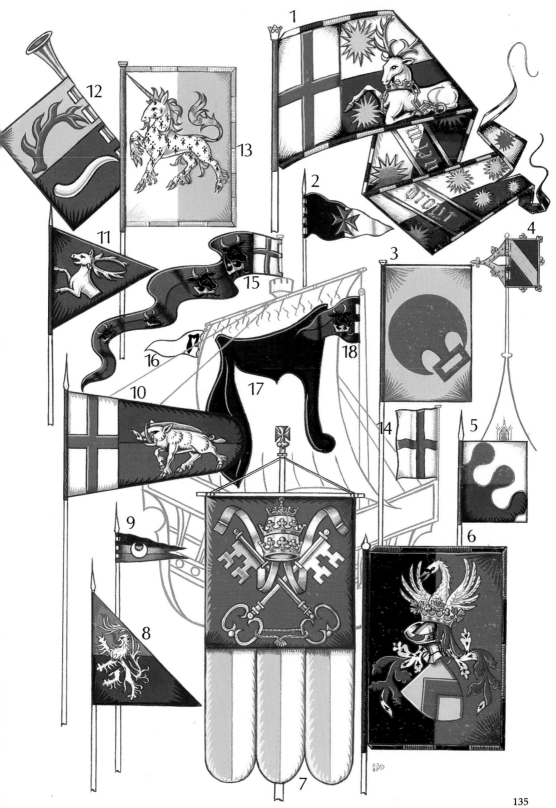

Emperor The sovereign of an empire, and considered to be superior to a king. The female form of the title is Empress. JC-K

Empire A large and composite state, sometimes unitary, sometimes a federation of free states, ruled over by an emperor. Examples have been the Roman, Russian, German (1870-1918), Austro-Hungarian and British. Some historians include the Assyrian, Persian and Macedonian, but the whole concept of empire (from the Latin *imperium*) was Roman in origin. The so-called Central African Empire of the late twentieth century was a short-lived travesty. JC-K

Enamelling Armorial achievements executed in enamel have been known since at least the thirteenth century — as adornments on horse-trappings, goblets, ciboria, jewel boxes, fibulae, chalices, lamps and many other metal items. Today, in addition, numerous examples may be found in cathedrals, public buildings, university colleges and so on, often enriching memorials in bronze, copper or silver, and depicting shields of towns and badges of regiments as well as arms of individuals.

Enamel is a vitreous glaze, or combination of glazes, fused on a metallic surface. The art itself is of great antiquity and probably originated in western Asia. The base substance of enamel is a clear, colourless, vitreous compound called flux, containing silica, red lead and potash. This material is coloured by the addition of metallic oxides while in a liquid state, so that the flux is stained throughout its entirety. The material is fired at varying temperatures into solid lumps, the higher the temperature the harder the enamel.

OPPOSITE, TOP LEFT A charming fragment of armorial glass at Athelhampton, Dorset. The vigorous treatment of the lion and the use of brown enamel for the detail of the figure suggest that it may be of late medieval origin. TOP RIGHT Sixteenth-century glass at Aldermaston Church, Berkshire, showing the arms of De La Mare *Gules two Lions passant Argent*, on red flashed glass with the lions abraided. The sable field of the impaled arms (attributed to Brocas quartering Roches) was obtained by painting black varnish on clear glass. The lions and division lines were then scraped away and the gold tincture effected by the application of silver oxide and re-firing. Clear glass may be seen in those areas where the varnish is damaged. BOTTOM LEFT Nineteenth-century glass in the style of the sixteenth century (though the shield itself may be original and much restored) at Aldermaston Court, Berkshire. The arms are those of Henry VIII impaling the arms of Queen Catherine (Howard). BOTTOM RIGHT Twentieth-century cartoon by Francis Spear ARCA, President of the Society of Master Glass Painters.

The brilliance of enamel depends on the materials — and their proportions — added to the flux, and the colour of enamels is affected by the constituents of the flux as well as by the added oxides. Turquoise blue, for example, is obtained from the black oxide of copper by using a large proportion of sodium carbonate in the flux, and a yellow-green is achieved from the same oxide by increasing the amount of red lead.

The process of enamelling begins by pulverizing the lumps of prepared enamel to fine particle size, the powders obtained being washed in distilled water to remove floury contaminants. The pulverized enamel is then spread in the desired pattern over its intended metal base — which has been carefully cleaned with acid and thoroughly dried. The piece is then gently warmed before being introduced into a furnace, which is then raised to the necessary temperature for vitrification. When the enamel shines all over — a process which takes but a few minutes — the item is removed from the furnace and allowed to cool.

There are many forms of enamelling, each using different artistic techniques and design elements in combination, such as raised metal ridges between sections of the design; shallow reliefs below the enamel layers; various processes using wire to enhance patterns; overlaying with transparent enamel glaze, and so on. All have been used in the depiction of armorial bearings. JC-K

Further reading
Siggert, J.P. *Enamelling* London, 1968.

Enarmes Straps for arm and hand on the back of a shield.

Encircled *see* **Attitude**

Endorsed *or* **Addorsed** (i) Back to back. *See* ATTITUDE.
(ii) A pale cotised is said to be endorsed.

Enfield The strange but elegant enfield is composed of parts of a number of natural animals. Its head and ears are those of a fox, but its chest is that of a greyhound. It has the talons of an eagle in the place of forefeet, whilst its hindquarters, back legs and tail derive from the wolf. It appears occasionally in modern heraldry, and is an obvious choice of the London Borough of Enfield, both as a charge on the shield and as a supporter. MY

Enfile An armorial term meaning to pass through. The plumes in the famous feathers badge of the heir apparent to the English throne pass through a coronet and therefore enfile it. The coronet is, therefore, enfiled by the feathers. Until recently the term was used to mean quite the reverse, and care should be

A crozier
enfiling a tower

exercised whenever it is met with in blazon or in heraldic reference books.

Enflamed *see* **Attributes**

England The term may be applied to any armorial field, ordinary or sub-ordinary which is gules and charged with gold lions passant guardant.
See also FRANCE

England, Royal Heraldry *see* **United Kingdom, Royal Heraldry**

Engrailed *see* **Lines, Varied**

Engrossing The writing out in formal script of a legal document, such as letters patent.

Enhanced An armorial charge or line of partition when raised above its normal position is said to be enhanced.

Enraged *see* **Attributes**

Ensign (i) In heraldry any armorial cognizance.
(ii) In armory a charge may be ensigned with an object, such as a crown or coronet, placed immediately above it.
(iii) A type of livery banner. A large square ensign or cornet was carried by the heavy cavalry in the Elizabethan period (*see* FLAG).
(iv) A term (pronounced ens'n) specifically to describe national and government flags other than armorial banners.

Ensign Banner A square or rectangular flag, on which is displayed the full achievement of arms. This practice is contrary to the spirit of armory, making this the least functional of all flags. The use of ensign banners should be avoided at all costs!
See also FLAG

Ensigned *see* **Ensign (ii)**

En Soleil Descriptive of an armorial charge environed by rays of the sun.

Entitlement to Arms To be entitled to arms, a person must establish his or her direct, legitimate, male line

descent from someone to whom arms have been granted or allowed by the kings of arms. If such a right to arms by descent is to be officially recognized, the pedigree proving it must be submitted to the Chapter of the College of Arms, through an officer of arms. Chapter will appoint two officers to examine the pedigree against evidences and then, if they report favourably, Chapter will order the pedigree to be recorded, thus establishing the unquestioned right of all members of the family included in that pedigree, to the arms, which may be evidenced by a certificate or certified painting of the arms.   JB-L

Entoured *see* **Attitude**

Entrance Porches The fabric of the main entrance to a country house often incorporates the arms of its builder. The original principal entrance of one period may have become a subsidiary one after subsequent additions and alterations. The arms are usually carved in stone and their position will depend on the scale of the property. At Haddon Hall, Derbyshire, they occupy a central position above the upper storey and against the skyline, but in most cases they will be found inserted in the stonework above the main door or surmounting a porch way. In classical buildings arms often decorate the pediment, and if the entrance is approached by stairs the balustrades may well support beasts with or without shields.   JET

Environed Surrounded or encircled by.

Envoy An official sent by one sovereign (or head of state) to another to transact high-level diplomatic business.   JC-K

Equipped *see* **Attributes**

Eradicated *see* **Attributes**

Erased *see* **Attributes**

Erased Close *see* **Attributes**

Erect *see* **Attitude**

Ermine, Ermines *and* **Erminois** *see* **Furs**

Escallop A scallop shell, usually depicted with the 'point' upwards.
Further reading
Cox, I. (Ed.) *The Scallop* London, 1957.

Escarbuncle *or* **Carbuncle** An armorial charge comprising eight ornamental spokes, each terminating in a fleur-de-lis, and radiating from a central boss. This charge almost certainly originated in the ornamentation of the central boss and studs of the early shield. An escarbuncle of more than eight projections is so qualified when blazoned.

Escartellé *see* Lines, Varied

Escheator In medieval law, when a tenant died in possession of his estate but without an heir, his land lapsed to his lord, who might even be the king if the vassal were eminent enough. Such a lapse was called an 'escheat'. An escheator was a properly appointed official who determined the course of action to be taken in the circumstances that pertained, and who certified them to the Exchequer.   JC-K

Escutcheon, Scutcheon *or* **Scotcheon** A shield. In armory, a single escutcheon borne as a charge is usually termed an inescutcheon.

Escutcheon of Pretence A small shield charged with the arms of an heraldic heiress and placed in the centre of her husband's arms where it is said to be in pretence. Correctly an inescutcheon of pretence, this method of marshalling can have alarming artistic consequences.
See also MARSHALLING; WOMEN BEARING ARMS

Esquire (i) In armory a single gyron is sometimes blazoned esquire.
(ii) In the Middle Ages, an attendant (*escutifer*, literally 'shield bearer') to a noble or knight. An esquire's traditional service required him to maintain his master's shield and armour, though his duties and responsibilities were considerably greater than this and were, in part, intended to train him in the martial and courtly arts and chivalric code. Many esquires were themselves of noble birth, and in practice pages tended to perform the more menial duties.

By the sixteenth century 'Esquire' had become a title appropriate to officers of the Crown and was considered to be superior to that of Gentleman, though only by association with a royal office which provided added distinction. In his *Order of Precedence* (1851) Sir Charles Young, Garter King of Arms, stated: 'It is extremely difficult to define accurately or satisfactorily the persons included by, or entitled to, this designation. Lord Coke, in his exposition of the Statute I Henry V, cap. 5, of *Additions*, said "The sons of all the Peers and Lords of Parliament in the life of their Fathers are in law Esquires, and so to be named". By this statute the Eldest Son of a Knight is an Esquire (2 Inst. 667).'

In modern usage, Camden's four classifications remain appropriate:

1. The Eldest Sons of Knights and their Eldest Sons in perpetual succession.

2. The Eldest Sons of Younger Sons of Peers, and their Elder Sons in like perpetual succession.
3. Esquires created by the King's (Sovereign's) letters patent, or other investiture, and their Eldest Sons.
4. Esquires by virtue of their offices; as Justices of the Peace and others who bear any office of trust under the Crown.
Interestingly, heralds are esquires by patent, pursuivants are not. In correspondence, it is for the writer to determine whether one should be addressed as Esquire or Mister. The former style, abbreviated to Esq., is now customary in Great Britain and Ireland and is used in social correspondence in the United States, particularly in the eastern states, though never in business circles. In the Department of State, the term is used in full for Foreign Service Officers serving abroad. Although considered to be old-fashioned, the form Esqre. is often adopted on stationery to indicate the writer's entitlement to the designation.

In armory, an esquire's helmet is steel and has a closed visor.

The rural 'Squire' is generally a lord of the manor or land-owner, and the term is entirely colloquial.
Further reading
Montague-Smith, P. *Debrett's Correct Form* London (revised 1976). For precedence and correct forms of address, etc.
Wagner, A. *English Genealogy* London, 1960. For the history of esquires and gentlemen.

Estoil A star of six wavy rays. Estoily is semy of such stars.

Ethnic Armory Among the tribal peoples of the world, symbolism remains an integral part of their art and religion. Certain peoples carried shields into battle, often decorated with designs of a ritualistic or personal nature. Although none can be construed as a true form of armory by European standards, many conform to certain conventions which facilitate recognition in battle. Many such shields are polychrome, the colours used being those at hand and having no significance apart from enhancing the appearance of the shield.

The warriors of the vast South African plains of the eighteenth century comprised men from different tribes and clans. The legendary early nineteenth-century leader Shaka was mainly responsible for moulding those constantly warring factions into a homogenous Zulu nation. The shield of the Zulu warrior was made from cowhide which had been soaked and stretched over a wooden frame, giving extra strength. The shield was carried over the left arm and measured about three feet (1 metre) across, covering almost the whole body of the bearer. Each regiment was designated a colour or combination of colours for easy recognition during battle and to act as a rallying feature when regrouping for further combat. The basic Zulu colours were black, white, red, red on white, and black on white. Shaka carried a completely white shield with a solitary black spot.

The three main cultures of pre-Colombian South America were the Incas of Peru, the Aztecs of Mexico and the Mayas of the Yucatan. In Peru the only army of paid soldiers was the royal Inca bodyguard, though every able-bodied man was trained and taught how to handle various weapons. In the event of war, the people were armed by the state from strategically placed repositories of weapons and equipment. Apart from his weapons and body armour, the auxiliary warrior carried a round or square shield made from wood and the hides of the deer and tapir. These shields were decorated with geometric devices which dictated the group in which each warrior would fight. In the Cambridge University Museum of Archaeology is a fifteenth-century warrior's poncho from the Chimú Empire (roughly Ecuador/Peru). This resembles very closely a tabard and is quarterly of white and black charged with fish counterchanged. With the poncho is a feather cap with, hanging from the rear, a woven 'mantling'. There is some evidence to suggest that in some indigenous nations of Peru such designs of identity and display were hereditary.

The Aztec warriors were extremely warlike, war being a quasi-religious act. Every able-bodied man was inducted into a form of military service where he learned to use arms. The only permanent warriors were the bodyguard of the Chief Speaker. The elite military leaders wore elaborate garb, whilst the soldiers from various clans wore distinctive tunics. Their shields, made of wood covered with toughened hide, were decorated with totemic and clan devices.

The Mayas were an agrarian nation, and warfare was usually timed for late in the year when the soldier-farmer could leave his land. The warrior leaders went into battle ornately dressed, their faces gaudily painted, and wearing huge wooden headdresses festooned with the feathers of exotic birds. All carried round shields made of wood, painted with different clan and totemic devices, and usually with a fringe of feathers hanging from the lower edge.

The plains indians of North America carried small round shields when they adopted the horse during the sixteenth century. These shields were made of buffalo hide stretched over a wooden frame. Magic played a great part in the symbolism of these indians, and the making of a shield was shrouded in esoteric secrecy.

Symbols representing nature or common artefacts were very popular amongst these nomadic horsemen, though the same motif could be differently interpreted by various clans. The zig-zag could be lightning or a snake, the triangle could be a mountain or a tent. The plains indians also relied on the use of ornate pictographs, including depictions of warriors, horses, buffaloes, trails, fish, birds and many other familiar things. The designs painted on the shields usually alluded to events in the life of each warrior. Someone finding a good horse, or considering himself a fast runner, would possibl paint a horse on his shield. Another warrior may have painted a symbolic turtle on his shield, believing that the armoured properties of the carapace may be transferred to his shield and protect him in battle.

Of the many different races inhabiting the huge South Pacific region, only three areas are populated by true shield-using peoples: the Solomon Islands, New Guinea and Australia.

The shields used by the Solomon Islanders are of an elongated oval shape, made of wood and covered with a vegetable gum into which small pieces of shell are pressed to form geometric patterns, usually surrounding an anthropomorphic symbol. The shields are usually red and black.

The southern coast of New Guinea was populated by the Asmat, a very fierce and warlike people. The warriors carried huge rectangular wooden shields, almost the size of the bearer, beautifully carved with symbolic designs and motifs curiously derived from large segments of the human body. The relief designs were generally painted white, with the odd black band, usually across the top. The ground inside the relief carving was painted in a very rich and unmistakable red pigment.

The Australian aborigines who inhabit the northern peninsula of Arnhem Land carried huge wooden shields painted and engraved with totemic devices.

Some other tribal peoples also carried small ceremonial shields which were an integral part of their dances, but their function could not be compared with that of the larger war shields.   BC

Further reading
Boas, F. *Primitive Art* 1955.
Morris, D.R. *The Washing of the Spears* London, 1965.
Von Hagen V.W. *The Ancient Sun Kingdoms of the Americas* London, 1962.

European Titles, Styles, etc. For forms of address, usage, etc., see Patrick Montague-Smith's *Debrett's Correct Form*, London, 1976.

Exemplification A pictorial example of. An exemplification of armorial bearings in a patent of arms ('as the same are in the margin hereof more plainly depicted') is intended to be an unambiguous representation of the arms as blazoned. However, it is important to remember that there is nothing definitive about this exemplification — only the blazon and the type of helmet (that appropriate to rank) are inviolable — and for all other purposes the arms may be depicted in any style or form which the artist and his client may agree upon.

Extended *see* **Attitude**

Eyed *see* **Attributes**

F

Fabrics *see* **Textiles**

Face *see* **Attitude**

Falchion A broad-bladed sword with a curved front edge.

Falcon In armory, the artistic treatment of falcons and other hawks is usually identical unless a blazon specifies a particular type of bird, e.g. a gyrfalcon, peregrine, goshawk, etc. Falcons are usually depicted as close or sometimes volant (when the position of the wings should also be given) and preying. They may also be belled and jessed (that is, with bells attached to their feet by thongs), or vervelled (when the thongs end in rings called vervels), or hooded.

Falcon, Order of Founded in 1921 this is the only Icelandic order. It has four classes, and may be conferred on Icelanders or foreigners for national or international achievement.   JC-K

Fald *or* **Fauld** Mailed crotch protection.

Falkland Pursuivant of Arms Extraordinary A current Scottish pursuivant extraordinary. First mentioned in 1493, this title is derived from the Royal Palace of the same name situated in Fife.   CJB

'Family' Silver *see* **Silverware**

Feathered *see* **Attributes**

Fer-de-Moline *see* **Mill Rind**

Fess An ordinary consisting of a broad horizontal band crossing the centre of the shield. The most notable characteristic of the fess is the complexity of conventions relating to it and to its diminutives. A fess embattled is crenellated only at the upper edge. If both edges are so depicted it is said to be a fess embattled and counter embattled (the term bretessé is rarely used but indicates that the embrasures of the upper edge are opposite those of the lower one). A fess may be couped and also wreathed when it is depicted as a series of bendwise twists of coloured material. The diminutive of the fess is the bar. It may be borne singly or in any number that avoids confusion with a barry field, which is composed of an *even* number of horizontal divisions. The bar may be positioned anywhere on the shield except adjacent to the upper edge, where it would have the appearance of a narrow chief. Bars themselves possess diminutives (barrulets), and when these are borne in pairs (as they invariably are) each *pair* is blazoned a bar gemel. Readers of romantic novels may be assured that there is no such charge as a bar sinister!

Diminutives: bar and barrulet
Parted field: per fess
Varied field: barry (barruly if more than ten divisions)
Disposition: in fess
Inclination: fesswise

Fess Point A charge depicted in the centre of the shield is said to be in fess point (also occasionally blazoned heart point).
See also ORDINARY *and* SHIELD, POINTS OF THE

Fetterlock A shackle for a horse, usually depicted as a barrel-lock with a hinged, elliptical clasp. The famous Falcon and Fetterlock badge of Edward IV derived from Edmund of Langley, Duke of York (1341-1402), who bore as a badge the silver falcon of Plantagenet confined within a gold fetterlock. His grandson, Richard Duke of York (1411-60) inherited both the Yorkist claim to the English throne and the badge, which he depicted with an open clasp in which the falcon was no longer confined: a clear allusion to his ambitions. Political verses of 1449 refer to the badge:

The Fawkon fleyth and hath no rest
Tille he witte wher to bigge his nest.

Field The surface of a shield or armorial flag on which charges are placed, also the surfaces of charges themselves. Parted or varied fields are assumed to be

Surely the most extravagant boasting match of all time took place in 1520, near Calais. Henry VIII, in the foreground, with Wolsey, took with him nearly 3000 horses and nearly 4000 people. A magnificent tent, painted to look like brick, housed a golden banqueting hall. Temporary palaces were constructed, as in the

foreground, for the reception of Henry and his queen, Catherine of Aragon. Francis I also brought 22 specially woven tapestries, and in the picture above he and Henry can be seen greeting each other in the circular tent centre background. At the right is the joust and the Tree of Nobility. This sixteenth-century painting, a contemporary record of the event, shows many armorial devices including, of course, Henry's great Welsh dragon.

flat surfaces, and lines of partition should not be depicted in relief, therefore.

Field of the Cloth of Gold The glittering gathering of the Field of the Cloth of Gold, held at Guisnes in June 1520, was intended as a summit meeting between Henry VIII of England and Francis I of France. Its objective: to guarantee the peace of Europe. Henry, who was less than thirty, and Francis who was twenty-seven, vied with each other in the richness of their retinues and the lavishness of their entertainment. Nearly three thousand tents were erected to accommodate the two courts, and a temporary palace was constructed for Henry's reception in which fountains spouted wine! Four weeks were entirely devoted to pageantry, festivities and jousting. The lists, which measured 900 x 320 feet (275 x 97 metres), were surrounded by a deep ditch to keep out the crowds of spectators. However, the most amazing feature was undoubtedly the Tree of Nobility, from which depended the shields of the participants with those of the two young kings above the rest, for both entered the lists with their knights. The trunk of the tree was of cloth of gold, its foliage green silk and the flowers and fruits it bore were of silver and Venetian gold. Regrettably, the burial of old animosities which was to be symbolized by this 'celebration of the rebirth of chivalry' was doomed from the start, and Wolsey, who had devised the entire affair, enjoyed only a transient triumph.

Parted Fields

Field, Parted A shield or charge may be divided into a variety of geometrical shapes based on the principal lines of partition, each defined by the name of the ordinary whose geometry it follows. When a shield or charge is divided in this way it is said to be parted, party or partitioned. When blazoned, each term is preceded by the word per (per fess, per chevron, etc.), excepting per cross which is quarterly, per pall which is tierced in pairle (a convention which should be dispensed with), and gyronny which is a combination of quarterly and per saltire. Partitions are flat surfaces and, therefore, never shown in relief. Colour may be depicted alongside colour and metal alongside metal, and charges placed on a parted field of both metal and colour do not infringe the tincture convention.
See also FIELD, VARIED

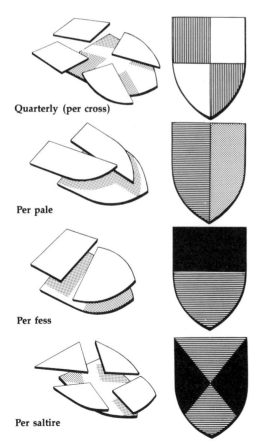

Quarterly (per cross)

Per pale

Per fess

Per saltire

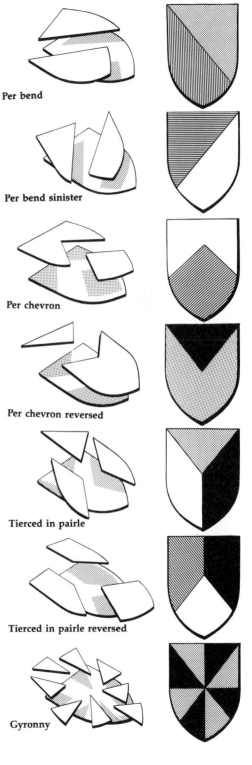

Per bend

Per bend sinister

Per chevron

Per chevron reversed

Tierced in pairle

Tierced in pairle reversed

Gyronny

143

Field, Varied The field of a shield or charge composed of a series of geometrical lines and divisions.

The majority of varied fields derives from palewise, fesswise, bendwise and chevronwise lines of partition, and combinations thereof. The divisions thereby created are always of an even number (to avoid confusion with diminutives of ordinaries) and are invariably six in number unless otherwise specified.

Other varied fields include:

Compony (or *gobony*) which is a single row of chequers (a double row is counter-compony) appropriate for use on ordinaries and sub-ordinaries where its geometry follows that of the space it occupies.

Gyronny of more than eight pieces, the number being specified, e.g. *gyronny of twelve Or and Vert* (gyronny of eight is a parted field and the number of pieces is not blazoned).

Pily, Pily bendy and *Pily bendy sinister* are varied fields composed of conjoined piles.

Lozengy is a varied field divided bendy and bendy sinister to give an over all pattern of lozenges.

Fusilly is similar to lozengy but the bendy and bendy sinister lines are nearer the horizontal and the lozenges thereby have an elongated appearance.

Although varied fields are deemed to have a plain surface, and are therefore not subject to the tincture convention, they are frequently composed of alternating metal and colour, the former normally depicted in the 'senior' position (i.e. dexter chief). Charges placed on varied fields of metal and colour do not contravene the tincture convention.

Figured *see* Attributes

Fillet Diminutives of the cross, pall and saltire ordinaries are blazoned fillet cross, etc. (*see* ORDINARY).

A fillet cross may be added to a quartered shield containing separate coats of arms, thereby making it an impartible or indivisible coat.

Fimbriated An ordinary when edged by a narrow band of metal or colour is said to be fimbriated. The

A pale fimbriated

144

tincture of the fimbriation should always comply with the tincture convention. This enables a red cross to be combined with a blue field when *fimbriated Argent*, for example.

Finland, Armorial Practice The Finnish republic was established in June 1919, the country of Finland having since 1809 been a semi-independent Grand Duchy within the Russian Empire. Prior to that date it was, from 1155, a province of Sweden. The bearing of arms in modern Finland is quite unregulated. In previous centuries there was a closely controlled system for the registration of the arms of the nobility, but all other 'coats' were merely assumed and not officially recognized.

Today some families display arms (in the Swedish and Russian styles) as true descendants of armigerous forebears, some because they believe they are so descended, still others because they simply wish to do so. The interest in heraldry thus remains alive, and there are several societies flourishing. One, the Suomen Heraldinen Seura (*see* ADDRESSES) maintains a register of arms   JC-K

Karjala Brigade badge

Finland, Military Insignia Current Finnish military insignia, uniform and flags, although often of strikingly original design, also possess characteristics of Russian and Swedish military insignia — an indication of their armorial ancestry. The Finnish armed forces are organized on a regional system and their insignia usually include an armorial charge taken from the arms of their location. The unit shoulder badge of the Vaasa Coast Artillery Battalion includes the device, usually interpreted as a vase or wheatsheaf, taken from the arms of Vaasa itself (this charge was borne in the arms of the Swedish royal dynasty surnamed Vaasa). Finnish army brigades wear regional or other territorial devices within an oval wreath on their shoulder insignia. The badge of the Karjala Brigade (illustrated) includes a curious charge taken from the provincial arms, consisting of two arms bearing swords. The arm on the left side is in armour and holds a straight sword, whilst that on the right is in chainmail and bears a curved sword or falchion. This device supposedly symbolizes the ancient conflict waged between the East and West: the old Swedo-Finnish territory of Karjala and the Russians. The Finnish arms of a lion trampling a scimitar is borne on the lower button of the armed

Varied Fields

1 Barry
2 Bendy
3 Bendy sinister
4 Paly
5 Chevrony
6 Chequy
7 A bend compony
8 A bend counter-compony
9 Lozengy
10 Barry bendy
11 Paly bendy
12 Gyronny of twelve
13 Pily
14 Pily bendy
15 Pily bendy sinister

forces' cockade and on officers' cap badges, whilst other ranks tend to wear the national cockade of blue and white.   SS

Finned *see* **Attributes**

Fireback *see* **Fireplaces**

Fired *see* **Attributes**

Firemarks The idea of insurance against fire damage originated in the seventeenth century, encouraged by the horrors of the Great Fire of London in 1666. The insurance companies established their own fire brigades in order to minimize losses, and it became the practice during the eighteenth and nineteenth centuries for the companies to identify insured property with a distinctive firemark. These early marks usually bore a number below the company's device, indicating the policy relating to a particular building. Plates (as these marks were called) were originally of lead, but in the early 1800s copper was used, to be superseded by iron or tin in the 1820s. Many of the independent companies introduced several variations of their device, which were not only useful as a means of identifying insured property, but also as a form of advertizing. Many examples may still be seen on the walls of houses today, and the Chartered Insurance Institute has two major collections of British marks in its museum, at 20 Aldermanbury, London EC2V 7HY.

Many British firemarks included armorial elements, such as the portcullis ensigned by three feathers and a crown of the Westminster Fire Office and the three silver leopards' faces on blue of the Salop Company, a clear armorial reference to the arms of Shropshire. The mark of the Star Insurance Company comprised what is essentially the star of the Order of the Garter, the garter itself and the cross of St George being inscribed with the company's name. The West of England Company device had a figure of King Alfred supporting a silver shield charged with a red dragon (of Wessex), and that of the Worcester Fire Office was an embossed representation of the arms of the City of Worcester in gold within a black and gold oval border. The London and Lancashire Fire Insurance Company used a blue shield charged with its name above two smaller shields, one depicting the arms of the City of London and the other the royal arms of England which, presumably, should be charged with a label of France for the Duchy of Lancaster. The Scottish Union Company, as one might expect, used a red lion rampant on a gold roundel from the Scottish royal arms, and the device of the Kent Invicta Company was a silver horse forcene on a red octagon. Other devices included a castle on a mount for the Alliance Company, a beautiful golden sun in splendour for the

Firemark of the Bath Sun Fire Company.

Sun Fire Company, a particularly appropriate phoenix for the company of that name, and a vigorous salamander for the Commercial Union Company.

Many of these devices have found their way into subsequent grants of arms, the castle of the Alliance Company for example: *Argent upon a Rock issuant from the base proper inscribed 1824 in Gold numerals a quadrangular Castle also proper Pennons flying to the sinister from each Tower Gules* (1933), and the phoenix of the Phoenix Insurance Company: *Azure upon a Billet fesswise Or inscribed 1782 in numerals Sable a Phoenix proper* (1936).

Fireplaces The gradual introduction of the enclosed chimney flue and fireplace during the Middle Ages was probably to have a greater effect on the social history of western Europe than any other factor. It resulted in a previously unknown luxury — privacy. Domestic rooms became smaller and, therefore, greater in number, and allowed for a variety of functions which the old communal hall had not. The fireplace became the focal point of a chamber and it is not surprising that it should become a principal domestic means of displaying armorial devices. Regrettably, few decorated fireplaces of the medieval period have survived, but those of later times are legion.

Hardwick Hall, Derbyshire, has a magnificent plasterwork achievement of the arms of Bess of Hardwick (born 1520) in the entrance hall with a similar, though not identical, design in the dining room, while in the High Great Chamber will be found the royal arms in plasterwork. Wood was also a popular medium during the Elizabethan and Jacobean periods.

During the eighteenth century armorial themes were less prominent, the fine fireplace of marble and gilt in the Double Cube Room of Wilton House, Wiltshire, being exceptional. This has an heraldic cartouche in the pediment and the so-called Prince of

Wales' Feathers above a painting of a family group.

The Gothic Revival produced many grand heraldic fireplaces. At Powderham Castle in Devon the fireplace has four shields of the Courteney family and is surmounted by the royal arms. It is based on a fireplace in the Bishop's Palace at Exeter, erected by Bishop Peter Courteney *c.* 1478. Arundel Castle in Sussex (the Drawing Room) and Carlton Towers, North Yorkshire (the Venetian Drawing Room) both have fine heraldic overmantels. At Oxburgh Hall in Norfolk there is a frieze of five shields beneath the mantleshelf, the tiled surround to the fireplace being decorated with armorial badges and cyphers.

Within such fireplaces armorial firebacks may also be found. These were effectively early storage radiators which not only reflected the fire's heat into the room but also stored it long after a fire was extinguished. Many designs are traditional and incorporate floral motifs, religious symbols and scroll-work. Many, however, are armorial, the royal arms being particularly popular. Many early firebacks were made for specific fireplaces, and included devices or even full achievements appropriate to the family who commissioned the work. However, care should be exercised, for it may not be assumed that a fireback has remained in its original location and the heraldry may not relate to the house in which it is found. Modern firebacks often have quasi-armorial designs, many of which are most attractive.

Fire-dogs and implements may also incorporate armorial features, some associated with a particular family.   JET

Fir Tree *and* Fir Twig *see* Lines, Varied

Fitchy, Fitché *or* **Fitched** Pointed at the foot. Usually applied to a cross, the lower limb of which is pointed. If a cross is depicted normally but a point is *added* to the lower limb, it is blazoned *fitchy at the foot*.
See also CROSS

Fitzalan Pursuivant of Arms Extraordinary This

pursuivant obtains his title from one of the baronies held by the Duke of Norfolk, Earl Marshal of England. The appointment was first made for the coronation of Queen Victoria (1837), and the first four Fitzalans all subsequently became Garter kings of arms. The badge

of office, assigned in 1958, is derived from a Fitzalan badge of the fifteenth century: *An Oak Sprig Vert Acorns Or* (also recorded as *A Sprig of Oak proper*).

Flag *And the children of Israel . . . pitched by their standards, and so they set forward, every one after their families, according to the house of their fathers* (The Book of Numbers 2 v.34). The antiquity of flags is evident in this passage from the Old Testament, and in the records of ancient Egypt, where every territorial district had its standard which was used both as a point of muster for military forces and as a device by which its authority was recognized. Here, too, are the origins of armory. The children of Israel assembled beneath household flags reminiscent of the nobility and their retainers in the High Middle Ages. Egyptian and Assyrian standards were, in fact, poles with cross-pieces to which were affixed various representational devices: the images of local gods, for example. Roman standards were similar and carried religious and martial symbols such as the open hand of military command and even portraits. Inevitably a system evolved and devices were adopted to represent both specific units of the Roman army and functional designations. After a long period of general use the eagle was adopted as the device of the legion, and this was accompanied on a legion's standard by its own honours and emblems. Cavalry used the *vexillum*, a large cloth flag suspended from a cross-piece at right-angles to the pole (an early gonfannon). The *labarum* or Imperial Standard was of purple silk fringed with gold and decorated with devices. Such standards became so large that it was often necessary to transport them onto the field of battle by means of a special chariot. During the so-called Dark Ages the popularity of the modelled or rigid standard declined, though even at Hastings (1066) the famous Wessex Dragon Standard (now defined as a wyvern) raised over Harold's command post was probably of this earlier 'vane' type. The *Anglo-Saxon Chronicle* tells of 'the conflict of banners' and how, at the battle of Brumby, 'the sons of Edward . . . hewed their banners with the wrecks of their hammers.' Bede also writes of King Edwin of East Anglia whose banners 'were not only borne before him in battle, but even in time of peace when he rode about his cities, towns or provinces, with his officers, the standard-bearer was wont to go before him.' Regrettably, few of the devices of this period have come down to us — only the Wessex wyvern, the Kentish horse and the raven of the Danes are familiar. The majority of flags depicted in the Bayeaux Tapestry are of cloth; small, square and with a number of 'tails' attached to the fly. That the devices borne on these flags were territorial or even personal symbols has long been a matter of dispute; however, by the time of the First Crusade, only thirty years later, the mass cavalry charge of mail-clad knights and men-at-arms was the standard tactic of warfare, and control was exercised in the ensuing mêlée by the use of mustering flags bearing the personal devices of commanders. Such flags were necessary in order that scattered members of a unit could reform around them. Clearly, these early command flags were sufficiently distinctive to be recognized, even in the heat of battle, and it is likely that they also possessed a peace-time function — that of marking territory and symbolizing authority. The anonymous author of the *Gesta Francorum*, a chronicle of the First Crusade, informs us that many of the nobles possessed their own banners. In the early Middle Ages command flags took the form of simple lance pennons, and by the end of the twelfth century senior commanders were using rectangular banners, twice as high as they were wide. By the fourteenth century these had become square, while the pennon remained the flag of those below the rank of knight banneret. These banners, bannerets and pennons were the personal flags of nobility and knighthood, indicative of a man's presence in the field and of his hereditary superiority. They bore the devices peculiar to him and his family — visible and outward symbols of power and authority — repeated on his shield, surcoat and horse caparison. The mustering and rallying functions were performed by the livery flags: the guidon and standard, livery pennon and streamer, which bore both the liveries and badges familiar to retainers and soldiery, and of which their uniforms were composed.

Unlike the components of a coat of arms, the flag has retained its original function and remains the supreme form of armorial display, as effective today as it was at the dawn of armory. And yet, England (one of the few remaining countries where armory is officially recognized) is appallingly deficient in its use of flags. This is undoubtedly a reflection of the national character which considers such matters to be excessively flamboyant, and even pretentious. It is also the result of obscure legislation which discourages the flying of national flags. The 'Stars and Stripes' of the United States of America is ubiquitous in that country. It expresses a nation's pride and patriotism in a form which is neither ostentatious nor chauvinistic. Civic and corporate banners bedeck the streets and public buildings of Europe's cities and ancient towns. Yet in England it is the cheap and tatty, the commercial and the vulgar which flutter from the flagstaffs of road-side petrol stations and city-centre shopping precincts. Employed with imagination and sensitivity, flags may enhance human experience: a solitary, fluttering banner can animate a landscape, ranks of civic flags provide diversity in the drab uniformity of a modern town. They are symbols of pride and allegiance *par excellence* and their use is entirely appropriate to the family, the community and the nation. The British should fly their national flags whenever they wish, the Union Flag being reserved for royal, state and ceremonial occasions. (The so-called 'rules' apply only to the Union Flag and military and departmental flags of government.)

In Scotland, armorial flags are subject to strict regulation and armigers wishing to fly an armorial flag must first seek the authority of Lord Lyon. Yet it does not follow that increased regulation would deter the English armiger — quite the reverse, for the Scots enjoy and appreciate their flags. Armigers and armigerous corporations should be encouraged to use their arms and badges on appropriate flags, and the College of Arms should *grant* livery flags to those who acquire badges, instead of simply depicting them in patents as mere decoration. Standards are rarely appropriate to personal armigers, and the guidon and livery pennon should be reintroduced for this purpose.

Armorial flags (all the following have their own entries). See colour page 135.

Personal flags denoting the presence of an armiger or that an armigerous corporation is in session:

Banner	Gonfannon
Banneret	Pennant (nautical)
Banneroll	Pennon
Burgee (nautical)	Pennoncelle
Ensign banner	

Livery flags denoting allegiance or service to an armiger or membership of an armigerous corporation:

Ensign	Livery pennoncelle
Guidon	Pinsel (Scotland)
Livery banner	Standard
Livery pennant (nautical)	Streamer (nautical)
Livery pennon	

The rules for hoisting flags on government and other public buildings are clearly set out in *Debrett's Correct Form* edited by Patrick Montague-Smith (applicable to UK and Commonwealth).

The study of flags is vexillology (Latin *vexillum* = standard). In several languages a distinction is made between flags used on land (French = *drapeaux*, German = *fahnen*) and those used at sea (French = *pavillons*, German = *flaggen*). No such distinction is made in English. Nautical flags are a complex and fascinating subject, the literature of which provides an extraordinary number of conflicting definitions and opinions even with regard to the interpretation of official regulations and conventions.

An excellent, inexpensive book on nautical flags is *Flags at Sea* by Timothy Wilson, HMSO 1986. The standard international reference book on flags is *Flags of the World* edited by W.G. Crampton, 1986,

published in Britain since 1897 and probably the definitive work on the subject. *Heraldic Standards and Other Ensigns* by Lt Col Robert Gayre, 1959, is by far the most comprehensive work on armorial flags. The book has an unashamed Scottish inclination, and as such is somewhat prescriptive, particularly when dealing with the complexities of rank and regulation in that country. Nevertheless, it should be compulsory reading for armorist and vexillologist alike. *Flags Through the Ages and Across the World* by Dr Whitney Smith, 1975, has 'added a new dimension to the study of flags'. Two specialist books are worthy of note: *A History of Irish Flags* by G.H. Hayes-McCoy, 1979, and *Military Flags of the World* by T. Wise, 1977. International and national flags are dealt with in *Flags of All Nations*, reprinted in two volumes in 1965 by HMSO; *Flags of the World* edited by E.M. Barraclough, 1978; *Guide to Flags of the World* by Mauro Talocci, revised 1982; *International Flag Book* by Christian Fogd Pederson, (Ed. English edition Lt Comm. John Bedells, 1971); *The New Observer's Book of Flags* by W.G. Crampton, 1984; and *The book of Flags* by G. Campbell and I.O. Evans, 1974.
Further sources of information: The Flag Institute, and The Flag Research Center (*see* ADDRESSES).
See also ARMORIAL BEARINGS, USE OF; FLAG, ECCLESIASTICAL; FLAG, NATIONAL

Flag, Ecclesiastical The gonfannon (or gonfallon) is the traditional flag of the Church, principally because of its suitability for carrying in procession. Its use is rarely armorial, however, and devices are usually of a religious or purely symbolic nature. The question of which flag is appropriate to the tower of an English church is a constant source of controversy, exacerbated by a Warrant of 1938 which permitted the Cross of St George with the diocesan arms on a shield in the first quarter of the flag to be used for this purpose in the provinces of Canterbury and York. This is a most unsatisfactory arrangement. Surely there is no reason why a diocese should not apply to the College of Arms for a badge which could then be flown by its churches on a livery flag — complete with the Cross of St George in the hoist? Some ecclesiastical foundations are armigerous and are, therefore, fortunate in possessing their own banners.

Flag, Ethnic and Cultural The best known ethnic symbol today is perhaps the flag of the Rastafarians: red, yellow, green and black, derived from that of Ethiopia, and often combined with the 'Lion of Judah'. These emblems became popular in Jamaica in the 1930s and have now spread throughout the world, having overtaken the original Afro-American colours of red, black and green invented by Marcus Garvey in the 1900s. Another well-known set of colours is

employed in the flag of the Palestine Arabs. This flag is in the colours first used in the Arab Revolt of 1917, and Arabs have been campaigning for a homeland in Palestine ever since then. Less well known is the Sikh flag, known as the *Nishan Sahib*, which represents Sikhs in all parts of the world. The Lapps, or *Sami*, who inhabit the northern parts of Norway, Sweden and Finland also have a flag, whose colours recall their colourful traditional dress. In the USA the Irish-Americans are well known for the exuberant use of green, whilst in Europe there is a flag for the gypsies.

Cultural minorities often wish to express their identity by means of traditional symbols, such as the Welsh Dragon, the Scottish royal lion, and the Saracen's head of Corsica. These emblems often become those of separatist movements, seeking autonomy or self-determination on the cultural plane if not on the political one. Examples are the Cross of Toulouse used by the Languedoc peoples of southern France; the flaming sun of the Kurds, and the golden sun of the Australian aboriginals. Quebec, Britanny, Cornwall, Scania, Friesland, and the Shetland Islands are all examples of places where flags and devices are used to express the wish to be recognized as 'different'. Sometimes, as in modern Spain, these expressions of individuality achieve the force of law and become the established emblems of well-defined cultural regions, whilst elsewhere they remain symbols of unfulfilled aspirations.   WGC

Flag, International The supreme international emblem is the badge of the United Nations, which was adopted in 1947. It contains several well-established 'international' elements: the globe, signifying universality, the wreath of olive-branches for peace, and the light blue colour of neutrality. Earlier international flags used white to stand for peace, like that of the Olympic Games with its five interlaced rings representing the five continents. The International Co-operative Movement has long used a flag representing the rainbow, of red, orange, yellow, green, blue, black and purple horizontal stripes. This refers to the legend of Noah and the Ark, as do the olive-branches and the dove, representing peace.

The European Economic Community (EEC) and the Council of Europe both have the same flag, of blue (the international colour) with a ring of twelve gold stars, whereas the Soviet-led Council for Economic Co-operation has a red flag with a white star emblem in the centre. The Organisation of African Unity has a green flag with a white, gold-edged band across the centre charged with a map of Africa. Maps are favourite ways of denoting an international association, as are rings of stars, links of chains, groups of flags or combinations of flag colours.

White for peace also occurs in the flags of the

Geneva Convention, the Red Cross and the Red Crescent; the red cross is derived from the flag of Switzerland and the crescent from that of Turkey. The flag of the Hispanic Race is also white, with three crosses representing the ships of Columbus and the setting sun of the West. It is flown extensively on the 'Day of the Race' (12 October).

The League of Arab States uses green and the crescent associated with Islam and a chain for unity. The South Pacific Commission has perhaps the most ingenious flag: a big C for 'Commission', an arc of stars and a palm tree all come together to make a stylized atoll and reef. The World Scout flag contains the famous fleur-de-lis emblem from Baden-Powell's arms, and the World Guide flag the golden trefoil of the guide movement. The internationally used flag of the Buddhists is in the colours of the 'aura' of the Buddha: the five horizontal segments signify an unknown composite colour. The flag symbolizing the international language Esperanto is green, the colour of Hope, and has a green star in its white canton. The flag of NATO is blue for the Atlantic, with a white compass rose denoting both North and the extensive commitments of the organization. There is no flag for the Warsaw Pact, nor for the Commonwealth.   WGC

Flag, National Western European armory is only one of the major sources of the designs of modern national flags. Of the 179 national flags of the world today only three are true 'armorial' banners: those of Austria, Kiribati and Switzerland, although the flag of Albania, without the red star it bears today, was also originally such a banner. On the other hand, many flags are composed of the armorial colours, i.e. the predominant tinctures of the field and charges of an original coat of arms, and the French Tricolor has clearly influenced the creation of other tricolours out of armorial colours, as for example in the cases of Hungary and Belgium (not of Germany, contrary to a once-popular theory). Poland, Spain, Luxembourg, Monaco, Malta, the Vatican City, Andorra and San Marino all have flags in the armorial colours, sometimes with added arms.

The oldest national flag in the world in continuous use is that of Denmark, which is a simple white cross on red. The flag was originally square, so that the cross was equal-armed, but over the centuries its shape became more oblong, extending the 'fly' arm of the cross to give rise to the distinctive form known today as a Scandinavian cross.

The Scandinavian cross of Denmark was not originally an armorial flag, but that used in Sweden is (it is in the colours of the arms). Norway combined the Danish flag with the French Tricolor, and Finland kept the form but in new colours. Sweden and Finland still use the 'swallow-tail with tongue' version of the flag for state purposes, a form of medieval

origin. The other famous flag derived from crosses is the 'Union Jack' (the popular name for the British Union flag). Its unusual combination derives from the need to combine the emblems of England and Scotland to make a distinctive mark for use at sea, and later from the need to add an extra cross to symbolize Ireland. This unique composition makes the flag very memorable and recognizable. The only other countries to use crosses today, apart from the Scandinavian countries, are Iceland, Switzerland, Tonga and Jamaica (a saltire). The flag of Switzerland is similar in origin to that of Denmark; that of Tonga is unrelated but also aims at declaring the country's Christian faith. The Dutch tricolour is also armorial in origin: it was created from the colours of William of Orange, Count of Nassau. Its original colours of orange, white, blue were later adopted in South Africa. The later form of red, white and blue was copied by Russia and inspired the 'Pan-Slav' colours still used by Czechoslovakia and Yugoslavia, and in amended form by Bulgaria. The French Tricolor, which is vertical as opposed to the horizontal Dutch one, gave rise to another large group of flags, including those of Italy and Ireland and of many South American countries. It is generally accepted that its colours are derived from the white of the Bourbon dynasty added to the blue and red livery colours of Paris. The idea of the Tricolor became associated with liberty and independence, hence its later popularity as a flag form. The 'Stars and Stripes' of the USA is also a very inspirational flag. Opinion is still divided about how it came into being, but it has had a similar influence to that of the French Tricolor. Flags immediately derived from it are those of Chile, Cuba, Liberia and Panama, but it could also be said to have influenced other flags with stripes, such as that of Malaysia.

In Africa, many flags are derived from the colours of Ethiopia (red, yellow, green) or from the colours of Marcus Garvey's Black Liberation Movement (black, red, green). In South America, the activities of the liberationists such as Bolivar, San Martin and Artigas had an influence on flags. Some say that the colours of the five Central American states (blue and white) are derived from the flag of Argentina, and the colours of Bolivar (blue, yellow, red) led to the flags of Ecuador, Colombia and Venezuela.

Two other major flag groups are those in the colours of the Arab revolt of 1917 (black, white, red, green, as in the flag of Jordan), and of the Arab Liberation Movement (red, white, black, as in the flag of Egypt). The crescent and star, now universally recognized as the emblem of Islam, first appeared on the merchant ensign of the Ottoman Empire. From there it was adopted by Tunisia, and in modern times by several Islamic states.

In the Communist world the Red Flag is not so

widespread as might be expected. Only the USSR, China, Vietnam and Kampuchea have all-red flags with gold devices. In East Europe the new régimes have merely added new emblems to existing flags (e.g. Romania, Bulgaria, Albania, Yugoslavia). After the troubles in Hungary in 1956 the Communist emblem was removed from the flag. In 1935 the Nazi swastika was the first political party flag to become a national flag, but since that time this process has accelerated. With the partition of India the flags of the Moslem League and the India National Congress were adapted for the new states of Pakistan and India, and after that new national flags which are derived from party flags have proliferated. This sometimes has the result that the flag is altered when the original party loses power, as has happened recently in the case of Lesotho.

A source of designs often overlooked, but which is also a significant trend, is public competition. Sometimes a single winning design is selected, as in the case of St Kitts, or else several might be composited, as in the case of Jamaica, or the winning design might be selected but modified by the judges, as in the case of Nigeria. Very occasionally flag designs are provided by expert vexillologists, as in the case of Guernsey and Guyana, although in both these cases the original design was modified. Graphic artists designed the flags of Zambia and Vanuatu. The College of Arms has had a certain influence on the designs of some modern flags of Commonwealth countries. Examples of flags which have been designed or processed by the College are those of Sierra Leone, Gambia, Uganda, Trinidad, the Solomon Islands, Botswana, and many now obsolete ones, such as those of Zanzibar and certain West Indian states. College of Arms flags are characterized by a central fimbriated stripe. The College has encouraged the use of indigenous shield forms, as in the flag of Kenya.

Modern flags are normally rectangular (only Nepal has one which is not), and can be in any proportion of width to length from 1:1 (Switzerland) to 11:28 (Qatar). It is becoming standard practice to specify the proportions of a national flag and the structure of its design, as well as the exact shades of the colours (which are more numerous than those used in heraldry), in official documentation. National flags are generally of simple design and do not often employ more than three main colours. Horizontal stripes tend to be more popular in Germanic areas than in lands influenced by France, and lines of partition are generally straight. Only the flags of the Seychelles and of Kiribati have wavy lines, but serrated divisions were once popular in the Persian Gulf and are to be seen in the flags of Qatar and Bahrein. The star is the most popular single emblem, usually of five points, as in the 'Stars and Stripes'. Fimbriated or voided stars

are common in Soviet and related heraldry. Only in one or two cases are whole coats of arms superimposed on a basic design, for obvious practical reasons; on the other hand, devices derived from arms are used in some cases (Zimbabwe, Dominica, Mozambique). Inscriptions are now very rare, and only two national flags (Saudi Arabia and Iran) include writing, in each case in Arabic. Nearly all national flags have the same design on the reverse as on the obverse, but there are some notable exceptions. Paraguay has a different badge on each side, and the Soviet flag omits the star, hammer and sickle from the reverse side.

To the vexillologist the term 'national flag' is an ambiguous one, in that many countries have more than one form of flag. Britain is an outstanding example of a country which uses a different form of the national flag on land (the Union Flag), at sea (the Red Ensign), for its navy (the White Ensign), and for government vessels (the Blue Ensign). In Britain no official definition has ever been given as to which of these (if any!) is the 'national' flag.

For further information contact The Flag Institute (*see* ADDRESSES). WGC

Further reading

Crampton, W.G. (Ed.) *The Orbis Encyclopedia of Flags and Coats of Arms* London, 1985.
— *Webster's Concise Encyclopedia of Flags and Coats of Arms* New York, 1985.
Furlong, W.R. and B. McCandless *So Proudly We Hail — The History of the United States Flag* Washington, 1981.
Perrin, W.G. *British Flags* Cambridge, 1922.
Smith, W. *Bibliography of Flags of Foreign Nations* Boston, Mass., 1965.
— *Flags Through the Ages and Across the World* New York, 1975.
Wise, T. *Military Flags of the World in Colour 1618-1900* Poole, 1977.

Flamant *see* **Attributes**

Flaunches *or* **Flanches** An armorial charge consisting of a *pair* of concave indentations, one on each side of the shield. A sub-ordinary, apparently

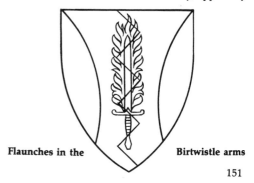

Flaunches in the   Birtwistle arms

possessed of two diminutives: flasques and (even narrower) voiders. Fortunately, both terms appear to be confined to the pages of reference books. Flaunches can be attractive when drawn with care and on a suitably shaped shield. Badly constructed they look awful! Flaunches can be plain, parted, varied or charged and their edges formed of any of the ornamental variations of line. However, some of these treatments would look decidedly odd, and they are usually depicted plain or charged but otherwise unadorned. To blazon a charge as being *between two Flaunches* is tautologous, *between Flaunches* being entirely adequate.
See also SUB-ORDINARY

Fleam *see* **Medical Heraldry**

The **Digby arms** *Azure a Fleur-de-lis Argent.*

Fleur-de-Lis *or* **Fleur-de-Lys** A common armorial charge in the form of a stylized lily — probably the Madonna Lily (*Lilium candidum*). The lily as a symbol of purity has long been associated with the Virgin Mary. As the emblem of France — the 'Flower of Louis' — it was first borne by Louis VII (1137-80) on a royal seal. The French arms *Azure Semy-de-Lis Or* (now termed France Ancient) were quartered with the lions of England by Edward III in his Great Seal of 1340 to emphasize the English claim to the throne of France. In *c.* 1405 Henry IV reduced the number of fleurs-de-lis to three, following the pattern set by Charles V (1364-80) in the French seals. The fleurs-de-lis were finally removed from the arms of the

British sovereign in 1801, though the French influence is still evident in the Scottish tressure. Both as an armorial charge and as a means of armorial ornamentation, the fleur-de-lis is ubiquitous — justifiably so, for it is possessed of a variety of forms unmatched by any other charge. The fleur-de-lis is the mark of cadency of the sixth son.
See also FLEURETTY, FLORY, JESSANT *and* SEMY-DE-LIS
Further reading
Ibbett, V. *Flowers in Heraldry* London, 1977.

Fleuretty *or* **Floretty** (i) A field or charge semy-de-lis, each fleur-de-lis being smaller and more closely disposed than in a normal semy field.
(ii) A charge (usually a cross) with fleurs-de-lis 'sprouting' from its limbs.
See also CROSS *and* FLORY

Fleury *see* **Flory**

Flexed *see* **Attitude**

Flighted *see* **Attributes**

Floor Tiles Decorated floor tiles from the fourteenth to the sixteenth century can be found in small numbers in many churches. They should not be confused with nineteenth-century reproductions made by Victorian restorers, who in some cases copied patterns found on medieval tiles in the church. Victorian tiles are very uniform in appearance, the result of mass production, while no two medieval tiles of the same pattern will be identical.

Patterns for the earliest tiled pavements were created by using different shaped tiles of different colours. Five colours were available by using a combination of glazes on either white slip or red clay. However, during the thirteenth century several methods were used to decorate the plain tile. The pattern could be carved in outline into the surface of the tile, or alternatively the tile could be stamped to produce the pattern in relief or counter-relief. In both cases the tile was then glazed and fired, producing a patterned tile of one colour. The final method was to impress the pattern with a stamp and then fill that impression with white clay. The tile was then glazed and fired to produce the brown and yellow 'encaustic' tile.

These early tiles are usually 5-6 inches (12½-15 cm) square, and one inch (2½ cm) thick, with the inlay to a depth of one-tenth of an inch (2 mm). In the middle of the fourteenth century a flourishing English tile manufacturing industry in the Chilterns may have modified this technique. The tiles were smaller, only 4½ inches (11½ cm) square, and three-quarters of an

Encaustic floor tiles of the thirteenth and early fourteenth centuries, each approximately 6 inches square and one inch thick. Such tiles were produced by 'stamping' the design into the malleable tile and filling the impression with white clay before glazing and firing. Very often an armorial design was carved correctly on the stamp, but the resultant impression was back to front, as in the arms of Fitzpayne *Gules three Lions passant guardant Argent over all a Bend Azure* and the lions of Eleanor of Castile (Queen of Edward I) *Quarterly Castile and Leon.* The un-identified griffin segreant is depicted correctly.

inch (2 cm) thick. It is probable that the operations of making the impression and filling it with the white clay were combined as one process. The stamp was dipped into the white slip clay before it was pushed into the red clay, and the white slip was left in the impression. This technique would explain why the slip is very thin, and some edges of the slip may be smudged or missing. The centre of this industry was at Penn, Buckinghamshire, and these tiles are thus frequently referred to as 'Penn' tiles. A later development of this technique was for the surface of white slip not to be flush with the main surface of the tile, but sunken slightly below it.

Early tiles were produced to decorate royal palaces and important religious houses, but during the fourteenth century their use spread to other buildings. Some designs required four or even sixteen tiles to complete a pattern.

Armorial devices were just one of many designs used on encaustic relief and counter-relief tiles. An early example from the second half of the thirteenth century is a roundel from Chertsey Abbey showing Richard, Coeur de Lion, on horseback bearing a shield of three lions passant. Beasts such as the lion and

griffin appear alone, as do single fleurs-de-lis. These may have heraldic significance, but were probably just popular designs. Frequently encountered are tiles bearing the shields of the nobility. Often a connection can be established between the family and the location, but this may not always be the case.   JET
Further reading
Eames, E.S. *Medieval Tiles: a handbook* London, 1976. A very good book providing an introduction and background to the subject. It has a comprehensive bibliography for further reading on more specific aspects.

Floretty *see* **Fleuretty**

Flory *or* **Fleury** Charges terminating in or ornamented with fleurs-de-lis. Not to be confused with fleuretty, which implies that the fleurs-de-lis have been added to the charge. *See also* CROSS

Flory Counter Flory Charges decorated with fleurs-de-lis alternately on either side, e.g. the double tressure flory counter flory in the Scottish royal arms. *See also* FLORY

Flotant *see* **Attitude**

Fluted *see* **Attributes**

Fly The main body of a flag — that furthest from the mast or pole. *See also* HOIST

Foliated *see* **Attributes**

Fonts Those in English parish churches survive for all periods from the Anglo-Saxon time to the present day. The majority are made from stone, although there are a few of lead (less than forty). Heraldry was not widely used as decoration, although a number of hexagonal or octagonal Perpendicular fonts have shields carved on the outside of the bowl. The lead font at Greatham House, Parham in West Sussex, has the Peveral arms repeated eight times, and in Dorset there is a series of fifteenth-century stone fonts characterized by four supporting pillars, often richly ornamented, those at Winterborne Whitechurch bearing shields with beautifully vigorous armorial carvings.   JET

Forcene *see* **Attitude**

Forester In medieval times a forester (sometimes 'fee-forester') was an officer of the king's forest (the vert), whose duty it was to preserve the animals and the forest for the king's sport. These officials were well-to-do, with wide powers, and were frequently armigerous.   JC-K

Heraldic and proper fountains

Fountain (i) A roundel *barry wavy of six Argent and Azure* represents a spring of clear water. In current practice blazoned as an *Heraldic Fountain*.
(ii) A representation of a water fountain used as a charge. If such a fountain is intended it should always be blazoned as such, e.g. *a Fountain playing proper* (in the arms of Brunner).

Fourché *see* **Attributes**

Fracted *see* **Attributes**

France The term may be applied to any armorial field, ordinary or sub-ordinary which is azure and charged with gold fleurs-de-lis, e.g. *a Bordure of France, a Label of France*, etc. When appropriate the blazon should specify whether it is semy-de-lis (France Ancient) or three fleurs-de-lis (France Modern).
See also ENGLAND

France Ancient *Azure semy-de-lis Or.* In *c.* 1405 Henry IV of England, following the pattern set by Charles V of France, reduced the number of fleurs-de-lis in the French arms to three, The 'new' arms are known as France Modern.
See also FLEUR-DE-LIS

France, Armorial Practice From proud and honourable medieval beginnings the bearing of arms in France grew in importance, went into farcical decline, was legally abolished in April 1791, reinstituted during the Napoleonic era (*c.* 1805), regulated under the Second Empire of 1852-70, then allowed to decline again. Today there is no legislation concerning armory in France, but theft of arms is recognized in law, and many families are justly proud to display armorial achievements, some of which are ancient indeed.

A case could be made that the art and science of things heraldic began in France, and certainly devices for *chevaliers* and *dames* were known in the twelfth century. By the thirteenth century the bourgeois classes were sporting arms and, by the fourteenth, the peasant class (the *roturier*) had also aspired to, and been granted, such distinctions. Corporate arms were being granted in the second half of the twelfth century. There seem to have been various attempts by successive kings to regulate the use of armorial bearings, but to little practical effect. By the fifteenth century French noblemen began to depict helms in

the pictorial representations of their arms, but the bourgeoisie soon followed.

In 1407 King Charles VI founded a 'College of Heralds' with three classes of officer — kings, heralds and pursuivants — but these appointees had no jurisdiction. Petitions for the granting of arms were submitted to the king, and many points of dispute were settled by parliament. Abuses continued, however. In 1489 the office of *Mareschal d'Armes des Francais* was created, with the power to compile details of the arms of the nobility, and to rectify any abuses of heraldic usage. The holder did not have any jurisdictional power, and in 1615 King Louis XIII found it necessary to appoint a *juge general d'Armes*, with the title *Conseillor du Roi*, who did have such power. In 1696 King Louis XIV bypassed this official and set up local functionaries with territorial responsibility for the registration of arms. In fact, this action was not what it appeared to be, but was a device by the sovereign to raise money from the fees demanded. It led to the granting of arms to all kinds and classes of people. In 1760 there was a campaign (to be backed by ordinance) aimed at regulating the situation, but the conditions were so severe that many worthy families would have lost their armigerous status, and the campaign came to nothing.

Then came the Revolution, the monarchy was abolished and in 1791-92 the symbols of royalty, *noblesse* and armory were abolished. In early Napoleonic times (1802) various titles reappeared, as did decorations — the Legion of Honour was created, and armory was again in vogue, the ancient nobility frequently being permitted to use their arms, having

Many wine labels are embellished with armorial devices, of which only a few, such as the above, may genuinely be associated with former aristocratic families whose vineyards continue to prosper.

French Air Force Base No 118

been granted new titles. The new arms were often over-elaborate and rather vulgar.

During the period of the Bourbon restoration, titles and arms of the *ancien régime* were reinstated, and although titles were again dispensed with in 1852 the bearing of arms continued. There followed fluctuations as republic succeeded republic, and today there is no heraldic authority although, as stated earlier, the law recognizes the theft of arms, and the Interior Ministry controls the arms of towns.

There is a Société du Grand Armorial de France, and a national heraldic society (*see* ADDRESSES).   JC-K

France, Military Insignia The French armed forces maintain a tradition of metal and enamel unit insignia which has its origins in the French Air Force squadrons of the First World War. By the start of the Second World War many units of all descriptions had adopted insignia, worn on the breast of tunic or shirt, usually suspended from a pocket button by a leather strap. Insignia are often of splendid design, and many incorporate armorial charges or complete coats of arms. When arms are shown, these tend to be from the region or town where the unit is based. The drawing shows the insignia of the French Air Force Base No. 118. The arms are those of the unit location Mont de Marsan, borne beside a wing and supported by a squirrel, an animal common to that region.

Many regiments of the French army are proud of their origins, which sometimes date from the period of Bourbon rule before the Revolution in the eighteenth century. The insignia of such units may include the regimental flag from the Royalist period. These flags are very simple in appearance, consisting of unit colours (often quarterly) and charged with a white cross, the medieval French device. Should the regiment have been accorded 'elite' status by the monarchy, then the flag is often decorated with gold fleurs-de-lis from the royal arms. Under the Bourbon kings some regiments were known by the name of their Colonel Proprietor, and even today this may be recalled in the insignia of the 1st Regiment of Hussars (now a paratroop unit) which bears the arms of the Unit's founder, Count Ladislas de Bercheny, on a cartouche. Today, all French military insignia have to be approved and registered by the Service Historique de l'Armée, and the insignia then become the property of the State. The Service applies various rules relating to the design of military insignia, one being that only certain units at army, corps or external intervention level should bear on their badge the colours of the French Republic.   SS

France, Royal Arms of The royal arms of France were *Azure semy-de-lis Or*, thought by many to have been one of the most beautiful of all shields, and now

called 'France Ancient'. From 1340 Edward III of England claimed the throne of France, and quartered England and France Ancient. Later he placed France in the first and fourth quarters and England in the second and third, giving France precedence as the 'senior' kingdom. In or about 1394 the king of France changed his arms to 'France Modern' — *Azure three Fleurs-de-lis Or*. This practice was followed by Henry IV of England in *c.* 1405. The arms of France remained part of the royal arms of the United Kingdom until after the fall of the French monarchy, and were finally removed in 1801.   KH

Freemen of the City of London, Guild of The arms of the Guild are *Argent on a Cross Gules enfiling in chief and base two Mural Crowns Or a Rose of the last slipped and leaved proper. Crest: A Mural Crown Or therefrom a Dove wings expanded proper* (granted 1912).
See also LIVERY COMPANY, MEMBERSHIP OF

Freiherr A German baron. A baroness was a 'freiherrin'.

Fret An armorial charge consisting of a mascle interlaced by a bendlet and a bendlet sinister. Unless more than one fret is borne (in which case the ends of the bendlets are couped at right-angles) the fret is depicted throughout.

Fretted Interlaced.

Fretty In effect, a field semy of frets conjoined to form a trellis pattern of interlaced bendlets and bendlets sinister. A similar pattern of pallets and bars (i.e. vertical and horizontal pieces) is *square* fretty. However, such a classification may be misleading, for many medieval fretty fields were depicted with just three pieces in each direction — in other words, a fret throughout. It is normally assumed that there are six pieces in each direction unless otherwise specified, as in the arms of Cave: *Azure Fretty of eight Argent four pieces one way and four the other*. The qualification 'four pieces one way, etc.' seems somehow superfluous.

Fringe An ornamental edging to a flag. Ceremonial banners are usually fringed with the armorial colours, as are gonfannons when used for armorial purposes. Standards and guidons are fringed with the livery or armorial colours, though modern practice seems to be entirely arbitrary. For outdoor use the fringe is usually of bunting, whereas the indoor or ceremonial flag is braided.

Fringed *see* **Attributes**

Fructed *see* **Attributes**

Fumant *see* **Attributes**

Funeral Certificate *see* **Funeral Heraldry**

Funeral Heraldry During the late Middle Ages, funerals of royalty and the nobility were magnificent occasions, not least the processions which preceded the committal in which the deceased's armorial accoutrements accompanied the cortège. These included the noble's spurs, gauntlets, helm and crest, shield (known in this context as a targe), sword, tabard, pennons and banner. At state funerals they were carried by heralds and kings of arms, just as the shield of arms was carried by Somerset Herald at the state funeral of Sir Winston Churchill KG in 1965. (On this occasion, the officers of arms wore black crepe sashes over their tabards.) After the service, the symbols of chivalry would be laid up in the church. Regrettably very few early examples remain, the best known being the helm, scabbard (without the sword), gauntlets, wooden shield covered with leather, and surcoat embroidered with the arms of France Ancient and England of Edward the Black Prince (d. 1376) at Canterbury Cathedral. These are kept near his tomb, those which hang above it being replicas. Several examples from the sixteenth century remain, and from these may be traced the gradual evolution of funeral heraldry from the practical accoutrements of war to the stylized helms, crests and tabards of the late Tudor period and the armorial substitute, the funeral HATCHMENT, of the seventeenth and eighteenth centuries. At St Mary Redcliffe, Bristol, the monument of Admiral Sir William Penn (d. 1620), father of the founder of Pennsylvania, is surmounted and flanked by his breastplate, helmet and crest, gauntlet, spurs, shield, banner and pennons. There are stylized funeral helms at St Michael's Church, Aldershot, Hampshire, complete with crests, for Sir John White (d. 1573) and for his son Richard (d. 1599), and a

Funeral helms with the *Griffin's Head erased Vert beaked Gules* crests of the ancient Fettiplace family at Swinbrook, Oxfordshire.

funeral tabard may be seen at Stoke d'Abernon, Surrey. Few funeral banners remain, though there are many examples of banners of the various orders of knighthood, released from the custody of the kings of arms of the orders, and hung in the parish churches of former knights. There are good examples at Minterne Magna, Dorset, High Wycombe, Buckinghamshire, Salisbury Cathedral, Tewkesbury Abbey and Aldermaston, Berkshire, though this last (the banner of Sir George Forrester) may not be contemporary with his death.

In the sixteenth and seventeenth centuries, the heralds were required to attend funerals of the nobility and gentry and the records of these events are contained in eighteen volumes in the archives of the College of Arms. These funeral certificates contain much interesting and useful information, for not only do they record the exact date and place of death of the deceased person, but they also give details of his or her descendants. Coats of arms are painted in the margin.

The funeral certificate of Sir John Sedley, Baronet, who died on 13 August 1638, records that he was attended by two officers of arms accompanied by divers baronets, knights, esquires and gentlemen of the county at his funeral in the parish church of Southfleet in Kent. The certificate was taken by William Ryley, Bluemantle, and was authenticated by Dame Elizabeth Sedley, the relict of the deceased.

Today the erection of heraldic memorials is subject both to the approval of Garter King of Arms and to the grant of a faculty from the diocesan authorities. The funeral of an officer of arms is not without its armorial accompaniment, for the custom is for his coffin to be draped with his tabard embroidered with the royal arms.   JET/SA

Furnished *see* Attributes

Furniture Hall chairs can be irresistibly attractive to collectors, or just admirers, of armorial furniture. These eighteenth and nineteenth-century seats were made for the halls and corridors of substantial houses, there to provide temporary and not too comfortable relief for visitors awaiting reception, and for footmen. Perhaps unique amongst armorial furniture, they could have been speculatively made, to stand in the cabinet-maker's workshop until a customer bought them and had his armorial devices painted in the panel provided for that purpose. The panel was often recessed and the painting will have suffered less wear than the chair, itself not sufficiently inviting to attract heavy usage.

Devices emblazoned on such chairs vary from a simple crest to a full achievement of arms complete with mantling, coronet and supporters. Whatever form it takes the heraldic decoration invites investigation. This can often be rewarded with a full revelation of the origin and provenance of the chairs. There were, of course, hall chairs commissioned from a maker who would design them round the patron's crest, which could be inlaid in coloured veneers or carved from the solid backplate. Chairs of such quality are more sought after than those above described, and are unlikely to be found 'going for a song'.

These chairs are a pointer to the general rule that such armorial furniture as exists was almost all commissioned, and therefore likely to be of firmer quality and greater artistic significance than items produced for the showroom. A minor exception is provided by the pieces produced in some quantity around the turn of the nineteenth century by cabinet makers who obligingly incorporated the occasional cartouche which the purchaser could complete if he was so minded.

The Victoria and Albert Museum in London displays a 1730 side-table of carved and gilded pine by Flitcroft. Its *scaglio* top is inlaid with an oval panel bearing the arms of George Lee, second Earl of Lichfield, impaling those of his wife Frances, daughter of Sir John Hales. The same museum houses a gilded table attributed to James Moore, the royal cabinet maker. Carving is used on the apron of this table to show the crest and coronet of Richard Temple, Baron Cobham of Cobham, Kent, signifying that the table was commissioned after 1714, when Temple was raised to the peerage, but before 1718, when he was created a viscount.

A silver panel inlaid into the wood's surface was sometimes engraved with the owner's arms, but perhaps the last word in armorial furniture must be given to furniture made, so far as was mechanically possible, in solid silver for the Crown and the nobility. Although little was made after the accession of Queen

Anne in 1702, a silver table was made between 1709 and 1718 for Edward Harley, second Earl of Oxford. Its top was engraved with his arms and showed 72 quarterings. A silver table was presented to William III by the City of London, with only the minimum of wood and iron being used in its construction. The top is magnificently engraved with the royal arms by an artist signing his work with the letters RH. It may be seen at Windsor Castle.   JA

Furs The two principal furs used in armory are ermine and vair.

Ermine consists of black ermine tails on a white field (the 'tails' may be depicted in a variety of forms according to artistic taste, and the field is white *not* silver). Of the variants, the most common are:

Ermines — white tails on black
Erminois — black tails on gold
Pean — gold tails on black

Ermine spots, in a variety of colours, are to be found as charges, either singly or as semy fields when the conventional variations of ermine are not appropriate, e.g. *Gules semy of Ermine Spots Or.*

Vair originates from the fur of a species of squirrel

Edward I wearing a cloak lined with minever.

(*varus*) which was popular in the Middle Ages as a lining for the garments of those not entitled to wear ermine. The animal was blue-grey on the back and white underneath. By sewing a number of these pelts together, with white and blue-grey alternating, an attractive design was obtained, one which easily translated into the stylized armorial form of Vair and its variants. (No doubt Cinderella's slippers were made of this fur, the word *verre*, glass, being erroneously translated from the French in place of *vairé*.) The most common variants are:

Counter vair (Contre vair)
Vair in pāle
Vair en point
Potent (so called because the pieces are T-shaped like crutch-heads: *potent* = OE crutch)
Counter-potent

Furs in the vair group are depicted with alternating white (*not* silver) and blue pieces, unless other tinctures are specified, e.g. *vairy Or and Vert* and *potenty Argent and Gules*. In such circumstances there appears to be no convention which would preclude the use of two metals or two colours, but a combination of metal and colour is usually chosen — a fur sometimes taking the place of one or other, e.g. *Vairy Gules and Ermine* (Gresley). It is also feasible that vair variations of three or more tinctures could be devised, known in Germany as *Buntfeh*. In British armory, furs of the vair group are usually depicted in five rows, though this is a recent convention and numerous examples may be found to contradict it. In European armory, vair is of three specific sizes: gros-vair (the largest, used when fewer than four rows are depicted), vair ('normal' size) and menu-vair (the smallest size), from which the term minever derives.

Not strictly furs but here classified as such are plumeté (also plumetty and plummete), and papelloné (also papillone). A field of the former comprises overlapping feathers, and the latter scales, apparently derived from a butterfly's wings, e.g. *Sable papillone Argent three Hazlenuts Or* (Holborn Law Tutors, London).

Furs are not confined by the tincture convention, though it is most unlikely that the kings of arms would allow, for example, a sable charge on a field of pean!

Fusil A somewhat spurious armorial charge consisting of an elongated lozenge. It may be that the fusil is nothing more than a segment of an indented ordinary, and as such should not be depicted singly but conjoined in fess, in bend, etc. If this is so, the term 'conjoined' is tautologous. *Fusilly* is descriptive of a varied field similar to *lozengy* but with elongated divisions.

A possible clue to the origin of the fusil may be found in the arms of Trefusis of Cornwall, which are clearly allusive: *Argent a Chevron between three Spindles Sable*. Perhaps the fusil is no more than a stylized spindle?

Fusilly *see* **Fusil** *and* **Field, Varied**

Fylfot A swastika (*see* CROSS).

G

Gad A steel billet.

Gamb *or* **Jamb** The lower part of a beast's leg cut off at the second joint.

Garb A wheatsheaf, unless the blazon specifies another type of grain. A garb is always banded, but this is not blazoned unless of a different tincture from the garb.

Garland *or* **Chaplet** A circular wreath of leaves depicted in conventional form. A chaplet also has four flowers in cross, and these are usually the armorial rose unless otherwise blazoned.

Garnished *see* **Attributes**

Garter, Principal King of Arms Garter is the *ex officio* principal of the corporation of officers of arms in England, and king of arms to the Order of the Garter. The office was created by Henry V in 1415, before which date there had not been a permanent *roy d'armes d'Angleterre*, the position being filled either by royal favour or seniority. It was also the first occasion on which a king of arms had been appointed to serve

**Arms of Garter
Principal King of Arms**

Furs

Ermine

Ermines

Pean

Erminois

Vair

Counter-vair

Vair in pale

Potent

Counter-potent

Vair en point

Potent en point

Plumeté

Papelloné

159

an order of chivalry. The arms of office are *Argent a Cross Gules on a Chief Azure a Crown enclosed in a Garter between a Lion passant guardant and a Fleur-de-lis all Or.* These have been in use since *c.* 1520, though for a short period Henry VII substituted a Tudor Rose for the crown within the Garter, and from 1536-84 and 1586-1606 a dove azure, with one wing open, was depicted in the dexter canton.

Garter, The Most Noble Order of the (Abbr. KG)
The premier British order of chivalry.

Even today there exists some doubt as to precisely when the Order of the Garter was created, for the original records, up to the year 1416, are lost. The fourteenth-century chronicler Jean Froissart asserted that the foundation was in 1344, but he is almost certainly wrong, for it is not likely that the Order would have been established prior to 1346, when the Black Prince and some of his founder-contemporaries were knighted. The treasury accounts for the Prince for November 1348 bear witness to his gift of '24 garters to the knights of the Society of the Garter', and a document published in 1905 for the Central Chancery of the Orders of Knighthood at St James's Palace inclines to the later date.

Several historians are of the view that at first the 'order' was quite casually formed, perhaps at a tournament — 24 knights in two bands of twelve, one under the king, the other under the prince, and only later did it become a permanent institution.

In 1348 the Black Prince was just eighteen years old, and several other founders not much more — the Earls of March and Salisbury were about twenty, Courtney and Burghersh were around twenty-two, and the king himself no more than thirty-seven. Thus, to begin with, the Order of the Garter, perhaps formally instituted on St George's Day 1348, was a brotherhood of young men, a fellowship, in which all were equal 'to represent how they ought to be united in all Chances and various Turns of Fortune, co-partners in both Peace and War, assistant to one another in all serious and dangerous Exploits and through the whole Course of their Lives to show Fidelity and Friendliness towards one another.'

The symbol of the blue garter seems to have been suggested by an incident at a ball at Calais in the autumn of 1347, when the young Countess of Salisbury, Joan of Kent (later to be Princess of Wales), dropped her garter, which the king picked up and tied round her knee with the now famous words, *Honi soit qui mal y pense,* 'Shame on him who thinks evil of it', and the promise that the garter would become highly honoured. And so it was. The informal creation of the Round Table after the great tournament at Windsor in 1344 was translated, in 1348, into the Order of the Garter — 24 young men plus the king and his eldest son — founder knights 'foreshadowing a distinguished

line of noble successors throughout the history of English chivalry.' No change in the numbers was made until 1786, when the sons of George III and his successors were made eligible even though the Chapter might be complete. A further change was introduced in 1805, when the lineal descendants of George II were also deemed to be eligible. In 1831 it was decided that all direct descendants of George I should be accorded the same privilege.

From earliest times, certainly from the late fourteenth century, ladies were received into the Order as 'honorary' members with the title of 'Dames de la Fraternité de Saint George', but this died out under Henry VIII who was, apparently, 'altogether un-genial' to the presence of ladies on such occasions. Queens of England were of course members as Head of the Order, and they wore the Garter on the left arm. However, it was not until the reign of Edward VII that the King's Consort was automatically a 'Lady of the Garter'. Foreign royalty have been appointed as members: 'Stranger Knights and Ladies of the Garter', and they are additional to the twenty-six companion knights. Membership was often used for diplomatic purposes, though today membership of both the Garter and the Thistle is in the personal gift of the sovereign.   JC-K

Insignia
The arms of the Most Noble Order of the Garter were in use from an early date and consist of the *Argent a Cross Gules* shield of St George within the Garter. The knights were ordered to wear a garter at all times on the left leg below the knee, and a dark blue mantle charged with the arms. The Garter was originally light blue, but has been dark blue since the beginning of George I's reign. It is edged, buckled and adorned in gold and bears the motto in gold. Henry VII added the magnificent collar consisting of twenty-six Garters each encircling a red enamelled rose, alternating with interlaced knots. The original roses may have been of the Tudor type: 'The collar shall be made . . . in fashion of Garters, in the midst of which Garters shall be a double rose, the one Rose red, and the other within white, and the other Rose white, and the other Rose within red. And at the end of the said collar shall be put and fastened The Image of Saint George.' This shows the saint mounted and killing the dragon. It is also enamelled and is known as 'The George'. Charles II introduced the broad blue riband worn over the left shoulder with a small device in plain gold, 'The Lesser George', as a clasp on the right hip. For ceremonial purposes, Knights Companion wear a dark blue velvet mantle, lined with white taffeta and with the Star of the Order on the left breast. This is an eight-pointed silver star with, at the centre, the St George's Cross encircled with the Garter. The mantle is worn with a hood of crimson velvet, lined with white taffeta.

The Tudor Garter Collar in a portrait (at Knowsley, Lancashire), reputed to be that of Thomas Stanley, Earl of Derby (d. 1504), though certainly not contemporary and probably based on the famous portrait of William Cecil, Lord Burghley (d. 1598).

The hat is of black velvet and has an ostrich feather plume and tuft of black heron's feathers affixed with a band studded with diamonds.

The Officers of the Order each possess insignia of office:

The Prelate wears a blue mantle with the shield of St George within a Garter on the right shoulder. His badge of office comprises the George and Dragon device encompassed by the Garter and ensigned by a mitre. The office is vested in the Bishop of Winchester.

The Chancellor wears a crimson mantle with the arms of the Order on the right shoulder. He carries a purse bearing the arms of the sovereign and wears a badge of office consisting of a red rose within the Garter.

The Registrar wears a crimson robe with the shield of St George on the left shoulder. His badge is a closed book charged with two quill pens saltirewise within the Garter.

Garter Principal King of Arms wears a crimson mantle bearing the shield of St George on the left shoulder. His badge of office is the shield of St George impaling the arms of the sovereign, all within a Garter. He carries a sceptre of office which has four facets, two of which show the shield of St George impaling the sovereign's arms, the other two the arms of the Order. It is ensigned by the Royal Crown.

Gentleman Usher of the Black Rod wears a crimson mantle with the shield of St George on the left shoulder. His badge of office consists of a double knot encircled by the Garter. The black rod is crowned by the Royal Lion bearing a shield of St George.

The Secretary wears a crimson mantle. His badge of office is a rose upon two quill pens saltirewise within the Garter.

Garter insignia may be seen at the Tower of London and the British Museum, where there are fine examples of early insignia.

When a new knight is invested, the sovereign presides over the Chapter of the Order in the Throne Room at Windsor Castle. This usually takes place on the nearest convenient Monday to St George's Day, 23 April. Knights Elect are presented to the sovereign by Black Rod, Garter King of Arms and two supporting knights. The sovereign personally secures the Garter, places the Riband and Lesser George over the left shoulder, affixes the Star and invests the knight with the Mantle and Collar. At the same time the Admonition is read. This takes the same form as in the time of the Tudors, and possibly earlier. The Admonition upon Putting on the Mantle, for example, is:

> Receive this Robe of heavenly colour, the Livery of this Most Excellent Order in Augmentation of thine Honour, ennobled with the shield and red Cross of our Lord, by whose power thou mayest safely pierce troops of thine enemies, and be over them ever victorious, and being in this temporal warfare glorious, in egregious and heroic actions, thou mayest obtain eternal and triumphant joy.

Instead of the three-day festivities of earlier times there is now luncheon in the Waterloo Chamber for knights and their wives and officers of the Order, after which is the procession (abandoned in 1805 but revived by George VI in 1948) to St George's Chapel. This is led by the Constable and Governor of Windsor Castle, followed by the Military Knights of Windsor and the officers of arms in full uniform of tabards and Tudor bonnets. They are followed by the Garter knights and officers of the Order, the sovereign and other members of the royal family following in procession with the Yeomen of the Guard at the rear. In the Chapel, each knight takes his place in his own stall, having been greeted on the steps of the Chapel by the clergy of the College of St George.

The occasion has not always been popular: in 1663 Daniel O'Neill recorded that the celebrations had been very disappointing, with a 'slender appearance of knights of the order, and other lords, and indeed all sorts of people.' O'Neill thought that this was probably due to King Charles II being attended both by his queen and his mistress, Lady Castlemaine, such behaviour rendering the king 'odious to His people'.

The public is not admitted to the investiture or to the service, but those who have obtained tickets may stand and watch the procession to St George's Chapel in the afternoon.   SS

Banners, Crests and Stall Plates (current procedure)

The 1522 Statutes of the Order of the Garter require every Knight Companion to display his banner, sword, helm and crest above his stall in St George's Chapel, Windsor. The banners and crests are of course made individually for each new knight, and they make a fine display. They remain above his stall during his lifetime and are taken down at his death. Modern banners are 5 feet square and thus an ideal shape for displaying the arms without distortion. They are made of heavy quality silk, on which the design is painted in oil colours with real gold in appropriate places, but owing to rising costs it may soon be necessary to try modern materials. A sleeve of a hard-wearing fabric such as nylon is attached to the side nearest the staff, and the other three sides are finished with a two-inch tasselled fringe of the colours.

The crests are carved from limewood or pear, but a stronger-grained wood such as pine is used for sections which are liable to break off, such as sword blades, tails and feathers and, like the banners, they are painted and gilded. They are placed above metal helmets and wooden swords which are stock items, and mantlings are added in appropriate colours.

The cost of preparing the banners, crests and stall plates is borne by the Order and not by the knight himself, and thus they become the property of Her Majesty the Queen. When the knight dies his crest and banner are taken down and by custom go to Garter as his perquisite, though often he presents the banner to the family if they have somewhere suitable to hang it. It has become traditional for the banner of a recently deceased knight to be offered up to God at the altar during evensong.

Unlike the crests and banners the stall plate remains in place after the knight's death, and these plates, now numbering over 700, constitute one of the finest collections of heraldic art in the world. Originally the plate was put up as a memorial after the knight's death, but since the sixteenth century the practice has been to erect it as soon as possible after his appointment. The plate is made of copper and usually measures about 6 inches high by 4 inches wide (15 x 10 cm), thus taking up less space than some of the huge eighteenth and nineteenth-century examples. Supporters are omitted and the brief inscription is traditionally in French (e.g. Hugues Denis Charles, Duc de Grafton, MCMLXXVI). Once the pencil design has been approved by Garter it is redrawn in black and white and etched with acid into the copper plate. The cavities are then filled with coloured enamel and the untreated copper surface receives a plating of hard gold in an electrolytic bath. After a final coat of lacquer the plate is ready to take its place in the stalls of St George's Chapel.   DHBC

Further reading

Ashmole, E. *History of the Order of the Garter* 1715.

Begent, P. *A Noble Place Indeed* Windsor, 1984.

Beltz, G.F. *Memorials of the Garter* 1841.

Fellowes, E.H. *The Knights of the Garter 1348-1939* London, 1963

Paget, J. *The Pageantry of Britain* London, 1979.

Pole, J. *History and Antiquities of Windsor Castle* 1749.

St John Hope, W. *The Stall Plates of the Knights of the Order of the Garter* 1901.

— *Windsor Castle* 1913.

Shaw, W.A. *Knights of England* 1905.

Garter Tower The official lodging of Garter King of Arms at Windsor Castle.

Gatehouse *see* **Lodge Gates**

Gates *see* **Lodge Gates** *and* **Metalwork**

Gemmed *see* **Attributes**

Genealogical Office, Dublin *see* **Ulster Office and the Genealogical Office**

Genealogies, Scottish Register of Located in Lyon Office this contains a number of pedigrees and birth-brieves from 1727 to 1796, and others from 1827 to the present day.   CJB

Genealogy and Armory The ancestry researcher at some point in his work is likely to encounter a branch of his family which bore arms. He will find that progress to earlier generations in Britain becomes a matter for library rather than record office searches, for such families will undoubtedly have been documented.

In the nineteenth century much help can be obtained from Burke's *Peerage* and *Landed Gentry*. These volumes were first published in 1826 and 1833-

35 respectively, and have appeared at intervals ever since. The *Landed Gentry* especially has undergone considerable change over the years, as families have been left out as their fortunes have declined and new families included. To assist the search, for it is unusual to find all editions under one roof, Burke's Peerage Ltd has published (1976) a small volume called Burke's *Family Index*. This is a comprehensive listing of all the families which have appeared in Burke's publications 1826-1976.

An older publication dating from 1713 is Debrett's *Peerage and Baronetage* (later to include the *Knightage and Companionage*). This has also appeared at frequent intervals to the present day, and gives information about living title holders and their relatives, and is useful for collateral branches. A very reliable account of the peerage and baronetage is contained in *The Complete Peerage* edited by G.E. Cokayne, in thirteen volumes, 1887-1940 (with addenda to the present day held at the House of Lords Record Office), and *The Complete Baronetage 1611-1800* by the same author, first published in six volumes from 1900.

Walford's *County Families*, published at intervals 1860-1920 should be consulted, for this gives details of individuals who were regarded as belonging to county families, some of whom may not be found in Debrett or Burke. Mention should also be made of the *Index to Pedigrees of English Families* by Charles Bridger, London, 1867 (reprinted by the Genealogical Publishing Company, Baltimore, 1969). This is a location guide to printed pedigrees of families of note. Covering similar ground is *A Genealogical Guide* by J.B. Whitmore, 1953, a continuation of Marshall's *Genealogist's Guide*, 1903.

In the late eighteenth and nineteenth centuries there appeared a considerable number of county histories which very often included details and pedigrees of important families. Examples of these are *The History and Antiquities of the County of Dorset* by Revd J. Hutchins, 1774, *The History and Antiquities of the County of Somerset* by Revd J. Collinson, 1791, E. Hasted's *History of Kent* 1797-1801, and J.E. Cussan's *History of Hertfordshire* 1880, amongst many others; quite a number of which have recently been reprinted and sometimes augmented, as in the cases of Hutchins and Collinson. Most of these county histories give details of the heraldry associated with those families important enough to be mentioned. A later, important county source is the series of some 150 volumes of the *Victoria History of the Counties of England*, launched in 1899 and with many volumes still to be produced. Although very wide in scope, this series gives some details, often over several generations, of families who had manorial status.

The volumes comprising the *Dictionary of National Biography*, in one alphabetical series from the earliest times to 1900, and with supplements issued thereafter, give excellent biographical details of individuals, with source references. Some periodicals which recorded genealogical details, almost amounting to social gossip, include the *Gentleman's Magazine* (1731-1907), *Notes and Queries, London Magazine, Monthly Magazine, Scots Magazine* and *Annual Register. Who's Who* and *Who was Who* may also be of use.

Details of the pedigrees of armigerous ancestors of the sixteenth and seventeenth centuries should be available from the manuscripts known as the heraldic visitations, many of which have been published. These are the records of official surveys made on a county basis by the heralds whose task it was to see that arms were being both legally and correctly used. The printed versions often contain additions to the originals, and not infrequently continue the pedigrees into the nineteenth century. The Harleian Society and other county record societies who have printed many of the visitations, have made available a wealth of material which otherwise would be relatively inaccessible and difficult to find. Other volumes in their lists may well provide additional source material.

Some words of warning will not be out of place, addressed to those tracing family histories by means of heraldry and heraldic artefacts. The last heraldic visitations were in the 1680s, so there have been three hundred years to the present day during which less rigorous control over the use of arms was possible. As a consequence it is certain that there are very many families who have used or have assumed arms to which, strictly, they are not entitled. This can create difficulties for the genealogist who is not aware of the possibility. In tracing the descent of families it is essential to work back from those ancestors personally known to those living at the present time, by using the recognized linking and location records. When sufficient information has been gathered the pedigree thus far compiled can be set against pedigrees found in the various sources of heraldic genealogy. If these match then the short cut can be taken. To assume that the present-day family is descended from that to whom the arms were originally granted or confirmed may well result in much wasted time and possibly money.

Similar remarks apply to the use of heraldic objects which may be thought to point towards ancestral origins, by being in the home, perhaps by inheritance from previous generations. Great-grandfather may indeed have received the heraldic signet ring from his forebears, but he could, equally, have bought it in a second-hand jewellery shop. A common source of confusion is provided by the heraldic painting or carving which may occupy pride of place in the hall or sitting room. Often the family surname is included below, or in place of, the motto. The item may indeed show the arms which belong to you or to an ancestor, but equally may have been purchased from a firm which supplied paintings of arms to go with a surname without implying any genealogical relationship. Such firms are in business today and were known even in the seventeenth century. No heraldic claim was ever intended, and the article was simply for decoration. The problems arise when the source of the item has been forgotten and the assumption made that the arms displayed *belong* to that family of the same name.

There are many books available dealing with the practical aspects of tracing ancestors. Especially to be recommended is the companion volume to this, the *Dictionary of Genealogy* by Terrick V.H. FitzHugh, Sherborne, 1985. This volume, both concise and readable, covers almost everything that the family historian is likely to come across or want to know about. Another indispensable aid is the *Atlas and Index of Parish Registers* Ed. Cecil Humphery-Smith, Chichester, 1985, which contains both parish and topographical maps of each county and a wealth of tabulated data on deposited and copied parish registers, marriage indexes and International Genealogical Index coverage, etc. Bibliographies of genealogy which can be recommended include *Guide to Printed Books and MSS Relating to English and Foreign Heraldry and Genealogy* by George Gatfield, 1892, *A Genealogist's Bibliography* by Cecil Humphery-Smith, Chichester, 1976, the first up-to-date replacement for Harrison's *Select Bibliography of English Genealogy* 1837, *A New Bibliography of British Genealogy* by M.J. Kaminkow 1965, and *Books for the Family Historian* by I.S. Swinnerton and P.A. Saul, Federation of Family History Societies, 1980. Two series of booklets published by the same Society will be found to be very useful: the first, by Eve McLaughlin, covers a number of topics of practical genealogy, such as *St Catherine's House Wills before 1858, Somerset House Wills from 1858, Illegitimacy, The Censuses 1841-1881*, etc. The other, by J.S.W. Gibson, comprises *Guides for Genealogists, Family and Local Historians*. These are location guides to wills, census returns, record offices, the International Genealogical Index, and other types of document.   DJ

Further reading
Begley, D.F. *Irish Genealogy* London, 1981.
Cox, J. and T. Padfield *Tracing your Ancestors in the Public Record Office* Public Record Office.
Currer-Briggs, N. et al *Huguenot Ancestry* London, 1985.
Gibson, J.S.W. and P. Peskett *Record Offices, How to Find Them* Federation of Family History Societies.
Hamilton-Edwards, G. *In Search of Ancestry* Chichester, 1983.
— *In Search of Scottish Ancestry* London, 1984.

— *In Search of Welsh Ancestry* London, 1986.
Moncreiffe, Iain of that Ilk *Debrett's Family Historian* London 1981.
Rogers, C.D. *The Family Tree Detective* Manchester, 1983.
Wagner, A. *Pedigree and Progress* London, 1975.
— *English Genealogy* London, 1983.
Willis, A.J. and M. Tatchell *Genealogy for Beginners* London, 1984.

Geneva Bonnet A flat black hat of the type associated with the reformer John Knox and granted in 1960 as part of the armorial ensigns used by the Moderator of the General Assembly of the Church of Scotland during his tenure of office.   CJB

Gentleman In the Middle Ages the word 'gentil' meant 'noble', and it has been argued that all armigers are, by their letters patent, deemed to be gentlemen and therefore junior members of the nobility. A statute of Henry V required that in certain legal documents the 'estate, degree or mystery' of a defendant must be stated, and the style 'gentleman' came into use to signify a condition between knight and yeoman. The term *les gentiles* was used in an act of parliament in 1429 to describe men holding freehold property of forty shillings a year or more. From the sixteenth century the term seems to have been applied to those who were not required to labour and who therefore employed servants. The son of a gentleman who laboured on his father's behalf pending inheritance was styled YEOMAN. In the early Middle Ages the designation yeoman implied knightly services as a retainer. In both instances a yeoman *may* have been armigerous, but by inheritance not by grant. Members of professions, military and naval officers, barristers, etc., were considered to be gentlemen, some of them being entitled to the designation ESQUIRE. Modern usage equates 'gentleman' with 'armiger' (a gentleman of coat armour), though John Brooke-Little (*An Heraldic Alphabet*) suggests that the term may apply also to anyone who is considered eligible for a grant of arms.

Gentleman Usher The principal orders of chivalry each have a gentleman usher who carries a rod of office and whose formal duty is to act as doorkeeper at meetings of an order's Chapter. The gentlemen ushers are named after the colour of the rods they carry:

Garter: Black Rod
Thistle: Green Rod
Bath: Scarlet Rod
St Michael & St George: Blue Rod
British Empire: Purple Rod

Gentlemen at Arms More properly Her Majesty's Body Guard of the Honourable Corps of Gentlemen at Arms and the senior of the three royal bodyguards. The other two are the YEOMEN OF THE GUARD and the ROYAL COMPANY OF ARCHERS.

The Corps of the Gentlemen at Arms was founded by King Henry VIII in 1509, and until 1834 was known as the Band of Gentlemen Pensioners (after the style of the French royal *pensionnaires*). They were required to provide a mounted and armed escort for the sovereign and to protect him at all times. This active role continued for centuries — the last occasion being the defence of St James's Palace in 1848 from possible attack by Chartist rioters. Today the duties are ceremonial — attendance on the monarch on numerous state occasions including the Garter service. The Corps consists of five officers and twenty-seven gentlemen. The senior officer, the Captain, is a peer and is now always the Government Chief Whip in the House of Lords.

The uniform of the Gentlemen at Arms is today very similar to that of an officer in the Dragoon Guards of the reign of William IV. This is a skirted red coat with Garter-blue velvet cuffs and facings, adorned with the portcullis badge of the Tudors. The uniform includes a gold pouch-belt and ornate gold epaulettes, the helmet carrying a plume of white feathers. Ceremonial swords are worn and the Gentlemen carry long ceremonial battleaxes. The officers wear gold aiguilettes and carry sticks of office — gold for the Captain, ivory for the Harbinger, and silver for the others. The standard of the Corps bears a cross of St George, the royal cypher and a portcullis with a Tudor crown. Two battle honours are displayed — the battle of the Spurs (Guinegatte) 1513, and Boulogne, 1544. Also embroidered on the standard are the words 'Gentlemen at Arms'.   JC-K

Further reading
Kearsley, H. *Her Majesty's Body Guard of the Honourable Corps of Gentlemen-of-Arms* 1937.
Legge-Bourke, H. *The King's Guards* 1952.

Gentlemen Ushers to the Sovereign The posts of Gentlemen Ushers date from the reign of King Edward IV (1461-83). There are at present ten Gentlemen Ushers and eighteen 'extra Gentlemen' who hold the title, as well as the Gentlemen Ushers of the Sword of State, and the Black Rod. All are members of the ROYAL HOUSEHOLD in the department of the LORD CHAMBERLAIN. Their duties are to attend the guests at important royal functions and to marshal royal processions. As required, these gentlemen, who are almost always distinguished former officers of the armed forces, wear the Household Coat — a tail coat of royal blue.   JC-K

George, The (i) The device of the Most Noble Order of the Garter, depicting St George slaying the dragon, when attached to the collar of the Order. That which is pendent from a blue riband worn over the shoulder is the Lesser George.

(ii) The English national ensign *Argent a Cross Gules* (colloquial).

Gerattie The distribution of small charges on a field or on a larger charge in such a way that the attributes of the principal charge are not obscured and the smaller charges not defaced.

This ancient term is worthy of a revival. Gerattie is a useful alternative to semy, for the distribution of gerattie charges is determined by the outline and the features of the charge on which they are placed and, unless the alternative term *sans nombre* is used, the number of charges may be specified; eg. *Gules, a Lion rampant Or gerattie of ten Fleurs-de-lis Azure.*

Gerattyng is the ancient practice of powdering shields with small charges to indicate differencing.

Germany, Armorial Practice The partitioning of Germany into East and West following the Second World War was but the latest in a series of upheavals dating from well before the reign of Charlemagne. In the tenth century Germany was united with Italy and, in the eleventh, with Burgundy. In the twelfth, and for many centuries afterwards, the Emperor was an elected figurehead, the rulers of the Marches, Principalities, Duchies, Counties and Landgravates being privileged and powerful.

With influences of this diversity, plus those of the Holy Roman Empire itself, the Papacy and the Teutonic Order, it follows that heraldry played important practical and ceremonial parts in national life. German armory became rich in the depiction of simple, positive charges — armed men, animals, and birds of prey. Elaborate crests were adopted (often several in one family to differentiate between cadet lines), the use of quartered arms was popular, as were symbols of station. The display of barred helms was, from the sixteenth century, reserved for the nobility, and the coronet of rank was introduced in the seventeenth. The implicit importance of SEIZE QUARTIERS was an important feature of German heraldic doctrine. Despite this rich tradition, the offices of the heralds themselves were extinguished in the eighteenth century. Today in the Federal Republic of Germany civic arms are generally regulated by departments of each federal state. Family arms are not so controlled, though they enjoy some protection under Section 12 of the Federal Law. There are several thriving heraldic societies (*see* ADDRESSES). The arms of the Republic comprise the single charge of an eagle displayed (which had its beginning in the symbols of the Holy Roman Empire) and are a modern rendering of the ancient Imperial arms, from the *Codex Manesse, c.* 1300.   JC-K

Germany, Imperial Arms of *An Imperial Eagle displayed Sable ensigned with the German Imperial Crown armed and beaked Gules* charged on the breast with a shield *Argent an Eagle displayed Sable armed beaked and crowned Or holding in the dexter claw a Sceptre Or and in the sinister an Orb Azure banded and with a Cross Or* (Prussia) over all an escutcheon *Quarterly Argent and Sable* (Hohenzollern).

Germany, Military Insignia of the Federal Republic
Within the recent past, units of the Federal German armed forces have adopted insignia in metal and enamel suspended from the pocket button in the French manner (termed in German *Interne Verbandsabzeichen*).   Heraldic authority failed to survive the fall of the German monarchies and principalities and consequently armorial practices and conventions are not always evident in military insignia. The Federal German Ministry of Defence has attempted to remedy this deficiency by issuing various instructions regarding the design and application of insignia, and has commissioned heraldic experts to publish guidelines in official military journals. Most insignia take the form of a metal and enamel shield charged with an emblem indicating branch and function, together with armorial charges taken from the arms of the unit location, one such example being the badge of the Army Topography Battery 600 (see drawing). The branch emblem appears in the base of the badge, whilst the other charges comprise the arms of Schleswig Holstein where the unit is based. Insignia also often include the divisional brigade badge which is worn in cloth on the tunic shoulder. These badges are armorial in nature, bearing devices from regional arms.   Insignia below army corps level are not supposed to include the eagle emblem of the Federal Republic. Should a national emblem be required by a unit for its insignia, the black Iron Cross may be used. This has its origins in the arms of the Teutonic Knights.   SS

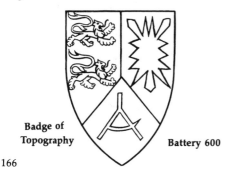

Badge of
Topography   Battery 600

Gifts of Superiors Armorial devices such as chapeaux, collars and badges given by members of royal and noble families to household officers, retainers, etc., in recognition of singular loyalty and service.

Gimmel Ring *see* **Annulet**

Glass Stained glass was used in church windows as early as the seventh century, but the earliest surviving examples date from the eleventh century in Europe and the twelfth century in England. Although the Romans produced slabs of coloured glass, the idea of holding pieces together with lead strips to form a patterned window may have come from the Byzantine Empire.

Glass windows produced prior to the sixteenth century were made by heating wood-ash and river sand together to form glass, which was then either spun on the end of a rod into a circular sheet, or blown into a long cylinder and cut longitudinally to produce a flat sheet. The former method was common in France, the latter was the more usual English practice. This glass, although not coloured, would have some tint which was the result of impurities in the raw materials.

The coloured glasses which were called pot-metals were made by adding different metallic oxides to the molten clear glass, e.g. cobalt for blue, copper for red, manganese for violet and silver salts for yellow. The colour produced also depended on the way the furnace was fired, and different results were achieved by varying the level of oxidation. The glass was thus coloured throughout. The red and blue glasses were very dark, and to make these colours more transparent the technique of flashing was developed, a thin layer of coloured glass being combined with a sheet of white glass.

The design (cartoon) of the window was drawn on a board or table and the pieces of coloured glass cut to the required shape. Until the diamond cutter was developed in the sixteenth century a hot iron was drawn across the glass, with cold water or other liquid run after it. The glass cracked along the incision and the piece so produced was then trimmed to shape. Details in the design such as faces, hair, arms, legs, linen folds, foliage, etc. were then painted in a brown enamel which was made permanent by firing the glass again in the kiln. The pieces were then reassembled and bound together with the familiar lead strips.

A fourteenth-century development was the use of silver oxide painted on to white glass and fired to produce gold designs. With coloured glass the 'flashed' surface could be removed (abraided) to leave a required pattern of clear glass. This then could be left plain and wholly or partly repainted with silver oxide and refired to produce a yellow pattern. This was very useful for heraldic glass. Silver or gold charges could be produced on a gules field by abraiding and applying (if required) silver oxide to red glass. This could be used to produce the Royal Arms of England (*Gules three Lions passant guardant Or*), for example.

Many heraldic charges, such as a fleur-de-lis or a lion, were not of a convenient shape to be surrounded by lead strip. Whilst large charges such as the lion were built up of several pieces of glass leaded together, the problem of small charges was overcome by using small pieces of coloured glass and then painting around the outline with brown enamel to leave only the shape of the charge as the unpainted surface. Alternatively, the whole sheet was painted with brown enamel and then the appropriate area scraped away to form the desired charge. The arms of France Ancient are just one example of arms produced in this way. The combination of diamond panels, bearing the gold fleurs-de-lis, with strips of blue glass for the field may produce a 'fretty' appearance, e.g. at Christchurch, Oxford.

Heraldic glass, like many other artefacts, has suffered greatly over the centuries for a variety of reasons. Whilst some is still in its original location some may have been moved several times and now be combined with other glass, centuries its junior or senior. Some twelfth-century biblical figures at Canterbury Cathedral are surmounted by heraldic figures of the fourteenth century, and at Salisbury there are six thirteenth-century shields at the base of the west window, which is composed principally of fifteenth-century and sixteenth-century glass. (The shields were formerly in the Chapter House.) Such considerations may be important when trying to identify arms.

The reasons for the erection of heraldic glass are various. People left bequests in their wills for the expenses of chantry priests to pray for their souls and for the souls of relatives, friends and others, including the king and important lords. The shields therefore might represent the people for whom prayers should be said. Ecclesiastics and magnates, guilds and fraternities often endowed money for the repair of a church, and their arms might be erected to record this gift. Also, a number of people would sometimes jointly finance certain building works, and arms erected to commemorate their benevolence are often found in tracery lights, particularly those of the fourteenth century. At Dorchester Abbey, Oxfordshire, the south window of the chancel contains twenty-one heraldic shields to record those who financed the extension of the sanctuary *c.* 1340. At Tewkesbury Abbey at least two windows were given by Eleanor de Clare *c.* 1340. One of these shows four knights in armour representing her two husbands and her ancestors. Frequently recurring examples are the

Plantagenet arms, either for the king or differenced for various sons or brothers of the monarch, who themselves were men of considerable substance and benevolence.

The decoration surrounding the shields may be of significance. At Arkesdon, Essex, a shield of Thomas FitzAlan, Archbishop of Canterbury, is set within three crowns. This was possibly erected during the period when he was Bishop of Ely (1374-88), because the arms of that see are *Gules three Crowns Or*.

Perhaps the greatest of all commemorative windows belongs to the fourteenth century. The magnificent east window at Gloucester Cathedral, constructed between 1347 and 1350, is thirty-eight feet wide and seventy-two feet high; the size of a tennis court, and the largest stone-traceried window in England. In its lower lights are the shields of arms of the Gloucestershire knights who fought at the battle of Crècy in 1346.

In the fifteenth century donor windows became more popular, and these often contained kneeling figures wearing cloaks or tabards bearing a benefactor's arms. Apart from armorial dress some knights may be wearing a Lancastrian, Yorkist or Tudor collar, e.g. Sir John Clopton at Long Melford, Suffolk. Whilst such figures are obvious, others may be hidden within the religious scenes displayed. At St Peter Mancroft, Norwich, the fifteenth-century east window displays forty-two panels depicting biblical subjects. However, one of the panels shows two figures kneeling at a prayer desk which has quartered arms on its end. Full achievements of arms, with crest and supporters, did not appear in glass until the fifteenth century. However, heraldic devices had been used as decoration earlier. Diamond-shaped quarries or panels in the border of a window were often decorated with badges, rebuses or cyphers.

Quarries depicting the crowned hawthorn and portcullis badges and cypher of Henry VII.

Victorian glass by William Burges at Cardiff Castle depicting Richard III and Queen Anne (Nevill).

The sixteenth century was to prove important for heraldic glass. It was during this time that enamel painting was first introduced, which meant that one sheet of glass could be painted with different colours, as on canvas, and designs were no longer limited by the need for lead strips to hold different coloured glass. The Renaissance brought about a change in style. Shields were surrounded by wreaths and later by strapwork. The latter was used well into the seventeenth century. The most significant change in England occurred at the Reformation. This brought about the destruction of many windows with allegorical themes, to be replaced with plain glass, for new windows could not include religious subjects. Heraldry was an obvious alternative at a time when memorials were acquiring heraldic decoration, and it was the fashion to display the multi-quartered coat. This fashion was to continue into the seventeenth century.

Some families must have expended substantial sums on glazing church windows. For example, Sir John St John of Lydiard Tregoze was responsible for the St John heraldic windows at Battersea, and also (probably in association with his uncle, Viscount Grandison) for the windows at Lydiard Tregoze. The visitation of Berkshire 1665/6 also shows that he was responsible for a more modest heraldic window at Purley-on-Thames, Berkshire, another manor held by his family.

There are occasional examples in the Tudor and Stuart periods of the Royal Arms of England being displayed in glass. Some were erected to meet the requirement to display the royal arms, e.g. at Acomb, York, but most were simply an act of loyalty on the part of a local nobility or gentry.

Erection of purely heraldic windows in the eighteenth century and first half of the nineteenth century was rare, but the arms of 'donors' would still be included in designs. Some nineteenth and twentieth-century glass was erected by lords of the manor, and often contained a series of shields showing the arms of predecessors. This practice seems to have been popular with those who acquired manors by purchase rather than by inheritance, e.g. at Puddletown, Dorset, and Aldermaston, Berkshire. Also during the nineteenth and twentieth centuries glass may have been installed as a memorial to an individual or family. Often small shields were included in the composition, which usually was a religious scene with an inscription at the base. Occasionally the family badge, crest or motto may be found within the design or in the tracery lights. In addition to the family arms, the arms of a school, college or regimental badge may be included. Many such memorials commemorate those who lost their lives in the world wars. At Cheriton, Hampshire, there are four windows to the memory of four cousins who were killed in action, each dressed in armour charged with their arms. At St Albans, Hertfordshire, there is a window, erected in 1925, displaying the emblems of all the allies of the last world war, and a window in the RAF chapel in Westminster Abbey incorporates the badges of the sixty-eight fighter squadrons that took part in the Battle of Britain.

Stained glass in domestic buildings was intended to be both decorative and to impress visitors. The heraldry of the owner and families with which he was associated were obvious subjects. At what stage and to what extent secular buildings were glazed is uncertain. Chaucer (before 1372) refers to his chamber which 'with glas were al the windows wel y glazed' in his own house. These windows told the story of Troy, and no doubt heraldry or heraldic figures featured in some designs from at least this date.

Shields with crests and supporters are usually of similar date to those found in churches. At Athelhampton House, Dorset, there are several superb examples of late fifteenth-century and early sixteenth-century coats of arms in the Great Hall and oriel windows, though some bays contain Victorian restorations. The importance of heraldic display to Tudor landowners can be seen in the magnificent armorial windows in the Library at Montacute House, Somerset, and at Charlecote Park, Warwickshire, which date from this period. As in other areas, the late sixteenth century saw an increasing desire to display acquired (or assumed) quarterings, and many examples of multi-quartered coats are to be found in houses of the period.

Visits by the sovereign to a house were often commemorated by displaying the royal arms of the monarch concerned. Aldermaston Court in Berkshire has the arms of both Henry VIII and Queen Elizabeth in glass, recalling Forster hospitality.

There was little room in the classic designs of Robert Adam and his successors for armorial windows, and it is not until the Gothic Revival of the nineteenth century that heraldic subjects again became popular. Often they were used to display the arms of previous generations. There was also a tendency for the owners of new houses to purchase miscellaneous shields, both native and foreign, to embellish the glass of their new homes. Today many of these prove difficult to identify.

Although fashions change, heraldic glass in homes has not suffered the same destruction as that in churches. Only destruction by fire is final, but if the house has been remodelled or a new one built then existing glass is often preserved and reused. Window glass of the late twentieth century is technically superior to that of any other period, and the armorial glass of such craftsmen as Francis Spear may reasonably be compared with the creative genius of the Middle Ages. (See colour page 136)   JET

Further reading

Archer, M. *Stained Glass* Andover, 1979.
— *English Stained Glass* 1985.
Baker, J. *English Stained Glass* London, 1960.
— *English Stained Glass of the late Medieval Period* 1978.
Brisac, C. *A Thousand Years of Stained Glass* London 1984. A comprehensive book, well illustrated, dealing with European glass; translated from the French.
Couteur, J.D. Le *English Medieval Painted Glass* London, 1926.
Cowan, P. *A Guide to Stained Glass in Britain* 1985. Includes a gazetteer.
Day, L.F. *Windows* London, 1909.
Drake, M. *History of English Glass Painting* London, 1912.
Harries, J. *Discovering Stained Glass* Aylesbury, 1980 (second edn.).
Nelson, P. *Ancient Painted Glass in England* London, 1913.
Read, H. *English Stained Glass* London, 1926.
Westlake, N.H.J. *History of Design in Painted Glass* (1881-84).

Glassware Armorial subjects have long provided a minor but by no means unimportant source of inspiration for the embellishment of drinking and other glass vessels. Armorial charges can be engraved on crystal, and enamelled or gilded to give a coloured decoration to clear or coloured glass.

A superb example of armorial table glass, engraved with the Stuart royal arms.

Giacomo Verzelini absconded from Murano, the ancient glass-making centre at Venice, where glass was enamelled with armorial bearings at the beginning of the sixteenth century, and settled in Crutched Friars in the City of London, where Elizabeth I granted him the privilege of making Murano-styled drinking glasses until he died in 1606. His work is rare and highly valued today, and one surviving glass, gilded by de Lysle, is embellished with the arms of the Vintners' Company of London and shows an almost predictable patronage of his period and craft.

Decoration by enamelling flourished in the prolific glass-making area of Bohemia when the technique went out of fashion in Venice. The arms of Bohemian families were important decorative features on many of the tall cylindrical drinking vessels, called *Humpen*, made in this part of Europe.

The arousal of a national appreciation of the quality of British engravers stems from the formation in 1966 of the Guild of Glass Engravers of England. New organization was brought to craftsmen who had hitherto earned their reputation as individuals. Corporate exhibitions stimulated an elevation of standards. Now the outstanding quality of its members' work has enabled armorially engraved crystal to replace the former ubiquitous engraved silver salver as a formal presentation piece. A crystal

169

bowl or goblet with an armiger's achievement finely engraved is a highly cherished possession in many households.

Laurence Whistler (born 1912) is regarded as the father figure of the modern resurgence of this ancient art, and David Peace, Peter Dreiser, Anne Cotton, Stephen Rickard, Peter Pullen and Denis Bustard are among the contemporary craftsmen whose bold and confident heraldic engraving attracts universal admiration.

For the Guild of Glass Engravers in England, *see* · ADDRESSES. JA

Further reading

Peace, D. *Glass Engraving, Lettering and Design* London, 1985.

Glissant *see* **Attitude**

Glory A halo.

Glory, in his *see* **Attributes**

Gobony *or* **Company** *see* **Field, Varied**

Golden Circle, Knights of Founded in 1861, the 'order' was a military secret society in the middle west of the United States of America. Its purpose was to end the civil war and to 'restore the union as it was.' In 1863 some of its secrets became known and it regrouped as the Order of American Knights, and, in 1864, as the Sons of Liberty. The order collapsed later that year, three of its leaders being captured and sentenced to death. Sentences were suspended, however, and in 1866 the offenders were released by order of the Supreme Court. JC-K

· **Golden Fleece, Order of** (La Toison d'Or) This great secular order was founded on 10 January 1429/30 by Philip the Good, Duke of Burgundy, to celebrate his marriage to Isabella of Portugal. The order was dedicated to the Virgin and St Andrew. Various theories have been put forward to account for the name — the Burgundian wool trade, the legend of Jason — but none has ever been accepted, the origin being in dispute from the very early days of the order. At its beginning, membership was limited to twenty-four knights plus the sovereign and the grand master.

In 1477 the mastership came by marriage to Maximilian, the Habsburg Duke of Austria, and then in 1504 to Spain by the accession of a member of that dynasty to the throne of Castile. When the bloodline became extinct in Spain, the Austrian Emperor, Charles VI, claimed sovereignty, and in 1713 instituted the order in Vienna. From that date the Fleece continued separately in the two countries, the Austrian branch allowing only Catholics but the Spanish order being granted also to Protestants.

The insignia of the order included the famous steel and flint badge, and its collar was composed of alternating steels (furisons) and flints with a pendant of the golden fleece itself — a horned ram depicted as if suspended from a hook by means of a broad sling. The herald of the order had his own collar of office, one of which may be seen at the Treasury Museum in the Vienna Hofburg. This splendid collar comprises a representation of the Golden Fleece and a double row of small gold plaques, each charged with the arms of a knight of the order. The sixteenth-century robes of the order included a murrey habit on which the Fleece was embroidered, and a huge bonnet. KH

Golden Rose, Order of The Papal Order of the Golden Rose originated in the eleventh century, when a single rose or spray of roses made of wrought gold and set with gems (usually sapphires) was presented to an individual or community by the Pope as an honourable award for devotion to the Roman Catholic Church. On the fourth Sunday in Lent (*dies dominica in rose*) the Rose was blessed by the Pope, anointed and sprinkled with incense, balsam and musk, and placed on the high altar throughout the Mass which preceded the presentation. If no recipient was found the Rose was retained at the Vatican until the following year. Although intended as a reward for religious devotion, it was often granted for purely political reasons, and its history is beset with intrigue, scandal and misery.

Gold Stick for Scotland A title held by the Captain-General of the Royal Company of Archers. The appointment was made in 1822 by King George IV, who presented the officer with the stick 'to pertain to his office'. The title was later confirmed by King William IV.

Golpe A purpure roundel (golpe = a wound).

Gonfannon *or* **Gonfallon** A personal flag, emblazoned with the arms, and supported by means of a horizontal pole suspended by cords from the top of a staff. Probably (in shape) a descendant of the Roman *vexillum*, and usually with 'tails' at the lower edge. Popular in Europe, especially in Italy, but less so in Britain where it has always been associated with the church or guilds and mysteries, and is now to be found in the vernacular form of ecclesiastical or trade-union 'banner', probably because of its suitability for use in processions and parades. *Gunn-fane* = war flag (Norse).

See also FLAG

Gore *see* **Abatement**

Gorged *see* **Attributes**

Gorget Neck armour, sometimes extending to the chest and shoulders. Usually of plate.

Goutte A drop.

Goutty, Goutté, Gutty *or* **Gutté** Semy of drops.

Grand Ecu A shield showing many quarterings, particularly those of sovereignty or dominion, of Spain, France and Austria. The many quarterings of the Spanish Royal House are still borne by HRH the Count of Barcelona, the father of King Juan Carlos of Spain. The French Grand Ecu appears more as an historical document than a shield in normal use. Austrian examples include the *Ecu Complet* of the Empress Maria Theresa, and the achievement of the Emperor Franz Josef II of 1915, the last of many bearing, in some fashion, the arms of the several parts of the Empire.

The term is also applied to the multiple quarterings of the higher nobility in the above countries and also in England.   KH

Grand Guard A large additional piece of plate armour, fixed to the left of the breastplate and intended to provide extra protection from an opponent's lance in the tilt.

Grand-Quarter *see* **Quartering** *and* **Blazon**

Grand Seigneur A great nobleman, or person of high rank.

Grand Serjeantry A system whereby a sovereign would grant to his favoured henchmen one or more royal manors in perpetuity, on condition that the holder should perform some specified service to the crown. The system pre-dates the Conquest, and although the few remaining HEREDITARY OFFICES are for the most part performed only at a coronation, Grand Serjeantry is enshrined in Section 136 of the Law of Property Act 1922.

Grant of Arms The act of conferring armorial bearings on a successful petitioner.

England and Wales (current procedure)

A grant of arms is a form of honour, but an unusual one in that it has to be applied for and paid for. Like any other award under the 'honours system' it emanates from the sovereign as the fount of honour, but the function of granting arms has long been delegated to the kings of arms, whose patents of appointment authorize them to make grants to 'eminent men', and this phrase covers corporate bodies as well as men and women.

The kings of arms are therefore not allowed to grant

arms indiscriminately, but must satisfy themselves as to the applicant's eligibility before the wheels can be set in motion. There are no rigid guidelines, but a personal petition is likely to be favourably entertained if the applicant has received some honour or decoration from the crown, held commissioned rank in the armed services, gained a university degree or professional diploma, made a worthwhile contribution to local or national affairs, charitable causes, and so on. In the case of corporate bodies, eligibility would extend to such categories as local authorities, schools and universities, and leading professional institutions. As for commercial enterprises, these are usually expected to be leaders in their field, to be financially sound, to have been reasonably long-established and to perform some function which is of value to the life of the nation.

Once the candidate's eligibility has been established the next step is the submission of a formal petition or 'memorial' addressed to the Earl Marshal. This will be prepared by the agent (i.e. the officer of arms handling the case) who will send it to his client for signature and then forward it to the Earl Marshal's Secretary, together with the grant fees, which are lodged in a special account. In due course the Earl Marshal issues his Warrant to the appropriate kings of arms, instructing them to proceed, and if he has not already done so the agent starts considering the design of the arms.

For this purpose he naturally asks the client's views, and may even compile a list of some five or ten items in order of importance which might be incorporated either directly or symbolically in the design. Such a list could include the applicant's birthplace, school, university, professional career, hobbies, pets, favourite shapes and colours, the occupations and places of residence of his ancestors, details of his children, his wife's family, his mother's family, and so on. However, the significance of the emblems in a coat of arms is a private matter between the grantee and his agent, and it is scarcely ever recited in the patent itself.

When the agent has worked out a provisional design, he makes searches to ensure that it is sufficiently distinct from the thousands of coats already on record, and if it is he prepares an 'approval sketch' which he sends for the client's consideration. If it is accepted he then seeks the agreement of the kings of arms, who must approve not only the pictorial elements of the design but also the 'blazon' or verbal description. Once all the details of the achievement have been settled to the satisfaction of the client and the kings of arms, the agent instructs an artist to start painting the letters patent, or more simply 'the patent', by which the arms will be granted. This is a vellum document measuring about 15 by 21 inches (38 by 53 cm) and embellished at the top with the royal arms flanked by those of the Earl Marshal and the College of Arms. The grantee's new achievement is painted in the top left-hand corner, and a scrivener engrosses the text which refers to the Memorial and the Earl Marshal's Warrant, as well as describing the grantee and his new arms (see colour pages 249 and 250). Both text and illustration must then be copied into the official registers of the College to the satisfaction of the Registrar. The patent is then endorsed by the Registrar, signed and sealed by the kings of arms and put into a red box adorned with the royal cypher in gold.

As the patent has to pass through so many processes, as well as taking its turn with others (there may be as many as 200 grants in a single year), its completion takes several months. However, once the design is settled the grantee is at liberty to make use of the arms and can commission drawings or paintings for specific purposes, for instance a finely illuminated 'library painting' on strained vellum to hang on the wall, a black and white line drawing for letterheads, a bookplate design or a drawing of the crest for cufflinks or a signet ring.

The fees for grants of arms are laid down from time to time by warrant from the Earl Marshal, and a large proportion of each fee goes towards the maintenance of the College of Arms, which is self-supporting and is not, like a museum or public library, subsidized by the taxpayer. The agent receives his share of the fee only at the end of the day when the patent has been signed and sealed. The basic fee for a grant of arms and crest to an individual and his descendants stands at present (1987) at £960 and there are also standard fees for grants to corporations, grants to women, grants of supporters, badges and so on. Sometimes the grantee may wish to have a more elaborate patent than usual, with a portrait of Garter King of Arms in the initial letter, or an illuminated border containing animals, birds, flowers or other objects which take his fancy. These embellishments must of course be paid for, and they are not normally copied into the College records.

There has been a revival in the granting of badges in recent years, and these are often depicted in the patent on a standard. Another recent development is the granting of honorary arms to eminent American citizens who have proved and registered at the College a legitimate descent in the male line from an English ancestor, or one living in America prior to independence in 1783.   DHBC

Ireland
see IRELAND, LAW OF ARMS

Scotland

The armorial prerogative of the United Kingdom has been assigned in Scotland to the Lord Lyon, who is empowered to grant arms to 'virtuous and well deserving persons'. Armorial bearings may also be constituted for and in memory of a deceased ancestor. A petition for arms can be done through an agent or in person. Armigerous persons, not subjects of the sovereign of the United Kingdom, can petition the Lord Lyon for a matriculation of their arms, if these are to be used while sojourning in Scotland.

By law of the Scottish parliament the armiger's heraldic property is fully protected from unregistered use. Unregistered arms are prohibited. The Procurator Fiscal, on behalf of the Crown, can raise an action in the Court of the Lord Lyon to prevent any but the armiger from using his registered arms, or anyone from using unregistered arms in Scotland. CJB

Great Marischal of Scotland Hereditary office held by the family of Keith from the twelfth century. Before 1458 the Great Marischal was created Earl Marischal, but the earldom was eventually attainted in 1715, the Earl having supported the Jacobite cause.   CJB

Great Offices of State The generic term for eight anciently established state appointments. The offices still exist, but in much modified and often ceremonial form. Their titles are LORD HIGH STEWARD, LORD HIGH CHANCELLOR, LORD HIGH TREASURER, LORD PRESIDENT OF THE COUNCIL, LORD KEEPER OF THE GREAT SEAL (*see also* LORD PRIVY SEAL), LORD GREAT CHAMBERLAIN, LORD HIGH CONSTABLE and EARL MARSHAL.

The great offices have their origin in the royal household of the Norman kings, and these were in turn modelled on those of the kings of France, as they existed in the tenth century. In time, as the government of England evolved and the functions of crown and parliament diverged, some of the early offices became (or mutated to) the offices of state as noted above, while others — such as the LORD CHAMBERLAIN and the LORD STEWARD — remained as offices of the ROYAL HOUSEHOLD.   JC-K

Great Seal of England Perhaps the first seal of England which may be termed 'great' is that of Edward the Confessor, but it is more practical to trace the history of the Great Seal from the reign of William I. This monarch used a seal, on one side of which was the majesty copied from that of Henri II of France, and on the obverse an equestrian style depicting him mounted and armed. Subsequently the faces were reversed, the majesty becoming the obverse and the equestrian the reverse. This style has remained almost unchanged to the present day.   JC-K

Great Seal of the United States of America From proposals submitted to Congress as early as 20

August 1776 by Benjamin Franklin, John Adams and Thomas Jefferson, the design of the Great Seal was finalized on 20 June 1782. The blazon adopted remains part of the law of the land today. The arms are *Palewise of thirteen pieces Argent and Gules a Chief Azure the Escutcheon on the breast of an American Eagle displayed proper holding in his dexter Talon an Olive Branch and in his sinister a Bunch of thirteen Arrows all proper and in his Beak a Scroll inscribed with the motto E Pluribus Unum. The crest is Over the Head of the Eagle which appears above the Escutcheon a Glory Or breaking through a Cloud proper and surrounding thirteen Stars forming a Constellation Argent on an Azure field. The reverse is A Pyramid unfinished in the Zenith an Eye in a triangle surrounded with a Glory proper over the Eye these Words Annuit Coeptois on the base of the Pyramid the numerical letters MDCCLXXVI and underneath the following motto Novus Ordo Seclorum.* JC-K

Great Steward of Scotland *see* **Wales, Prince of**

Greave *or* **Jamb** Armour for the lower leg.

Greece, Royal Arms of *Azure a Cross couped Argent and over all an escutcheon of pretence Or semy of Hearts Gules three Lions passant Azure crowned Or.*

Green Rod, Gentleman Usher of the One of five officers attached to the Order of the Thistle. The first appointment was Sir Thomas Brand in 1714. The staff of office carried by the Usher is of silver gilt enamelled green with a finial in the form of a unicorn supporting a shield bearing the St Andrew's cross. The Usher wears a blue silk mantle bearing a shield with the cross of St Andrew on the left shoulder. CJB

Greyhound The greyhound of armory is effectively the greyhound of nature. It may be depicted in any of the armorial attitudes and is often gorged with a plain collar.

Equestrian figure and diaper of Yorkist suns and roses on the Great Seal of Edward IV.

Griffin Of the animals in mythology the griffin or gryphon is the most magnificent. The lion is the king of the beasts and the eagle the king of the birds, but in the griffin the majesty of the two creatures is joined together. Its head, wings and talons are those of an eagle, to which are added a pair of sharp ears, as it has very acute hearing. Its body, hindquarters and tail are like a lion, and thus it combined the strength and vigilance of both animals in one.

The griffin was associated with the Gods in Minoan, Greek and other civilizations of the Near East. It was an animal of the sun, and pulled Apollo's chariot across the sky, but it had a double role, and also pulled the chariot of Nemesis, the God of Justice. Griffins guarded the gold mines in the mountains of Scythia, and were always at war with the one-eyed Arimaspians, who tried to steal the gold to adorn their hair. These people always rode horses on their raids into the mountains and engendered hatred in the griffins who, ever since, have regarded horses with great hostility. The griffin is one of the Royal Beasts of England, and Cardinal Wolsey, amongst other great men, used them as supporters.

There are many medieval stories about the griffin, its claw was believed to have medicinal properties, and one of its feathers could restore sight to the blind. It was also sculpted on churches to denote the union of the divine and human natures. The griffin is reputed never to have been captured and its attributes have made it a popular heraldic emblem since the fifteenth century. Appropriately it appears in the arms attributed to Alexander the Great, as four of these animals were used to carry him in a specially designed basket in flight above the earth.

There is in armory a separate animal called the male griffin, which has sharp spikes protruding from its body instead of wings. However, there is no suggestion of this version amongst legendary griffins, and in these stories there does not appear to be any distinction between male and female, and in armory both creatures possess the usual male attributes.

When depicted in the rampant attitude, the griffin is said to be segreant. MY

Gringoly *see* **Attributes**

Guardant *see* **Attitude**

Guarded *see* **Attributes**

Guardian In the present context, the guardian of a minor who held his lands by knight-service. Guardianships were much sought after since they permitted the generation of wealth, and the arrangement of worthwhile marriages. They were frequently traded for large sums of money by all levels of nobility, the king himself not being exempt from the practice. JC-K

Guidon A medium-size livery flag with a full, rounded fly bearing the national device in the hoist (e.g. the Cross of St George) and the livery colours and principal badge in the fly. In effect, the guidon is a miniature standard, made more suitable for carrying into battle before a troop of men by the removal of the subsidiary badges and motto bends which adorn a STANDARD. The national device was, of course, intended to be a clear indication of the allegiance of a particular troop, the badge and liveries being those of the magnate by whom they were retained and whose uniform they wore. The modern cavalry standard is a direct descendant of the guidon and is often described as such. However, its fly is usually split and so cluttered with regimental devices that it cannot possibly be identified at a distance. Guidons are still granted by Lord Lyon according to strict armorial regulations. In England, however, where livery flags appear more often in patents that on flag-staffs, the guidon is something of a rarity. This is regrettable, for it is a singularly attractive and practical flag. As with the standard, the national device in the hoist is usually replaced by the arms.
See also FLAG

Guige A shoulder strap for a shield.

Guisarme A pole arm with curved sword-head and straight hook.

Gules (Abbr. Gu.) The armorial tincture red. Pronounced to rhyme with 'rules', the G being either soft or hard, though armorists generally prefer the latter. In the early Middle Ages no distinction was made between red and purple, both being considered the colours of princes.
See also TINCTURES

Gumphion A seventeenth-century non-armorial banner used at funerals, charged with symbols of mortality and fringed with the livery colours.

Gurges *or* **Gorge** A whirlpool depicted as a spiral.

Gusset (i) An armorial charge, similar in shape to a small escutcheon, rarely employed (in Scotland) as an abatement to indicate adultery, when it is depicted in sinister chief, abutting the upper edge of the shield and debruising the field.
(ii) Attachment of mail used to protect the joints of plate armour.

Gutty *see* **Semy**

Guze A sanguine roundel, named after the eyeball.

Gyron *also* **Esquire** A fairly unusual armorial charge comprising half of a quarter.

Gyronny *see* **Field, Parted** *and* **Field, Varied**

H

Habited *see* **Attributes**

Hafted *see* **Attributes**

Haketon, Aketon *or* **Gambeson** Stuffed and quilted body armour, especially as worn under a hauberk, with or without sleeves.

Halberd A pole arm with axe-head, point and spike.

Hallmark A stamp applied to an article of gold, silver or platinum after test by assay at an official assay office.
    The word hallmark is derived from Goldsmiths' Hall, the City of London headquarters of the Worshipful Company of Goldsmiths. The Company received a royal charter dated 30 March 1327, giving them power to enforce in England consumer-protection legislation similar to measures introduced

in Paris in 1260. The death penalty for counterfeiting the British hallmark was changed to fourteen years' transportation to a penal colony as recently as 1773. The maximum penalty is now ten years' imprisonment.

The date of assay, the identity of maker or sponsor, the carat standard of gold or fineness of silver employed and the town of assay, may be determined from a full set of assay marks.

The townmark of the assay office both in Great Britain and overseas frequently has an armorial quality. Amsterdam, Augsburg, Utrecht and Copenhagen have used their respective city arms for this purpose. In Great Britain the former assay offices of Bristol, Exeter, Newcastle, York, Norwich, Chester and Glasgow used their civic arms as a townmark while they were active, as Edinburgh does today. The other active assay offices in Great Britain are Birmingham, which uses an anchor, and Sheffield which used a crown for two hundred years but today uses a Yorkshire rose.

The leopard's head affronty now used as the townmark for London was actually introduced to denote the sterling standard of silver. It was established by statute in 1300 and was later legally referred to as the King's Mark, probably because it was taken from the royal arms. The leopard's head has been used as a charge in the arms of the Goldsmiths' Company since 1470.   JA

Further reading
Touching Gold and Silver The Worshipful Company of Goldsmiths, 1978.

Hamade A bar couped. Originally borne in threes.

Hanover, Royal Arms of The arms of Hanover were included in the arms of the sovereign of the United Kingdom from 1714 to 1837. Until 1801 they occupied the fourth quarter, but from that date they were placed in pretence, being ensigned with an electoral bonnet until 1816, and thereafter by a royal crown. The arms are *Tierced in pairle reversed 1 Gules two Lions passant guardant Or* (Brunswick cf. Henry II of England) *2 Or semy of Hearts Gules a Lion rampant Azure* (Luneburg) *3 Gules a Horse courant Argent* (Hanover) *over all on an inescutcheon Gules the Crown of Charlemagne* signifying the office of High Treasurer of the Holy Roman Empire.

By Salic Law, a woman could not succeed to the throne of Hanover, and on the accession of Victoria to the throne of the United Kingdom her uncle, the Duke of Cumberland, became King of Hanover. Hanover remained a kingdom until 1918. The arms, still used by the present Prince of Hanover, are the Royal Arms of Great Britain with the escutcheon of Hanover in pretence and ensigned with the Royal Crown of Hanover.   KH

Harleian Society, The Founded in 1869 for the purpose of publishing manuscripts of the heraldic visitations of the counties of England and Wales, and other unpublished manuscripts relating to genealogy, armory and heraldry in its widest sense. Since its inception the Harleian Society has published ninety-one volumes of parish registers, fifty-four volumes of heraldic visitations, and sixty-five volumes drawn from other sources. The publications of the Society are available by subscription. Subscribers receive one copy of each new publication without any additional charge, and as a bonus a new subscriber will also receive free of charge one copy of any publication he chooses from the current list of publications in print. Enquiries should be addressed to the College of Arms (*see* ADDRESSES).   JB-L

Harpy A mythical creature used in armory, having the body of a vulture and the head and breasts of a woman.

Hatching *see* **Petra Sancta** *and* **Tincture**

Hatchment A diamond-shaped armorial panel, usually found affixed to the wall of a church above the arcade, though many have been removed to ringing chambers, vestries and other inaccessible quarters. The word 'hatchment' is a corruption of 'achievement' and suggests that its origins may be found in the FUNERAL HERALDRY of the medieval nobility. Hatchments are known to have been used in the Low Countries before they first appeared in England during the early seventeenth century. Several Dutch paintings of the period show hatchments hanging on church walls and pillars, and in Ghent are two churches in each of which may be seen no fewer than one hundred hatchments which have survived the ravages of time. In England the hatchment has survived on a smaller scale, but regrettably research indicates that many continue to be lost through decay and neglect.

The precise function of the hatchment remains unclear, indeed it may be that it possessed a variety of functions, depending on the practices of a particular locality or period. If indeed it is a direct descendant of the medieval funeral achievement (the crested helm shield, spurs, sword, etc., carried in the funeral procession) then it is not unreasonable to assume that the hatchment was also carried in the procession to the church, in which it remained following interment. However, there is ample evidence to suggest that it was hung on the front of a house during the period of mourning, and thereafter placed in the church. In Scotland, two hatchments were painted, one to be hung above the front door of the deceased's house, and the other over the place of interment. There are also several examples in England of hatchments for

175

the same individual being erected at different churches where he held estates. In *Doctor Thorne*, by Anthony Trollope, a hatchment is erected over the doorway of Hatherley Court as mourners return from the funeral, which suggests that it may have been returned from the church following the arrival of the cortège. It is uncertain how long the hatchment remained outside a house. Exposure to the elements for a long period would have caused substantial damage.

A hatchment normally comprises a full armorial achievement painted on a wooden panel or on canvas within a wooden frame. Early examples are small, two to three feet square, the narrow frames being decorated with hourglasses, mortheads, crossbones and other symbols of mortality. Late eighteenth and nineteenth-century hatchments are larger, the wider frames often covered in black cloth with rosettes at the corners. Early hatchments were executed in a vigorous style, unlike those of the nineteenth century which are, for the most part, of poor artistic quality.

It is the treatment of the background which makes the hatchment unique, for it was intended to convey to the observer the identity of the deceased, through a system of black and white divisions which correspond to the appropriate parts of the shield of arms or (for women) the lozenge.

Bachelor: personal arms on shield with all-black background.
Spinster: personal arms on a lozenge with all-black background.
Husband: impaled arms of husband and wife on a shield, dexter background black, sinister background white.
Wife: impaled arms of husband and wife on a shield, sinister background black, dexter background white.
Widower: impaled arms of husband and wife on a shield, all-black background.
Widow: impaled arms of husband and wife on a lozenge, all-black background.

Where a wife is an heraldic heiress the arms are in pretence, though they are sometimes found impaled or even both in pretence and impaled. The appropriate background is still used.

If the crest contains sable or argent elements, then the background may be modified at this point to allow for a clear representation.

The rules of background were well established by 1700, and were in general use before that time. In some early instances the all-black background was used with impaled arms even though one partner was still living. An unusual example, at Marnhull in Dorset, is that of a nine-year-old girl whose initials and date of death are shown at the top of the hatchment above the impaled arms of her parents.

The impalement of a blank half shield is sometimes used when a wife is not armigerous, or alternatively no impalement is shown but the background is divided accordingly. Care should be exercised when interpreting such hatchments, for it is possible to find an apparent bachelor who is in fact the head of a family, and whose death followed that of his non-armigerous wife.

Several methods are used to indicate two or more wives. The sinister impalement may be divided per fess with the arms of the first wife in chief and those of the second in base. Alternatively the shield may be divided per pale into three with the husband's arms in the centre, the first wife to the dexter and the second wife to the sinister. This practice can cause confusion with a similar one whereby the husband's arms are to the dexter and his wives successively to the sinister. In each case the background corresponding with the arms of the deceased is painted black. Again, the armorist should be aware of these alternatives and should not attempt to apply the conventions of marshalling to the interpretation of hatchments.

A third method of dealing with this situation was to show the husband's arms alone on the shield of a central achievement, and the impaled arms of each of his wives on smaller shields, set in separate panels, on either side. The background of each of these panels would be appropriately coloured to show which of the marital partners had died. In many ways this is a more satisfactory method and is certainly less confusing when adopted for the purpose of identifying several wives! At Moulton, Lincolnshire, the hatchment of Henry Boulton (d. 1828) impales the arms of his fifth wife in the central achievement. A small shield is placed in each of the corners of the hatchment and each impales the arms of one of his previous four wives. Less commonly, similar practices were adopted by ladies who had two or more husbands.

Knights of the orders of chivalry use two shields accollé, the dexter being the personal arms within the Garter or appropriate insignia, and the sinister being the impaled arms of husband and wife. Where personal arms are impaled with those of an office, e.g. archbishop, bishop, college warden, etc., then the background behind the arms of office is usually painted white to indicate that the office continues after the death of the holder. Occasionally, as in the hatchment of Jane, wife of the Rt Revd George Henry Law, Bishop of Bath and Wells, a husband's arms of office are shown accollé with his deceased wife's impaled arms (in this instance on oval 'shields'), the background being coloured black only behind the wife's arms, indicating that the hatchment is for her. (This hatchment may be seen at Babraham, Cambridgeshire.)

Non-armorial devices appear on hatchments of all periods. Cherubs' heads are frequently found in place

Hatchment of Jane Law

of crests in the hatchments of women, skulls fill the lower corner beneath the motto scroll, and flags may be found in the hatchments of prominent naval and military men.

Another trap for the unsuspecting armorist is the funeral motto. These often refer to mortality, e.g. *Resurgam* or *In Coela Quies*. They should not be confused with the family motto which may also appear, but infrequently so.

The number of hatchments which survive today is only a small proportion of those made. Evidence for this is provided by eighteenth and nineteenth-century illustrations and engravings of church interiors, together with records in antiquarian county histories. Wood and canvas are unlikely to survive centuries of damp and neglect, and many hatchments fell victim to the 'restorations' of the nineteenth century. The use of hatchments was at its peak at the beginning of Queen Victoria's reign, but then declined rapidly. Of the 4500 hatchments recently recorded in England, only 120 are of the present century.

Hatchments are found somewhat haphazardly. Most churches, if they have any, have perhaps one or two to a local squire or parson. To possess five or more is, in England, unusual. The five at Marnhull in Dorset form a splendid collection from the seventeenth century, with no two being of the same family. At Wootton, Bedfordshire, there are thirteen of members of the Monoux family, and Breamore in Hampshire has twelve of the Hulse family. One of the largest collections in England is at Shrewsbury, where two churches have twenty and twenty-one respectively.

Hatchments in Scotland are few, and follow north European funeral practice by surrounding the achievement with small escutcheons representing the probative branches of the deceased.

Hatchments may also be found in secular buildings. Peter Summers, author of the magnificent series *Hatchments in Britain*, has discovered them not only in country houses, but in a seaside hotel, a village inn, two girls' schools, a tea shop and a cave, though the last, commemorating a Dashwood baronet, has sadly perished. It hung over a pool in one of the caves at West Wycombe, Buckinghamshire, a haunt of the notorious Hell Fire Club.

Royal hatchments are, of course, rare. William IV (d. 1837) is commemorated by four surviving examples, and there are several others, painted on both canvas and silk, in the parish church at Kew. These should not be confused with the ubiquitous ARMORIAL BOARD, painted with royal devices, which may easily be mistaken for a hatchment. So, too, the MEMORIAL BOARD, erected to the memory of an individual and bearing both arms and inscription. However, the majority of these are square or rectangular, which hatchments are not, and inscriptions on hatchments are rare and usually confined to initials or a date. No diamond-shaped hatchment has been recorded of an earlier date than 1627, whereas memorial boards are of sixteenth-century origin.   JET/SF

See also MONUMENTS

Further reading

Summers, P.G. *Hatchments in Britain* Chichester. This work, to be completed in ten volumes, will record all the hatchments traced in Britain since Peter Summers began his survey in 1952. Counties are grouped together in each volume, eight of which will have been published by December 1987.

Hauberk Mailed body armour split fore and aft for horse-riding, usually worn over quilting or padding. The principal Norman body defence at the Battle of Hastings.

Hauriant *see* **Attitude**

Hawk *see* **Falcon**

Head Unless otherwise blazoned, a head is couped and faces the dexter.

  Blackamoor's negroid

  Child's young boy with fair hair

  Englishman's fair complexion, fair hair and beard

  Forester's bearded and rugged

  Maiden's usually affronty with long fair hair

  Moor's Arabian with dark hair and beard

  Saracen's swarthy with long dark hair and beard

  Savage's bearded, long haired and usually
    wreathed about the temples with leaves

Saxon's   beardless and fair hair
Wodehouse's   bearded and with green hair
Woodsman's   bearded and rugged

A head may be *wreathed about the temples* with a torse of specific tinctures or a wreath of leaves.

Heater Shield The most popular shield for armorial display, having the shape of the base of a flat iron.

Hedgehog *see* **Urchin**

Heir One who has inherited, and enjoys possession of, a title, property or arms. Frequently confused with heir apparent.

Heir Apparent One whose right of succession is inalienable.

Heiress An heiress is a daughter who has inherited arms from her deceased father, there being no brothers or surviving issue of brothers. The arms of an heraldic heiress are marshalled on an escutcheon of pretence at the centre of her husband's arms. Both her arms and those of her husband are transmitted to their issue as quarterings, her husband's arms occupying the first quarter.

Where there is more than one daughter, all inherit and each is a co-heiress, all transmitting their father's arms on equal terms.

An heiress in her issue is one through whose issue

arms descend when all male lines of her father have failed. It is possible, therefore, for descendants of the daughter of an armiger to inherit arms several generations after her death.

Heir Presumptive One whose right of succession is dependent on the absence of an heir apparent.

Helm Correctly a particular pattern of helmet used in the tournament, but universally adopted as an abbreviation for the word 'helmet' and so used here.
See also TILTING HELM

Helmed *see* **Attributes**

Helmet (i) Representation of the helmet above the shield in a coat of arms has usually reflected the armorial requirements of a particular period.

In the thirteenth and fourteenth centuries, when the helmet was an essential component of a knight's equipment, the cylindrical barrel or great helm, with a flat or rounded top, eye slits (sights) and ventilation holes (breathes) was invariably used for armorial display.

From the end of the fourteenth century, when theoretical eligibility for the aristocracy depended on possession both of a suitable pedigree and the resources necessary to participate in a tournament and the attendant festivities, the tilting helm was widely used to display the ornate tournament crests, which effectively signalled the bearer's rank both in the lists and symbolically in his arms. This was permanently 'closed' except for an eye-slit, and was only effective when leaning forward in the tilting position.

However, following the Tudor period (when, encouraged by the heralds' visitations, crests were widely adopted by members of the 'new gentility'), the nobility perceived the need for further differentiation, and from the early seventeenth century a variety of helmets has been used to indicate rank.

Not surprisingly, these also derived from the TOURNAMENT. However, the manner in which they are depicted in coats of arms suggests that they were not the true mêlée helm (with its wide aperture for the

A tilting helm from Melbury Sampford church, Dorset. Probably erected as a funeral helm in memory of William Browning, Lord of the Manor (d. 1472). The helm weighs 18½ pounds, and is one of only three of this type known to be extant in England. Notice the 'breathes' in the side of the helm, the hole in the crown through which the crest was secured, and the attachments for the mantling and wreath.

The Armorial Helmet

Since the seventeenth century, stylized forms of medieval tournament helms have been depicted with crests to indicate rank: the mêlée helm for peers (1), the barriers helm for baronets and knights (2), and closed barrel helms (3 and 4, both fourteenth century) and tilting helms (5 and 6, both fifteenth century) for esquires and gentlemen. The armet (7, late fifteenth century), and the sallet or salade (8, late fifteenth century) are also used, the latter in Scottish civic and corporate arms. Above is the stylized helm of the British sovereign.

face and protective bars or latticed grille) and the barriers helm (the fifteenth-century visored bascinet, which was also to be found on the battlefield, or its sophisticated successor the armet), but rather the stylized 'parade' versions which were used purely for the display of tournament crests during the preliminary pageantry and ceremonial (*see* HELMSCHAU). The tilting helm was retained for the use of esquires and gentlemen.

In Germany, two types of helmet were adopted for armorial purposes: the open helmet with bars or grilles was reserved for use by the older families of prominent position, the lesser, closed helm being used by the new nobility. Likewise, in France, the grilled helm was appropriate to the ancient noblesse, newly ennobled families being denied its use until the third generation when they became 'bon-gentil-hommes'. French heralds delighted in devising complex rules governing the number of bars relating to each rank, but it seems that these were never strictly observed and the practice was generally that of English armory: a gold helm for the sovereign, silver for the peerage and steel for all other armigers.

The depictions of helmets during the Tudor period, when the accoutrements of war still retained some relevance in the lists if not in the battlefield, gradually declined through the 'heraldry of the decadence' until the most bizarre and impracticable headgear began to appear in achievements of arms towards the end of the sixteenth century. It is appropriate that the current enthusiasm for medieval armory should have encouraged a return to the use of fourteenth and fifteenth-century helmets in late twentieth-century achievements, for it was in the high Middle Ages that the crest flourished and no other helm is more suited to its display. Of course, it is essential that the type of helmet depicted should be of the same period as the shield, and of the correct proportions. Regrettably, in English armory today, helmets are depicted much too small, thereby reducing the height of the crest which should be equal to that of the shield. .

Since the Stuart period the position of the helm has also been regulated. This convention has often forced crests into the most ridiculous contortions. Imagine, for example, an esquire's helm in profile with *a Lion sejant affronty* crest perched at right angles to it! Fortunately, the kings of arms today take a far more lenient view and permit the helm and crest to be depicted in positions which are more compatible and aesthetically pleasing; the only condition being that there should be no ambiguity with regard to the blazon of the crest. The current requirement that all new crests should be capable of being borne on a real helmet has facilitated this relaxation of an unnecessary convention.

It is strictly incorrect for the crest and its accessories to be depicted without the helmet to which they are attached. However, the convention is frequently broken, even by the College of Arms who, on letters patent, depict their own arms *sans* helmet and with the crest coronet neatly positioned on the upper edge of the shield. This is certainly an effective device when the crest coronet is used, but it is rarely successful when a crest is borne on a wreath, and should be avoided.

British armorial helmets currently in use are:

British Sovereign and Princes of the Blood A stylized gold helm in the affronty position with bars, the number of which may vary according to the sovereign's wishes. (The Queen's helm has five, and that of the Prince of Wales seven.) The Royal Helm is also used in the arms of some Commonwealth countries, e.g. Jamaica, granted in 1661.

Peers A stylized silver mêlée helm (see above) facing the dexter with gold bars (usually five visible) and garnished in gold.

Knights and Baronets A stylized steel barriers helm (see above) in the affronty position and with the vizor raised. In Scotland, a tilting helm may be used, this being of steel garnished with gold.

Scottish Feudal Barons A tilting helm of steel, or a steel helm with one or three grilles, both garnished with gold.

Esquires In England, a closed helm of steel facing the dexter, usually but not necessarily a tilting helm. In Scotland, a tilting helm is considered appropriate only to those of 'tournament rank' (i.e. not esquires or gentlemen) and a steel barrel helm, garnished with gold, is used. (This is sometimes termed a pot helm.)

Gentlemen In England, the helm is that of an esquire. In Scotland, an ungarnished steel barrel helm is used.

Corporations In England, a tilting helm facing the dexter. In Scotland, a steel sallet affronty is used by corporate bodies who have registered their arms since 1966.

(ii) An armorial charge. The type of helmet may be blazoned, also the position of the vizor and the colour of the padded lining which is otherwise assumed to be red, though there is no convention regarding this.
Further reading
Wilkinson, F. *Arms and Armour* London, 1978.

Helmschau Literally, a 'helm-show' which preceded a tournament, particularly in fifteenth and sixteenth-century Germany from where the term derives. It was, in fact, a display of crests and its original purpose was to eliminate those not considered to be of 'tournament rank' by the judges, who were assisted in their deliberations by the heralds. To be 'of tournament rank' one required not only a noble pedigree but substantial resources in order to maintain armour, equipment and a horse, and to participate in the attendant festivities and pageantry. From the late fifteenth century the names of the same men recur time and time again in the tournament rolls and jousting cheques of the heralds, and clearly only a privileged few were able to consider themselves 'of tournament rank'. The acquisition of a crest, therefore, was indicative of membership of a true élite, almost synonymous with nobility, and it is hardly surprising that the newly established Tudor gentleman was so anxious to register a crest at the visitations.

Ladies were also expected to play their part in these colourful proceedings. According to King René (*Traité de la Forme et Devis d'un Tournoi, c.* 1465) the ladies were led four times past the participants' helms and crests, which were placed in rows in the *helmschau.* If any of the knights had been overheard making unchivalrous remarks about the women, a lady would touch his crested helm and he would be disqualified.

Henry VIII, Royal Augmentations

Henry VIII of England, who married six times, conferred coats of augmentation on the four of his wives who were not royal by birth.

Anne Boleyn was created Countess of Pembroke before her marriage to the king, and at the same time was granted a coat of six quarterings. Although her father was created Viscount Rochford, Earl of Wiltshire and Earl of Ormonde, it is notable that the arms of Boleyn did not appear among the quarterings, which alluded to her mother's more illustrious descent.

Quarterly of six: 1 *England with a Label of France* (for the Duchy of Lancaster) 2 *France Ancient with a Label Gules* (for Anjou-Naples) 3 *Gules a Lion passant guardant Or* (Aquitaine) 4 Quarterly 1 and 4 *Or a Chief indented Azure* (Butler of Ormonde) 2 and 3 *Argent a Lion rampant Sable crowned Gules* (Rochford) 5 *England a Label Argent* (Thomas of Brotherton) 6 *Checky Or and Azure* (Warrenne).

Jane Seymour's marriage to the king was heraldically recorded by a new grant of arms to her family.

Quarterly of six: 1 *Or on a Pile Gules between six Fleurs-de-lis Azure three Lions of England* (Coat of Augmentation) 2 *Gules two Wings in lure Or* (Seymour) 3 *Vair* (Beauchamp of Hache) 4 *Argent three demi-Lions rampant couped Gules* (Sturmy) 5 *Per bend Argent and Gules three Roses in bend counterchanged* (McWilliam) 6 *Argent on a Bend Gules three Leopard's Faces Or* (Coker)

Catherine Howard was granted two coats of augmentation, making a coat of four quarterings.

Quarterly: 1 *Azure three Fleurs-de-lis in pale Or between two Flaunches Ermine each charged with a Rose Gules* (Coat of Augmentation) 2 *England a Label Argent* (Brotherton) 3 *Gules on a Bend between six Cross-Crosslets fitchy Argent an Escutcheon Or charged with a demi-Lion shot through the mouth with an Arrow all within a double Tressure flory counterflory Gules* (Howard with the augmentation for Flodden) 4 *Azure two Lions passant guardant between four demi-Fleurs-de-lis issuant from the edges of the shield Or* (Coat of Augmentation).

Catherine Parr was also given a Coat of Augmentation making a coat of six quarters.

1 *Or on a Pile between six Roses Gules three Roses Argent* (Coat of Augmentation) 2 *Argent two Bars Azure within a Bordure engrailed Sable* (Parr) 3 *Or three Water Bougets Sable* (Ros of Kendal) 4 *Vair a Fess Gules* (Marmion) 5 *Azure three Chevronels interlaced and a Chief Or* (FitzHugh) 6 *Vert three Stags at gaze Or* (Green). KH

Herald An officer of arms of the middle rank. Correctly a herald of arms. Frequently and erroneously used as a generic term for all officers of arms.

Herald Extraordinary An honorary officer of arms, either a herald or pursuivant, correctly termed an officer of arms extraordinary. In England the officers of arms extraordinary are not members of the corporation of the College of Arms, and their duties are entirely ceremonial, as are those of their Scottish counterparts. Appointment of an officer of arms extraordinary is no longer dependent on the occurrence of a major ceremony of state, such as a coronation, and appointments are generally made *honoris causa.* Full-time officers of arms are termed officers of arms in ordinary.
See also OFFICER OF ARMS

Heraldic Arts, Society of A society formed in 1987 to serve the interests of heraldic artists, craftsmen, designers and writers, to provide a 'shop window' for their work and a forum for the exchange of ideas and information (*see* ADDRESSES).

Heraldic Offices Victorian offices which offered spurious armorial and genealogical services in return for a fee. The following advertisement appeared in the newspapers in 1860:

For family Arms, Crest of Pedigree, send Name and County, and in 3 days you will receive a correct copy of your Armorial Bearings. Plain sketch 3/- In heraldic colours 6/- Family Pedigrees with original grant of Arms, to whom and when granted, the origin of the family, traced from authentic records at the British Museum, fee 21/- By T. Culleton, Genealogist, Royal Heraldic Office, 25 Cranbourn Street (corner of St Martin's Lane)

See also BOGUS HERALDRY, BUCKET SHOP HERALDRY *and* SPURIOUS HERALDRY

Heraldic Visitations *see* Visitations

Herald Painter An heraldic artist is one who specializes in designing, drawing or painting everything connected with armory. If he or she works exclusively for the officers of arms the title of Herald Painter is used. The artists working at the College of Arms are in effect self-employed, each one having an officer or group of officers for whom he or she habitually works. The senior herald painters take on trainees as and when they need them, who start with the most elementary tasks and progress to more complicated work as their skill and knowledge increase. In due course they may graduate to become herald painters themselves, though some do not remain at the College for very long but prefer to freelance and develop a wider range of work and styles.

The primary work of the herald painter is involved with the process of granting arms. An approval sketch is prepared on the instructions of an officer of arms, acting on behalf of a client, and the design sent to Garter for his approval. If it is acceptable the sketch is returned to one of the herald painters to make a finished painting of the arms on the vellum document which will, in due course, become the patent of arms. For the grantee who wishes it the herald painter will also paint the arms of the Earl Marshal, the sovereign and those of the College at the head of the patent, instead of their being printed. An increasing number of people also ask and are willing to pay for patents with elaborate decorative borders, which may also include the grant of a badge, often exemplified on a standard.

When the herald painter has made a grant painting, it is customary for any subsequent art work resulting from the grant to go to him. The fees paid to the artist for a patent are on a fixed scale, but for subsequent work he can charge within reason what he wishes. If he asks too much the officer, albeit reluctantly, may go to another artist. Such additional work usually comprises of certificated or library paintings, more elaborate versions of that done on the patent and whose limits are set only by good taste and by the amount the client is willing to pay. A design drawn only in line is often required for bookplates or illustrations for books or magazines. From time to time the senior herald painters have produced three-dimensional designs for use on seals, coins, furniture or sculpture. The herald painter also undertakes additional works for the officers of arms, such as designing and painting flags or the armorial devices in a family tree or pedigree.

Senior herald painters at the College are under contract which precludes their producing heraldry in any form for anyone other than an officer of arms. They are self-employed in that they are paid commission only on the work they do, but they have the advantage of a continual flow of work and the security of an assured living. Some have studios on the top floor of the College, while others prefer to work at home.

It has been the practice at the College of Arms for well over half a century for the herald painters to concern themselves solely with heraldry, and for the scriveners to do all the writing necessary on documents. Now, as more young artists are being trained outside the College in heraldic art, calligraphy and manuscript illumination, the practice of allowing one person to produce an entire document is coming back into favour, with what ultimately can only be a beneficial result. Rigidly dividing the layout involved in producing a patent of arms, or indeed any other heraldic document, between several artists working in isolation must result in a lack of artistic unity. As if to emphasize this further, blue box lines have for many years been drawn on patents, physically dividing the painting from the text. When the beauty and artistic wholeness of the two earliest surviving patents in England, made to the Drapers' Company in 1438 and to the Tallow Chandlers' Company in 1456, both Guilds of the City of London, are compared with nineteenth and twentieth-century examples, the advantages of using one artist or several working closely and harmoniously together become obvious.

The College of Arms style has tended for many years to have perhaps too great an influence on English heraldic art, partly because more sheer volume comes out of the College than from any other source and partly because of a general lack of understanding as to precisely what function a grant painting is intended to perform. It is designed to illustrate the arms concerned in as unambiguous a way as possible, so that any artist or craftsman or woman subsequently working in any medium can understand clearly what each part of an achievement consists of and can interpret it accurately and intelligently. Unfortunately there are still many people who are afraid of armory, believing it to be full of mysteries which only the initiated can understand, and are in consequence unwilling to depart from the grant painting by so much as a whisker.

The work done by the herald painters, excellent though much of it is, is far from being the only way in which armory can be interpreted, and the best of the work done outside the College is as good as that done

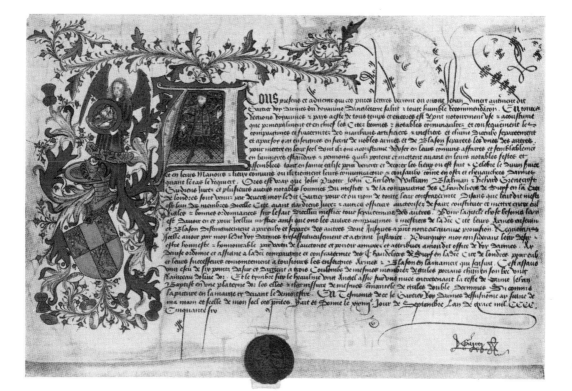

Patent of arms to the Worshipful Company of Tallow Chandlers of the City of London, incorporated in 1463. Uniquely among the livery companies, the Tallow Chandlers have two crests, the first *An Angel issuant from Clouds proper holding a Platter Or thereon the Head of St John the Baptist*, and the second *On a Charger proper rayonné Or the Head of St John the Baptist*. The arms and original crest were granted in 1456, and the second crest and supporters in 1603.

within it, albeit sometimes very different in style and technique. Whatever style is employed and for whatever purpose the design is to be used, the basic test of its soundness, with regard both to the nature of the arms which have been granted and the manner of their visual interpretation, is whether it has visual impact and can instantly be read even from a distance. After all, the life of a knight in a medieval battle may well have depended on it. However well the heraldic artist interprets them, the herald must contrive arms which are simple, which make a satisfactory design and have immediate visual impact.   AW

Heraldry (i) All matters relating to the duties and responsibilities of officers of arms. The term is frequently and erroneously used as a synonym for ARMORY, which is but one of the herald's many duties.
(ii) The art of depicting armorial devices in paint, line, stone, glass, etc.

(iii) 'Vernacular heraldry' is concerned with non-armorial devices used for the purposes of identification and communication (*see* SEMIOTICS).

Heraldry, Bucket Shop *see* **Bucket Shop Heraldry**

Heraldry, Bogus *see* **Bogus Heraldry**

Heraldry of the Decadence The late and post-Tudor period when armorial and heraldic practice was in a state of rapid degeneration, the practical application of heraldry having been replaced by exaggerated ceremonial.

Heraldry Society Founded in 1947 by John Brooke-Little, now Norroy and Ulster King of Arms, as The Society of Heraldic Antiquaries, its name was changed to The Heraldry Society in 1950. It was incorporated in 1956 and is a registered charity. The principal object of the Society is to extend interest in and knowledge of heraldry, genealogy, precedence and related disciplines. It maintains a library and an extensive library of slides. It mounts exhibitions, organizes the English Heraldic Congress, holds regular meetings at the Society of Antiquaries and arranges various social events. It also published *The Coat of Arms*, a quarterly magazine, and *The Heraldry Gazette*, which is quarterly and contains Society news

Badge of the Heraldry Society

and comments on events and news of an heraldic nature.

By letters patent dated 10 August 1957, arms, supporters and a badge were granted to the Society: *Quarterly Azure and Gules a Lion's Face crowned with an Ancient Crown within a Tressure flory on the outer edge Or.* The supporters are two black unicorns *armed unguled crined and tufted Or wreathed about the neck with a Torse Argent and Gules,* from the arms of the Society's founder. The badge, *A Lion's Face crowned with an Ancient Crown within an Annulet flory on the outer edge Or,* is depicted on the mantling in the arms and on the Society's standard. JB-L

See also ADDRESSES

Heraldry, Spurious *see* **Spurious Heraldry**

Heralds' College *see* **College of Arms**

Heralds' Museum at the Tower of London Opened in the old Waterloo Barracks in the Tower of London in 1981, it is run by the College of Arms Trust. The museum is open from the beginning of April to the end of October, admission being included in the price of a ticket to visit the Tower. Exhibits include treasures from the College of Arms, and artefacts borrowed from other sources, and some exhibits are changed each year. JB-L

Heralds of the Nobility From the very earliest times heralds took their titles of office from their masters' names, styles, mottoes, devices or mere fancies. The list which follows, drawn from a number of sources, is inevitably incomplete, for no doubt many manuscripts mentioning heralds have not survived or are still awaiting discovery. The following abbreviations apply: K, King of Arms; H, Herald; P, Pursuivant; E, Extraordinary. A date after a bracket, e.g. (1403, indicates the earliest known mention of the office; N/D indicates no date.

English Heralds

Antelope P (temp. Henry V); Arundel H (1413, to Earl of Arundel); Aulet P (1383, to Sir Peter Courteney?); Bardolf H (1368, to Lord Bardolf); Bath K (1725, to serve Order of the Bath); Bedford H (1428, to the Duke of Bedford); Bellesme P (*c.* 1420, to Earl of Salisbury); Bensilver P (*c.* 1440); Berners P (1562, to Lord Berners, also called Barnes P); Berwick P (temp. Edward IV); Besoure P (1380); Beul P (fl 1446, to Matthew Goff); Bien Alaunt P (*c.* 1450, to Earl of Warwick); Biencele P (1434, to Duke of Bedford, also called Biendelle); Bien Colier P (1444); Blanc Coursier H (1725, to Prince William); Blanch Lyon P (*c.* 1465, initially to the crown, then to Duke of Norfolk); Blanchlyverer P (1418, to Mauleverer family); Blanche Sanglier P (1480, to Duke of Gloucester); Blanquefort P (1463, to Lord Duras KG); Bonaventure P (1445, to Lord Hoo); Bonespoir H or P (*c.* 1460); Bon Rapport P (1448); Bontemps P (1434); Bordeaux H (temp. Richard II); Boulogne P (1544); Broke P (1489, to Lord Broke); Brunswick H (1725, to Prince William); Buckingham H or P (1447, to Duke of Buckingham); Bucky P (1490); Cadran H (1414, to Earl of Dorset); Calais H (temp. Henry VIII); Calveley H (1382, to Sir Hugh Calveley); Cambridge H (1380); Carolina H (1705); Chandos H (1360, to Sir John Chandos); Chateaubleu P (1465, to Lord Mountjoy); Clarence H (*c.* 1419, to Duke of Clarence); Coller P (*c.* 1436); Condé P (1428); Corbin P (1431, to Sir Richard Gethin); Cornwall H (1398, to Prince of Wales); Crescent P (N/D, to Lord Percy); Croyslett P (*c.* 1380); Derby H (1384, or (H)Erby, to Henry Bolingbroke); Derväll H (1361, to Sir Robert Knolles); Desirous P (*c.* 1450); Devoir P (1439, to Lord Hungerford); Dieu Y Pourvoye P (1430); Diligent P (*c.* 1431, to Sir Ralph Neville); Dorset H (to Earl of Dorset; Dublin P (1502, recreated as H 1783); Eagle P (1389, to Earl of Derby?); Eagle Vert P (1429, to Earl of Salisbury); Esperance P (1438, to Earl of Northumberland); Esperance Herbert P (1523, to Lord Herbert); Espoir P (1442, to Sir John Lisle); Etoile Volant P (1515, to Sir Richard Wingfield); Exeter H (*c.* 1416, to Duke of Exeter); Falcon P (temp. Henry VI); Fitzwalter P (1485, to Duke of Bedford); Fleur de Lis H (1435); Gloucester H (*c.* 1400, to Earl of Gloucester); Groby H or P (1425, to Marquis of Dorset); Gryphon P (*c.* 1385, to Earl of Salisbury); Guisnes P (temp. Edward IV); Hampnes P (1360); Harrington P (1475, also Harington, to Marquis of Dorset); Hastings P (1480, to Lord Hastings); Hembre P (1435); Herbert P (1514, to Lord Herbert); Hereford H (1369, to Earl of Hereford); Huntingdon H (1441, to Duke of Exeter); Il Faut Faire P (1443, to Sir John Fastolf); (1415, to Lord Bonville); Joye P (*c.* 1453, to Lord Scales); Kendal H (1430): Kildare P (*c.* 1512, to Lord Kildare. The title also appears corruptly as Gardare); Lancaster H (1347, to Earl of Lancaster); Leicester H (1386, to John of Gaunt); Leon d'Or P (1446, to Lord Dudley); Leopard H (1467); Le Sparre

P (1449, to Earl of Worcester); Lisle P (1513, to Sir Charles Brandon); Longchamp P (1433); Louvre P (1430, to Duke of Bedford); Loveyn P (1445, to Henry Bourchier); Loyaute P (c. 1440); Lyon P (1429, to Thomas Burgh); Maine H (1428); Maltravers P (c. 1540, to Lord Maltravers); Maltravers HE (1887); March K and H (1337, to Earl of March); Marenceux P (c. 1463); Marleon de Aye P (1522, to Sir Charles Brandon E.M.); Merlyne P (c. 1470); Montacue P (c. 1470); Montorgueil P and H (c. 1495); Mortain H (1450); Mouncells P (c. 1470); Mowbray H (c. 1390); Mushon K? (1353); Nazers H (14th century); Newhaven P (c. 1544); Nogent P (c. 1460); Noir Lion P (1498, to Viscount Wells); Noir Taureau (?1475, to Duke of Clarence); Norfolk HE? (1539, to Duke of Norfolk); Norfolk H (1538); Northampton H (1370, to Earl of Northampton); Northumberland H (c. 1473, to Earl of Northumberland); Nottingham H (1398); Nucells P (1446, to Earl Rivers); Papillon P (1423); Passavant P (1431, to Sir Thomas Stainer); Patiens P (c. 1470); Pembroke H (1424, to Duke of Gloucester); Percy H (c. 1385, to Earl of Northumberland); Pisore or Pisow P (1379); Portcullis P (c. 1490); Portsmouth PE (1604); Purchase P (c. 1470); Rasyn P (1435, to Duke of Bedford); Richmond H (1412, to Duke of Bedford); Risebank P (c. Edward IV); Rivers H or P (c. 1466, to Earl Rivers); Rose Blanche P (1482); Rouge Dragon P (c. 1485); Rutland H (1395, to Earl of Rutland); Salisbury H (1388, to Earl of Salisbury); Sans Repose P (c. 1430); Scales P (c. 1445, to Lord Scales); Segret or Secret P (c. 1425, to Sir John Fastolf); Serreshall P (c. 1490, to Sir Richard Nanfant); Shrewsbury H or P (1403, to Earl of March); Somerset H (1448, to Duke of Somerset); Stafford H (1355, to Earl of Stafford); Suffolk H (1385); Talbot H (1456); Thury P (1428); Torrington P (1431, to Earl of Huntingdon); Tyger P (1477, to Lord Hastings); Verrey P (c. 1475); Volant or Vaillant K (14th century); Villebon P (1449); Wales or Waleys H (1393, to Earl of March?); Wallingford P (temp. Henry VI); Wark P (1454, to Lord Grey); Warwick H (1435, to Duke of Warwick); Wexford P (1436, to Earl of Shrewsbury); Worcester H (1449, to Earl of Worcester); York H (1484, to Duke of York).

Scottish Heralds

Albany H (1398, to Duke of Albany); Alihay, possibly Islay? P (c. 1426, to the Lord of the Isles, if the spelling were truly Islay); Angus H (1490, to Earl of Angus); Armyldoun, possibly Hamilton? P (1482); Bruce H (1401, to, possibly, the Earl of Carrick); Buchan H (?1409, to Earl of Buchan); Carrick H (1364, perhaps as early as 1306, to the Earl of Carrick); Darnaway P (1499, to the Earl of Moray); Dingwall P (1460, perhaps to the Earl of Ross); Douglas H (1327); Endure P (1454, to the Earl of Crawford); Garioch P (1501, to the Earl of Mar and Garioch); Hailes P (1488,

to Earl of Bothwell); Hamilton P (see Armyldoun); Islay H (1493); Kintyre P (prior to 1494, to the lords of the isles); Lennox H (c. 1419, to Earl Buchan); Lindsay H (1398, to Earl Crawford); Montrose P (1488, to Earl of Montrose); Marchmont H (1438); Orkney H (1581, to Earl of Orkney?); Ormonde P (1487, to. Marquess of Ormonde); Ross H (1475, to Earl of Ross); Rothesay H (?1370, to Lord High Steward); Slaines P (1404, to Earl of Errol).

European Heralds

During the Middle Ages there were numerous heralds throughout Europe. Many held high office, others were hardly better than vagabonds, travelling from tournament to castle, to battle, looking for employment — as was never the case in England. Perhaps the most famous were Toison d'Or and Montjoie, although the latter was the title of a royal officer in the time of Charles V (1364-80). Toison d'Or (the Golden Fleece) was founded in 1430 by the Duke of Burgundy who, at the same time, appointed a king of arms of that name to serve the order. It is, from the English sources available, difficult to distinguish royal from non-royal heralds in France, for the style *roy d'armes des Franchois* rotated between different offices at different times. Offices of note are Alençon K; Berry K; Bourbon K; Calabré K; Champagne K; Charolais K (c. 1425, to Duke of Burgundy); Dampier H; Guesclin H; Horne H; Jerusalem H; Navarre H (c. 1368); Normandy H (1347); Orleans H; Sealand H (c. 1393); Sicily H (to Aragon and Sicily); Swethe H (c. 1393); Voulévrier H. JC-K

See also ROYAL HERALDS

Further reading
Cokayne, G.E. *The Complete Peerage* Vol XI, App C.
Godfrey, W.H. (and others) *The College of Arms* London, 1963.
Wagner, A. *The Heralds of England* London, 1967.

Heralds' Tract *see* **Treatises**

Heraudie, de *see* **Treatises**

Herb *see* **Poland, Armorial Practice**

Hereditary Champion of England An office borne by a member of the Dymoke family since the coronation of Richard II in 1377. The first of the Norman-English line was Robert Marmion, Champion to King William I, whose ancestors had been Hereditary Champions to the Dukes of Normandy. In the fourteenth century the title passed to Sir John Dymoke (who had married the Marmion heiress), and the office has been exercised by his descendants ever since.

The duty of the Champion is to 'ride completely armed upon a barbed horse into Westminster Hall after the coronation and there to challenge to combat with whomsoever should deny the monarch's right to the Crown.' This ceremony was observed through the centuries, but after the confusion it caused at the coronation of King George IV it was never again performed, subsequent champions bearing the ensign of England (1901 and 1911), and that of the Union (1937 and 1953), in substitution for the robust events of earlier days.

The badge of office of the Hereditary Champion of England is a *Sword erect hilt and pommel Or* and this may be found quartered on a sable field with the arms of Dymoke *Sable two Lions passant Argent ducally crowned Or*. The Dymoke motto 'Pro Rege Dimico' (I Fight for the King) is a canting reference to the family name. The family's punning crest of two 'moke's ears' (donkey's ears) was considered to be rather too much of a good thing, and the ears were changed to those of a hare, though some branches of the family still use the original crest.   JC-K

Hereditary Chief Butler of Ireland Theobald FitzWalter was created Chief Butler of Ireland in 1177. His son, the second Butler, assumed the name of le Botiler (or Butler) in 1221. The head of the Butler family is now the Marquess of Ormonde, the present marquess being the 32nd holder of the hereditary post. The office of Butler (anciently in charge of the wine butts) is marked in the second quarter of the Ormonde arms *Gules three covered Cups Or*.   JC-K

Hereditary Cup Bearer In 1297 the noble family of De Argentine held land in Cambridgeshire by grand serjeanty of serving the king at his coronation with a silver cup. The office became the prerogative of the family and the ancient office is alluded to in their arms: *Gules three covered Cups Argent*, and their crest, *a demi-Lion Gules holding a covered Cup*.   JC-K

Hereditary Grand Almoner of England Not to be confused with the High Almoner, who is always a bishop, this post is attached to the Manor of Bedford and is held in the family of Cecil, marquesses of Exeter. Anciently the Grand Almoner was responsible for the royal charities, but today his only duty is to collect the offering from those present at a coronation.

Hereditary Grand Falconer of England There was for many centuries a King's Falconer, but the present office of Hereditary Grand Falconer, held by the Dukes of St Albans, was conferred on the first of the present creation, Sir Charles Beauclerk KG, natural son of King Charles II and Nell Gwynne, around 1690. The arms of St Albans do not allude to the office, although several holders have been known to have

had special 'uniforms' made to mark their tenure. The present Duke is the 13th Grand Falconer.   JC-K

Hereditary Grand Master of the Household in Scotland This office is vested in the Duke of Argyll who may place a baton gules, semy of thistles and tipped with an Imperial Crown, bendwise behind his shield of arms.

Hereditary Justice-General of Scotland This office is vested in the Duke of Argyll who places a sword proper, hilt and pommel gold, bend sinisterwise behind his arms.

Hereditary Keeper of St Fillan's Crozier An office which is an honour of the Dewar family. The insignia of office are two croziers of St Fillan proper placed saltirewise behind the shield of arms.

Hereditary Lord Great Seneschal of Ireland This office is vested in the Earl of Shrewsbury, who may place a white wand palewise behind his shield of arms.

Hereditary Lord High Constable of Scotland The office of Lord High Constable of Scotland (*see* CONSTABLE) has been held by the Earls of Erroll since 1314, when Sir Gilbert Erroll was created such by charter, as a reward for his adherence to Robert the Bruce, and on the forfeiture of his Comyn cousins. The present Earl of Erroll is the 28th Hereditary Lord High Constable. The armorial symbols of office are *on either side of the Shield an Arm gauntleted proper issuing out of a Cloud and grasping a Sword palewise Argent hilt and pommel Or behind the Shield saltirewise two Silver Batons tipped with Gold at either end*.   JC-K

Hereditary Marshal of Ireland The office is now in abeyance, if not entirely extinguished. The insignia of office were two batons placed saltirewise behind the shield of arms.

Hereditary Offices One of the characteristics of feudalism was the creation of numerous hereditary (or heritable) offices with which service to the nobility or the Crown was recognized and rewarded. It should not be imagined that all such offices were sinecures, for although many have since become ceremonial and others extinguished, their origins were very much concerned with the day-to-day administration of society, and in particular those aspects of it which appertained directly to the Crown. Such offices are legion, and it is possible here to provide only an indication of their diversity.

In the eleventh and twelfth centuries the Earls of Chester were Honorary (H.) Viscounts (*vicecomes*) of Avranches, Vau de Vire, and Bayeaux. In 1119 Robert, Earl of Gloucester, was H. Governor of Caen and H.

Banner-bearer of Bayeaux Cathedral; in 1152 the Earl of Northampton was H. High Farrier to the king; in 1189 the Earl of Norfolk was H. Steward to the (Royal) Household; in 1199 the Earl of Hereford was H. Constable of England. During the same period the Earl of Arundel was H. Chief Butler of England and H. Patron of Wymundham Abbey. The Earl of Derby was H. Patron of four religious houses — two abbeys and two priories. In 1148 the Earl of Pembroke was H. Marshal of England, while in 1148 the Earl of Oxford was H. Steward of the Royal Forests in Essex.

Several hereditary offices became the prerogative of one man. Around 1270, for example, the Earl of Norfolk and Suffolk was H. Marshal of England, H. Steward of the Household, H. Bearer of the Banner of St Edmund, H. Forester of Farnedale and H. Warden of Romford Forest. A little later the Earl of March was H. Constable of two castles and H. Patron of two religious institutions. Also in the thirteenth and fourteenth centuries the Earls of Derby were H. Lord Sewers to the king, Enguerrand de Courcy, Earl of Bedford, was H. Grand Butler of France, the Earl of Salisbury was H. Advocate of Montacute Priory and H. Steward of Chester.

There were many other h. stewardships, posts of h. constable, and h. keepers of castles, woods and palaces, and many of these were endowed with INSIGNIA OF OFFICE.

An examination of the records of the fifteenth to nineteenth centuries shows the pattern continued, with some interesting additions. In 1479 the Earl of Pembroke was H. Chief Justice and Chamberlain of South Wales; in 1451 Baron de Sale was H. Warden of the Cinque Ports; in 1525 the Earl of Cumberland was H. Sheriff of Westmoreland. Other titles of note are: H. Master-Marshal and Surveyor of Hawks (the Earl of Carnarvon, 1643); H. Chief Avenor of the Crown (the Earl of Carnarvon, also 1643); H. Collector of Alnage on Woollen Cloths in England and Wales (Duke of Richmond and Lennox, 1626); H. Admiral of the Isle of Man (Earl of Derby, 1651); H. Sheriff-Principal of Dumfriesshire (Duke of Dover and Queensberry, *c.* 1715); H. Registrar of the Court of Chancery (Duke of St Albans, 1751); H. Master Falconer of England, also styled H. Grand Falconer (Duke of St Albans, also 1751).

Among numerous hereditary titles still extant are Earl Marshal and H. Marshal of England (Duke of Norfolk); H. Abbot of the Exempt Jurisdiction of Newry and Mourne (Earl of Kilmorey); H. Governor of Repton School (Earl of Loudon); H. Thane of Lennox (Earl of Perth); Joint H. Lord Great Chamberlain of England (Earl of Ancaster); H. Grand Almoner (Marquess of Exeter); H. Champion (and Standard Bearer) of England (the head of the Dymoke family); H. Lord Great Seneschal of Ireland (Earl of Shrewsbury); H. Justice-General of Scotland (Duke of Argyll); H. Ranger of Whittlebury Forest (Duke of Grafton); H. Chief Butler of Ireland (Marquess of Ormond); H. Lord High Constable of Scotland (head of the Dewar family); H. Keeper of Raglan Castle (Duke of Beaufort); H. Grand Falconer of England (Duke of St Albans). The foregoing are merely examples selected to illustrate both the range of offices and their often flamboyant titles. The list is by no means definitive. JC-K/SS

See also GRAND SERJEANTRY; LORD WARDEN OF THE CINQUE PORTS; ROYAL FORESTERS, WARDENS AND VERDURERS

Hereditary Squire to the Royal Body and Royal Armour Bearer in Scotland A hereditary office held by the family of Hay-Seton of Abercorn since 1488, when a charter was granted to Sir Alexander Seton by James IV of Scotland.

Hereditary Standard Bearer of Scotland An office held by the family of Scrymgeour-Wedderburn of Cupar at least since the accession of James VI (and I of England) in 1603.

Herr This German word could mean 'lord', 'master', 'ruler' and 'gentleman', depending on circumstances. In much the way that the English words 'gentleman' and 'esquire' have become debased, Herr is now merely the equivalent of the English Mr. JC-K

Herse A barrel-shaped metal cage placed over an EFFIGY and originally intended to support a pall cover, which was removed from the tomb only on special occasions. One of the most magnificent examples is that on the tomb of Richard Beauchamp at St Mary's church, Warwick.

High Sheriff *see* **Sheriff**

Hilted *see* **Attributes**

Hippocampus A marine sea-horse.

Hippogriff A monster comprising the foreparts of a griffin and the hind parts of a horse.

Hoist That part of a flag adjacent to the mast or pole. *See also* FLY

Holy Ghost, Order of the The first Order of the Holy Ghost was founded in 1190 as a hospital order; its badge was a knot. The same name was given to the second most important order of France, founded in 1578. The badge was an eight-pointed gold cross, edged in green and white, with a dove on the obverse and St Michael on the reverse sides. KH

Holy Roman Empire An 'empire' which existed from AD 962 to 1806. The foundation was substantially that of Pope John XII, who invited King Otto I of Germany to revive the Roman Empire which had been preserved *by* the church as a concept and *in* the church as a fact of organisation. There was to be the philosophy of a single Christian Church, with Christ as its head, an emperor as a sign of its secular indivisible unity, and a doctrine of realism demanding that Europe should be a single political entity.

Otto achieved the crown of Italy in addition to that of Germany and was annointed 'emperor' on Candlemass Day 962. The Pope and Emperor stood as equal joint sovereigns of what they regarded as the commonwealth of Europe.

In time the Holy Roman Emperors (Otto's line and its successors) assumed the degree of feudal overlords of mere kings and princes, whilst from the mid-twelfth century, the popes claimed for themselves the overlordship of the whole world, with the emperor as their chief vassal. The resultant struggle between popes and emperors was protracted. Italy was lost and a new Germany arose, but its kings, even after 300 years, continued as 'emperors', although this title meant very little more than the presidency of the German federation. With the Reformation, the 'presidency' came to mean less and less, the unity of the Christian church had been lost, there was no 'empire' outside Germany, and even within it only a legal fiction.

The coming of Napoleon in the wake of the French Revolution saw the end of what was neither Holy, Roman nor an Empire. In the face of his formidable Corsican adversary, Francis I resigned as emperor in August 1806, assuming the title of Hereditary Emperor of Austria, leaving Napoleon to be Emperor of the French.

As Arch Treasurers to the Holy Roman Empire, the kings of England from George I to William IV bore in the centre of the Hanoverian arms a representation of the crown of Charlemagne on an inescutcheon gules.   JC-K

Holy Sepulchre, Venerable Order of the Tradition assigns the foundation of this order to Godfrey de Bouillon, Duke of Lower Lorraine (*c.* 1090), a dedicated crusader who is reputed to have given the accolade of knighthood to persons of noble degree making a pilgrimage to the church of the Holy Sepulchre in Jerusalem. It is, however, far more likely that it was founded by Pope Alexander VI (the Borgia) in 1496 as a military order whose duty it was to protect the site of the Holy Sepulchre.

The right to nominate to the order was shared by the pope (as grand master) and the guardian of the *Patres Minores* in Jerusalem. By the sixteenth century the guardian of the Franciscan monastery on Mount Sion had assumed this duty, and later still, in the middle of the nineteenth century, the Latin Patriarch in Jerusalem took over. In 1905 the last-named was nominated grand master, but the pope reserves the right of joint nomination. Today the order is concerned mainly with acts of teaching and the maintenance of the fabric of buildings in the Holy Land.   JC-K

Holy Water Sprinkler A short pole arm with spiked head and point.

Honorary Armorial Bearings Although arms cannot be granted to foreign nationals the kings of arms may grant honorary armorial bearings to citizens of the United States of America, on the same conditions as they grant to a British subject, except that the grantee must be descended in the direct, legitimate, male line from a subject of the Crown, and must enter in the records of the College of Arms a pedigree proving this descent. Honorary arms may also be granted to an American citizen who is in receipt of an honour from the British Crown, such as an honorary membership of the Order of the British Empire or an associate member of the Most Venerable Order of St John. Naturally, such arms cannot be protected in America unless the grantee has recourse to the protection afforded by the federal copyright laws, but the grantee can be certain that a similar coat has never been granted before and never will be granted in future to any person or institution over whom the English kings of arms have armorial jurisdiction.   JB-L
See also DEVISAL OF ARMS

Honourable *see* **Courtesy Title**

Honourable Ordinary *see* **Ordinary**

Honour Point *see* **Shield, Points of the**

Honours and Investiture Honours, in recognition of singular service to the sovereign or state, are bestowed in countries throughout the world. Very few do not make provision in their constitutions for some form of recognition, Switzerland and the Republic of Ireland being two such countries. In Britain, some 4500 individuals are awarded honours each year. These consist of peerages, membership of the various orders of chivalry and merit, knighthoods and decorations for service or gallantry. They are published in two 'honours' lists, one on the sovereign's official birthday in June and one in the New Year, though recipients are invited to confirm acceptance of their honour some time before the publication of the lists.

Peers are introduced at a special ceremony in the House of Lords, attended by two fellow peers acting as 'supporters' and Garter King of Arms in tabard and carrying his sceptre. All three peers wear the parliamentary robes of their degree, often borrowed for the occasion. The Lord Chancellor enters first in wig and black tricorn hat and is seated at the Woolsack on which is placed the Purse containing the Great Seal. Black Rod then escorts the new peer and his supporters into the Upper Chamber, where he shows himself to his fellow peers so that in future he may be recognized. He bows three times to the Cloth of Estate on the throne, which symbolizes the royal presence, and going down on one knee presents to the Lord Chancellor his Writ of Summons and Letters Patent of Creation, which are than read aloud by the Reading Clerk to the House of Lords. In February 1987 Prince Andrew, the second son of Elizabeth II, was introduced as Baron Killarney, Earl of Inverness and Duke of York: 'Know Ye that We of Our especial Grace certain knowledge and mere motion do by these Presents advance create and prefer the said Prince . . . to the state degree style dignity title and honour of Duke of York and by these Presents do dignify invest and enoble him by girding him with a Sword and putting a Cap of Honour and a Coronet of Gold on his head and by giving into his hand a Rod of Gold . . .'

The letters patent are issued by warrant under the Queen's sign manual. The peer then takes the oath of allegiance to the Queen and signs the Test Roll. Before being greeted by his fellow peers he undertakes the ceremonial doffing of hats three times with the Lord Chancellor. The origin of this strange little ceremony is unknown.

Members of the ancient orders of chivalry are installed at special ceremonies at Windsor Castle (Order of the Garter) or Edinburgh (Order of the Thistle).

Members of other orders and recipients of decorations attend one of the fourteen or so investitures held each year, usually in the ballroom of Buckingham Palace. These are attended by the Queen in person, or another senior member of the royal family if she is abroad. The investiture is attended by three (no more) relatives or friends of the recipient. The sovereign stands on a dais in front of the throne, attended by five Yeomen of the Guard and two of the Queen's Gurkha officers. Four Gentlemen Ushers to the Queen also attend, and the Master of the Household or a member of the Lord Chamberlain's Office hands the Queen the insignia to be presented to each recipient. As the name is announced, he or she steps forward (having entered from 'the wings, stage right', where the recipients wait in an ante-room) and is invested with the insignia. Knights receive the accolade by kneeling on one knee to be dubbed on each shoulder with the sword. This simple ceremony has been the custom for many centuries, knights being dubbed both on the field of battle and off. King George knighted several military commanders in the field, and Sir Francis Chichester was knighted at Greenwich after his single-handed voyage round the world in 1967, the Queen using a sword which had once belonged to Sir Francis Drake. Investitures are also held in Edinburgh and overseas when the sovereign is visiting a Commonwealth country.

There is, of course, continuing controversy regarding the honours system, and in particular hereditary honours. (It should be remembered here that a grant of arms is a form of hereditary honour emanating from the sovereign.) Much of the controversy is, of course, political and in practice very few hereditary peerages have been created in recent times. However, there are those who regularly advocate the reform of the system, arguing that it is susceptible to political manipulation: 'Time for Parliament to clean up the great British gong show' was the caption for a feature article in *The Times* in the New Year of 1987.

Further reading

Brooke-Little, J. *The British Monarchy* Poole, 1976.

Walker, J. *The Queen has been Pleased: the British Honours System at Work* 1986.

Honours of Scotland, The These are the crown of Robert the Bruce, the Sword of State presented to James IV of Scotland by Pope Julius II in 1507, and the Sceptre, an elaborate version of the coronation wand of the Dalriadic Scottish kings. The Honours were originally used in the coronation of Scottish kings, the last occasion being that of Charles II in 1651 (as King of Scotland, not of England). In 1953, they were escorted from Edinburgh Castle by an officer and ten archers of the Royal Company, and were carried in front of Elizabeth II during her Progress in St Giles' Cathedral. The Honours of Scotland are the oldest crown jewels remaining in Britain, and may be seen on daily display in the Castle of Edinburgh.

Hooded *see* **Attributes**

Horned *see* **Attributes**

Horse When shown rearing, a horse is said to be forcene, otherwise the various attitudes conform to other beasts. A horse's head is often termed a nag's head.

Horse Bells, Pendants and Brasses One of the first representations of a horse bell in use occurs in Caxton's *Game and Playe of Chesse* (1476), the earliest illustrated book printed in English. A knight is shown fully armed, his horse caparisoned and 'coveryd with hys armes' and wearing, up-ended on its crupper, a large bell.

189

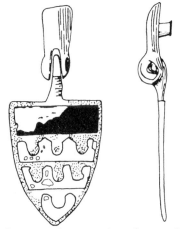

Fourteenth century horse pendant, front and side view, bearing the Stoke arms.

By the early seventeenth century, horse bells were well established as prizes at the races, and in 1610 a superb set of three was presented by the Sheriff of Chester at a meeting in that city. The first was of silver double gilt and bore the arms of 'the Kynge' (James I) and one of the others the arms of 'the Princes'. The practice of ornamenting horse bells with armorial bearings appears to have continued for many years.

Metal pendants for enhancing horse harness have a very ancient history, specimens are known dating from the late Bronze Age (about 500 BC), and they appear, in the light of further archaeological evidence, to have had a continuous application from that time onwards. Most of the early ones were extremely plain, but by the medieval period pendants were cast to a high quality and richly decorated with armorial devices in coloured enamel. All kinds of motifs are known — lions, resplendent birds, crowns and coronets. Some armorial pendants are able to be dated precisely. Two fine examples, now in Salisbury and South Wiltshire Museum, may be cited. The first shows the arms of Sir Robert Fitzpaine, Governor of Corfe Castle in. 1304, and the other depicts, on opposite faces, the shields of St Maur and Lovell — presumably marking the union of Nicholas St Maur and Muriel Lovell in 1351. Another pendant, illustrated actual size, which may also be dated to the fourteenth century, was excavated in 1983 in Dorset. The arms are those of Stoke, or Estoke (*Vair a Chief Gules*), later adopted by the Clavell family of Smedmore.

Although some modern scholars believe that the medieval use of enamelled pendants on horse harness was not quite as widespread as was at one time believed, by the eighteenth century it was the fashion to decorate carriage-horse harness with finely made precious metal family crests — on the brow bands, blinkers, side-straps, martingales and saddles. By

contrast, heavy-horse brasses of the now-popular variety were never particularly fine to begin with (when judged against the above), nor do they have a long history. It is extremely rare to discover a brass dating from earlier than the mid-nineteenth century, and a difficult task to find any textual references. As late as 1855 the *Encyclopaedia of Agriculture* made no reference to harness brasses. Nonetheless, when they were finally produced in quantity (around the 1860s) they quickly displayed pseudo-armorial designs such as unicorns, lions, eagles and other heraldic beasts. In the early years of the twentieth century, ceramic enamels were called into service to lend areas of solid colour to horse brasses, and many were made by hand by a repouseé technique rather than by sand casting and fettling. Occasionally German silver 'brasses' were made, and sometimes nickel was used, and in the 1930s aluminium was preferred by some manufacturers. With the passing of carriages and work-horses, harness brasses have become the province of the collector. For the National Horse Brass Society *see* ADDRESSES.   JC-K

Further reading
Hartfield, G. *Horse Brasses* 1956.
Keegan, T. *The Heavy Horse, its Harness and Harness Decoration* 1973.
Vince, J. *Discovering Horse Brasses* 1972. Contains a useful bibliography.

Horseshoe Unless otherwise blazoned, the armorial horseshoe has its points downwards.

Hospitallers *see* **St John of Jerusalem, Orders**

House Flag The flag of a shipping company, airline, commercial organization, etc., usually composed of the company's colours and logo. Rarely armorial.

Household Badge *see* **Badge**

House of Commons The lower of the two houses of parliament of the United Kingdom of Great Britain and Northern Ireland. Members are elected by the citizens in accordance with specific procedures under the law. The House of Commons has the exclusive right to institute legislation to originate the provision of supplies to the service of the state and for the imposition of taxes.   JC-K

Further reading
Hasler, P.W. *The House of Commons 1558-1603* 3 vols, 1981.

House of Lords The upper of the two houses of parliament of the United Kingdom of Great Britain and Northern Ireland. Membership is not elective, but by right or elevation (hereditary peers and life peers, the 'lords temporal'), or by custom (senior bishops, the 'lords spiritual'). The members of the house form a permanent council to the crown, and, when lawfully assembled, the highest court of judicature in the land. Until the Parliament Act of 1911, the House of Lords was co-equal with the House of Commons, and no laws could be made without its consent, but this is no longer the case.   JC-K

Further reading
Pike, L.O. *Constitutional History of the House of Lords* 1951.

Humetty Couped at the ends.

Hungary, Armorial Practice The Hungarian Peoples' Republic has, by a decree of 1947, abolished all aristocratic ranks and forbidden the use of titles of nobility, coats of arms and devices of like kind. There are, however (1076, State Regulation No.3, Paragraph 13), a number of awards, the most senior or which is Hero of Socialist Labour.

The Hungarian people derive from the fifth to ninth-century confederation of the Magyars, called *On-Ogur* (Ten Arrows), from which the name 'Hungarian' descends. Over the dark, and later the medieval, centuries, they were subject to Saxon, Turkish, Bohemian, Austrian and other influences. They have lived under tyrants, kings, emperors and regents.

The general adoption of arms dates from the early fifteenth century, initially by personal will, but later by letters patent. These latter were predicated under local government seals, and after the first quarter of the sixteenth century matriculated in a national register, the *Libri Regii* (since published). The archives in both Budapest and Vienna contain thousands of documents illustrating the designs of Hungarian arms over the centuries.   JC-K

Hurt, Heurt *or* **Heurte** A blue roundel, possibly derived from the hurtle-berry or whortle-berry, commonly known as the bilberry. The Old French word *hurte* means a knock or bruise, which (presumably) turns blue! The modern word 'hurt' meaning pain or damage derives from the same source.

Hurty *or* **Hurte** Semy of hurts.

Hydra In heraldry the hydra is depicted as a dragon with a multiplicity of heads, sometimes three, sometimes seven. When one of its heads was cut off three would grow in its place. The hydra dragon was believed to live on the Island of Lerna, or in the marshes of Arcadia.   MY

I

Ibex An heraldic antelope with serrated horns pointing forwards.

Iceland, Armorial Practice The republic of Iceland was proclaimed on 17 June 1944, having been since 1918 an independent state under the king of Denmark. Prior to that date it had been, from the thirteenth century, a vassal dominion. It had no hereditary nobility of its own, although a number of its people had held Norwegian or Danish titles. Few details are known of their arms, but these are certain to have conformed to Danish practice. As might be expected the arms of Iceland have been changed several times in the course of its history, and are now *Azure a Cross Argent charged with a Cross Gules* supported by four legendary beasts from the Norse sagas.   JC-K

Ilk (Scotland) A word meaning 'the same' in the context of being the chief of the name, e.g. Moncreiffe of that Ilk is the chief of the name Moncreiffe, and could be written Moncreiffe of Moncreiffe.   CJB

Illumination A manuscript which is described as illuminated is one which is decorated in colours and gold, and sometimes silver. When the page is bent, and the precious metals are caught by the light, it appears to possess a lustrous quality unequalled by other forms of decoration. The great proportion of heraldry is illuminated in this way, except in instances where, either for reasons of economy or for photographic reproduction, yellow and white have been substituted for gold and silver.

Because armory requires the juxtaposition of metals and colours, it has always had a high decorative value which artists have been quick to exploit. Also, because of its timeless nature (notwithstanding style or period), it remains visually one of the richest and most intrinsically satisfying forms of manuscript decoration.

The gilding on three-dimensional work (on artefacts, buildings, etc.) is done with gold or aluminium leaf, using oil-bound varnish as a base, particularly when prolonged exposure to varying weather conditions is expected. The gilding on manuscripts is done in quite a different way. Gold and silver, or more often aluminium, can be applied in the form of a powder mixed with a suitable water-based medium and used as a pigment. It has the double advantage of being comparatively easy to do and having a wider range of possible treatments. It can also to some extent be burnished. This is the method used by the herald painters at the College of Arms.

These metals can also be applied in the form of leaf, either directly to the working surface or on a ground which is composed of deactivated calcium sulphate, lead carbonate, an animal glue and sugar, called by Cennino Cennini 'Gesso sottile'. The plaster ground is either applied with a quill pen or painted on, and dries hard, flexible and raised. The leaf is then applied and polished or burnished with an agate burnisher. This process is difficult to do and is unpredictable, sometimes wasting much time and expensive materials. But the raised and brilliantly burnished gold which results when it is done skilfully holds an extraordinary fascination, and has captured people's imagination since it was first used.

In a succession of fifteenth-century manuscripts, heraldry formed the central theme of the decoration of some pages, and raised gilding always played a major part. Some of the most impressive examples are in the British Library, although the College of Arms also has its share. John, Duke of Bedford, brother of Henry V, commissioned a book of hours to be made as a wedding present for his bride, Anne of Burgundy. It was executed in 1423 by a team of artists working under Pol de Limbourg, one of three brothers who were some of the finest book illuminators of their day. The Bedford arms and badges, the silver eagle, the black antelope and the gold tree stump of Woodstock appear as decorative motifs throughout the book, as do the arms of Burgundy (Additional MS 18850).

A book of French romances presented by John Talbot, Earl of Shrewsbury, to Henry VI's bride, Margaret of Anjou, in 1445 has a magnificent heraldic page. It contains a genealogical table in the form of a large fleur-de-lis, showing the French and English royal descents from St Louis, uniting at the base in the figure of Henry VI of England. The page abounds with lions, fleurs-de-lis, shields of arms, banners, badges, garters and motto scrolls, all glittering with burnished gold. This is heraldic illumination at its best (Royal MS 15.E.VI.,f.3.). Gilding of this kind is still very much in evidence, and may be used to great effect on heraldic subjects.

One of the most beautiful examples of modern heraldic illumination is a manuscript book in the library of Canterbury Cathedral. The *Canterbury Book of Arms* was commissioned just before the Second World War by friends of the cathedral to record the medieval arms carved on the cloister roof bosses, so that in the event of the cathedral being damaged or destroyed by enemy action they could be restored. It was carried out under the guidance of Professor E.W. Tristram by a team of three graduates of the Royal College of Art. One of them, William Gardner, the only student ever to take an A.R.C.A. in heraldry, has since become eminent in the field of seal and coin design and is one of the leading calligraphers in

Britain. It is a large book, 13½ by 19 inches (34 by 48 cm), written on vellum, designed so that each page contains three columns. The first consists of the names of the armigers, the second their shields of arms illustrated in a large size in burnished gold and colour, with the blazons of the arms forming the last. The columns of shields are offset from the centre of the page so that when the book is closed they lie side by side, avoiding wear on the gilding and excessive strain on the binding.

It is a tradition in England that only metallic gold and not silver or a substitute is used by the herald painters. Silver looks equally rich, but will have tarnished badly within about seven years, depending on the atmospheric conditions in which the work is kept. Aluminium or platinum are sometimes employed as substitutes, but in spite of the very high cost of the latter, neither have the sharpness or brilliance of silver.

The use of raised and burnished gold in heraldry does impose limitations on the size in which work can be done, and on the amount of detail which can profitably be included. But when it is well used it imparts a brilliance and richness to the work which cannot be achieved by any other means. AW
See also ARMORIAL STYLES; ART WORK AND MATERIALS; CALLIGRAPHY

Imbrication An armorial charge, added to an original shield of arms in order to denote cadency, abatement, augmentation, etc. Usually a sub-ordinary, e.g. bordure, canton, chief, etc. A rarely used, but useful, generic term.

Imbrued *see* **Attributes**

Impalement The division of a shield per pale to incorporate two different coats side-by-side. A husband may impale his wife's arms to the sinister of his own, unless she is an heraldic heiress, in which case they are placed on an escutcheon of pretence. Holders of certain offices which carry with them armorial bearings may impale their personal coats with those of their office, the latter being placed in the dexter. These are known as Arms of Office. The system of impalement known as DIMIDIATION is no longer used except in the case of bordures, orles, tressures and charges in orle, all of which are dimidiated at the paler line in impaled arms.
See also MARSHALLING

Impartible Arms Two or more coats combined permanently in one shield by the addition of a bordure or other charge which renders them indivisible.

Imperial Service Order (Abbr. ISO) Founded in

Illuminated manuscript by Anthony Wood (1980).

1902 (and revised 1908). The order recognizes the contribution of members of the civil service abroad.

Impersonal Arms *see* **Arms of Community**

Incensed *see* **Attributes**

Incised Slabs Engraved stone memorials date back at least as far as ancient Egypt. In the early centuries of the Christian era incised gravestones occur in the Catacombs, usually taking the form of a simple inscription sometimes accompanied by symbols of the Faith. Among early examples in the British Isles is a collection at Clonmacnois in Ireland of over two hundred of the eighth to the tenth centuries. It is not until the early medieval period that incised slabs become numerous. From the eleventh century to about 1350 the majority are coffin-shaped, usually incised only with a cross. Most are of hard sandstone, but other regional stones are used, for example gritstone in Derbyshire and Northumberland, Purbeck and other marbles in the south of England,

Bath and Ham stone in the south-west, while the mica-schist of the west Highlands of Scotland provided material for a vigorous school of Celtic artists. By the time of the Reformation, alabaster was much used in the Midlands.

Human figures, often of priests, appear from the twelfth century onwards, including an early military figure of a knight with pot helm at Sollers Hope, Herefordshire. One of the earliest armorial slabs is that at Gilling-in-Rydale, Yorkshire, on which are incised a cross and a knight's gauntlets and shield of arms. Incised slabs showing heraldic figures are not common in the British Isles, though there are two early examples at St Brides Major in Glamorgan (Sir Johan le Botiler *c.* 1285, holding a shield and upraised sword) and at Bromyard, Herefordshire (a man in armour *c.* 1260, holding a plain shield). Later examples of armory are mostly confined to coats of arms on small shields, though there are occasional examples of figures wearing heraldic mantles. On the slab for John Foljambe (d. 1499, monument *c.* 1515) at Sutton Scarsdale, Derbyshire, the figure is depicted wearing armour, over which is a tabard of the Foljambe arms. His head rests on a helm bearing a crest, and his feet on a chatloup, a chimerical beast granted to the Foljambe family as a badge in 1513.

Memorials of this type, often laid in the church floor, were obviously liable to wear and thus their heraldry does not have the same chance of surviving as does that on monumental brasses. Some were set on tomb chests. At Ashbourne, Derbyshire, the incised slab of John Cockayne (d. 1505) is badly worn but is now raised on a modern base. Others may have been lifted and set upright against a wall.

Some incised slabs may have been decorated with inlaid materials, particularly those imported from the Low Countries. Occasionally brass is found, but pitch and painted lead or, occasionally, enamel were used for colouring figures. Regrettably little of this has survived to the present day.

Slabs with incised effigies are prolific in northern France and Belgium, followed closely by Holland, Germany and Cyprus. Many of these are heraldic and range in date from the mounted knight bearing a lozengy shield (*c.* 1250) at Notre-Dame Saint-Omer in France, to a 'restored' example with heraldic jupon (1800) at Monfavet in France.

During the seventeenth century incised slabs depicting full-length figures were replaced by what is known as the ledger stone. These bore no depiction of the deceased, but an inscription and a deeply incised roundel of the armorial achievement, the slab usually being of black marble and laid in the floor. The ledger stone remained popular to the nineteenth century. A few examples are to be found on tomb chests, both inside the church and in the churchyard. Very little research has been undertaken and the armorial ledger stone represents a fertile field for the enthusiastic armorist.   JC/JET

Further reading
Creeny, W.F. *Illustrations of Incised Slabs on the Continent of Europe* Norwich, 1891.
Greenhill, F.A. *The Incised Slabs of Leicestershire and Rutland* Leicester, 1958. This contains a very useful 'Brief Manual of Incised Slabs'.
— *Incised Effigial Slabs* 2 vols, London, 1976.

Inclination The angle at which a charge is depicted or the posture of an armorial beast. *See also* ATTITUDE

Increscent A crescent with the 'horns' facing the dexter.

Indented *see* **Lines, Varied**

Indian Empire, Most Eminent Order of Instituted in 1878 in three classes: Knights Grand Commander, Knights Commander, and Companion. It was enlarged in 1887, 1892, 1897 and 1903. The collar of the order is gold and adorned with Indian roses, peacocks and lotus flowers, linked by double chains.

At the centre is an imperial crown flanked by two elephants. The badge is an heraldic rose with scarlet petals and green sepals, carrying an imperial crown in gold. The centre carries the likeness of Queen Victoria, also in gold. The circlet is royal purple edged in gold, with the motto 'Imperatricis Auspiciis'. The order has not been awarded since 1947.   JC-K

Indivisible Arms A coat of arms granted by virtue of a royal licence which combines two or more coats as though they were one. The component coats of indivisible arms may not thereafter be borne independently and subsequent quarterings are marshalled with the indivisible arms occupying one grand quartering.

Indult A special privilege granted (often by the pope) to authorize an act not commonly permitted.

Inescutcheon In armory, a small shield usually depicted in fess point unless otherwise specified. A sub-ordinary, invariably employed for the purposes of marshalling, etc. An inescutcheon may be plain, parted, varied or charged, and its edge formed of any of the ornamental variations of line, though such treatment is rare. Smaller shields used as minor charges are *escutcheons*, though in current practice the terms appear to be interchangeable.
See also ESCUTCHEON OF PRETENCE

Infant *or* **Infante** A son of the king and queen of Spain or Portugal, not the heir to the throne. The feminine form is Infanta.
See also PRINCIPE

Inflamed *see* **Attributes**

Inheritance of Arms In English law armorial bearings are a form of property held and enjoyed by an armiger on two conditions: he shall not have the power to assign them to another party (alienation), and they may be inherited only by heirs who are lineal descendants of the original armiger. During the Middle Ages arms were occasionally granted to heirs general and there is some evidence of alienation, though the validity of surviving documentation is questionable. In armorial descent, male issue always has precedence, and of males otherwise equal in their hereditary relationship the eldest has precedence. When no male heir of direct lineage exists a female succeeds to the arms, and if there are several such females, all of whom are equal in their hereditary relationship, they all succeed on equal terms as heraldic co-heirs.

In general, then, armorial bearings are inherited by legitimate male line descendants of an armiger. Sons use the arms and crest, daughters use the arms only.

Hereditary peers transmit their supporters to their successors in the title. An unmarried daughter displays her father's arms on a diamond-shaped figure called a lozenge. When she marries her arms are impaled with those of her husband. If her husband has no arms she cannot use her own unless and until her husband takes steps to become armigerous. An armigerous woman who has no brothers living, and no nephews or nieces from deceased brothers, becomes her father's heir (or co-heir if she has sisters) upon his death. While he lives her arms are impaled with her husband's, but when her father dies they are displayed on an escutcheon of pretence. After her death, her children can quarter her arms with their paternal arms. Her husband, if he has survived her, ceases to bear the escutcheon of pretence. A married woman can become an heir or co-heir in her issue if her brothers die without issue or if any issue becomes extinct. A woman who is armigerous in her own right (i.e. by grant) may transmit her arms, impaled by those of her husband and within a bordure, as a quartering to her descendants. Should she become an heir or co-heir in her issue she would transmit her arms as an undifferenced quartering with those of her husband.   SF/SA

See also MARSHALLING

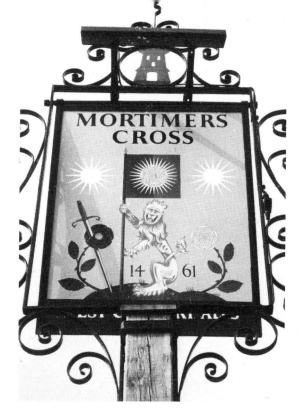

Heraldic inn sign at Mortimer's Cross, Herefordshire. Before the battle of Mortimer's Cross (1461) the nineteen-year old Edward, Duke of York, saw the sun 'like three sunnes, and suddenlie joined altogither in one; at which sight he took such courage that he, fiercelie setting on his enemies, put them to flight' (Holinshead). The 'sun in splendour' was a Yorkist badge and was often combined with the white rose 'en soleil'.

Inn Signs Inn signs are found in large numbers in every English town, and most villages have one example, if not more. These signs are the principal survivor of the medieval practice by which shop-keepers declared their function to an illiterate populace. The dairyman, the butcher, the baker, would each have his own sign, as did the taverner. Other twentieth-century survivors are the barber's pole and the three balls of the pawnbroker.

For taverns the sign was more than just advertising. Before the end of the fourteenth century there was a legal requirement, at least in London, to display a sign: in 1393 a landlord was taken to court for non-compliance. Many such signs must have been very large, as in 1419 their encroachment above the roadway was restricted to 7 feet (just over 2 metres).

The origin of the names used by inns is often difficult to establish. The Romans used the sign of a bush, which was often reduced to a garland of evergreens, and the hoop in names such as 'The Eagle on the Hoop' is probably derived from this garland. Also, the expression 'a good wine needs no bush' dates from this practice. Many inn signs have an obvious armorial origin: they are simply called 'the so-and-so arms'. Reference to the monarchy is widespread: there are numerous examples of the 'King's Arms' and 'Queen's Arms', and the 'Duke of Edinburgh', 'Duke of York' and 'Duke of Cambridge'

all take their names from younger sons of monarchs. The 'Royal Arms' displayed on the sign are frequently those of the Tudors or the current royal arms. Stuart and Hanoverian examples are also to be found. At Winchester the 'King's Arms' displays *Gules three Lions passant guardant Or*, and the pub claims to date from the time of Henry III. However, the arms should *not* be taken to date the pub; signs are regularly repainted and the owner or painter may choose to 'update' the arms concerned — for example, the royal arms from 1837 are much easier to paint anew than to repaint an existing Hanoverian coat. Royal allegiance is found in many other signs: royal badges and beasts are common, such as the 'White Hart', 'The Rising Sun', 'The Rose and Crown' and 'The Feathers'.

Other heraldic signs are usually the family arms of a past or present lord of the manor, or of a guild or other institution which at one time had a local connection. Again, badges or crests of the family may be found instead of the arms. Notable examples are

'The Bear and Ragged Staff' (Earls of Warwick), and 'The Blue Boar' (De Vere, Earls of Oxford). If the sign displays a crest on a wreath, the heraldic connection is obvious. If there is no wreath then the association of, for example, 'The Eagle and Child' (St Giles, Oxford) and the Earls of Derby is lost to most except the armorist (the device was a Derby badge). Signs such as the 'Red Lion', 'White Lion' and 'The Chequers' may have an armorial background. The chequers, for example, is reputed to be based on the arms of the de Warenne family *Chequy Or and Azure*, but many signs have different coloured chequers and research would be necessary to establish whether the tinctures have been changed or if the arms are simply those of another family.

To determine the correct armorial origin of a pub sign may require research into the heraldry of many local families and lords over several centuries, and the pub sign may survive long after the family has died out. For example 'The Hind's Head' at Aldermaston, Berkshire, is the crest of the Forster family, lords of the manor before 1711. To trace such connections for inn signs in towns is even more difficult.

Inn signs may not portray exactly the pub's name: 'The Prince of Wales' may have a sign of three ostrich feathers; at Sonning, Berkshire, that of 'The Bull' shows the full coat of arms of the Marquis of Abergavenny, the name being derived from the bull supporters and crest.

Evidence of the origin of inn signs is gradually being lost through the repainting of signs and the renaming of inns. The magnificent sign of 'The Tabard' in Gloucester was recently saved from destruction at the eleventh hour and now graces the Heralds' Museum at the Tower of London.

During the nineteenth and twentieth centuries the number of new public houses which have non-heraldic names has increased. Nevertheless, the practice is still popular: a modern example is 'The Tylers' Rest' at Tilehurst, Berkshire, built in the 1980s and proudly displaying the arms of the Tylers and Bricklayers Company. JET

Further reading
Delderfield, E.R. *Introduction to Inn Signs* Newton Abbot, 1969.
Hill, B. *Inn-signia* 1949.
Larwood J. and J.C. Hotten *English Inn Signs* 1866 (reprinted 1984).

In Orle *see* **Orle**

In Point Converging, e.g. of piles.

Insignia Devices which may be incorporated in an achievement of arms but which are not essential to it. These may include INSIGNIA OF OFFICE (e.g. the SS collars of kings and heralds of arms); mitres and ecclesiastical hats, episcopal crosses and croziers; collars and badges of the orders of chivalry, and decorations such as the Victoria and Military crosses. Campaign and commemorative medals are not insignia. Some insignia are associated with HEREDITARY OFFICES such as that of Earl Marshal.

Orders of chivalry possess insignia appropriate to the different classes and divisions into which members are admitted. Ancient orders such as the Garter and the Thistle have only one class of membership (that of Knight Companion), others may have civil and military divisions and several classes of membership (typically, Knights and Dames Grand Cross, Knights and Dames Commander, Commanders, Officers and Members). Most orders also have a number of offices, holders of which possess their own distinctive insignia, such as King of Arms, Chancellor, Prelate, etc.

All orders have a badge which is usually depicted within a circlet bearing the order's motto. If there are civil and military divisions each will possess its own variation of the badge. Knights and Dames Grand Cross will normally wear a mantle in the colours of the order, charged on the left shoulder with the Star, which is usually of faceted silver, charged with the badge or similar device. From the collar of the order depends the badge, and a sash of the order's colour is worn over the left shoulder with the badge pendent at the hip. In some of the more ancient orders a ceremonial hat is worn, usually of velvet with an ostrich feather plume. Commanders wear the badge pendent from a neck ribbon in the colours of the order, Officers and Members having similar badges suspended from a ribbon on the breast in the manner of a medal. Mantle and hat are clearly ceremonial, other insignia being worn on appropriate formal occasions. Baronets and (since 1926) knights bachelor possess insignia consisting of a badge, and this is worn about the neck by an appropriately coloured ribbon. The badge of the knight bachelor may alternatively be worn on the left breast.

Such insignia may be worn only by those upon whom they have been conferred. It therefore follows that these may only be represented in the achievement of arms of the recipient, and not in a marital coat. With the exception of the insignia of baronetcies and hereditary officers, they are not transmitted to descendants.

Insignia, Marshalling of Insignia are personal to the armiger, and when marshalled in armorial bearings there should be no doubt as to the identity of the person to whom they appertain. With the exception of peers' coronets and insignia which are reserved for men (and about which there can be no ambiguity) it is customary in a marital achievement to depict two shields accolé (i.e. side by side), that to the dexter being the husband's arms and that to the sinister the marital arms. The husband's insignia are depicted with the dexter shield, and those of his wife with the sinister, marital shield. If either shield is depicted within a circlet of one of the orders of chivalry, the other may be shown within a conventional garland to balance the design. Helm, crest, wreath and mantling ensign the combined shields, which are flanked by supporters when appropriate.

Theoretically, it is possible to marshall the insignia of more than one order about or below the shield. However, armigers who are entitled to the insignia of several orders should incorporate only the circlet of the senior order to which they belong. Below the shield, the badge of the senior order should be placed centrally, other badges being to the dexter and then the sinister according to seniority. If collars are to be depicted, that of the senior order should be next to the circlet and that of the lesser order outside.

Coronets of rank, helmets and supporters are dealt with elsewhere, but there are certain other insignia which may be incorporated in a coat of arms, such as the SS chain of office of the kings and heralds of arms, the coronet of office of the kings of arms, ecclesiastical insignia, decorations (though not campaign or commemorative medals) and arms of office, which are impaled with the personal arms of the holder of the office. The marshalling of such insignia is a matter of common sense rather than prescription, a coronet ensigning the arms, a chain encircling them and decorations pendent below the shield, for example.

A baronet of the United Kingdom charges his shield of arms with the badge of the BARONETCY either on an escutcheon or (more rarely) a canton, though since 1929 he has been permitted to depict it pendent from a ribbon beneath the shield, which is a far more satisfactory practice. A baronet of Scotland also depicts his badge pendent from an orange ribbon, though occasionally it will be found as a canton in the shield. Knights bachelor are not members of an order and, prior to 1926, possessed no insignia. In that year George V sanctioned the use of a badge and this is now suspended below the shield on a vermillion ribbon with gold edging. Decorations and medals awarded by the sovereign are suspended from their appropriate ribbons, the senior being in the central position, others being to the dexter and sinister according to seniority. This also applies to insignia authorized 'by the sovereign's leave' but not conferred by the Crown, such as the insignia of foreign orders.

The insignia of the Most Venerable Order of the Hospital of St John of Jerusalem (*see* ST JOHN OF JERUSALEM, ORDERS OF) may be incorporated in armorial bearings. Bailiffs, Knights, Dames and Chaplains may display their shields on the white Maltese Cross badge of the Order, while other

members may show the badge pendent from its appropriate ribbon below the shield. Bailiffs and Dames Grand Cross may add a chief of the arms of the Order *Gules a Cross Argent in the first quarter a Representation of Her Majesty's Crest* to their own shield of arms.

Insignia, Military Devices used on uniforms, flags, vehicles, etc., to identify military units.

The military or defence attaché's office of western embassies will usually supply by mail details of military insignia or the addresses of collectors' clubs and societies in their own country. Supreme Headquarters Allied Powers in Europe (SHAPE), which is based at Casteau, Mons, Belgium, has an excellent public relations department which will supply details of NATO command insignia or the addresses of individual commands from which information may also be obtained. The American Society of Military Insignia Collectors (ASMIC) maintains coverage of all forms of United States military insignia, and its quarterly journal *Trading Post* often includes articles on military heraldry. Membership of ASMIC includes a yearly subscription to *Trading Post*, and a list of members' interests (*see* ADDRESSES).   SS

Insignia of Office Throughout the centuries it has been the practice in many countries to augment armorial bearings with symbols of office. These may refer to non-hereditary or hereditary offices, and may take the form of arms of office or devices incorporated in the armorial bearings of the holder. Such devices may represent objects actually carried or worn, such as the baton of the Earl Marshal, the crozier of a bishop, or the black cap of the President of the Royal French Parliament. Other devices may be in symbolic allusion to the office, such as the wolf's head of the Grand Wolf-hunter of France, or the anchor of the Admirals of Castile and of the Indies.

See entries prefixed HEREDITARY, *also* ROYAL FORESTERS, WARDENS AND VERDURERS, *and* various offices as individual entries. *See also* INSIGNIA, MARSHALLING OF. For the insignia of office of the Royal French Court see *Complete Guide to Heraldry* by A.C. Fox-Davies.

Insigniis et Armis, De *see* **Treatises**

Institute of Heraldic and Genealogical Studies Founded in 1961, the Institute promotes research, study and training in all aspects of family history, including heraldry (*see* ADDRESSES). Courses may be undertaken by full-time students, through a series of evening classes combined with other studies, and by a correspondence course. Those who complete approved courses may sit the Diploma examination, after submitting adequate evidence of practical experience. Those who hold the Diploma and produce an acceptable dissertation or thesis can qualify as Licentiates of the Institute (L.H.G.). This is accepted as equal to honours degree qualification. Students, armorists, genealogists and family historians are able to make use of the extensive collection of books and manuscripts in the Institute's library, which is open on Mondays, Wednesdays and Fridays from 10.00a.m. to 4.30p.m. Free access is a privilege of membership. The general public is charged for whole-day or half-day admission and bookings should be made in advance through the Librarian. The Institute is particularly proud of its heraldic collection; there is also a number of genealogical and heraldic indexes, some in manuscript, others on microfilm. Associate membership of the Institute is available to those who support its objectives.

In 1982 armorial bearings were granted to the Institute: *Azure a Cross patonce within an orle of eight Acorns cups inwards Or*. No crest was applied for. The Institute's motto, taken from Psalm 95, is 'Tentaverunt Me Patres Vestry' — 'your fathers put me to the test'. A badge, *A Crane's Leg Couped a la quise surmounted by an Ancient Crown Gold* was also granted. (The earliest form of genealogical table, in which the names of forebears were written in groups of circles joined by curving lines, was thought to resemble a crane's foot or *pied de gru*.)   CRHS

Instruments, Musical *see* **Musical Heraldry**

Intelligence Organizations, Insignia of Both the CIA and its Russian counterpart, the KGB, use insignia of a quasi-armorial nature. The seal of the Central Intelligence Agency bears an orange shield symbolizing earthly wisdom charged with a gold compass rose. The KGB (Committee for Internal Security) uses an emblem consisting of a shield charged with a sword palewise and the hammer and sickle. The arm badge of KGB troops consists of a shield of royal blue (the branch colour) edged with gold and bearing a red star also edged in gold, superimposed on a gold wreath, the star charged with a gold hammer and sickle.   SS·

Interlaced Interwoven. *See also* BRACED

Invected *see* **Lines, Varied**

Inverness, Earl of Peerage title first granted in 1718 by Prince James Francis Edward Stuart, the Old Pretender. The first creation in Britain was in 1801, to Prince Augustus Frederick, sixth son of George III, who died in 1843. The second creation, 1892, was to George, Duke of York, later King George V. The third creation, 1986, was to Prince Andrew, second son to the present sovereign, Elizabeth II.   CJB

Inverted *see* **Attitude**

Investiture *see* **Honours and Investiture**

Involved *see* **Attitude**

Ireland, Armorial Practice Heraldic practices in Ireland have closely followed those of England, and there is very little difference with regard to the use of coronets, insignia of knighthood, supporters and other appurtenances of rank. This is entirely due to the fact that the English Crown exercised *fons honorum* authority first in the Lordship, and subsequently in the Kingdom of Ireland. Indeed, with regard to coronets of rank the Irish peerage use and display precisely the same designs as their English peers. It is worthy of special note that the use of coronets by the Irish baronage rests on the authority of a Royal Warrant of James II as *de jure* and *de facto* King of Ireland in 1689, after his 'abdication' of the crown of England. However, during that period of history, constitutional theory held that the crown of Ireland depended on that of England, so it is interesting to note that the first Dublin-held parliament of William III nonetheless confirmed the validity of the warrant, while at the same time declaring the other actions of James as King of Ireland between the years 1688 and 1690 null and void.

A special convention applies regarding the use of the 'crest coronet' in Ireland. This is reserved for families of established gentility and is thus allowed in confirmations of arms (*see* IRELAND, LAWS OF ARMS). It is never granted to petitioners for new grants of arms. It must be remembered that in addition to the Irish peerage there are still many extant Gaelic chiefly families who are indigenous to the island and who enjoy titles of much greater antiquity than the vast majority of the former. Some of these chiefs, particularly those who represent houses which previously held sovereignty, use coronets in their armorial achievements. The O'Conor Don, Chief of the Name and Head of the Ancient Irish Royal House of Connaught, has for several centuries surmounted his arms with an Antique Coronet, as has The Mac Carthy Mor, Chief of the Name and Head of the Ancient Irish Royal House of Munster. The O'Neill of

Clanaboy, Prince of Clanaboy, surmounts his arms with a Ducal Coronet, being derived from the old form of a crown of sovereignty.

Armorial supporters are now reserved to the Chiefs of the Name, peers, baronets, and certain old armigerous corporate bodies, such as the Royal College of Surgeons.

Before the establishment of the Republic the rules governing the heraldic display of the insignia of British orders followed the practices of England or Scotland. However, since the state does not bestow any decorations whatsoever, the Chief Herald has not been obliged to make any rulings on this matter. In practice, Irish citizens who enjoy a proven right to arms are permitted to display the insignia of any order to which they belong, in the manner ordained by its statutes. Thus Knights of Malta, and Knights of the Military and Hospitaller Order of St Lazarus of Jerusalem, at their own discretion adorn their arms in the appropriate manner. In such cases, and particularly when an Irish citizen has received a recognized foreign or international order, the Chief Herald may, with the consent of the President, allow the insignia to be displayed on patents issuing from his office.

The Irish convention regarding cadency marks is the same as that of England, although in practice this system is little used, but is still technically obligatory. Patents of arms issued by the Chief Herald still stipulate, in fact, that the armorial bearings in question should be borne 'according to their due differences' by the descendants of the grantee. MCM

Ireland, Association of Professional Genealogists in This association was founded in 1986 as a scrutinizing body certifying the standards of genealogists practising in Ireland, its founders being recognized by, or being members of, the Association of Genealogists and Record Agents, London. The Patron of the Association is Norroy and Ulster King of Arms. Applications for admission are carefully examined by a panel of senior members. The Association does not do genealogical research, but individual members may be commissioned to do specific studies. Names of members may be obtained from the Secretary (*see* ADDRESSES). MCM

Ireland, Clans Unfortunately, the clan system in Ireland has not developed along Scottish lines and very few have any form of formalized structure. After the collapse of the quasi-independent Gaelic lordships in the late sixteenth and early seventeenth centuries, and the emigration of a large number of chiefs to continental Europe, the English administration made every effort to Anglicize the customs of the native Irish. The few great Gaelic families who

survived the Tudor and Stuart Plantations were almost entirely ruined by the anti-Catholic legislation enacted by the Dublin Parliament after the victory of William III. These laws forbade Catholic gentlemen from devising their estates by primogeniture and obliged them to divide them amongst all their children. One result of this measure was that the surviving Gaelic aristocracy, almost all of whom were Catholic, were, over several generations, gradually reduced to the standing of small freeholders. Because the chiefs were unable to maintain the system of patronage within their clans there was an erosion of the whole social system. For all intents and purposes the Irish clan system was completely dormant by the late seventeenth century. Whilst the local peasantry continued to hold the chiefs in esteem, the bonds of patronage and dependence had been severed.

In recent years several Irish chiefly houses have attempted to found clan societies, with varying degrees of success. The O'Donnels, O'Doghertys, Mac Sweeneys, O'Neills and Mac Egans all have functioning clans and hold gatherings and other cultural events.

Unfortunately, Irish heraldic development, having followed English practice, has not taken any notice of clans. Furthermore, tartan has never been used in Ireland in the manner familiar in Scotland. Those Irish clans which do function do not, therefore, make use of any heraldic device (such as the Scottish plant badge or crest within a strap and buckle) or tartan within their memberships. Perhaps in time the chiefs concerned will, with the co-operation of the Genealogical Office, make some provision whereby recognized clan badges can be registered by the Chief Herald for use by their clansmen. Hopefully such an innovation would discourage over-zealous and well-intentioned people from adopting as their own property, contrary to the Law of Arms, the arms appertaining to the chief of their particular surname. MCM

Ireland Kings of Arms Although most armorists are at least acquainted with the existence of the Office of ULSTER KING OF ARMS, very few indeed realize that a much older kingship of arms had, at least in theory, enjoyed heraldic jurisdiction in the Lordship of Ireland. In 1392, almost exactly 160 years prior to the establishment of Ulster Office, King Richard II of England created the first of a succession of Ireland kings of arms. Froissart, although reporting the creation of *Chandos le Roy d'Ireland*, did not provide any idea why the crown called such an office into being. It is evident, however, that this act was related to King Richard II's Irish policy in general, that is his desire to re-establish English control in those areas of the colony where the native Irish had reasserted their independence, and his military policy in particular.

Thus the creation of Chandos as Ireland King of Arms can be seen as part of the necessary preparation following the appointment of the Duke of Gloucester as Lieutenant of Ireland in 1392. Richard intended the Duke to lead a major military operation to Ireland in order to restore some semblance of order within the colony. Such a campaign necessarily involved the attendance of heralds, not only to marshal the arms of the various knights but to give advice and evidence in the case of heraldic disputes.

The campaign of 1392 never materialized, but in 1394 King Richard, accompanied by a large army, did disembark in Ireland. The king was accompanied by one John Othelake, who had succeeded Chandos as Ireland King of Arms, probably in 1393. Othelake had some previous connection with Ireland, for he had attended the Earl of March as a private herald during the latter's Lieutenancy in 1381. On March's death he had passed into the king's service and he was one of the heralds who visited France in order to arrange the marriage of Isabel de Valois to Richard II. No details of Othelake's career as Ireland, other than those given, are known, and indeed we are not even certain how long he enjoyed that office.

The next Ireland king of arms known to historians was one John Kitley, who was appointed to the office by King Henry V at the instigation of James Butler, 4th Earl of Ormond. His exact date of creation is unknown, but he already enjoyed this office in 1420, since he was listed in this capacity as one of the heralds attending a Chapter meeting at the siege of Rouen. The only other documented reference to Kitley is the fact that he attended the requiem of Queen Catherine de Valois at Westminster Abbey in 1421. There is no evidence to suggest that he was either born in Ireland or even visited it, but the fact that he was a protegé of the Earl of Ormond is of interest.

Kitley would appear to have been succeeded by Thomas Collyer, who had served as Clarenceux and Lancaster heralds. Nothing is known of his career, except that he enjoyed the office during the reign of Henry VI. In his *History of the College of Arms* Noble states that he was succeeded by Thomas Ashwell, who had also acted as Clarenceux and as Lancaster herald, but his statement that Ashwell attended the funeral of Edward IV in his capacity as Ireland King of Arms is obviously incorrect, as one Walter Bellinger enjoyed this office from at least as early as 1468. This succession is proven beyond all doubt, since on 3 June 1469 King Edward IV granted Bellinger a pension of £20 per annum for his service as Ireland. The same writ states that he had been appointed on 'the IX day of Juyn the VII yere' of Edward's reign (1468).

It has been established that Bellinger was a native of Dieppe and, according to a manuscript prepared at his request by his servant, Jehan Pellisser, had served as a herald for fifty-five years by 1477. He certainly had no known connection with Ireland and never visited his titular province. Only three grants of arms are known to have been made by him, and none at all by any of his predecessors, in the office of Ireland King of Arms. None of Bellinger's grants was made to residents in Ireland and all provoked serious disputes among the other kings of arms, and resulted in two of them being disallowed completely on the grounds that they had been made within the provinces of the English heralds. The third, made to one Jehan Baret of Picardy on 13 July 1475, was permitted to stand. This would seem to imply that Bellinger was not considered as having any lawful authority within England nor as being an English herald. There is, however, no evidence to suggest that he ever attempted to exercise authority in Ireland.

In 1475 Bellinger accompanied King Edward IV to France and acted as an ambassador from him to the French Court in the discussions preceding the treaty of Picquigny. He apparently played a very important roll in these negotiations, as a document in the State Papers of Milan states that he was in personal discussion with King Louis for two hours and 'the King gave him the value of two hundred silver marks' for his services in representing his English opponent.

Bellinger appears to have continued to hold office until the reign of Henry VII, but was deprived at that sovereign's accession. He was the last Ireland King of Arms, as Henry VII and Henry VIII did not appoint any successor to this office. Edward VI's creation in 1552 of Bartholomew Butler as the first Ulster King of Arms can, to some extent, be regarded as a revival of the more ancient position. Between the suspension of Bellinger and the appointment of Butler there was an intervening period of sixty to seventy years. Although no king of arms connected with Ireland existed in this inter-regnum there are several references to Irish pursuivants. Shortly after his coronation Henry VII created Dublin Pursuivant of Arms, who appears to have been based at the court of the Lord Deputy in Ireland. In 1501/2 a Dublin pursuivant escorted prisoners from Ireland into England. No subsequent references to this office have survived.

The Earl of Kildare, the most powerful of the Irish peers of the fifteenth and sixteenth centuries, would also appear to have retained the services of a pursuivant. There is a reference to such an officer in 1487 when Kildare, having crowned Lambert Simnel, the Yorkist Pretender, as King of England and Lord of Ireland, sent 'a herald in his cote of arms to Waterford' to demand the city's surrender. The fact that this herald wore Kildare's arms certainly suggests that he was that peer's private servant, and yet this is contradicted by the fact that this same officer was allocated mourning clothes from the royal wardrobe when he attended the funeral of Henry VII. This privilege was normally reserved to royal heralds. It is possible that this was conceded either because Kildare was Deputy Lieutenant of Ireland at that time, and thus enjoyed vice-regal powers, or, quite simply, Kildare's pursuivant was one and the same officer as Dublin Pursuivant.

Although there was a succession of Ireland kings of arms from the fourteenth to the fifteenth century, and evidence proving the existence of heralds and/or pursuivants in Ireland in the early sixteenth century, there are no surviving records to indicate that such officers exercised any real heraldic authority in that lordship. It was only following the creation of Ulster Office that a real heraldic jurisdiction effectively existed in Ireland.   MCM

Further reading
Butler, T.B. 'The Officers of Arms in Ireland' in *The Irish Genealogist* vol.II, No.1, 1943.
Noble, M. *A History of the College of Arms* London, 1805.
Wagner, A. *Heralds of England, a History of the College of Arms* London, 1967.

Ireland, Law of Arms The only persons who enjoy an automatic and legal right to bear arms (which can be simply defined as a right which would be acknowledged by the Chief Herald of Ireland, or Norroy and Ulster King of Arms) in Ireland are those who have obtained a grant of the same from the competent offices, or who descend in proven and unbroken male line from an ancestor who enjoyed arms granted, or acknowledged, by them. Such armigers may bear their ancestral or granted devices, without let or hindrance, on their stationery, seals or silver or in any other manner which they deem suitable. Their right to do so is unquestionable and is in accordance with heraldic law. Unfortunately, however, and all too frequently, many people now use armorially headed notepaper, or otherwise make use of arms, in a personal sense, who have no right whatsoever to do so. Normally such abuses proceed from an imprecise understanding of the nature of 'Sept' or 'Clan' arms, with no intended trespass (for as we shall see, in law such usage constitutes an offence) against the armiger entitled to, and actually legally enjoying the arms in question.

The theory of Sept Arms was first advanced by Dr MacLysaght, a former Chief Herald of Ireland, in 1957, in the preface to the first edition of his *Irish Families* series. It was MacLysaght's contention that persons descended from Irish clans, or rather septs, might without committing any impropriety display, in the form of a plaque, the arms of the Chief of the Name of their patronymic. The arms in question could never, however, be used in the personal sense, which pertains to armigers alone. As MacLysaght firmly

maintained, any person 'wishing to bear arms in the true heraldic sense' required either a grant or confirmation of arms from the Chief Herald of Ireland, or Norroy and Ulster King of Arms, unless they were already recognized as being armigerous. By contrast, Sept arms convey no social status to the bearer (other than to the Chief of the Name and his family), nor can they be considered as, nor used in place of, a personal grant or entitlement to arms.

Unfortunately, at the present time, Ireland does not possess an heraldic court in which armigers can bring law suits for trespasses committed against their own rights. Indeed, the only functioning heraldic court of any authority in Europe is that of the Lord Lyon King of Arms in Scotland. Lyon is, indeed, a judge in his own court and has both powers of fine and imprisonment vested in him by the Crown of Scotland. England, too, possesses a Court of Chivalry, but this has sat only once since 1735 (in 1954) and must be considered to be in desuetude pending legislation by the Westminster Parliament. In the seventeenth century a form of heraldic court, or rather council, did exist in Ireland and was convoked by the Lord Deputy in order to enforce particular heraldic enactments when necessary. Such meetings were, however, extremely rare since, under the letters patent of their creation, the Ulster kings of arms had wide powers of search and entry to prevent the usurpation, or other misusage, of arms. They had, for example, the right to enter any castle, church or house in Ireland and to deface, burn or pull down any representations of arms illegally borne. It is to be doubted if such methods would be employed today by their successors, the Chief Herald of Ireland and Norroy and Ulster King of Arms, but these powers remain vested in these officers within their respective jurisdictions. The Irish Constitution does in fact make indirect provision for the protection of arms granted by the Chief Herald, or registered in his office (or that of his predecessors) on government authority. Clause 40, III, II guarantees that 'The State shall . . . in the case of injustice done, vindicate the life, person, good name and property rights of the citizen . . .'

Arms recorded in the Office of Arms, Dublin, as pertaining to an individual or corporate body do, in fact and in law, constitute an intangible form of feudal property, protected by the government of Ireland in the person of its Chief Herald, and clearly come within the scope of the above clause. The Irish state could, if it deemed it necessary, establish a special heraldic court to try breaches of the law of arms. Provision is made for this type of institution by Clause 38, III, II of the Irish Constitution: 'Special Courts may be established by law for the trial of offences in cases where it may be determined in accordance with such that the Courts are inadequate to secure the effective administration of Justice.' With respect to Northern

Ireland, over which the Norroy and Ulster King of Arms of the College of Arms, London, has authority, it is doubted if arms can be protected even in theory. Certainly the Court of Chivalry, which is convoked by and presided over by the Duke of Norfolk as Hereditary Marshal of England, would have no authority whatsoever in the Province.

Despite the creation of the Irish Free State in 1922, the British crown continued to appoint and maintain Ulster King of Arms, and Deputy Ulsters, to the Office of Arms, Dublin Castle. This anomaly was the result of the ambiguous position of the Irish Free State vis-a-vis the Crown. On 1 April 1943 Mr De Valera, then Prime Minister of the Free State, authorized the creation of the office of Chief Herald, and on 24 July 1943 Dr Edward MacLysaght was appointed to that office. The terms of his appointment were such that he assumed all of the old rights, powers and privileges of the Ulster King of Arms, which the Chief Heralds thereafter have continued to enjoy without a breach in succession or legal form. As a result the Chief Herald claims heraldic authority over all persons of Irish descent, irrespective of their country of domicile. After some hesitation the British crown merged the old office of Ulster King of Arms with that of Norroy in England, who is responsible for the northern part of England. The merger of these offices might in fact be questioned, since it has in effect subjected a Superior and National Kingship of Arms to a Junior and Regional Kingship in the English College of Arms. Norroy and Ulster King of Arms is subject to the authority of the Earl Marshal of England, and can only grant or confirm arms on his authority and with the consent of Garter and Clarenceux kings of arms. The Chief Herald of Ireland certainly enjoys more fully the old privileges of Ulster's office, since he is not subject to any controlling authority and acts in respect of all his heraldic and genealogical duties 'of his own mere motion'.

Coats of arms are still granted and confirmed by the Chief Herald to persons of Irish descent, domiciled in any state, who fulfil the qualifications necessary in such cases (see colour page 251). It is difficult to define precisely what these are, but, according to tradition, the petitioner should have reached the 'Port of Gentry'. This can be interpreted as meaning that he, or she, should enjoy a position in society where a grant of arms would not be incongruous with his or her status. A confirmation of arms is made on an entirely different basis, simply because it does not initiate a right to arms but confirms that such a right exists. Confirmations are only made to persons who can prove, to the satisfaction of the Chief Herald, that their family have borne arms for over one hundred years, or three generations, whichever being the greater. It should be stressed that both grants and confirmations of arms are a form of honour, and the number made in any one year is small, certainly amounting to less than two dozen.

Norroy and Ulster King of Arms grants to persons domiciled in Northern Ireland. The fees involved are more than double those charged by the Chief Herald's office. In both jurisdictions, petitions can take more than a year to progress through all of the administrative processes to the point where the letters patent receive their seals. Faults in the form of the initiating petition, and a lack of knowledge of heraldic terminology on the part of the petitioners, can further delay applications.   MCM

Ireland, Royal Arms of Although there has never been a separate title for the King of Ireland, from the accession of James VI of Scotland as James I of England, the royal arms have included a quarter for Ireland: *Azure a Harp Or stringed Argent*. The Irish harp has occupied the third quarter for almost the whole period since, even during the Commonwealth when the other quarters were completely changed. The royal crest for Ireland is *a Tower triple-towered Or with a Hart Argent unguled and attired Gules springing from the Portal*.   KH

Ireland, Royal Houses of The Irish royal houses are acknowledged by most genealogists to be the oldest traceable dynasties in Europe, descending as they do from kings who were regnant before the conversion of Constantine the Great in AD 311. Prior to the Norman invasion of Ireland in the late twelfth century the island was divided into a number of provincial kingdoms (rather like those of Anglo-Saxon England), all of which, in theory, were subject to the High King who ruled from Tara. In reality the position of the High King was more sacerdotal than magisterial, although a few individual holders of the High Kingship, such as Brien Boru, did almost succeed in converting it into a real over-lordship. Although the number of provincial kingships varied, five principal ones came to have a permanent existence, namely those of Ulster, Munster, Leinster, Connaught and Meath (this latter kingdom being the appanage of the High King, and including his seat at Tara). For several centuries the High Kingship was disputed between the kings of the Ui Niall (Ulster) and the kings of the Eoghanaghta dynasty (Munster), before the former succeeded in obtaining a more or less secure monopoly of this title. The idea of a vacillating right of succession to the High Kingship did, however, remain a reality, and as late as the eleventh century Brien Boru, a Dalcasian Prince who had succeeded to the Throne of Munster, claiming descent from the Eoghanaghta, successfully contested the High Kingship.

Upon the arrival of Henry II in Ireland the

Contemporary map of sixteenth century Ireland showing the territories of the native chiefs. By a masterly piece of diplomatic strategy, Henry VIII (1509-47) persuaded the Gaelic chiefs to acknowledge the supremacy of the English Crown, surrender their lands to it, and receive them back as lieges of the King. The proposal was so plausible that most of the chiefs accepted it readily, but it was to be insidious in its weakening effects on their sovereignty.

following royal houses enjoyed the sovereignties of their respective kingdoms:

High Kingship Roderick O'Connor, King of Connaught, now represented by The O'Conor Don.
Ulster O'Neill, now represented by The O'Neill Mor and The O'Neill of Clanaboy.
Munster Mac Carthy, now represented by The Mac Carthy Mor.
Leinster MacMorrough, dormant.

Connaught O'Connor, now represented by The O'Conor Don.

These dynasties continued to rule as independent princes, under the lordship of the kings of England, for several centuries and were repeatedly recognized as such by that Crown. Following upon the Reformation, and the determined process of Anglicization pursued by the English government in the later fifteenth and early sixteenth centuries, the Gaelic principalities finally collapsed. All but the royal house of Leinster have continued to exist down to the present time, and their respective chiefs are recognized as such by the Chief Herald of Ireland, acting on behalf of the Irish government. According to the received principles of international law, these chiefs are entitled to use the style of Prince, and indeed some do. As recently as the 1890s the Holy See recognized The O'Neill of Clanaboy as a 'Most Serene Highness'.   MCM

Further reading
Byrne, F.J. *Irish Kings and High Kings* London, 1973.

Irradiated *see* **Attributes**

Islay Herald of Arms A Scottish herald of arms prior to 1867. The office was first mentioned in 1493. Islay is an island off the west coast of Scotland and was the headquarters of the Lord of the Isles. When the influence of that powerful noble was broken by the King of Scots during the fifteenth century, several place names associated with the Lord of the Isles were absorbed and used by the Crown.   CJB

Isle of Man, King of Henry de Beaumont, grandson of John de Brienne, King of Jerusalem and Emperor of Constantinople, was made King of the Isle of Man for life, in 1310.

Isles, Lord of the *see* **Wales, Prince of**

Issuant *see* **Attitude**

Italy, Armorial Practice Until recent times a kingdom, Italy has been a republic since 1946 and as such takes no official account of former rank or armory, nor does it inhibit the assumption, misuse or appropriation of arms, styles or, indeed, titles. The governing body in such matters, the *Consulta Araldica*, no longer exists.

The modern kingdom of Italy dates from February 1861, when the Turin parliament declared Victor Immanuel to be monarch of the state it regarded as a continuation of the ancient kingdom of Sardinia. Prior to that the Italian peninsula had seen many invaders, many rulers — Austrian, Spanish and French, among others — and, during the high-centuries of armorial display, had comprised many sovereign states, including Tuscany, Naples, Lombardy and Venice. It thus had a rich heraldic tradition and a proud, finely bred nobility. An organization called the Collegio Araldica founded in 1858 is now supported by members of the Italian aristocracy and publishes *Il Libro d'Oro dell Nobilità Italiana* (Golden Book of the Italian Nobility). In 1928 the Collegio edited, in five volumes, the *Nobiliario e Blasonario del Regno d'Italia*.

Today there exists a National Heraldic Council and a separate Central Heraldic Commission, both of which are recognized by the ex-king of Italy who has, in his entourage, a 'Secretary for Heraldic Affairs'. It seems fair to suggest that in modern Italy ancient and more recent philosophies, ideals and institutions, exist side by side in a mainly tolerant climate.   JC-K

Italy, Military Insignia Mountain troop units usually wear coloured pocket badges which often include municipal arms in their design. The gilt feather-holder worn by officers on their caps also bears the Cross of Savoy, a reminder of the former Kingdom. Troops of the Lagunari (a unit trained for amphibious warfare, mainly in the lagoons of the Venice area) wear badges bearing the winged lion of St Mark.   SS

Italy, Royal Arms of *Gules a Cross Argent.*

The Palio of Siena, an annual pageant at which liveried citizens of seventeen *contrades* (districts) contend for the honour of possessing the *palladium*, an ancient flag bearing the image of the Virgin Mary.

J

Jack (i) In armory a rare alternative to the pike (fish).
(ii) A small flag flown at the bows of a ship.
(iii) Colloquial term for a medieval retainer.
(iv) A sleeveless coat worn especially by the medieval archer.
(v) A rough canvas garment, strengthened with plates of metal or horn, worn by infantrymen.

Jamaica, Orders of Jamaica has the Order of the National Hero, the Order of the Nation, the Order of Merit, the Order of Jamaica, and the Order of Distinction, all of which were established by the National Honours and Awards Act (Act No. 21 of 1969). The Governor-General is the Chancellor of each order, membership of which is conferred by the Governor-General upon the advice of the Prime Minister. The sovereign is not, however, the sovereign of these orders, as in the case of the Order of Canada, the Order of Australia, and so on. In a sense, therefore, they are somewhat analogous to those distinctions awarded by certain of the Canadian provinces.   CS

Jamb *see* **Gamb** *and* **Greave**

Japanese Armory Japan, like western Europe, once existed under a feudal system, and like Europe developed a system of hereditary armorial devices during the twelfth and thirteenth centuries. The Japanese equivalent of the European armorial device is the *mon*. Unlike European armory, which became increasingly complex, the *mon* has retained a simplicity of form unsurpassed by the devices of any other civilization. The Japanese did not have the equivalent of European heralds to grant or control the use of devices. Their system evolved informally and like most things Japanese its development was essentially aesthetic and functional. The *mon* was used by the Japanese nobleman as a means of identification on clothing, banners and other accoutrements, and also appeared on his furniture and domestic artefacts and fabrics.

During the sixteenth century the *mon* was displayed on the breast (twice), sleeves and back of a garment. Later the Japanese nobleman restricted its use to just three points: the back (just below the collar), and on the sleeves. Occasionally it would be worn on the front of a war helmet. From the seventeenth to the nineteenth century, Japan isolated itself from the rest of the world — this was the age of the feudal lord and the *Samurai*.

Confusion inevitably arose from the indiscriminate method of selecting a device to be used as a *mon*, and unrelated clans were often found to have adopted the same symbol. In the mid seventeenth century a law was passed which compelled all aristocratic families to register their *mon*; they were required to register two symbols, from which they could not deviate. Among the nobility two forms of *mon* were used: the *jomon* was the more important, and the *kayemon*, or lesser *mon*, was reserved for more mundane use.

The *mon* had also been adopted by the merchant classes, scholars and priests. As with their European counterparts, the *mon* was also used as a mark of ownership.

During the *Maiji* era (equating to the Victorian and Edwardian period in England) all Japanese were obliged to take a surname, and many at this time also adopted a *mon*. When the head of a family or clan died, the eldest son would inherit the *mon* of his father, along with the leadership of the clan. Other sons were expected to adopt symbols of their own, and for this reason variations of the family *mon* were created.

The range of objects from which *mon* were drawn is as varied as the subjects of their European counterparts, with one notable exception. Due to the influence of Buddhism there is a paucity of the larger animal subjects so popular in British armory. Flowers, vegetables and inanimate objects of every description abound, including helmets, fans, bells, keys, swords, tools and simple geometrical shapes. Botanical subjects cover much of Japan's wide and rich plant life: bamboo, ivy, cherry blossom, wisteria, cloves, wood sorrel, gentian, grapes and even the humble radish. Insects are another popular theme: dragonflies, beetles, centipedes and butterflies, either solitary or in groups. Other popular motifs are the lobster, fish of many kinds, shells, the dove, crane and phoenix.

The most famous Japanese symbol, however, is the chrysanthemum, which is the Imperial device. The Emperor bears a sixteen-petalled chrysanthemum, whilst the fourteen-petalled variety is borne by his imperial brothers and sons. It is considered improper for any non-royal person to use the flower as a *mon*.

The subject of the *mon* frequently made reference to

Japanese mons

the name of the bearer, in a similar manner to the canting arms of European armory. BC

Further reading

Adachi, F. (trans.) *Japanese Design Motifs* 1980.

Dower, J.W. *The Elements of Japanese Design* New York, 1982. A handbook of Japanese armory.

Hawley, W.M. and K.K. Chappelear *Mon: The Japanese Family Crest* London, 1976.

Ito K. *Nihon no Monsho* (Crests of Japan) Tokyo, 1965.

— *Monsho* (Crests) Tokyo, 1969.

Turnbull, S.R. *The Samurai — a military history* London, 1977.

— *The Book of the Samurai* London, 1983.

— *Samurai Warriors* London, 1987.

Jelloped *see* **Attributes**

Jerusalem, King of The title of the rulers of the Latin Kingdom of Jerusalem which existed from 1100 to 1291 during the period of the first CRUSADES. JC-K

Further reading

La Monte, J.L. *Feudal Monarchy in the Latin Kingdom of Jerusalem* 1932.

Riley-Smith, J. *The Feudal Nobility and the Kingdom of Jerusalem 1174-1277* 1973.

Runciman, S. *A History of the Crusades. Vol II: the Kingdom of Jerusalem* Cambridge, 1952.

Jessant An armorial charge enfiling the face of a beast. The most common form is jessant-de-lis, in which a fleur-de-lis enfiles a leopard's head as though thrust upward through its mouth to emerge from the top of the head.

Jessed *see* **Attributes**

Jolly Roger Popular in schoolboy literature, the term has come to mean a black pirate flag charged with a white 'skull and cross-bones'. In reality, the term dates from the early eighteenth century and may be applied to any nautical flag used by pirates to obtain a psychological advantage over their intended victims. Such flags were used during the seventeenth and eighteenth centuries, and were often charged with symbols of death, such as the black death's head on white used by French pirates who attacked an English ship west of Madeira in 1717, and the 'Black Flag with a Pourtrature of Death having an Hour-Glass in one Hand, and a Dart in the other, at the end of which was the Form of a Heart with three Drops of Blood falling from it' — the 'Old Roger', which was fixed to the gallows at Rhode Island for the mass execution of pirates in 1723. The Barbary pirates were reputed to have flown a red flag, charged with a winged hourglass, an arm brandishing a sword, and a skull and cross-bones. Some pirates used plain signal flags — black for death and red for battle (the 'Bloody Flag'). However, one suspects that recognition and identification were, on most occasions, unwelcome, and that the majority of pirate vessels would have flown a variety of false flags, the element of surprise being essential to a successful skirmish. The Jolly Roger is now the (unofficial) prerogative of the submariner, exploits and 'kills' being denoted by the addition of appropriate minor charges.

Joust A combat between two knights, either mounted or on foot. Infrequently the contest was to the death — *à l'outrance* — but more usually for sport, as in a TOURNAMENT, the bout being described as *à plaisance*. JC-K

Jousting Cheques A piece of paper upon which a herald noted the score at a tournament. These varied from hastily marked scores pricked on scraps of paper to carefully drawn diagrams, often embellished with the emblazoned arms of the combatants. A remarkable collection of sixteenth-century jousting cheques is in the possession of the College of Arms. By that century the tournament had developed into the stylized form of combat one now associates with fencing and the martial arts. Pageantry and ceremonial dominated the proceedings, all carefully marshalled by the officers of arms.

The tilt, tourney and barriers (*see* TOURNAMENT) was each recorded on a differently designed cheque. That for the tilt (fig. 1) showed the courses run (on the projecting line), the taints or attaints (direct hits) on the top line, the lances broken on the centre line, and those disallowed on the bottom line. The tourney cheques (fig. 2) show the swords 'broken in passage' (i.e. when the contending parties first met), and 'at the joining' (during the ensuing mêlée). The scoring for barriers was similar (fig. 3): on the upper line were marked the swords broken, on the centre line the pikes broken, and on the lower line 'faults' (disallowed advantages). A cross indicated that a participant had been forced to the ground.

Elizabethan jousting cheques also provide evidence of the identity of combatants, and it is clear that at that time only a comparatively small number of nobles was able to afford the rapidly increasing expense of maintaining costly armour and equipment, and of participating in the attendant pageantry and festivities.

Judiciar This officer was the chief political and judicial authority of the Norman and Plantagenet kings. He acted as regent when the king was absent abroad.

Jupon The successor to the surcoat, the jupon was a short, sleeveless coat worn over armour and emblazoned with arms. Popular from the mid fourteenth to the mid fifteenth century, at which time plate armour had become so highly embellished and valuable that it was fashionable for it to be worn without a covering. The later tabard was worn for purely armorial purposes.

Justice of the Peace An office which arose in medieval times as that of an inferior magistrate responsible for preserving the peace in a county, town, or other district. Sometimes called a 'Justicer'.

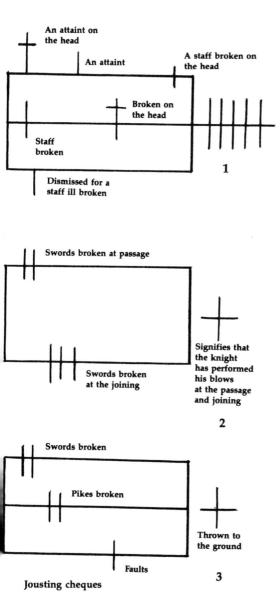

An attaint on the head

An attaint

A staff broken on the head

Broken on the head

Staff broken

1

Dismissed for a staff ill broken

Swords broken at passage

Swords broken at the joining

Signifies that the knight has performed his blows at the passage and joining

2

Swords broken

Pikes broken

Thrown to the ground

Faults

3

Jousting cheques

Key (i) A common armorial charge usually symbolic of security, household management, property and education. Often borne in pairs saltirewise to represent the Keys of St Peter. When blazoned, not only should the inclination of the key be specified but also that of the ward, e.g. *a Key palewise ward downwards and outwards Gules* (see colour page 51).
(ii) The ornamental bows of keys provide a rich source of armorial information, as do ornamental lock plates. Elaborate cyphers and ornamentation in the form of coats of arms, crests and badges were popular from the fifteenth to the eighteenth century.
Further reading
Eras, V.J.M. *Locks and Keys Throughout the Ages* Folkestone, 1974.

King The word 'king' comes from the Saxon 'cyning' and may be related to 'kin', perhaps thus indicating that the man so described was the head of his tribe. It is now applied to the male sovereign ruler of an independent state, the position being hereditary, elective, or a mixture of the two. The rank is considered to be inferior to that of an emperor.   JC-K

King of Arms The senior rank of officer of arms. Only a king of arms has authority to grant armorial bearings, and in England this is subject to the formal approval of the Earl Marshal in the form of a warrant. The English and Scottish kings of arms are the only officers of arms to have a distinctive coronet of office, used for ceremonial purposes.

Kings of Arms Certificate of Confirmation Letters patent confirming a right to arms by virtue of an unconsummated grant. In 1978 Mr Rodney Dennys, then Somerset Herald, discovered an Elizabethan docket of a grant of arms to the Corporation of Mint Officers. In fact, neither the Corporation nor its successors the Royal Mint had ever used the arms blazoned in the docket, which was part of a College of Arms manuscript (Harvey's Grants ICB No. 101 at Folio 77), but which had not been signed or sealed. The grant was, therefore, effectively in abeyance. Consequently, the kings of arms issued by letters patent a certificate of confirmation dated 1982 which recited the proofs of intent by which confirmation was allowed:

Whereas upon examination of the Records and Collections of Her Majesty's College of Arms it appears that about the year 1561 or 1562 William Hervey, Esquire, Clarenceux King of Arms...

caused to be put in preparation Letters Patent thereby intending to assign, ratify, confirm, give and grant unto the Company and Fellowship of the Queen's Majesty's Mint . . . that Armorial Ensigns in perpetual memory of King Edward II their founder and patron . . . might be borne and used by the said Company and Fellowship as a Corporation . . . and by their successors forever.

Further reading
Challis, D.A. and D.P. Dyer *The Arms of the Royal Mint* Llantrisant, 1986.

Kintyre Pursuivant of Arms A current Scottish pursuivant of arms, first mentioned in the Treasurer's Accounts in 1494. Another of the titles associated with an area of the west coast of Scotland formerly within the control of the Lord of the Isles.

The badge of the office is *Two Dolphins hauriant addorsed Azure enfiling a Coronet of four Fleurs-de-lis and four Crosses paty proper.* CJB

Knight Bachelor The lowest degree of knighthood, but perhaps the most ancient. In a medieval army the knight bachelor would command the smallest unit, perhaps consisting of only a few personal retainers. He was not a member of an order of chivalry, and until 1926 possessed no insignia of his degree. The medieval knight bachelor displayed his arms on a pennon, the tails of which would be removed to form the banner of a banneret if he were promoted in the field of battle.

Badge of a knight bachelor

Today, the knight bachelor (who is addressed as Sir) is permitted to wear his insignia either as a breast badge or pendent from a vermillion ribbon, lined gold, about the neck. This badge, sanctioned by George V in 1926, consists of an oval medallion of vermillion enclosed by a scroll, thereon a cross-hilted sword, belted and sheathed, the pommel upwards, between two spurs, rowels upwards, the whole set within the sword belt, all in gold. Originally, this was borne without a ribbon on the left breast, but by a warrant of 1973 knights bachelor may *alternatively* wear the badge pendent from the neck ribbon, and it is with this that a newly created knight is invested when he receives the accolade.

If he is armigerous, the arms of a knight bachelor would include a helmet with open vizor and the badge pendent from its ribbon below the shield. Conventionally, the helmet should be affronty, but greater flexibility is now allowed so that crests and helms may more easily face the same direction.
See also KNIGHTS BACHELOR, IMPERIAL SOCIETY OF

Knight Banneret The highest degree of knighthood during the medieval period. A knight banneret could be a knight of great renown who personally served the sovereign, or one who had shown outstanding service and bravery on the battlefield. The knight banneret was permitted to lead troops in battle under his own banner, a right normally reserved for the highest nobility in the land. Lesser knights were only permitted to fly a pennon on the battlefield, and it therefore was the custom for the military commander when upgrading a knight to banneret degree to take the pennon and remove its tails, thus making it into a square or oblong banner. Sir John Froissart, a great chronicler of chivalry in the medieval period, recorded an incident of the above ceremony which took place on the battlefield of Najera in 1367. Sir John Chandos, a knight under the command of Edward, Prince of Wales (The Black Prince), was raised to the status of knight banneret on the eve of the battle. The actual cutting of the pennon's tails was performed by Pedro of Castile, whom the Black Prince was assisting during a period of dynastic warfare. Sir John, upon being handed his new 'banner', paraded it in front of his troops, exhorting them to defend it well.

Knight-errant A medieval knight who travelled in search of adventure.

Knighthood and Chivalry, Orders of The early chivalric orders were fraternities of like-minded men of the appropriate social class, bound together in common purpose. That of the Knights Hospitaller, for example, was to succour pilgrims in the Holy Land, the Trinitarians ransomed Christian captives, and the knights of the Most Noble Order of the Garter pledged themselves to 'a Society, Fellowship, College of Knights' of equal status 'Co-partners in Peace and War, assistant to one another in all serious and dangerous Exploits: and thro' the whole Course of their Lives to shew Fidelity and Friendliness towards one another.'

Of course, many members of the early crusading orders were simply adventurers, no doubt motivated as much by the security of fellowship and the concept of exclusive pre-eminence as by religious or chivalric idealism.

Several chivalric orders lay claim to very early dates of foundation: the Order of Constantine St George, for example, claims a fourth-century foundation and reconstitution in 1190. However, the majority of the early orders can justifiably claim to have been founded during the period of the first crusade (1096-99), though papal recognition may have been considerably later. The Knights Hospitaller received recognition of Pope Pascal II in 1113, though their foundation undoubtedly pre-dates it by some thirty years.

Many of the later medieval orders of chivalry were exclusive foundations, membership being strictly limited and usually in the gift of a sovereign. Although modelled on the concepts of chivalric egalitarianism and humility, these orders were essentially élitist, membership being the ultimate reward for service to the sovereign or utilized for the purposes of international diplomacy.

Post-medieval orders, for the most part, confer membership in recognition of distinguished or meritorious service to one's country. Although some of these orders originated in earlier orders of chivalry, their application is now of a more general nature, and several have been divided into classes in order to accommodate a rapidly increasing membership.

Many orders have, of course, disappeared: some of the early fraternal orders outlived their usefulness or were suppressed, and with the rise and fall of kingdoms, principalities and dukedoms, orders came and went. The French Revolution and the advent of the Napoleonic era saw the demise of the Order of St Michael (1469), the Order of the Holy Ghost (1578), and other dignities, to be replaced by the Ordre National de la Legion d'Honneur (1802). The destruction of the German Empire saw the dissolution of nearly fifty orders, and the upheavals following the Second World War were such that in the Federal Republic of Germany there remains just one order: that 'of Merit' (1955) in eight classes. The granting of independence to the Indian sub-continent in 1947 saw the end of the Star of India and the Indian Empire orders. In other countries the development of republican government brought many changes. Nevertheless, there still exist some five-hundred

orders worldwide, including at least fifty ORDERS OF MERIT. These may be found, listed by country, in *Debrett's Peerage*. Many important orders dating from an earlier age and now defunct are described under the heading Knighthood and Chivalry in the fourteenth edition of the *Encyclopaedia Britannica*. Information concerning both orders of knighthood and decorations extant in the mid nineteenth century may be found in *The Book of Orders of Knighthood and Decorations of Honour* by Sir Bernard Burke (1858). This rare book contains a wealth of detail and numerous coloured illustrations of insignia and decorations of the period. Any reader who requires details of current orders is recommended to write to the embassy of the country concerned. Without exception useful information will be forthcoming, sometimes with photographs of insignia, etc.

It should be noted that neither the Republic of Ireland nor Switzerland grant national honours of any kind. Indeed, Article 40.2.1 of the Irish Constitution states that titles of nobility shall not be conferred by the state, and no title of nobility or honour may be accepted by any citizen without the approval of the government.

The following orders are detailed in this dictionary, each under its own heading: Alcantara (Spain), Annunziata (Italy, Savoy), Australia, Barbados, Bath (British), Brethren of the Sword (Livonia), British Empire, Calatrava (Spain), Canada, Christ (Portugal), Collar of St Agatha of Paterno (Aragona), Columbus, Knights of (USA), Companions of Honour (British), Constantine St George (Byzantium), Cross of Liberty (Finland), Crown of India (British), Dannebrog (Denmark), Distinguished Service (British), Dove (Castile), Dragon (Hungary)', Elephant (Denmark), Falcon (Iceland), Garter (British), Golden Circle (USA), Golden Fleece (France/Spain), Golden Rose (papal), Holy Ghost (France/Castile), Holy Sepulchre (papal crusader), Imperial Service (British), Indian Empire (British), Jamaica, Legion of Honour (France), Legion of Merit (USA), Lion of Finland, Merit (British), Merit (French), Merit (German), Merit (Italian), New Zealand, Royal Victorian (British), St Benedict of Aviz (Portugal), St Hubert (Bavaria), St Iago (Portugal), St Jacob of the Sword (Spain), St John of Jerusalem (crusader), St Lazarus of Jerusalem (crusader), St Maurice and St Lazarus (crusader), St Michael (France), St Michael and St George (British), St Olav (Norway), St Patrick (Ireland), St Stephen (Tuscany), Seraphim (Sweden), Star (French medieval), Star of India (British), Swan (Bavaria), Sword of Cyprus (crusader), Tankard (Aragon), Templars (crusader), Teutonic (crusader), Tower and Sword (Portugal), Thistle (British), Victoria and Albert (British), White Rose of Finland.

The British orders of chivalry each have their own insignia, chapels and officers. The officers for each order are broadly the same: the sovereign is Head of the Order and its administration is the responsibility of a Chancellor, Registrar or Secretary. A bishop, dean or canon is appointed as Prelate and the order's king of arms is invariably a herald who is responsible for matters armorial and genealogical. Some orders also have a genealogist who is usually a herald. A Gentleman Usher, who carries a rod after which his office is named, is responsible for ceremonial.

The orders of the Garter and Thistle have only one rank, that of the Garter being Knight Companion and of the Thistle, Knight. However, in other orders there are several classes, usually: Knights or Dames Grand Cross, Knights or Dames Commander, Commanders or Companions, Officers or Lieutenants, and Members.   JC-K/SF

Further reading

De la Bere, I. *The Queen's Orders of Chivalry* 1961.

Shaw, W.A. *The Knights of England* 1906 (reprinted 1971). A complete record of the knights of the orders of chivalry in England, Scotland and Ireland and of knights bachelor.

Knighthood and Chivalry, Origins of The word 'knighthood' is the modern form of the Old English *cnihthád*, the period between youth and maturity; the word 'chivalry' derives from the Old French *chevalerie* meaning men-at-arms, gallant horsemen equipped for battle, a company of honourable men. By the middle of the twelfth century the two words were virtually synonymous, as describing both personal attributes and a code of conduct.

To begin with in England, *cnihthas* were, perhaps, the retainers of Anglo-Saxon magnates; young landholders who, in the time of King Edward the Confessor, had pledged themselves to the service of some 'lord' (ealdormen, bishop or greater thegn). After the Conquest the term seems to have been applied to military tenants who, as vassals of earls, major barons and bishops, held their estates (or manors) in return for service on the field of battle when called upon, for forty days a year, with specified arms and armour. Analogous practices pertained abroad. Also in pre-Conquest times, and particularly in Europe, there appears to have grown up some ceremony of importance which, on attaining adulthood, a young man of noble birth would undergo on admission to the ranks of the warriors. This certainly involved being presented with a sword, or a lance and shield. The coming together of these customs within the military systems which were established, together with the gradual emergence of the paid man-at-arms replacing service by land-tenure saw, at the time of the crusades, the establishment of seasoned warriors able and willing to fight in any cause.

It was perhaps only to be expected that in this climate of holy war, augmented by a release from feudalism, a concept of knighthood with codes of honour should gain ground and find expression in both military and religious orders of chivalry. The first group, under the command of a king or royal nominee, often richly endowed, evolved into such orders as the Garter, the Golden Fleece, and the Annunziata. The second fraternal group comprised orders under 'grand masters', of which the Knight Templars and the Knight Hospitallers were the pre-eminent examples.

Coming now to the progress of a youth from boyhood to knighthood, it seems reasonably clear that there were four progressive stages: page, squire, knight bachelor and, for some men, knight banneret, of which the last was of considerable distinction. From their very earliest years boys of the appropriate social class were schooled, through military exercises, in the arts of war; every feudal court and castle was, in effect, a school of chivalry and the knight-to-be progressed from toy weapons made of wood to more demanding tilting exercises as he moved from the first stage to the second. The conditions of page and squire were passed through during boyhood and early teens, and the stage of knighthood was reached at the very threshold of maturity. Pages were never combatant, but squires were, and some men (by reason of poverty) stayed as squires all their lives, voluntarily serving knights — looking after their horses and armour and following them into battle, or aiding them in tournaments. More generally, however, knighthood was attained after a suitable period as a squire.

There were, from the times of earliest record, two methods by which knighthood could be conferred on an aspirant. The first was extremely simple, and was used mainly in time of conflict. The candidate knelt before a senior knight or field commander who struck him three times with the flat of a sword. The second procedure was much more elaborate. The historian, John Selden, writing in 1614 said, 'The ceremonies and circumstances at the giving of this dignity in the elder time were of two kinds especially, which we may call courtly and sacred. The courtly were the feats held at the creation, giving of robes, arms, spurs and the like. The second were the holy devotions and what else was used in the church at or before the receiving of the dignity.' These elaborate solemnities seem to have been superseded at an early stage by the practice of 'dubbing' alone, so much so that Garter Segar in the reign of Queen Elizabeth I wrote, 'He that is to be made a knight is stricken by the prince with a sword drawn upon his back or shoulder, the prince saying Soys Chevalier.' Segar does not mention a holy vigil, the presentation of golden spurs or any form of complex ceremonial event.

The degree of knight banneret appears to have been based on personal distinction; one kind being

for a deed of valour done on the field of battle in the king's presence, the other being a request for promotion by the knight himself to the commander of the army. If, because of some signal service, the applicant was judged to be worthy of preferment, the heralds were called upon to cut the tails from his pennon, thereby transforming it into a small banner. The dignity of banneret fell gradually into disuse, and the last occasion on which it was conferred was at the Battle of Pinkie in 1547, when the Lord Protector Somerset advanced Sir Francis Bryen and two of his comrades to the rank of knight banneret.   JC-K
See also KNIGHTHOOD AND CHIVALRY, ORDERS OF
Further reading
Keen, M. *Chivalry* Yale, 1984.

Knight of the Shire In the thirteenth century and later, one of the twelve knights 'elected' to represent a shire in parliament. These knights had little political power and their activities were minor.

Knights Bachelor, Imperial Society of Formed in 1908, the Society received royal recognition in 1912 and its patron is Her Majesty Queen Elizabeth. It is a registered charity and seeks to uphold the dignity and rights of the degree at all times, to register every duly authenticated knighthood and to advise members on matters relating to the degree. Its charitable objectives include the relief of poverty, the advancement of education, support for hospitals, the elderly and the needy. A particular objective is to encourage knights bachelor within the Commonwealth to develop understanding and co-operation between the citizens of the Commonwealth. In 1962 the Society established its own chapel in the Priory Church of St Bartholomew the Great, Smithfield, London. The Society's badge may be worn in the form of a brooch by wives and daughters of knights.
See also ADDRESSES

Badge of the Imperial   Society of Knights Bachelor

Knights of Christ *see* **Templars**

Knot Intertwined cords in the form of slackened, symmetrical knots are widely used in armory, and are particularly effective as badges. Clearly the origins of many knots are practical, though others may be traced to the interlaced patterns of Celtic art and decoration. Knots are generally named after the families who

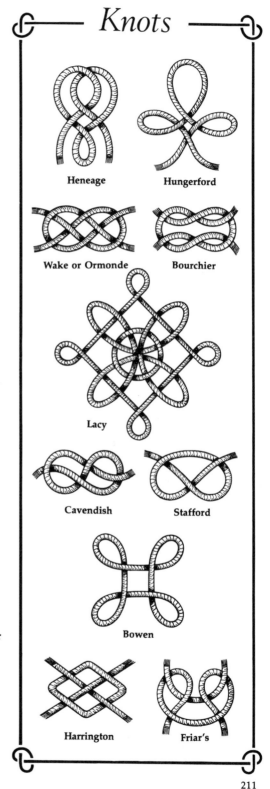

Knots

Heneage

Hungerford

Wake or Ormonde

Bourchier

Lacy

Cavendish

Stafford

Bowen

Harrington

Friar's

adopted them, and are often used in conjunction with badges acquired through marriage or inheritance, the badge of the lords Hastings, for example, in which the sickle of Hungerford is united by a knot with the garb of the Peverels. Regrettably, several well-known household badges have assumed spurious territorial designations as the result of their use as charges in the civic heraldry of a particular locality. The best known example is that of the so-called 'Staffordshire Knot', originally the badge of the earls of Stafford, but now ubiquitous as a charge in the heraldry of that county.

The translation of mariners' knots and Celtic interlacing to armorial representations is a fertile field for those armorists who enjoy devising charges. Two excellent (and inexpensive) books for this purpose are *The Harrison Book of Knots* by P.P.O. Harrison, Glasgow, 1964, and *Celtic Art: The Methods of Construction* by G. Bain, London, 1986.

L

Label A sub-ordinary consisting of a horizontal band, from which depend three or more short pieces. These may be straight (as in current practice), slightly splayed or dovetailed. The label is a brisure (mark of cadency) borne in the upper part of the shield by the eldest son during the lifetime of his father. All members of the British royal family, both male and female, bear labels in their arms. That of the heir apparent is argent of three points, others also being argent, the points variously charged. Grandchildren of the sovereign bear silver labels of five points. If a label has more than three points this should be specified in the blazon.

Lady Originally the female equivalent of a lord. The word is now used as the title prefixing the names of consorts of the lower ranks of the nobility.   JC-K

Lambrequin *see* **Mantling**

Lancaster Herald of Arms in Ordinary The title of Lancaster Herald first occurs in 1347 at Calais, and to begin with this officer was a servant to the noble house of Lancaster. As a retainer to John of Gaunt (1377-99) Lancaster was advanced to the rank of king of arms, and was later promoted to the royal household of King Henry IV (Gaunt's son), and made king of the northern province.

This arrangement continued until 1464, when Lancaster reverted to the rank of herald. Since the reign of King Henry VII (1485-1509) Lancaster has been a herald in ordinary. The badge of office is a red rose of Lancaster, royally crowned.   JC-K

Landgrave *or* **Landgraf** A German count with jurisdiction over a territory; also the title of certain German princes.

Landgravine The wife of a landgrave, or a female ruler of a landgraviate such as a territory, jurisdiction or province.

Langued *see* **Attributes**

Largesse A word meaning 'munificence', generally applied to money or gifts bestowed by great persons on occasions of rejoicing. It was shouted by heralds at medieval tournaments and at coronations, when it was their privileged custom to ask for gifts of money for their services.   JC-K

Law of Arms in England and Wales The basis of the Law of Arms is that no-one may bear and use arms without lawful authority, and that arms are in the nature of an incorporeal hereditament and are inalienable, being inherited in accordance with the laws and usages of arms. Many of these basic laws are of great antiquity, but they are constantly being augmented either by rulings of the kings of arms or by warrants from the Earl Marshal. Thus, the ecclesiastical hats that may be used as insignia by the Roman Catholic and Anglican clergy were recently established by Earl Marshal's warrant. On the other hand, the use by a bishop of a mitre in place of a crest is an ancient and traditional use. The kings of arms recently ordered what mark of difference should be used on the arms of legitimated bastards granted their paternal arms under the terms of a royal licence. The difference between these two types of ruling is that an Earl Marshal's warrant can only be upset by a further warrant, whereas the kings of arms are at liberty to alter their rulings, or those of their predecessors, as and when they please: while having a healthy respect for precedents they are not bound by them.

These laws, rules, conventions — call them what you will — are principally for the guidance of officers of arms. If they were ignored or flouted a case could be brought before the Court of Chivalry, but the result of such a case could not safely be anticipated, as the Court has never been called upon to deal with a minor breach of heraldic law, as from time to time promulgated by the Earl Marshal or the kings of arms.

Thus there is the Law of Arms as deduced from judgements in cases that have come before the Court of Chivalry, and the laws of arms as detailed above, whose validity has not so far been challenged before the Court and probably never will be, as the authority of the Earl Marshal and the kings of arms in matters heraldic is everywhere accepted.　　　　JB-L
See also CHIVALRY, COURT OF *and* ENTITLEMENT TO ARMS
Further reading
Squibb, G.D. *The Law of Arms in England* Heraldry Society (revised 1967).

Leathered *see* **Attributes**

Leaved *see* **Attributes**

Lecturers Beware the pseudo-armorist! To many people heraldry is such an abstruse subject that anyone who appears to be acquainted with a few armorial terms is immediately regarded as an 'expert'! Engaged as lecturers, such 'experts' may do more harm than good. By far the best sources of information regarding experienced and authoritative speakers are the national heraldry societies. Many professional officers of arms undertake speaking engagements and lecture tours both within their own jurisdictions and as guests in other countries. Enquiries should be addressed to the various heraldic authorities (*see* ADDRESSES).

Ledger Stones *see* **Incised Slabs**

Legate (i) An ecclesiastic deputed to represent the pope.
(ii) The deputy governor of a province or the governor himself.　　　　JC-K

Legged *see* **Attributes**

Legion of Honour (L'Ordre National de Légion d'Honneur) The senior French national order, created

by Napoleon Bonaparte on 19 May 1802 as a reward for military service. The decoration consists of a five-pointed star in white enamel hanging from a red moiré ribbon. The centre of the star is surrounded by a crown of oak and laurel leaves. The order is divided into five ranks: Grand Croix, Grand Officier, Commandeur, Officier and Chevalier.　　JC-K

Legion of Merit (United States of America) Established in 1942 and amended in 1955, the Legion of Merit is awarded to citizens of any nation who 'have distinguished themselves by exceptionally meritorious conduct in the performance of outstanding services' since 8 September 1939, the date of proclamation of a state of emergency following the outbreak of war in Europe.

It is the first United States award to have different degrees, there being four in all. The highest rank is Chief Commander and is bestowed on heads of foreign states or government. The insignia of this degree is a large breast-worn star of five points with V-shaped ends. It is finished in white enamel bordered in crimson and trimmed with gold. Behind the star is a green laurel leaf, and at the centre a blue enamel field with thirteen white stars. Within the wreath in the angles of the star are outward-pointing crossed arrows.

The second rank is that of Commander and is bestowed on senior military commanders (such as the British Chief of the Imperial General Staff); the insignia is a smaller version of the Chief Commanders' star, and is suspended around the neck from a ribbon of crimson moiré edged with a narrow white stripe.

The rank of Officer is awarded to foreign military attachés and senior members of armed forces. The insignia is a medal, on a ribbon, the design being the same as the star already described. The lowest rank, Legionnaire, is granted to deserving persons of all nationalities, the medal of the degree being as for Officers, but without the distinctive ribbon.　JC-K
Further reading
Korrigan, E.E. *American War Medals and Decorations* New York, 1974.

Leopard In early armory, any lion that was not rampant was a *lion leopardé*. The term leopard was later applied to the lion passant guardant, hence the expression 'the leopards of England'. In current practice, the term leopard is properly applied only to the zoological creature.

Letters Patent An open letter (Latin *patere* = to open) addressed 'To All and Singular to whom these Presents shall Come'. Armorial bearings are granted by means of a PATENT OF ARMS, the form of which varies from one heraldic authority to another (see colour pages 249-51).

Early patents were splendidly vigorous works of art, each endowed with a character of its own by the vitality of the artist's imagination and his skill with brush and pen. Regrettably, the modern patent rarely transcends the status of a finely executed document, and is unlikely to do so until the constraints placed upon composition and artistic interpretation are relaxed.

The text is generally executed in copper plate or foundation hand by a skilled calligrapher, the initial letters 'TO' being illuminated and the blazon often in a contrasting colour. Above the text, in English patents, are (from left to right) the arms of the Earl Marshal, the sovereign and the College of Arms, occasionally depicted in their entirety with crests and supporters. In the left (dexter) margin is the painting of the coat of arms and, when granted, the badge or badges beneath and sometimes a standard above. (There is some flexibility with regard to an exemplification of a badge, which may be painted within the text if preferred.) In the right (sinister) margin of more elaborate patents may be found the arms of the granting kings of arms, whose signatures and seals are always appended at the foot: Garter and the appropriate provincial king for grants to individuals resident in England, Wales and Northern Ireland, and all three kings for grants to civic and corporate bodies or armigers resident abroad. In English patents the blue margin line, which separates the paintings in the margin from the text, is now optional and its omission greatly improves the appearance of the patent. On the reverse of the vellum is the signature of the Registrar and the date of registration. It is also possible to record here the rationale of the arms and the identity of the artist who executed them.

Of course, elaborate and highly illuminated margins and additional embellishments must be paid for, and most armigers are more than satisfied to receive a simple patent of arms in its red box with gold royal cyphers.

Opinion is divided as to whether letters patent should be displayed or whether they should remain in their box. Advocates of the latter insist that the public display of armorial bearings is somehow pretentious and 'bad form'. By their very nature letters patent are 'open' and intended to be seen, and the term pretentious in such a context is strictly inaccurate: an armiger is *de facto* an armiger! (The opposite of Letters Patent are Letters Close, which are of a personal nature and closed with a seal.)

Consideration should be given both to the mounting and siting of a patent of arms. Adhesives should not be applied to the vellum, neither should it be punctured. The most satisfactory answer is to engage an experienced picture framer and have the patent 'double framed'. In this way the vellum is secured within a small inner frame which allows it to respond to atmospheric changes, the glass of this inner frame keeping the patent in place without recourse to adhesives or pins. This is mounted on a stout, velvet-covered board (material of a contrasting colour is best), drilled to admit air, and itself mounted within a stout, outer frame. This solution also provides the most satisfactory method of dealing with the seals and attractive seal-box covers which may be affixed to the lower section of the backing board through the velvet, with the seal ribbons passing beneath the lower section of the inner frame. This 'double frame' method also prevents dust particles and insects from reaching the vellum. It is also advisable to use ultra-violet light-proof perspex instead of glass, in order to conserve the paint colour, but this material should be treated with respect for it is easily scratched. In any event, it is best if the framed patent is hung away from direct natural light, otherwise the colours may fade. Green, blue and purple are particularly susceptible; gold, on the other hand, is not but may react to excessive heat, as will the vellum if placed too near a radiator. A library painting of the armorial bearings may be commissioned through the College of Arms. This is usually executed by the same herald painter who painted the arms in the original patent, and is authenticated by the officer of arms responsible for the grant. Complete copies of patents of arms may also be obtained, but these have only one seal: that of the College itself.

See also ARMORIAL BEARINGS, USE OF

Library Painting *or* **Certificated Painting** A copy of the armorial bearings emblazoned on letters patent, painted on vellum or line and wash board and certified by an officer of arms. A library painting may be commissioned by an armiger and received well in advance of the letters patent. Naturally, an additional fee is required.

Liechtenstein, Royal Arms of Quarterly 1 *Or an Eagle displayed Sable beaked and membered Gold charged with a Crescent trefoiled at the extremities and crowned Or* (Silesia) 2 *Barry of eight Or and Sable a Crown of Rue arched bendwise Vert* (Kuenking) 3 *Per pale Gules and Argent* (Troppau) 4 *Or a Harpy Sable visage Argent crowned Or* (Schellenberg) on a point in base *Azure a Buglehorn stringed Or* (Jägendorf) over all an escutcheon of pretence *Per fess Or and Gules* (Liechtenstein).

Lieutenant (i) A banner.
(ii) The officer responsible for the maintenance of a banner.

Life Peerages The creation of life peers has been a practice since 1377, when the Earldom of Huntingdon was conferred for life on Guichard d'Angle. However, the right to sit in the House of Lords seems not to have been accorded to the holders of the dignity until the third quarter of the nineteenth century. In 1856 there was an attempt to create a precedent to allow the House of Lords to be enriched by the talents of men whose income was insufficient to enable them to support a hereditary dignity, and on 16 January of that year Sir Thomas Parke was created Baron Wensleydale for the term of his natural life. However, on 22 February 1856 the Committee of Privileges ruled that the grantee could not 'sit and vote' in the Upper House. In 1869 an attempt was made to introduce a bill for the wider creation of Life Peerages, but this was defeated. In 1876 the Appellate Jurisdiction Act was passed, by which powers were taken to create certain dignitaries Barons for Life (Lords of Appeal in Ordinary).

In the second half of the twentieth century hereditary peerages are seldom granted, and following the Life Peerages Act of 1958 the majority of advancements to that degree, with the right to sit in the House of Lords, have been for life only. The armorial achievement of a life peer includes supporters, though these are personal to the grantee and not inherited at his death.   JC-K

Limitation Clause A grant of arms by letters patent contains a limitation clause specifying to whom the armorial bearings are granted and how they are to descend. Thus, for example, arms may be granted to 'X' and his descendants and to the other descendants of his father or grandfather, or brother or uncle, who are named in the patent. Armorial bearings cannot be granted to deceased persons (though they can be placed upon their monuments), but their descendants may benefit from such a clause.   HPB

Lined *see* **Attributes**

Line of Partition A line dividing the surface of a shield or charge. There are four principal lines of partition: one vertical, one horizontal and two diagonals, each passing through the centre of the shield, thereby creating eight 'radii'. These provide the geometrical basis for the principal PARTITIONS and ORDINARIES by which they are named.

Lines of partition also separate DIVISIONS in a varied field, and are subject to a number of decorative variations.

See also LINES, VARIED

Lines, Varied Lines of partition and the edges of geometrical charges such as ordinaries may be ornamented by the use of variations. Care should be exercized when depicting or blazoning engrailed and invected. The 'points' of the former point outwards and those of the latter point inwards. The fess, chevron and bend may be embattled only at the upper edge. If both edges are so depicted they are 'embattled counter embattled', the (rare) term bretessé being used when the embrasures are opposite each other. The dimensions and frequency of indentations should be compatible with the size and disposition of other charges, and are matters best determined by the artist. The most common variations of line are illustrated overleaf.

Lion The lions of mythology have magic in their tails. By sweeping them over their tracks they obliterate their footprints and make their ways unknown. By swinging them over their bodies they render themselves invisible. Thus the longer the tail, the greater the magic.

The lion is always alert and sleeps with his eyes open. It was also believed that the cubs were born dead and remained so for three days, whereupon their father came and breathed into their faces to give them life. Many other strange beliefs concerning the lion have come down the ages: if he is sick, he is cured by eating a monkey; he is of such a noble and

One of four carved lions on a twelfth-century font at Shobdon, Hereford and Worcester. The mid-twelfth century Hereford school of sculpture derived its distinctive style from Scandinavian, Byzantine and Celtic art, and although the lions are not armorial, their influence on later heraldic art is undeniable. Sadly the church at Shobdon was dismantled in the eighteenth century and replaced by a 'Strawberry Hill Gothic' building. Fortunately, the font has survived.

Varied Lines

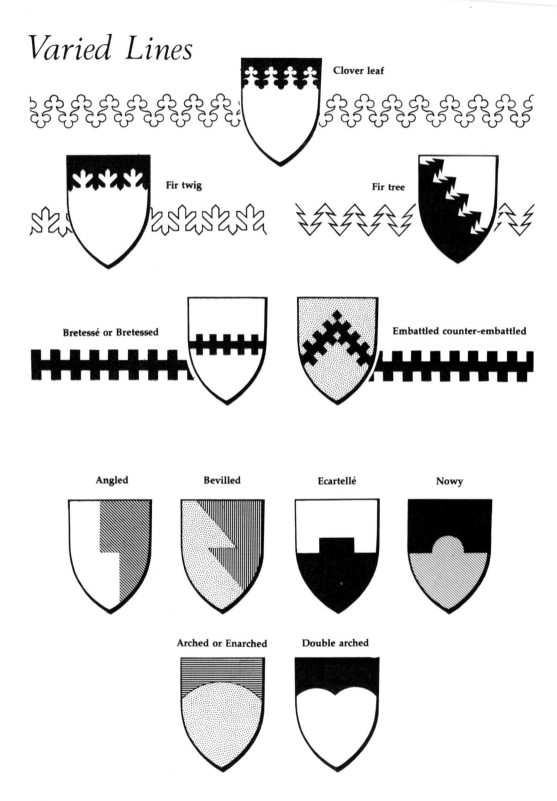

Clover leaf

Fir twig

Fir tree

Bretessé or Bretessed

Embattled counter-embattled

Angled   Bevilled   Ecartellé   Nowy

Arched or Enarched   Double arched

Varied Lines

Engrailed

Indented

Dancetty

Invected

Nebuly

Wavy or Undy

Raguly

Embattled

Crested

Dovetailed

Rayonné

Urdy or Vallary

Embattled grady

Potenty

Saxonised

Lion

compassionate nature that he will not attack a fallen man and does not get angry unless wounded; he is so courageous that he fears nothing, except a cock, especially a white one. The lion is regarded as the embodiment of courage, strength and nobleness. He is the King of the Beasts, and a fitting symbol of kings and kingdoms.

Since the beginning of armory the lion has appeared with great frequency in arms, and was greatly favoured by kings and the great lords of the Middle Ages. One of the earliest known examples of hereditary arms is that of William Longespee, natural son of King Henry II of England, who bore six golden lions on a blue shield, this being the same as that of his grandfather, Geoffrey of Anjou.   MY

Lioncel A small lion. Used in blazon when more than one lion is depicted. Like the similarly tiresome eaglet, this term has at last been abandoned.

Lion-Dragon An unusual monster having the foreparts of a lion and the hind parts of a dragon.

Lion of Finland, Order of Founded in September 1942, the order recognizes outstanding merit in both the military and civil spheres. It can be awarded to non-nationals. There are five classes, plus the Medal of Finland.   JC-K

Liver Bird Familiar as the cormorant in the arms of the City of Liverpool, but not to be found elsewhere.

Liveries *see* **Livery Colours**

Livery The term is derived through the French *Livrée* from the Latin *liberare*, meaning to liberate or bestow, and originally meant the dispensing of food, provisions, clothing, etc., to retainers and domestic servants. Later the term was applied to the uniforms, badges and other indications of patronage and partisanship of those who accepted the privileges and obligations of livery and maintenance.

Livery and Maintenance *or* **Badge and Livery** *or* **Maintenance** *or* **Embracery** The practice of maintaining and protecting large numbers of retainers in return for domestic and military services. Maintenance was common throughout Europe in the Middle Ages, and particularly so in England during the fourteenth and fifteenth centuries, when a magnate's influence was judged by the number of men wearing his badge and livery and his ability to protect them when necessary in the courts of law. Some retinues were little better than brigands terrorizing their lord's neighbours, seizing lands and bearing false witness against them in law suits.

With the parallel development of guilds, confraternities and mysteries, following the granting of special privileges by Edward II, came a demand that every guild and mystery should have its special colours and uniforms (hence the livery companies), and as a result throughout the land there grew a competition both in the bestowal and acceptance of liveries.

Historians, who seem by common consent to terminate the Middle Ages at Bosworth Field (1485), overlook one characteristic of the period which is unique in English history, and without which the turmoil of the Wars of the Roses would have been impossible: the ability of a magnate to summon to the field of battle large retinues of men whose allegiance was bought through the practice of livery and maintenance. This was recognized by successive medieval kings who attempted to legislate against the abuses of the system: Richard II in 1392 and 1396 (at the same time increasing his own liveried Cheshire retinue); Henry IV in 1399 and 1411; Edward IV in 1468. Ultimately it was the Tudors who were successful, though by then livery and maintenance included several distinct offences and so it is doubtful whether any one act actually solved all the problems. The Tudors were also aware that, with judicious application of the law, the system could be exploited for financial purposes. However, by the statutes of 3 Henry VII *c.* 1 (which set up the Court of Star Chamber primarily to suppress maintenance); 19 Henry VIII *c.* 14 (which provided penalties for giving liveries to retainers); and 32 Henry VIII *c.* 9 (against maintenance and embracery), the practice of bestowing a patron's liveries on retainers other than household servants was suppressed, the private army effectively abolished and thereby the Middle Ages brought to a close.

Further reading
Holdsworth, W. *A History of English Law* Vol.III pp.395-400, Vol.IV p.521, and Vol.V p.202.

Livery Banners (i) (also Badge Banner) A square livery flag of the Tudor period, probably originally a livery pennon with the tails removed, divided per pale of the livery colours and charged with a badge. In this form too easily confused with the personal banner to be effective.
(ii) A square livery flag used throughout the medieval and Tudor periods divided per fess of the livery colours and (usually) fringed of the armorial colours, e.g. the *Beau Sant* (*Per fess Sable and Argent*) of the Knights Templar.
See also FLAG

Livery Colours The colour or colours in which a lord clothed his retainers (usually in conjunction with a badge) for the purpose of identification and as an outward and visible indication of allegiance. In modern usage they are the colours used by armigerous corporations and institutions for the same purpose — to mark property and for the uniforms of members and employees. There are ample precedents to suggest that livery colours do not necessarily have to be the conventional tinctures of armory. Few individual armigers have need of livery colours. In armorial bearings the livery colours should be depicted in the fields of livery flags and in the mantling when charged with badges. In practice, however, modern English standards (which often accompany grants of badges) are rarely composed of livery colours, the fields being selected for artistic rather than armorial reasons. The crest-wreath and the fringe of a standard are occasionally used for this purpose, but this is contrary to medieval practice and is to be regretted. In Scotland, the use of badges, liveries and livery flags is regulated and specified in patents. Caution should be exercised when interpreting the term 'on a wreath of the liveries', which is to be found in numerous heraldic reference books. Scottish armorial and livery colours are generally the same, and the crest-wreath may indeed be of the livery colours. However, in England this is not necessarily so and the tinctures of the wreath are now specified in order to avoid ambiguity. Fox-Davies, in his *Heraldic Badges* (1907), demonstrates that few medieval nobles dressed their retainers in the colours of their shields of arms. For example, the armorial colours of John Mowbray, Duke of Norfolk (d. 1476) were silver and red (*Gules a Lion rampant Argent*) and yet his livery colours were dark blue and 'tawny'. Not all the troops who fought at Agincourt or Bosworth wore full livery. Many were conscripts or mercenaries, and their 'livery' was often no more than a simple jupon charged with a badge, or even a coloured scarf no different from those worn by the Khmer Rouge in Vietnam or the Philippine revolutionary of 1986. They would march and muster beneath the great standard of the noble who had enlisted them and follow his guidons into battle. These were the livery flags, composed of the livery colours, charged with the national device and the badges worn by the attendant soldiery.

The practice of dressing domestic servants and retainers in livery continued through the eighteenth and nineteenth centuries, though today there are few examples to be found outside the British royal household. Generally muted colours were used: grey for silver, oatmeal or tawny for gold, murrey for red, etc., the proper colours being reserved for 'full dress' occasions. (See *Concise Encyclopedia of Heraldry* by Guy Cadogan Rothery, 1915 reprinted 1985, for intricate details of Victorian and Edwardian practice.)

See also BADGE *and* FLAG

Livery Companies of the City of London derive their twelfth-century origins from the religious fraternities which grew up around a church, monastery or hospital to which they attached themselves, and which the members used as a meeting place and whose saint was adopted as their patron. Members of those fraternities who lived together often worked together in a common trade or craft, and they developed into mutual protection societies making provision for the poor, sick and needy in their communities and promoting the interests of their crafts, including apprenticeship and the power of search which gave each company the right to inspect all goods handled by its members. This gave the guilds an effective weapon against competition from strangers to the city, and a constructive measure to keep their own members in line, to maintain high standards of work and so make the guilds stronger.

Part of the mystique attached to the idea of livery companies is caused by the fact that it is so difficult to lay down hard and fast definitions of exactly what they are. A guild obtains its charter from the monarch, but its grant of livery since 1560 comes from the Court of Aldermen, who have to be satisfied that 'a number of men of good repute from some trade or mystery not already represented by an existing guild have joined together for a time sufficiently long to justify the belief that they will continue to hold together and are not likely to fall apart from lack of interest or support.'

Evidence that the early medieval guilds were a development from religious fraternities is to be found in the symbolism of many of the companies' coats of arms, reflected in the pious tenor of their mottoes, and by direct reference in the letters patent to religious allegiance. Of the twenty-five patents to the London guilds during the period 1439 to 1500, five are composed wholly of religious symbols. A further five combine religious and trade allusions, and the remainder refer only to the respective trade or craft. The earliest mention of the Mercers is the appointment of the fraternity, in about 1190, as patrons of the Hospital of St Thomas of Acon, a brotherhood of crusader knights which had settled in the city. The Mercers' arms show the figure of a virgin issuing from and within a border of clouds, and may have been adopted by the Mercers from the Hospital Order after it had been dissolved. The Drapers' grant of 1439 is not only the earliest grant to a city company, but is also the oldest to survive and still in the possession of the company, its three crowns representing a heraldic tripling of the imperial crown of Our Lady. Within the versal letter with which the Drapers' 1439 patent begins is a representation of the Virgin being crowned at her Assumption by God the Father and God the Son, who are also triple-crowned.

The grant of Sir William Bruges states in old French that 'I Garter King of Arms . . . have devised a coat of arms under the form of a blazon to remain to the said honourable Mistery as a perpetual memorial. That is to say, in honour of the very glorious Virgin and Mother Mary who is in the shadow of the sun and yet shines with all clearness and purity, I have devised . . .'. The doves in the arms of the Tallow Chandlers were probably inspired by John i.32: 'and John bare record, saying I saw the Spirit descending from Heaven like a dove and it abode upon him.' The crest of the head of St John the Baptist in a charger is an allusion to the origins of the company as a religious fraternity of St John. The motto is taken from the Gospel of St John i.29: 'Behold the Lamb of God, which taketh away the sin of the world.' The arms are supported either side by an angel vested, winged and crowned with stars. (See illustration page 183.)

The cross keys in the chief of the Fishmongers' arms are symbols of St Peter. Members were required, under an ordinance of 1426, to attend each year a solemn mass in the worship of God and St Peter. The three lilies in the chief of the Coopers' arms symbolize the company's incorporation in 1501 as a fraternity in honour of the Blessed Virgin Mary, while the eagle in the arms of the Scriveners and the Stationers may suggest a common origin in a religious fraternity of St John the Evangelist, whose ancient symbol of a rising eagle is said to have been assigned because his gaze pierced further into the mysteries of Heaven than that of any man. The Stationers' shield is supported by *two Angels proper vested Argent mantled Azure winged and blowing a Trumpet Or*. The Company of Parish Clerks, who received their first charter in 1442 (and who have never applied for a grant of livery, since they prefer the distinction of the surplice to livery gowns), bear as a main charge a fleur-de-lis, a symbol of the Holy Trinity and the Blessed Virgin. There was a fraternity of Girdlers at St Lawrence in St Lawrence Jewry in 1332 devoted to the Blessed Virgin Mary and to St Lawrence. The arms of the Girdlers Company are *On a field of six pieces Azure and Or three Gridirons Or*. The crest depicts the patron saint, St Lawrence, who was martyred by burning over a gridiron. This was the earliest (1454) grant of a crest to a corporate body.

Much of the religious symbolism found in the arms of the early guilds was, however, suppressed and removed during the Reformation, to be replaced by more conventional devices reflecting the trade or craft of the companies.

Of the ninety-five City of London livery companies bearing arms in 1986, thirty-six make use of the chevron as a main charge, six of which are engrailed, between three minor charges. In fourteen instances the chevron itself is charged, thirteen with three charges and one, the Masons, with a single pair of compasses. In three coats the chevron has been chosen to allude to the craft or trade. The Carpenters' arms are *Argent a Chevron engrailed between three Pairs of Compasses Sable*. Whilst the compasses are obvious tools of the carpenter, the chevron may also be allusive to his trade. The French term for rafter is *chevron*, and the charge in the Carpenters' arms may be intended to represent one of the products of the carpenter — a roof support. Not so obvious is the allusive use of the chevron in the Cordwainers' arms *Azure a Chevron Or between three Goat's Heads erased Argent horned and bearded Or*, until it is remembered that the French *chevron* has its roots in the Latin word *caper*, for goat. The Furniture Makers' arms, granted 1954, are *Argent a Chevron dovetailed counterdovetailed Gules between three Braces and Bits each palewise with bits downwards Sable*. The arms of the Pewterers contain a curious charge, the stryke or strake, which has yet to be positively identified.

Two companies use a party field of per chevron, the Salters *Party per chevron Azure and Gules three Covered Salts Argent garnished Or the Salt shedding on both sides of the Salt Argent* granted 1530, the Actuaries *Per chevron chequy Argent and Gules and Gules each chequer Gules charged with a Bezant in base a Cross potent Gold*. The Actuaries were incorporated in 1979 and granted arms in 1980. The chequer board in the traditional red and white colours of the City of London symbolizes the medieval counting board, the red squares charged with a gold coin whilst the cross potent in base comprizes four crutches allusive to the support given to the sick and needy. The crest of three hour-glasses, in varying stages of running out, reflects the company's interest in mortality.

Six companies use a quarterly shield. The first and fourth quarters of the Painter-Stainers' shield contain three escutcheons, which are said to refer to the painters' claim to pursue the craft of painting of escutcheons of arms independently of the College of Arms. The company has as supporters two heraldic panthers. In the past these beasts have been called 'panters', an English phonetic rendering of the Latin *panthera*, or the old French *pantère*: a pun on the word painter the heraldic artist would find hard to resist.

Three companies — Tallow Chandlers, Girdlers and the Glovers — have shields divided into six pieces. All three received their grants from John Smert, Garter (1450-77), that of the Tallow Chandlers being *On a field of six pieces Azure and Argent three Doves Argent membered Gules each holding in its beak an Olive Branch Or*.

The heraldic lion is included in the arms of nine companies and royal patronage is alluded to by this favoured charge. In the arms of the Merchant Taylors the lion is the lion of England and may be connected with royal favours, as the company was granted a number of royal letters patent and included many royal personages in its list of members. Several kings

Engraving by Wenceslaus Hollar of the arms of the Twelve Great Livery Companies in 1667.

of England have been Freemen of the Company. Both the Merchant Taylors and the Haberdashers received in charters granted by Henry VII the distinctive epithet of 'Merchant'.

The London Assay Office is at Goldsmiths Hall. The Company of Goldsmiths is the oldest hallmarking authority in the country, having being assigned the right of assay of gold and silver by an Act of 1300. The word hallmark derives from the official mark or stamp of the Goldsmiths Company, to denote the standard of precious metals assayed by them and marked with the leopard's head. Assay of new coin of the realm is also the responsibility of the Goldsmiths. The Trial of the Pyx is an examination of the coinage to ascertain that the gold, silver and cupro-nickel coins made by the Royal Mint are of the proper weight, diameter and composition specified by law. The Trial is convened annually in the presence of a jury consisting of

221

Freemen of the Goldsmiths Company sworn in and presided over by the Queen's Remembrancer. The verdict of the jury is delivered in writing in the Goldsmiths' arms. The leopard's head of the hallmark is charged in the first and fourth quarters of the shield, whilst the touchstone, used for testing the quality of gold and silver, in the crest refers to the assay of metals, the balance representing the Trial of the Pyx.

King James I gave the Musicians Company their first charter, and this may be the reason for the inclusion in 1604 of the double tressure flory-counter-flory in the arms of the company. The lions and rose in the chief of the arms may be a relic of the early association — A Fellowship of Minstrels of London — whose members had formerly been controlled by the king's minstrels.

Exclusive use of an ermine field is exercised by the Guild or Fraternity of the Body of Christ of the Skinners of London. Ermine was reserved by the sumptuary laws of the Middle Ages to the use of royalty and nobility, and because of its importance the Skinners Company adopted ermine as a badge of the craft. No fewer than six kings have been members of this corporation.

In England the right to bear supporters is confined to those to whom they have been granted or recorded, and today they are only granted in special cases, including grants to eminent corporate bodies. The Leathersellers Company were first granted arms in 1479, and in 1505 were the first corporate body to be granted supporters, of roebuck and ram. The Vintners Company bears as supporters *On either side a Swan the dexter a Cob the sinister a Pen both nicked in the beak with the Mark of the Company . . .*, a reference to the royalty of a game of swans of the Thames, held in common with the Dyers Company. Each July, led by the Queen's Swan Keeper, the Swan Master of the Dyers Company and the Swan Marker of the Vintners Company, six Thames skiffs set off on a Swan Voyage up the Thames as far as Henley. The cygnets are marked with two nicks in their beaks by the Vintners, while those of the Dyers have one nick, and the Queen's swans are not marked at all. The Marten supporter of the Skinners Company is a typical heraldic pun: sable is produced from the fur of the marten, a species of the weasel family, and is blazoned as *a Marten sable.*

The Weavers Company is described as the oldest chartered craft in the City and is mentioned in the Pipe Roll of 1130. The guild's earliest charter was granted in 1155. The company's arms and crest were granted in 1490, and the supporters, granted 1616, are wyverns, originally blazoned as *Wyvers*. The choice of the beast as supporters would seem to rest solely on the phonetic resemblance of the word wyvers to the name of the company. The dexter supporter of The

Worshipful Company of Fuellers, granted 1984, is a caretyne, an heraldic monster with gold spots, cloven hoofs, horns, tusks, mane and tufts. Flames issue from its mouth and one ear.

The mantling of two companies deviates from normal practice. That of the Fishmongers is *Gules doubled Or* on the dexter side, and *Azure doubled Argent* on the sinister, as shown in the patent of 1575 when supporters were granted. The original grant of 1512 blazons the mantling as *Gules doubled Argent*, and apparently the use of either is admissible. The mantling of the Parish Clerks is *Gules and Azure doubled Ermine on the dexter and Or on the sinister.*

The type of helm laid down for use by a corporate body is that used by a gentleman, a closed tilting helm in England and a sallet in Scotland. But five livery companies boast the use of a peer's helm — the Apothecaries, Clockmakers, Fishmongers, Goldsmiths and, until recently, the Gunmakers. The Gunmakers' device of two guns saltirewise was borne on a shield with a motley collection of banners and weapons on either side. No mantling was shown, but ostrich feathers decorated the helm, above which floated a wreath and crest. The Gunmakers have recently obtained both English and Scottish grants of arms in which these devices have been incorporated in a more conventional manner (see colour page 251). In the case of the other four companies the peer's helm is shown in the paintings in the margin of their patents, although the patents themselves are silent on the subject and no explanation has been offered for this particular distinction.

The Poulters are alone among the livery companies in the use of a crest coronet, that of a mural crown in lieu of the wreath.

Many phrases in common usage have originated from the livery companies of the City of London: 'on tenterhooks' from the double-ended hook in the Clothworkers' arms; 'baker's dozen' in the efforts of the Bakers' provision of the vantage loaf to avoid all risks of incurring a fine for short weight; 'all at sixes and sevens' some say originated in the struggle of the Merchant Taylors and the Skinners Companies for six and seventh place in the table of precedence; 'hallmarking' from the marking of precious metals at Goldsmiths Hall; and at the completion of his apprenticeship the aspiring smith submits to the Wardens of the Company of Goldsmiths his 'masterpiece'. The word has come to mean a work of art of exceptional merit, but originally it meant only the first piece of craftsmanship made by the apprentice entirely on his own to prove that he had mastered his craft. The Haberdashers found a commercial winner in the pin. It is said that £50,000 was paid annually to import this little item, but by the end of the reign of Elizabeth I the Haberdashers were making it themselves. Essential to the well-dressed woman, whose husband made her suitable allowance, the trade soon gave rise to the expression 'pin money'.

Thirty-eight companies have livery halls within the City of London, including that of the Master Mariners — the sloop *Wellington*, moored at Temple Stairs on the Thames. The halls are private property and cannot be entered except on certain open days, details of which can be obtained from the City of London Information Centre (*see* ADDRESSES).   LGP

See also LIVERY COMPANY, MEMBERSHIP OF

Further reading

Bromley, J. and H. Child *The Armorial Bearings of the Guilds of London* London, 1960.

City of London Directory and Livery Companies Guide contains details of the masters, wardens, clerks, beadles, freemen and livery of each company. Published annually and available from City Press Directory, Fairfax House, Colchester, Essex CO1 1RJ.

Kennedy Melling, J. *Discovering London's Guilds and Liveries* Aylesbury, 1978.

The Livery of the City of London is a free pamphlet printed by the Corporation of London in conjunction with the Livery Committee and the Livery Consultative Committee in 1986, and is available on request from the City of London Information Centre. The following is a list of the present livery companies.

In the *first column* is the year of the company's first charter of incorporation as a guild from the Crown, or the year of its grant of livery from the Court of Aldermen, whichever is the earlier. (Many companies were known to exist long before they obtained a charter from the Crown; others did not receive a grant of livery until long after incorporation.)

In the *second column* are the names of the companies in alphabetical order. Those with livery halls are indicated by an *asterisk*, and the order of precedence is given *in brackets*.

In the *third column* are the colours of the livery.

Date of charter or grant of livery	Company	Livery colours
1979	Actuaries (91)	
1955	Air Pilots (81)	blue and cerise
1606*	Apothecaries (58)	yellow and blue
1981	Arbitrators (93)	
1453*	Armourers and Brasiers (22)	white and black; yellow and blue
1307*	Bakers (19)	olive-green and maroon
1462*	Barbers Surgeons (17)	white and black
1568	Basketmakers (52)	yellow and black
1571	Blacksmiths (40)	yellow and black
1621	Bowyers (38)	white and black
1437*	Brewers (14)	white and red
1564	Broderers (48)	white and blue
1972	Builders Merchants (88)	red and blue
1606*	Butchers (24)	white and blue
1657	Carmen (77)	white and red
1477*	Carpenters (26)	white and black
1977	Chartered Accountants (86)	hoods: maroon and orange; gowns: scarlet and grey
1977	Chartered Secretaries and Administrators (87)	blue and gold
1977	Chartered Surveyors (85)	black, gold and red
1631	Clockmakers (61)	yellow and black
1528*	Clothworkers (12)	white and black
1677	Coachmakers and Coach Harness Makers (72)	yellow and blue
1482	Cooks (35)	white and red
1501*	Coopers (36)	yellow and red
1438	Cordwainers (27)	yellow and blue
1606	Curriers (29)	yellow and blue
1415*	Cutlers (18)	white and red
1638	Distillers (69)	white and blue
1364*	Drapers (3)	yellow and blue
1471*	Dyers (13)	white and black
1983	Engineers (94)	red and gold
1986	Environmental Cleaners (97)	medium blue, cornflower blue and gulf blue
1709*	Fanmakers (76)	yellow and red
1952*	Farmers (80)	yellow and brown
1684	Farriers (55)	white and black
1604	Feltmakers (63)	white and red
1364*	Fishmongers (4)	white and blue
1536*	Fletchers (36)	yellow and blue
1614*	Founders (33)	yellow and blue
1657	Framework Knitters (64)	white and red
1606	Fruiterers (45)	white and green
1984	Fuellers (95)	red and gold
1963	Furniture Makers (83)	
1605	Gardeners (66)	white and green
1448*	Girdlers (23)	yellow and blue
1664	Glass Sellers (71)	royal blue and maroon
1631*	Glaziers (53)	white and black
1639	Glovers (62)	white and black
1693	Gold and Silver Wyre Drawers (74)	yellow and blue
1327*	Goldsmiths (5)	white and red
1345*	Grocers (2)	white and red
1637*	Gunmakers (73)	

1448*	Haberdashers (8)	white and blue
1638	Horners (54)	white and black
1515*	Innholders (32)	white and blue
1454*	Ironmongers (10)	white and red
1979	Insurers (92)	gold and light blue
1571	Joiners and Ceilers (41)	white and red
1978	Launderers (89)	
1444*	Leathersellers (15)	white and red
1984	Lightmongers (96)	
1712	Loriners (57)	white and blue
1628	Makers of Playing Cards (75)	white and red
1977	Marketors (90)	blue and green
1677	Masons (30)	white and black
1929*	Master Mariners (78)	royal blue
1393*	Mercers (1)	yellow and red
1326*	Merchant Taylors (6 and 7)	white and red
1604	Musicians (50)	blue and red
1656	Needlemakers (65)	white and blue
1467*	Painter Stainers (28)	white and blue
1442	Parish Clerks	yellow and blue
1671	Patternmakers (70)	white and red
1480	Paviors (56)	white and black
1473*	Pewterers (16)	yellow and blue
1501*	Plaisterers (46)	silver and turquoise
1611	Plumbers (31)	yellow and black
1504	Poulters (34)	white and blue
1272*	Saddlers (25)	yellow and blue
1559*	Salters (9)	white and blue (or blue and red)
1964	Scientific Instrument Makers (84)	
1617	Scriveners (44)	yellow and blue
1605	Shipwrights (59)	yellow and blue
1327*	Skinners (6 and 7)	white and red (or yellow and red)
1944	Solicitors (79)	
1629	Spectacle Makers (60)	green and gold
1556*	Stationers and Newspaper Makers (47)	yellow and blue
1462*	Tallow Chandlers (21)	white and blue
1671	Tinplate Workers (67)	yellow and black
1960	Tobacco Pipe Makers and Tobacco Blenders (82)	
1604	Turners (51)	yellow and blue
1568	Tylers and Bricklayers (37)	yellow and blue
1626	Upholders (49)	white and black
1437*	Vintners (11)	white and black
1155*	Watermen and Lightermen of the River Thames	white and blue

1483*	Wax Chandlers (20)	white and blue
1184	Weavers (42)	white and blue
1670	Wheelwrights (68)	yellow and red
1484	Woolmen (43)	white and red

Livery Company, Membership of To belong to a guild or livery company one must first be sponsored and then accepted by the Court of Assistants, the governing body of a company. This can be achieved in one of three ways: Patrimony, an ancient system of hereditary privilege, Servitude, by serving the company as an apprentice, or Redemption, by purchase with the approval of the Corporation of the City of London. After the oath of loyalty, one receives the certificate of the freedom of the company. Once free of a company the next step is to attend the Chamberlain's Court in the Guildhall, to receive the freedom of the City of London. After taking the oath of loyalty, the Roll is signed, the right hand of friendship extended, and the certificate of freedom received. This is taken back to the livery company to apply for the livery itself — but freedom of a company and of the City does not lead immediately to election of the livery. Usually there is a period of waiting until a vacancy occurs, and this may be one or many years. In some companies the livery consists only of the more senior members. A fine is paid by the freeman on election to the livery, and he is 'clothed' with the company's livery in a simple ceremony. Nowadays he disrobes again almost immediately, as in most companies only the Master and Wardens wear their gowns when engaged in the company's business. In due course, by seniority, he is eligible for the Court of Assistants, and thereafter can go through the various degrees of Warden to Master. LGP

Livery Flag A generic term for mustering flags of various sizes and designs, charged with livery badges on fields of the livery colours.
See also FLAG

Liveryman A liveryman is a freeman of the City of London, entitled to wear the livery of his company and to exercise other privileges. During the Middle Ages the LIVERY COMPANIES OF THE CITY OF LONDON began to restrict the wearing of livery to the elders of each guild, and from 1560 the Court of Aldermen decreed that no further companies should assume a livery without its consent. LGP
See also LIVERY COMPANY, MEMBERSHIP OF

Livery Pennant *see* **Pennant**

Livery Pennon *see* **Pennon**

Livery Pennoncelle *see* **Pennoncelle**

Livre des Faits d'Armes et de Chevalerie, Le *see* **Treatises**

Lizard Usually depicted in its natural form, but the term has been used to describe the lynx.

Llyfr Dysgread Arfau *see* **Treatises**

Lodged *see* **Attitude**

Lodge Gates A lodge, or pair of lodges sometimes linked by a masonry arch, was often built in a similar style to the main residence — an architectural hors d'oevre. Its purposes are unambiguous: they are to impress the visitor and to remind the estate community of its position in life. Within the fabric of such buildings the coat of arms and other devices of the owner may be discovered, carved in stone and intended as a declaration both of his prosperity and gentility, and of·his authority. Large country houses, surrounded by parkland, invariably possessed a number of entrances and at each would be a lodge or gateway suitably embellished in a manner appropriate to its use. Today, many gates are no longer in use, though, somewhat incongruously on occasions, their finery remains.

Gate pillars provide an excellent opportunity for heraldic display, and may bear a supporter or other beast from the family arms, or a distinctive charge, such as the magnificent fire basket crest of the Phelips family who built Montacute House in Somerset.

The gates themselves are often of the finest METALWORK and incorporate armorial devices within scrollwork and other motifs, or display the arms, often a full achievement, on an enamelled plaque above.

Impressive gateways are not restricted to country houses and estates. Some of the finest examples are to be found at the entrances to ancient cities such as York, colleges and cathedral precincts. One of the finest gatehouses is that of St John's College, Cambridge. This commemorates the College's founder, Lady Margaret Beaufort, Duchess of Richmond (d. 1509), and includes the Beaufort arms with yale supporters, and the Beaufort badges of the portcullis and red rose, the whole strewn with daisies and borage, Lady Margaret's flowers. Another fine example is the gatehouse to Sherborne School, Dorset, over which are the gilded arms of the school's founder, Edward VI (1550).

Logo *or* **Logotype** *see* **Semiotics**

Lord (i) The abbreviated style of a peer below the rank of duke.
(ii) An honorary prefix used by the younger sons of dukes and marquesses.
(iii) The style of Scottish Lords of Session.

Sherborne School, Dorset.

Lord Chamberlain The senior office in the royal household of England, and quite separate from that of the LORD GREAT CHAMBERLAIN. The holder is a privy councillor, a peer, and a member of the government. The ensigns of his office are a golden or jewelled key and a white staff. The ceremonial duties of the Lord Chamberlain include the organization of all state functions involving the monarch other than those within the province of the Earl Marshal. The Lord Chamberlain has responsibility for a number of departments including the Gentlemen at Arms, Yeomen of the Guard, Gentlemen Ushers, Serjeants at Arms, numerous constables, and keepers of royal premises and their contents. The Master of the Queen's Musick and the Poet Laureate are within the Lord Chamberlain's department. The Lord Chamberlain of the household may depict a gold key palewise behind his shield of arms.   JC-K

Lord Chancellor, The *see* **Chancellor**

Lord Chief Justice of England The only judicial officer now entitled to the collar of SS, previously worn by the chief justices of the common law courts. The office may be traced to that of the first minister of the crown under the Norman kings — *capitalis Angliae justiciarius*. The Lord Chief Justice is next in rank to the Lord Chancellor, and is now appointed by the Crown on the recommendation of the prime minister.   JC-K

Lord Great Chamberlain One of the English great officers of state whose earlier title of Master Chamberlain dates from the times of the first dukes of Normandy. The Chamberlain may be considered as the financial officer of the household (and the implication of the terms used to describe him — *camerarius* and *cubicularius* — is that the royal treasure was kept in the bedchamber), but soon after the Conquest this work passed to the Treasurer, and the duties of the Chamberlain evolved over the centuries into the running of the royal palaces and the conduct of ceremonies in the House of Lords. Between the years 1133 and 1779 the office (which had come to be called Lord Great Chamberlain) was held by the earls of Oxford, but it then passed to other peers, and in 1901 the Committee of Privileges of the House of Lords resolved that the office would in the future be held in alternate reigns by the Marquesses of Cholmondeley (who provide the present officer) and the Barons Carrington.

Since 1966 the role of the Lord Great Chamberlain is ceremonial only, being confined to attending the state opening of parliament, state funerals and, in due course, coronations. He also attends the introduction of new peers into the House of Lords. The Lord Great Chamberlain of England may incorporate the golden keys of his office saltirewise behind his shield of arms.   JC-K

Lord High Chamberlain of Scotland The holder may depict two golden keys saltirewise behind his arms.

Lord High Constable *see* **Constable**

Lord High Steward In the household of the Norman kings the stewards (who had charge of all the departments concerned with food) were considered to be the chief officers, and there is some evidence that there was a similar office of high rank in the reign of Edward the Confessor.

However, as early as the twelfth century it was the custom in England to appoint magnates of the highest rank to discharge these duties on special occasions such as great festivals and coronations, and for a time the office of Lord High Steward (which is not the same as LORD STEWARD) became hereditary, but after 1415 no permanent steward was again appointed.

On the accession of King William IV (1830) the imposing coronation ceremonies in which the Lord High Steward played an important part were abandoned or transferred to a senior nobleman appointed for the occasion. He now carries the St Edward's crown in front of the bearer of the bible, who immediately precedes the sovereign.   JC-K
Further reading
Vernon-Harcourt, L.W. *His Grace the Steward and the Trial of Peers* 1907.

Lord High Treasurer This English office dates from 1216, and by the end of the reign of Henry III was the third greatest office of state, the holder acting as keeper of the royal treasure (*see* LORD GREAT CHAMBERLAIN) and receiver of the sheriffs' accounts. The officer was styled Lord High Treasurer and Treasurer of the Exchequer. In 1612, on the death of Lord Salisbury, the office lapsed for a while but was filled sporadically until 1714, when the then holder the Duke of Shrewsbury resigned the post, and the office ceased. Since that time the prime minister of the day has usually been the First Lord of the Treasury, presiding over a board of Lords Commissioner, but in practice the responsibility for the country's finances is vested in the Chancellor of the Exchequer.   JC-K
See also GREAT OFFICES OF STATE

Lord Justice Clerk An officer of state for Scotland, a commissioner responsible for the safety of the royal regalia, and the judge next in rank to the Lord Justice-General who is head of the justiciary. The insignia of office are two swords borne saltirewise behind the shield of arms.   JC-K

Lord Keeper of the Great Seal An English great office of state which lasted from the time of King Edward the Confessor (1042-66) until 1772. The Lord Keeper had the right of discharging all duties connected with the Great Seal of England. He was usually a peer, and in Elizabethan times (1558-1603) had the same authority as the Lord Chancellor. The office afterwards declined in importance and was not filled when the then holder, Sir Robert Henley, died in 1772.   JC-K
See also LORD PRIVY SEAL

Lord-Lieutenant As a part of the process of strengthening royal control over the counties of England, the post of lord-lieutenant was created in the mid-sixteenth century. This officer, originally the monarch's 'lieutenant', was usually a nobleman, and came in time to be known as the 'lord-lieutenant'. He took over the military duties of the sheriff and gradually assumed the headship of the county, together with the older post of custodian of the rolls. The Crown continues to appoint lord-lieutenants 'of and in' the counties of the United Kingdom. Each is the sovereign's representative in his county, and is responsible for such matters as confirming the appointment of justices of the peace. For some counties the Crown also appoints one or more lieutenants, styled Her Majesty's Lieutenant for . . . . . shire, and for his period of office a lord-lieutenant may himself appoint a vice-lieutenant from among his deputy lieutenants (abbr. DL), who hold their offices for life. In Scotland, the Lord Provosts of Aberdeen, Dundee, Edinburgh and Glasgow are also ex-officio lord-lieutenants.

Lord Lyon, Court of This operates on a daily basis at HM New Register House, Edinburgh, and numerous cases concerning heraldry or succession to arms have been heard, the most recent being recognition of the right to the title Lord Borthwick in 1986. There is a procurator fiscal who is responsible for deciding on which cases to lay before the Court, and a macer who precedes the Lord Lyon when acting as a judge in matters armorial.   CJB

Arms of Lord Lyon

Lord Lyon, King of Arms The Right Honourable the Lord Lyon King of Arms of Scotland is head of the heraldic executive in Scotland, and has been the principal officer of arms since at least 1377. (The Right Honourable title has been borne since 1554; the description as Lord Lyon being formally recognized by the Scottish parliament in 1663.) He is an Officer of State and holds his office immediately of the sovereign. It is still high treason to strike or deforce the Lord Lyon. He has general jurisdiction in Scottish matters armorial and is a Judge of the Realm. From the end of the sixteenth century until 1867 the Lord Lyon had a Depute. As Controller of Her Majesty's Messengers of Arms he is head of the Executive Department of the Law in Scotland. He personally appoints officers of arms and, apart from granting arms, he decides on 'Name and change of Name', on questions relating to family representation, pedigrees and genealogies. He conducts and supervises all state ceremonial in Scotland, and is King of Arms of the Order of the Thistle. Since 1913 the Chancery of the

Order has been located in Lyon Office, and since 1926 the Office of Secretary and King of Arms have been combined in his person.   CJB

Lord of Appeal in Ordinary This is a life peer who is not 'created', as is the usual case, but who is 'nominated and appointed to be a lord of appeal in ordinary by the style of baron'. The first lords of appeal in ordinary were appointed in 1876 as permitted by the first Appellate Jurisdiction Act, which was expressly passed for the purpose of enabling a high judicial officer to sit for life in the House of Lords and adjudicate on cases brought before it.   JC-K

Lord of Parliament *see* **Peerage**

Lord of the Manor After the conquest of 1066 England was divided among the followers of King William I, who remained, in theory at any rate, the owner of the kingdom. The smallest holding within the granted estates has come to be called the 'manor'. There were several levels of tenancy; the highest, held of the king, was the tenancy-in-chief (the chief lordship of the fee). Magnates in this category sometimes let to lesser lords (mesne tenants), who on occasion let to *their* followers who thus became the actual tenants-in-demesne. The 'lord of the manor' in any specific instance could be from any of the categories mentioned, but was always the tenant on whom the actual feudal obligation fell. In succeeding centuries overlordships (or chief lordships) of manors tended to become forgotten and, after 1290, when the statute of *Quia Emptores* forbad new subinfeudation, qualifying clauses were inserted into conveyances against future demands by people claiming 'overlordship'.

Tenants of all levels can frequently be identified from the *Book of Fees* (or *Feudal Aids*), or from the *inquisito post mortem*. These records, although sometimes unreliable, should state by whom and what service fees (manors) were held. Since 1926 the possession of all manorial records (and changes in their ownership) have to be reported to the Master of the Rolls. The Royal Commission on Historical Manuscripts (National Register of Archives) maintains a two-fold *Manorial Documents Register* giving the names of manors within each vill (parish), and the location of any manorial records which may have survived.

In the late twentieth century, 'lordships' of manors have become extremely marketable commodities, despite the fact that few bring with them more than a meagre bundle of documents and an archaic title. At the time of writing, they appear to be a sound enough financial investment, but it is to be hoped that purchasers are aware that their acquisition brings no substantial 'feudal' or social standing, much less the right to use any armorial devices borne by any previous holders of the fees.

For The Manorial Society, *see* ADDRESSES.   JC-K

Further reading
Bennett, H.S. *Life on the English Manor* Cambridge, 1937.
Calendar of Inquisitions four vols. published 1806 to 1828 by the Record Commission. Available at PRO and many county record offices.
Jolliffe, J.E.A. *The Constitutional History of Medieval England* London, 1937.
Postan, M.M. *The Medieval Economy and Society* London, 1972.

Lord President of the Council One of the great officers of state in England. The duty of the office (which was made permanent in 1679) is to preside over meetings of the Privy Council. The officer is invariably a member of the House of Lords and a member of the cabinet. The office is frequently held in conjunction with other ministerial responsibilities.
      JC-K
See also GREAT OFFICES OF STATE

Lord Privy Seal In medieval times the privy seal (which was a quite different instrument to the Great Seal of England) was used principally in the execution of the monarch's private business, being first mentioned in the reign of King John. The custody of the seal became increasingly important, and from the sixteenth century the keepers were noblemen. As government grew in complexity the importance of the office waned, the actual seal and the office itself being abolished in 1884. The title of the Lord (keeper of the) Privy Seal was retained and is now that of a government minister who usually holds it in plurality.   JC-K
See also LORD KEEPER OF THE GREAT SEAL

Lord Steward One of the great offices of the royal household in England. The holder is always a peer, a privy councillor and a member of the government. Up to 1782 the office was of cabinet rank, and to this day the steward received his appointment from the sovereign in person, his symbol of office being a white staff. He presides at the Board of Green Cloth, the committee which audits the royal accounts. The Steward has a number of ceremonial functions, including the organization of state banquets.   JC-K

Lord Warden of the Cinque Ports The highest officer of the Cinque Ports, the name given to an association of maritime towns in the south of England which, until the reign of King Henry VII, had the duty to furnish the bulk of the ships and men for the king's service.

Prior to the Tudor period the authority of the Lord Warden (who is also Constable of Dover Castle) was considerable, but is now minimal. The present Lord Warden is Her Majesty Queen Elizabeth the Queen Mother, whose armorial flag of office is *Per pale Gules and Azure three Lions passant guardant conjoined to as many Ships' Hulls in pale Or on a Panel Azure nearest the fly the Cypher of Her Majesty the Queen Mother ensigned by a Royal Crown.*

The archives of the Cinque Ports are in depositories in New Romney, Dover and Rye. The original five ports were Hastings, Romney, Hythe, Dover and Sandwich, the 'ancient towns' of Winchelsea and Rye being added later.   JC-K

Loutfut's Book *see* **Treatises**

Lozenge An armorial charge shaped like a diamond. The shield of a spinster or widow is lozenge-shaped. The field of a shield is said to be lozengy when divided bendy and bendy sinister, thereby creating a pattern of lozenges. Elongated lozenges are termed fusils, though the distinction is somewhat pedantic.
See also FIELD, VARIED

Lozengy *see* **Lozenge** *and* **Field, Varied**

Lucy, Luce *or* **Ged** A pike (the fish). Shakespeare caricatured Sir Thomas Lucy of Charlecote, Warwickshire, in his character Justice Shallow, whom he describes as 'the old pike', a clear reference to the arms of the Lucy family in whose park the young Shakespeare is said to have been discovered poaching. The Lucy arms are *Gules semy of Cross Crosslets and three Luces hauriant Argent.*

Lure, in *see* **Attitude**

Luxembourg, Armorial Practice The Grand Duchy of Luxembourg is ruled by the senior branch of the House of Nassau. Grants of arms are the prerogative of the Grand Duke, and are made but infrequently.

Luxembourg has had a complex history, having at different times been ruled by Burgundy, France, Austria and Spain, becoming independent in 1860. The National Archives contain registers of arms and titles as well as details of grants and are now to be found, for historical reasons, in Brussels in the Department de la Noblesse of the Archives de Royaume. There is an heraldic council, the *Conseil Heraldique de Luxembourg* (see ADDRESSES).   JC-K

Luxembourg, Royal Arms Quarterly 1 and 4 *Azure billety Or a Lion rampant crowned Or armed and langued Gules* (Nassau) 2 and 3 *Barry of ten Argent and Azure a Lion rampant queue fourché Gules armed langued and crowned Or* (Luxembourg).

Medieval vessel from which the lymphad charge is derived, depicted on the seal of Richard, Duke of Gloucester, as Admiral of England.

Lymphad One of the most common charges in armory associated with the west coast of Scotland. This is a boat having both a forecastle and stern castle, each often bearing a flag pole. Oars are shown if these are blazoned *in action* with the sails furled. Lymphad has only one mast. CJB

Lyon Clerk and Keeper of the Records (Scotland) The holder of this office is appointed by the Crown, and like LORD LYON receives an annual salary. Lyon Clerk's duties are to conduct and assist with the preliminary business of application for a grant of arms, including the scrutiny of documents supporting the application. As Keeper of the Records the duties consist of allowing inspection of the PUBLIC REGISTER OF ALL ARMS AND BEARINGS IN SCOTLAND and other records, and issuing certified extracts when required. Until 1867 there was a Lyon Clerk Depute, and in 1986 the first woman to hold the office of Lyon Clerk and Keeper of the Records was appointed. CJB

Mace A club-like weapon of various designs, most of which had a short handle and spiked or ribbed head. The favourite weapon of military churchmen who were anxious not to draw blood with a blade, but had no such reservations about bruising and maiming with the equally vicious mace. An early illustration of such a piece is in the Bayeux tapestry, where Bishop Odo, the

Conqueror's half-brother, bears a mace instead of a sword. In the twelfth century the bodyguards of the kings of England and France (the serjeants-at-arms) carried maces, which by the fourteenth century had become more ceremonial than practical, being richly decorated and chased with precious metals.

Although no examples survive, the civic mace made its appearance in the thirteenth century, and grew in importance in local ceremonial until the point in 1344 when parliament decreed that only the king's serjeants were important enough to have richly ornamented maces. However, this privilege was soon allowed to the serjeants-at-mace of London, and, by 1506, York, Norwich and Chester were similarly honoured.

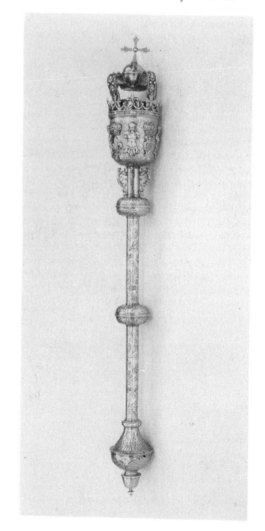

Mace presented to the Royal Society by Charles II (1660-85). Visible at the head are the Stuart badges of a crowned fleur-de-lis and harp.

Mace

The silver-covered mace became the vogue, being used by Exeter in 1387/8, Norwich in 1435/6, and Launceston in 1467/8. By the sixteenth century silver maces were used almost to the exclusion of other varieties. The large mace (as borne before mayors and other local dignitaries) was brought into general use c. 1650, when the smaller serjeants' mace fell into disfavour.

The mace currently in use in the House of Commons was made in 1649 during the Commonwealth, the original head being replaced by one with royal symbols at the restoration of Charles II. The earliest mace still in use in the House of Lords dates from the reign of King William III.

The historic silver maces of England have their counterparts in overseas countries with British connections past and present. The American House of Representatives has a mace surmounted by an eagle; the mace of Norfolk, Virginia, dates from 1753, and that of South Carolina from 1756. The New Zealand parliament uses a silver-gilt mace. Other maces of note are the silver mace with crystal globe used by the Lord High Treasurer of Scotland (made about 1690), and that of the Lord Mayor of London which, dating from the fifteenth century, is of crystal set with pearls, the mounts of the shaft being early medieval. The great mace of Winchester measures 5 feet 3 inches (1.6 m) in length, and, with that of London, is the largest in the country.

Several members of the peerage display maces in their arms as symbols of offices formerly held by them or by their ancestors. Viscount Hailsham's arms have supporters, one of which holds the mace of the Lord High Chancellor. The Speaker's mace appears in an escutcheon around the necks of the supporters of Lord Peel, and the ancient crystal mace of Norwich is used in the crest of Lord Mancroft.   SS

See also WANDS, STAFFS AND RODS OF OFFICE

Magistrate A civil officer responsible for administering the laws, a justice of the peace. In medieval times a magistrate could also be a member of the executive government.

Magnate A great and influential man, often a nobleman. In Hungary and Poland the term was applied to members of the Upper Houses in the legislature. Nowadays, and especially in the USA, a 'magnate' is one who runs a large and profitable business enterprise.

Maintenance *see* **Livery and Maintenance**

Male Griffin *see* **Griffin**

Malta, Order of *see* **St John of Jerusalem, Orders of**

Maltravers badge

Maltravers Herald of Arms Extraordinary The present office was created in 1887 by the Earl Marshal, the Duke of Norfolk and Baron Maltravers. The office is known to have been held by a pursuivant to Lord Maltravers when he was Deputy of Calais 1540-44. The badge, *A Fret Or*, was officially assigned in 1973, though it had been assumed by two Maltravers heralds in the 1930s. It derives from the arms of Maltravers *Sable a Fret Or and a Label of three points Ermine*, and was the badge of John, Earl of Arundel (d. 1435) through which family the barony passed to the Howard dukes of Norfolk.

Man Antelope An heraldic antelope with a man's face.

Man-at-Arms A Middle English term for a heavily armed and mounted soldier, frequently a knight.

Mandrake *see* **Medical Heraldry**

Maned *see* **Attributes**

Man Lion A lion with a human face.

Manorial Court *see* **Baron Court (Scotland), Court Baron, Court Leet** *and* **Lord of the Manor**

Mantle *or* **Manteau** Correctly a Robe of Dignity or of Estate. A ceremonial or parliamentary robe worn by sovereigns, royal princes and dukes, members of the nobility, the baronage of Scotland and certain orders of chivalry.

Widely used in European and Scottish armory as a constituent part of the achievements of arms of those who are entitled to Robes of Dignity and Estate, the mantle forms a background on which the coat of arms is placed and is usually ensigned by an appropriate crown, coronet or Cap of Dignity or Estate. It is retained in the 'open' position by coloured cords and tassels, like the entrance flaps of a tent, and it is perhaps because of its canopy-like appearance that the term is frequently confused with the Pavilion, which is often used in conjunction with the mantle but is reserved for use by sovereigns.

European mantles are of a variety of colours and furs, depending on nationality, rank and period; those of dukes during the French Empire being *Azure lined Vair*, for example. Mantles were not used in England until the late eighteenth century, when the arms of peers were often depicted on hatchments and door panels of carriages on a background of a red and ermine mantle with gold cords and tassels. Unlike its European counterpart, this type of mantle is purely decorative and has no other significance. Mantles continue to be used in the arms of European nobility and in those of the baronage of Scotland, but are rarely found in English armory, and are not granted by the English kings of arms.

A blue mantle, lined with ermine, is the badge of Bluemantle Pursuivant of Arms.

Mantling *or* **Lambrequin** A protective cloth affixed to the helmet. In a coat of arms the mantling is depicted as flowing from beneath the crest, sometimes terminating in tassels and scalloped or 'slashed' in a stylized form. Unlike the WREATH or torse, the mantling is considered to be an essential component of the crest, and therefore endowed with some armorial significance, the nature of which remains obscure. Almost certainly, the mantling originated in the Holy Land where it was worn by crusading knights to absorb the sun's heat, thereby preventing the helmet from becoming intolerably hot. The current convention that the mantling should be depicted with the lighter coloured material on the *inside* may appear to contradict this theory until it is noted that the convention is a comparatively recent one.

Although the mantling is now considered to be an essential adjunct to the crest, its use, both for practical purposes and as a component of a coat of arms, predates the crest and there are numerous examples of arms in which mantling is depicted but a crest is not. Mantlings of specific tinctures, unrelated to either arms or crest, were often used by succeeding generations and different branches of the same family, suggesting that the choice of tinctures was not entirely arbitrary. However, the diversity of practice in the medieval period suggests also that the mantling possessed no single prescribed armorial function, and

that it was adopted simply for purposes not provided for by other components of the coat of arms. For example, it may be that the red and ermine mantlings which predominate in the Plantagenet Garter stall plates at St George's Chapel Windsor, were adopted when a ceremonial chapeau was not compatible with an existing crest, or as an indication that the bearer was considered to be above the sumptuary laws of the period. Other mantlings are charged with badges and may have been composed of the livery colours with which they were associated. Others are semy of charges from the arms or even charged with the arms themselves.

A most attractive practice was the continuation of the material of the crest (often in the form of fur or feathers) into the mantling, the black Benedictine monk in the crest of Stourton and the swan's head of Thomas Beauchamp, third Earl of Warwick, being two notable medieval English examples.

Often a variety of colours was chosen, the mantling on either side the helm being of the tinctures of subsidiary quarterings, even when these were not depicted in the accompanying arms.

Thus, during the Middle Ages, armigers appear to have selected the most appropriate mantling from a range of recognized options, the only common rationale being the enhancement of armorial display. In the second half of the sixteenth century the majority of mantlings exemplified in patents of arms were *Gules doubled Argent*, irrespective of the colours of the shield or crest. This practice may have been an attempt by the kings of arms to regularize the situation at a time when grants of crests were in great demand and all aspects of armory were being subjected to increasing prescription and regulation, the choice of red and white perhaps reflecting the 'national colours'. From the end of the eighteenth century the principal metal and colour of the arms were used for this purpose (i.e. those first mentioned in the blazon), and this continues to be the practice in Scotland, where only peers may vary their mantlings by the use of gules and ermine. Elsewhere the tinctures of mantlings are now specified in patents and are, therefore, unalterable.

Today, mantlings may be of any colour doubled (on the inside) with either metal, or may be parted of two colours on the outside and/or of two metals on the inside. Whilst this allows for an artistically pleasing composition the selection of tinctures is entirely arbitrary. There are also modern instances of mantlings semy of badges, though there is no corresponding requirement that the mantling should be of the livery colours of the armiger. Since Elizabeth I the mantling of the sovereign and of royal princes has been *Gold doubled Ermine*, and those of British peers *Gules doubled Ermine*. Style, of course, reflects the taste of a particular period, the simple scalloped and tasselled mantlings of the early Middle Ages (when mantlings were still used

17th-century ledger stone to the memory of Sir John Fitzjames, showing elaborate mantling and unusual crest of *A Dolphin Argent devouring the top of an Antique Cap Azure lined Ermine.*

for practical purposes) giving way to ever more elaborate and fanciful styles, romantically 'slashed' as if by an opponent's sword, culminating in the grotesque 'seaweed' mantlings of the Victorian period. Today, when no other style is requested by an armiger, it is that of the medieval period which is preferred by the heraldic authorities, either in its simple, early form or in the slightly more elaborate style of the later Middle Ages. Current terminology favours 'mantling' to 'lambrequin', and for this reason it is used throughout this book. This is an unfortunate development, for the ancient alternative is less easily confused with MANTLE, which has an entirely different function and definition.

Mantygre *or* **Manticora** The mantygre is a strange beast which was believed to live in the Indies. It had three rows of teeth, reaching from ear to ear. Its face was that of a man, but its eyes were blood-red. It had a lion's body with the sting of a scorpion at the end of its tail. Its voice was very shrill, though sweet-sounding. It

was always ravenous and particularly craved human flesh. It was extremely swift and agile, and could not be captured. In spite of its apparent unpleasantness, the mantygre was popular in armory from the fifteenth century. It is usually depicted as having the body of the heraldic tyger, an old man's head with beard and flowing hair and two spiral horns. Occasionally the monster may be found with human feet and without horns, and several nineteenth-century examples depict the mantygre as a lion with human features.   MY

Maps Unfortunately, little survives of medieval cartography. However, the finest examples from the sixteenth century are brilliant works of art, 'gifts fit for a prince' and not merely tools for a seaman. These delineate coastlines, as accurately as knowledge allowed, the blank spaces 'blossoming into a pictorial and heraldic geography', full of fantasy and legend (R.V. Tooley).

The first county maps of England and Wales appeared in the late sixteenth century, the oldest known series being that of Laurence Nowell (1559-76), though these remain unprinted. Christopher Saxton, the 'father of English cartographers', produced an entire series of English and Welsh counties during

John Speed's map of 'Hantshire' 1610 (1612-14 edition). To the right are the coats of arms of various earls of Southampton, and to the left those of earls and one marquess of Winchester. Top left is a town plan of Winchester, with its arms.

the period 1574-9 by the authority of Thomas Seckford, Master of the Court of Requests and Surveyor of the Court of Wards and Liveries under Elizabeth I. These maps were both plain and hand-coloured, and the margins contained shields of arms. The most notable of his later works was a magnificent large-scale map of England and Wales on twenty-one sheets and with a scale of eight miles to the inch. One edition of this map was enclosed within a broad engraved border of eighty-three coats of arms of the nobility and gentry. Philip Lea published a revised edition in 1687 in which many of these coats were changed.

Several heralds of the period were also cartographers: Robert Glover, Somerset Herald, produced a manuscript map of Kent in 1571, and William Smith, Rouge Dragon Pursuivant, compiled a *Description of England* in 1588, illustrated by a general map and plans of various cities, as well as maps of Cheshire (1585) and Lancashire (1598).

Camden's *Britannia* was first published in 1607, with a Latin text and a series of county maps. This was re-issued in 1610 and 1637 with the same maps but an English text. The maps were engraved by William Kip and William Hole from Saxton's maps of 1579, though reduced in size to 14 x 11 inches (35 x 28 cm).

Perhaps the most attractive maps for the armorist are those of John Speed. These were again based on Saxton's work but included much new material, including plans or views of principal towns and a great deal of heraldry, particularly the arms of royalty and nobility, and civic arms such as those of the Cambridge colleges. Maps for the counties of England and Wales and general maps of each kingdom (including Ireland and Scotland) were issued in 1611 in the form of an atlas. This was followed by a 'pocket' atlas which, because of its reduced size, contained less heraldry. Both were particularly popular and ran to many editions. Speed's maps were generally uncoloured, though some contemporary owners commissioned hand-coloured versions.

J. Bleau published his first atlas of the counties of England and Wales in 1645 as part IV of *Theatrum Orbis Terrarum*. These were superb maps and included the arms of the principal nobility and gentry. Many of Bleau's maps contain blank shields, perhaps indicative of 'vanity' publishing, the cost of producing the atlas being met in part by the financial contributions of those whose arms appeared in the maps. Jan Jansson's *Atlas of England and Wales* of 1646 also contained royal arms and the shields of county nobility and gentry. Jansson was a rival of Bleau and his work is very similar.

Several maps in Richard Blome's *Britannia* (1673) include arms. These are mostly civic coats; for example, those of the Livery Companies in W. Hollar's plan of London.

From the end of the seventeenth century armory is less in evidence, the maps of the prolific Robert Morden containing very little decoration of any kind. A series of county maps, published by Bowen and Kitchin (1750-80) contain some heraldry within title-pieces, but it was not until Thomas Moule's maps, published during the reign of William IV, with further Victorian editions, that armory is again featured, usually the arms of major towns and cities, diocesan arms and those of the county nobility, e.g. the Beauforts in his map of Gloucestershire in *The English Counties Delineated* of 1836.

Today there are numerous colourful, attractive and inexpensive heraldic maps, the best of which is undoubtedly Bartholomew's *Map of Scotland of Old* by Sir Iain Moncreiffe of that Ilk, and Don Pottinger, published some years ago but still a classic of its type.

Further reading
Chubb, T. *The Printed Maps in the Atlases of Great Britain and Ireland: A Bibliography 1579-1870* London, 1927 (reprinted 1968).
Morland, C. and D. Bannister *Antique Maps* London, 1983.

Marcher Lord A march was a tract of land on the border of a country. In medieval England such tracts were given into the care of powerful barons charged with defensive measures against invasion, and sometimes with aggressive forays into the neighbouring state. These barons became known as Marcher Lords.

Marchioness The wife of a marquess, or a lady who holds a marquisate in her own right. The robe of a marchioness is similar to that of a DUCHESS, except that it is trimmed with three and a half rows of ermine, the edging being 4 inches broad, the train 1¾ yards (10 cm by 1.6 m) on the ground. The coronet of a marchioness is also similar to that of a duchess, except that it is composed on the circle of four strawberry leaves, and four silver balls (representing pearls) raised upon points of the same height as the leaves, alternately, above the rim. The arms of a marchioness in her own right are similar to those of a duchess, but surmounted by the coronet of her own degree.   JC-K

Marchmont Herald of Arms A current Scottish herald of arms. The office was first mentioned in 1438, and the title is derived from the royal castle of Marchmont or Roxburgh in the Borders.

The badge of office is *A Tower of three castellations Vert masoned Argent the dexter Castellation Azure charged of a Saltire Argent the sinister Castellation Argent charged of a Cross Gules all ensigned of the Crown of Scotland proper.*   CJB

March Pursuivant of Arms Extraordinary A current Scottish pursuivant extraordinary. First mentioned in 1515-16, this title is associated with that part of the Border area known as the marches.   CJB

Margin Lines The blue lines separating the text from the armorial bearings ('in the margin hereof more plainly depicted') in English patents of arms. An armiger may request that the margin lines are omitted from his LETTERS PATENT.

Margrave A German title, originally of a border province, later the hereditary title of certain princes in the Holy Roman Empire. The wife of a margrave was a margravine.

Marine A suffix formerly applied to monsters, e.g. a sea-dog was blazoned as a hound marine.

Marks of Difference *see* **Difference, Marks of**

Marks of Distinction *see* **Distinction, Marks of**

Marquess *or* **Marquis** The second rank in the British peerage, introduced in 1385. In this sense the word was introduced from Europe, although from an early date lords of the Welsh and Scottish marches had sometimes been called *marchiones*.

The robes of a marquess are similar to those of a DUKE, with the exceptions that his coronation robe has three and a half rows of ermine, and his parliamentary robe of estate has four guards of ermine on the right side and three on the left. The coronet of a marquess has, on the circlet, four gilt strawberry leaves and four silver balls alternately, the latter a little raised on points above the rim. The armorial privileges of a marquess are as those of a duke. The wife of a marquess is known as a marchioness.   JC-K

Married Women, Use of Arms *see* **Women Bearing Arms**

Marshalling The discipline of assembling the constituent elements of a coat of arms, and the various devices of which each is composed, in a manner which is in accordance with accepted armorial practice and convention. In particular, the correct ordering of combinations of armorial devices in a single coat of arms to signify marriage, inheritance or office.

During the latter part of the thirteenth century armory assumed a significance additional to that of personal identification. Armorial devices were ordered and displayed in such a way as to denote marriage alliances, the acquisition or inheritance of lordships and the holding of an office with which arms or insignia were associated. Historically, the most interesting of these was the practice of combining two or more shields of arms to indicate the union of lordships. However, it should be remembered that not all such arms are indicative of actual possession, some (the best known being the quartered arms of France and England from Edward III in 1340) represent only a *claim* to possession.

The earliest form of marshalling was the practice of grouping together two or more shields to indicate marital alliances, etc., on seals. These usually consisted either of a figure, often in armorial costume, between separate shields bearing arms of alliance, or a geometrical design in which were incorporated a number of related shields, that of the principal house being at the centre.

Another early method of marshalling was by compounding charges from a number of shields to form an entirely new shield of arms. An example may be found in the arms of John de Dreux, Duke of Brittany and Earl of Richmond, whose mother was a daughter of Henry III. At the siege of Caerlaverock in 1300 he bore *Checky Or and Azure* (de Dreux) *on a Bordure Gules eight Lions passant guardant Or* (England) *over all a Canton Ermine* (Brittany).

From *c.* 1300, coats were marshalled in the same shield of arms, at first by means of DIMIDIATION, by which the arms of husband and wife were each cut in half by a vertical line and then joined to form one shield, the husband's arms being to the dexter. This practice often resulted in somewhat alarming visual ambiguities and was eventually abandoned in favour of simple IMPALEMENT, though vestiges of the system may be discerned in the treatment of impaled bordures, tressures and orles today.

Arms were also quartered, that is divided into four with the principal arms in the first (dexter chief) quarter and other coats in the remaining three in order of acquisition. The earliest known example in England of quartered arms are those of Eleanor, queen of Edward I (1291) *Quarterly Castile and Leon*, though the

first truly English arms to be quartered are believed to be those of Sir Symon de Montagu, *Quarterly 1 and 4 Argent a Fess dancetty Gules 2 and 3 Azure a Griffin Or* as recorded on a roll of *c.* 1310. When only two coats are represented, the principal coat occupies the first and fourth quarters and the secondary coat the second and third. In the case of three, the principal coat would again occupy the first and fourth quarters, and the other two coats, according to seniority, would be in the second and third. Once the number of coats depicted exceeds four, further quartering becomes necessary and other coats are added in the correct order, with the principal coat in the first quartering and, if the number is an odd one, in the last also. Quarterings are numbered from dexter to sinister, and from top to bottom. Of course, quartered coats may themselves be quartered. In such cases the principal quarterings are termed grand quarters and the subsidiary ones sub-quarters. This method of marshalling, called counter-quartering or sub-quartering, is retained in Scotland but not in England. It is not necessary to include all the coats acquired by marriage, etc., and it is often impracticable to display more than four. However, if a selection is made it is necessary to include those coats by which the selected ones were acquired. For example, if an armiger were able to prove (say) Mowbray descent through a fairly humble ancestor called Smith, and thereby entitlement to the Mowbray arms, it would be necessary to include the Smith coat in order to justify the use of the more illustrious arms of Mowbray.

Armorial badges, invariably in the form of chimerical and other creatures, were also acquired through inheritance, etc., and these were often translated into crests and, from the fifteenth century, into supporters. There are numerous medieval examples of crests being adopted purely to indicate alliance with an ancient noble house, and it would appear that there were no conventions relating to the marshalling of the armorial accessories, only to the shield of arms. It seems likely, therefore, that it was not until the Tudor period and the first visitations that crests and supporters became subject to systematic marshalling, probably as a result of the wholesale adoption of crests by the 'new' gentility and the (then) innovative use of supporters as symbols of nobility.

Current practice

Temporary and non-hereditary combinations of arms, such as arms of office and the arms of a husband and a wife (who is not an heraldic heiress but whose father is armigerous) are marshalled by straightforward impalement, the official arms or those of the husband being placed in the senior (dexter) position.

Permanent and hereditary combinations of coats are somewhat more complex. An armigerous woman who has no brothers living and no nephews or nieces from

deceased brothers becomes her father's heraldic heiress (or co-heiress if she has sisters) upon his death. While he lives her arms are impaled with her husband's, but when her father dies they are displayed on a small shield (an escutcheon of pretence) in the centre of her husband's shield. After her death her children may quarter her arms, with the paternal arms in the first and fourth quarters. Her husband, if he survives her, ceases to bear the escutcheon of pretence. Thereafter, further inherited arms may be added in similar fashion. However, in England when quartered arms are inherited they are no longer depicted as sub-quarters within a grand quarter, but are incorporated in the correct sequence as quarterings following those of the paternal coat.

Today, many more women are armigerous in their own right. Providing that her husband is also armigerous, a woman may transmit her arms, impaled by those of her husband and within a bordure, as a quartering to her descendants. If, however, she should become an heiress in her issue (i.e. if there were no surviving male heirs of her father) she would transmit her arms as an undifferenced quartering with those of her husband.

Crests are hereditary but are not usually transmitted through heiresses. There is a small number of crests which have been allowed by royal licence, as augmentations of honour for example, which have been transmitted in addition to the paternal crest, and there are several examples of crests acquired through heraldic heiresses recorded in the visitations, which are still regarded as authoritative. When two crests are used, the principal crest (i.e. a crest of augmentation or that relating to the first quartering) is placed in the dexter. The helms on which they are placed may both face the dexter or each other. When three crests are used, that in the centre is the principal crest, followed by that to the dexter.

Supporters are hereditary only when granted to peers other than life peers. In effect they descend with the peerage itself. The sons of peers, even though they may use one of their father's junior titles, do not use his supporters, except in Scotland where the heir apparent is permitted to do so.   PF/SF

See also INSIGNIA, MARSHALLING OF
Further reading
Fox Davies, A.C. *A Complete Guide to Heraldry*, for the complexities of marshalling.

Martlet This strange little bird has been an extremely popular charge since the early days of heraldry. In appearance it is similar to the house martin, swallow and swift, but it is always depicted with its legs terminating in two tufts of feathers without feet or claws. In medieval times it was believed that these birds lived their whole lives in the air, without ever having any need to touch the ground, even that they slept whilst still on the wing. Therefore they would have no need of feet and were deemed to have none. It is said that martlets in a man's arms signified that he had raised himself to a position of nobility by his own endeavours, rather than that he had any inheritance, the martlet's lack of feet being a symbol of one having no foundation on which to stand. Similarly the martlet is used as a cadency mark for the fourth son — one who would not be likely to enjoy a great inheritance and would need to make his own way in the world.

In spite of all this the martlet is found in armory in high places as well as low. The attributed arms of Edward the Confessor are charged with martlets, although his shield in Westminster Abbey depicts birds with feet. Martlets appear in the arms of both East and West Sussex, and in other civic heraldry in those counties, perhaps having a connection with the true swallows (*hirondelle*) of the Arundel family of Sussex. The arms of William de Valence may be an example of one who used martlets, and was originally 'without foundation', since he was the son of Hugh de Lusignan, Count of La Marche, and settled in England having received land and wealth from his half-brother, Henry III.   MY

Mascle A voided lozenge. A divorced woman may use her maiden arms charged with a mascle.

Masculy Composed of conjoined mascles.

Masoned *see* **Attributes**

Masons' Marks These are not armorial, but were devices used by stone masons to mark their work. Each mason had his own mark which could be passed from father to son. The medieval masons formed themselves into guilds, and registers were kept of the marks used. Wood carvers also used a similar system, as on some of the misericords at Ludlow church, Shropshire. Marks found on wooden panelling and pews may have a similar purpose. However, these items were often marked at a workshop to help correct assembly. JET

See also WINDOW MARKS

Master General of the Ordnance By a warrant of Charles II, the Master General of the Ordnance may depict a field-piece (a piece of artillery) on either side of his arms.

Master of a College He may impale the arms of his college with his own to form ARMS OF OFFICE.

Master of the Horse The title of this office of the ROYAL HOUSEHOLD dates from *c.* 1360 and was introduced by King Edward III, although the fore-runner — the *horsthegn* — was known in Saxon times. In the beginning the office of Master may have been hereditary in the family of Brocas, but an early holder (Sir Bernard) was beheaded in 1400 and the post moved to others. Since its inception there have been seventy-six masters, many of them distinguished noblemen. The duties are now largely ceremonial, the Master being 'the senior personal attendant to the sovereign on those occasions when the horses are used.' JC-K

Further reading
Reese, M.M. *The Royal Office of Master of the Horse* 1976.

Master of the Revels in Scotland The arms of office are *Argent a Lady rising out of a Cloud in the nombril point richly apparelled on her head a Garland of Ivy holding in her right hand a Short Sword crowned in her left a Vizard all proper standing beneath a Canopy Azure garnished Or in base a Thistle Vert.* (A vizard is a human mask.)

Master of the Rolls Originally known as the Vice-Chancellor, the title of Master of the Rolls was accorded to this officer in 1519/20. His duties included custody of all the rolls, writs, patents and grants under the GREAT SEAL. In time he sat as a judge in chancery and lost the keepership of the records. This was restored to him in 1838. Since Acts of 1875 and 1876 he is a member of the Court of Appeal, whose decisions can be questioned only by the House of Lords. The Master of the Rolls is sworn to the Privy Council. JC-K

Masterpiece *see* **Livery Companies of the City of London**

Matriculation of Arms In Scotland it is an offence to bear arms unless they have been matriculated with Lord Lyon King of Arms, and entered in the Public Register of All Arms and Bearings in Scotland.

A Scottish matriculation of arms. Miss Gaylor's arms are those of her grandfather, differenced for her own use and distinguished from those of her brother and younger sister by the addition of a crescent.

Matriculation is not simply registration. The process requires the correct marshalling of the arms, together with appropriate marks of difference indicating relationships within a family. Younger sons have no right to bear their father's arms until they have been re-matriculated, and even male heirs are recommended to re-matriculate their arms every third generation. Arms emanating from the College of Arms may be matriculated with Lord Lyon for use in Scotland.

Maunch *or* **Manch** An ancient sleeve, cut off at the shoulder and with a long lappet pendent from the cuff. The best known example is that of Hastings *Argent a Maunch sable*. The maunch may be depicted in a variety of forms, the female breast being implied by the folds of material below the shoulder.
See also DEXTROCHÈRE

Mayors Mayors and lords mayor may impale the arms of the corporation of which they are head with their own to form ARMS OF OFFICE.

Medals and Decorations Medals and decorations are legion and beyond the scope of this work, except where they impinge in armorial display or may be considered integral to the insignia of the orders of chivalry or merit. The insignia of orders of chivalry and decorations such as the Military Cross may be depicted as suspended beneath the shield of arms. Commemorative and campaign medals are not so depicted.
See also MERIT, ORDER OF for bibliography, and the various orders of chivalry and merit under individual entries. *See also* Orders and Medals Research Society in ADDRESSES.

Medical Heraldry There are some charges which nearly always refer to the medical profession and which are seldom met with in other connections. Probably the best known (and most overworked) is the serpent, a symbol of healing and a sign of wisdom and knowledge. Throughout the Middle East temples were frequently used as early hospitals. As a cure for certain diseases it was often customary to use a harmless variety of snake, whose forked tongue was thought to have healing properties when applied to diseased parts. The snake represented eternal life

because it appears reborn when it casts its skin. The snake may be depicted on its own, but is usually shown entwined about a rod or staff. These were the attributes of the Greek god Aesculapius, and when depicted in this fashion are blazoned as a Rod of Aesculapius. This should not be confused with the Caduceus, which has two snakes entwined about a rod. Near the top are two wings, while the rod itself is surmounted by a cone, ball or similar object.

The mythical Greek monster, the opinicus, is very similar to the griffin, but whereas only two of the griffin's legs are those of a lion, all four of the opinicus are so depicted. Its tail is thin and short, similar to that of a camel. An opinicus was granted as a crest in 1561 to the Company of Barber Surgeons, but has seldom been granted since. One recent example is that of the opinicus rampant in the arms of the British Association of Oral Surgery, granted in 1962.

Mystic objects found as charges include the Egyptian ankh, symbol of life, and utchat (eye) symbol of health, the Nordic acorn of longevity and the semitic sacred tree of life. In oriental symbolism, the unicorn, bat, tortoise and bell represent health. The horn of the unicorn and rhinoceros are traditionally believed to possess miraculous powers of healing, and the narcotic properties of the mildly poisonous mandrake plant were highly thought of in the Middle Ages. Its knobbly root resembles the human figure and it was believed to utter a shriek when pulled from the ground, driving all who heard it mad. The pomegranate (apple of Granada) was generally regarded as an armorial symbol of fertility by reason of its numerous seeds.

Inanimate objects to be found as charges in medical heraldry include the fleam, an ancient form of blood-letting instrument used by barbers and depicted in armory as an elaborate figure seven. When encountered as a charge some connection with surgery may be assumed. The red cross, symbol of St George, conqueror of evil, and since the 1863 Berne Convention the device of international medical aid (non-Christian countries have adopted the red crescent for the same purpose), has its origins in the crosses of the Crusades and the Swiss national emblem of a white cross on a red field, adopted in 1339. The white Maltese Cross on a black field of the St John Ambulance Brigade also originated in the Crusades as the device of the hospitaller knights of St John. The mullet or star represents the Natal Star of Bethlehem, or Morning Star, and is favoured by midwives and gynaecologists and is to be found in the arms of the Royal College of Obstetricians and Gynaecologists *Per pale Azure and Sable a Mullet of eight points the lowest point extended Towards the base Argent*, granted in 1931. The supporters, granted in 1950, are a representation of a woman holding a staff ensigned with an Egyptian ankh (blazoned as *a Crux ansata Or*) and the figure of

Aesculapius holding his staff. The sun is also a popular medical device, its rays representing healing. *Azure a Fountain radiating Or* are the arms of the Royal Society of Health (1949), and the arms of the Association of Public Health Inspectors *Per fess Azure and Gules a Pentagram Or*. The Ancient Roman or Antique Lamp has been granted as a symbol of nursing, as in the crest of the Royal College of Nursing: *In front of an open Book proper a Roman Lamp Or inflamed also proper*. The arms are *Azure a Sun in Splendour and in chief three Mullets Or* (1945). Several of the foregoing devices appear in the arms of the Royal College of Physicians: *Sable a Hand proper vested Argent issuing out of Clouds in chief of the second rayonné Or feeling the pulse of an Arm proper issuing from the sinister side of the shield vested Argent in base a Pomegranate Or between five demi Fleurs-de-lis bordering the edge of the escutcheon of the last*.

Colours also have significance: argent expresses hygiene, azure is associated with midwives (and the Virgin Mary), vert is the colour of spring and the season of gestation in nature, murrey is occasionally used to represent blood and the combination of argent and sable to symbolize day and night, and thereby vigilance and watchfulness.

Supporters in medical heraldry are frequently representations of human figures, saints and mythological deities. The Greek god of medicine and healing, Aesculapius was the son of Apollo and Corinis. Legend tells us that he was such an expert physician that he was able to bring the dead back to life. This resulted in Hell becoming depopulated and Pluto, the God of the Underworld, complained to Jupiter, head of the gods, who obliged by slaying Aesculapius with a thunderbolt! Apollo, God of Light and patron of medicine and science, slaughtered Phython, the formidable dragon which guarded Delphi, and is depicted holding a bow and arrow astride a dragon in the arms of the Society of Apothecaries of London. Aesculapius had six daughters, one of whom, Hygeia, was the Goddess of Health, both physical and mental, and also of the prevention of disease.

Cosmos and Damian are the patron saints of surgeons and featured as supporters in the arms of the Fellowship of Surgeons in 1492. Strangely, they were not adopted for the arms of the Royal College of Surgeons, but reappear as supporters in the arms of the Royal Society of Medicine, granted in 1927: *Per pale Vert and Gules the Serpent of Moses Or entwined round a Tau Cross Argent*. The Society's crest includes three sprigs of the herb 'All Heal'. The Royal College of Surgeons have, as supporters, Machaon and Podalivius, two brothers who served as surgeons in the army of the King of Greece at the siege of Troy. The king was wounded by an arrow and was saved by Machaon, who is represented armorially holding a broken arrow. Somnus and Morpheus are, appropriately,

A Caduceus between the arms of the Royal College of Physicians (left) and the Royal College of Surgeons (right) and here used as the device of the Imperial Cancer Research Fund.

supporters in the arms of the Association of Anaesthetists of Great Britain and Ireland. Somnus was the ancient Roman god of Sleep, son of Night and twin brother of Death. His son, Morpheus, was the God of Dreams. The Association's arms (1945) are *Gules a Rod of Aesculapius proper in chief two Poppy Heads Or*, and the crest *Two Mandrakes pilewise Or*.

Among actual people represented as supporters are William Harvey, physician and discoverer of the circulatory system. He is the sinister supporter in the arms of the British Medical Association. Benjamin Golding, vested as a Doctor of Medicine of St Andrew's University, is the dexter supporter in the arms of Charing Cross Hospital, which he founded in 1818.

Birds are found as supporters in the arms of St Thomas' Hospital, London. The chough or 'Becket Bird' and a nightingale represent the association of St Thomas à Becket and Florence Nightingale with the hospital.

Possibly the earliest, and certainly the most beautiful arms to be used by a medical body are the *Per pale Argent and Sable a Chevron counterchanged* of St Bartholomew's Hospital in the City of London. The first seal of the hospital to bear the present arms was in use in 1423. William Wakering was Master of the hospital from 1423 to 1462, but he has left us no clue, armorial or otherwise, as to why these most distinctive arms came to be used. The College of Arms did not grant them to either William or his family, or to the hospital. They are, however, recorded as the arms of the hospital in a sixteenth-century roll at the College of Arms. Presumably, continued use from the early fifteenth century had established a right. The Priory Church of St Bartholomew-the-Great and the hospital were founded by Rahere in 1123.

The ancient guilds and livery companies of the City of London were possibly the first institutions with early medical connections to have armorial bearings. The sale of drugs was originally under the control of the Grocers' Company and the Society of Apothecaries did not become an independent body until 1617. A grant of arms was made just six days after their incorporation: *Azure Apollo the Inventor of Physic proper his head radiant holding in his left hand a Bow and in his right hand an Arrow Or supplanting a Serpent Argent*. The crest is *A Rhinoceros statant proper* and the supporters gold unicorns. The Company of Barbers were first granted arms in 1451, and their charter gave them the right to control the practice of barbery and surgery in the City. An unincorporated body, the Fellowship of Surgeons of London, had used an armorial badge since 1492, and an act of parliament of 1540 united these two bodies as the Worshipful Company of Barber Surgeons of London. Their separate devices were incorporated in a new grant of arms which includes *three Fleams Argent* and a spatter or spatula. The crest is an opinicus and the supporters two lynx *semy of Hurts Torteaux Pomeis Bezants and Plates*.

Armorial bearings have been granted by the College of Arms and by Lord Lyon in Scotland to numerous medical bodies both in Britain and overseas. These include hospitals, colleges, medical associations and institutions, royal societies, regional health authorities and several private hospitals, clinics, etc. Included in these are grants to the Institute of Hospital Administrators (1966) *Or a Cross couped Gules on a Chief Sable an Ancient Lamp Or inflamed proper between two Ankhs Or* and the Institute of Hospital Engineering (1969) *Or on a Bend between two Cocks Sable three Cog Wheels Or.* ENT

Melusine A mermaid with two tails.

Membered *see* **Attributes**

Memorial A formal petition addressed to the Earl Marshal by a prospective grantee requesting that a warrant be issued to the kings of arms thereby enabling them to grant armorial bearings to the petitioner. The memorial is generally prepared by an officer of arms acting on behalf of the petitioner. A typical example would be:

To The Most Noble Miles Francis Stapleton, Duke of Norfolk, Knight of the Most Noble Order of the Garter, Companion of the Most Honourable Order of the Bath, Commander of the Most Excellent Order of the British Empire upon whom has been conferred the Decoration of the Military Cross, Earl Marshal and Hereditary Marshal of England

THE MEMORIAL OF . . . .
of
in the County of . . . . , Gentleman

SHEWETH THAT
being desirous of having Letters Patent of Armorial Bearings
granted and appointed unto him for . . . .
Your Memorialist has the honour to request the favour of Your Grace's Warrant to the Kings of Arms for their granting and assigning such Arms and Crest as they deem suitable to be borne and used by Your Memorialist and by his descendants with due and proper differences and in accordance with the Laws of Arms

And Your Grace's Memorialist will ever most humbly pray

. . . .

Memorial Board These boards are an inexpensive form of WALL MONUMENT painted on wood or canvas, and date principally from the seventeenth century. They are usually square or rectangular and between 2 and 6 feet (60cm - 2m) in size. Diamond-shaped panels may also be found and these can be confused with HATCHMENTS. A hatchment has either no inscription or one limited to the name or initials of the deceased and the date of death, whereas the memorial board is a memorial intended for display in the church, and usually the text includes such phrases as 'Near here lies buried' or 'In loving memory of'.

In addition to the achievement and the inscription giving biographical details of the deceased there may be a biblical quotation or a verse praising the character of the individual. Symbols of mortality such as hourglasses, mortheads or cross-bones may be used as decoration. At Whitchurch Canonicorum, Dorset, the memorial board of Elizabeth Floyer (d. 1668) conforms with this pattern. The small shield, which displays her husband's arms impaling her paternal arms, has the sinister background painted black and the dexter white, to indicate she predeceased her husband — a practice usually associated with hatchments. JET

Merchant Jack A flag flown at the bows of a merchant ship. The British merchant jack is the Union flag with a white border.

Merchants' Marks These marks were used in medieval times to indicate ownership of all manner of trade goods. In a society which was in broad terms illiterate, it was important to have such a simple system of symbols. For safety reasons a consignment of items for dispatch by sea was often dispersed between a number of vessels. In such circumstances it was essential properly to mark the cargo to avoid any confusion and, within the Hanseatic League, merchants' marks on trade items were regarded as proof of legal ownership.

The use of marks by merchants was not unique to them; there were related classes of marks indicating places of origin and craftsmanship. Such marks were made on furniture and pottery, for example, and were employed by goldsmiths, masons and armourers, among others.

The nature of a merchant's mark was threefold: it had to be recognizable, unambiguous and capable of being drawn, painted or scratched quickly. At first sight many marks seem somewhat runic in nature, the majority being built on the foundation of a vertical line:

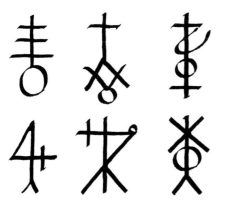

while a variation was based on the initials of the individual merchant concerned.

Merchant marks were used by non-armigerous men in much the same way as coats of arms were used by gentlemen and, indeed, members of the same family would frequently difference their marks just as cadet branches of gentle families differenced their arms.

In time, as they became more prosperous, certain merchants displayed their marks in window glass and on tombs, and on the interiors and exteriors of buildings. Then, as one might expect, when a merchant was granted arms he sometimes incorporated his mark into his shield as a charge, particularly if he were Swiss or German. Instances are also on record where a non-armigerous merchant married an heraldic heiress and impaled his mark with her arms. An example is known (on the magnificent Canynge tomb in St Mary's Redcliffe church in Bristol) of the family arms being flanked on each side by their merchant mark, not quite close enough to be mistaken for supporters but carrying equal pride of place.

Although considerable research has been carried out, no-one has been able to show a logical system (and hence perhaps the existence of a 'register') underlying the design of merchants' marks. Nor has there been any proof forthcoming of any relationship between the marks of members of particular guilds, merchants of a single town, or indeed any given group of traders.   JC-K

Further reading

Elmhurst, E.M. *Merchants' Marks* Harleian Society, 1959.

Merit, National Order of (L'Ordre National de Mérite) The junior French National Order, created on 3 December 1963. The decoration is a six-pointed star suspended from a blue ribbon. The order has five ranks: Grand Croix, Grand Officier, Commandeur, Officier, and Chevalier.

Merit, Order of There are currently about fifty orders of merit. In a few cases the orders are chivalric in nature but most are awarded for distinction of service in a specific field. Apart from Britain, the following countries award these distinctions: Austria, Brazil (National, Military, Naval, and Aeronautic orders), Cambodia, Cameroon, Columbia (Industrial), Cuba (Agricultural, Industrial, Commercial, Military, Naval, and Political), Czechoslovakia, Dominica, Ecuador, France (Naval, and Maritime), German Federal Republic, Guatemala (Military), Haiti (Honour & Merit), Hungary, Italy (of the Republic, and of Labour), Korea (National Foundation, Military, Civil, Service, Diplomatic, Cultural, and Industrial), Laos (Civil), Lebanon, Liechtenstein, Luxembourg, Malagasy Republic (of Madagascar, and of Agriculture), Malaysia, Norway, Paraguay, Peru, Romania (Scientific, Cultural, Military, and Sporting), Sudan, United Arab Republic, United States of America, and Venezuela. (For Orders and Medals Research Society *see* ADDRESSES.)

Further reading

Dorling, H.T. *Ribbons and Medals* new edition, 1983.
Hall, D. *British Orders, Decorations and Medals* 1973.
Hieronymussen, P. *Orders, Medals and Decorations of Britain and Europe* Blandford, 1975.
Rosignoli, G. *Ribbons of Orders, Decorations and Medals* 1976.
Werlich, R. *Orders and Decorations of all Nations* 1974.
For British insignia see *Spink's Catalogue of British and Associated Orders, Decorations and Medals* by E.C. Joslin, 1983. Information concerning both orders and decorations extant in the mid-nineteenth century may be found in *The Book of Orders of Knighthood and Decorations of Honour* by Sir Bernard Burke, 1858.

A number of countries produce books (some in

English and illustrated in colour) describing their own orders and decorations. Typical of these are *The National Orders of Finland*, 1975; *The Monarchy, Symbols and National Anthems* (of Denmark), 1980; *Orders and Awards of the Netherlands*, 1985; and *Condecoracions Españolas*, 1953. Details of foreign orders are almost always available (in printed form and in English) through the embassies of the countries concerned.

JC-K

Merit, Order of (Britain) This important British order was founded by King Edward VII on the occasion of his coronation. It carries no title and is awarded sparingly. Its members include those who have given distinguished public service or have achieved eminence in a particular field. The membership is limited to twenty-four British members, with such foreigners as the sovereign shall deem appropriate. It is awarded to both men and women.

The badge is a cross of red and blue enamel surmounted by an imperial crown with, on a central medallion, the words 'For Merit'. The medallion is surrounded by a laurel wreath. The badge of military and naval members also carries two crossed swords. The ribbon is blue and crimson and is worn around the neck. (Abbr. OM)

Merit, Order of (Federal Republic of Germany) The national order of the Federal Republic of Germany, created in 1955 in eight classes: Grand Cross Special Class, Grand Cross 1st Class, Grand Cross 2nd Class, Knight Commander's Cross, Commander's Cross, Officer's Cross, Cross of Order of Merit, Medal of Order of Merit.   JC-K

Merit, Order of (Ordine al Merito della Repubblica) The principal Italian order, founded on 3 March 1951. Insignia comprise a badge in white and gold, a star and, in the senior grade, a gold collar. The order has five classes: Knight Grand Cross, Grand Officer, Commander, Officer and Knight. For the highest meritorious deeds or service the Grand Cordon may be awarded to Knights Grand Cross. The Grand Master of the Order is the President of the Republic.

JC-K

Mermaid The upper half of a maiden with flowing hair, and the lower half a fish's tail. Many mermaids are depicted admiring themselves in a mirror and are so blazoned.

Merman *see* **Triton**

Metals The armorial tinctures Or (gold) and Argent (silver). Although modern blazons have included copper, iron, steel and other products of the industrial age, the classic metals of armory are Or and Argent.

Both are given other names such as Sun and Moon in fanciful blazons of the fifteenth and sixteenth centuries. The common-sense tincture convention, that metal may not be placed upon metal, can be dated to the late thirteenth-century tract De Heraudie, and continues through the treatises and manuals, citing the papal banner and the arms of the Crusaders' Kingdom of Jerusalem as the only exceptions. However, the armorist Msgr Bruno Heim has located many hundreds of coats with Argent upon Or or vice versa in the course of his studies. In blazon the terms Gold and Silver may be substituted in order to avoid repetition of Or and Argent, e.g. *Out of an Ancient Crown Or a male Griffin segreant Sable armed beaked and rayed Gold*. For artwork, gold (which will retain its brilliance) is generally used in documents such as letters patent and fine quality illumination, yellow ochre being an acceptable substitute for normal use. Unfortunately, silver tarnishes rapidly and is usually represented by white.

See also TINCTURES

Metalwork An early application of metalwork was in the furniture of doors and chests, much of which was both functional and decorative, and sometimes incorporated armorial devices. However, these were not normally of a personal nature until the fifteenth century, when cyphers, creatures and badges became popular forms of ornamentation in lock plates and the bows of KEYS.

Effigies were often enclosed in an ornamental metal framework (a hearse) such as that on the tomb-chest of Richard Beauchamp in the magnificent Beauchamp Chapel at St Mary's church, Warwick (a veritable Mecca for armorists!). Many of the great heraldic tombs of the late sixteenth and early seventeenth centuries were surrounded by ornate railings.

Mayoral sword-rests such as that at St Peter Mancroft, Norwich (nineteenth century), may incorporate armorial devices or the arms of a mayor. Sword-rests are the stands for the sword and mace, used when a lord mayor attends ceremonial and state occasions. The churches of the City of London possess many such rests and there are splendid examples at St Mary Abchurch near Cannon Street.

Over three thousand medieval bells are still rung in English belfries, and many are inscribed in beautiful lettering with dedications to saints, with foundry marks and other fanciful devices, some of which are heraldic in nature. After the Reformation, such inscriptions took the form of secular dedications, often in rhyme, and incorporated the name of the foundry.

Items associated with the Sacrament are not usually embellished with personal or armorial devices, though the occasional chalice or paten may be found so engraved. Such decoration is usually indicative of a bequest of church plate and is, to modern tastes,

The life-size gilded bronze effigy of Richard Beau-champ, fifth earl of Warwick (d.1439 at Rouen), on a Purbeck marble tomb at the centre of the magnificent Beauchamp chantry chapel in the Collegiate Church of St Mary, Warwick. The Earl's head rests on a helm with a swan crest and at his feet are the bear of Warwick and the griffin of Salisbury. Niches in the four sides of the tomb chest contain bronze angels and 'weepers', each of the latter identified by armorial shields below, including that of Richard Nevill.

singularly pretentious. The Boleyn Cup at Cirencester church, Gloucestershire, originally belonged to Queen Anne Boleyn and was later given to the church. The cover is surmounted by her crest.

Other items of metalwork, both ecclesiastical and domestic, may have armorial motifs incorporated in their decoration. Wrought iron *corona lucis*, circlets suspended by chains on the rim of which are candleholders and their drip-pans, are often decorated with heraldic devices or enamelled shields and crests. Candlesticks, bier lights, candelabra, chandeliers, flagons, tankards, tableware, cutlery, etc., may be engraved with heraldry. However, beware! The 'family' silver may have been purchased as a job-lot by a late relative and the arms engraved thereon of no significance whatever to you or your ancestors. FIREBACKS and HORSE BELLS, PENDANTS AND BRASSES are also rich sources of heraldry.

Ironwork GATES are a constant source of information

to the armorist. Most large residences possess a pair of entrance gates and these are often decorated with armorial work and surmounted by an enamelled coat of arms intended to announce the owner's status to the world, and particularly to his guests. Universities and colleges, especially those of Oxford and Cambridge, are endowed with an abundance of armorial gates. At Magdalen College, Oxford, even the lead drainpipes are charged with the college arms.

Perhaps the finest armorial doors are those to the chapel of Henry VII in Westminster Abbey. These are of bronze (1509) and are decorated with lions and fleurs-de-lis and royal badges: the sunburst, portcullis, falcon and fetterlock, crowns and HR cypher.
See also SILVERWARE

Further reading

Catalogue of *Victorian Church Art* Victoria & Albert Museum, 1971.

Cotterell, H. *Old Pewter its Makers and Marks* London, 1929.

Hollister-Short, G.J. *Discovering Wrought Iron* Aylesbury, 1970.

Lindsay, J.S. *Anatomy of English Wrought Iron* London, 1964.

Oman, C.C. *English Church Plate 597-1830* London, 1968.

Peal, C.A. *Old Pewter and Britannia Metal* London, 1971.

Midas's Head A man's head with long hair, beard and ears like those of an ass.

Miles A knight. This word appears in medieval documents from the eleventh century onwards, sometimes as a personal description (e.g. Guy de Bryen, miles), sometimes in a more generally descriptive context. Examples are *miles agrarius* (holder of a knight's fee), *miles argentarius* (an exchequer official), and *miles parliamentalis* (knight of the shire).   JC-K

Military Knights of Windsor Originally dubbed the 'Poor Knights' this order was founded by King Edward III and comprised eighteen *milites paupers*, gentlemen who were 'decayed in wars, and indigent', and for whom the king provided honourable lodgings at Windsor Castle. It was the presumed intention of the king that the Company should be twenty-six in number, equalling the Garter in that respect. In succeeding reigns the order became oppressed by the 'crafty set of religious men' at Windsor who sought to appropriate its assets. King Henry VIII materially re-established the order on a firm basis with thirteen members, and gave them the title of the Knights of Windsor; he also left the Company the yearly sum of £600 in his will. In the reign of Charles I (1625-49) the number of knights was increased to eighteen, 'two by the foundation of Sir Peter le Maire and three by Sir

Francis Crane'. Today, however, their number is again thirteen, and by command of King William IV they have, since 1833, been known as the Military Knights of Windsor.

In return for the hospitality provided by King Edward III, the Poor Knights were required to represent the Knights of the Garter at daily mass in St George's Chapel. To begin with they wore the same habits as the Garter Knights, but this was changed in 1833 to the uniform as worn today: a scarlet swallow-tail coat, white cross sword-belt, crimson sash and cocked hat which, in the nineteenth century, had been the dress of 'unattached officers and officers on half pay'. Military Knights have almost always been distinguished former warriors, and over the centuries their ranks have included many famous soldiers.

In addition to attending daily service in the Garter Chapel, their duties now include leading Garter processions and mounting watch over the coffin before a royal funeral service at Windsor.   JC-K
See also NAVAL KNIGHTS OF WINDSOR

Mill rinds

Mill Rind The iron centrepiece of a millstone, similar in appearance to the decorative plate at the end of a tie-beam. Usually depicted palewise.

Miniatures The miniature modern knight of today probably finds its origins in a 2½ inch (6 cm) mounted knight of lead, moulded in detail on one side and flat on the other, the horse supported on two quatrefoil stands. These first toys or ornaments were known in the thirteenth and fourteenth centuries, and a fine specimen in bascinet and jupon, bearing a shield with fimbriated cross, astride his fan-crested palfrey may be found in the Musée de Cluny. The model knight has traditionally been produced in lead, a cheap and malleable material. There are fabulous exceptions in silver and gold, but the most popular figures in modern productions are of pewter. The product of painstaking heraldic research and eye-straining miniaturism, they are made by casting molten metal into rubber or brass moulds, and painting in enamels.

What usually separates the model knight from the toy is scrupulous research combined with more careful modelling and painting, the finest specimens being no more than two or three inches tall. This is the province of the artist craftsman whose individual ability distinguishes his work from the studio-produced

figure. The most successful maker of toy knights was an Englishman, Roy Selwyn-Smith, whose Knights of Agincourt series, designed in 1951, is still unsurpassed. The greatest maker of the model knight was another Englishman, Richard Courtenay (1892-1963), who produced some seven thousand figures in thirty-five years. Courtenay concerned himself with the fighting knights and the retainers who served their monarchs at the battles of Crécy and Poitiers. These were the men who contested the right to the crown of France during the Hundred Years' War. The English were supported by the Gascons and the Welsh; the French found their allies amongst the Scots and the mercenary armies of Germany, Austria and Italy. Today 'Courtenays' are produced in pewter by Peter Greenhill of Bournemouth.

For further information, contact the Guild of Master Craftsmen, the British Toymakers' Guild, and the British Model Soldier Society (*see* ADDRESSES).   PG
Further reading
Blum, P. *Military Miniatures* London, 1964.
Garratt, J.G. *Model Soldiers: A Collector's Guide* 1965.
— *Collecting Model Soldiers* Newton Abbot, 1975.
— *The World Encyclopedia of Model Soldiers* 1981.

Minister This word has had a variety of meanings applied to it. The ones most relevant in the present context are: an officer charged with the administration of the law; a high officer of state; a person sent as a political agent by one sovereign state to another.

Minnesängers In Germany, as in Provence, the notion of romantic love coloured the poetry of the 1100s, and the Minnesängers, like the TROUBADOURS, sang of love. They tried to express the thoughts of women as well as those of men, so that the women appear more real and less remote than those of the troubadours.   KH

Minstrels It has been argued that many early heralds were recruited from the ranks of the minstrels and TROUBADOURS and, therefore, from the heart of the brilliant and imaginative society of the twelfth-century renaissance. There is certainly evidence that several thirteenth-century 'Kings of Heralds' were also in receipt of royal largesse as 'Kings of Minstrels', and clearly minstrels who specialized in reciting the legendary deeds and noble ancestry of their patrons (in the manner of the Celtic bards) were literate, intelligent and ideally suited to the rapidly expanding role of the medieval staff officer.

Misericord A hinged wooden seat which, when tipped up, presents a corbel for the user to rest on when in a standing position. Generally found in the choir stalls of Gothic cathedrals and churches. Often

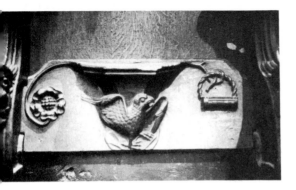

Yorkist badges: the white rose, falcon and fetterlock on a misericord originally at Fotheringhay church but now at Tansor, Northamptonshire.

elaborately carved and always a possible source of armorial devices.

Further reading

Anderson, M.D. *Misericords* London, 1954.

Laird, M. *English Misericords* London, 1986.

Misericorde A thrusting dagger, especially for the 'coup de grace'.

Monaco, Royal Arms of *Argent three Bars of five Fusils Gules.*

Monarch Once the sole and absolute ruler of a state, now a sovereign carrying the title of emperor, empress, king or queen.

Monogram Two or more letters interwoven to form a symbol. *See also* CHRISTIAN SYMBOLS

Monseigneur A style at different times applied to princes, cardinals, dukes and bishops.

Monsieur A gentleman. Used in medieval England, when the language of the nobility was French, as a form of address or style. Some Garter stall plates in St George's Chapel, Windsor, bear witness, e.g. 'Mons Guy de Bryen' (created 1369).

Monsters *see* **Beasts** *and individual entries*

Montenegro, Royal Arms of *Gules an Eagle displayed Argent armed and crowned Or holding in its dexter claw a Sceptre and in the sinister an Orb all proper* charged on the breast with an escutcheon of pretence *Azure on a Base Vert a Lion passant Or armed and langued Gules.*

Monuments The term may embrace all forms of memorial erected to perpetuate the memory of an individual. Monuments bearing armorial devices are a common feature of most churches, and a rich source of information for the armorist.

Monuments developed from the practice of carving designs on coffin lids and slabs which were exposed in the church floor. The earliest surviving lids date from the eleventh century and the designs, usually in shallow relief, were initially of a purely decorative nature, incorporating foliage, beasts and Christian symbols, particularly the cross.

It is likely that the depiction of the human form was reserved, in the twelfth century, for ecclesiastics, the earliest known example in England being that of Abbot Gilbert Crispin (d. 1117), whose tapering coffin lid may be seen in the cloister of Westminster Abbey. In these early memorials the image was 'sunk' into the slab and was effectively a two-dimensional EFFIGY. By the beginning of the thirteenth century the figure was depicted proud of the slab, and by the middle of that century effigies were assuming a more three-dimensional form.

One of the earliest knightly effigies is that of William Longespée, Earl of Salisbury (d. 1226) in Salisbury Cathedral. Monuments such as this provide evidence of the early systematic use of hereditary devices centred on the shield: the six lioncels (small lions) depicted in Longespée's shield appear to be those of his paternal grandfather, Geoffrey, Count of Anjou (d. 1151) whose enamelled plate, originally on his tomb at Le Mans Cathedral, also bore a number of small lions.

During the following centuries church monuments developed in diverse ways. The three-dimensional effigy continued to be a major feature and was normally placed on a TOMB CHEST. In addition, two-dimensional figures were depicted on INCISED SLABS and monumental BRASSES. The development of armour and costume may be traced through such figures, though it should be remembered that many memorials were prepared well in advance of the demise of those whose memory they were intended to perpetuate or were erected retrospectively in a later style. Tomb chests, with a two or three-dimensional effigy, could be free-standing or placed against a wall, and in either case could be surmounted by a CANOPY. Canopied, free-standing tomb chests are clearly the precursors of the CHANTRY chapels.

Early monuments depicted only a stylized image of the deceased, but it became the practice to place man and wife (or wives) side by side. Children were not usually represented, except as weepers around the base of the tomb, or by shields illustrative of marital alliances. Armory was generally shown as it was used in real life, and although a frequent element in the design it was not, at this time, a predominant one.

The Renaissance period saw the emergence of the reclining, kneeling or standing figure, and children of the deceased appeared more prominently. This period also produced the WALL MONUMENT which had no tomb chest. Whilst this tended to be smaller than earlier monuments, it nevertheless followed the same artistic development as the effigy. Two distinctive types of memorial which date from the late sixteenth and early seventeenth centuries are the TRIPTYCH, which consisted of three painted panels hinged together and which probably originated in the portable altars of the medieval nobility; and the obelisk, a tall, four-sided, tapering pillar, usually placed on a plinth, that of Lady Margaret Hoby (d. 1605) at Bisham, Berkshire, being one example. This consists of a single obelisk surmounted by a heart, and with four swans at the corners of its base, and four coats of arms, one at each side of the plinth. The swan was the crest of Lady Margaret's father, Henry Carey, Lord Hunsdon.

During the seventeenth century, the effigy was often omitted from the wall monument to produce the wall tablet and its cheap and simple precursor, the MEMORIAL BOARD.

During the late sixteenth and early seventeenth centuries, armorial display on monuments reached its height and occasionally became the dominant feature of memorials, reflecting the changing nature of armory itself from the practical to the ceremonial and symbolic. It was now necessary to provide 'reproduction' helms, gauntlets, tabards and other items of FUNERAL HERALDRY which, in the previous century, would have been readily available. It was at this time that the HATCHMENT was introduced, possibly as a substitute for the elaborate (and expensive) trappings of the heraldic funerals of the nobility. The seventeenth century also saw the rise of purer classical influences in English domestic architecture which naturally affected the design of church monuments. Columns and pediments became prominent and the tomb chest less popular. The kneeling effigy remained in hanging monuments, but in general figures were depicted in more natural poses and the grief of a surviving spouse was often shown. This culminated in the Baroque period, when figures became much grander and often appear to capture a moment of the deceased's life, and the tomb chest was now rarely used. Carved fruit, flowers, garlands and cherubs' heads became part of the decoration and were common on wall monuments.

In the early eighteenth century there was a reaction against the Baroque and a reversion to a more classical style. Indeed, many figures of this period are depicted in classical costume. The two-dimensional pyramid was a common element, particularly in wall monuments, and the tomb chest was now replaced by the sarcophagus which often had the deceased, his family or allegorical figures sitting or leaning against it. The area at the base of the monument was often devoted to biographical or genealogical details or a carving of a scene from the deceased's life, particularly of those who had enjoyed successful military or naval careers.

The nineteenth century saw two contrasting styles: the classical Roman art form was replaced by the classical Greek, usually in black and white marble, and the two-dimensional pyramid was replaced by the 'stele', a rectangular slab surmounted by a low triangular pediment. The size varied from the small tablet with only an inscription, to the hanging monument with the inscription in the base and a carved sculpture shown in relief. Such figures were depicted in classical Grecian dress and were often of angels or the deceased shown resting against an urn or sarcophagus.

The Greek revival continued into the second half of the century, when it was overtaken by the Gothic Revival, the origins of which may be traced from the mid-eighteenth century. This brought with it the return of the tomb chest with an effigy, sometimes surmounted by a canopy. However, these were designed to provide an overall effect and frequently combined a variety of medieval influences rather than being copies of a specific style or period. In most cases the effigy was recumbent, but occasional examples of a kneeling representation may be found. There was also a revival of the figured monumental brass. This medium spread to wall monuments with the familiar 'Gothic' lettering and illuminated capital letters.

The end of the nineteenth century saw a close of the era of grand funeral monuments. Memorials took the form of wall tablets, window GLASS and memorial panels, or the provision of church furniture and fittings as bequests 'in memoriam'.

Modern heraldic memorials are, for the most part, discreet and tasteful and often beautifully executed. In England the erection of armorial devices for this purpose is subject to the approval of Garter Principal King of Arms, and in Scotland to the control of Lord Lyon. It is also necessary to obtain a faculty from diocesan authorities for the erection of a memorial in a church and this may involve much paperwork before approval is given.

For The Royal Commission for Historic Monuments, the Church Monuments Society and the Monumental Brass Society, *see* ADDRESSES. JET

See also CHURCHYARD MONUMENTS *and* STALL PLATES

Further reading

Collinson, H. *Country Monuments, Their Families and Houses* Newton Abbot, 1975.

Esdaile, K. *English Church Monuments* London, 1946.

Foster, J. *Some Feudal Coats of Arms* 1902 (reprinted

Magnificent canopied monuments to (left) Thomas Winston (d.1609) and (right) Sir John Fitzjames (d.1625) at Longburton church, Dorset.

1979). Contains over eighty illustrations of heraldic effigies and brasses.

Heraldry from Military Monuments before 1350 in England and Wales Harleian Society, 1946, Vol.XCVIII.

Kemp, B. *Church Monuments* Aylesbury, 1984. A sound introduction.

— *English Church Monuments* London, 1980. An excellent book, well illustrated, and covering the whole range of English church monuments. Good bibliography.

Physick, J. *Designs for English Sculpture 1680-1860* HMSO, 1969.

Morion *or* **Morian** A helmet with a brim raised fore and aft and a high, often ridged, crown.

Morning Star A heavy battle mace with spiked, cylindrical head.

Morthead A death's head or human skull.

Motto *or* **Mot** An aphorism, the interpretation of which is often obscure and known only to the armiger who adopted it. The motto is usually (though not necessarily) included in a coat of arms, where it is depicted either below the shield or (as in Scotland) above the crest, generally on a scroll. Scottish mottoes and CRIS-DE-GUERRE are subject to armorial control, are specified in patents and must be re-matriculated with arms. In Irish patents the motto is also specified but not so in England, where it may be included in the exemplification of arms (and on the motto bends in the fly of a standard if one is depicted), but is not actually granted. It follows, therefore, that English armigers may both change their mottoes at will and add to them.

Quite often a motto may refer to a charge in the arms, the crest, a badge or the name of the armiger. 'We Are One', the motto of Johnson of Alabama, USA, neatly refers to the *Gules a Chain in Cross Argent* of his arms, as does 'I Support My Beliefs' to the arms of Pundyke *a Chevron embattled ensigned with a Celtic Cross* (see colour page 251). 'As Man Sows So Shall He Reap' is an allusion to the name Asman in a recent grant.

Mottoes may be in any language. In the past, Latin has been favoured but there is now a growing preference for native languages, for example *Umlimu Lelizwe* ('God and Country') in the Sindebele language of the Matabele tribe of Zimbabwe in the arms of Cooper of Pietermaritzburg.

The colour of the scroll is a matter for artistic taste. Some mottoes may be found encircling the shield in the manner of insignia — which they are not.

Mottoes accompanying signatures are commonly found on medieval documents and manuscripts. They first appeared in achievements of arms in the fourteenth and fifteenth centuries, but were not in general use until the seventeenth century when the coat of arms became more decorative and stylized. Armorists should beware the motto when attempting to identify a coat of arms. By using appropriate works of reference one may obtain a 'pointer' in the right direction, but because they were frequently changed and are not required to be unique, mottoes can be very misleading.

Further reading

Elvin, C.N. *Handbook of Mottoes* Heraldry Today, 1860 (reprinted 1986).

Pine, L.G. *A Dictionary of Mottoes* 1983.

Mount A grassy hillock.

Mulberry A murrey roundel, named after the fruit.

Mullet *or* **Molet** An armorial charge from the French *molette*, meaning a spur rowel. In practice, the mullet is a stylized star of five points (unless more are blazoned) and it may be pierced, in which case the tincture of the hole should also be blazoned unless it is that of the field.

Muniment A document such as a title deed, letters patent (or closed) preserved as evidence of rights or privileges.

Mural Crown *see* **Crest Coronet**

Murrey (Abbr. Mu.) An uncommon armorial tincture of mulberry colour, more often employed as livery than for armorial purposes. Considered by some to be a 'stain', and by others (erroneously) to be synonymous with sanguine.

See also STAINS

A clarion

Musical Heraldry Musical instruments and symbols used as charges are commonly found in armory, the best known (and the most controversial) being the clarion. Unknown in European armory, the earliest depiction in Britain is in thirteenth-century tiles from Neath and Margam abbeys in South Wales, and Keynsham Abbey near Bristol. The arms *Gules three Clarions Or* have been attributed to Henry I's bastard son, Robert Earl of Gloucester (d. 1146), and Gilbert de Clare (d. 1230) adopted a clarion as his badge, clearly in allusion to his name. The term occurs in print for the first time in the fourth edition of Guillim's

An English patent of arms, granted in 1985 to the Worshipful Company of Engineers. The arms are blazoned *Azure on a Fess between in chief a Sun in Splendour and in base a Rack and Pinion in mesh Or a representation of Tower Bridge London in outline Sable*, and for the crest *On a Mount Vert a representation of Smeaton's Lighthouse proper supported by two Lions rampant guardant each crowned with a Mural Crown Gules the faces Or*. The supporters *Standing upon a representation of the Iron Bridge proper* (Telford's bridge at Iron Bridge, Shropshire, built 1779) *a Pegasus forcene Gules winged maned tailed and unguled Or its dexter hoof resting on a Measuring Stick proper and suspended from a Collar Gold the Company Badge* and on the sinister a *Wyvern proper its sinister paw resting on a Shovel*

proper and suspended from a Collar Or the Badge of the Lord Mayor of London also proper. The wreath and mantling are gold, azure and sable and the badge *On a Sun in Splendour a representation of the Iron Bridge Sable*.

The use of specific buildings or artefacts as charges is generally discouraged by contemporary heraldic authorities, and yet the Engineers' arms successfully include several such references. Note also the affronty position of the helm which facilitates the accurate depiction of the crest. Until recently such a relaxation of the convention relating to the position of helmets would not have been possible.

Contrast this simple and attractive patent with that of the Police Federation (see POLICE).

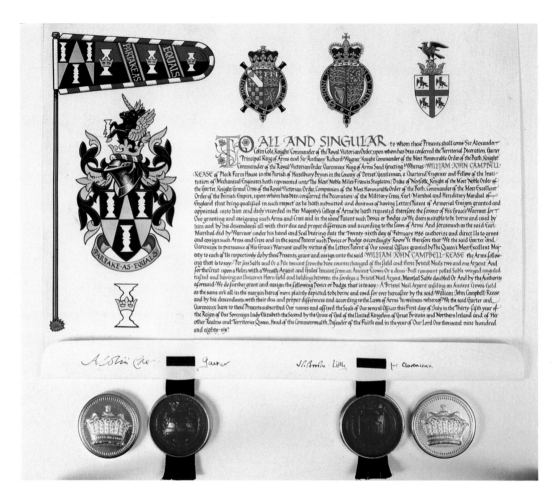

ABOVE English patent of arms granted in 1986 to John Campbell-Kease of Dorset. The arms are blazoned *Per fess Sable and Or a Pile issuant from the base counterchanged of the field three Bristol Nails two and one Argent* and for the crest *Issuant from an Ancient Crown Or a demi-Bull rampant polled Sable winged unguled tufted and having an Unicorn's Horn Gold and holding between the forelegs a Bristol Nail Argent*. Beneath the exemplification of arms is the badge, *a Bristol Nail enfiling an Ancient Crown Or*, and this is repeated on the standard. The Bristol Nail is unique in armory.

OPPOSITE, TOP Patent of arms, in Gaelic and English, granted in 1983 by the Chief Herald of Ireland to Kenneth Pundyke of County Antrim. The arms, which allude both to the name and motto, are *Per chevron Sable and Or a Chevron embattled counterchanged ensigned with a Celtic Cross of the last*.

OPPOSITE, BELOW Confirmed in 1982 by Lord Lyon, the Scottish arms of the Mistery of Gunmakers of the City of London incorporate two Scottish shotguns saltirewise between the conjoined letters GP (the Proof Mark of the Gunmakers) and the letter V (the View Mark), each ensigned with the Royal Crown. Above the shield is a sallet affronty, appropriate in Scotland to the arms of a corporation. At top right are the arms of office of the Master of the Gunmakers, and below is the banner, 'sustained' by one of the supporters. The standard, specified as being '8 yards in length', is charged with the Proof and View marks on a background of argent and gules liveries. The patent illustrates current Scottish heraldic style, charges and traditional elements such as the helm, mantling and compartment being reduced to their simplest form. Until recently the Gunmakers' Company used arms without authority, but have now obtained both English and Scottish patents.

earl of worcester

1427 1470

non son pense

non son pense

sir john tiptofte

non son pense

non son pense

A cruel man but a scholar
he held high state offices
under Edward iv. He was
executed when temporarily
he lost the king's protection.

Display of Heraldry in the middle of the seventeenth century. The numerous alternatives by which this device may be found blazoned provide ample evidence of the controversy which has surrounded both its origin and its function: bracket, clavicimbal, clavichord, psaltery, organ, organ rest, rest, lance, lance rest, horseman's rest, fewter, rest of arms, sufflue, gubernacle or rudder have all been ascribed to the figure at one time or another. Armorists are now generally agreed that it represents a musical instrument, probably a portable organ or Panpipes, and that the lance rest and rudder, which are sometimes depicted in a similar fashion, are entirely different charges. Clearly, many of the other alternatives have resulted from confusion, organ rest, for example, suggesting that the herald was hedging his bets!

The psaltery, lyre and harp are often found in the arms of musical organizations. The harp is often used as the device of Saint Cecilia, the Virgin Martyr of the third century and patroness of church music. The tincture of the strings of the harp must always be mentioned if different from that of the frame, for example *Azure a Harp Or stringed Argent*, being one of the attributed arms of Saint Cecilia.

Wind instruments of many forms are found as charges and include trumpet, bugle, recorder and horn. An early use of the armorial trumpet is found on the Trumpington brass at Trumpington, Cambridgeshire: *Azure crusily two Trumpets palewise Or*.

A rare musical crest was granted in 1982 to Keith Lovell in the form of *a demi-Figure of a Youth habited in an alb and amice and playing a Recorder at the note B Flat all proper* — a fitting device for a music teacher who has spent much time with the instrument in question.

Since very early times the horn has been used as a signal for hunting, and it is no surprise to find horns as charges in the arms of the Worshipful Company of Horners of the City of London. In the Netherlands the town of Hoorn uses a horn as a canting charge, as does the family of Horn in Finland. In Finland, horns were sometimes made of birchbark and these appear in the civic arms of Tuupovaara and Pielavesi. It is said that the Gamekeeper to the King of France was, through his position in the court, allowed two bugle horns attached to and hanging from the end of the mantling on his helm.

When bells appear in a blazon their type should be specified, as both church bells and hawk's bells are fairly common charges. If the blazon just refers to a bell, it is usually safe to assume that it is a church bell. In European armory the clapper is sometimes of a different tincture to that of the bell. The arms of Puolanka in Finland have introduced a third type of bell to armory — a cow bell!

Organ pipes can be used to good effect as heraldic charges and may appear side by side, palewise and graded in size, the shortest on the dexter and the number stated in the blazon. They are sometimes placed saltirewise and often stand alone. Not surprisingly the Royal College of Organists has such charges on its arms.

The violin and fiddle are sometimes confused in armory, but both can be blazoned correctly. For instance *Gules three treble Violins transposed Argent stringed Sable* are, according to Papworth, the arms of the family of Sweeting, and *Azure three Fiddles Argent* the arms of Sueting.

In 1977 the Royal Philharmonic Orchestra was granted arms and it was part of a violin that inspired a most interesting coat of arms: *Per pale Or and Azure three Stradivari Violin Bridges each ensigned with an Ancient Crown counterchanged*. Until this grant a violin bridge had never been used before in armory.

In Finnish civic heraldry the kantele, a string instrument of the zither type, has been used in the arms of Halsua and Ilomantsi.

It was a chance discovery of a book on heraldry that inspired the composer Sir Arthur Bliss to write his 'Colour Symphony', following an invitation by Sir Edward Elgar in 1921 to write a new work for the Three Choirs Festival the following year. Each movement of the work is given an armorial colour and expresses its symbolism.

It is not uncommon now for musical organizations to obtain a grant of arms, and rather fitting that in 1947 the Performing Rights Society, which protects the rights of composers, was granted *Per fess embattled Argent and Azure in chief five Barrulets surmounted to the dexter by an Alto Clef Sable over all a dexter Hand proper the cuff erased Or holding a Baton erect also proper*.   MGM

OPPOSITE **A magnificent illuminated painting by Anthony Wood of the arms of John Tiptoft, Earl of Worcester K.G. (*c.* 1427-70). Sometime Constable of England, scholar, humanist, patron of Caxton and avant-courier of the Renaissance, Tiptoft's bestial cruelty and ruthlessness earned him the sobriquet 'Butcher of England'. A Yorkist, whose services to Edward IV included the impaling of captured rebels in 1470, he was beheaded during the readeption of Henry VI in the same year. The Tiptoft arms *Argent a Saltire engrailed Gules* are quartered with those of his mother, heir of Edward, Lord Chorleton, feudal Lord of Powis *Or a Lion rampant Gules*. On an escutcheon of pretence are the arms of his first wife Cecily, daughter of Richard Nevill (4 *Gules a Saltire Argent and a Label gobony Argent and Azure*) Earl of Salisbury, by Alice, daughter and heir of Thomas Montacute, Earl of Salisbury (1 *Argent three Lozenges in fess Gules*) and heir to Monthermer (2 and 3 *Or an Eagle displayed Vert*).**

Mutilé *see* **Attributes**

Muzzled *see* **Attributes**

N

Nag's Head A horse's head.

Naiant *see* **Attitude**

Naissant *see* **Attitude**

Name and Arms Clause A clause in a will requiring a beneficiary to assume the name and arms of the testator as a requirement of inheritance. To comply, the beneficiary must apply to the Crown for a royal licence within a year of the testator's death. Both name and arms may then be used in addition to, or instead of, his own.

Name, Change of (through the College of Arms)
An officer of arms can effect a change of name for a client by means of a deed poll, for which the College of Arms is an official registry. A change of name can also be effected by means of a royal licence from the Sovereign, but only if a change of arms is involved as well.

For the purpose of a deed poll, a statutory declaration has to be made by an acquaintance of some years' standing, and a birth certificate is also required. When the deed has been executed, a notice of it is published in the *London Gazette*, and then the deed is recorded in the College.

It is not desirable to link a forename to a surname, thus causing the loss of a forename. If, for example, John Smith Robinson wishes to take the additional surname of Smith, he should call himself John Smith Smith-Robinson, not John Smith-Robinson.

In the case of a change of name and arms, which is usually required under the terms of a will, the Home Secretary is acquainted with the facts of the case by the officer of arms dealing with it. If he agrees to accept a petition to the Sovereign, the officer of arms draws this up for the applicant's signature and then forwards it to the Home Office. In due course the royal licence is received and a notice is published in the *London Gazette*. Finally, the royal licence is recorded in the College of Arms.   SA

NATO North Atlantic Treaty Organisation. The various commands of NATO have pocket insignia which often include armorial emblems, e.g. HQ LandSouthEast (Allied Land Force South East Europe) has a shield quartered with the arms of Greece and Turkey, HQ AFNorth (Allied Forces Northern Europe) has a blue shield with a splendid Viking ship.   SS

Naval Crown *see* **Crest Coronet**

Naval Knights of Windsor A college of seven naval knights instituted at Windsor in 1798 by King William III from a bequest by Samuel Travers, Auditor General. It was the intention to establish a foundation similar to that of the Poor Knights (now MILITARY KNIGHTS OF WINDSOR), but for naval veterans. It was laid down that members should be 'superannuated or disabled lieutenants of English men-of-war', who should also be 'single men, without children, inclined to lead a virtuous and devout life.' The college was disbanded in 1892 by Queen Victoria because of the 'irredeemable discord' between the military and naval groups.   JC-K

Nebek A particularly hairy heraldic tyger.

Nebuly *see* **Lines, Varied**

Neptune A crowned merman, armed with a trident.

Netherlands, Armorial Practice The Kingdom of the Netherlands has no laws relating to armorial bearings, any citizen being able to assume them, and there is no official register of the arms of untitled persons.

The arms of the nobility are, however, a different matter. These are governed by the Supreme Court of the Nobility, which has responsibility to the Queen on matters of title, flags, public arms, badges and emblems for the armed services, and other related matters.

There is a Royal Society for Genealogy and Heraldry, and a Central Bureau for Genealogy, which publishes the *Yearbook of the Dutch Nobility* (*see* ADDRESSES).   JC-K

Netherlands, Military Insignia Ships and units of the Royal Dutch Navy and Marine Corps use insignia consisting of crossed anchors surmounted by emblems within a loop of rope and ensigned with a naval crown. The emblems are often armorial in character and bear the arms of naval heroes or those of provinces, towns, etc.   SS

Netherlands, Royal Arms of *Azure billety a Lion rampant crowned Or armed and langued Gules holding in the dexter forepaw a Sword and in the sinister a Sheaf of Arrows proper.*

New Zealand Herald of Arms Extraordinary Known as the 'Antipodean Herald', the office was created in 1978. The badge of office is *A complex Maori Koru coloured in the traditional manner proper ensigned by a representation of the Royal Crown also proper.*

The Koru design is used to decorate the rafters of Maori meeting houses, where important ceremonies take place, and is also found on a number of objects used at these ceremonial gatherings. The loops and

coils of the Koru also represent the complex Maori genealogical tree of Whakapapa. Maori genealogy is based for the most part on oral evidence and tradition, and in art the Koru is used to symbolize this.

New Zealand Herald Extraordinary represents the College of Arms in New Zealand, is deputy in that country to Garter King of Arms, and is *ex officio* a member of the royal household.

New Zealand, Order of Instituted by the Queen on the advice of her New Zealand ministers on 6 February 1987, to recognize outstanding service to the Crown and people of New Zealand in either a civilian or military capacity. Members are designated as Members of the Order of New Zealand, and may add ONZ after their names. The Badge of the Order is worn after the insignia of Knights and Dames Grand Cross and that of the Order of Companions of Honour, but before that of all Knights and Dames Commander and Knights Bachelor. CS

New Zealand, Queen's Service Order Instituted by the Queen on the advice of her New Zealand ministers on 13 March 1975, to recognize valuable voluntary service to the community and meritorious and faithful public services, both in a civilian capacity. There are two sub-divisions to the single class of Companion of the Order — 'For Community Service' and 'For Public Services' — both of whom can add QSO after their names. Members are designated as Companions of the Order; they rank equal to OBEs but the insignia is worn before that of the OBE insignia. CS

Niadh Nask The Niadh Nask is a nobiliary fraternity which developed from the old warrior-guard of the

Kings of Munster. It restricts admission to armigers, entitled to bear arms of nobility, and to persons holding noble offices. Although not an order of chivalry or knighthood, the Niadh Nask has been listed as a nobiliary association by the International Commission for Orders of Chivalry, and its arms have been recorded in a number of heraldic offices. Admission is not restricted to persons of Irish descent, and the present membership includes Scottish chiefs and peers, English and Irish peers, and European noblemen. The fraternity undertakes charitable work and in particular the relief of suffering amongst the very young and the elderly. The fraternity bears the following arms: *Vert a Cross pommé Argent fimbriated Or inset with a Greek Cross of the first*. Its crest is *An Antique Crown Or enclosing a Cap of Maintenance Vert*, and its motto is 'Divina Faventia Clementia'. MCM

Nimbed *see* **Attributes**

Noble (i) In England a peer who, by his letters patent of creation, is 'really ennobled' by the Crown. A grant of arms in England recognizes gentility but does not create nobility, therefore.
(ii) In Scotland, the term nobility is synonymous with gentility and a Scottish grant of arms is, therefore, effectively a patent of nobility.
(iii) An English gold coin first minted in the reign of Edward III.

Nombril Point *see* **Shield, Points of the**

Norfolk Herald of Arms Extraordinary From 1539 this officer was a herald to the dukes of Norfolk, though the first holder, John James, was paid a salary by Henry VIII. Subsequent Norfolk heralds have been officers of arms extraordinary, though the office has not always been filled but rather revived when required. The badge of office, assigned in 1958, *Two Ostrich Feathers saltirewise each charged with a Gold Chain laid along the quill*, derives from the ostrich feather badge granted by Richard II in *c.* 1387 as a mark of special favour to Thomas Mowbray, Duke of Norfolk, Marshal of England and first to be styled Earl Marshal.

Norroy and Ulster King of Arms Norroy and Ulster is the junior of the two provincial kings of arms, the office combining two former appointments. There is a case to be made that the office of Norroy is the older of the two English territorial offices, there being a reference as early as 1276 to a 'King of Heralds beyond Trent in the North', the precise area to come under the later kings specifically nominated 'Norroy'. The office of Ulster King of Arms (and principal herald of Ireland) was established in 1552 by King Edward VI to replace the post of Ireland King of Arms, which had lapsed in 1487.

In 1943 the office of Ulster was combined with that of Norroy, and the King of Arms now has jurisdiction over the counties of Northern Ireland as well as England north of Trent.

The arms of Norroy and Ulster date from 1980: *Quarterly Argent and Or a Cross Gules on a Chief per pale Azure and Gules a Lion passant guardant Or crowned with an open Crown between a Fleur-de-lis and a Harp Or.* JC-K

Norway, Armorial Practice Apart from national, civic and corporate heraldry, arms are seen but little in Norway. The social, military and political history of the country is very different from that of nations in the main land mass of Europe, and the institutions of knighthood and chivalry played little part in Norwegian affairs. Notwithstanding this, and although never widely used, armorial bearings were borne by royal, noble and knightly persons from at least the thirteenth century. In later years, Norwegian armorial designs were influenced by Scottish and French conventions, but stark pagan charges were also used. From the mid-fourteenth century the ties with, and then the dominion by, Denmark brought a closer similarity to mainstream armorial practice.

Excepting royal and noble armory, most of the arms known today date from the seventeenth century, when commercial life expanded, bringing into being merchant and trading classes. There have been no titled families since 1814, the registration of private arms was abolished in 1821, and only national arms are fully protected by law. There is, however, a developing interest in heraldry, and a corresponding increase in the number of heraldic and genealogical societies (*see* ADDRESSES). JC-K

Norway, Military Insignia In recent years the unit insignia of the Norwegian army have undergone considerable change. Unit badges, which formerly took the form of non-armorial designs on a diamond-shaped cloth backing, now consist for the most part of very simple armorial devices in one metal and one colour on a shield. The illustration shows the arm badge of the Norwegian ABC Defence School. On certain types of headgear the royal cypher within a wreath is worn, whilst on other forms of cap Norwegian army officers wear a badge bearing the lion of St Olaf. The national cockade of red, white and blue is worn by all ranks on the ski cap. Officers and men of the King's Guard wear on their curious 'bowler hats' (parade hats) a combination of national cockade and royal cypher. SS

ABC Defence School

Norway, Royal Arms of *Gules a Lion rampant crowned Or holding in his paws a long-handled Axe (of St Olaf) blade Argent handle Or.*

Nova Scotia, Baronetcy of *see* **Baronetcy**

Nova Scotia, Baroness of Certain of the Nova Scotia baronetcies were granted with a destination which has allowed ladies to inherit the title. For example, the Dunbar of Hempriggs baronetcy (10 December 1706) granted by Queen Anne to heirs whatsoever is now held by Dame Maureen Dunbar of Hempriggs, Baroness. CJB

Nowed *see* **Attitude**

Nowy *see* **Lines, Varied**

Nuncio Strictly a 'messsenger', but more usually a permanent official representative of the Vatican at a foreign court.

O

Octofoil An armorial charge, similar to a cinquefoil but with eight petals.

Officer in Waiting At the College of Arms, this is the officer of arms in attendance during a particular week to deal with enquiries other than those which may be directed to specific officers of arms by established clients. The banner of arms of the officer in waiting is displayed at the entrance to the College.

Officer of Arms A person appointed by a sovereign or state with authority to perform one or more of the following functions:
1. to control and initiate armorial matters
2. to arrange and participate in ceremonies of state
3. to conserve and interpret heraldic and genealogical records.

Traditionally, officers of arms are of three ranks: kings of arms, heralds of arms, and pursuivants of arms. Officers of arms whose appointments are of a permanent nature are known as officers of arms in ordinary; those whose appointments are of a temporary or occasional nature are known as officers of arms extraordinary.

The medieval practice of appointing heralds or pursuivants to the establishment of a noble household is still common in European countries, particularly those in which there is no official heraldic control or authority. Such appointments are purely advisory.

In England, the authority of the thirteen officers of arms in ordinary who form the Corporation of the Kings, Heralds and Pursuivants of Arms extends throughout the Commonwealth, with the exception of Scotland where Lord Lyon King of Arms, three heralds and four pursuivants control matters armorial within a strict legal framework not enjoyed by their brother officers of arms in London. Lord Lyon is appointed by the Crown, and, with the Crown's authority, himself appoints the other Scottish officers. The officers of arms in ordinary who form the College of Arms are members of the royal household and receive a nominal salary (a herald's salary is £17.16p!).

In the Republic of Ireland, matters armorial and genealogical come within the authority of an officer designated as Chief Herald of Ireland.

Officers of arms in ordinary at the College of Arms are:

Garter Principal King of Arms
Clarenceux King of Arms
Norroy and Ulster King of Arms

Chester Herald of Arms
Windsor Herald of Arms
Richmond Herald of Arms
Somerset Herald of Arms
York Herald of Arms
Lancaster Herald of Arms
Portcullis Pursuivant of Arms
Bluemantle Pursuivant of Arms
Rouge Croix Pursuivant of Arms
Rouge Dragon Pursuivant of Arms

Officers of arms in ordinary in Scotland are:

Lord Lyon King of Arms
Marchmont Herald of Arms
Albany Herald of Arms
Rothesay Herald of Arms
Dingwall Pursuivant of Arms
Kintyre Pursuivant of Arms
Carrick Pursuivant of Arms
Unicorn Pursuivant of Arms

English officers of arms extraordinary are:

Arundel Herald Extraordinary
Beaumont Herald Extraordinary
Fitzalan Pursuivant Extraordinary
Maltravers Herald Extraordinary
New Zealand Herald Extraordinary
Norfolk Herald Extraordinary
Surrey Herald Extraordinary
Wales Herald Extraordinary

and in Scotland:

Falkland Pursuivant Extraordinary
March Pursuivant Extraordinary

All the above have individual entries.
See also ROYAL HERALDS

Offices of State, Origins of Many of the great English offices of state have their origins in the households of the dukes of Normandy well before the Conquest of 1066, and there is little doubt that the ducal establishment itself was modelled on that of the kings of France which maintained the five great offices of Steward, Butler, Chamberlain, Constable and Chancellor. The Conqueror's officers served both the dominions of Normandy and England until 1133, when Henry I began to distribute the duties so that there were separate establishments for his two states. The offices of Steward and Constable were already divided among several holders, and it seems reasonable to assume that where possible offices were so arranged as to prevent the holders from becoming too powerful. However, this does not seem always to have been the case in England, for before the end of the twelfth century each office was held by a single noble, even though the post of Steward hovered uneasily between the earls of Norfolk and Leicester. Perhaps the definitive account of the early years of the great offices of England is that contained in the *Constitutio Domus Regis*, compiled for King Stephen at the beginning of his reign. This document indicates that there were then four principal ranks of officer:

First: Chancellor, Steward, Master Butler, Master Chamberlain and Constable.
Second: Master Dispenser of the Bread, Master Dispenser of the Larder, Master Dispenser of the Buttery, Master of the Writing Desk, Clerk of the Spence of the Bread and Wine and Duty Chamberlain (deputy to the Master Chamberlain).
Third: Deputy Constables, Master Marshal (whose duties are unclear), and Chamberlain of the Privy Purse.
Fourth: Dispenser of the Pannetry, Dispenser of the Larder, Keeper of the Butts, Chamberlain of the Candle and four Marshals of the Household.

The Norman dukes did not at first have chancellors, but soon after his arrival in England William promoted his chaplain to be chancellor, to be head of the royal chapel, responsible for the king's seal, and to supervise secretarial work.

The stewards were, at the outset, in charge of the hall and those departments connected with food over which the butler had no jurisdiction. As might be expected, the chamberlain was in charge of the royal bedchamber and, in the days after the Conquest, was also the royal treasurer. Towards the end of the Norman period a separate office of treasurer was created.

The master butler of the English royal house was in charge of the butlery, wine selection, dispensers and so on, but in France the office was much more important, the butler controlling the royal vineyards, collecting taxes from certain abbeys and also sitting as a judge in the king's court.

The holder of the new office of treasurer came to be in control of liquid financial assets and some others. By the time of Henry I (1100-35) the post of treasurer was a very important one and the holder was paid at the same rate as the chancellor and other officers of the first rank.

The constables initially controlled the stables (from whence their name derives), the kennels, the mews and, indeed, anything to do with the king's sporting activities. They were responsible for paying the more junior officers who tended the horses, hounds and hawks, and also the king's soldiers.

It will be noted that the marshal was to begin with an officer of the third rank, and although his duties were unclear it is likely that they were related to the royal horses (to which the word 'marshal' almost certainly relates), and that under the constables he had command of the stables. It was only later that the office became transformed and elevated to the important

function exemplified today in that of Earl Marshal (and Hereditary Marshal of England), to the holder of which must be addressed all memorials for the granting of arms.   JC-K

Officio Militari et Insigniis Armorum de *see* **Treatises**

Ombrellino The emblem of the basilica. Granted as an augmentation in the arms of those families who gave a pope to the Church, or in recognition of signal service to the Catholic Church. Often described as a pavilion.

Open *see* **Attitude**

Opinicus *see* **Medical Heraldry**

Oppressed *see* **Attitude**

Or The armorial metal gold, often represented by yellow-ochre. *See also* TINCTURES

Orange A tenné roundel, named after the fruit.

Orders and Medals Research Society This was founded in 1942 with the aim of encouraging interest in orders of chivalry and decorations. The patron of the society is HRH The Prince of Wales. The society publishes a quarterly journal which is sent to all 2000 members worldwide. An annual convention, exhibition and dinner is held, usually at Grosvenor Hotel in London.
See ADDRESSES

Ordinary *or* **Honourable Ordinary** A principal charge of bold rectilinear shape by which the geometry of other armorial figures is regulated.

It is extraordinary that a term which has defied definition and to which can be ascribed no apparent function should have survived for so long in the armorial vocabulary. Every heraldic text book contains a different selection of ordinaries: few attempt a definition. Indeed, some armorists conclude that there is no difference between a so-called ordinary and any other principal charge.

The prefix 'honourable' implies precedence and suggests that it is the charge's position in the sequence

Ordinaries
and their diminutives

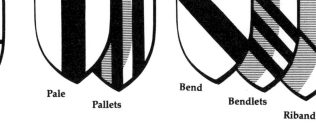

of blazon which is the determining factor. If the honourable ordinary is, therefore, to be defined as a charge which *always* precedes other charges (i.e. a principal charge) then both the CHIEF and the BORDURE must be omitted from the classification. Of course, this definition may also apply to *any* principal charge, rectilinear or otherwise. The ordinaries, therefore, must exercise a function *in addition* to that of a principal charge.

The ordinaries as here defined also possess a *regulative* function (Latin *ordinare* = to regulate). The geometry of each corresponds with the four principal

Fess

Bars

Barrulet

Pale

Pallets

Bend

Bendlets

Riband

Bend sinister

Bendlets sinister

Chevron

Chevronels

Chevron reversed

Chevronel reversed

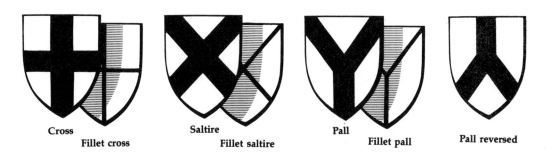

Cross

Fillet cross

Saltire

Fillet saltire

Pall

Fillet pall

Pall reversed

lines of partition, and their disposition within the armorial field is unalterable: for these reasons the terminology of blazon is determined by reference to them, i.e.:

Parted fields (e.g. *per chevron*);
Disposition of charges (e.g. *five martlets in saltire*);
Attitudes (inclination) of charges (e.g. *a Spear fesswise*).

The ordinaries so defined are: fess, pale, cross, bend, bend sinister, saltire, chevron, chevron reversed, pall, pall reversed.

Of these the pall is generally assumed to have ecclesiastical connotations, and the chevron reversed and pall reversed are rare in British armory. The PILE, by this definition, is a principal charge, though many armorists would consider it to be an ordinary.

Ordinaries may be parted, have varied, semy or gerattie fields and their edges are subject to variations of line. They are always depicted *upon* a field, and therefore in relief. When an ordinary is itself composed of a varied field the geometrical lines and divisions are generally depicted as they would be on the surface of the shield — company and counter-company being exceptional in that they follow the geometry of the ordinary. Charges placed on ordinaries are normally depicted in the upright position except on the bend and bend sinister.

Specific proportions have been proposed for each of the ordinaries, but the impossibility of such a proposition is best demonstrated by considering the entirely different requirements of, for example, *a Cross between four Eagles displayed* and *on a Cross four Eagles displayed*. Clearly decisions regarding the dimensions of the ordinaries are best left to the artist!

Many writers also suggest that only certain of the ordinaries may be cotised. This again seems unreasonably restrictive.

Ordinaries are borne singly unless the arms are subsequently debruised to indicate augmentation, cadency, bastardy, etc. However, several are possessed of diminutives which may be borne in pairs or in any number which cannot be confused with a varied field:

Fess: bar
Pale: pallet
Chevron: chevronel
Bend: bendlet (and bendlet sinister)

The bar also possesses a diminutive, the barrulet, and the bendlet the riband. Narrow versions of the cross, the pall and the saltire are theoretically diminutives but, because of their geometry, can only be borne singly. These are termed the fillet cross, fillet pall and fillet saltire, all of which are rare and rather unattractive.

Several theories regarding the origins of the ordinaries have been propounded, the most popular being that they were simply the decorated raised framework of the early shield. Equally plausible is the suggestion that distinguishing devices first appeared on flags, and that bold rectilinear figures were simple to sew together, were highly effective as a means of identification, and eminently attractive.

Ordinary of Arms An armorial reference book which lists the blazons of shields of arms alphabetically by the charges they contain. Proficiency in the use of blazon is essential if an ordinary is to be used to identify arms.

The best-known ordinary of arms is J.W. Papworth's *Ordinary of British Armorials* (known simply as 'Papworth' by armorists), first published in 1874 and reprinted in 1977.

Oriflamme The sacred flag of the Abbey of St Denis and the battle flag of the kings of France. Last carried in war at the battle of Agincourt (1415), the Oriflamme was a gonfannon of considerable size, with five points, coloured scarlet diapered throughout with flames of gold, fringed and tasselled in green. It is believed to have originated in the tenth century, and to have been destroyed during the French Revolution. One of the few known contemporary illustrations is 'St Augustine, The City of God' (*c.* 1445), a miniature in the Royal Library of Belgium (see *Medieval Miniatures* by L.M.J. Delrisse 1965).

Orle A narrow border running parallel to the edge of the shield but not adjacent to it. A sub-ordinary. In early armory the orle was blazoned *a false escutcheon* or *an escutcheon voided*. It is generally considered to be too narrow to carry charges, but there are rare instances of orles charged with, for example, fleurs-de-lis. Variations of line are also possible but, again, examples are rare.

Minor charges arranged *in orle* follow the inner edge of the bordure rather than the line of the orle. The term *an orle of* (e.g.) *eight Martlets* (meaning *eight Martlets in orle*) is strictly incorrect though widely used. In impaled arms the orle is truncated at the line of impalement, as with the bordure.

The diminutive of the orle is the tressure, which is frequently double. A.C. Fox-Davies (*A Complete Guide to Heraldry*) insists that the tressure is, in effect, an *orle*

Single tressure flory in the Lawrence arms

gemel (i.e. a *pair* of narrow orles), and that it cannot, therefore, be borne singly. However, there are several examples to contradict this and clearly the narrower tressure is better able to accommodate the popular flory (having fleurs-de-lis at the outer edge) and flory counter-flory (ornamented with fleurs-de-lis alternately on either side). A recent example of a single tressure flory is that in the arms of Edward G. Lawrence of London: *Ermine on a Cross Gules a Catherine Wheel Or a Tressure flory Gules counterchanged on the cross Argent*. It will be noticed that a tressure may be superimposed on an ordinary (the cross) as may an orle. The royal arms of Scotland are the best known example of a double tressure flory counter-flory, a device which is strictly controlled because of its royal associations. (The fact that the fleurs-de-lis are not depicted in the central 'void' of a double tressure lends credence to Fox-Davies' suggestion.) As with the orle, the tressure is truncated at a line of impalement and it is a convention that the bend and bend sinister should not surmount it but be confined within it, as within a bordure.

See also SUB-ORDINARY

Ormonde Pursuivant of Arms A Scottish pursuivant of arms prior to 1867. The title was probably created on the elevation of James Stewart, Earl of Ross, second son of King James III, to Duke of Ross and Marquess of Ormonde on 20 January 1487-8.   CJB

Over All *or* **Surtout** Used to describe a charge which is superimposed on other charges.

Overt *see* **Attitude**

Owl Unless otherwise blazoned, the owl is depicted at rest, viewed from the side and guardant.

P

Pakenham Tract *see* **Treatises**

Paladin One of the twelve peers of Charlemagne's household. A paragon of knighthood.

Palatine A term meaning 'of the palace'. In practice a chamberlain or other public officer, sometimes a person with royal privileges or having territorial powers on behalf of his monarch.

Pale An ORDINARY consisting of a broad vertical band in the centre of the shield and normally about one-third of its width. When the pale is cotised it is termed endorsed. The shield may be divided into six (anciently *a Shield of six pieces*) by means of *per fess a Pale counterchanged*. This is a particularly useful device when, for example, a coat of three charges (two and one) requires to be differenced. However, it should be noted that the pale is a charge *upon* the field and should, therefore, be depicted in relief, whilst the per fess line of partition is not. *Quarterly of six*, used to marshal six separate coats in one shield, is not depicted in this way, the two central vertical lines being merely lines of partition. A recent innovation is the Canadian pale — a vertical band occupying the central *half* of the field and named after its incorporation in the Canadian flag in 1965.

> Diminutive: pallet
> Parted field: per pale
> Varied field: paly
> Disposition: in pale
> Inclination: palewise

Palisado Crown *see* **Crest Coronet**

Pall *and* **Pall Reversed** The pall is an ORDINARY consisting of a broad Y, its limbs extending to the edges of the shield. The pall reversed is likewise an ordinary, though it is rare in British armory. A.C. Fox-Davies (*A Complete Guide to Heraldry*) suggests that 'there can be little doubt that originally the pall itself was the heraldic symbol in this country [i.e. England] of an archbishop.' Its shape is certainly that of the PALLIUM, and its application often ecclesiastical. However, the pall and (in particular) the pall reversed are sufficiently rare for their use in non-ecclesiastical armory to be encouraged. By doing so an entirely fresh range of options is available — to signify the amalgamation of three organizations in one, or the confluence of rivers, for example. Neither the cross nor the saltire are exclusively religious symbols, so why then should the pall be considered essentially ecclesiastical? Few examples of the pall reversed exist, that in the arms of Frederick Stewart Hindmarsh of New Zealand (1969) being one of the most recent: *Vert a Pall reversed wavy between three Hinds lodged Argent*.

When all three limbs are couped to conform to the edge of the shield the pall becomes a shakefork. It is in this form that the pall may be depicted as a minor charge, the limbs being couped horizontally or at right angles.

Diminutive: fillet pall or fillet pall reversed

Parted field: tierced in pairle or tierced in pairle reversed

Varied field: none (though there is no reason why there should not be such a field)

Disposition: in pall or in pall reversed

Inclination: pallwise or pallwise reversed (rare)

Pallet The diminutive of the pale.

Pallium An armorial charge in the form of an ecclesiastical vestment, similar in shape to the PALL but with the lower limb couped and fringed. The upper limbs always extend to the corners of the shield, and the pallium is usually edged in gold and charged with crosses fitched to resemble the pins by which it attached to the chasuble. Often blazoned as a pall, which is ambiguous.

Pallium

Paly *see* **Field, Varied**

Paly-bendy *see* **Field, Varied**

Panache A fan of feathers, generally in three rows. Most frequently found in crests.

Pantheon Unlike most other mythical animals the pantheon does not seem to be of great antiquity, nor are there any legends appertaining to it. It is, however, a very decorative creature which appears to have been invented by the heralds of Tudor times, when it was used in a number of grants of arms. A painting in *Prince Arthur's Book* depicts it as a star-spangled hind with a bushy tail like a fox. It gradually deteriorated into a somewhat nondescript creature, but has been used again to great effect in the present day as supporters to the arms of the Atomic Energy Authority, where the points of the stars on the two animals add up to 92, which is the number denoting uranium in the table of physical elements.   MY

Panther

Panther The heraldic panther is always termed incensed, that is with flames issuing from its mouth and ears. It is depicted with spots of various colours on its body, although in appearance it is much like the natural animal. However, this fiery creature seems to derive from a much more peaceful one. In medieval bestiaries it is described as being both beautiful and kind, its body being streaked with a variety of colours. Only the dragon regards it as an enemy. It sleeps for three days after dining, and when it awakes 'a lofty sweet singing comes from his mouth and with the song a most delightful stream of sweet-smelling breath, more grateful than all the blooms of herbs and blossoms of the trees' (*Exeter Book*, translated by Stopford Brooke). All other animals follow the sound because of the sweetness of the scent, except the dragon, who runs away from it and hides in fear, as the smell overcomes it and makes it torpid. The sweet breath depicted streaming from the panther's mouth in early pictures was later changed to fire and smoke.

Another story, told by Pliny, says that the panther entices animals by its sweet breath, but its looks are so hideous that it hides its head until they are near enough for it to spring on them and kill them.

Their many-coloured spots make panthers appropriate supporters for the Painter-Stainers Company in London. A very different panther is a supporter of Henry VIII's third wife, Jane Seymour. This delightful

Pantheon

creature, though blazoned incensed, appears to be much more like the animal in the bestiaries, with breath, not fire, issuing from its mouth and its body striped with various colours, instead of being spotted.

MY

Pantler A medieval domestic office, sometimes rendered as 'panter' or 'panterer'. In 1439 the Duke of Warwick was described as the Hereditary Pantler of England. The office was akin to that of Butler.

Papal Arms The papal arms are borne in front of St Peter's keys saltirewise: that in bend (gold) representing the power of the Church extending to heaven, and that in bend sinister (silver) power over the faithful on earth. The arms are ensigned by the papal tiara as a symbol of dignity (see colour page 135). It is believed that some form of special headgear was worn by the popes from the seventh century. The first crown was added to the papal cap at some time between the ninth and eleventh centuries, and the second at the time of Pope Boniface VIII (1294-1303). Together they came to symbolize temporal and spiritual power. The third crown was added in the early fourteenth century.
Further reading
Galbreath, D.L. (Ed. Briggs) *Papal Heraldry* Heraldry Today, 1972.
Heim, Archbishop Bruno *Heraldry in the Catholic Church* Gerrards Cross (revised 1981).

Papal Orders of Chivalry Papal Orders were re-modelled in 1905 by Pope Pius X. Pronouncement was made with regard to both constitution and precedence. The Order of Christ is the supreme pontifical order and has only one class. The Order of Pius was founded in 1847 by Pius IX. The Order of St Gregory the Great (1831) has two divisions — civil and military. The Order of St Sylvester (formerly the Golden Spur) was established as a military body in 1559, reorganized in 1841, and divided into three classes in 1905. A separate Order of the Golden Spur (or Golden Legion — *Militia Aurata*) was formed at the same time with a single class, and limited to one hundred members. The Venerable Order of the Holy Sepulchre is, strictly speaking, not a papal order, but the pope reserves the right of joint nomination with the Latin patriarch of Jerusalem who is Grand Master.   JC-K
See also KNIGHTHOOD AND CHIVALRY, ORDERS OF
Further reading
Cardinale, Archbishop *Orders of Knighthood, Awards and the Holy See* 1983.

Papellloné *or* **Papillone** Overlapping scales, apparently derived from the wings of the butterfly. *See also* FURS

Parted *see* **Party**

Partition A geometrical shape resulting from the division of a shield or charge by the principal lines of partition.

Partition, Lines of *see* **Lines of Partition**

Parts of the Shield *see* **Shield, Points of the**

Party *or* **Parted** Divided. A term used to describe the division of a field or charge by lines of partition, e.g. party per pale, party per saltire, etc. It is now considered so superfluous, however, the simpler per pale, per saltire, etc. being preferred. A party field is one which is divided by lines of partition. Mantling may be blazoned as party of two colours and/or two metals.

Paschal Lamb *or* **Agnus Dei** A CHRISTIAN SYMBOL. A lamb passant with a halo or nimbus behind the head, and holding a staff at the upper end of which are both a cross and a white pennon charged with a red cross. The nimbus or halo are often themselves charged with a cross formy throughout.

Passant *see* **Attitude**

Passion, Symbols of the *see* **Christian Symbols**

Patent *see* **Letters Patent** *and* **Patent of Arms**

Patent of Arms LETTERS PATENT granting armorial bearings. Often erroneously described as a 'grant of arms'. Usually referred to simply as a patent in armorial circles.

Patriarch Chief or head of a tribe or family. An honorary title for early bishops. In medieval times the title of the Latin bishops of Alexandria, Antioch, Constantinople and Jerusalem.

Patrick's Book *see* **Treatises**

Patrimony *see* **Livery Company, Membership of**

Pavilion *or* **Tabernacle** (i) A circular or rectangular tent supported on a central pole, the canvas or material of the outer skin being of the armorial colours of the occupant and often decorated with personal badges. During the medieval and Tudor periods pavilions were much in evidence at tournaments, pageants, the scenes of diplomatic negotiations and, of course, military camps.
(ii) A tent as an armorial charge, the central pole being visible between the open tent flaps. The tinctures are normally specified and form broad vertical bands of alternating metal and colour. Often depicted with a pennoncelle flying from the head of the tent pole.

263

(iii) A canopy-like structure within which the arms of sovereigns are sometimes displayed in an achievement of arms. Supposedly invented by Philip Moreau in France in the late seventeenth century, but more likely to have originated in seals of the late medieval European sovereigns which depict just such awnings. Widely adopted by the sovereigns of France, Germany and other central European states, but never used by the British monarchy. The pavilion used with the arms of the German Emperors was *Gold semy of Imperial Crowns and Eagles Sable lined Ermine*, ensigned by the Imperial Crown and a banner of the national colours: red, silver and black. That of the kings of France was *Azure semy-de-lis Gold*. The alternative term Tabernacle suggests that the origin of the pavilion was the tent-like drapery surrounding the throne to form a sanctuary in which the sovereign's person was both sacred and inviolable.
See also MANTLE

Pavise *or* **Tallevas** etc. A large standing shield for archer or cross-bowman, often decorated with badges. A paviser was a man who carried the shield for the archer. PG

Pavon *see* **Pennon**

Peacock Depicted facing the dexter with the tail closed. If blazoned 'in his pride' the peacock is shown in the affronty position with the tail displayed.

Pean *see* **Furs**

Pedigree This is the term for a chart, also called a Family Tree, which summarizes the ancestry of a person through his father to his father's father, and in like manner to whatever point in history is appropriate. Because it is concerned with male line descent only, all members of the pedigree will usually carry the same surname, handed down from father to son. It is customary to record the brothers and sisters of each generation, but not to continue their lines down. An

Extended Family Tree shows the descendants from all sons and gives rise to collateral branches. This rapidly produces difficulties in accommodating all the information on one sheet of paper. A good method of solving this problem is to use overlays, of different sizes, bound together at the left in book form, so that the common ancestors remain in view when each collateral branch is laid in turn on top of the lower parts of the tree.

A chart which displays all the direct line ancestors, both male and female, is termed a Birth Brief, Blood Descent or Total Descent, and may be of circular, horizontal or vertical form. Because the number of ancestors doubles in each generation further back, it is usually convenient to record up to five generations on the same sheet. Additional sheets can then be utilized to display the earlier ancestry of a chosen family member in the same way.

Another method of showing relationships is the so-called Paragraph or Narrative Pedigree. The information is displayed by using numbered paragraphs, with a different numbering style for each generation and employing different sized indentations, so that the details of the most recent members of the family are set furthest from the left-hand margin, and siblings are identified by the similarity in style of their identifying numbers and by their equal distance from the margin. This is the method adopted in Burke's *Peerage* and *Landed Gentry*. Whilst overcoming the problems of space when relating collateral lines, it does suffer from the drawback of being less immediately clear than pedigrees in chart form.

In Britain, the only authoritative armorial pedigrees are those of the College of Arms, London, and Lord Lyon in Edinburgh.

The word Pedigree is said to have originated in the earliest form of genealogical table, in which names of forebears were written in groups of circles joined by curved lines which were thought to resemble the imprint of a crane's foot, the French word for which is *pied de gru*. A Crane's Foot surmounted by an Ancient Crown is the badge of the Institute of Heraldic and Genealogical Studies at Canterbury. DJ
See also GENEALOGY AND ARMORY

Pedigrees, Proof and Registration of The College of Arms is the official registry of English, Welsh, Northern Irish and Commonwealth pedigrees, the equivalent in Scotland being the Court of the Lord Lyon. Genealogies are of course recorded in many other places, including the library of the Society of Genealogists, and in reference books such as Burke's *Landed Gentry*. However, pedigrees registered at the College have a special degree of authenticity for reasons which will be explained presently.

A major component of the College's genealogical archives is the series of heraldic VISITATIONS which took place between about 1530 and 1685. There are other important post-visitation categories, such as the pedigrees of peers and baronets, and those with such titles as D14, Arundel, Norfolk and Surrey, as well as the extensive collections left by former heralds which are not classed as official records. Our present concern, however, is with current practice as regards the official registration of pedigrees. These are recorded for three main purposes: to establish a right by descent to an existing coat of arms; to prove a right to a dignity such as a peerage or baronetcy; and simply to record the results of a programme of genealogical research regardless of any entitlement to arms or dignities.

The first step is, of course, the actual research, which may be undertaken by an officer or arms, by the inquirer himself or by a third party. Once the pedigree is considered to be more or less 'finished', it is redrafted in the appropriate form for entry in the College records. In the interest of uniformity, entries follow a standard pattern. There is not space to recount the full procedure here, but a typical sequence would be: (a) full names, (b) place of residence, (c) rank, if appropriate (e.g. knight, baronet, clerk in holy orders), (d) orders (e.g. OBE), (e) decorations (e.g. TD), (f) degrees (e.g. Master of Arts of the University of Bristol), (g) occupation (e.g. barrister at law), (h) date and place of birth or baptism, (i) date and place of death or burial. It is important to note that the *place* of an event must always be given, and this is an element usually lacking in pedigrees published in such works as Burke and Debrett. Sons are traditionally listed before daughters; the date and place of marriage is usually shown in the wife's 'block', and she is further identified by the full names and usual place of residence of her father.

Once the draft pedigree is more or less complete it is sent to the client for careful scrutiny, correction where necessary, and the addition of any missing details, particularly in the later generations. He or she then signs it in the presence of a witness and returns it to the College. It is customary to accept a person's word for details back to his or her grandparents, provided these are known with certainty and supplied in full, but beyond the grandparents, proof is necessary for every item.

The attested pedigree is then 'referred' at a meeting of the College Chapter to two independent examiners, who are normally officers of arms who had no part in the research. The junior examiner subsequently works painstakingly through the pedigree, calling for proof of each item or event, and if he is not satisfied he may call for additional evidence. If one is trying to prove, for example, the parentage of John, son of Thomas Bloggs, it is not sufficient simply to produce an appropriate baptismal entry. The examiner will want to know who undertook the search, whether the registers are complete, whether burials have been examined as well as baptisms, whether other Bloggs families were flourishing in the area at that time, whether the registers of neighbouring parishes and non-conformist records have been searched, whether the subject is mentioned in any wills, and whether his age at death or burial corresponds with his supposed date of birth or baptism. Only when the examiner is thoroughly satisfied that the point has been proved beyond reasonable doubt will he underline it in red ink, which is the signal to the College Registrar that it may be entered in the records. When the junior examiner is satisfied he signs the draft and passes it to the senior examiner, who likewise signs it once he considers everything to be in order.

The draft pedigree is then 'reported' at a subsequent meeting of Chapter, and passed to the Registrar who arranges for it to be engrossed by hand in the official registers of the College.   DHBC

Peerage In the twentieth century, and for some time earlier, the word 'peerage' has been used as a convenient one to describe the British degrees of duke, marquess, earl, viscount and baron. Strictly speaking, the word, as derived from the medieval Latin *paragium*, means simply a company of equals. A bishop, for example, had his peers in other bishops, a feudal tenant his peers in others of like station. However, the word 'peers' was soon employed to describe those senior barons of England who were accustomed to receive a writ of summons to parliament, and first occurs in 1321 in the records of the proceedings against the Despencers.

The term 'peers' is also used to describe the 'lords spiritual' — the two archbishops and twenty-four senior diocesan bishops of the Church of England. These dignitaries, together with temporal peers and peeresses in their own right (except Irish peers) may, since 1963, sit in the House of Lords. (It may be noted at this point that under the 1963 Peerage Act peerages may be disclaimed.) It is important to recognize that the British peerage is, in fact, five separate peerages, those of England, Scotland, Ireland, Great Britain and the United Kingdom. The first two mentioned continued until 1707, when the two countries were joined by the Act of Union. The separate peerages were then combined as the Peerage of Great Britain. The separate peerage of Ireland continued until 1801, when a further Act of Union saw the now combined peerages of the countries termed 'of the United Kingdom'. The peerage of Ireland did not entirely disappear after 1801 and occasionally creations are made in that dignity, but the recipients do not as of right sit in the House of Lords. However, if an Irish peer holds a rank of a lower grade than his senior title, and which allows him to take a seat in the House of Lords, then he may be admitted within the dignity of the lesser rank.

In the Scottish peerage there is no title of 'baron', the equivalent rank being termed a 'lord of parliament' (*see* BARONAGE OF SCOTLAND).   JC-K/SS

See also HONOURS AND INVESTITURE *and* ROBES
Further reading
Cokayne, G.E. *The Complete Peerage* 1910 (reprinted 1984).
Gadd, R.P. *Peerage Law* 1985.
— *The Peerage of Ireland* 1985.
Leeson, F. and C.J. Parry *A Directory of British Peerages* 1984.
Pine, L.G. *New Extinct Peerage 1884-1971* 1972.

Peerage, Disclaiming and Surrender of A peerage of the United Kingdom may, under the Peerage Act of 1963, be disclaimed. However, there remains the unanswered question of whether a former peer may retain the use of his armorial supporters having divested himself of 'all right or interest to or in the peerage and the precedence attaching thereto.' The grant of supporters to a peer specifically states that they shall be inherited by those upon whom the peerage shall descend, and there is no provision in law by which an armiger may disclaim part of his inherited arms, even though he may disclaim the peerage by which he has obtained them.

The surrender of a peerage up to the time of Charles I was not at all unusual. A few examples will illustrate the point: in 1232 the Earldom of Leicester was conferred on Simon de Montfort on the resignation of his brother Amaury; in 1493 the Dukedom and Marquessate of Suffolk (but not the Earldom) were surrendered by Michael de la Pole; in 1660 the Earldom of Buckingham and the Viscountcy of Purbeck were surrendered by Robert Villiers. In the twentieth century, three examples of disclaimer are the Viscountcy of Stansgate (Anthony Wedgwood Benn, 1963), the Earldom of Home (Sir Alec Douglas-Home, later Lord Home of the Hirshel, 1963), and the Barony of Beaverbrook (Sir Max Aitken, 1964).

Peer, Introduction of *see* **Honours and Investiture**

Pegasus The beautiful flying horse of Greek mythology was captured by Bellerophon, the hero of Corinth, when it came down to drink from the spring at Pirene. The gods helped Bellerophon to tame and use the spirited Pegasus and, rising into the air on his winged steed, Bellerophon destroyed the monster, Chimera, with his bow and arrows. Later he incurred the wrath of the gods by attempting to fly to heaven on Pegasus. Zeus sent a gadfly to sting the horse, which cast off his rider and then flew to the stables of Zeus, whose thunder chariot he has drawn ever since.

At one time Mount Helicon began to rise, but Pegasus kicked it to stop it, and from the side of the mountain the waters of the fountain Hippocrene gushed forth.

Pegasus has become the symbol of fame, eloquence and contemplation, and thus is a worthy emblem to be used in heraldry. He was the badge of the Knights Templar, and is to be found in the arms of the Inner Temple.   MY

Pelican The heraldic pelican is transformed from the clumsy natural bird into one of great beauty and religious significance. It is sometimes depicted like an eagle, and sometimes more like a swan, and although it always has a much longer beak than either of these two birds, this is much more slender and graceful than that of the real bird.

It was once believed that although pelicans were extremely devoted to their young, these would rebel against their father and provoke his anger, whereupon he would strike back and kill them. Three days later the mother bird would return to the nest, and piercing her own breast would bring them back to life by pouring her blood on them. Thus the pelican became the mystic emblem of Christ, whose blood was shed for mankind. It is the symbol of charity, love and piety.

There are armorial terms which apply only to the pelican who is depicted with her wings raised, her neck embowed, pecking at her own breast, from which drops of blood are falling. In this posture the bird is blazoned as 'vulning herself'. But if she is standing on her nest and nourishing her babies with her blood she is described as being 'in her piety'.

Pelican vulning herself

The pelican is used quite frequently in armory both in the arms and as the crest. Its association with Christ makes it a particularly appropriate charge in the arms of the two colleges of Corpus Christi, one at Oxford and the other at Cambridge. At Oxford the shield is divided into three and on the dexter part is a pelican vulning herself. At Cambridge the shield is quartered, the first and fourth quarters bearing a pelican in her piety for Christ. MY

Pellet, Gunstone *or* **Ogress** A black roundel. Derived from an ancient cannon-ball: Chaucer uses the word in 'As swift as pelet out of gonne.' The alternative term ogress may have been fourteenth-century slang, but its origin is uncertain.

Pellety Semy of pellets.

Pendant An ornament or device hung from a chain round the neck.

Pendent (i) In armory: dependent or hanging from.
(ii) Pendent, pendant: alternative spellings for pennant, a nautical flag. (Always pronounced 'pennant' irrespective of spelling.)

Pennant A generic term applied to any tapering nautical flag. This may be long and narrow, swallow-tailed or blunt-ended. Personal armorial pennants bear the arms in the hoist. Livery pennants are divided of the livery colours and charged with the badge.
See also FLAG

Penner and Inkhorn A charge consisting of a stylized pen case and ink bottle joined by a cord.

Pennon (i) A medium-sized personal flag, about three feet (1 metre) in length, swallow-tailed or triangular, charged with the arms and carried on a staff by medieval military commanders below the rank of banneret. Like the banner, the pennon indicated the physical presence of an armiger. Unanticipated promotion on the field of battle to the rank of banneret could be signified by the removal of the pennon's tails to form a small banner (banneret). Both Sir John Chandos (1367) and Sir Thomas Trivet (1380) were

promoted in this way. A pavon pennon is triangular with a right-angle at its lower edge adjacent to the staff.
(ii) A livery pennon is similar to the personal pennon in size and shape but is charged with a livery badge on a field of the livery colours.
(iii) A military pennon (naval pennant) is similar in form to the armorial pennon but is used to signify the presence of a military or naval commander, e.g. the white swallow-tailed pennant with red upper and lower borders of a squadron commander in the Royal Navy. Some yacht clubs use a nautical pennant to denote the presence of a senior official.
See also FLAG

Pennoncelle, Pencell *or* **Pensell** A small pennon, usually no more than 18 inches (45 cm) in length, triangular or swallow-tailed and carried at the head of a lance. There are three types:
(i)Personal, charged with the arms.
(ii) Livery, charged with a livery badge on a field of the livery colours.
(iii) As (ii) above, but without a device and divided, usually per fess, of the livery colours. Familiar as a lance-head flag used by cavalry.
See also FLAG

Perched *see* **Attitude**

Per *see* **Field, Parted**

Petardier A medieval grenade comprising a petard filled with inflammable materials and explosives which was thrown in the face of the enemy. When it exploded prematurely, the unfortunate soldier would be 'hoisted with his own petard'.

Petra Sancta A seventeenth-century Jesuit writer on armory, who devised a system of hatching to represent the armorial tinctures. Hatching is generally reserved for uncoloured illustrations where an indication of the tinctures is considered essential and 'tricking' inappropriate (*see* TRICK). A knowledge of hatching is essential in the identification of armorial silverware, bookplates and carvings in wood and stone, where this method has frequently been employed. The tinctures were entirely ignored in all matters of handicraft until the seventeenth century, and it is doubtful if hatching has ever been used in official armorial records. There is general agreement with regard to the method of depicting the common tinctures, but not to the treatment of the so-called stains, and they are shown overleaf in a manner which conforms to the majority (though certainly not all) of the heraldic reference books.

Petra Sancta

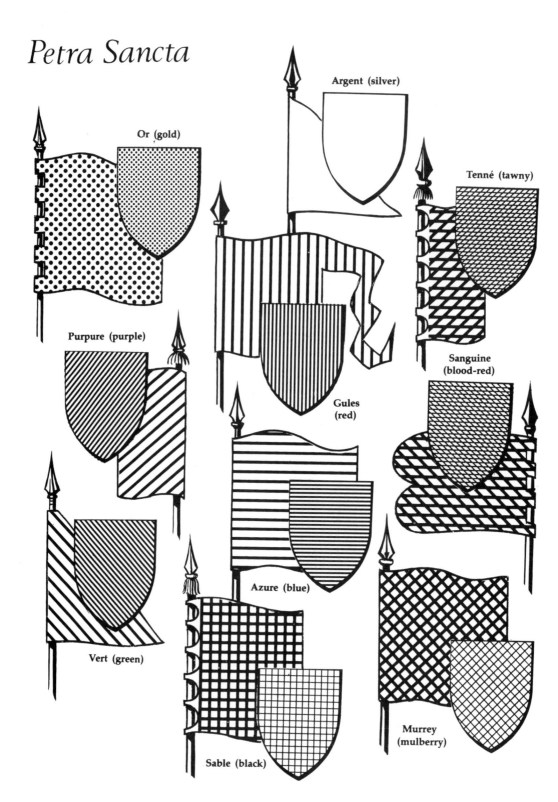

Argent (silver)

Or (gold)

Tenné (tawny)

Sanguine
(blood-red)

Purpure (purple)

Gules
(red)

Vert (green)

Azure (blue)

Sable (black)

Murrey
(mulberry)

Pewter Touch Marks Pewter is an alloy of tin with lead or other metal.

In the year 1348, a number of reputable pewter-makers, anxious to maintain the high standards of their craft, formed themselves into a guild which for 150 years regulated the lead content in pewter. Legislation was later introduced stating that each pewterer should have his own distinguishable mark, which was to be officially recorded on a 'touch plate' lodged at the Pewterers' Hall. Unfortunately, the original plates were lost during the Great Fire of London in 1666. A new series of plates was struck in 1668, with many established pewter-makers re-striking their touches.

A touch mark should not be confused with a hallmark found on silver and other precious metals. A pewter mark usually consists of the maker's name and place of manufacture and some form of pictorial device. The earlier examples of touches were usually small, often within a palmate or beaded border.

Many heraldic devices are incorporated into these touches, and lions, roses, eagles, coronets, griffins, stars, crosses and fleurs-de-lis are quite common. Coats of arms are also to be found, as well as numerous rebuses; for example, Samuel Cox had two cockerels, George Bacon a pig, John Belson a bell over a sun. Samuel Hancock had a cockerel resting on a hand, and a man in the act of bowling was used by Henry Bowler. BC

Further reading
Cotterell, L. *Old Pewter, Its Makers and Marks* 1929.
MacDonald-Taylor, M. *A Dictionary of Marks* 1962.

Pheon An arrowhead with the barbs engrailed on the inner edge. Borne with the point downwards unless otherwise specified.
See also BROAD ARROWHEAD

Phoenix The splendour of the phoenix is said to be greater than the eagle, although in modern heraldry the legendary phoenix is very much the same as the eagle of nature. In earlier times it appeared to be more like a peacock, with a crest of feathers on its head and a long sweeping tail, and in this form it is found in the London Blacksmiths' Company's Charter of 1571. It is always shown as rising from flames. Like the eagle it was a bird of the sun and was believed to be reddish purple in colour. In classic times it was the emblem of people in Paradise who enjoyed eternal youth.

The phoenix was thought to live until it was five hundred years old, when it became young again. Only one was alive at any one time. It lived in Egypt but when its time came for renewal it flew to Arabia and hid itself in a nest it made of the rarest sweet-smelling spices, which rose in flames when fanned by the bird's wings in the heat of the sun. The bird was burnt to ashes, but after three days a small worm appeared which gradually grew and became the new phoenix, fresh in life and vigour. This became an obvious symbol of resurrection and immortality in Christianity. The phoenix was used as a badge by King Henry VII of England and later by his grand-daughter Queen Elizabeth I. It was also a badge of Mary Queen of Scots. A phoenix in flames was painted as a symbol for Jeanne d'Arc in the Gallery of the Palais Royale in Paris with the motto 'Her death itself will make her live.'
MY

Pierced *see* **Attributes**

Piety, in its *see* **Attitude**

Pile An armorial charge composed of a triangular 'wedge' normally depicted as issuing from the top of the shield, or, when so blazoned, from the sides or base (fig.1).

The pile is generally classified as an ORDINARY, but possesses few of the characteristics or functions of the ordinary as here defined. However, it is frequently encountered as a principal charge.

Early piles were evidently variations of the pale or pallet and were depicted singly, or in twos or (most often) threes, always issuing from the top of the shield and converging in the base following the tapering of the shield. They were exceedingly graceful, for example the *Or three Piles Azure* of Sir Guy de Bryan (fig.2).

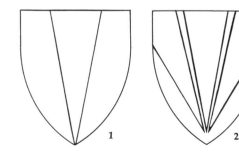

1   2

Pile

3

However, as the result of two entirely unrelated developments, the pile was to become one of the least attractive armorial figures. As armorial design became more complex, so the geometry of the pile altered to accommodate an increasing number of minor charges. It grew shorter and wider until, by the Victorian period, it was hardly distinguishable from *per chevron reversed*. When more than one pile was depicted, the blazon often had to include the term 'in point' in order to differentiate between the medieval converging piles and the new variety of stubby, erect triangles. The second development concerned the chief, many of which were indented, often to indicate differencing, and of these several were erroneously translated into three piles, again of the ugly vertical type (fig.3).

There can be little doubt that piles which 'issue' from the sides of the shield or so-called pily fields (e.g. barry pily, pily bendy, etc.) are likewise developments of early misinterpretations of indented lines of partition, and have little affinity with the true pile.

An interesting variant, not uncommon in Britain, is the *two piles in chief and one in base* disposition, e.g. *Erminois three Piles Azure two issuant from chief and one in base each charged with a Leopard's Face Or* (Shropshire County Council).

When a single pile issues from base (i.e. reversed or transposed) it should always be depicted in relief and narrower than the per chevron partition with which it may be confused.

Charges are sometimes blazoned as 'pilewise' or 'in pile', in which case they follow the geometry of the pile. There is no diminutive of the pile.

Pily, Pily bendy etc. *see* **Field, Varied**

Pinsel *or* **Pinsil** In Scotland, a triangular flag containing the crest within a strap and buckle bearing the motto, and within a gold circlet inscribed with the Chief or Baron's title, ensigned with a coronet or cap. In the fly, which is of the livery colours, is the plant badge and a scroll having the slogan or motto. Used by a Chief's local commander or *Tosheadeor* exercising his authority in the absence of the Chief. In his book *Heraldic Standards and Other Ensigns* Lt Col Robert Gayre suggests that the length of the pinsel is 4½ feet (1.5 m). CJB

See also FLAG

Pipe Banner In Scotland, a small banner suspended from the drone pipe of bagpipes. Correctly, this should be emblazoned with the arms throughout of the Chief, or, in the case of military pipes, the company commander. The use of any other device is considered to be improper.

Pizzled *see* **Attributes**

Plantagenet The name given to the House of Anjou and to the Angevin kings of England who reigned from 1154 to 1399. The Plantagenet device was the punning *planta genista* or broom pod, and their colours white and red, later the tinctures of the opposing roses in the civil wars of the fifteenth century, in which the last descendants of the Plantagenets fought each other to extinction. The last English king of Plantagenet descent was Richard III, killed at Bosworth Field in 1485.

Further reading
Tuxton, W.H. *The Plantagenet Ancestry* London, 1928 (reprinted 1984).

Planta Genista A sprig of the broom plant depicted with leaves and open pods. See also PLANTAGENET

Plate A silver disc. Like the bezant, the plate probably originated as coinage — the coins of ancient Barbary and Spain were known as plates.

Platinum The marks for platinum are similar to those for sterling silver, except that the lion passant or other sterling mark is replaced by an orb surmounted by a cross and encompassed by a pentagon. The town mark remains the same as for silver.
See also HALLMARK

Platy *or* **Platé** Semy of plates.

Plenipotentiary An envoy or ambassador representing his sovereign ruler, and with full discretionary powers.

Plenitude, in her *see* **Attributes**

Plumed *see* **Attributes**

Plumeté, Plumetty *or* **Plumette** A pattern of over-lapping feathers. *See also* FURS

Point (i) *See* ABATEMENT.
(ii) When unqualified, the term implies the base of the shield.
(iii) Piles are said to be 'in point' when their points meet.

Poland, Armorial Practice It is a characteristic of Polish heraldry that whole groups — or clans — of the *szlachta* (hereditary nobles), although of different family names, frequently share undifferenced arms. Each such is called a *herb* (from the Czech word *erb*, German *erbe* or *erben*, meaning 'to inherit'). In the Polish sense it simply means a particular coat of arms or blazon. Each *herb* has its own name, and in many cases this is identical with a clan's pre-heraldic war cry (or *proclamatio*) which, in turn, would appear to be derived from the name of an ancestor or place name which served as a species of clan name. In other words, the names of most *herbs* are based upon *proclamationes* which, in turn, were of ancestral or regional origin.

Examples of well-known *herbs* are: *Trąby* (fig.1), meaning Horns — although in this case the *proclamatio* was Brezezina; *Jastrzębiec*, Sparrowhawk (see colour page 52) and *Lis*, Fox (fig.2). Other names have no such linear significance, as with *Gozdawa* (*Gules a Fleur-de-lis Argent*) and *Pomian* (*Or the Head of an Ox caboshed Sable transfixed with a Sword bendwise point downwards proper*); in the latter case *Pomian* is an old Slavonic first name and is a good example of how a *proclamatio* has been preserved as the *herb* name. By and large, linear and chromatic characteristics remain constant, although some rare modifications are known within a given *herb*.

The use of the same arms by families of different surname apparently stemmed frequently from the necessity for branches of common male-line descent to differentiate the one from the other. This they did by adopting a territorial designation in their name in the sense of being 'of' this or that among their estates; and so the frequent suffix of —ski or —cki, as in Czosnowski, meaning 'of Czosnowo', a property near Warsaw. On the other hand, not all names with such suffixes signify designation by estate. Some, such as Wolski and Górski ('of Wola' and 'of Góra' respectively) refer not to family properties but simply to place names. As a result such families can only be identified if one knows their original heraldic clan or *herb*.

The situation is complicated by same-name families bearing two or more *herbs*. Such came about, for example, at the Union of Horolds, 1413, between the Kingdom of Poland and the Grand Duchy of Lithuania, upon the final Christianization of the latter when the Lithuanian-Bylorussian Bojars were adopted into Polish *herbs* (as with the families of Radziwell and Saphia). This pattern was followed, for instance, by the newly ennobled Laczynskis. Such apparently was the result of a decision to ally themselves with families of a different *herb* for various reasons, as when the Laczynskis received in 1574 permission from Albert Czarnkowski to be adopted into the *Herb Nalecz* (*Gules a Bandeau with two tails Argent*), confirmed by King Stephen Batory on 2 January 1580. Indeed, entry into a clan through marriage, adoption (for centuries the normal way of acquiring noble status) or military service within a particular clan were methods of admission, all known to history.

In a sense, these arrangements all contain characteristics of a clan system, as was also demonstrated at the decisive battle of Grunweld in 1410 against the Teutonic Knights, when members of particular *herbs* fought under banners of their arms (*herbs*).

However, there are obvious radical Polish peculiarities, quite apart from the fact that those bearing one undifferenced *herb* are *not* organized into tribo-feudal groupings under duly recognized Chiefs — as with Scots, for example.

A further distinguishing attribute of Polish heraldry is its extreme simplicity of design. Ordinaries, sub-ordinaries and lines of partition are extremely rare. One or two charges is all one expects to find in typically Polish arms. Arrows, horseshoes, different crosses and charges peculiar to the Polish system, at times alone, upon other occasions in combination with another charge, is an arrangement found again and again. In some cases, the designs are based upon pre-heraldic marks of property, which were transformed into arms in the thirteenth and fourteenth centuries when the old clans adopted heraldic insignia under the influence, by way of Silesia, of Western chivalry.

In short, such clan characteristics as pertain to Polish heraldry have military rather than social orientations. Accordingly, one should not press too far the analogy with such highly developed clan systems as that of the Scots.   CS

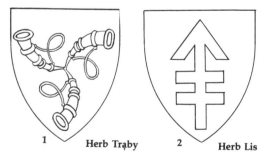

1   **Herb Trąby**   2   **Herb Lis**

Poleyne Knee guard.

Police Although many of Britain's police forces are not armigerous, and for that reason use the standard star and Royal Cypher device on uniforms, vehicles, etc., an increasing number are obtaining arms, and the public relations officers at regional headquarters are generally pleased to provide illustrated information in response to enquiries from armorists. The uniform currently worn by the British police was standardized by the Home Office in 1934, though regional variations of helmet and insignia are permitted.

The armorial bearings of several police authorities are clearly indicative of amalgamations of earlier forces, reflected in the charges and composition of the arms. Many were granted shields of arms without crest or supporters, that of the Leicester and Rutland Constabulary, for example: *Per fess Azure and Vert on a Fess Argent between in chief two Cinquefoils pierced Ermine and in base a Horseshoe Or a Fox courant proper*, which contains elements from the former forces of Leicester City (the cinquefoil of the Beaumont earls), Rutland (the gold horseshoe), and Leicestershire (the fox). Only six years after these arms were granted, local government reorganization in 1974 resulted in the formation of an entirely new force (the Leicestershire Constabulary), and the new authority was permitted to retain the earlier shield of arms on payment of the necessary fees.

The uniform of the Leicestershire Constabulary also provides a good example of applied armory: the arms appear in white metal on the uniform collar, at the centre of the star-shaped helmet-plate and in the centre of the cap badge. As with most forces, there is a distinctive cap badge for senior officers comprising a circlet of blue enamel inscribed in silver and with the arms on an eight-pointed star surmounted by a crown. The ranks of constable and sergeant wear a white metal circlet bearing the force title, within which is the shield ensigned by a crown. The arms are also displayed on patrol vehicles, stationery, premises, etc. Armorial bearings which include a crest have been granted to several police authorities, and some also possess supporters. Two Alsatian dogs support the arms of the former Nottinghamshire Combined Police Authority, and the hart and ox supporters in the arms of the Thames Valley Police are gorged with blue and white duty arm bands. The livery colours of the City of London are used by the City of London Police, who wear red and white duty arm bands. The blue and white check cap bands, which are now used by English and Welsh police forces, as well as in Scotland where they originated, appear in the arms of the Scottish Lothians and Border Police in the form of a saltire chequy. All Scottish police forces wear the same cap badge of a crowned thistle and motto 'Semper Vigilo', and the Royal Crown of Scotland is used as a rank badge by senior officers. Unlike the ambulance services, which now use a uniform crown badge (*see*

PUBLIC SERVICES), several police authorities have obtained grants of badges which are both more appropriate than shields of arms and better suited to display within the standard star. However, some of these, such as that of the West Midlands Police Authority, are simply circular versions of the arms within a distinctive roundel: *On a Bezant between two Bars vallary as many Barrulets dancetty of three points interlaced Sable the whole environed by an Annulet embattled at the outer edge Gold*. Others are more imaginative; for example the *Mullet Argent fimbriated Azure behind a Crown Palisado Or* of the Thames Valley Police, and the cap badge of the UK Atomic Energy Authority Police, *a Lion passant guardant Gules supporting a Pile Sable*, granted with arms to the Authority in 1955. Palisado and vallary crowns, and vallary (also urdy) variations of line are particularly popular in the armory of police authorities, undoubtedly because of their defensive and protective connotations: the arms of the West Midlands Police Authority include both a field of two bars vallary and a crown vallary in the crest.

Mottoes are, for the most part, self-explanatory: 'Always Vigilant', 'Protect And Serve', etc. Both Welsh and Gaelic are also used, the motto of the North Wales Police being 'Goreu Camp Cadw' (The best feat of arms is to guard) for example.

The compartments of both the Metropolitan Police and the Police Federation contain paving stones, indicative of the policeman 'pounding the beat', and the arms of the latter include bees, symbolic of vigilance and derived from the personal arms of Sir Robert Peel who, as Prime Minister, founded the world-famous Metropolitan force in 1829. The arms of the 'Met' contain both the portcullis of the City of Westminster and a double tressure flory counter flory similar to that in the royal arms of Scotland, though argent, and a reference to the force's home at Scotland Yard.

Sharp-eyed armorists may also spot one of the many ingenious (though strictly unheraldic) ties sported by members of the various specialist police groups when off duty; for example, members of the Obscene Publications Squad wear ties charged with a pair of scissors cutting through the blue pages of a book.   SS

Political Symbols In modern times combats occur not between knights in armour with emblazoned shields, but between political parties and movements with badges, stickers and logos; but nevertheless fixed symbols and colours still play an important part in political life.

Modern political symbols are often used as lapel badges, car-stickers (decals), insignia on leaflets and other printed material, and in many countries in the form of flags. In Britain there is a long-standing

The elaborate patent of arms of the Police Federation, granted in 1982: *Per pale Gules and Vert a Balance between three Bees volant Or.* **At the top are the achievements of the Earl Marshal, the Sovereign and the College of Arms, complete with supporters, and to the right those of the granting kings of arms: Cole, Garter; Wagner, Clarenceux; Brooke-Little, Norroy and Ulster.**

tradition of the use of 'campaign colours' by the parties, which are used in rosettes and favours and as the colour scheme for literature. The Conservatives are today associated with the colour blue (hence the expression 'True Blue'), the Labour Party with red, and the Alliance parties with gold, the Liberals' orange colour dating back to the Reform Act of 1832. The Red Flag of socialism is perhaps the best-known political flag, and one which has formed the basis of several national flags.

Among the best known political symbols in history have been the Tricolor cockade of the French Revolution, the Red Star of the Russian Revolution, the *fasces* (the badge of Italian fascism), the Jewish Shield of David, and the Crescent and Star which has often been used to represent Moslems. The Nazi swastika was once equally well-known.

Symbols that have become popular in modern times

273

include the flaming torch (often held by a muscular hand), broken or linked chains, the cogwheel (denoting industry), and the hoe (a popular emblem in Africa denoting agriculture). A more sinister article is the Kalashnikov rifle, which has replaced the heraldic sword; and a more peaceful one, the well-known symbol of unilateral nuclear disarmament.

Some political symbols become the national emblems of their country. Examples are the elephant, which represents the dominant parties in Guinea and the Ivory Coast; the spread eagle of the Egyptian revolution of 1952 (now used in the arms of Egypt and of many other African countries); and the flaming torch emblem of the *Mouvement Populaire de Libération* of Zaire, which now features on the flag of that country. Some political emblems have still to make this transition and are used by movements still campaigning for freedom and self-determination, such as the four-spoked wheel of the African National Congress, or the rising sun of the Tamil Separatists. These may one day be transformed from political badges to national emblems. WGC

Polled *see* **Attributes**

Pomeis, Pomey *or* **Pomme** A green roundel. The term is derived from the French *pomme*, meaning apple. It has been argued that the singular form is correctly pomme, pomeis being the plural.

Pommé Descriptive of an armorial charge, usually a cross, having each limb ending in a ball.

Pommell The boss as the end of the hilt of a dagger or sword. These were often embellished with armorial devices.

Pommelled *see* **Attributes**

Pommety Semy of pomeis.

Pontiff A bishop. The pope is sometimes referred to as the 'sovereign pontiff'.

Pope The bishop of Rome as head of the Roman Catholic Church. A parish priest of the Greek Church in Russia and Serbian countries.

Popinjay A parrot. When depicted with green feathers and red beak and legs it is said to be proper.

Portcullis Usually depicted with four horizontal and five vertical bars with points, it was originally a Beaufort badge adopted by Henry VII. When chains ending in rings are attached, it is blazoned 'chained'. A crowned portcullis is the badge of the Palace of Westminster.

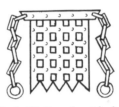

Portcullis Pursuivant badge

Portcullis Pursuivant of Arms in Ordinary Named from the *Portcullis chained Or* badge of the Beauforts, and a favourite device of Henry VII, whose mother was Lady Margaret Beaufort. The office was instituted *c.* 1485, probably at the time of Henry's coronation. The badge of office is very similar to that of Somerset Herald, the latter being ensigned with the Royal Crown.

Portugal, Armorial Practice The ancient kingdom of Portugal was rich in the practices of chivalry, and a controlling body of heralds was established by King Joao I (John) in the fourteenth century. Before that time the assumption of arms was an entirely private affair. With the coming of regulation, only nobles were allowed the use of metals in their arms, and in 1512 King Manoel I decreed that untitled families not classed as noble were forbidden to display arms. There was some relaxation later, and it was judged that arms descended to all heirs in blood of an armiger's family, so individuals were free to display the arms of any of their true ancestors. With the coming of the Republic in 1910, the heralds were disbanded and the control of personal arms ceased, though corporate armory is supervized by the Heraldic Commission of the Associação dos Arqueàlogos Portugueses. There remain several bodies interested in heraldry, of which the most notable is the Instituto Heráldica de Portuguese (*see* ADDRESSES). A useful volume, *Manuel de Heráldica Portuguesa*, appeared in 1940. JC-K

Portugal, Royal Arms of *Argent five Escutcheons in cross Azure each charged with five Plates in saltire all within a Bordure Gules charged with seven Castles Or.*

Postcards Amongst the subjects printed on postcards since the late nineteenth century, armorial devices continue to be very popular. As they are extremely colourful, some printers and publishers have been able to experiment with metallic inks. One of the most popular and highly collectable series of heraldic postcards was published by the Halifax firm of Stodart & Co. Ltd, in their *Ja Ja* series. The cards were printed in full colour, including gold and silver, on a white ground with the arms contained in an ornate gold border.

An interesting heraldic series was produced by S. Oates & Co. of Halifax, in conjunction with the ornamental porcelain producers, William Henry Goss Ltd. The cards presumably acted as advertisements for these small 'crested' pottery items which were produced in large quantities at the Falcon Pottery, Stoke on Trent. Goss cards offer the collector a wide range of arms, crests and seals, both British and foreign.

Postcards depicting the arms of the Oxford and Cambridge colleges were produced by various printers and publishers. A fine series entitled *Arms of the Oxford Colleges*, and a second series depicting a view of each college as well as the coat of arms, was published by Alfred Savage Ltd. Many other publishers issued cards depicting the university arms surrounded by those of the colleges, including a set by the London firm of E. Wrench Ltd.

Each card in the Twiss Bros.' *County Arms* series displays a local view above two coats of arms, the one on the left being the arms of the county, the one on the right the appropriate town arms.

Amongst family heraldry, Scottish clan tartans and badges were produced on a wide scale. W. & A.K. Johnston of Edinburgh were famed for their *Clansman* series depicting a tartan strip and the appropriate clan crest. Johnstons also produced two other similar series, one showing the arms of the clan and a map showing its location on a tartan background, the other simply a tartan background on which was displayed the relevant clan badge. Both Stodart and Brown & Rawcliffe published postcards of tartan backgrounds, overprinted with clan crests and civic arms respectively. R. Tuck & Sons produced four different series entitled *Scottish Clans*, each card depicting the clan seat and coat of arms on the relevant tartan background.

Other armorial postcards produced during the Edwardian period include ecclesiastic arms, civic heraldry and some quaint forms of rustic heraldry such as the Moonrakers' badge, and the arms of the Yorkshiremen, which depicts a flea, fly, magpie and flitch of bacon.

Regimental badges proved a very popular subject for the postcard producer, the best known of which was the Aldershot publisher and printer, Gale & Polden Ltd. Their fine series of *Regimental Badges* covers in excess of a hundred badges. An unusual series of embossed regimental badges was produced by Birn Bros Ltd, of London.

Silk embroidered cards often bore regimental badges or flags. These cards were only made during the years of the First World War, and many were made in France by women as a cottage industry. Today some of these highly coloured cards, with their poignant messages, badges and other forms of insignia, still command a high price in the auction room or the postcard dealer's shop.   BC

Potent Crutch-shaped (OE = a crutch). (i) A variety of the armorial fur vair (*see* FURS).

(ii) A cross potent has crutch-shaped limbs (*see* CROSS).

Potenty (i) An ornamental variation of line (*see* LINES, VARIED).

(ii) A variation of the fur potent, the tinctures of which have to be specified (*see* FURS).

Precedence, Order of The placing of persons in order of degree or rank within society. In the United Kingdom, 'Tables of Precedence' exist which clearly list the placing in society held by members of the Royal Family, members of the Church, the peerage, nobility and knighthood, the judiciary, etc. Tables of General Precedence may deal separately with England, Scotland and other countries within the Commonwealth, and can be further divided into tables for both ladies and gentlemen.

Although importance is still given to placing the above persons in a correct order at formal and ceremonial functions (especially at court), the tables of precedence are much less complex than they were in former times. Attempts at regulating position at court and in society had been attempted by various monarchs since the fourteenth century, but it was not until 1539 that an act was passed defining precedence in England. Since that date other statutes have been added to include new degrees of rank.   SS
Further reading
Debrett's Peerage for Tables of Precedence and Precedence in Scotland.
Complete Peerage Vol.I, App. C for Precedence of Peers in Parliament by Royal Prerogative.
Complete Peerage Vol.I, App. D for Precedence Anomalously Allowed.
Squibb, G.D. *Precedence in England and Wales* Oxford, 1981.

Precedence, Royal Warrant of A Royal Warrant of Precedence varies the normal rules of honour. If a peer succeeds to a peerage from someone other than his father, he may petition the Crown through the Secretary of State for the Home Department for a royal warrant to allow his brothers and sisters to be styled by a courtesy title according to rank (e.g. Lord, Lady or

Honourable), as if their father had succeeded to the peerage. Included in the royal warrant is an order by the sovereign to the Earl Marshal to direct that the royal warrant is recorded at Her Majesty's College of Arms.   HPB

Premier Peer The name given to the living holder of the oldest established peerage of each rank.

The premier royal dukedom is that of Cornwall, created on 17 March 1337.

The premier dukedom is Norfolk of the creation of 1514, but with precedence of 1397. The explanation for this is that the Howard family was first granted the dukedom of Norfolk on 28 June 1483, but after the battle of Bosworth in 1485 the duke, being a prominent Yorkist, was stripped of his honours. Then, on 1 February 1513/14, the family regained the title with precedence over any previous duke of Norfolk. In practice this meant 29 September 1397, the date on which an ancestor of the Howards (Thomas Mowbray) had been created the first duke. The Mowbray dukedom became extinct on 16-17 January 1475/76.

The premier marquessate of England is that of Winchester, which dates from 12 October 1551.

The premier earldom on the roll is that of Shrewsbury, dating from 20 May 1442. However, the distinction of 'premier earl' is accorded to the later dukes of Norfolk by virtue of their descent from Philip (Howard) Earl of Surrey, who in 1580 inherited the medieval earldom of Arundel, which is deemed to be more anciently granted than 1442, and hence is the 'premier earldom'.

The premier viscountcy is Hereford (2 February 1549/50), barony is De Ros (14 December 1264), and baronetcy (which is *not* in fact of peerage rank) is that of Bacon, and dates from 22 May 1611. The premier baronet of the UK creation is de Saumarez (1801).

The Duke of Hamilton (1643) and Brandon (1711) is the premier peer of Scotland; the premier marquess is Huntly (1599); the earl is Mar (1404); the 'Earl on the Union Roll' is Crawford and Balcarres (1651); the premier viscountcy is that of Fentoun (1606) held by the Earl of Mar and Kellie; and the premier lord of Scotland is Forbes (1442 or earlier). For Ireland, the Duke of Leinster is premier duke (1766), marquess (1761), and earl (1316). The premier baron, with precedence of 1397, is Kinsale.   JC-K

Pretence, In *see* **Escutcheon of Pretence**

Preying *see* **Attitude**

Pride, in its *see* **Attitude**

Prince A term of rank applied at different periods to monarchs, sovereigns, rulers and kings, as well as provincial governors, senior commanders, chiefs, or

any person pre-eminent in a specified class. Gradually, in medieval times, the title was allowed to rulers of principalities bearing feudal allegiance to a king or emperor. The title came to be used by the male members of royal families; in Great Britain by the sons and grandsons of the king or regnant queen. In the Holy Roman Church the title is applied to cardinals, and in the English Church to archbishops and certain bishops.   JC-K

Princess A female sovereign, the wife of a prince, a daughter of a sovereign, and a daughter of a sovereign's son.

Principal Charge The most prominent charge (or group of charges) on a shield of arms, and that first mentioned in a blazon following the description of the field and any semy charges thereon.

Principe (fem. Princesa) The heir(ess) apparent to the throne of Spain or Portugal.

Privy Councillor A member of Her Majesty's Most Honourable Privy Council, an institution of central government descended from the *curia regis* of the Norman kings. The *curia* was composed of tenants-in-chief, officials of the royal household, and anyone else the sovereign chose to advise him. By the late fifteenth century, the privy council was an instrument comprising members proper and advisers, and was known as the 'Council at Court'. Members were drawn from the clergy, the peerage and commoners.

Today the Privy Council is a formal body transacting formal constitutional business. There are more than 300 'right honourable' members, most of whom hold, or have held, high political, judicial or ecclesiastical office in Britain. Tenure of office lasts for the life of the sovereign plus six months.   JC-K

Privy Seal The *privatum sigillum* was, in England, a twelfth-century innovation, and was kept by the clerks of the king's chamber. It was used to seal chancery and exchequer business documents other than the mundane. By the fourteenth century the privy seal had come to nearly equal the GREAT SEAL OF ENGLAND in importance, and in the reign of Edward II a *secretum* was introduced for the king's personal use. · JC-K

Proclamations In England the term 'proclamation' is that given to two kinds of formal public announcement: those which are royal, and those made by private persons under customary or other valid authority.

Royal proclamations are made under the Great Seal, and are announcements which the monarch wishes to make known to the subject people. Examples of such are the declaration of war, the summoning of parliament, the dissolution of the same, or the attainment of peace. Examples of proclamations issued by private persons are those of the accession of a new sovereign, made on behalf of the Privy Council, or of some new legislation by the High Commissioner in a protectorate. In 1952, on the accession of Her Majesty Queen Elizabeth II, proclamations were made in London (by Garter King of Arms), Edinburgh (by Lord Lyon King of Arms), Windsor, York and other places. In London the Earl Marshal accompanied by heralds and two serjeants at arms proclaimed from the balcony of St James's Palace, trumpets were sounded, heads bared, and Garter read from the scroll sealed with the Great Seal: 'Whereas it has pleased Almighty God to call to his Mercy our Late Sovereign Lord . . . ', and ended by beseeching God, 'by whom Kings and Queens do reign, to bless the Royal Princess, Elizabeth the Second many long and happy Years to reign over us. God save the Queen.' The National Anthem was played and gun salutes fired at the Tower of London and in Hyde Park. The proclamation was made again, as is the custom, at the statue of Charles I at Charing Cross, and in the City of London.

In Scotland the proclamation of accession was executed in Edinburgh and other principal cities. In Edinburgh the sites were Mercat Cross, the Gate of the Castle, Holyroodhouse, and the Pier and Shore at Leith. It is interesting to note that proclamations are made in Edinburgh seven days later than in London — this being the traditional time taken for news to be carried by a horseman riding between the two capitals. At Mercat Cross the proclamation was made twice, first by the Lord Provost to the citizens of Edinburgh, and then by the Lord Lyon to the people of the Kingdom of Scotland.

The proclamation of other matters of great moment follow slightly different courses, but are, in essence, similar.

Proclamations made under statutory authority have the force of law.   JC-K

Pronomial Coat The paternal quartering in a shield of arms, usually the first quartering.

Pronunciation The golden rule is to pronounce armorial terms as they are spelt. Even those (numerous) words derived from the French are so pronounced: vert rhymes with skirt, for example. Many words may properly be pronounced in more than one way: Gules rhymes with rules, and the G may be either soft or hard (most armorists prefer the latter); saltire begins as in 'salt and pepper' but the ending may rhyme with either 'tire' or 'tier' — each is correct.

Proper (Abbr. Ppr) A charge when depicted in its natural colour. The tincture convention does not apply to charges so blazoned, though in practice the kings of arms would rule against any application which they consider confusing. Unlike the tinctures, the term is not endowed with a capital letter when blazoned. The use of charges proper is not popular in armory at the present time.

Provence In this part of southern France the romantic ideals of chivalry flourished in the songs and poems of the TROUBADOURS. They sang of romantic love, the joy of physical love and the pain of unrequited love, and the idealized figure of woman became the object of adoration. Eventually the philosophy of the Provençals came to be regarded as heretical by the church, and its brief flowering ended in the blood and slaughter of the Albigensian Crusades of the early thirteenth century.
                                                            KH

Provincial King of Arms A king of arms who exercises control over matters armorial within a specific geographical area.

Public Register of all Arms and Bearings in Scotland Established by Act of the Scottish Parliament in 1672, this is held in the Lyon Office and contains every grant of arms since that date. Now consisting of over eighty volumes of parchment and illustrated by a succession of the greatest heraldic artists working in Scotland. As a public register, it can be seen by anyone on application, and on payment of a statutory fee.   CJB

Public Services The uniformed public services of the fire brigades, ambulances and POLICE employ a variety of armorial and quasi-armorial devices. Best known are the international devices of the red cross and the red crescent, symbols of medical care, the white 'Maltese' cross on black of the St John Ambulance Brigade, and the white cross on red of the ambulance and hospital services of the Order of Malta, all direct descendants of the crusading hospital orders.

In Britain, most of the county fire services adopt the whole or some portion of the arms of the local authority to which they belong, these being displayed on equipment, vehicles, uniforms and, occasionally, on buildings. There are, however, some exceptions. In Scotland, for example, several brigades use a device the basic element of which is a fountain (*A Roundel barry wavy Argent and Azure*) bearing an armorial pile carrying a tongue of flame flanked by a thistle. In Tyne and Wear, the device consists of a five-pointed gilt star bearing concentric roundels, the inner charged with a blue castle tower together with a stylized representation of a water pump impeller.

The devices used by county ambulance services are equally varied, but frequently incorporate a cross paty and/or the Rod of Aesculapius, and sometimes a wheel to further symbolize the duties of the service.

Badge of the British NHS Ambulance Service

The Scottish Ambulance Service has for several years had its own device known as the 'Crown Badge'. This was designed by the office of Lord Lyon and comprises a roundel bearing the saltire of St Andrew on a blue background, within a half wreath of thistles ensigned by the Scottish Crown. In 1985 the ambulance service of the National Health Service in England received a new badge designed by the College of Arms and approved by Her Majesty the Queen. It comprises a cross paty in gold charged with a blue circlet encircling a gold wheel, around the centre spoke of which is entwined a red serpent. The cross is within a wreath of laurel proper and ensigned by the Royal Crown. The circlet may be inscribed with the title of the local body as the new device is adopted for new equipment and uniforms.   SS

Pulpits It was not until 1603 that it was compulsory for churches to have a pulpit, though many had them before this date. In the Middle Ages stone was frequently used where it was available locally, but wood was increasingly employed from the sixteenth century. The panels of a wooden pulpit offer the wood

Detail of a fifteenth century carved pulpit, a gift of Edward IV, at Fotheringhay church, Northamptonshire. The royal arms are flanked by badges: the black bull for Clarence and the white boar of the Duke of Gloucester.

carver an excellent medium for his craft, as was recognized in the Jacobean period when many new pulpits were erected because of the legal requirement mentioned above. Heraldic devices or complete shields may form part of this decoration and may be found on the sides and tester. The arms displayed are frequently those of a benefactor of the church. At Croscombe, Somerset, for example, the pulpit was a gift of Bishop Lake and displays his personal arms and those of his diocese on the sides and canopy.   JET
See also WOOD CARVING

Punctuation In blazon there is no punctuation other than capital letters for charges and tinctures, and apostrophes to indicate possession; e.g. *Sable a Chevron engrailed between three Bear's Gambs erased Or* (Barfett).

Purfled *see* **Attributes**

Purple Rod *see* **Gentleman Usher**

Purpure (Abbr. Purp) The armorial tincture purple, usually (though not necessarily) with imperial or ecclesiastical connotations.

Pursuivant An officer of arms of junior rank. Correctly a pursuivant of arms.

Pursuivant Extraordinary *see* **Herald Extraordinary** *and* **Officer of Arms**

Python In armory a winged serpent.

Quadrate A CROSS, the limbs of which project from a square or rectangular centre, is blazoned quadrate.

Quarrel A metal dart fired from a small cannon.

Quarter A SUB-ORDINARY occupying one quarter of the shield. Its diminutive, the canton, is far more common than the quarter itself. The quarter may be plain, parted, varied or charged, and its edges formed of any of the ornamental variations of line, though such treatment is rare. Not to be confused with quartering, which has an entirely different function.

Quartering The method whereby the shield is divided to display more than one coat of arms. Not necessarily, as the name implies, into four parts, although the shield is always divided into equal sections, and if it is desired to display an odd number of quarterings, as they are called, the first and most important coat is repeated at the end, and the whole is read like the page of a book.

Whilst a many-quartered coat is of historical interest, it is often not practical to display more than four, on a printed letterhead for example. Armigerous persons are at liberty to select which quarterings they display, but they must show inheritance; humble coats should not be omitted if it is through them that a noble and famous coat has been inherited.

A quartering itself may be quartered to show two or more coats, and it is then called a grand-quarter. The modern practice is to use grand-quarterings only where an indivisible coat has been granted by royal licence, although grand-quartering is still used in Scotland.

During the medieval period, arms were often associated with lordships and quarterings frequently illustrated inheritance of property rather than blood, though of course the two were often coincidental.   PF

Quarterly A field parted per cross. *See also* FIELD, PARTED

Quatrefoil In armory, a charge similar to the cinquefoil but with four petals.

Queen The wife or consort of a king. A lady who is chief ruler of a state, and having the same rank as a king.

Queen's Beasts *see* **Beasts**

Queen's Colour A British royal ceremonial flag used by the Royal Navy since 1924, and consisting of the White Ensign charged with the crowned royal cypher surrounded by a Garter.

Queen's Messengers The Corps of Queen's Messengers is responsible for the over-all safe custody of British diplomatic mail worldwide. The dress badge of office is an oval pendant suspended from a Garter-blue neck ribbon. The pendant bears a gilt cypher of the monarch ensigned by the Crown of St Edward. Surrounding the cypher is a gilt and enamel representation of the Garter, and hanging from the Garter buckle is the symbol of the Corps — a silver greyhound courant.   SS

Queen's Personal Flag In 1960 the Queen of England adopted a personal flag for use when the royal banner may be considered inappropriate. The flag is a square livery banner of blue, fringed gold, and charged with the Queen's initial E, ensigned by the

Royal Crown, within a chaplet of roses all gold. During visits to Commonwealth countries, the Queen adopts the government flag of those countries with this personal motif in the centre.

Questing Beast The Questing Beast of Arthurian legend had a serpent's head, the body of a leopard, the hind-quarters of a lion, and the feet of a hart. 'Questing' means baying, and the Arthurian beast made a noise like sixty hounds baying wherever he went.

Queued *see* **Attributes**

Queue Fourché *see* **Attributes**

Quilled *see* **Attributes**

Quintain A tall board, fixed in the earth, and used as a target for tilting practice.

Quintin *or* **Quintal** An upright pole with pivoted cross-beam, at one end of which was affixed a shield and on the other a log of wood or sand-filled sack, suspended from a chain. Used for tilting practice — the target being the shield and the punishment for tardiness being a firm clout on the back of the head!

Quise, á la A bird's leg when cut off at the thigh is erased or couped á la quise.

R

Raguly *see* **Lines, Varied**

Raised *see* **Attitude**

Rampant *see* **Attitude**

Rayed *see* **Attributes**

Rayonné *see* **Lines, Varied**

Rebated *see* **Attributes**

Rebus *(non verbis sed rebus)* A pictorial pun on a name. Rebuses were particularly popular in medieval ecclesiastical circles and were widely used as personal

Rebus

Rebuses of William Bolton and Thomas Goldstone

devices and to decorate stonework of buildings, chapels and tombs. Writers on heraldry are unanimous in dismissing the rebus as being outside the scope of armory. However, simple punning devices are to be found on early seals such as that of the Swinton family (a single boar's head), long before they appear in true armorial form as coats of arms (Swinton eventually bore *A Chevron between three Boar's Heads*). They were adopted and discarded at will without reference to heraldic authority — but so, too, were badges in the Middle Ages. Many of the best known armorial badges are, indeed, rebuses: the talbot of the Talbot family, and the *hirondelle* (swallow or martlet) of the Arundels, for example. Even the *Bottle Argent suspended from a Cord Azure* badge of the de Vere Earls of Oxford has all the attributes of a perfect rebus — *de verre* being 'of glass'. The tun (a barrel) was undoubtedly a favourite of those whose name ended in '—ton'. At Winchester, in the chantry of Bishop Langton, a musical note called a 'long' protrudes from a tun; an ash tree grows out of a tun for the name Ashton at St John's, Cambridge; and the rebus of William Bolton, Prior of St Bartholomew's, Smithfield, shows a bolt piercing a tun. Other rebuses were no less ingenious: Thomas Goldstone, Prior of Christchurch, Canterbury, used a gold flint-stone ensigned with a mitre; Sir John Peché a peach charged with a letter e; and in Canterbury Cathedral an eagle, standing over an ox branded with the letters NE stands for John Oxney. It may be argued that it is the inclusion of lettering which distinguishes the rebus from true armorial devices, but there is no denying their heraldic significance.

The term is also applied to the fanciful devices sometimes adopted by participants in a tournament who wished to 'keep the audience guessing' as to their identity, and to identification marks such as those used by printers and masons.

Redemption *see* **Livery Company, Membership of**

Reflexed *see* **Attitude**

Reguardant *see* **Attitude**

Relief *see* **Shading**

Re-Matriculation *see* **Matriculation of Arms**

Remembrancer An officer of exchequer, e.g. The Queen's Remembrancer, whose duty it is to collect debts due to the sovereign; and the City Remembrancer, who represents the Corporation of the City of London before parliamentary committees.

Replenished *see* **Attributes**

Rerebrace *or* **Monion** Armour for the upper arm.

Respectant *see* **Attitude**

Retainer One who is retained by a magnate, thereby enjoying patronage and protection in return for domestic, administrative or military service.

Retainers upon whom liveries were bestowed as tokens of maintenance were not necessarily menials, but were drawn from all classes of medieval society. To hold office in the household of an influential magnate was a recognized means of advancement for the sons of the minor nobility, and even the humble cleric could ascend the ecclesiastical ladder in the service of a spiritual lord. Even the sons of the sovereign and of the nobility were expected to receive their education in the service of a noble household other than their own, and to wear the livery and badge of their patron.
See also LIVERY AND MAINTENANCE.

Retrospective Arms *see* **Limitation Clause**

Reversed Turned upside down (as with an armorial charge).

Riband A narrow bendlet. *See also* BEND

Richard III (1452-85) He was the last Yorkist king of England (1483-85), and the last of the Plantagenets. Tudor propaganda depicted him as a villain, a view adhered to by Shakespeare in his play *Richard III*. Loyal to his brother Edward IV while he lived, Richard became Protector to his young nephew Edward V in 1483. There followed a period of ruthless elimination of possible opponents to his rule, especially among the despised supporters of Elizabeth (Woodville) the Queen Mother, culminating in seizure of the throne and the incarceration of Edward V and his brother in the Tower. A growing belief that the princes had been murdered by his order fuelled the flames of rebellion, and on 7 August 1485 Henry Tudor, Earl of Richmond, landed near Milford Haven in west Wales with 2000 troops and a decidedly fragile claim to the English throne. Richard and Tudor met at Ambion Hill near the village of Sutton Cheney in Leicestershire, on 22 August 1485. Treachery and procrastination ruled the

The Battle of Bosworth by Andrew Jamieson. King Richard (centre right) leads his knights in a final desperate charge against the 'accursed Tydder' (lower left). 'Jerking his horse about, Henry Tudor precipitately recoiled. It was the most dreadful moment of his life. The slight figure wielding a battle-axe with the strength of Hercules was death itself; yet he dared retire not a foot farther lest his army see and lose heart from its leader's cowardice.' (Charles Ross)

day, and Richard was finally hacked to death at Tudor's feet, having staked his crown on a final heroic charge aimed at direct confrontation with the 'accursed Tydder' himself. Richard III is undoubtedly the most enigmatic and, to many, charismatic of sovereigns and his death at Bosworth Field represents the dénouement of the Age of Chivalry.

Richard's badge, both as Duke of Gloucester and as king, was 'the wretched, bloody and usurping boar' (Shakespeare), *blanc sanglier* — the silver boar with gold tusks and bristles after which he named his personal herald. In addition, he would have used the white rose en soleil badge of York with the blue and murrey livery of his house.

It was by his hand and seal that the Corporation of the Kings, Heralds and Pursuivants of Arms received its charter on 2 March 1484: for us a tangible link with the Middle Ages. It therefore seems strange that the officers of arms should now wear the Lancastrian Collar of SS and not the Yorkist collar of suns and white roses.

For The Richard III Society *see* ADDRESSES. Note also the Bosworth Battlefield Visitors' Centre at Ambion Hill Farm, Sutton Cheney, Market Bosworth, Leicestershire: the site of the battle is now a country park and there is a comprehensive visual interpretation of the battle and an extensive visitor centre close to the village of Sutton Cheney. As one would expect, heraldry is much in evidence at the Centre, and the standards of the participants are often flown from their positions about the battlefield. An excellent official guide *The Battle of Bosworth* by Dr D.T. Williams (1984) is available.

Further reading

Hammond, P.W. and A.F. Sutton *Richard III, the Road to Bosworth Field* London, 1985.

Kendall, P.M. *Richard III* London, 1955.
More, Sir Thomas *History of King Richard III* 1557 (reprinted London, 1965).
Seward, D. *Richard III — England's Black Legend* Twickenham, 1983.
Ross, C.D. *Richard III* London, 1981.
Walpole, H. *Historic doubts on the life of King Richard III* 1768 (reprinted London, 1965).

Richmond Herald of Arms in Ordinary From 1421 to 1485 Richmond was a herald to the Honor (estate) of Richmond. However, on the accession of Henry VII (1485) Richmond became a king of arms and remained so until 1510, when the office became that of a herald in ordinary to the Crown. The badge of office is the red rose of Lancaster dimidiating the white rose en soleil of York, ensigned by the royal crown. Although this device has all the characteristics of a Tudor invention, it is likely to be of fairly recent derivation.

Ringed *see* **Attributes**

Rising *see* **Attitude**

Ritter A German term for a mounted warrior or knight. The word became a title of some nobility, and its derivative *rittmeister*, literally the leader of a troop of cavalry, also passed into the language as a title for some members of the aristocracy. A most notable example was Manfred von Richtofen, 'The Red Baron'. JC-K

Road and Rail Devices The use of emblems and decorations on vehicles has a long and honourable history, from the panels on the hunting chariots of Assyria to the artistic motifs of twentieth-century automobiles. In this span of some 5000 years, the use of armory plays a small but significant part. The greatest period was undoubtedly the eighteenth century when, with the coming of good roads, the coach makers' art rose to considerable heights.

In the English-speaking world the two most famous surviving coaches are those of the Lord Mayor of London, and the Royal State Coach. The first of these is richly carved and the different panels and doors contain allegorical groups of figures and heraldic devices of great boldness of both colour and treatment. The Royal State Coach, 'the most superb carriage ever built', has paintings by Cipriani. It is most richly

One of a series of milestones in Cambridgeshire, dated 1728 and said to be the first to be erected since the Roman occupation. Each bears the arms of Trinity Hall, Cambridge, *Sable a Crescent and a Bordure engrailed Ermine* (the tinctures have mistakenly been reversed), and this example also impales the arms of Dr Mowse, a former Master of the College.

adorned and is crowned on the centre of the roof by three figures holding the Sceptre, the Sword of State and the ensigns of knighthood.

At a more plebeian and commercial level, horse-drawn stage coaches of the eighteenth and nineteenth centuries were very heraldic in their decoration. The doors of mail coaches bore the royal arms, and the panels carried renderings of the stars of the orders of the Garter, Bath, Thistle and St Patrick. The Ross-Chepstow coach had door panels with a portcullis device, and many stage coaches bore the arms of the towns they served.

The advent of the horseless carriage and its successor the modern automobile saw a rapid decline in the use of true heraldry as decoration, and a gradual adoption of badges of identity, some, it is true, of heraldic character. Alfa-Romeo, for example, impale the arms of the city of Milan with those of its ancient dukes. The Morris company of England (now part of the Rover Organisation) used the arms of the city of Oxford where, in the early days of the twentieth century, the firm began. In France, the Citroen company employs two chevrons as its motif; Germany's BMW organisation displays blue and white quarterings, thus honouring its Bavarian connection. In England, the SS car company's leaping jaguar badge became so famous the firm changed its name to Jaguar Cars. Motoring organisations which were founded in the wake of the industry also adopted heraldic or quasi-heraldic symbols, perhaps the purest being the saltire of the Royal Scottish Automobile Club, although the English Automobile Association had a pleasing badge of interlaced initials until a 'modern image' was demanded of them by the market place.

Manufacturers of steamrollers also used heraldic devices to decorate and advertize their products: the rampant horse of Kent and its related motto 'Invicta' was used by Aveling of Rochester. Clayton and Shuttleworth of Lincoln sported the arms of the city, *Argent on a Cross Gules a Fleur-de-lis Or*, while Marshalls of Gainsborough adopted the famous seated figure of Britannia after the name of the factory in which the rollers were made.

Second only to the use of heraldry on horse-drawn carriage panels was its adoption by railways in England. This great, proud Victorian industry was quick to proclaim its aspirations and status by the assumption of armorial bearings — sometimes quite illegally. The application of arms was widespread; on locomotives and rolling stock, station façades, tunnel keystones, and windows. Most achievements sported by British railway companies incorporated the arms of the towns they sought to serve; the Great Eastern system, for example, adopted a radial design composed of the arms of Middlesex, Malden, Ipswich, Norwich, Cambridge, Hertford, Northampton and Huntingdon. North of the border the Highland Railway used the coats of Inverness and Perth held by an eagle, while the Caledonian appropriated the Royal Arms of Scotland.

In continental Europe the railways themselves very seldom employed heraldry, although the Swiss Federal Railways have, since the 1950s, borne on their locomotives the arms of towns, cantons and communes. Further afield in the Americas, the Antipodes, India, Africa and the Far East, rolling stock has carried quasi-heraldic devices, often of great beauty and certainly of great variety, but little has been seen of true armorial bearings. Today the trend is towards logotypes of the trade mark variety — in much the way that British Rail now use parallel lines with opposed arrowheads indicative of bi-directional travel.

Finally, an area of land transport where heraldry survives (albeit somewhat tenuously) is on omnibuses, which often carry the arms of the places they serve, although once again the need for aggressive marketing, particularly in England, has necessitated the development of logotypes, acronyms and slogans to catch the customers' attention and raise the awareness thresholds of the travelling public to the identities of the fleet operators.   EP-T

Further reading

Burridge, F. *Nameplates of the Big Four* Oxford, 1975 (reprinted 1985). This excellent, inexpensive book includes a wealth of illustrated information on the 'splashers', or locomotive nameplates, of British railways, many of which carry armorial devices.

Dow, G. *Railway Heraldry and Other Insignia* Newton Abbot, 1973.

Hyman, S. (Ed.) *Railway Art* 1977.

Whitehouse, P. (Ed.) *Railway Relics and Regalia* Twickenham, 1975.

Wright, I.W. *Locomotive Nameplates on Public Display* 1986.

Robe of Dignity *and* **Robe of Estate** *see* **Mantle**

Robes In the Middle Ages, members of the royal court and important retainers received numerous payments in kind for their services, as well as money. Of these, the robe must have been the most welcome, for it was 'an all enveloping garment of thick cloth suitable to protect the wearer from the draughts in contemporary halls and churches' (D.M. Stenton). Of course, the quality of the materials used reflected the status of the wearer and conformed, to some degree, with the SUMPTUARY LAWS of the period.

Garments of such fine quality lent themselves to embellishment and, eventually, to regulation, so that certain colours, styles, etc., became the perquisite of specific ranks of nobility or office and ultimately part of the insignia of the peerage and orders of chivalry. An illuminated manuscript of 1446 shows peers wearing robes of scarlet lined with miniver, and by the

time of James II (1685-88) noblemen had crimson velvet robes of estate comprising a long gown, a mantle lined with ermine and a hood and tippet. In this century, robes are still worn by peers (see individual entries) on great occasions of state, and in connection with certain parliamentary ceremonies.

Peers may be identified by the number of ermine bands on the tippet: Duke, 4 rows; Marquis, 3½ rows; Earl, 3 rows; Viscount, 2½ rows; Baron, 2 rows.

Senior members of the orders of chivalry wear mantles of the following colours: Garter, dark blue; Thistle, green; Bath, crimson; St Michael and St George, Saxon blue; Royal Victorian, dark blue; British Empire, rose pink (before 1937, purple).

Rods of Office *see* **Wands, Staffs and Rods of Office**

Roland The best known of the Paladins of Charlemagne, he is immortalized in the *Song of Roland*. He was in command of the rearguard of Charlemagne's army withdrawing from Spain when he was ambushed by the Moors in the Pass of Roncesvalles. Although urged by his great friend and fellow paladin, Oliver, to call Charlemagne back to his aid, he refused to do so. Only after the death of Oliver and being himself mortally wounded did he order the horn to sound, too late to bring help. Romantic chivalry sees the heroic gesture transcend defeat and death.   KH

Rolls of Arms Any collection of coats of arms, whether written in the language of heraldry (blazon), painted or tricked on drawings, listings or even carvings of shields (as in the great cloister vault at Canterbury Cathedral), constitutes a roll of arms. Such compilations are usually arranged in rows of shields on strips of vellum or parchment sewn together and rolled up or bound into books. The identity of the person bearing each particular coat normally appears above each shield or accompanies the description. The term is generally applied to manuscripts of the medieval period, but with so many having been lost, a closer study must also include an appreciation of similar compilations throughout Europe. These illustrate the mobility of the knightly classes and the development of the use of armorial devices.

Rolls may be classified as:

Occasional Those relating to an event such as an expedition, tournament or siege, e.g. the Bigot Roll *c.* 1354-5, compiled during the campaign of Charles of Anjou in Hainault, and the Caerlaverock Roll of 1300. In the present century, Adam-Even was the first to note their importance in biographical enquiry and historical interpretation, as well as a means of dating or even of identifying the compiler or artist of a roll.

Institutional Rolls associated with foundations, orders

Two pages from Powell's Roll of *c*.1345-51. Of particular interest is the use of the bend to indicate cadency in the arms of Grandison (lower right). To the original arms *Paly Argent and Azure* were added *a Bend Gules* variously charged with, for example, eagles displayed, escallops and cinquefoils in gold to differentiate between cadet branches of the family.

of religion and chivalry, and possibly compiled over many generations, e.g. the Armorial of the Members of the Confraternity of St Christopher of Arlberg, begun in 1390 and continued until the end of the eighteenth century; the Parliamentary Roll of 1312-14, though divided regionally, effectively falls into this category; Bruges' Garter Book of 1430 and the Armorial Equestre de la Toison d'Or of 1440-5.

Regional It is almost peculiarly English to have regional or local rolls (for example, the County Roll of the fourteenth century), though throughout Europe there were compilations made on a regional basis for general purposes.

Illustrative Some rolls are simply illustrative of stories or chronicles and may therefore contain imaginary coats, as for ancient kings or knights of the Round Table, and the Matthew Paris Shields from the first half of the thirteenth century (which are the subject of a part of 'Aspilogia II, Rolls of Arms of the Reign of King Henry III', London, 1967), and the Tournament at Chauvency 1285, by Jacques Bretel.

General General rolls were clearly combinations of many collections, though it is often possible to detect the previous sources of such rolls and perhaps hazard a guess at their dating from style and content, based

upon the elements of occasional rolls or groupings of identified relations within them. The Fitzwilliam Roll, for example, possesses elements of all the above, and compares with the Armorial Wijnbergen of *c.* 1280-5; Zurich of *c.* 1335-45; le Héraut Navarre of *c.* 1368-75; Bellenville of *c.* 1370-85; Gelre of *c.* 1370-90, and Conrad Grunenberg 1483. Compilers would often arrange shields in such a way that they might be easier to read or find in their rolls, in fair library copies and as ordinaries (e.g. Cooke's and Cotgrave's ordinaries *c.* 1340), where the arrangement was perhaps by colour and design combinations.

Some two dozen rolls have survived in England from the thirteenth century (*see* C.R. Humphery-Smith *Anglo-Norman Armory* (1976) and *Anglo-Norman Armory Two* (1985) in which several renderings of each roll are brought together in armory and ordinary form). For the medieval period as a whole there are perhaps 350 known surviving armorial rolls, of which 130 are English (see colour page 335), 80 French, 60 German, 30 Flemish, and 20 Spanish and Italian. Little appears in other regions before sixteenth-century copies of allegedly earlier material.

The study of rolls of arms dates to the thirteenth century, when heralds recorded events and exchanged such listings in order to compile their own armories. This practice has developed over the centuries and by the sixteenth and seventeenth centuries many 'editions' of the earlier rolls were known. To these were being added the listings made by heralds, and local heraldic antiquaries and artists of the collections derived from events of the Wars of the Roses, Tudor progresses and heralds' VISITATIONS. In the early seventeenth century, in fear of the 'impending conflict', a group of antiquaries under William Dugdale, Christopher Hatton, Edward Dering and others clubbed together to transcribe faithful editions of the rolls of arms from the mid-thirteenth century onwards. A remarkable collection of painted copies was made and is now kept at the Society of Antiquaries in London. From these beginnings the scholarly study of English rolls of arms began with the greater part of the work being left to Greenstreet, Walford, Russell, Barron, St John Hope, Collins, Wagner, London, Tremlett, Humphery-Smith, Denholm-Young and Brault, in the nineteenth and twentieth centuries.

Such work has not been limited to English rolls. In the 1870s and 1880s the work of Sir David Lyndsay of the Mount was recognized, and magnificent publications appeared of Scottish armorial rolls, under the editorship of David Laing and Stodart. Stodart turned also to Scottish coats found in the armorial of the herald Gelre, dating from about 1334 to 1369, and kept in the Bibliothèque Royale at Brussels. He had been preceded in his study of continental European rolls of arms by Bouly de Lésdain and Prinet, and followed in more recent decades by Adam-Even, Jéquier, de Vaivre, von Berchem, Galbreath, Hupp and others. Even the work of Siebmacher, Rietstap, Edmonson, Robson and Burke in the compilation of their enormous general armories must not be discounted in relation to rolls of arms. General armorials of this kind, however, may be but hotchpotches of material from many sources, often without any reference to the original right to use arms.

Fairly comprehensive bibliographies for most countries are to be found in *Archivum Heraldicum* (published since 1957 by Archives Héraldique Suisses), in Gatfield's *Guide to Printed Books and Manuscripts relating to English and Foreign Heraldry and Genealogy* (London, 1892), and Saffroy's *Bibliographie Généalogique, Héraldique et Nobiliaire de la France* (Paris, 1968). Max Prinet, Paul Adam-Even and Anthony Wagner set the tone for later twentieth-century scholarship with the appearance of their catalogues of medieval armorial rolls. Adam-Even developed a classification which was simplified by Wagner, who initiated the important *Aspilogia* series published jointly by the Society of Antiquaries and the Harleian Society.

Until the pioneer work of those mentioned above, to which may be added the more recent studies of Jan Raneke and Michel Pastoureau, there had been no demonstration of the enormous value of these sources (in company with SEALS) as an aid to historical and etymological studies, to an understanding of the use and laws of armory, the military role of colours and charges, and the political and social aspects of the armorial system. Much research still needs to be done on such aspects as language, rules, cadency, dating, compilation and provenance of the rolls, as well as the heraldic aspect of symbolism and allusion. CRH-S

Further reading

Adam-Even, P. *Catalogue des Armoriaux Francais Imprimés* 1946.

Berchem, E. von, D.L. Galbreath and O. Hupp 'Die Wappenbucher des Deutschen Mittelalters' in *Beitrage zur Geschichte der Heraldik* Berlin, 1939.

Brault, G.J. *Eight Thirteenth-century Rolls of Arms* 1973.

Foster, J. *Some Feudal Coats of Arms* 1901 (reprinted 1984).

Galbreath, D.L. and L. Jéquier *Manuel du Blason* Laussanne, 1977.

Humphery-Smith, C.R. 'New Lights on Old Rolls' in *Proceedings of XV Congress and Internacional de las Ciencias Genealogica y Heraldica* Madrid, 1982.

Pastoureau, M. *Trétise d'Héraldique* Paris, 1979.

Vaivre, J-B. de *Cahiers d'Héraldique* Paris, 1974.

Wagner, A.R. *A Catalogue of English Medieval Rolls of Arms* London, 1950. (See *Aspilogia II* 1967, pp 255- 81.)
— *Heralds and Heraldry in the Middle Ages* London (2nd ed. 1956).

Roman Catholic Church, Clergy of Roman Catholic clergymen are permitted to use their personal shield of arms ensigned by an ecclesiastical hat, the cords and tassels of which descend on either side of the shield and, by colour and number, signify degree. Unlike the non-episcopal clergy of the CHURCH OF ENGLAND, Catholic clergymen may not use helm, crest or motto, and there are strict rules which effectively prohibit the use of insignia of temporal dignity or nobility. In 1969 Pope Paul VI ordered that mitres and croziers should no longer be used. However, a diocese may use the mitre with cross and crozier, and an abbey may use a mitre with a crozier.

	Colour of ecclesiastical hat	Number and colour of tassels each side	Insignia accompanying the shield
Cardinal	scarlet	15 scarlet interlaced with gold	according to degree, e.g. bishop
Patriarch and Primate	green	15 green	patriarchal cross palewise
Archbishop (not a Primate)	green	10 green	patriarchal cross palewise
Bishop	green	6 green	Latin cross palewise
Abbot and Provost	black	6 black	veiled crozier palewise
Abbot and Prelate Nullius	green	6 green	veiled crozier palewise
Prelate Fiocchetto	violet	10 scarlet	
Apostolic Protonotary	violet	6 scarlet	
Domestic Prelate	violet	6 violet	
Privy Chamberlain and Privy Chaplain to the Pope	black	6 violet	
Canons Ordinary	black	3 black	
Dean and Minor Superior	black	2 black	
Priest	black	1 black	
Abbess	none	none	veiled crozier with rosary encircling the shield

There are several variations within each degree.

Further reading
Heim, Archbishop Bruno *Heraldry in the Catholic Church* Gerrards Cross (revised 1981).

Roman Lamp *or* **Antique Lamp** *see* **Medical Heraldry**

Rompu Broken, interrupted or displaced. Any armorial charge which is broken may be described as rompu, though the term is usually applied to geometrical charges and lines.

A chevron rompu   in the arms of Bernard C. Martin

Roofs *see* **Ceilings**

Rook The bird. However, the term is also applied to the chess-piece, though rarely so.

Rose The armorial charge has five petals and is of the dog-rose variety. When blazoned *barbed and seeded proper* the sepals between the petals are green, and the centre of seeds gold. It is incorrect to depict an inner set of five petals unless blazoned as a *double rose*, or when a Tudor Rose is intended.

Roses, Wars of the The period of internecine strife between the houses of York and Lancaster lasting from the St Alban's incident in 1455 to the battle of Stoke in 1487, the last occasion on which the reigning English king was required to take the field in person against a rival claimant to his throne. It has been calculated that during these thirty-two years of dynastic turbulence, actual fighting occupied no more than thirteen weeks, the longest campaign (that of 1471, from Edward IV's landing to the battle of Tewkesbury) lasting only seven and a half weeks. The idea that the two sides adopted their respective roses in the Temple Garden belongs entirely to Shakespeare (*Henry VI Part 1*), and the term 'Wars of the Roses' may be attributed to Sir Walter Scott's *Anne of Geierstein*, written in 1829.

The golden rose had been a royal badge since its introduction into English armory by Eleanor of Provence, Henry III's queen. It was the badge of the three Edwards and was used both by the Black Prince and Richard II. The red rose was a 'cousin' of the gold rose. It was associated with the title of Lancaster since its adoption by the second son of Eleanor of Provence, Edmund Crouchback, and descended to John of Gaunt through his marriage to the Lancastrian heiress,

Blanche. Thus it became the distinctive device of the Lancastrian kings and of Gaunt's illegitimate Beaufort line. (The Beauforts were later legitimated by act of parliament confirming a patent issued by Richard II, though their half-brother, Henry IV, added the words *excepta dignitate regali* to the patent, thereby debarring them from succession to the throne. However, he failed to make the disqualification law by a further act of parliament, and in later years it was argued that a royal patent could not alter one confirmed by parliament and the Beauforts therefore enjoyed a rightful claim to succession.)

A white rose was a badge of Roger Mortimer (2nd Earl of March, died 1360), grandfather of Richard II's heir, also Roger (4th Earl of March, killed 1398). It was by his Mortimer descent that Richard Plantagenet, Duke of York, could claim the throne, and it seems likely that he selected the white rose from his numerous badges to emphasize the point.

It is interesting to note, in retrospect, that the two roses came to represent the principles of parliamentary sanction by which the Lancastrians held the crown, and 'strict legitimism' which was the basis of Yorkist rule. In more recent times, the red rose has been adopted by European political parties as a symbol of democratic socialism.

The proliferation of the red and white rose devices in the civic armory of the counties of Lancashire and Yorkshire is of doubtful validity, for both are essentially dynastic symbols and are inappropriate when adopted in a territorial context.

The badges and livery colours of the principal

Following the battle of Towton (1461), the largest and bloodiest battle of the Wars of the Roses, the Lancastrians retreated in dense mist across the Cock Beck where thousands were slaughtered, among them Lionel, Lord Welles, whose effigy (at Methley, Yorkshire) bears his arms: *Or a Lion rampant double queued Sable.*

participants in the Wars of the Roses may be found in *Heraldic Badges* by A.C. Fox-Davies, 1907, and in abbreviated form in *The Wars of the Roses* by Terence Wise, 1983, which also includes details of arms and armour of the period, genealogical tables and accounts of the various battles.

Further reading

Chrimes, S.B. et al *15th Century England 1399-1509* Manchester, 1972.

Clive, M. *This Sun of York* London, 1973.

Cole, H. *The Wars of the Roses* London, 1973.

de Walden, Lord *Banners, Standards and Badges from a Tudor Manuscript in the College of Arms* 1904 facsimile for the de Walden library.

Gillingham, J. *The Wars of the Roses* London, 1981.

Goodman, A. *The Wars of the Roses: Military Activity and English Society* London, 1982.

Jacob, E.F. *The Fifteenth Century 1399-1485* Oxford, 1961.

Kendall, P.M. *The Yorkist Age* London, 1967.

Lander, J.R. *The Wars of the Roses* London, 1965.

— *Crown and Nobility 1450-1509* London 1976.

— *Politics and Power in England 1450-1509* London, 1976.

McFarlane, K.B. *The Nobility of Later Medieval England* Oxford, 1973.

Ross, C. *The Wars of the Roses* London, 1973.

Seymour, W. *Battles in Britain* London, 1975.

Ross Herald of Arms A Scottish herald of arms prior to 1867. The office was first mentioned in 1476, and the title is derived from the earldom of Ross conferred on James Stewart, second son of King James III, on 28 January 1480-1, promoted Duke of Ross in 1487.   CJB

Rothesay, Duke of The first ducal title created in Scotland on 28 April 1398, and granted to David, eldest son of King Robert III. The title has been enjoyed by the eldest son of the sovereign since the middle of the fifteenth century to the present day. Along with this dukedom the heir to the throne has the following titles: Earl of Carrick, Baron of Renfrew, Lord of the Isles, Prince and Great Steward of Scotland.   CJB

Rothesay Herald of Arms A current Scottish herald of arms. Created after 1398 when the dukedom of Rothesay was conferred on David, eldest son of King Robert III, on 28 April 1398. This was the first ducal title ever granted in Scotland.

The badge of office is *Two Fleurs-de-lis Gules surmounted of a three point Label chequy Azure and Argent and ensigned of the Crown of Scotland proper*.   CJB

Rouge Croix Pursuivant of Arms in Ordinary Said to be the oldest of the four offices of pursuivant in ordinary, but there is no record of the office earlier

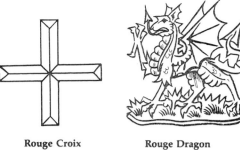

Rouge Croix Pursuivant badge	**Rouge Dragon Pursuivant badge**

than 1418/9. The name is taken from the red cross of St George, which is both the badge of the Order of the Garter and for centuries England's national device. The badge of office is a red cross, either couped or set on a white roundel.

Rouge Dragon Pursuivant of Arms in Ordinary Founded by Henry VII in 1485 immediately before his coronation, the title of this pursuivant in ordinary is clearly a reference to the red dragon of Cadwallader from whom the Tudor dynasty claimed descent. The badge of office is *a Dragon passant Gules on a Mount Vert*, the royal badge for Wales.

Roundel A flat coloured disc. In armory, roundels have names according to their colour, all of which may be found as individual entries.

> Or: bezant
> Argent: plate
> Gules: torteau
> Azure: hurt
> Sable: pellet
> Vert: pomeis
> Purpure: golpe
> Sanguine: guze
> Tenné: orange
> Murrey: mulberry
> Barry wavy Azure and Argent: fountain

In medieval armory several of the above terms were used generically, e.g. *a Bezant Gules*. Likewise, in French armory all roundels are blazoned *torteau*, and

Rothesay badge

those which are depicted as spheres *boules*. Some confusion exists in British armory regarding the depiction of roundels. Some armorists argue that bezants, plates and fountains should always be flat discs, whilst others may be depicted as spheres if required. Medieval roundels were invariably flat and no equivalent of the French *boules* is available to us. This is most regrettable, for the introduction of such a term into British armory would remove any ambiguity with regard to the nature of roundels and would create a stimulating range of new and distinctive charges, each possessed of a fresh symbolism.

Roundels may be depicted as semy charges.

Round Table *see* **Arthur, King**

Rousant *see* **Attitude**

Royal Arms The arms of sovereigns are, in most cases, also ARMS OF DOMINION. They descend to, or are adopted by, successive monarchs, who cease to use their personal or family arms.
See individual entries by names of country. The royal heraldry of England will be found under UNITED KINGDOM, ROYAL HERALDRY.
Further reading
Burke's Royal Families of the World Vol.I. Europe and Latin America, 1977; Vol.II Africa, Arabia and the Middle East, 1980.
Louda, J. and M. Maclagan *Lines of Succession* London, 1981. An excellent, fully illustrated book giving the genealogies and arms of all the European royal dynasties.

Royal Arms in Churches The royal arms are to be found prominently displayed in many English churches as tokens of loyalty to the crown and obedience to the sovereign as head of the Church. Consequently, all examples date from after 1534, when Henry VIII assumed the title of 'Supreme Head on Earth of the Church of England'. At all periods, however, royal devices have appeared in glass, furnishings, memorials, etc., their function being mainly commemorative.

Proclamations of Henry VIII or of his successor Edward VI regarding usage of the royal arms have not been traced. However, there is evidence from church-wardens' accounts and other sources to suggest that it was common practice for the royal arms to be erected on top of the chancel screen in place of the rood during these reigns. The initiative may have been taken by zealous churchwardens, for during the reign of Edward VI the curate and wardens of St Martin's, Ironmonger Lane, London, were ordered to restore the crucifix to the rood screen and remove the royal arms they had erected.

The succession of the Catholic Queen Mary I resulted in the removal or destruction of all but a very few examples, such as those at Rushbrooke, Suffolk, and Westerham, Kent, which are both attributed to her predecessors. The process was again reversed by her half-sister and heir, Elizabeth I, for whom several examples are to be found. Most surviving examples of this period are painted on wooden panels or directly on to plaster, and some are still to be found above the chancel arch.

The early Stuart kings maintained the practice. In 1614 Archbishop Abbot, the then Archbishop of Canterbury, instructed a painter-stainer to 'survey and paynte in all the churches and chappells within the Realme of England, the Kinges Majesties Armes in due form, with helmet, crest, mantell, and supporters as they ought to be, together with the noble young princes.' This directive concerning the arms of the young prince (the future Charles I) may have encouraged the appearances of boards bearing the so-called 'Prince of Wales' Feathers' (i.e. the badge of the heir apparent to the English throne), rather than the prince's coat of arms. However, the example at Sherborne Abbey, Dorset, for Henry, Prince of Wales, dated 1611 shows that the practice existed before this directive was issued. The undated example with the initials CP at Bramley, Hampshire, is for either Prince Charles, later Charles I, or his son Charles, later Charles II. There are several examples of the royal arms surmounting Jacobean chancel screens with the 'Prince of Wales' Feathers' occupying a similar position on the screen over the north aisle, as at Hurst, Berkshire, and Wash, Devon. Archbishop Abbott in 1631 gave further instructions that the royal arms should once again be painted or repaired, together with the Ten Commandments and 'other holy sentences'.

During the Commonwealth, 1649-60, many examples of the royal arms were destroyed or defaced. Some must have been taken down and hidden, only to be re-erected later. A few were turned round and the Commonwealth arms painted on the reverse!

The restoration of Charles II in 1660 resulted in a statute requiring that the royal arms should be displayed in all churches, and this caused a large number of arms to be prepared or old ones repainted. Although the marshalling of the royal arms changed several times after 1660, royal arms in churches were to suffer only once more from the changing dynastic fortunes of monarchs. So concerned were the early Hanoverians with the claims of Stuart Pretenders that many Stuart arms in churches were repainted with those of Hanover. This work was often done incorrectly, with only the fourth quarter being over-painted with the Hanoverian quartering. At Cirencester, Gloucestershire, the Stuart arms had a new 'Hanover' canvas painted and fixed over the top. Both canvases are now on display.

Square or rectangular boards and canvas were the most popular forms of display, though carved wood, cast iron and plaster-cast examples are to be found. The writer has also seen one painted on sheet metal. Examples for all reigns from James I to Victoria are quite common, but there are few for the twentieth century, that at Remenham, Berkshire, for Queen Elizabeth II being exceptional.

The dating of arms may prove difficult. Those which have no dates or initials can only be dated from the marshalling of the various quarterings, and even this may not always be conclusive. One form of arms used by Queen Anne was applicable for only seven years, but after her death in 1714 the Hanoverian royal arms were to remain unchanged of eighty-seven years. Examples with initials and/or dates must be regarded critically, as these may have been altered. The initials on Stuart arms are usually floriated and, although the J (James) or C (Charles) may have been changed to a G (George), the floriated shape will suggest a Stuart origin. Likewise those which bear dates may show the date of the alteration rather than the original painting. With careful examination one may be able to make out the old date underneath the new. Often more information about their construction, repair or re-painting may be found in the appropriate surviving churchwardens' accounts. (For identification of royal arms *see* UNITED KINGDOM, ROYAL HERALDRY.)   JET

Further reading

Hasler, C. *The Royal Arms* London, 1980.

Munroe Cautley, H. *Royal Arms and Commandments in our Churches* 1934.

Royal Beasts *see* Beasts

Royal Company of Archers

The Royal Company of Archers form the sovereign's Body Guard for Scotland, the equivalent in England being the Gentlemen at Arms. The Company was formed in 1676, for the practice of archery, then 'for many years much neglected' by an 'influential body of Noblemen and Gentlemen'. They received a royal charter in 1704 from Queen Anne, and assumed the style 'royal'. Their appointment as royal Body Guard in Scotland was granted by King George IV in 1822, their sole right to the honour was confirmed in 1830 and again (after much dispute) by Queen Victoria in 1842.

The archers number over 450 at the present time, and are under the command of a Captain-General, who from the year 1822 has had the title of Gold Stick for Scotland. The duties of the archers are now ceremonial — providing guards of honour to the sovereign when in Scotland, mounting parades and attending investitures, and royal proclamations.

The dress of the Company is a field-green uniform, the bonnet carrying eagle feathers, three for the Captain-General, two for officers and one for archers.

The Secretary of the Company wears a bonnet with a feather of a Himalayan Condor, the plume being 28 inches (70 cm) long. This custom dates from the mid-nineteenth century, when a former Governor General of India presented such a feather as a commemoration of his office.   JC-K

Further reading

Blair, A. *The History of the Royal Company of Archers 1951-76* 1977.

Hay, I. *The Royal Company of Archers 1676-1951* 1951.

Royal Consorts

The wife of a reigning king becomes queen for the lifetime of her husband, but the husband of a reigning queen does not automatically receive any particular title. The title of Prince Consort was bestowed upon Prince Albert by Queen Victoria. Philip, Duke of Edinburgh, husband of the present Queen, is not a Prince Consort. He was born a prince of Greece and Denmark, but on 28 February 1947 he became a naturalised British subject, renounced his foreign titles, and assumed the name Philip Mountbatten. On 19 November 1947 (the eve of his wedding to the Princess Elizabeth, later Queen Elizabeth II), he was created a Knight of the Garter (and was thus for a few hours Sir Philip Mountbatten KG), Duke of Edinburgh, Earl of Merioneth, and Baron Greenwich. In 1957 he was granted the status and dignity of a Prince of the United Kingdom.   KH

Royal Cypher

The Royal Cypher is formed from the initial of the sovereign combined with R for Rex or Regina, and, if appropriate, the number of the monarch of that name, ensigned by the imperial crown. The cypher has been in general use in Britain since the reign of George III, but there are numerous earlier examples of similar devices used in conjunction with the royal arms in churches, and from the medieval period, in costume, jewellery, fabrics, manuscripts and the architectural features of buildings.

Royal Dukedoms, British

The title of Duke of Lancaster has been borne by the English sovereign from the reign of Henry IV. The eldest son of the sovereign is Duke of Cornwall and Duke of Rothesay. Other contemporary royal dukes are York, Gloucester and Kent. Edward VIII, after his abdication, was created Duke of Windsor. Other dukedoms which have been held by members of the British royal families of the past have included Albany, Cambridge, Clarence, Connaught, Cumberland, Kendal and Sussex.   KH

Royal Foresters, Wardens and Verdurers

During the medieval period armorial devices allusive to these offices began to appear in the arms of those who held them. These included bugles, stags' heads and woodsmen's and foresters' heads, and hunting horns, of which the last were by far the most common. Such a horn, carved in stone, may be seen on the roof of St Briavel's Castle in Gloucestershire, which was the administrative centre of the Hundred of St Briavel's and the Royal Forest of Dean. As early as 1246 Matthew Paris painted a hunting horn beside the arms of John de Nevil, Chief Forester of the King (Henry III) in a roll of arms. The Kingsley family, sometime hereditary foresters of Delamere Forest in Cheshire, adopted an 'escutcheon of office' comprising *Argent a Bugle stringed Sable*. Two further examples, both from the county of Dorset, will illustrate the custom: the le Brets, hereditary fee foresters of Blackmore (*c*. 1260) bore *Argent three Hunting Horns stringed Sable*, and the De Forestereshegh (Forsey) family of Marshwood bore *Argent three Forester's Heads Sable*, a form of canting arms some fifty years later. Richard, Duke of York, as Justice of the Forests this side of Trent, adopted a device of a stag's head with his personal shield of arms between the antlers. Although there are too many exceptions to suggest a common practice, arms associated with foresters, wardens and verdurers were frequently argent charged sable.

See also HEREDITARY OFFICES *and* INSIGNIA OF OFFICE

Royal Heralds In the following text, these abbreviations apply: K, King of Arms; H, Herald; P, Pursuivant; E, Extraordinary. A date after a bracket indicates the earliest known mention of the office. N/D = no date.

English heralds There remains uncertainty as to when the first English royal herald was appointed; the earliest known reference occurs in 1276, when 'a King of Heralds North of Trent' is mentioned. This officer is unlikely to have been the first, for William the Marshal, an English nobleman who died in 1219 was 'a patron of heralds' and it seems unreasonable that there was no holder of a royal post at that earlier time. The first occasion that a herald's name of office occurs is in 1327, when Carlisle herald was created by King Edward III; even then it is not possible to state that the office was exclusively royal.

Identification is further complicated by the fact that early officers of arms moved from private to royal service (and back again), titles disappeared and were then revived, and some royal and non-royal heralds possessed similar titles. Early names and descriptions also tend to confuse the issue — as witness John Arundel alias Mowbray, Clarenceux King of Arms (died 1428), who was also known as John Clarenceux, John Mowbray Clarenceux, and whose son was called Richard Arundel. It was not unusual for names of offices to be drafted into service as family names. The widow of a Lancaster king of arms called herself Katherine Lancaster in 1436; the son of another officer

was styled Nicholas Norrey. (In 1851 the wife of a provincial king described herself as Norroy Queen, but that is merely amusing.)

It is recorded that around 4 July 1415, King Henry V created the office of Garter King of Arms and appointed to that position William Bruges, Guyenne King of Arms, who had previously been Chester Herald. In 1420 Bruges composed a document referring to the following kings of arms who in their time had been *premieres et chiefz de l'office* in England: Vaillant (1358), Marche — and Norroy? (*c*. 1394), Lancastre (1418), and Faucon (*c*. 1395). Research indicates that these officers had, in fact, taken turns to act as principal king.

In the time of King Edward III (1327-77), kings of heralds are recorded as Claroncel or Clarencell (1334), Norreys (1338), Volant or Vaillant (1354), Falcon (1359), Aquitaine (1366), and Guyenne. Some authorities regard Claroncel as king of the southern province of England, but others believe the jurisdiction (*c*. 1380-1419) was that of Leicester King of Arms — the title Clarenceux Roy d'arms des Clarenceux appearing in 1420. A similar uncertainty applies to the northern province. The title Roi d'Armes de North is applied to the officer called Norreys (1338, above), but the northern king (Rex Noreys) in 1384 was, in fact, March King of Arms. In the reigns of Henry V and Henry VI (1413-66) the king of the northern province was Lancaster, and it is likely that 'Norroy' became the *title* only from 1467. The late Stanford London (Norfolk Herald Extraordinary, and a distinguished historian) has suggested that prior to 1420 in the south, and 1467 in the north, the governing kings used their own personal titles although the provinces themselves were known as 'of the Clarenceux' and 'of the Norreys'.

Heralds identified in the reign of Edward III are Carlisle (1327, already mentioned), Windsor (1364), and Nazers (1369). In the reign of Richard II (1377-99) recorded names are Ireland K (1382, who with Guyenne, Clarenceux and Norreys completed the senior officers), Bordeaux H (1389), Chester H (1393) and Cornwall H (1398). In the reign of Henry V (1413-22) there were, in addition to the senior kings already mentioned, Agincourt K (1415), Rouge Croix P (1418) and Antelope P (1415). From the days of Henry VI (1422-71) there are references to Fleur de lis H (1435), Collar P (1436) and Bluemantle P (1448).

Other royal offices of arms are: Anjou K (*c*. 1425, to the Duke of Bedford, later to the crown. The title lapsed in 1436); Aquitaine K (1366, to Prince of Wales, a royal officer from 1380. It has been suggested the title was an alternative to Guyenne K); Arundel PE (1727); Beaumont HE (1982); Berwick P (*c*. 1460, appointed for service on the Scottish Marches); Blanche Lyon P (temp. Edward IV, and PE 1602); Blanc Sanglier P (1480, to Duke of Gloucester, then to the same as

Richard III. After Bosworth, Blanc Sanglier rescued the king's body and took it to the Grey Friars.); Boulogne P (1544, lapsed 1550); Calais P (1462, to serve holdings in Picardy. The office lapsed in 1558.); Carlisle H (1327, as mentioned earlier. It seems to have lasted until 1370, and was revived in 1483 before lapsing again in 1554. In 1703 it temporarily restored as HE.); Carnarvon PE (1911, for investiture of Prince of Wales); Chandos H (1360, to Sir John Chandos. In 1370 Chandos H was declared by Richard II Roy d'armes d'Engleterre, and in 1381 the officer, whose name is unknown, was made Ireland King of Arms.) Collar P (1436, perhaps named from the collar of SS); Comfort P (temp. Edward IV); Conk, more properly Concarneau P (1489 *ad partes Franciae*); Dublin H (1502, was perhaps a royal officer); Falcon K H and P (1359. The title was again bestowed, but as HE in 1813. The name comes from a royal badge.); Fitzalan PE (created for the coronation of Queen Victoria, and employed at the coronations of Edward VII and George V); Gloucester K (*c.* 1400, a royal officer previously in the service of the Earl of Gloucester. In 1726 the office was revived when the Bath King of Arms was given this additional title with jurisdiction over Wales. The title and authority were soon dropped.); Guisnes P (before 1476, to serve English possessions in France. The title lapsed temp. Elizabeth I, having by then become PE); Hambres P (perhaps Hampres, temp. Henry VIII); Hameltue P (1562); Ich Dien P (1476, to the 'princes in the Tower'); Lancaster K (*c.* 1347 to Earl of Lancaster. On accession of Henry IV, a royal officer, and for a time king of arms of the northern province. In 1464 the rank reverted to H.); Leicester H (originally to John of Gaunt but, *c.* 1398, a royal appointment. It has been suggested that, before Clarenceux, Leicester was king of arms of the southern province.); Maltravers HE (1887); March (before 1377, to Earl of March, then a royal H. In temp. Edward IV and Henry VII there was a March K.); Mowbray HE (1623); New Zealand H (1978); Norfolk H (1539, initially to Duke of Norfolk. At later revivals ranked as HE.); Northampton H (1370, to Earl of Northampton, then *c.* 1372/82 a crown officer); Northumberland H (*c.* 1375, to earls of Northumberland, but *c.* 1527 treated as a crown HE); Nottingham P (*c.* 1525 the office was granted crown status and shared fees as PE. In 1778 the office was designated PE.); Portcullis P (prior to 1490); Richmond H (1421, a royal officer from 1485 when the then private Richmond Herald was made a king of arms. The post reverted to H in 1510.); Risebank P (temp. Edward IV, a French garrison P); Rose P (1561, perhaps an error for Rose Blanche); Rose Blanche P (temp. Edward IV); Rouge Dragon P (1485); Rouge Rose (1604); Somerset H (possibly 1485, certainly from 1536); Suffolk HE (1707); Surrey HE (1856); Surroy K (a doubtful title. From time to time encountered as applied to the office

of king of arms south of Trent. It is not mentioned in any of the authoritative reference books, and may be discounted as a recognized title.); Ulster K (1552, the title replaced that of 'Ireland King of Arms', which had lapsed in 1487. The title was combined with that of Norroy in 1943 with jurisdiction over the six counties of Northern Ireland.); Wales H (1393) HE (1963); Wallingford P (1489); Windsor H (?1338); York H (1484). JC-K

Scottish heralds Until 1867 there were six royal heralds and six royal pursuivants in Scotland. Their titles, with the earliest recorded date for each office, were: Albany H (1401); Marchmont H (1438); Snowdoun H (1448); Ross H (1476); Rothesay H (1479) and Islay H (1493); Carrick P (1364); Unicorn P (1426); Dingwall P (1460); Bute P (1488); Kintyre P (1494) and Ormonde P (1501). In addition, two current pursuivants extra-ordinary may be noted: Falkland P (1493) and March P (1515). CJB

See also HERALDS OF THE NOBILITY *and* OFFICER OF ARMS (for current offices)

Royal Household From the time of the Conquest it has been the custom of English sovereigns to maintain a royal household of officers responsible for important duties. In the beginning the most important were the stewards, the master butler, the master chamberlain, the treasurer, the constables and the chancellor. Many of the offices still exist in modified form and, over the centuries, new ones have been created. Also over a period, as the functions of monarchy and government diverged, so too did the offices, some becoming GREAT OFFICES OF STATE, others remaining as offices of the royal household. Today, the sovereign's household in England contains many departments, the most impor-tant officers being Lord Chamberlain, Lord Steward, Master of the Horse, Treasurer, Comptroller, Vice-Chamberlain, Mistress of the Robes, Ladies of the Bedchamber, and Women of the Bedchamber. The officers of arms are members of the royal household.

The royal household in Scotland is headed by the Hereditary High Constable, followed by the Hereditary Master of the Household, Lord Lyon King of Arms, Hereditary Standard Bearer, the hereditary keepers of various palaces and castles, and the Captain-General of the Royal Company of Archers.

Details of the offices within the royal households appear in the *Peerages* of Debrett and Burke. JC-K

Royal Licence A Royal Licence varies the normal Laws of Arms. It is usually required to comply with a 'name and arms' clause in a will, whereby property is bequeathed on condition that the inheritor changes his surname and arms to include the surname and arms of his benefactor with his own. Either the surname is completely changed or the benefactor's surname is added to that of the inheritor; likewise the arms are similarly changed either completely, or as an added quartering. Arms thus quartered are an indivisible quartering, i.e. no intervening quartering can be placed between the arms thus quartered. An indivisible quartered coat can of course be marshalled with others, but must remain undivided as the first quartering. The Royal Licence with the Earl Marshall's Warrant must be recorded at the College of Arms, otherwise it is of no effect. A Royal Licence is also known as a Royal Sign Manual or Sign Manual.   HPB

Royal Society of St George The premier patriotic society of England. It is incorporated by Royal Charter and its patron is Her Majesty the Queen. The principal objects of the society are to foster the love of England and to strengthen England and the Commonwealth by spreading knowledge of English history, traditions and ideals, and to keep fresh the memory of those in all walks of life who served England or the Commonwealth (*see* ADDRESSES).   AHH-H

Royal 'Standard' The BANNER of the royal arms of the sovereign of England. Erroneously termed a 'standard' even in official documents. In England and Wales the first and third quarters are those of England (*Gules three Lions passant guardant in pale Or*), the second contains the arms of the sovereign of Scotland (*Or a Lion rampant within a double Tressure flory-counter-flory Gules*) and the fourth is charged with the *Harp Or stringed Argent* on an azure field for Ireland. When in Scotland, the quarterings of the royal banner are changed so that the Scottish arms are in the first and third quarters, and the English arms in the second. The present Queen has a series of banners appropriate to the various countries of the Commonwealth of which she is sovereign. The flying of the royal banner is the sole prerogative of the sovereign, and the flag should not be flown (or waved!) by any other person.

Royal Titles The titles accorded by tradition and honour to the present ruler of England are 'Elizabeth II by the Grace of God of the United Kingdom of Great Britain and Northern Ireland and of Her Other Realms and Territories Queen, Head of the Commonwealth, Defender of the Faith.'

These are but the latest in a long line of titles held over the centuries by English and British monarchs, and reflect changes dictated by twentieth-century political reality, while retaining the niceties of their sixteenth-century origins. They also observe the convention that some monarchs rule *countries*, while others (like the King of the Belgians) rule *peoples*. William the Conqueror, for example, was styled *Ducis Normannorum et Regis Anglorum* (Duke of the Normans and King of the English). His successors bore other titles, depending on their lineage, political aspirations,

actual dominion or method of acquiring the throne. For several centuries they were kings of France, at others dukes or counts of Aquitaine, Blois or Anjou. The consort of Mary I was also King of Spain (and for a brief span 'king' of England). King William III was Prince of Orange, the German Georges were Electors of Hanover. George V and his two reigning sons were Kings of Ireland and Emperors of India, as well as monarchs of the British kingdoms.

There is a long history of rulers being granted (or assuming) additional titles or elevated modes of address. Around AD 732 the father of Charlemagne was granted, by the pope, the style *patricius Romanorum*, granting him the duty of defending the church and some authority in Rome. There were early medieval 'kings' of Jerusalem, and of the Isle of Man. There were 'emperors' of Constantinople. Nearer our own time Napolean Bonaparte referred to himself as 'Emperor of the French and Hereditary Emperor of Austria'.

In the twentieth century, monarchs have been deemed Excellent, Serene, Sublime, and so on — the Japanese Emperor was the 'Son of Heaven'. The Nizam of Hyderabad was, until 1947, 'His Exalted Highness'; the Emperor of Ethiopia, until his post-war downfall, 'Lion of Lions and Elect of God'; the Shah-in-Shah of Persia was holder of 'the Peacock Throne'. No doubt such titles will last as long as there are sovereigns.   JC-K

Further reading
Fryde, E.B. et al. *Handbook of British Chronology* 1986.
Pinches J.H. and R.V. *The Royal Heraldry of England* London, 1974.

Royal Victorian Order, The Founded in 1896 by Queen Victoria, this order is normally bestowed on members of the royal household and those who have rendered personal service to the sovereign. It is very much a private order, entirely in the gift of the sovereign, and its investitures reflect this and contain little pageantry. The chapel of the order is the Queen's Chapel of the Savoy in London, which is a Royal Peculiar. The chapel is small and there is no display of banners, though Knights and Dames Grand Cross have stall plates.

The present sovereign of the order is, of course, the Queen, and the Grand Master is H.M. Queen Elizabeth, the Queen Mother. There are five classes: Knights and Dames Grand Cross (GCVO), Knights and Dames Commander (KCVO, DCVO), Commanders (CVO), Lieutenants, formerly Members Fourth Class (LVO), and Members, formerly Members Fifth Class (MVO).

The badge of the order consists of a white enamelled Maltese Cross with a central oval medallion in crimson enamel bearing the Imperial and Royal Cypher of Queen Victoria within a blue circlet, with the motto 'Victoria' and ensigned with the Imperial Crown. The Star for Knights and Dames Grand Cross is of chipped silver and is charged with the badge. The Star for Knights and Dames Commander is composed of a silver Maltese Cross with silver rays issuing from the angles of the cross. This also bears the badge of the order, but with the cross in frosted silver instead of white enamel. Commanders of the order wear the badge on a ribbon of dark blue with narrow edges of three stripes: red, white and red. Lieutenants and Members of the order wear a badge on a chest ribbon or bow. The Collar of the order is of gold, composed of octagonal pieces and ornately pierced oblong frames linked with gold. Each octagonal piece bears a blue enamel plaque, in the centre of which is a gold rose charged with an escarbuncle. The oblong frames each contain a portion of the inscription 'Victoria — Britt — Reg — Def.Ind — Ind.Emp'. The letters are in white enamel edged in gold. The badge is pendent from a central octagonal piece which is highly ornamented in blue enamel, edged with red and charged with a white saltire, on which is a gold medallion of Queen Victoria. The mantle is of dark blue silk.

The Royal Victorian Chain, instituted by Edward VII in 1902, is bestowed only rarely and for singular circumstances.   SS

Royal Warrant Holders Henry II is believed to have granted the first Royal Warrant or charter in recognition of personal service to the sovereign or to members of his family or household. From the mid-twelfth century such charters were granted collectively to trade guilds such as the weavers, drapers and mercers. The practice seems to have been well-established during the reign of Elizabeth I, and it is likely that the royal arms were first displayed by tradesmen in the eighteenth century. The majority of these tradespeople were in the cities of London and Westminster, and in other towns with royal associations, such as Windsor and Edinburgh. In the late eighteenth century the use of the royal arms for advertising purposes was discreet: by means of small advertisements in the press and in books, and on trade cards. As the nineteenth century progressed warrants were granted for specific products as well as general services to the sovereign and his family. Such warrants were granted under oath and by the Board of the Green Cloth, but the system was revised during Victoria's reign. Responsibility for the granting of warrants passed to the Lord Chamberlain's office, aided by the Royal Household Tradesmen's Warrants Committee and the Royal Warrant Holders' Association, which received a royal charter in 1907. A Royal Warrant lapses at the death of the member of the royal family in whose name it was granted, though the grantee may continue to use the phrase 'By appointment to His (or Her) Late Majesty', but not the arms. Today about one thousand firms enjoy the privilege of displaying the royal arms, and they are listed in Debrett's *Alphabetical List of Royal Warrant Holders.*

Strictly speaking, the use of a coat of arms for this purpose is contrary to good armorial practice, a royal badge (as used by Warrant Holders to H.R.H. The Prince of Wales) being a more appropriate device.
Further reading
Whittington, B. *A Short History of the Royal Warrant* 1961.

Romania, Royal Arms of Quarterly 1 *Azure an Eagle displayed crowned Or armed and langued Gules holding in the dexter claw a Sword and in the sinister a Sceptre proper in its beak a Cross paty and in dexter chief a Sun in Splendour Or* (Wallachia) 2 *Gules a Bull's Head cabossed a Mullet between the horns and in sinister chief a Crescent Or* (Moldavia) 3 *Gules a demi-Lion rampant crowned issuant from a Coronet and holding in the forepaws a Mullet Or* (Banat) 4 *Azure two Dolphins respectant heads in base Or* (Dobrudja) over all an escutcheon of pretence *Quarterly Argent and Sable* (Hohenzollern).

Rules of Armory In armory there are no rules, only conventions. *See also* BLAZON *and* TINCTURE CONVENTION

Russia, Armorial Practice There had been an ancient nobility in Russia since earliest civilized Viking and Slav times, but there emerged no equivalent of what European nations were to regard as 'knighthood and chivalry'.

The right to arms in Russia was introduced by Tsar Peter the Great (1689-1725), and a House of Nobles under a Herald Marshal was instituted as late as 1722. The Tsar in effect *created* a new nobility, entry to which was attained by signal services to state and realm, and in time all important posts were held by 'noblemen' who were, by definition, armigerous.

A register of the old nobility (called the *Rodoslovnoia Knega*) had been started around the year 1550 in the reign of Ivan IV, and was copied several times prior to 1680. The innovations of Peter the Great included European-style titles and arms, but it was left to Tsar Paul (1796-1802) to initiate a record of armorial bearings, not only for families of what is generally regarded as Russia but also for the countries which came into the Empire: Estonia, Finland, Georgia, Latvia, Lithuania, and so on.

Heraldic records are kept in various museums in the Soviet Union, but many were destroyed, and others found their way abroad. Today armory as here defined has no place in Russia, but there are many national awards analogous to modern orders of chivalry, typical styles being the orders of Alexander Nevsky, the Red Banner, the Patriotic War, the Glory of Motherhood, and so on.   JC-K

Russia, Imperial Arms of *Or a double-headed Eagle displayed Sable beaked langued and membered Gules each*

head royally crowned Or holding in the dexter claw a Sceptre and in the sinister an Orb all Or charged on the breast with the arms of Moscow *Gules the Figure of St George mounted slaying the Dragon all proper*, the shield encircled by the Collar of the Order of St Andrew.

The wings of the eagle charged with eight shields four to the dexter and four to the sinister. Dexter: 1 Kazan *Argent a Basilisk* (or dragon) *Sable winged Gules crowned Or* 2 Poland *Gules an Eagle displayed Argent crowned Or* 3 Tauria *Or a double-headed Eagle displayed Sable* charged on the breast with a shield *Azure a Cross triple-traversed within a Bordure Or* 4 tierced in pairle reversed: Kiev *Azure the Archangel Michael proper* Vladimir *Gules a Lion rampant guardant Or armed and langued Azure crowned and holding in the forepaws a Long Cross-crosslet couped at the base Argent* Novgorod *Argent a Throne Or cushioned Gules surmounted by Candles flamant proper on the seat of the throne a Sceptre and a Sword saltirewise Or supported by two Bears Sable on a base Azure two Fishes naiant respectant Argent* Sinister: 5 Astrakan *Azure in chief a Royal Crown Or in base a Scimitar fesswise point to the dexter proper* 6 Siberia *Ermine two Martens Sable* (or *Sables*) *counter rampant supporting a Royal Crown Or behind them two Arrows saltirewise and a Bow fesswise Gules* 7 Georgia (otherwise quarterly: Kabarda, Iberia, Kartalinia and Armenia, in point Circassia, over all Georgia) *Or St George proper mounted on a Horse Sable slaying a Dragon also Sable winged Vert* 8 Finland *Gules semy of Roses Argent a Lion rampant crowned Or brandishing in the dexter forepaw a Sword and holding in the sinister forepaw a Scabbard all proper* the whole ensigned with the Imperial Crown.   KH

The great Russian double-headed eagle, holding a sceptre in the dexter claw, and an orb in the sinister.

Sable (Abbr. Sa.) The armorial tincture black.

Sagittarius *or* **Sagittary** A centaur with a bow and arrow.

Sail In the Middle Ages a singularly effective means of displaying arms on warships. Modern racing yachts also sport highly colourful spinnakers but, as yet, these are rarely used for armorial purposes. Also an armorial charge.

St Benedict of Aviz, Order of A Portuguese order of knights following monastic rules, founded *c.* 1144. The badge was a green Latin Cross, the limbs ending in the letter M for Mary.   KH

St Benet, The Guild Church of St Benet in Queen Victoria Street, London, has been the church of the College of Arms since 1555, when Philip and Mary I gave Derby House, at the northeast corner of the churchyard, to the heralds. Since that time they have had their own seats in the church. The burial of at least twenty-five officers of arms, starting with Sir Gilbert Dethick in 1584, is recorded in the registers together with a large number of domestic staff. There are several memorials in the church — one to the memory of John Charles Brooke, Somerset Herald, who was one of sixteen people who suffocated in the press when George III and Queen Charlotte visited the Theatre in the Haymarket in 1794. It was to this church on 2 March 1984 that the kings, heralds and pursuivants of the College of Arms, together with the Duke of Norfolk (the Earl Marshal), the Earl of Arundel (Deputy Earl Marshal), and the heralds extraordinary, processed from the College to give thanks on the occasion of the Quincentenary of their Incorporation as a College in 1484. The flags hanging in the church are the personal arms of the thirteen current members of the College, with the Duke of Norfolk's banner completing the set. On the east wall there is a seventeenth-century carved and painted coat of arms of the College, while on the north wall is the Garter Board — the personal arms of each Garter Principal King of Arms since the inception of the office in 1398. (Church Guide by Revd. A. Pryse-Hawkins)

Armorial spinnaker of the Bank of New Zealand: *Azure on a Chevron Or voided of the field between four Mullets Argent three in chief and one in base five Bezants.* **The Bank was the principal sponsor of New Zealand's challenge for the 1987 America's Cup,**

St George, Society of the Friends of The Society of the Friends of St George's and Descendants of the Knights of the Garter was formed in 1937 with the object of maintaining the ancient chapel of St George at Windsor Castle, home of the Most Noble Order of the Garter. It has two kinds of members: Friends and Descendants. Applications for the latter category must include proof of descent from a Knight of the Garter through the distaff side. *See* ADDRESSES.

St Hubert, Order of Founded in Julich-Berg in 1444, and also known as the Order of the Hunting Horn. The badge, suspended from a collar of horns, was an eight-pointed cross, edged with beads, with rays between the arms of the cross and charged in its centre with a picture of St Hubert. KH

St Iago, Order of (Ordem Militar de St Iago da Espada) The Portuguese branch of a Spanish order (see below) founded in 1170 for the succour of pilgrims to Santiago de Compostella, where the bones of the saint (Jacob the Elder) were found in the year 829. The Spanish and Portuguese branches were formed in 1290, and confirmed as separate orders in 1320. The Spanish order was eventually abolished, but the Portuguese order was secularized in 1789, re-organized in 1862 and reconstituted on 24 November 1963. The order has five classes: Grand Cross, Grand Officer, Commander, Officer and Knight. The badge of the order is a red enamelled cross fleury of gold. The star is multi-pointed and carries at its centre the badge of the order on a white background, surrounded by a laurel wreath. Both the Collar and the Grand Collar are gold embellished with laurel wreaths, shells, and badges of the order.

St Jacob of the Sword, Order of A Spanish order of religious knights, formed in 1170. The badge was a red cross with fleur-de-lis on three arms and a sword point at the foot, known as the *cross espada*.
See also ST IAGO, ORDER OF

St John of Jerusalem, Orders of The Sovereign Military and Hospitaller Order of St John of Jerusalem, called of Rhodes, called of Malta (generally known as the Order of Malta), came into existence between *c.* 1080 when a hospital for pilgrims was established in Jerusalem by the abbey of St Mary of the Latins, and 1113, when the hospital, its administrators and dependencies were recognized by the papacy as an Order of the Church, dedicated to the care of the sick poor. Half a century after its foundation it assumed military as well as hospitaller functions, and by 1200 it was playing a major rôle in the defence of the Christian settlements in Palestine and Syria which had been set up by the Crusaders. From its origins it was endowed on a massive scale in western Europe and it

developed an international structure to manage these properties for the benefit of its work in the East. Driven from Palestine with the rest of the Catholics in 1291, the Hospitallers of St John took over the island of Rhodes, off the coast of Asia Minor, which became their base for naval operations against Muslim shipping. They ruled the island as a semi-independent state until 1522. They were then given the island of Malta, which they held until 1798. During the centuries of the Order's government of Rhodes and Malta it became recognized as a sovereign power.

With the loss of Malta the order's military functions ceased, and hospitaller work again became its only duty. It moved its headquarters to Rome in 1834. It is still regarded by many states (though not by all) as a sovereign subject of international public law. The seat of the Grand Magistry in Rome (*see* ADDRESSES), under the present Grand Master, HMEH Fra' Angelo de Mojana di Cologna, has the right of extra-territoriality recognized by the Italian state.

The members of the order are divided into various classes. The brothers of the first class are professed religious, in terms of canon law, being members of an Order of the Church, recognized as such by the Holy See. But there are only about thirty of them. The vast majority (*c.* 10,000) of the members, in the second and third classes, are laymen who in other orders would be called *confratres* or tertiaries. They are grouped in five grand priories, three sub-priories, and thirty-seven national associations. Among its other activities, the headquarters in Rome runs the AIOM, an international campaign against hunger, misery, sickness and ignorance, which regularly sends medical stores to many Third World countries, as well as providing special help to Portugal and Poland; the CIOMAL, in the forefront of the struggle against leprosy, with an emphasis on the rehabilitation of lepers; pilgrimages to Lourdes; an institute of hospital study and research; and a School of Paediatrics. Each of the national associations organizes charitable activities within its region, and the work of strong associations, including those in Germany (where the *Malteser-Hilfsdienst* has over 66,000 active workers), Austria, Brazil, Great Britain, France, Switzerland, Ireland, Italy and the west coast of the United States, is outstanding.

There are also four independent Orders of St John, which are not Orders of the Church — indeed they are not Catholic Orders — but are Christian Orders of Chivalry, recognized by the sovereign authorities in their respective states. They are more overtly Christian than most present-day Orders of Chivalry because of their traditions as religious confraternities of laymen. Three of them originated in the Bailiwick of Branden-burg, a province of the medieval order, which broke away, adopted Protestantism and retained its identity after the Reformation.

Die Balley Brandenburg des Ritterlichen Ordens

Sankt Johannis vom Spital zu Jerusalem was recognized by the crown of Prussia in 1852, and since the fall of the German monarchy it has been recognized by the Federal German Republic. Besides seventeen associations in Germany, the order has four outside (the Finnish, French and Swiss, which are officially recognized in their respective countries, and the Hungarian in exile). Its headquarters are in Bonn (*see* ADDRESSES); its head, styled *Der Herrenmeister*, is HRH Prince Wilhelm Karl of Prussia. It runs thirteen hospitals with 3,200 beds in the Federal Republic, together with fourteen old peoples' homes with 1,500 places. It manages the Johanniter-Unfall-Hilfe, with 16,000 active workers, and the Johanniter-Hilfs-gemeinschaft with 1,650 participants. It co-operates with the German associations of the Order of Malta, and it engages in work in Africa as well as in Germany.

Johanniter Orde in Nederland, originally subject to Die Balley Brandenburg, was founded as an independent order in 1946. Its headquarters are in The Hague (*see* ADDRESSES), and its head is HRH Prince Bernhard of the Netherlands. Its foundations include a hospital and homes for disabled elderly people and spastic children. It co-operates with the Dutch association of the Order of Malta and with the Commandery of Utrecht of the Teutonic Order.

Johanniterorden i Sverige, also once part of Die Balley Brandenburg, was embodied by royal charter in 1946. Its headquarters are in Stockholm (*see* ADDRESSES), and the High Patron is HM King Carl XVI Gustaf. It supports many Swedish Christian charitable organizations, particularly those in cities involved in the care of the old and the sick.

The fourth non-Catholic order, The Grand Priory of the Most Venerable Order of the Hospital of St John of Jerusalem (generally known as The Order of St John), came into existence in 1831 as a result of initiatives taken by some French Knights of Malta, who intended to set up a non-Catholic priory in England, along the lines of the Bailiwick of Brandenburg and of a short-lived Russian Orthodox Grand Priory, which was in existence for a few years around 1800. The French knights' activities were disowned by the Grand Magistry in Rome, but the English priory remained in being, attracted the support of the royal family, and in 1888 was incorporated by royal charter. Its headquarters are in London (*see* ADDRESSES), and its Sovereign Head is HM Queen Elizabeth II. It has six priories, two commanderies, and forty St John Councils throughout the English-speaking world; there is also a St John Society in the United States of America. It manages two foundations: the St John Opthalmic Hospital in Jerusalem, and St John Ambulance Service in about fifty countries throughout the Commonwealth. The latter provides ambulance units — there are *c.* 60,000 members of the Ambulance Brigade in

England alone — and training in first aid. Through a joint committee with the Red Cross it is active on behalf of disabled ex-servicemen.

These five orders have friendly relations and accord each other recognition. There are also about twenty very small Orders of St John, most of which claim descent from the former Russian Orthodox Grand Priory, but are not recognized by the five orders listed above.   JR-S

The arms of the Grand Priory in the British Realm of the Venerable Order of the Hospital of St John of Jerusalem are *Gules a Cross Argent in the first quarter a representation of the Royal Crest of England*. Granted in 1926, these arms are an augmented version of the arms of the medieval order *Gules a Cross Argent*. The insignia of the order may be displayed in association with armorial bearings. Bailiffs, Knights, Dames and Chaplains, may display their shields on the badge of the order, while others may show the badge suspended below the shield by an appropriate ribbon. The badge of the British order is a white cross of eight points (the Maltese Cross), embellished in the four principal angles alternately with a lion passant guardant and a unicorn passant. Again, the white Maltese Cross was the original badge of the order and is always associated with its sable livery. The badges of other national orders and associations are similarly embellished with appropriate figures in the principal angles. Bailiffs and Dames Grand Cross may bear, as a chief of augmentation to their own arms, the arms of the order, and are entitled to supporters, though these are not hereditary.

Bailiffs and Knights of Justice and Grace do not receive the accolade, and membership of the Order does not confer any rank, title or precedence. Post-nominal letters signifying membership are used only for correspondence within the order (*see* ABBREVIATIONS OF THE CLASSES OF BRITISH AND COMMONWEALTH ORDERS).

Further reading
Cole-Mackintosh *A Century of Service to Mankind. A History of the St John Ambulance Brigade* 1986.
King, E. *The Knights of St John in the British Realm* London, 1967.

For the Rhodes period:
Luttrell, A.T. *The Hospitallers in Cyprus, Rhodes, Greece and the West (1291-1440)* London, 1978.
— *Latin Greece, The Hospitallers and the Crusades, 1291-1400* London, 1982.

For the Malta period:
Cavaliero *The Last of the Crusaders* 1960.
There is no general history for the period since 1798, although a start was made by M. de Pierredon *Histoire politique de l'Ordre Souverain de Saint-Jean de Jérusalem (Ordre de Malte) de 1789 à 1955* 2nd edn., 2 vols. to date (1956-).

Riley-Smith J.S.C. *The Knights of St John in Jerusalem and Cyprus c. 1050-1310* London, 1967.

St Lazarus of Jerusalem, The Military and Hospitaller Order of The foundation of the Order of St Lazarus and the evolution of the Italian commandery is described under the heading of ST MAURICE AND ST LAZARUS.

Following the fall of Acre in 1291, some members of the Order of St Lazarus moved to France, where a branch house already existed. The Grand Master of the order settled his seat at the commandery of Boigny and attained the protection of the French crown. In 1604 King Henri IV of France proclaimed himself supreme sovereign of the Order of St Lazarus but was unable to obtain the pope's agreement to restore the many privileges lost in 1573, when the Italian commandery had been merged with that of St Maurice. In 1607, however, he was granted a papal bull to found a new order to Our Lady of Mount Carmel and, in 1608, he combined this with the French section of the Order of St Lazarus. The united orders continued until the time of the French Revolution, at which point the Mount Carmel portion became dormant and the Order of St Lazarus achieved, in France, independence under the protection of the House of Bourbon. Following the flight of Charles X the order was placed, in 1837, under the spiritual protection of the uniate patriarch of Antioch, Alexandria and Jerusalem of the Melchite Rite until 1935, when Don Francisco de Borbon y de la Torre, Duke of Seville, obtained permission of his cousin King Alfonso XIII to accept the office of Grand Master.

In the 1960s the English Tongue of the order was revived with the blessing of the Grand Master (*see* ADDRESSES). The arms of the order *Argent a Cross Vert* were matriculated by Lord Lyon King of Arms (the order having previously enjoyed many properties in Scotland, including St Giles Cathedral, Edinburgh), and recorded by the Chief Herald of Ireland.   JC-K

St Maurice and St Lazarus, The Order of (SS Maurizio e Lazzaro) This order is a combination of two ancient foundations. The more ancient, St Lazarus, was established as a military and religious community at the time of the Latin Kingdom of Jerusalem around AD 1090. From its inception the order was concerned with the relief of leprosy, and many of its members were lepers who had been knights in other orders. It became very rich, its practices dubious and its funds much abused. With the fall of Acre in 1291 the knights of St Lazarus fled the Holy Land and Egypt and settled in France and, in 1311, in Naples.

In the sixteenth century the order again declined in credit and wealth, and the Duke of Savoy took over as Grand Master in 1571. Two years later Pope Gregory XIII merged the Italian foundation of the order of St Lazarus with that of St Maurice, and the new community was charged to defend the Holy See as well as to continue to assist lepers. The war galleys of the order fought against the Turks and the Barbary pirates and when leprosy again broke out the order founded, in 1773, a hospital in Aosta.

The order of St Maurice dates from 1434 and was founded by Amadeus VIII, Duke of Savoy, who became Pope Felix V. The order declined, but in 1572 was re-established by Pope Pius V at the instigation of the then Duke of Savoy. As noted above, the order merged in 1573 with the Order of St Lazarus. The combined order still exists as an Italian dignity and is granted, in the twentieth century, to persons eminent in the public service, science, art, letters, trade and charitable works.   JC-K

St Michael and St George, The Most Distinguished Order of The order was founded by the Prince Regent in 1818 on behalf of George III, with the aim of bestowing royal favour on the people of Malta and the Ionian Islands in reward for their outstanding loyalty during the Napoleonic War. The order was reorganized in 1864 following the ceding of the islands to Greece, and became an honour for British subjects serving overseas, particularly in the diplomatic service. Ladies have been admitted since 1965 and there are now approximately 2,400 members: Knights or Dames Grand Cross (GCMG), Knights or Dames Commander (KCMG, DCMG), and Companions (CMG).

The mantle of the order is Saxon blue satin, lined with scarlet silk. The silver faceted star of the order is embroidered on the left shoulder. This is charged with a plain red cross on which is a representation of St Michael suppressing Satan, within a blue circlet bearing the motto of the order 'Auspicium Melioris Aevi' (Token of a better age). The collar of the order consists of eight alternating gold lions and white enamelled Maltese crosses of eight points, four, monograms of St Michael and four of St George. Pendent from a centrepiece (composed of two winged lions counter passant guardant, each with a nimbus and holding a book and seven arrows, the whole ensigned with the crown) is the badge of the order. This is a gold cross of fourteen points of white enamel, edged with gold, having in the centre on one side St Michael encountering Satan and on the other St George on horseback slaying the dragon, within a blue circlet on which is inscribed the motto of the order. The cross is ensigned by the Imperial Crown, and is worn by the Knights Grand Cross pendent from the collar or a Saxon blue sash with a red stripe. The Sovereign of the order is HM the Queen, and the Grand Master is HRH the Duke of Kent. Knights and Dames Commander wear the badge suspended from a neck ribbon and a star of the order on their left side.

Companions wear the badge pendent from a neck ribbon of Saxon blue and scarlet.

The service for the order is held annually in its chapel, established at St Paul's Cathedral in 1904, and the banners and stall plates of the twenty-one Knights and Dames Grand Cross are displayed there. Interestingly (and uniquely) the banners are carried in procession at the annual service by relatives and friends, who thereby become retainers for the occasion. SS

St Michael, Order of A French order formed in 1469. The badge, suspended from a collar of shields and cords, was a gold oval medallion bearing the picture of the Archangel Michael. KH

St Olav, Order of The only Norwegian order of chivalry now awarded. Founded on 21 August 1847, it now has five classes: Grand Cross, Commander with Star, Commander, Officer and Chevalier. The principal badge is a silver star with eight points. For the rank of Grand Cross this has at its centre a white enamel cross with a royal lion on a scarlet enamel convex circle. The sash is of watered scarlet, with blue and double white edges. At the discretion of the Grand Master, holders of the Grand Cross may be awarded a collar. JC-K

St Patrick, The Most Illustrious Order of 'Quis Separabit, MDCCLXXXIII' (Who will sever us, 1783), the motto of The Most Illustrious Order of St Patrick, refers directly to the political considerations which led to its institution by King George III on 5 February 1783. The foundation of the order followed within only a few months of the declaration of the legislative independence of the Irish parliament from that of Great Britain, after which, in theory, the two kingdoms were linked only in the person of their common sovereign. The constitutional independence of Ireland, largely won by Henry Gratton and the Volunteer Movement, was to prove illusory and ended in 1801 when the Act of Union abolished the Dublin legislature, but for almost two decades Ireland was, in theory, a separate kingdom. The Order of St Patrick was founded at this point as an overtly political act of the crown to stress that although Ireland had indeed established its legislative independence it remained inseparably linked to Great Britain! At the same time as providing Ireland with a national order of chivalry, mimicking the much older orders of the Garter of England and Thistle of Scotland, the unique relationship between the three kingdoms was stressed both in the motto 'Who will sever us' and in the insignia which cleverly used the shamrock, the Irish symbol par-excellence, to carry the sub-charges of three crowns. This allusion was well understood in Ireland where St Patrick, the national saint to whom the new order was dedicated, had used the three-leaved shamrock to explain the greatest mystery of the Christian faith: the distinction in personalities but union in essence of the Holy Trinity. The parallel to the kingdoms of England, Ireland and Scotland was obvious.

According to the statutes promulgated in 1783, and revised in 1905, the order was to consist of the Sovereign, a Grand Master who was the Lord Lieutenant of Ireland pro-tem, and twenty-two knights with an additional number of honorary knights and officers. One of these officers was Ulster King of Arms (predecessor of the Chief Herald of Ireland). There was no chapel of the order *per se*, but until the disestablishment of the Church of Ireland investitures were normally held in St Patrick's Cathedral, Dublin. After disestablishment the ceremonies were conducted in St Patrick's Hall, Dublin Castle. The banners and stall plates of former knights can still be seen on display in both buildings.

The insignia of the order consisted of a collar, a breast star, and a neck badge. The official insignia was of pure gold and was issued by the chancery of the order to recipients, whose heirs were obliged to return it on the holder's death. The collar was composed of seven roses, alternately enamelled with white leaves enclosed by red ones and vice versa, alternating with six harps being tied together by elaborate open-work knots. The final harp of the collar was surmounted by the Imperial State Crown, and pendent therefrom was the badge of the order which displayed a shamrock or trefoil of green enamel, each of its leaves charged with an Imperial State Crown resting on the so-called 'Cross-saltire of St Patrick', in red enamel on a white field. This device was encircled with a motto strap of sky-blue enamel bearing the inscription 'Quis Separabit, MDCCLXXXIII' which was itself enclosed by a wreath of shamrocks, enamelled in their proper colours, on a gold field. The badge, which was oval in shape, was detachable from the collar and could be worn as a neck decoration on a ribbon of sky-blue watered silk. The star of the order repeated the design of the badge (only without the wreath of shamrocks) on a silver star of eight points. In addition to this insignia all knights possessed mantles which were worn at investitures and specified formal occasions. These were of sky-blue satin or poplin, lined with white silk, and displayed the star of the order embroidered on the right side. According to the statutes, only materials manufactured in Ireland were to be used in making them. MCM

Further reading

Galloway, P. *The Most Illustrious Order of St Patrick* 1983.

St Stephen, Order of One of the last of the orders of religious knights, founded in Tuscany in 1554, it bore an eight-pointed Maltese Cross with gold lilies between the arms. KH

Saints, Attributes of *see* **Christian Symbols**

Salade *see* **Sallet**

Salamander The salamander of nature is a harmless little amphibian which in fables was invested with fabulous powers which commended it to heraldry. It was thought that if a fire burned for seven years a salamander would be born. Also it was believed to be the most poisonous living creature. A salamander, if frightened, will exude a milky substance which makes its skin very moist, and so it was believed to be able to withstand any amount of heat and even to put out fires. Therefore as an armorial device it is always surrounded by fire, and in early heraldry was depicted somewhat like a short-legged dog. One writer, owning some of its supposed hair, says, 'I have several times put this in the fire and made it red hot and after taken out, which being cold, yet remaineth perfect wool or fine downy hair.' Marco Polo disbelieved all this, saying that the true salamander was an incombustible substance found in the earth, and in fact a substance known as Vein of Salamander found in the mountains of Tartary is asbestos. Pliny believed the creature to be a kind of lizard which sought great heat in which to breed, but that it could quench fire with the frigidity of its body. He experimented with it, but the salamander was reduced to ashes from which he made medicine.

The salamander has become the symbol of enduring faith which triumphs over the ardour of passion. It was the badge of Francis I of France, with the motto 'I nourish [the good] and extinguish [the bad]', and is beautifully portrayed, much more lizard-like, in the Chateau of Blois, Loire-en-Cher, France. It is used by some insurance companies in their arms with an obvious reference to its fire-fighting attributes.   MY

Salient *see* **Attitude**

Sallet *or* **Salade** A metal helmet rounded over the skull. It rested entirely on the head and was not attached to the body armour. Popular at the end of the fifteenth century, it took several forms and was often 'tailed' at the rear and visored.

Saltire An ORDINARY. A diagonal cross on which St Andrew, the patron saint of Scotland, is said to have been crucified, hence its popularity in that country where a silver saltire on a blue field is the national device. However, its use in Celtic art clearly pre-dates Christianity, and the saltire is the foundation of most circular knotwork of Scottish and Irish Pictish interlacing panels.

The word itself may derive from the Old French *saultoir* and the Latin *saltare*, meaning to leap. The notion that the saltire was granted to those who successfully besieged the walls of towns is an attractive one, but difficult to substantiate. Use of the saltire for armorial purposes is not confined to Scotland, of course. A saltire was attributed to the ancient kingdom of Mercia, for example, and *Gules a Saltire Argent* are the famous arms of the ubiquitous Nevill family. The saltires in the arms of such towns as Amsterdam, Nieuwer-Amstel and Bergen-op-Zoom are taken to be symbols of justice, and those in the arms of Hereford, *Gules three Lions passant guardant Argent within a Bordure Azure charged with ten Saltires also Argent*, represent the insurgent Scots who, in 1645, besieged the city and its Royalist forces.

Charges borne on a saltire are depicted in an upright

OPPOSITE **Painting by the late Dan Escott of the principal knights and nobles who fought at the Battle of Crecy in 1346. This was the first major English victory of the Hundred Years War. An invading English army under Edward III was attacked in a strong defensive position near the village of Crecy in Ponthieu by a French force of considerable size. English long-bowmen wrought havoc in the ranks of the mounted French knights, whose reckless and undisciplined charges made little impact on the English lines. After repeated assaults, lasting well into the night, the French retreated in confusion leaving thousands of their dead on the field, to be identified and recorded on the following morning by the English heralds. The valley below the ridge is still called *La Vallée aux clercs*, the Valley of Clerks. The chronicler Froissart tells us that King Edward established his command post in a windmill and it was from there that he watched his sixteen-year-old son, Edward Plantagenet, later called the Black Prince, win his spurs. Incredibly, the English seem to have lost less than fifty men.**

Dan Escott's spirited style and his sometimes enigmatic interpretation of armorial subjects are among the joys of twentieth-century heraldic art.

position unless otherwise specified. The saltire may be subject to all the variations of field and line, and may be couped, either to conform to the outline of the shield or flag within which it is depicted, or vertically, horizontally or at right angles to its limbs. It may be employed as a principal charge or as minor charges and there is no reason why there should not be as many variations of the saltire as there are of the cross, though examples are surprisingly uncommon.

> Diminutive: fillet saltire
> Parted field: per saltire
> Varied field: none
> Disposition: in saltire
> Inclination: saltirewise

Sangliante *see* **Attributes**

Sanguine A rare armorial tincture of blood-red colour (*see* STAINS).

Sans Nombre A gerattie field of an unspecified number of charges.

Sans Wings *see* **Attributes**

Satyr A mythological creature, half man and half goat.

Satyral A monster with the face of an old man, a lion's body and an antelope's horns and tail.

Savage *or* **Wild Man** A long-haired, bearded man, wreathed with leaves about the loins and temples, and carrying a club.

Saxon A demand for armorial devices to represent Saxon associations, particularly in civic arms, has

---

OPPOSITE **The arms of Francis, Viscount Lovel K.G. (1454-87?) Painting by Anthony Wood based on Lovel's Garter Stall Plate at St George's Chapel, Windsor. The Lovel arms,** *Barry nebuly of six Or and Gules***, are quartered with those of Deincourt** *Azure billety a Dance Or***, Holand** *Azure fleuretty a Lion rampant guardant Argent***, Grey of Rotherfield** *Barry Argent and Azure a Baston Gules***, and charged with an inescutcheon for Burnell** *Argent a Lion Rampant Sable crowned Or***.**

Lovel's loyalty to Richard III was much resented by the king's opponents. A contemporary political broadsheet contained a number of armorial allusions, including one to Lovel's crest, a silver wolf-dog (*lupellus***) allusive to his name:**

> 'The Cat [Sir William Catesby], the Rat
> [Sir Richard Ratcliffe], and Lovel our Dog
> Ruleth all England under an Hog [the King].'

The mantling in his arms is purple lined ermine, powdered with the Lovel badge of a gold padlock.

---

resulted in the development of several charges to which have been attributed the term 'Saxon'.
(i) Saxon Cross: a cross pommé, the limbs of which are slightly tapered.
(ii) Saxon Crown: a type of crest coronet.
(iii) Saxon Head: beardless and with fair hair.
(iv) Saxonized: a variation of line consisting of alternating tapered projections and counter-projections, each terminating in a 'knob' similar in appearance to the projections of a Saxon crown.
(v) Saxon Sword: a seax.
(vi) Saxon Wheel Cross: a plain cross within an annulet, the outer edge of which is indented.

Saxonized *see* **Lines, Varied**

Saxony, Royal Arms of *Barry of ten Or and Sable over all a Wreath of Rue bendwise Vert*. The shield ensigned with the Royal Crown of Saxony.

Scaling Ladder A ladder with hooks to secure it to that which is to be scaled.

Scarlet Rod *see* **Gentleman Usher**

Schools Many privately owned schools are armigerous; most state schools are not. Regrettably, most armigerous schools do not possess an armorial badge and are obliged to use their arms on uniforms, which is not good practice. Even worse are the quasi-armorial devices on shields worn by many other schools. In a small number of instances, a school has adopted the arms of its founder. At Steeple Aston in Oxfordshire, Dr Radcliffe's Church of England primary school uses the arms of its sixteenth-century founder, Dr Samuel Radcliffe, *Argent a Bend engrailed Sable with a Mullet charged with a Martlet for difference*. A bold representation of the arms, carved in stone and surmounted by a very strange academic cap, has been incorporated in the exterior of the school's new buildings.

Schools, Heraldry in the curriculum The idea of using heraldry in school is attractive. The subject is colourful, links easily to history, local studies or art, and appeals strongly to pupils. Nevertheless many teachers are hesitant about using it; usually because they are uncertain of how much technical language will be needed. There is, in fact, no need for this hesitation. Many aspects of heraldry can be studied without using armorial terms; moreover most teachers will find that, once started, they become interested and pick up all the technicalities they need with little difficulty.

Four possible approaches are suggested; the first two at least needing little or no use of technical language.

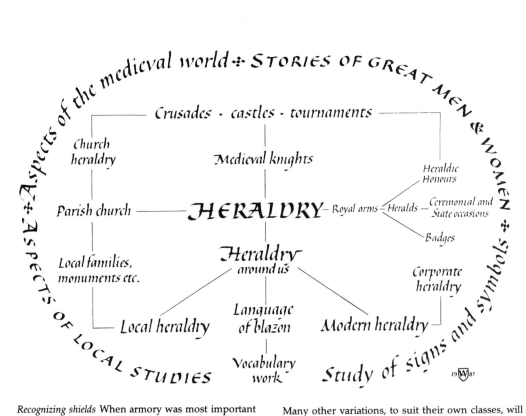

Aspects of the medieval world ✢ STORIES OF GREAT MEN & WOMEN ✢ Symbols ✢ Study of signs and symbols ✢ OF LOCAL STUDIES ✢ Aspects of

Crusades · castles · tournaments

Church
heraldry

Medieval knights

Heraldic
Honours

Parish church ——— HERALDRY — Royal arms — Heralds — Ceremonial and
State occasions

Badges

Heraldry
around us

Local families,
monuments etc.

Corporate
heraldry

Local heraldry

Language
of blazon

Modern heraldry

Vocabulary
work

19 87

Recognizing shields When armory was most important and widespread, in the Middle Ages, few people can have known its conventions and technicalities. Most must simply have recognized the shield or badge of their own feudal lord, much as people today recognize a road sign, a trade mark or a national flag.

Modern pupils can learn armory in the same way. They can, for example, learn to recognize the coat of arms of their own city or county; make drawings of it, look for it on public buildings, list places where they have seen it, discuss whether it includes symbols of local industry or alludes to events in local history, etc. Shields particularly suitable for this approach include those with special local interest, and also the royal arms, which can be studied in any area.

Heraldry as an aspect of other subjects Those who do not feel ready to embark on a project on heraldry itself may well feel able to include it as one aspect of some other topic, such as the following:

In a project on a foreign country, e.g. France, collect arms of different provinces (usually easy to find on tourist literature) and use them in a display.

In a project on church history — collect arms attributed to the saints and discuss reasons for the symbols used, e.g. keys of St Peter, shells of St James, St Catherine's wheel, etc.

In connections with a school play or a local pageant, research and design correct heraldic costumes for historical characters, or banners of craft guilds.

Many other variations, to suit their own classes, will occur to teachers.

Heraldic monuments This approach — perhaps most suited to older pupils — is useful where a number of heraldic monuments is available in a local church. Given a very few simple rules (difference between shield and lozenge, how arms are combined on marriage, etc.) pupils can look at monuments and answer questions for themselves, working out, for example, that one monument shows a third son and the next his married sister. This approach, with its emphasis on problem solving and field work, can make a good introduction to the study of local history, architecture, etc.

A project on heraldry A project on heraldry can be organized in a variety of ways. Some themes are suggested on the accompanying diagram. A few possible approaches are listed here.

Through local studies: this has the merit of giving opportunity for much activity and field work. It can include a visit to a church or historic house, or simply a walk round to look for shields on public buildings. This last will normally yield a number of modern arms (banks, insurance companies, etc.), and so can lead into work on modern uses of armory.

Through history: this usually means an emphasis on medieval armory (though it need not do so). It can be a good plan to concentrate on the shields of a particular group of men, e.g. those who besieged Caerlaverock in 1300 or fought at Agincourt in 1415. This lends itself both to the making of a class frieze of their arms, or to written compositions about the events involved. Alternatively, there could be an emphasis upon tournaments, including the costume of knights and of their ladies, the work of heralds, etc.

Through augmentations: since these were normally given for special service they provide a rich fund of good, adventurous stories, and many opportunities for pupils to work on individual topics of their own choice.

Through heraldic art: which does not mean simply drawing shields! This may be a good approach with older pupils, with whom it can involve discussion of design, colour schemes, stylization, etc. It can include comparison of medieval heraldic art with that of the eighteenth century, or with modern poster art. It may mean considering the use of a visual language in a non-literate society, and so raise a variety of questions about language in general.

Teachers will have plenty of ideas about other possibilities. Whatever approach they adopt a project centring upon heraldry is likely to include some work on the special language of blazon. Many fear that this may be difficult, but it need not be so. Pupils often like the idea of a 'secret' language. Moreover the terms of blazon can lead into useful language work. There can, for example, be discussion of the various technical and non-technical meanings of words such as chief, bend, sable, sinister, etc. The need to consider not only words but word order in a blazon can awaken interest in a more precise use of words in other connections.

Heraldry is a fascinating subject, and can become a life-long hobby. That alone is a good reason for teachers to introduce their pupils to it.   YW

Further reading
Brooke-Little, J.P. *Heraldry* London, 1977. The best introductory book for youngsters.
Manning, R. *Heraldry* London, 1966.
Priestly, A.E. *Learn about Heraldry* Loughborough, 1974.

Schwenkel A long projecting piece of cloth at the upper edge of a banner. Popular in medieval Europe, though not in Britain, the red schwenkel in Germany was considered to be a special privilege or honour.

Scimitar A broad-bladed, curved sword, sometimes with a serrated back edge.

Scotland, Armorial Practice The principal function of heraldry, whether personal heraldry or corporate heraldry, is to symbolize the identity of the owner of the armorial bearings. In Scotland the Clan, the Family and the Name have survived as significant entities in the social organization of Scottish society. The Clan, the Family and the Name are also of significance and interest to people of Scots descent throughout the world. In determining the right to the undifferenced armorial bearings, Lord Lyon King of Arms either in his ministerial capacity or in his judicial capacity decides who is Head of the Clan or Chief of the Family or Name. In Scottish heraldry there is no such thing as 'a family coat of arms' — junior members of a family are assigned due and congruent differences and by assigning the scientific and relevant differences to the armorial bearings of younger members of families, Lyon has a vital and continuing influence on the family organization in Scotland. Armorial bearings are succeeded to by the heir, and the heir may be the heir male, the heir female, or the heir of tailzie (an heir nominated within the blood relationship).

An interest in clan and family heraldry is not confined to those who have recorded armorial bearings in the Statutory Public Register of All Arms and Bearings in Scotland, and many clansmen and clanswomen display the heraldic crest badge (crest of chief within strap and buckle bearing chief's motto) in bonnet or as a brooch. Many thousands of loyal followers of the various chiefs in all parts of the world thus demonstrate their loyalty. The scientific simplicity of the Scottish system of differencing, allied to the statutory regulation and protection of Scottish armorial bearings, and the system of appeals from Lyon's judicial decisions to the Superior Courts, has resulted in the Scottish heraldic administration being regarded as a socially useful and effective system.   MRI

Further reading
Balfour Paul, J. (Lord Lyon) *Heraldry in Relation to Scottish History and Art* 1899.
— *An Ordinary of Scottish Arms* 1977.
— *The Scots Peerage 1904-1914* 9 vols.
Gayre, R. *The Nature of Arms* Edinburgh, 1961.
Grant, F.J. (Lord Lyon) *Memorial Catalogue of the Heraldic Exhibition* 1891.
Innes, T. (Lord Lyon) *Scots Heraldry* revised 1978.
Lindsay, D. (Lord Lyon) *Heraldic Manuscript of 1542* 1878.
Macdonald, W.R. (Carrick Pursuivant) *Scottish Armorial Seals* 1904.
Mackenzie, G. *Science of Herauldrie* 1680.
Nisbet, A. *System of Heraldry* 1816 (reprinted 1984).
Ordinary of Arms in the Lyon Register Vol.1 (1672-1901), Vol.2 (1902-1973).

The ceiling at Earlshall Castle, Fife, includes coats of principal Scottish families, fabulous beasts and moral maxims.

Seton, G. *Law and Practice of Heraldry* 1863.

Stevenson, J.H. (Marchmont Herald) *Heraldry in Scotland* 1914.

— and M. Wood *Scottish Heraldic Seals* 1940.

Stodart, R.R. *Scottish Arms (1370-1678)* Edinburgh, 1888.

Urquhart, R.M. *Scottish Burgh and County Heraldry* 1973.

— *Scottish Civic Heraldry* 1979.

There are various articles of heraldic interest to be found in the *Proceedings of the Society of Antiquaries of Scotland*.

Scotland, Heraldic Art From the fourteenth to the seventeenth century, heraldry was the major decorative element to be found in Scottish architecture. The pattern of charges and marshalling, coupled with the kinship information contained within that combination, provided economical and prestigious decoration in a country which was not wealthy. Interior schemes of heraldic decoration, using tempera paint, were popular in the sixteenth and seventeenth centuries and several examples remain. The finest heraldic scheme of the early sixteenth century is in St Machar's Cathedral, Aberdeen, where the ceiling bears shields showing the political and religious composition of Scotland and Europe *c.* 1525.

There are several very fine buildings which incorporate heraldry: Thistle Chapel, St Giles' Kirk Edinburgh; Scottish National Portrait Gallery, Queen St, Edinburgh; Scottish National War Memorial Edinburgh Castle; Kelvingrove Museum and Art Gallery, Glasgow; St Andrew's Episcopal Cathedral, Aberdeen; Old Town Council Chamber, Aberdeen; Aberdeen Market Cross; Huntly Castle, Aberdeenshire; Mars Wark, Stirling.

Very little pre-Reformation glass remains in Scotland apart from four roundels in the Magdalen Chapel, Cowgate, Edinburgh. However, the Burrell Collection in Glasgow contains glass dating from a number of centuries, and there are fine collections of Victorian heraldic glass in the following Edinburgh locations: Great Hall, Edinburgh Castle; St Mary's Episcopal Cathedral; George Heriot's School; St Giles' Kirk, Royal Mile; St John's Episcopal Church; Signet Library.

At Glasgow Cathedral and Marischal College, Aberdeen, further examples of Victorian heraldic stained glass can be found.   CJB

Scotland, Royal Arms of The red lion was probably a device of King William I (1165-1214), known as 'The Lion'. A lion rampant within a bordure of fleurs-de-lis first appears during the reign of his son, Alexander II (1214-49), and the lion rampant within a double tressure flory counter-flory was first used in the Great

Seal of Alexander III in 1251. The lion crest was introduced during the reign of David II (1329-70), and unicorn supporters were adopted in 1440. For a period between 1471 and 1500 that part of the double tressure above the lion rampant was omitted. The lion crest became sejant *c.* 1502, with a sword and saltire flag held by the lion. At the same time a collar of thistles was placed round the shield. The unicorn supporters held a banner of the royal arms instead of the saltire. The oldest motto 'In My Defens God Us Defens', was first used by James III *c.* 1480. This was quickly shortened to 'In Defens' and this is found with the spelling 'In Defence' by the end of the sixteenth century. The second motto 'Nemo Me Impune Lacesset' (No one will assail me with impunity) was derived from the phrase *nemo me ledet* which occurred on a coin of James V in 1579. By 1617 the 'Nemo Me Impune Lacesset' motto had become incorporated in the royal arms. Variations of spelling can be seen, e.g. 'Nemo Me Impune Lacessit' (No one assails me with impunity), which is currently in use.

The Scottish arms were quartered with those of England, France and Ireland by James VI, when in 1603 he succeeded to the English throne as James I.

The royal arms currently used in Scotland are *Quarterly 1 and 4 Or a Lion rampant Gules armed and langued Azure within a double Tressure flory counter flory of*

The Royal arms above, as feudal superior, and on the lintel beneath the achievements of the Marquess of Huntly (right) and the Duke of Lennox (left), father of the Marchioness of Huntly. Huntly Castle, Fife.

the second (Scotland) 2 *Gules three Lions passant guardant Or* (England) 3 *Azure a Harp Or stringed Argent* (Ireland). Encircling the shield is the Collar of the Most Ancient and Most Noble Order of the Thistle. The crest is *An Imperial Crown proper surmounted by a Lion sejant affronty Gules imperially crowned holding in his dexter paw a naked Sword and in the sinister a Sceptre both proper.* On *a Compartment Vert with Thistles proper* are the supporters: dexter *a Unicorn Argent armed tufted and unguled Or imperially crowned proper and gorged with an open Crown chain reflexed over the back Or and supporting a Banner of St Andrew,* sinister *a Lion rampant guardant Or imperially crowned proper supporting a Banner of St George.* On an escroll above is the motto 'In Defens', and in the table of the compartment 'Nemo Me Impune Lacessit'. The royal badges are the Crowned Thistle and the Regal Saltire (a silver saltire enfiling a gold open crown). CJB/SF

See also; UNITED KINGDOM, ROYAL HERALDRY
Further reading
Godman, J. and I. Moncreiffe *Debrett's Royal Scotland* London, 1983.

Scottish Civic Coronets *see* **Crest Coronet**

Screens The medieval chancel screen was made of wood or stone and in many instances was surmounted by the rood, a cross or crucifix, in which case it is known as a rood screen. Sometimes the figures of the Virgin Mary and St John stand on either side of the rood, supported by a sturdy rood beam which itself rests on corbels. The chancel or rood screen should not be confused with the pulpitum which was constructed east of the chancel screen but west of the choir. This usually spans the church and has a gallery. The parclose screen separates a chapel or tomb from the chancel or nave, and the tower screen separates the tower from the nave.

Screens are usually divided into bays with pierced openings. The outer bays are generally panelled at the base and open between the central and top rails, except for the vertical members known as muntins or, in the case of the outer frame, stiles. The heads of the openings or lights are usually of carved tracery. There is sometimes a gate providing access through the screen, though many of these have now been lost.

Screens were usually carved and painted but there is little surviving evidence of armorial decoration from the medieval period. Jacobean screens were usually of carved wood and incorporated heraldic devices. A common feature of this period was the inclusion of the royal arms surmounting the centre of the screen, flanked by the arms of a patron of the living or benefactor and those of the bishop impaling the arms of his diocese. A good example of this practice is the screen at Abbey Dore in the county of Hereford and Worcester. This is located at the rear of the main body of the church. The early Renaissance Salkeld screen at Carlisle Cathedral is surmounted by the royal arms, flanked by shields bearing the so-called Prince of Wales' Feathers badge.

Larger churches and cathedrals often have several screens, and these, whether in wood or stone, will reflect the style of the period of their erection and may include armorial features.

Few medieval domestic screens have survived. The screens passage ran the full width of the medieval hall, and separated the kitchens and domestic quarters from the main hall. Often space above formed a minstrels' gallery. Such screens, eminently suited to armorial display, continued in use for a period of well over five hundred years, one of the latest examples being that at Montacute House, Somerset, constructed 1588-1601. The secondary functions of the screens passage, the conservation of heat and prevention of draughts, were transferred to the screened porch and hall-way of the Jacobean period, and, eventually, to the similar arrangement found in most Victorian and Edwardian houses.

The highly patterned and coloured glass lights of the Victorian hall screen are often composed of armorial devices, fleurs-de-lis being particularly popular. It is most unlikely that these designs possess any armorial significance, however, and many stained-glass coats of arms of the period are entirely bogus.

Modern architectural practices and building techniques have made the screen superfluous in most domestic buildings, though the wide, glass-fronted entrances to shops and public and commercial buildings are a twentieth-century equivalent and many have been engraved and embellished with armorial devices. An encouraging development is the modern use of glass screens within ancient buildings, particularly churches, both to provide greater flexibility in the use of internal space and to conserve heat. Such screens represent a potential for armorial display which has attracted the attention of many leading engravers.

Sea-dog *or* **Hound Marine** A talbot with webbed feet, scales, a dorsal fin and otter's tail.

Seals The precursors of armorial seals were without recognizable heraldic devices such as the ordinaries, but did nevertheless sometimes show figures having canting allusions to their owners' names. Thus a man called Raven might have used a raven on his seal. These figures did not, however, appear upon shields.

With the appearance in the twelfth century of armorial seals proper, showing devices on shields, the shape of the shield depicted on the seal was to become an important factor in its dating. The early shields were elongated, but in the thirteenth century the heater-shaped shield came into vogue and persisted

Seal of William, Lord Hastings (d.1483) showing his arms, *Argent a Maunch Sable*, 'supported' in the spaces between the achievement and the legend by two beast badges of a 'blake boull hed rasid, horns and bout the neke a croune gold' [MS. College of Arms 2nd M 16].

throughout that century and the next. In the fifteenth century, shields showing quartered arms became common, and of necessity these became broader, in order to accommodate the quarterings.

Early in the twelfth century, seals came to be used for authenticating documents, thereby fulfilling the same function as a signature. With the continued use of the same armorial seal by the later generations of a family, the hereditary element of armory came into being.

In the same century a man of the rank of knight or above would show on his seal an equestrian figure of himself in armour. Upon the shield borne by this figure would appear the personal device which the knight had adopted. In such a form we see the first occurrence of a shield of arms on the seal of an English sovereign. The second seal of Richard I (1189-99),

Signet ring of Richard Nevill 'the Kingmaker' (d. 1471), engraved with the bear and ragged staff badges of the Beauchamps and their successors in the earldom of Warwick.

which was produced some time after 1191, shows on the reverse side an equestrian figure bearing a pointed shield charged with three lions. As time went on, sovereigns and other people of high rank used a personal seal called a *secretum* as well as an official seal.

In the course of the fourteenth century, a crest upon a helm would be added to the shield shown on the seal. Since there was inevitably an empty space between the outline of the shield and the inner edge of the legend running round the seal, engravers began introducing small figures of animals and depictions of foliage to fill the gap. Some of these figures may have been purely ornamental, while others may have been included for a particular reason at the request of the person who commissioned the seal. At all events, these devices were almost certainly the forerunners of the heraldic figures called supporters.

In England the Great Seal of the Realm has always been two-sided, like the coinage, with a different device on each side. It was in the reign of Edward III (1327-77) that heraldry began to come into its own on the Great Seal, and in 1340 two shields appeared showing France (Ancient) and England quarterly.

Edward IV (1461-83) also used France (Modern) on his second seal, and he made an innovation by interspersing the words running round the edge of the seal with roses and fleurs-de-lis. He also made use of diapering for the background of the front of the seal, introducing roses and suns for this purpose.

An interesting point in connection with the legend on the Great Seal is that the second seal of Richard I, referred to above, was the last to describe the king as *Rex Anglorum*. Thereafter the king was to be *Rex Anglie*, and this description continued until the reign of James I (1603-25), who was *Rex Angliae*. His son and successor Charles I (1625-49) used this form only in 1625 and 1626, and then *Magnae Britanniae* was substituted for *Angliae*.

The story of the Great Seal is a study of its own and no more can be said about it in an article of this length, save perhaps for saying that Henry VIII (1509-47) made use of a golden bulla showing on the reverse side the royal arms surrounded by the Collar of the Order of the Garter. A bulla was a disc of metal, originally lead, which was attached to documents, particularly those emanating from the pope. Hence the expression Papal Bull, meaning the actual document.

Where arms of office are combined with personal arms, as, for example, on an episcopal seal, the arms of office are shown on the dexter. Patents granting armorial bearings now carry wax impressions only of the arms of office of the kings of arms who have signed these documents. Until recent times the personal arms of the kings of arms were combined with their arms of office.

In conclusion it should perhaps be pointed out that we use the word 'seal' rather loosely. Do we mean the piece of stone or metal or other hard substance often set in a gold or silver case, upon which the design is engraved (the matrix), or do we mean the piece of wax which has received the impression? Items in the first category can be used, in addition to their primary function, as official or personal ornaments or symbols of authority, and it is worth noting that today many 'seal impressions' are now ready-made in moulded plastic complete with full ornamentation. Such 'seals' will, theoretically at any rate, last for ever.   SA

See also PRIVY SEAL

Further reading

Ellis, R. *Catalogue of Seals in the Public Record Office* 1978-1981.

Williams D.H. *Welsh History through Seals* 1982.

Sea Monsters With the exceptions of the sea-dog and sea-wolf, which are peculiar to themselves, sea monsters may be created by joining the upper half of a creature or monster to the tail of a fish. Sometimes a dorsal fin and webbed feet are also depicted. Such creatures were at one time blazoned, e.g. a bull marine, but this is no longer the practice. Examples are the sea-dragon, sea-bull, sea-unicorn, etc. Sometimes wings are also depicted. The sea-horse may cause confusion, the natural sea-horse being blazoned *a sea-horse (hippocampus)*.

Sea-wolf *or* **Wolf Marine** A wolf with webbed feet, scales and a dorsal fin.

Seax A broad-bladed, curved sword, similar in appearance to the scimitar but with a semi-circular notch in the back. Traditionally the emblem of the East Saxons who, according to legend, derived their name from the seax. A common charge in the arms of places associated with the ancient kingdoms of the East and Middle Saxons.

Secretum *or* **Secret Seal** The *secretum sigillum* was adopted by the kings of England in the fourteenth century (when the use of the Privy Seal expanded) to authenticate private documents, the Great Seal being reserved for official documents.

Seeded *see* **Attributes**

Segreant *see* **Attitude**

Seigneur A feudal lord, a lord of the manor.

Seize Quartiers A European phenomenon (though more often encountered in text books than in practice), proof of seize quartiers (i.e. that all sixteen of an armiger's great-great-grandparents were entitled to bear arms in their own right) was sometimes proposed as a means of defining genuine ancestry, 'true blood' and, therefore, undisputed gentility. The principle was considered to be of some importance in German armory but, fortunately, has always been regarded with great suspicion in Britain where instances of genuine seize quartiers are rare. The College of Arms instituted in 1766 two series of folio volumes called *Howard* (later *Norfolk*) and *Arundel*, for the registration of large pedigrees. *Arundel* was reserved 'for documents certified under the Common Seal and later for Royal Descents, Seize Quartiers and other specially elaborate entries.' Fox-Davies (*A Complete Guide to Heraldry*) states: 'It should be distinctly understood that there is no connection whatever between the list of quarterings which may have been inherited, which it is permissible to display, and "Seize-Quartiers", which should never be marshalled together or displayed as quarterings.' In the late twentieth century, the concept is archaic and irrelevant.

Sejant *see* **Attitude**

Semiotics The science of non-linguistic sign systems. Armory is such a system, though it possesses a diversity of functions and attributes which are not necessarily found in other semiotic systems: it is hereditary, for example.

Semiotics is used in government: national and local, departmental, civil and military. It is used by administrative, commercial and service organizations and by individuals. Symbols are used to identify authority, ownership and origination. They are also used to inform. The international system of traffic signs is an outstanding example, and it is interesting to note that with only one exception (that of the restrictive parking group of signs) all signs comply with the tincture convention of armory. The system's weakness is in the prohibitive signs, in which the 'bend sinister' is not applied uniformly.

The majority of public information systems are in the true spirit of armory: bold, easily recognized figures displayed on backgrounds of contrasting colours. Many commercial logotypes are equally effective and are akin to armory because their function is to identify. Many logotypes demonstrate qualities of artistic ingenuity and perception unequalled since the flowering of the heraldic imagination in the Middle Ages. Logotypes used for commercial purposes are usually protected by trade or service mark legislation or by copyright; and any device which is borne on, or associated with, a shield falls within the jurisdiction of the heraldic authorities.

For the International Association for Semiotic Studies *see* ADDRESSES.

Further reading

Guiraud, P. *Semiology* 1975.

Hall. E.T. *The Silent Language* 1959.

Semiotics

Many logotypes are in the true spirit of medieval armory: bold, explicit and essentially memorable.

Seventeenth-century rat-catcher

Semy, Aspersed, Poudré, Powdered, Replenished, Semé, Strewed *or* **Strewn** An indeterminate number of small charges evenly distributed over a field to form a pattern. Semy charges are defaced both at the edges of the shield or ordinary which they occupy and by larger charges placed upon them. For this reason it is not possible to specify the number of charges so depicted or to arrange their disposition to accommodate, for example, the attributes of beasts which may themselves be defaced (gerattie charges are better suited to this purpose). Semy fields are blazoned, e.g. *Azure semy of Garbs Or a Pile Argent* (Allen). However, certain forms of semy have their own terms, although some are currently out of favour.

Roundels (discs)
or: bezanty (bezanté)
argent: platy (platté)
gules: semy of torteaux
azure: hurty (hurté)
vert: pommety
sable: pellety

Gouttes (drops)
or: goutty d'or
argent: goutty d'eau
gules: goutty de sang
azure: goutty des larmes
vert: goutty d'huile (also d'olive)
sable: goutty de poix
NB Current practice is to blazon the above as goutty gules, goutty vert, etc., and the fashionable spelling *gutty* will also be encountered.

Charges
annulets: annuletty
billets: billetty
cross-crosslets: crusily
estoils: estoily
fleurs-de-lis: fleuretty or semy-de-lis
fret: fretty
Fretty is formed from interlaced bendlets and bendlets sinister to create a trellis pattern. A similar pattern of pallets and bars is termed square fretty.

Semy-de-lis A field semy of fleurs-de-lis.

Seneschal Based on two linguistic elements, *seni* = old, and *skalkoz* = servant, the title 'seneschal' was applied to a variety of anciently established officials. Sometimes a seneschal was a member of a royal household and in charge of all the domestic arrangements; on other occasions he was the governor of a city or province. Today the title is that of an officer in the Channel Islands.   JC-K

Sept A division of a tribe or clan, especially in Ireland.

Sequier's Book *see* **Treatises**

Seraphim, Order of the A Swedish order formed in 1748, but with traditions going back to 1280. The badge is a Latin Cross with the letters IHS and three royal crowns, originally on an oval medallion, but now on a lozenge at the centre of a gold eight-pointed cross enamelled in white and beaded at the ends.   KH

Serjeant In early times a person of less than knightly rank in the service of a lord; a knight in attendance on the king; an officer of parliament charged with enforcing its commands. In the United States of America both the Senate and the House of Representatives have serjeants.

Serjeant at Arms The title given to a number of officers in the ROYAL HOUSEHOLD. Tradition has it that the serjeants ('knights and gentlemen of high degree') formed the bodyguard to King Richard I during the first crusades. Their symbol of authority is a mace, the maces in use today being of Stuart origin. The serjeants also wear collars of SS. In the twentieth century there are three serjeants personal to the sovereign, one in the House of Lords (represented by Black Rod), and one in the House of Commons who attends the Speaker. The serjeants are present at coronations, and also attend Garter King of Arms and heralds at the reading of proclamations.   JC-K

Serpent *or* **Snake** The serpent was regarded with great veneration in ancient Greece. It was the guardian of temples and the source of all wisdom. During a pestilence in Rome, Aesculapius, son of Apollo the god of medicine, appeared in the form of a serpent to drive out the scourge, and his rod is always entwined with a serpent as a symbol of healing. Mercury, with his Caduceus — a winged rod entwined with two snakes — could give sleep to whomever he chose. Both these symbols appear in armory and the rod of Aesculapius is used extensively in medical heraldry.

In Christian times the serpent became a symbol of evil from its association with the story of the fall of man, and is often depicted beneath the feet of various saints. The runic knot which is entwined in Celtic crosses is a Scandinavian version of the Byzantine image of a crushed snake curled around the cross. St Hilda of Whitby is said to have turned all the snakes in the area into stones. These are, in fact, ammonites, which are plentiful on that coast, but the legend is of such fame that the fossil is named *Hildoceras*. Three coiled snakes appeared in the arms of both the former Whitby urban and rural councils.   MY

Service Mark *see* **Trade Mark**

Servitude *see* **Livery Company, Membership of**

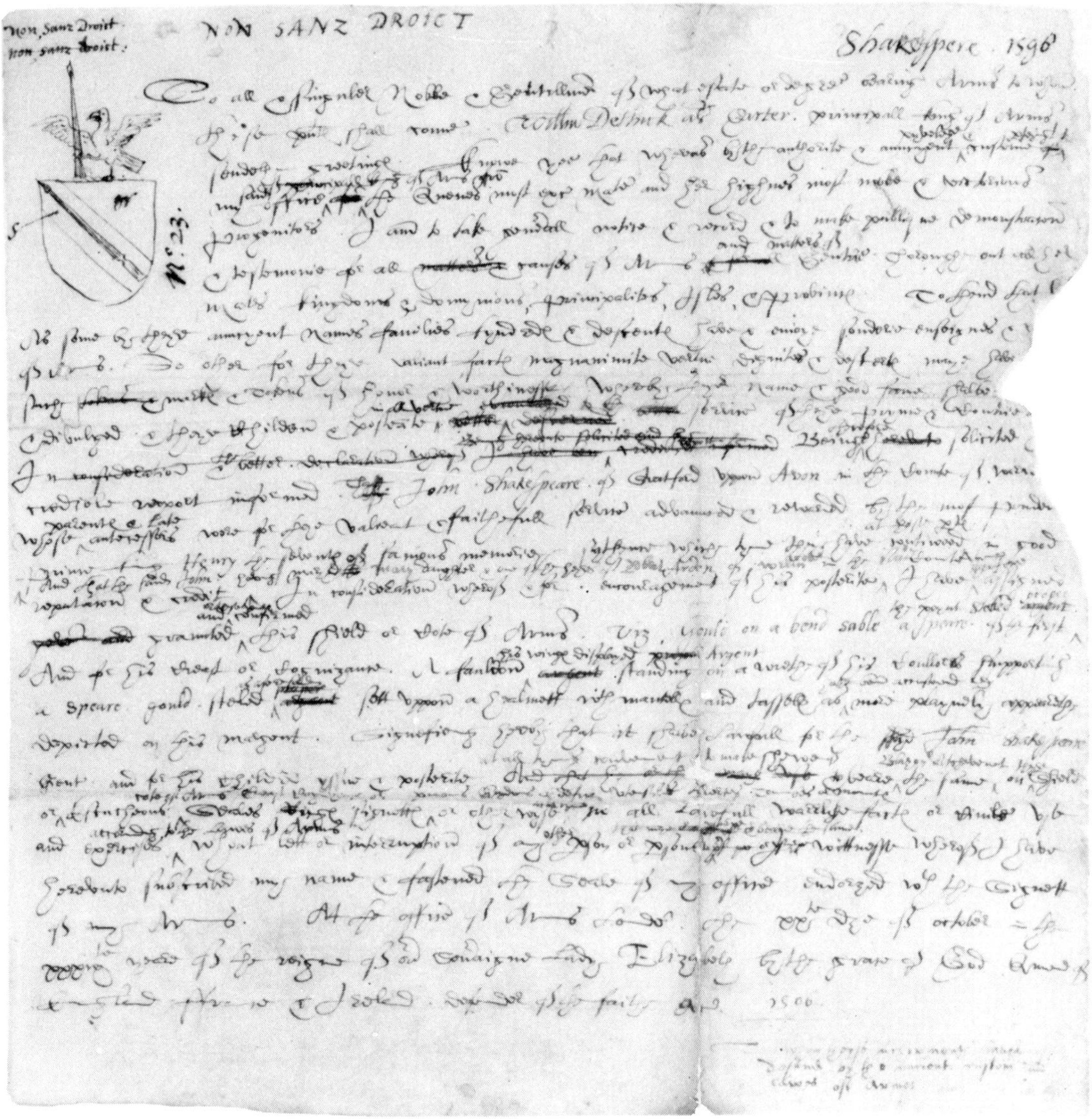

Sewer In medieval times an attendant responsible for arranging table, determining the seating of guests, and overseeing the tasting and serving of food, and until the fifteenth century an officer of the royal household. In 1254, for example, the Earl of Derby is described as Hereditary Lord Sewer to the King. In later centuries the sewer was an officer at coronations.

Sexed *see* **Attributes**

Shackbolt A manacle.

Shading Armorial bearings should be depicted as though illuminated from dexter chief.

First draft of the grant of arms to John Shakespeare, 1596, father of William Shakespeare.

Shafted *see* **Attributes**

Shakefork *see* **Pall**

Shakespeare and Heraldry Shakespeare's knowledge of medieval heraldry was considerable. The brilliance of his heraldic imagination illuminates every page of the history plays, though he acknowledges the paucity of his company's wardrobe when he reminds his audience, 'For 'tis your thoughts that now must

313

deck our kings . . .'. Current theatrical practice rejects armorial realism for abstruse symbolism. The best one may expect is a token fleur-de-lis or gauze lion to represent 'the vasty fields of France' or the English court. However, the armorial imagery remains, a source of delight and fascination for the armorist, an entirely new perspective for the Shakespeare enthusiast and medievalist. By far the best available guide is *Shakespeare's Heraldry* by C.W. Scott-Giles. Shakespeare's numerous heraldic textual references are analysed; genealogies explained with unusual clarity, and detailed descriptions of armorial costumes, flags, etc., are accompanied by simple blazons and excellent illustrations. There is a brief introduction to medieval and Tudor heraldry, and a chapter is devoted to the development of Shakespeare's personal armorial bearings. In his Foreword, the author states that his book is not only a companion to Shakespeare but also 'a Shakespearean introduction to heraldry'. Many armorists have acquired a fascination for heraldry through Shakespeare and through this book. Despite the occasional inaccuracy, it is a brilliant celebration of medieval pageantry, and a fitting tribute to the Bard's heraldic imagination.

The arms of William Shakespeare, which are much in evidence at properties in the care of the Birthplace Trust at Stratford-upon-Avon, were those of his father, John, viz. *Or on a Bend Sable a Spear Gold the point steeled proper*. The controversy concerning Shakespeare's armorial bearings is dealt with in detail in the above book. Both arms and pun are beautifully simple.

Sheffield Plate Marks Sheffield plate is the term given to articles made from sheet copper to each side of which has been applied a thin foil of silver by means of a fusion process, the name coming from the city in which the process was perfected by Thomas Boulsover (or Balsover) around 1743.

So famous and desirable did articles made from the new material become that from 1784 they were 'hallmarked', much to the irritation of the London silversmiths. Many of the 'hallmarks' used were of an armorial nature. The eight fretted arrows from the arms of Sheffield were employed by the Creswick brothers, the Hatfields used a fleur-de-lis, and the Holland Company a unicorn's head. Henry Wilkinson's products showed a shield with cross keys, and those of William Woodward a mill rind.

Further reading
Bradbury, F. *Guide to Marks of Origin on British and Irish Silver Plate* 1928.
Buck, J.H. *Old Plate, Its Makers and Marks* 1903.

Sheriff Before the Conquest of 1066, the sheriff (or shire-reeve) was the senior representative of the king in a shire. He was responsible for enforcing the law and looking after the royal estates within his territory.

So it continued for a number of centuries, and by the year 1300 the office was either vested in the Crown or was hereditary. In modern times, the sheriff (high sheriff) of a county (shire) is appointed by letters patent on an annual basis and is, in theory at any rate, responsible for a wide range of matters including presiding over parliamentary elections.

In the United States, the office of sheriff is normally an elective one at both county and town levels. The holder has an administrative and some judicial authority.   JC-K

Shield A weapon of defence carried on the arm to deflect the blows of an enemy's weapon, and a means of displaying armorial devices. When used as an armorial charge, a shield is blazoned escutcheon.

The shield is the only essential element in a coat of arms and, with the banner, the principal means of displaying arms. Any device borne on a shield *is* a coat of arms and is, therefore, subject to heraldic authority in those countries where such authority exists. The shield therefore distinguishes armory from other forms of pictorial symbolism.

Shields used in armory may be of any shape. Much depends on the style of painting required and on the blazon of arms, *a Cross between four Lions passant* fitting better a shield with a wide base than *Gules a Lion rampant Argent*, which is best suited to a slender shield, for example.

The shield may also be *couché* — that is, depicted as though suspended beneath the helmet by the sinister chief corner in the manner of a shield hanging naturally from a peg. This is a purely artistic device, popular in the fifteenth century and enjoying a revival of popularity today (see colour pages 50 and 252).

In the eleventh century and at the beginning of the twelfth century shields were long, narrow and kite-shaped, covering most of the body. They had rounded tops and were made of wood covered with tough boiled leather. Such shields were used both in the First Crusade and at Hastings, where raised edges, studs and bosses were often picked out in colour. During the twelfth century the tops of shields became flatter and decoration more personal. By the fourteenth century, the shield used by nobles and knights had become very much smaller, this heater-shaped shield being roughly one third longer than it was broad. The increasing efficiency of the long-bow and cross-bow, and the rapid development of plate armour, effectively altered the principal function of the shield from a means of defence to a vehicle for the display of armorial devices, and by the fifteenth century its use had been abandoned except for ceremonial use and at tournaments, pageants, etc. It was at this time that the bouché-shaped shield was most in evidence. This had a small piece cut out from the dexter side to allow for the free movement of the lance in the tournament.

The Shield

1 twelfth century
2 twelfth century
3 thirteenth century
4 fourteenth century
5 fourteenth century
6 mid-fifteenth century
7 late fifteenth century
8 early sixteenth century
9 sixteenth century
10 sixteenth century
11 seventeenth century
12 eighteenth century
13 eighteenth century

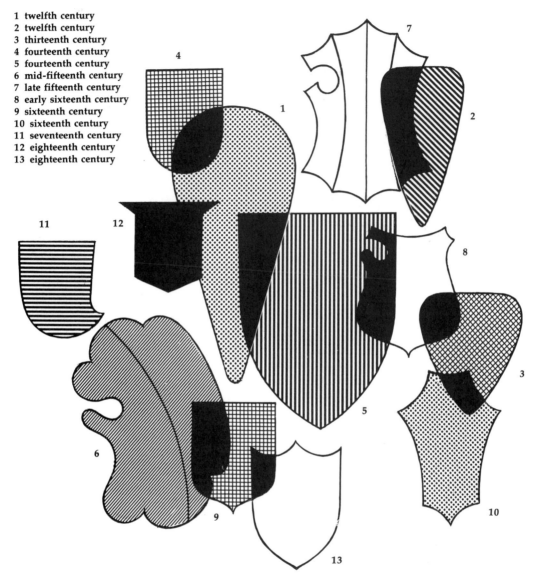

After the sixteenth century, when the instruments of war and tournament were to be found only in the stylized coat of arms, numerous fanciful shields appeared which could never have found their way on to the battlefield. These reflected the architectural and decorative tastes of the seventeenth, eighteenth and nineteenth centuries, just as the present-day preference for the early fourteenth-century shield is indicative of the twentieth-century rejection of the Heraldry of the Decadence in favour of the functional beauty and simplicity of the Middle Ages.

The fourteenth-century 'heater' shield, shaped like the base of a flat iron, is that which is now most commonly used for armorial purposes. Current practice in English patents is to draw it with a slightly convex upper edge. Also popular are the more fanciful fifteenth-century tournament shields, said to be *à bouche* when depicted with a 'notch' which allowed for the free movement of a lance.

315

Arms of the founder of Seedorf monastery, on Lake Lucerne. The top of the shield was probably rounded, but cut off to match the prevailing style in the early thirteenth century.

An interesting recent innovation is the African War Shield, used for depicting the arms of newly created African states such as those of Tanganyika, granted in 1961.

Shield, Points of the Precise points on an armorial field identified for the purpose of expressing the position of a charge in blazon. The three points are: Honour point (A), Fess point (B) and Nombril (or Navel) point (C).

In practice other interpretations may be encountered. All of these relate to the following terms;

Chief: upper part of the shield

Base: lower part of the shield

Dexter: left-hand side of the shield when viewed from the front.

Sinister: right-hand side of the shield when viewed from the front.

Combinations of these terms provide four 'parts' of the shield, e.g. dexter chief, sinister base, etc.

European armory provides for a further two terms and, thereby, a total of nine 'parts'. These are derived from the pale and fess (ordinaries whose geometry they follow) to give, for example, base pale and dexter fess. These are rarely encountered in British armory, neither are the terms middle chief point and middle base point, which are to be found in some reference books.

Clearly, the terms dexter and sinister originated in the right-hand and left-hand of the knight who actually held the shield before him. For the armorist, however, 'reading' a shield of arms is rather like reading the newspaper of a fellow traveller who occupies a seat opposite — 'top to bottom and left to right' is a rule worth remembering. Charges, crests, helmets, etc., always face the dexter unless otherwise specified, and blazons always proceed from the dexter chief. A charge qualified by the term 'sinister' proceeds from or faces the sinister.

Shipping Devices From little later than the fourth millenium BC, shipbuilders around the Mediterranean were beginning to decorate their vessels. The Egyptians, Cretans, Phoenicians and, later, the Greeks and Romans adorned the sails and hulls of their ships with all manner of devices, and flew masthead flags in order that their identity and authority should be known. Sails were painted with eyes for the vessel to find its way, prows and sternboard were carved and decorated with the likenesses of fabulous beasts, and by 1500 BC, when the function and design of ships began to diverge into merchantmen and fighting ships, many devices began to assume military and governmental significance.

In Scandinavia, around 300 BC, the people of the northern lands had begun to carve the raised ends of their primitive longships, and by the time of the great Viking states this practice had evolved into magnificently rendered heads of mythical creatures and Norse deities. The sails, too, bore all manner of devices which were both decorative and a means of identification and probably also possessed religious significance.

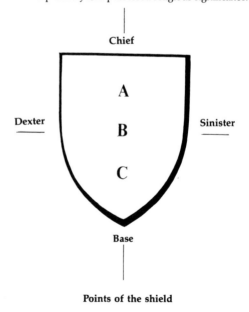

Points of the shield

316

The ships depicted in the Bayeux Tapestry appear to be painted with longitudinal stripes, and the sails decorated with roundels and interlaced and diagonal stripes of colour, though it is difficult to attribute any armorial significance to these.

The evidence provided by medieval seal impressions, paintings and drawings shows us that from the early days of armory the SAIL bore heraldic devices, often the arms of a military commander or in some cases the royal arms. Battle shields were ranged on the bulwarks, mastheads bore armorial streamers and pennants, and by the sixteenth century both the fore and after castles were decorated with representations of shields of arms. Ships of war, trade and exploration flew flags which often bore the devices of their captains, patron saints and national insignia. Many of these evolved into national ensigns, often with elements carried over from the previous tradition, as in the ensigns of England, Czarist Russia, Portugal, Spain and Sweden.

The growth of European trade in the Middle Ages saw the rise of fleets of merchantmen which flew FLAGS of identity. The Hanseatic League, for example, used the colours white and red and the Dutch East Indiamen adopted the arms of Amsterdam, their home port.

With the coming of steam propulsion and iron hulls, much of the decorative beauty of ships was lost, though the importance of flags as a means of identity increased. Merchant flags adopted house or home port insignia; the flag of the free port of Danzig, for example, was a striking armorial design comprising a red field charged with a gold crown above two white crosses palewise. Crosses, crowns, stars, diamonds, annuli, anchors, lions, globes and numerous other devices familiar to the armorist were called into service as mercantile flags, many of which were in fact armorial; for example, the burning castles of Dublin on the steam packet ships of that city, and the winged lion of St Mark, the patron saint of Venice, on the vessels of the Italian Adriatic Line.

Funnel and hull markings, whilst rarely armorial, generally conform to the conventions of armory. In the · nineteenth century a large house flag flown at the mainmast was used to identify a vessel at a distance. Today the funnel provides a larger, more prominent area for the display of colours and devices. Flags and funnels are frequently of the same design, and the corporate logotype of the late twentieth century is now preferred to the earlier combinations of stripes and letters. Some of these logotypes are armorial in character: the *Quarterly Or and Azure a Cross per quarterly counterchanged* on a black funnel of United Carriers Ltd (Monrovia), the Gold escallop shell on a red funnel of Shell Tankers (UK) Ltd, and the black 'indented' chief on a white funnel of Helmsing and Grimm of Bremen, for example. As with AIRLINE DEVICES, shipping flags and funnels are subject to

constant change as merchant fleets are amalgamated and re-formed, often with a new 'corporate image' and livery.

There is a legal requirement that ships should display identifying names, numbers and a civil ensign. In addition there are approximately twelve hundred different commercial liveries used in house flags and funnels, and countless pennants, burgees and banners of individuals and clubs. These private flags are correctly flown from the mainmast, and ordinaries of shipping flags, which list them by colour to aid identification, are available.   EP-T

Further reading

Lloyds Book of House Flags and Funnels London, 1904.

Loughran, J.L. *A Survey of Mercantile House Flags and Funnels* 1979.

Stewart, C.F. *Flags, Funnels and Hull Colours* London, 1953.

Styring, J.S. *Brown's Flags and Funnels of British and Foreign Steamship Companies* Glasgow, 1971.

Wilson, T. *Flags at Sea* HMSO, 1986.

Shop Signs Several generations ago, few of the common people could read or write, and the large display window of today was a feature unknown. The only way a tradesperson or craftsman could advertize his wares or a particular service was by hanging a suitable pictorial representation above the door to his premises. A locksmith might hang a huge lock or key from a suitable bracket, or a hosier a large wooden stocking and a glover a golden glove.

Many familiar signs abounded and the high streets of most towns became ridiculously overcrowded (and also dangerous, as signs which had suffered the ravages of the elements collapsed on to the innocent passerby). It took an act of parliament in the middle of the eighteenth century to regulate the conditions governing the size and usage of signs. Only inn-keepers were obliged by law to erect suitable INN SIGNS above the door to their hostelries. The familiar free-standing wooden figure of a highlander taking a pinch of snuff, or a Red Indian, would announce a tobacconist's shop. A huge pair of spectacles, sometimes with painted eyes, would grace the frontage of an optician. On a wrought iron bracket above the fascia of a mercer would hang a golden fleece.

A diversity of shop signs survives to this day, perhaps the most familiar being the red and white painted barber's pole. In former times, when blood-letting was considered a restorative, barbers were allowed to practice phlebotomy. The patient about to be bled would be given a pole to grip, so promoting the flow of blood. When not in use the pole was hung up with the bandage twisted around it, hence the red and white symbolism of the barber's pole today.

Some shop signs have heraldic connections, for example the three golden balls of the pawnbroker.

With the barring of Jewish merchants in the early thirteenth century, the Lombards took their place. Like their predecessors they were also money-lenders and bankers, the bezants in their arms forming the basis of this once very common street sign. The grasshopper crest of Sir Thomas Gresham, founder of the Royal Exchange, who carried out his business in a house which was later to become Martin's Bank, is still retained by that company for its trademark.

A red shield was once used as a sign by the Rothschild family of Frankfurt; in German, *roth schild* (red shield) is a fine example of a canting arms.

Other traders, especially if affiliated to a guild or a similar body, might use the device of that organization: a large grocery store in Hull, long ago demolished, had on the topmost pediment a huge stone camel laden with sacks of cloves, the crest of the Worshipful Company of Grocers.   CBC

Shut *see* Attitude

Signatures, Archbishops and Bishops Archbishops and bishops of the Church of England, the Church of Ireland, the Episcopal Church in Scotland and the Church in Wales sign, after a representation of the Cross, by their Christian name followed by their province or see. Where more than one diocese is designated, the first named only is used for this purpose. These are accorded the normal spelling, with the following exceptions:

> *Archbishops*
> Canterbury: Cantaur
> York: Ebor
> Wales: Cambrensis
>
> *Bishops*
> Carlisle: Carliol
> Chester: Cestr
> Chichester: Cicestr
> Durham: Dunelm
> Edinburgh: Edenburgen
> Ely: Elien
> Gloucester: Gloucestr
> London: Londin
> Norwich: Norvic
> Oxford: Oxon
> Peterborough: Petriburg
> Rochester: Roffen
> Salisbury: Sarum
> Truro: Truron
> Winchester: Winton

Signet A small seal or the impression of such a seal.

Sign Manual (i) A signature, especially that of a sovereign. (ii) A royal licence.

Silverware For some collectors the most highly prized pieces of antique silver are not those items originally bought from stock in a showroom and subsequently taken to an engraver for the customer's crest or achievement to be engraved, they are those items designed and made for a particular patron, bearing the patron's identity, symbolized by his arms. The arms are integral to the design of the piece, and will have been incorporated from the very first sketches on the silversmith's drawing board. Contemporaneous literature may describe the circumstances in which the piece was commissioned. Approval sketches by the smith for the patron may still exist. Ideally, the piece should have been preserved in pristine condition in its purpose-made case, and a photocopy of the account in the smith's ledger would complete the corpus. The arms may well be cast in solid silver and embodied as the centre piece of the design. An excellent example is the charger made by Paul de Lamerie (1688-1751) for the Worshipful Company of Goldsmiths in 1741 and often displayed in the Company's Hall in the City of London.

The crest, too, may be cast in silver and incorporated in the design, as illustrated by items of domestic silver by Paul Storr and his contemporaries during the Regency period, and by Leslie Durbin's commission for both personal and corporate patrons since 1950. The three-dimensional, solidly magnificent heraldic beasts and monsters have lent themselves to this form of artistry, as evidenced by English silversmiths like Kandler and Omar Ramsden (1873-1939).

An inventory of Sir John Falstolf (d. 1459) records him possessing 13,000 ounces of domestic silverware, with a further 1200 ounces in his private chapel. The quantities of such silver used in royal and noble households in the Middle Ages have regrettably not survived the melting down that was particularly associated with the Dissolution of the Monasteries and, later, the English Civil War, but the few pieces that do survive show the medieval craftsmen's mastery of, and fondness for, the use of heraldic charges in cast forms of decoration. These, now anonymous, craftsmen incorporated owls, boar's heads, sejant lions, and other heraldic charges associated with their client, into the ends of spoon handles, and a few of these items, once considered to be trivial, survive to remind present-day collectors of an early form of personalized table silver.

Enamelling the client's arms, to show the full colour of the armorial achievement, can equal, in decorative terms, the earlier three-dimensional form. The Cressener Cup, for instance, was made in 1503 for John Cressener of Hinckford Hundred in Essex. He was knighted by Henry VIII in 1513 for his services at the siege of Tournai. The button-shaped finial on his font cup bears the arms of Cressener quartering Mortimer, with Ferrers in pretence, in champlevé

A magnificent silver gilt sideboard dish by Paul de Lamerie, acknowledged master of British goldsmiths. The dish has a diameter of 31 inches, and bears the arms of the Worshipful Company of Goldsmiths by whom it was commissioned in 1741.

enamel. The cup remained in the Cressener family until 1908, when it was bought by the Goldsmith's Company, who exhibit it in Goldsmith's Hall today.

Raising the client's armorial insignia in low relief by chasing a flat sheet of a slender-gauge silver from its lower surface with numerous small punches and hammers, is an alternative way of incorporating heraldic designs into silverware. This time-consuming technique is most easily executed, and seen at its best, on large expanses of metal such as the 25 inch (63.5 cm) alms dish made for Westminster Abbey in 1685.

The technique was used again in a more modern idiom when B.J. Colson chased the shields of the 'Twelve Chief Livery Companies' and the City of London on the silver gilt rosewater dish they gave to the City of New York to mark the World Fair of 1939. The dish is now in New York City Museum.

When the owner's arms are engraved on silver, it would be wrong to assume they have necessarily been added as an afterthought. The delicacy and variety of line which a skilled and talented craftsman can engrave into the highly polished surface of heavy-gauge metal offers an attractive design alternative to casting, chasing and enamelling. The finest work has almost invariably been carried out on wares that were intended more for ornament than use, for fair wear and regular polishing soon blurs the initial appealing crispness of an engraver's work. Worn engraved

319

heraldic decoration also handicaps the collector intent on tracing the provenance of a piece of silver.

There is deep satisfaction to be gained from tracing the origin of an armorially marked piece of silver. One starts the task with two priceless advantages: silver and gold items originating in the United Kingdom are invariably hallmarked. The HALLMARK includes a date-letter which identifies the year of manufacture. In this respect the silver collector is much more fortunate than his counterpart in most of the other applied arts, who has to rely upon subtleties in stylistic design, and then make allowances for regional and provincial variation when attempting to date, for example, a piece of furniture or porcelain. The second tool at the hand of an armorial detective is the wealth of printed material at his disposal. Unreliable and discredited much of it may be, but it is probably true to say that some record of the pedigree of every British family that was genuinely armigerous before about 1850 will have found its way into print, and the numerous compendia of genealogical information laboriously compiled in the Victorian age give an amateur researcher an encouraging start in his enquiries.

The most frequently encountered armorial decoration on Georgian and Victorian silver spoons or forks is an engraved crest like a lion's or unicorn's head on a wreath. However, one would be rash to draw any conclusion from this. Fairbairn's *Book of Crests*, from its first publication in 1859, was sold in great numbers to jewellers and engravers, for whom it provided a wealth of artistic models. Although some clients chose to have their silver marked with a monogram or cypher, the prevailing fashion was to copy the illustration of a crest once used by a person of their own surname. It certainly was not the engraver's place to enquire into the propriety of his customer's order. He may have felt his duty to have been done if he edged a novice customer towards the choice of a ubiquitous crest, such as a lion's or a unicorn's head in his pattern book, and steered them away from a more rarely occurring model. The results of this lamentable heraldic free-for-all are with us to this day; there are still well-intentioned people who justify their use of a crest because 'it is engraved on the family silver'.

There is a greater chance of tracing heraldic decoration to its source with every further item of armorial information; a salver engraved with a shield bearing only a lion rampant offers no prospect of identification. The engraver's incorporation of cross-hatching (*see* PETRA SANCTA) on the lion to show that it is black leads to the blazon *Argent a Lion rampant Sable*, and although this narrows the field of possible claimants the range unfortunately now embraces what could be described as half the population of Wales, for among those who used this coat was Madoc ap Meredith, last Prince of Powys-Fadoc, from whom many claim descent!

A motto associated with the shield may perhaps help the hunt towards a conclusion, but as mottoes may be adopted or changed at whim in England, any conclusions would not be decisive. The motto 'Pro Magna Charta', unlikely for a descendant from a Welsh prince, is shown in Fairbairn's to have been used by the Dashwood and the Stapleton families, and although the Stapleton family bears *Argent a Lion rampant Sable* it also used the motto 'Dide Sed Cui Vide'. A crest above the shield would be a valuable corroborative piece of evidence, and as Fairbairn's *Book of Crests* records six used by the Stapletons, the inclusion of any one of these would serve to narrow the field to a particular branch of the Stapleton family.

This is as far as many armorial enquiries can go in the hands of the amateur, but the detection methods employed do not differ from those used in identifying the bearer of a coat of arms on a piece of English porcelain, for instance, or an architectural structure. But a hallmark (for London) and a secure dating (for, perhaps, 1770) given by that hallmark is the additional evidence available to the silver sleuth. Now if the shield on the salver bears also the red-hand device of a baronet it is tempting to conclude that the shield on the salver bears the arms of Sir Thomas Stapleton of Rotherfield Greys, Baronet (1727-81). However, the conclusion would not be justified without further support. To follow the example already given, Sir Thomas Stapleton married Mary Fane in 1765, and a 1770 salver bearing the arms of Stapleton, Baronet, impaling Fane justifies the conclusion that it was engraved *with* the arms of Sir Thomas. But it is not yet justifiable to conclude that the salver was engraved *for* Sir Thomas. It is not unknown for a piece of silver hallmarked with one date to be engraved with a shield that shows a marriage that did not take place until a decade or more later.

The stylistic fashions followed by engravers have changed at regular intervals. It was fashionable between about 1650 and 1685 to support an engraved shield on a pair of vigorously engraved crossed plumes. Towards the end of the same century the mantling from a helm hung around the shield. Armorial engraving from about 1705 until 1740 followed the Baroque fashion, with a cartouche replacing the shield and the surrounding decoration following a symmetrical architectural form. This was replaced by a rococo style with rocaille or foliate decoration around an asymmetrical cartouche. This lasted until about 1770, when the neo-classical style popularized by Robert Adam was in full swing. This was soon replaced by deep-cut engraving, by which silver was literally carved away by cuts made at an angle to reflect the light.

The process of electro-plating had not been invented at this time, but its precursor, now known by the name of Old Sheffield Plate, had been accidentally discovered. In this process a sheet of sterling silver too thin to be engraved without revealing what lay underneath was fused on to a thicker sheet of copper, and worked as if it were silver sheet. To accommodate the armorial engraving that society insisted should still be displayed, a recess was cut into the fused plate and a disc of pure silver burnished in. Such inserts can still be detected today by breathing on the engraving on a suspect piece of Old Sheffield Plate. An inserted silver disc will tarnish differently from the area around it, and immediately show a whiter colour.

Almost concurrent with bright-cut engraving came the entirely unadorned shield, spade-like in the 1790s, becoming square with extended triangular lugs on the chief line until about 1810.

It is not unknown for a piece of silver whose hallmarks show one date to be engraved with an armorial of another period, either to keep abreast of changing tides of fashion or, just occasionally, with intention to deceive. A Georgian goblet may have been thought unattractive by a person acquiring it in the mid 1800s. But to have the piece embellished and decorated with a shield of arms in the Victorian style reduces its interest to the collector and its value in the silver trade today. Similarly, an attempt to increase the value of, for instance, an unmarked Queen Anne two-handled cup by giving it some sort of spurious personality with the later engraving in appropriate style of the arms of a personage of Queen Anne's reign, is unscrupulous if not illegal, beside being, when detected, counter-productive.

With such snares and pitfalls awaiting him there is small wonder that a serious collector places such value on a ledger entry in which the goldsmith records the manufacture of a commission for his patron.

Apart from the rather grand items of silver discussed above, there are other and humbler pieces that have a claim to be, in the current phraseology, collectable. Among the most modern and popular are souvenir teaspoons. Some can be over-decorative and show all the stamps of mass-production. These bear an enamelled shield at the end of the handle, displaying the arms of their town of origin. They are the younger cousins of higher class counterparts cast in silver and bearing the shields of towns in the Netherlands, but nonetheless collected in Great Britain.

In another class of collectable armorial silver are the mementoes for liverymen and their guests at dinners of the City of London guilds in late Victorian and Edwardian times. Preserve spoons and tea caddy spoons were often specially made in silver for these occasions and usually bear the guild's arms. Livery dinner presents did not stop at spoons. A pomander engraved with the Cordwainers' arms, small dishes with the Goldsmiths' arms and standing salts with the Salters Company's arms are among the items noted by the collectors of such small objects.

A collection of livery buttons can also look most attractive, each item of fused plate stamped with the crest of the family for whom it was made.

Silver menu-holders stamped or engraved with a family crest are a twentieth-century phenomenon, but wine labels or bottle tickets as they are also called can be considerably older. They were much used in the eighteenth and nineteenth centuries, and in 1947 Dr N.M. Penzer classified into twenty categories these decorative silver tags held by a chain around the neck of a decanter. The armorial variety were specially commissioned from silversmiths. They show the owner's crest, pierced and engraved in silhouette, or shown in high relief by repoussé work above the name indicating the contents of the bottle. JA

Further reading

Chessyre, H. *The Identification of Coats of Arms on British Silver* 1978.

Fairbairn *Book of Crests* 1905 (4th edn reprinted Baltimore 1968).

Oman. C.C. *English Engraved Silver 1150-1900* London, 1978.

Papworth *Ordinary of British Armorials* 1874 (reprinted Bath 1977).

Taylor, G. *Silver* Harmondsworth, 1963.

Whitworth, E.W. *Wine Labels* London, 1966.

Sinister The right-hand side of the shield when viewed from the front. In armory, the sinister is considered to be inferior to the dexter or left-hand side.
See also SHIELD, POINTS OF THE

Sinople *see* **Vert**

Sir A reduced form of 'sire', this word forms the distinctive title of address of a British baronet or knight. At one stage (*c.* 1635) it was also placed before the names of ordinary priests. In the nineteenth century it was used with the surname of a person to designate him as a graduate of a university.

Sire Within the context of this dictionary a form of address appropriate to the crowned male ruler of a country or state.

Siren The siren of mythology has the upper half of a woman, the lower half of a web-foot sea bird, and large wings, and thus it should be depicted in armory, though it is often wrongly shown as a mermaid.

Sledging Flags Throughout history, symbolic flags have accompanied expeditions of conquest and exploration. Many of these flags have been armorial in character, such as the guidons attached to the sledges of Captain Scott's ill-fated expedition to the South Pole of 1910-13. Photographs of the expedition (particularly those entitled 'Mid-Winter's Day Dinner 1911', 'The Motor Party' and 'At the South Pole') clearly show small but correctly proportioned armorial guidons composed of the national flag in the hoist and devices on livery colours per fess in the fly, each being associated with an individual member of the expedition party.

Further reading
Ponting, H.G. *The Great White South* London, 1921.

Slipped *see* **Attributes**

Sloane Tract *see* **Treatises**

Slogan Also known as slughorn. The battle cry of the chief of a Scottish clan or house. It may be identical with the MOTTO.

Snake *see* **Serpent**

Snowdoun Herald of Arms A Scottish herald of arms prior to 1867. The office was first mentioned in 1448. The title is derived from a part of Stirling Castle which bore the name.   CJB

Soaring *see* **Attitude**

Solleret *or* **Solaret** Soleless foot armour, usually with overlapping plates to allow articulation.

Somerset Herald of Arms in Ordinary In the year 1448/49 Somerset Herald is known to have served the Duke of Somerset, Edmund Beaufort, but by the time of the coronation of King Henry VII in 1485 his successor appears to have been raised to the rank of a royal officer.

By 1525 Somerset was again in private service, on the staff of the Duke of Richmond and Somerset, Henry Fitzroy. On the death of that nobleman in 1536 the herald returned to the service of the Crown, and all later officers called Somerset have been members of the royal household as heralds in ordinary. The badge of office is *A Portcullis Or Royally Crowned* (a version of the Beaufort badge).   JC-K

Sovereign One with rank, jurisdiction or authority; the supreme ruler of a country, or a people with monarchical government.

Spain, Armorial Practice The development of armory in Spain began in the eleventh or twelfth centuries, probably with the great military orders, such as CALATRAVA in 1158 and ALCÁNTARA in 1178, and continued with the GOLDEN FLEECE in 1429.

Surprisingly, no body comparable to the College of Arms or the Court of Lord Lyon existed in Spain, and the heralds themselves seem to have been thought of little account. Indeed, even the posts of kings of arms were of but small moment, and the certificates the officers issued carried little legal weight.

In the twentieth century things improved somewhat. In 1915 it was decreed, through the Ministry of Grace and Justice, that only qualified men could be appointed kings of arms. In 1951 further legislation was enacted, and the new title Cronistas de Armas (Chronicler of Arms) was introduced to replace the more ancient one. Armorial certificates, recognition of titles and related issues are thus properly controlled by ministerial edict, and armorial bearings are protected by law.

Spanish armorial practice varies in minor details from the English, but there was in former centuries abuse of conventions such as those governing the display of coronets of rank and decorated helms. Such improper practices have been eliminated.   JC-K

Spain, Royal Arms of Quarterly 1 *Gules a Castle Or portalled Azure* (Castile) 2 *Argent a Lion rampant Gules armed langued and crowned Or* (Leon) 3 *Or four Pallets Gules* (Aragon) 4 *Gules a Cross Saltire and Orle of Chains linked with an Annulet Or stoned Vert* (Navarre) on a point in base *Argent a Pomegranate Gules stalked and leaved Vert* (Granada) over all an escutcheon of pretence *Azure three Fleurs-de-lis Or a Bordure Gules* (Bourbon-Anjou) behind the shield *two Ragged Staves saltirewise Gules* (the Cross of Burgundy) and below the shield dexter *a Yoke Gules* and sinister *a Sheaf of five Arrows* (badges of King Ferdinand and Queen Isabella).

Spancelled *see* **Attitude**

Spelling Numerous variations of spelling will be found in armory, the most common being exemplified by the goutty, goutté, gutty and gutté variants. Throughout this book, where such alternatives exist, the Y ending is preferred to é, except where ancient blazons are quoted verbatim.

Splendour, in his *see* **Attributes**

Sporting Heraldry The need for accurate, immediate, long-distance recognition of ally and opponent plays as important a part in fast-moving team sports today as it is said to have done in medieval warfare, where armory originated. Indeed, in today's commerce-oriented world the critical factor which can dictate the

A tabard embroidered with the arms of Spain.

funding of a sport is the television camera's power to relay a sponsor company's symbol right into the viewer's consciousness. It will come as no surprise, therefore, that both legitimate armory and what, for want of a better term, may be called 'pseudo-heraldry' are to be found in the world of sport.

The Football Associations of England, Scotland and Wales, granted arms in 1949, 1951 and 1953 respectively, are among a number of governing bodies to receive such a dignity. There is a remarkable conformity between the three shields despite the origin of two of them at the College of Arms and one at the Court of the Lord Lyon. The three leopards on the shield of the English F.A., red dragon on the Welsh and lion rampant on the Scottish shield respectively, assert their national importance. Closer inspection reveals eleven leeks on the Welsh shield, eleven thistles on the Scottish, but — strangely — only ten Tudor Roses on the English shield. One of the team has perhaps been sent off!

In the arms of the Welsh Rugby Union there is a red dragon, depicted taking a drop-kick, while the rugby ball in the crest of the Rugby Football Union (England) nestles under the paw of a demi-lion. The principal charges in the arms of the R.F.U. come from the arms of Lawrence Sheriff and his foundation Rugby School where the game had its origin. Both the Scottish Rugby Union and the Scottish Bowling Association have been granted arms.

A former Lord Lyon indicated the proper course for acquiring arms for sports clubs of Scottish Academies with the words: 'If armorial bearings are to be used at all the Club must petition for a grant, when some version of the superior's arms suitably differenced will be assigned.' Thus the arms granted to Ardrossan

Academy, Ayrshire, are differenced with a gold bordure for the Academy's Rugby Club. A cheaper and historically equally correct course commended by the Lord Lyon is the use of 'a round disc displaying per pale the superior's livery colours, and across this his motto on a scroll. The name of the Institution should surround this on a circlet or strap and buckle.

The Swimming Teachers' Association's arms resolve the interesting armorial complexity presented by a corporate sporting body operating in both England and Scotland. Its shield is an entertaining translation into heraldic idiom of the enticing 'Sea, Sun and Nudity' package-holiday advertisement. It is blazoned *Per fess wavy Azure and barry wavy of four Argent and Azure rising in chief a Sun in splendour issuant Or over all a Merman and a Mermaid embracing each other their tails counterchanged*. There are *Two Dolphins embowed head downwards* in the crest, but whereas in England the dolphins disport themselves between an oak and a rose branch, the oak branch is replaced by thistles in the crest granted by the Lord Lyon for use in Scotland.

Legitimate armory often has a strong influence on a club or a sportsman's racing colours. The arms of the sponsoring New Zealand Bank were used on the spinnaker of one of the ocean-racing yachts in the America's Cup in 1987.

Light and dark blue rowing blades of Oxford and Cambridge Universities appeared in the arms granted in 1966 to the London Borough of Richmond on Thames, and crosses crosslet, humetty, formy and fitchy are to be found on the oar-blades of some of the crews who race at Henley. They come from the arms of the schools and colleges the crews represent.

Among 12,000 racing colours in the Jockey Club's

register are a host of geometrical designs in numerous subtle shades. Many derive from armory: the colours of Lord Abergavenny, for example, 'Scarlet with white crossbelts', echo the arms of Nevill, *Gules a Saltire Argent*; and the Duke of Atholl's registered colours, 'Black and gold stripes', reflect his arms *Paly of six Or and Sable'*.

A review of the points of contact between sport and armory would not be complete without reference to the pseudo-heraldry that unfortunately abounds in the world of sport. A host of clubs invent arms for themselves, or shamelessly, and perhaps unknowingly, misappropriate arms legitimately granted to some other body. The Surrey County Cricket Club actually used the Prince of Wales' Feathers for its badge because the club leases the Oval Cricket Ground from the Duchy of Cornwall. Gloucester County Cricket Club uses the arms granted in 1569 to the City of Bristol Corporation, and in 1972 both Manchester City and Manchester United football clubs found ways to difference the arms of that city, which misuse was the subject of the celebrated action in the High Court of Chivalry only twenty years earlier. The irregularity of this practice is beyond doubt, and the missed opportunities for original and novel new grants of arms cause equal disappointment.   JA

Further reading
Colours of Riders supplement to 'The Racing Calendar', The Jockey Club, 1985.

Springing *see* **Attitude**

Spurious Heraldry An extreme form of BUCKET SHOP HERALDRY practised by armorial charlatans who provide dubious heraldic services in return for a substantial fee. Such firms offer 'genealogical research' leading (inevitably) to a confirmation of the right to bear arms. Some even offer to devise arms for clients in the manner of spurious academic degrees, or offer hereditary 'offices' associated with ancient or defunct European families to those of 'suitable character and achievement'.
See also BOGUS HERALDRY

Spurred *see* **Attributes**

Square Fretty *see* **Fretty**

Staffs of Office *see* **Wands, Staffs and Rods of Office**

Stained Glass *see* **Glass**

Stains The TINCTURES sanguine and tenné. These were supposedly used in abatements which 'stained' the gentility and honour of those who bore them.

However, both are known to have been used as livery colours during the Middle Ages, together with a third tincture, murrey, which is considered by some to be a stain and wrongly by others to be synonymous with sanguine. Today, instances of sanguine or tenné used in arms are rare indeed, though tenné remains the livery of the Berkeley family (whose arms are argent and gules) and is worn in modified form by members of the Berkeley Hunt. Murrey is occasionally granted and is particularly appropriate to educational establishments, providing an alternative to the exclusive royal livery of scarlet.

Staircases The staircase of a large house is, with the entrance hall, the main thoroughfare and its geometry and architectural features are often ideally suited to armorial display. Walls may be decorated with paintings, tapestries and frescoes which may contain armorial elements. Both stone and wooden newel posts may be surmounted with carved beasts, sometimes bearing shields and other devices. The structure of the ceiling or wall panelling may lend itself to armorial display, and some of the finest heraldic window glass will be found illuminating stair-wells, as at Godiston Park, Kent, for example.   JET

Stall Plates A metal plate emblazoned with the armorial bearings (though not usually the supporters) of a knight of an order of chivalry, and fastened over his stall in the chapel of his order. In the larger orders, the use of stall plates is restricted to the most senior members, such as the Knights Grand Cross of the Order of the Bath, and certain officers (see colour page 52). Early plates were erected after the death of the knight, and it was not until the reign of Henry VIII that they were erected during his lifetime. Unlike his banner, helmet and crest, which are removed from above the stall at his death, a knight's stall plate remains in perpetuity. For this reason the collection of stall plates of the knights of the Garter at Windsor is unparalleled as an armorial record of six centuries of chivalric nobility. Originally, such plates were enamelled on gilt or silver copper. From the end of the seventeenth century the arms were painted on copper until enamelling was reintroduced at the beginning of the present century. Had all the Garter plates been preserved there would now be well over nine hundred at Windsor, but some two hundred have been lost, stolen or removed following degradation, including all those of the founder Knights. The earliest remaining plate is that of Ralph, Lord Basset (c. 1390-1400) *Or three Piles Gules a Quarter Ermine* with a crest of *a Boar's Head Sable* issuing from a gold coronet and, on a separate roundel, *per pale Gules and Azure*, his badge *an Escarbuncle Or charged with a Bleeding Heart Azure*. One wonders how many contemporary plates, now missing, also depicted badges so prominently. Correctly, all the plates face the High Altar, the decanal helms and crests thereby breaching the armorial convention by facing the sinister. The Garter Knights are generally referred to by number in chronological order, the Founder Knights being 1-26.

The chapels of the principal orders of knighthood in Britain are: The Most Noble Order of the Garter: St George's Chapel Windsor; The Most Ancient and Most Noble Order of the Thistle: St Giles Church, Edinburgh; The Most Honourable Order of the Bath: King Henry VII's chapel, Westminster Abbey, London; The Most Distinguished Order of St Michael and St George: St Paul's Cathedral London; the chapel of the Most Illustrious Order of St Patrick (now virtually obsolete) is at St Patrick's Cathedral, Dublin, Eire.

At St David's Cathedral, Dyfed, Wales, where the sovereign is a member of the cathedral chapter, the arms of Elizabeth II appear both on her stall and its embroidered cushion.

See also KNIGHTHOOD, ORDERS OF

Further reading
Begent, P.J. *A Noble Place Indeed* 1984. An heraldic tour of St George's Chapel, Windsor Castle.

The stall plate of Walter, Lord Hungerford KG, elected to the Order of the Garter in 1421. Contrary to armorial convention, the arms are depicted facing the sinister and, therefore, the high altar.

Beltz, G.F. *Members of the Most Noble Order of the Garter from its Foundation to the Present Time* London, 1841.
de la Bere, I. *The Queen's Orders of Chivalry* 1964.
Fellowes, E.H. *The Knights of the Garter 1348-1939* and *Supplement 1939-1963.*
St John Hope, W. *The Stall Plates of the Knights of the Order of the Garter 1348-1485* London, 1901. A rare but magnificent book.

Stamps, Postage The first postage stamps to be issued were those by Great Britain in 1840 — the famous penny black and two-penny blue. Three years later the first stamps which could be called heraldic were issued in the canton of Geneva in Switzerland, and showed the cantonal arms, but it is understood that they were not valid outside the canton. In 1850 Switzerland issued a stamp which showed the national arms, although only in black and white. During the 1850s a number of other countries and states in Europe issued stamps which depicted the appropriate national or state arms. These included Austria 1850, Saxony 1851, Norway 1855, Wurtemburg 1857 and Luxembourg 1859. The earliest stamps in full colour appear to be those issued by Switzerland in 1918. They were the first two stamps in a set which appeared over a period of twelve years showing the arms of the various cantons.

Although a stamp is an ideal shape for the reproduction of a shield of arms or even full armorial bearings, the size is small and skill is needed on the part of the stamp designer to accurately portray a full achievement, or a complicated coat, on a small scale. Many heraldic stamps do show the full achievement but probably the majority only show the shield of arms. Some stamps show the heraldry as the main feature, but on others it is merely a small part of the total stamp design. With improved printing techniques most stamps in recent years have been printed in full heraldic colour rather than the monochrome used in the early issues.

In addition to heraldic designs on the actual stamp, heraldry will be found in two further areas of philately. Firstly, part of the national arms, often the crest, will be included in the watermark in the paper used for printing the stamps. Secondly, a number of the special handstamps used in the United Kingdom and elsewhere for cancelling mail for special events incorporate appropriate heraldry, usually a shield or achievement of the organization or town which has sponsored the special cancellation.

Most of the countries in the British Commonwealth have issued at least one stamp which shows their national arms. Some have included their arms in a special set issued at the time they gained their independence, for example Gambia in 1965, Guyana in 1966 and Bahamas in 1973. Some of the early stamps issued by Barbados showed the badge of the

Scottish heraldic stamps. Top left to bottom right: arms of Lord Lyon; Duke of Rothesay; Royal Scottish Academy of Painting, Sculpture and Architecture; Royal Society of Edinburgh.

Colony, but in 1966, at the time Barbados gained its independence, it issued a set of four stamps, one of which showed the arms of Barbados in full colour. Mauritius issued a number of stamps between 1895 and 1900 showing the arms then in use, which appear to have been based on an Admiralty badge. After arms were granted in 1906 by Royal Warrant, these have appeared on a number of stamps, including one in full colour in 1968 at the time of independence. An interesting set of four issued by the Falkland Islands in 1975 showed the devices used over the years — the 2p value showed the old seal and flag badge, the 7½p stamp the coat of arms granted by Royal Warrant in 1925, the 10p value the arms granted in 1948, and the 16p value the arms granted to the Falkland Islands Dependencies in 1952.

Heraldry has not appeared on many of the stamps issued by Great Britain, but the royal arms were included on the 5d values in the sets issued in 1887 and 1902, on the 2/6d and 5/- stamps issued in 1939, and the £1 stamp issued in 1951. The arms of the City of York appeared on a commemorative stamp issued in 1971. In 1974, a set of four stamps appeared to commemorate Great Britons — Robert the Bruce, Owain Glyndwr, the Black Prince and Henry V. In 1984, a further set of four heraldic stamps was issued to mark the 500th anniversary of the granting of the first charter to the heralds of the kings of England. The arms shown were those of the College of Arms, Richard III, the Earl Marshal and the City of London. A further set of heraldic stamps was issued in summer 1987 with a Scottish theme to mark the tercentenary of the revival of the Order of the Thistle.

Although most heraldic stamps which have been issued show national or civic arms, occasionally personal arms are shown. Examples include the arms of Sir Humphrey Gilbert on a stamp issued by Newfoundland in 1933. In 1974 the Cayman Islands issued two stamps to commemorate the centenary of the birth of Sir Winston Churchill: one showed his arms, and the other the banner he flew as Lord Warden of the Cinque Ports. Perhaps the most interesting set of personal arms is a set of twenty-one issued by Jersey in 1981 showing the arms of Jersey families.

An example of one country issuing a stamp showing the arms of another country is that issued by the United States of America in 1967, showing the arms of Finland, to mark the 50th anniversary of Finland's independence.

In 1963 Tonga issued an unusual set of circular stamps, printed on card rather than paper, showing the country's arms.

One stamp which is of particular interest to armorists is that issued by France in 1964, showing the tomb of Geoffrey of Anjou. Among sets of stamps which will appeal to armorists are those issued by France between 1942 and 1960, Cape Verde Islands in 1961, Spain between 1962 and 1966, Angola in 1963, as well as many issued by Liechtenstein and Switzerland.   PDE

Further reading

Holyoake, C.J. *Heraldic Notes on the Issue of Postage Stamps* 1976.

Standard A long, tapering flag, originally split or swallow-tailed but now usually rounded at the end.

The standard was the greatest of the medieval livery flags and served as a mustering point for feudal retainers during military campaigns and at tournaments, its household liveries and badges being more familiar to the populace than were the personal banners of the nobility. Also known as an ancient, maintenance of the standard was the responsibility of an officer of that name. In battle, it was second only in importance to the banner (also called a lieutenant) which, because it represented the physical presence of the owner, could never be relinquished without shame: 'The Lieutenant is to be saved before the Ancient' (Shakespeare's *Othello*). Several similar standards, guidons and other livery flags would be in simultaneous use, but only one banner.

In medieval terminology, 'standard' was a generic term for the livery flags. In the hoist of the standard was displayed the national device (e.g. the Cross of St George). This removed any ambiguity regarding the allegiance of a particular magnate and his retinue. The fly was composed of the livery colours (or colour) on which were displayed the principal livery badge and the badges of subsidiary territories from which a noble's retainers were drawn. Each retainer would wear a uniform of similar liveries and badge. Often (though not always) the tail of the fly would carry the Cri de Guerre, though on English standards this is more often found on 'motto bends' separating the badges. The flag was also fringed with the armorial or livery colours.

The late Tudor heralds characteristically determined that they should set down the size of standards, which by that time were used only for pageantry and ceremonial, and were ostentatiously large. 'The Great Standard to be sette before the Kinges pavilion or tent — not to be borne in battel' was 33 feet long. A duke's standard was 21 feet in length, and that of a humble knight 12 feet long. The shape of the fly was also specified according to degree, and crests were sometimes incorporated — a dubious practice which is sometimes in evidence today though many officers of arms actively discourage it. In the medieval period the battlefield standard was about 8 feet long, those used for tournaments and ceremonial being slightly longer.

In England today, standards are often depicted in patents which include a grant of a BADGE. However, there seems to be no requirement that the field should be of the LIVERY COLOURS with which a livery badge is properly associated, and the colours of the fringe are often those of the wreath in the arms (see colour page 250). All this is contrary to medieval practice, and the standard has assumed a purely decorative function which is regrettable. In Scotland, where standards and guidons still grace flagstaffs, Lord Lyon grants standards of varying dimensions for use by Chiefs of the Name and Barons of Scotland. The Scottish standard is reminiscent of that of the Tudor period, for it is forked

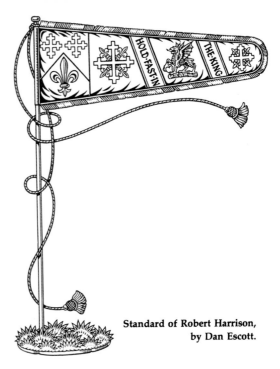

Standard of Robert Harrison, by Dan Escott.

or rounded at the end depending on rank, which also determines the length: sovereign 8 yards; duke 7 yards; earl 6 yards; lord 5 yards; knight or baron 4 yards. The ground colour is of the liveries, usually in tracts, and charged with the crest or badge and the motto inscribed in one, two or three ribands drawn bendwise across the fly.

In England, with the decline of military heraldry, the demise of the large estate and no equivalent of the Scottish clan system, the practice of allowing standards to all and sundry is rarely appropriate and frequently pretentious. The standard should be reserved for corporate bodies whose members and employees are the present-day equivalent of medieval retainers and where an obvious requirement for corporate identity exists. The livery pennon and guidon (a most attractive flag) could then be re-introduced for those armigers for whom a standard might be considered inappropriate, or organisations who use a badge 'under licence'. Such flags should be specified in the patent together with livery colours. In England, and on occasions in Scotland, the national device has been replaced by the personal arms in the hoist. This too is most regrettable: livery flags have never been used to denote the physical presence of their owners (this is the function of the banner) and to combine the two functions in one flag is both illogical and ambiguous.

See also ARMORIAL BEARINGS, USE OF; FLAG

Star of India, Most Exalted Order of Founded in 1861 (and enlarged 1876, 1897 and 1901). It has three classes: Knights Grand Commander, Knights Com-

327

mander, and Companions. The collar of the order is composed of alternate links of lotus flowers, red and white roses, and palm branches enamelled on gold; an imperial crown appears at the centre. The badge depends from the collar and takes the form of a five-pointed star adorned with diamonds. The badge of Knights Commander and Companions is of chipped silver. The ribbon of the order is light blue edged with white. The order has not been awarded since 1947.

JC-K

Star, Order of A French order of knighthood, formed in 1351 by John II in response to the founding of the English Order of the Garter. The order was to have consisted of five hundred knights who wore red mantles, lined with fur, and badges of a black star charged at its centre with a golden garland. The knights of the order were to have formed the nucleus of a national army, but following a crushing defeat at the battle of Mauron in 1352, Charles V allowed the order to die out.

Statant *see* **Attitude**

Steeled *see* **Attributes**

Stone Carving The carving of armorial devices in stone into the fabric of castles, churches, palaces and family homes has a history almost as old as heraldry itself. The rapid development of armory in the early medieval period coincided with the great flowering of the art of stone carving, and throughout Europe limestones and sandstones were quarried and carved into armorial devices to enhance the prestige of the already rich and powerful.

Stone carving is an art of reduction, of taking away excess material to expose the required form underneath. The stone should be fine-grained, consistent in both colour and texture, and able to take finely detailed work. A wide range of stones has been used, from limestones and sandstones to marbles, slates and alabaster (though little of this last is quarried in Britain).

Most armorial work in stone is carved in relief. The outline of the device to be carved is first drawn on paper and traced through on to a prepared flat face of suitably sized stone. All material outside this outline is then cut back to a predetermined background line, leaving the device raised but unfeatured. On to this 'blank' the main parts of the design are then carved as required: shield, helm, crest, mantling, etc. The good carver will always work all parts of the design at the same time, never, for example, finishing one supporter on one side before starting the other. An eye for the balance of the complete design is most important.

The tools used in stone carving are still very much as they were centuries ago: steel chisels and gouges, iron

Staircase tower and armorial doorway erected 1602 at Huntly Castle. Above the impaled arms of the Marquess of Huntly and the Marchioness (Lady Henrietta Stewart) is a central panel containing the royal arms of King James VI impaling those of Denmark.

hammers and fruitwood mallets. Some modern chisels are now made with tungsten carbide tips which, being very hard, can be useful with hard or abrasive sandstones.

The charges on the shield are left to last and being in low relief usually require the most intricate and careful carving. When all the carving is completed the background is 'sparrow pecked' or roughened with small chisel marks. This has the effect of making the design stand out against the background, giving a greater three-dimensional appearance to the work.

A well carved coat of arms in stone can be a beautiful work of art in its own right, coloured or not. The rhythmical curves of the mantling, boldness of the supporters or exquisite detail of the charges on the shield, can be a joy both to carve and to look at. Within

Arms of the governors and magistrates of the Bargello Palace, Florence. The courtyard below this wall was a place of execution until 1782 when, by order of Grand Duke Leopoldo, the instruments of torture and gallows were burned.

Fine armorial carving on a doorway in Bonifacio, Sicily.

the conventions of armory there is a surprisingly large scope for the individual's artistic flair and imagination, and each carving has its own character and style.   SW

See also CAPITALS; FONTS; ROOFS
Further reading
Priestly, H. *Heraldic Sculpture* 1972.

Stooping *see* **Attitude**

Strangway's Book *see* **Treatises**

Strap and Buckle In armory, a belt with ornamental buckle, cusp, eyelets and edging usually picked out in a distinctive tincture, and depicted as an annulet with the strap passing through the buckle and turned back through itself and pendent from the bottom edge. Usually inscribed with a motto or slogan and particularly common in Scottish armory where it is associated with a variety of badges. Perhaps the best known example is that of the Order of the Garter (see colour page 252).

Streamer (i) A long, tapering flag, the nautical equivalent of the standard, used to identify the allegiance of troops on board a medieval warship. Without motto or fringe, the field of the streamer is of the livery colours charged with livery badges.
(ii) Any very long, tapering flag, used either for decoration or as an additional means of identification when divided lengthways of the livery or armorial colours.

Stringed *see* **Attributes**

Studded *see* **Attributes**

Sub-Ordinary An armorial charge of geometrical shape subordinate to the ORDINARY or PRINCIPAL CHARGE.

The reader of heraldic reference books may search in vain for some clue as to the function of the sub-ordinary. Lists are varied and arbitrary — enlightenment minimal. Many writers conclude that the sub-ordinary is simply a minor geometrical charge — why, then, is a separate classification necessary? As with the ordinary, there seems little point in retaining terminology which cannot be defined and has no distinctive purpose.

If a function is to be ascribed to the sub-ordinary (and thereby a definition), it would seem that it is the sequence of BLAZON which is most likely to provide it. The term 'honourable' when applied to the ordinary implies precedence, and it is not unreasonable to suggest that the sub-ordinary is so named because it is consistently blazoned *after* the ordinary. This is not a matter of mere convention: because of its position on the shield it is impossible to blazon a sub-ordinary as though it were a principal charge (except in the absence of other charges). Those charges which are blazoned fifth, following the minor charges borne on the ordinary or principal charge, are by this definition sub-ordinaries: bordure, canton, chief, flaunches, inescutcheon, label, orle (and tressure), quarter.

Several of the above sub-ordinaries are employed for the purposes of augmentation, differencing, etc., when they are placed last in the sequence of blazon. When used for these purposes they are, in effect, extensions of the shield, placed either upon it (e.g. a canton) or adjacent to it (e.g. the bordure and chief). It is in these circumstances that they may appear to infringe the tincture convention or debruise the field.

Sumptuary Laws Laws intended to limit or control the private expenditure of the citizens of a community. Sumptuary laws existed in ancient civilizations, particularly that of Rome, and in medieval Europe the first important legislation was in Italy that of Frederick II, in Aragon that of James I, in France that of Philip IV, and in England that of Edward II. Charles V of France, for example, forbade the use of long-pointed shoes, a fashion vehemently opposed by the Church. In England, fourteenth-century writers tell us of the extravagance of dress and cuisine of the period, and in 1336 Edward III attempted to legislate against such luxurious living. In 1363 costume was regulated by law, and a further Act of 1444 sought to control clothing when it formed part of the wages of servants, specific allowances being permitted to bailiffs and overseers (5 shillings a year), principal (4s.) and ordinary servants (3s.4d) for example. A further

Statute of 1463 (Edward IV) legislated for the control of clothing of persons of all ranks. Indeed, a succession of English laws from that year up to 1532 sought to limit the splendour of apparel by forbidding untitled people to wear such things as purple silk, gold chains and collars, cloth of gold and crimson velvet. Of interest to armorists is the fact that at least six of these sumptuary laws specifically exempted both heralds and pursuivants.

Similar Acts were passed in Scotland: in 1433 (James I) the manner of living of all orders in Scotland was prescribed, and in particular the use of pies and baked meats was forbidden to all below the rank of baron. In 1457 (James II) an Act was passed against 'sumptuous cleithing', but in the Acts of 1471 and 1581 officers of arms were, following the English practice, specifically exempted. The Scottish sumptuary law of 1621 was the last of the kind in Britain.

Of further interest to armorists were the controls applied to the use of furs, ermine being reserved for the nobility and, as a token of royal favour, by concession to other magnates close to the Crown. It may be that the extensive use of ermine in the mantlings of many Garter knights was therefore intended to indicate their privileged position in society.

Sunburst An armorial charge comprising rays of light issuing upwards from behind a cloud. The sunburst was a badge of Edward III and Richard III and now, ensigned by the Royal Crown, it is the badge of Windsor Herald.

Supporters (i) Figures, usually beasts, chimerical creatures or of human form, placed on either side the shield in a coat of arms to 'support' it. Single supporters, standing to one side of or behind the shield, are rare in English armory but popular in Europe, where the eagle displayed is particularly suitable for this purpose. In Scotland, too, there are examples of single supporters. The Royal Burgh of Perth formerly used a double-headed eagle to support its arms, and the arms of the former Burgh of Falkirk were held by a *Lion rampant affronty Gules crowned with a Mural Crown Argent*. The arms of Campbell of Craignish and Askomel and of Campbell of Inverneill are supported on the mast of a galley. Instances of three supporters are not unknown, the third often taking the form of some inanimate object behind the shield. In French armory a distinction is drawn between human supporters (*tenants*) and beasts (*supports*), inanimate objects being *soutiens*.

Unlike other elements in a coat of arms supporters have no practical origin — unless, as has been suggested by some armorists, they originated in the flamboyant practice of dressing retainers as beasts and creatures to stand guard over their master's shield of

Sub-Ordinaries

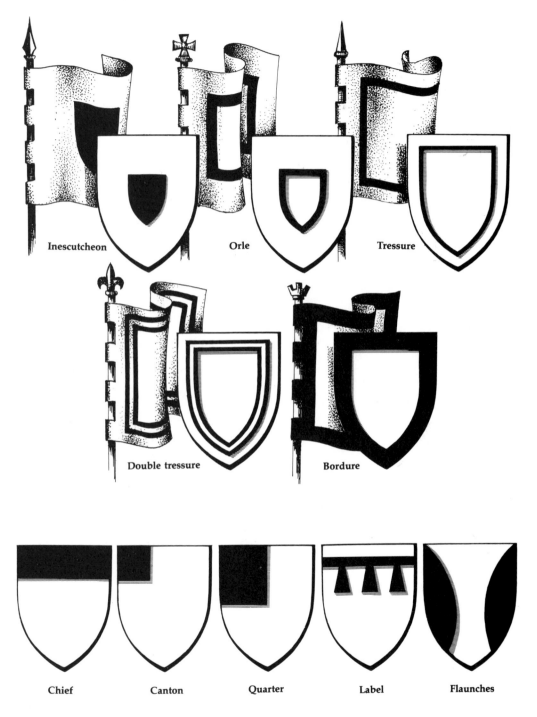

Inescutcheon

Orle

Tressure

Double tressure

Bordure

Chief

Canton

Quarter

Label

Flaunches

331

Griffin supporters of the arms of Baden. Otto Hupp, 1928.

arms at pageants and tournaments. The true armorial supporter cannot be traced with certainty before the fifteenth century. Its origin is to be found in a combination of factors, in particular the development of armorial badges, usually in the form of beasts, which were popular with the nobility of the fourteenth and fifteenth centuries. It should be remembered that by the fifteenth century, the nobility would have accumulated many armorial devices other than those which could be displayed by quarterings in the arms: badges acquired as the result of inheritance and marriage which needed to be depicted in some new way. To the medieval mind armorial devices were either displayed on a shield or they were not, hence the uninhibited translation of badges to crests, crests and badges to

supporters, and so on. The use of such devices in seals predates their depiction in armorial bearings, indeed numerous early seals bear beasts and chimerical creatures *instead* of shields. Many beast badges were incorporated into the seals of the fourteenth and fifteenth centuries to occupy the spaces between the helmet and the outer decorative border. However, few appear to 'support' the shield and whilst they may be considered as precursors of the true supporter their use was essentially decorative. Other seals show a shield of arms resting against or pendent from a creature, the swan badge of the earls of Hereford in the seal of Humphrey de Bohun (1322), for example. Often the *guige* (strap) of the shield was used as a means of support, as in the seal of Thomas Holland, Earl of Kent (1380) in which the shield is supported by a white hart gorged with a crown, the badge of his half-brother, Richard II.

As the practical application of armory in the field of battle and the tournament declined, so the adoption of the stylized coat of arms as a symbol of authority and eminence increased, and by the late Tudor period the use of crests and supporters was subject to regulation and control. Whereas the 'supporters' in medieval seals were invariably depicted as pairs of creatures, from the Tudor period dissimilar supporters appear with greater frequency, often diminishing the attractive symmetry of an achievement.

Today, supporters are symbols of eminence granted only to peers, knights of the Garter, Thistle and (formerly) St Patrick, and to knights of the first class of the British orders of chivalry and of the Most Venerable Order of St John of Jerusalem. With the exception of hereditary peers, supporters are personal to the grantee and are not transmitted. The sons of peers do not use their father's supporters, the eldest son of an hereditary peer inheriting them with the arms. In Scotland, supporters are granted on the authority of Lord Lyon to peers, baronets, Knights Grand Cross of the orders of chivalry, Chiefs of Clans, certain knights and the heirs of minor barons who sat in parliament prior to 1587 as of right. Also in Scotland, the heir apparent may use his father's supporters. In both England and Scotland a royal warrant may be obtained enabling supporters to be granted to someone who would not normally be entitled to them, and certain families may claim an ancient right to include supporters in their arms. Supporters may also be granted to corporate bodies. The policy of the College of Arms with regard to applications from corporations is not fixed, eminence and permanence being criteria. County, city, metropolitan and district councils, nationalized corporations, bodies incorporated by royal charter, eminent national societies, etc., would not normally be denied supporters. Supporters may also be incorporated in a devisal of arms emanating from the College of Arms, such as that to the Cathedral Church of the Advent, Alabama, USA (see page 126). Supporters are often depicted standing on some form of COMPARTMENT, though the current practice in England is to include these only when specified and blazoned in the patent.

See also IRELAND, ARMORIAL PRACTICE

(ii) A beast, chimerical creature or human figure used to support or 'sustain' an armorial flag in an achievement of arms. Such supporters are usually already associated with the armiger (e.g. a crest creature, badge, etc.) and are not considered to be part of the armorial bearings. This type of supporter is sometimes termed a bearer.

Suppressed *see* **Attitude**

Surcoat A long coat of linen, split at the sides to facilitate movement, especially on horseback, and originally intended to protect mail from heat and rain. Dating from the crusades of the twelfth century, the surcoat provided an obvious means of displaying armorial devices. Also known as coat armour, a 'Gentleman of Coat Armour' was an armiger — hence 'coat of arms'. By the middle of the fourteenth century the surcoat had become shorter and was, in effect, a jupon.

Sur le tout *see* **Attributes**

Surmounted When an armorial charge is laid over another in an original design, the second is said to be surmounted of or by the first. Not to be confused with debruised.

Surrey Herald of Arms Extraordinary This office was created in 1856 and a badge of office assigned in 1981: *Within a representation of a Herald's Collar of SS Argent a Tabard chequy Or and Azure*. These were the arms of John de Warenne, Earl of Surrey in the late thirteenth century, from whom the earldom descended through the Fitzalans to the Howard dukes of Norfolk and earls marshal.

Surtout Placed over all.

Swan, Order of the A Bavarian order of knights, also known as the Society of Our Dear Lady, formed in 1440. The badge was a swan in a twisted scarf, surmounted by a picture of the Virgin on a medallion surrounded by rays.   KH

Swans *see* **Livery Companies of the City of London**

Sweden, Armorial Practice Sweden's armorial tradition, like that of Denmark, is medieval and contains Germanic influences. Members of the Swedish nobility were originally untitled, but two titled ranks, those of count and baron, were introduced by Eric XIV (1560-68), and these are recognized armorially by the use of coronets, multiple crests, inescutcheons and quarterings. The Riddarhus, constructed in Stockholm towards the end of the seventeenth century as the official headquarters of the Swedish nobility, contains a magnificent collection of arms: some 2300 escutcheons fill the walls of the great hall, and many patents of nobility are held in the archives.

Of particular interest are the 'coats of arms of provinces', which were introduced in *c.* 1560. These were intended to proclaim the extent of the Vasa territories (Gustavus Vasa, otherwise Gustavus I Eriksson, 1496-1560, King of Sweden), and as 'arms for the people' of the various provinces. These arms have maintained a special place in the public consciousness and are widely and enthusiastically used today. Officially, their most important function has always been the identification of military units raised in the different provinces. More recently, many of these arms have also been incorporated in the arms of Sweden's administrative districts.

In the eighteenth century there was a reaction against the adoption of arms by the middle classes and a royal decree of 1762 prescribed penalties for the use of certain armorial insignia, which were considered to be more properly the privilege of the nobility.

From the seventeenth century, responsibility for matters armorial was vested in a state official, the Riksheraldiker, though ultimate authority rested with the state, as it does today. In the 1950s two heraldic authorities were created: the Statens Heraldiska Namnd and an heraldic department of the Royal Archives. The Keeper of the Royal Archives and the Royal Antiquarian are automatically members of the Heraldiska Namnd, other members being appointed by the government.

Ennoblement ceased in 1902 and personal arms have been recognized only for members of the Order of the Seraphim, Sweden's premier order of chivalry, though these are not hereditary. The arms of Knights of the Seraphim are displayed in the Riddarholm's chapel in Stockholm.

For the most part, armory in Sweden is now primarily concerned with civic, corporate and ecclesiastical arms which, as 'evocative symbols for local government and community life', are protected by law.

Sweden, Military Insignia All the Scandinavian armed forces currently use heraldry in their insignia. The Swedish army has used armorial bearings associated with regions, districts and municipalities from the seventeenth century onwards. Indeed, it was the Swedish army that set the trend for a proper system of regional infantry and cavalry regiments, which still forms the basis for many national armies.

Swedish regiments have long used such arms on their flags, and in 1960 many units began wearing small metal badges on their shoulder straps, and some on side caps. For the most part the *förbandstecken*, as these badges are known, consist of stylized angular armorial emblems taken from the arms borne in unit flags and are made in stamped gold or silver metal. For example, the regimental badge of the Västerbottens Regiment (20th Infantry Regiment) consists of the Wild Man of Lappland, taken from the arms of that province. In 1977 each Swedish army regiment was given its own arms. These consisted of the arms associated with the unit location (district, province, etc.) ensigned by the Royal Crown and placed in front of certain emblems relating to that branch of the army to which the unit belonged. These emblems included crossed rifles for the infantry, crossed cannons for the artillery, etc. In the devices of the Skaraborgs Regiment (4th Armoured Regiment), the arms in armour indicate that the unit is armoured. The unit arms were intended for use on stationery, vehicles, etc., but not on uniforms. Such devices are authorized after consultation between the Swedish State Heraldic Office and various defence departments, notably the Swedish Army Museum in Stockholm. In 1981 various military units down to and including company level began wearing cloth insignia on field uniform. The small arms of Sweden (three gold crowns on a blue background) are used on the cockade for officers, whilst enlisted men normally use the national cockade of blue and yellow. One interesting variation of the cockade is worn by certain regiments and consists of a piece of plaited straw worn behind a button bearing

---

OPPOSITE **John Rous was a chantry priest and an antiquary whose many works included a history of England and what is now known as the Rous or Warwick Roll, a vellum manuscript 11 inches wide and nearly 25 feet in length (28 cm x 7.5 m), compiled between the years 1477 and 1485 as a chronicle of the Earls of Warwick. Each of the 63 principal characters is described in detail and the accompanying drawings provide a wealth of armorial information, as in this section devoted to George, Duke of Clarence (1449-78). He it was who was supposedly put to death in a butt of Malmsey wine. Brother of Edward IV and Richard of Gloucester (later Richard III), George was created Duke of Clarence in 1461 and a Knight of the Garter. He differenced the royal arms and crest with a silver label of three points each charged with a canton gules. On his banner, these arms are impaled with the multiple quarterings of his wife, a daughter of Richard Nevill, Earl of Warwick, the 'Kingmaker'. These include the arms of Beauchamp, Clare, Montacute, Monthermer, Nevill, Newburgh and Despencer. Clarence is depicted standing astride a black bull, which was his badge.**

Rous compiled the first version of the Roll in English during the reign of Richard III. It included a laudatory passage to Richard, but following the accession of Henry VII this was replaced, in a second Latin version, by a vilification of his former king.

HERZOGTUM SACHSEN MEININGEN

Reihenfolge der souveränen herzöge:

Bernhard
geboren 17. Dezember 1800 / folgt feinem 1803
geftorbenen Dater / tritt die Regierung an 1821 /
dankt ab 1866 / † 3. Dezember 1882.

Georg
geboren 2. April 1826 / folgt 1866.

Bernhard
Erbprinz / geboren 1. April 1851.

The Münchener Kalendar was published annually in Munich from 1888-1936 as a desk calendar for the business community. After the third year of publication, each page of every issue contained a different heraldic design, devised and executed by Otto Hupp, Professor of Design at Munich Polytechnik.

336

Arms of the Skaraborgs Regiment   **Badge of Vasterbottens Regiment**

the three crowns. This commemorated the bravery shown by these units at the battle of Lund in 1676, when Swedish troops fought the Danes with only a wisp of straw in their hats as a cognizance.   SS

Sweden, Royal Arms of *A Cross paty throughout Or between 1 and 4 Azure three Crowns Or* (Sweden) *2 and 3 Azure three Bendlets sinister wavy Argent over all a Lion rampant crowned Or* (Folkunger) *over all an escutcheon Per bend Azure and Gules a Bend Argent over all a Vase Or* (Vasa) *impaling Azure an Eagle displayed Sable in chief seven Stars Or and in base a Bridge with two towers over Water Argent* (Bernadotte).

Switzerland, Armorial Practice As in the rest of Western Europe there is evidence in Switzerland of the use of armorial devices from as early as the twelfth century. However, there is no armorial authority, but the Swiss Heraldic Society (*see* ADDRESSES), founded in the late nineteenth century, has a wide membership and publishes authoritative literature. Switzerland abounds in armorial glass, its museums contain rolls of arms and seals illustrating its heraldic heritage, and the arms of the Confederation, cantons, town and villages are widely displayed.

There are no Swiss noblemen, no Swiss orders of chivalry, and nationals are forbidden by the Federal Constitution to accept foreign orders and decorations. Nevertheless, armory both personal and civic is universal and unrestrained.   JC-K

Sword Unless otherwise specified, a long, straight-sided sword is depicted erect. Often the pommel, handle and cross-guard (quillons) are of a different tincture and may be blazoned as hafted or hilted.

Sword of Cyprus, Order of the Also known as the Order of Silence, this was formed c.1187, and bore as its badge a sword environed with the letter S.   KH

Sword Rests *see* **Metalwork**

T

Tabard A dress coat worn over armour from the late fifteenth century to the mid sixteenth century. Similar to the jupon but reaching below the thigh and with broad sleeves to the elbow, the tabard was emblazoned front and back and on the sleeves, and served a purely armorial purpose. In general use only during the reigns of Henry VII and Henry VIII, the tabard was at first waisted, later ones falling straight from the shoulders. It has been suggested that heralds of the period wore cast-off tabards as a form of livery, indicative of their special relationship with a particular noble. The tabard continued to be used by heralds long after it ceased to be worn by the nobility. At first it was actually worn as a garment, thereafter it was used as a peculiar form of insignia, particularly at funerals, when it was carried on a pole before the heralds.

Today it is once again worn, the tabard of a king of arms being of velvet, that of a herald satin, and a pursuivant's damask-silk. All are embroidered with the royal arms of England or Scotland. Originally pursuivants wore their tabards with the sleeves front and back, but this practice ceased during the reign of James II.

Heralds in their tabards in the Garter procession at Windsor, 1982.

Tabernacle *see* **Pavilion**

Talbot The conventional dog of armory, having a mastiff's body, a hound's head and the long, drooping ears of a bloodhound.

Tankard, Knights of the Founded in Aragon in 1410 as Knights 'de la Jara', for warfare against the Moors, this order bore a device consisting of a picture of the Virgin, suspended from a chain of pots of lilies alternating with griffins. It was also known as the Order of Lilies, or the Order of Griffins.   KH

Tapestry Marks Tapestries were both decorative and functional. They served to brighten the drab uniformity of large areas of stonework and reduced draughts by covering doorways and open fenestrations. Most surviving medieval tapestries were woven in the Low Countries, Flanders and France, there being no significant workshops in England until the mid-sixteenth century.

Many tapestries originally carried some form of identification mark woven into the selvage, though subsequently this was often removed and the mark lost. Tapestry marks were often armorial and usually depicted devices from the arms of the workshop owner or the town of manufacture as well as cyphers and complex merchants' marks.

Antwerp tapestries had two hands on a shield, Florence a fleur-de-lis, and Brussels a red shield between two letters B. Tournai usually used a castle, and Enghien (also in the Low Countries) a shield gyronny of eight. Delft used a pale cotised between the letters H and D, and Oudenaarde a shield barry of six. The Royal Manufactory in Madrid adopted a con-joined M and D beneath a coronet. Tapestries from the workshops of the Gobelins family in the Faubourg St Marcel in Paris (established *c.* 1660) were among those supplied to the Palace of Versailles. The Gobelins mark was a fleur-de-lis and a letter F with a right-angled 'tail' at the lower end. Another seventeenth-century French workshop, that at Aubusson, used a mark of a coronet with the conjoined letters A and P above, and the letter A beneath. The seventeenth-century Paris mark was a fleur-de-lis between two letters P.

In England, several workshops had been established by the early seventeenth century, notably that at Mortlake in Surrey, identified by a series of marks comprising a red cross on white shields of varying shapes. By the eighteenth century, London had become the centre of the English tapestry industry, and celebrated workshops at Soho and Fulham flourished at that time, though no marks are recorded for them. However, tapestries woven at Hatton Garden (established *c.* 1679) bore the arms of the City of London, a white shield charged with a red cross and a sword in the first quarter, confusingly similar in appearance to those of Mortlake.   BC

Target *or* **Targe** (i) A fixed shield for the purpose of marksmanship or set upon a staff for display.
(ii) A circular shield, especially as used by the Scots, leathered and studded, often with a removable spike projecting from the boss point.

Tartan Although woven checked material has been worn in Scotland since at least the seventeenth century, there is little evidence that particular combinations of checks and colours had any early significance. Indeed, portraits exist in which the wearer sports several different tartans at the same time.

Nevertheless, following the 1745 Jacobite Rising, tartans were prohibited, and if it had not been for the raising of Highland Regiments in the British Army, it is possible the wearing of tartan would have ceased forever after 1745. Sir Walter Scott was instrumental in obtaining the repeal of the Act of Prohibition. This was followed several years later, in 1824, when George IV became the first sovereign to pay an official visit to Scotland for over two hundred years. The visit acted as a stimulus for highland lairds who wished to appear at the Palace of Holyroodhouse in 'traditional' highland dress.

As a result, enterprising firms, such as Wilsons of Bannockburn, produced tartan designs to order, and most tartans now in use date from this period. Clan tartans therefore have a tradition of over one hundred and fifty years, long enough for authenticity to be established.   CJB
Further reading
Innes of Learney, Sir Thomas (Lord Lyon) *Tartans of the Clans and Families of Scotland* 1949 (5th edn).
Sutton, A. and R. Carr *Tartans, their Art and History* 1984.

Tassel (i) In armory, a charge which has tassels attached to it is blazoned tasselled.
(ii) Mantling about the helmet may be depicted as terminating in a tassel on either side. In the sixteenth century these were blazoned in the patent of arms, but they are now considered to be artistic embellishments and are usually (though not necessarily) painted gold.
(iii) Mantles, pavilions, etc., are frequently depicted with cords and tassels.

Tasselled *see* **Attributes**

Tasset Movable upper thigh armour.

Templars, Poor Knights of Christ and of the Temple of Solomon The Templars were probably the greatest military knights ever known. Together with the HOSPITALLERS and the TEUTONIC KNIGHTS they formed the three most powerful orders of chivalry to come from the crusades.

The Knights Templar were founded in 1118/19 by a Burgundian knight, Hugues de Payns, and Godeffroi de St Omer, a knight from northern France, to undertake the protection of pilgrims who came to Jerusalem and other sacred places in the Holy Land. King Baldwin II of Jerusalem gave them quarters near the Temple of Solomon, and they lived to 'fight with a pure mind for the supreme and true king.' They quickly achieved the sanction of the church.

The head of the order was Master of the Temple (at Jerusalem, and then, after 1291, in Cyprus). The Templars became established in almost every Latin kingdom, and received massive grants of land — Paris became the European headquarters and King Stephen and his queen gave the order estates at Cowley near Oxford. By the end of the thirteenth century the Templars were powerful indeed.

Their widespread influence soon attracted enemies in high places, strange stories circulated about their secret rites, and King Philip IV of France moved against them. He obtained the support of Pope Clement V and in just a few months in 1307/8 most European rulers arrested high officials of the order; in France many were tortured and at least thirty-eight died during 'examination'. In 1310, sixty-seven Templars died at the stake and in 1312 the pope transferred much of the wealth of the order to the Knights Hospitaller. In 1314 the Grand Master of the order was burnt alive in front of Notre Dame in Paris on the bidding of King Philip the Fair.

Although in several countries the order continued, things were never the same again. In Portugal, where King Dionysius had granted the members a refuge, they continued as the Knights of Christ. In England the order was suppressed but without undue cruelty. The headquarters still stand, as Temple Church in Fleet Street, London. This building, based on the Holy Sepulchre in Jerusalem, remains as a monument to the order which had given sanction to the ideal of *homo legalis*, the chivalrous man, beginning in a spirit of piety and ending in devouring flame.

The habit of the order was white with a red cross of eight points worn on the left shoulder. This cross was also depicted on lance pennons and guidons, together with the badge of the Agnus Dei and a strange device consisting of two knights riding on one horse, presumably an allusion to the original poverty of the order. (This emblem was later translated into a pegasus in the arms of the Inner Temple, London.) The banner of the order was the famous Beau Seant, *Per fess Sable and Argent.*   JC-K

See also KNIGHTHOOD AND CHIVALRY, ORDERS OF

Further reading
Barber, M. *The Trial of the Templars* Cambridge, 1983.
Burman, E. *The Templars, Knights of God* Wellingborough, 1986.
Howarth, S. *The Knights Templar* London, 1983.
Partner, P. *The Murdered Magicians: the Templars and their Myth* Oxford, 1982.
Prawer, J. *Crusader Institutions* Oxford, 1980.
Riley-Smith, J. and L. *The Crusades: Idea and Reality 1095-1274* London, 1981.
Runciman, S. *A History of the Crusades* 3 vols., West Drayton 1965 (reprinted 1985).
Seward, D. *The Monks of War: the Military Religious Orders* London, 1972.

Tenné A rare armorial tincture of tawny colour. *See also* STAINS

Tenterhook *see* **Livery Companies of the City of London**

Territorial Designation (Scotland) The owner of a piece of named land outwith a burgh can incorporate the name of the land in his own name, e.g. Brown of Sharnydubs, and this territorial designation becomes part of his name for all legal purposes.   CJB

Teutonic Order (Teutonic knights of St Mary's Hospital in Jerusalem) The Teutonic Order was founded during the third crusade, and was one of the three great orders of chivalry which sprang from the Holy Wars. The other two were the HOSPITALLERS and the TEMPLARS.

Starting as a shipboard hospital set up in 1190/91 by merchants from Lubeck and Bremen the 'brethren of the German Hospital of St Mary in Jerusalem' were raised to the rank of knights in 1198. The order developed into a military society and in 1228/9 began the conquest of heathen Prussia at the request of its Christian bishop. By 1234, the order was responsible only to the Holy See and began the subjugation of large areas of Eastern Europe on behalf of Christendom. It lost any real connection with the Holy Land and,

Seal of a Landmaster of the Teutonic Order, 1244-55.

Seal of the last Prussian Grand Master, Albrecht of Brandenburg.

when Acre fell in 1291, the Grand Master went from that city to Venice and then, in 1308, to Marienburg. The statutes of the order were altered, and the members moved from caring exclusively for the sick and the zeal of crusading to, in effect, governing large tracts of land on behalf of Rome. The Grand Master maintained a magnificent court at Marienburg and five great offices were created: the Grand Commander, the Marshal, Hospitaller, Treasurer and Master of the Wardrobe. There was a Landmaster for Livonia (Latvia and Estonia) and a similar officer for the German province. Twenty districts were established, each under a Commander.

The order achieved beneficial relationships with the powerful towns and principalities of Eastern Europe and the merchants of the Hanseatic League, but in the fifteenth century this alliance broke down. The greatest blow to the Teutonic Order was, however, the crushing military defeat inflicted on the knights by King Ladislaus of Poland in 1410. Ulric von Jungingen, the Grand Master, and some six hundred members of the order were killed. The new Grand Master, Henry of Plauen, attempted to rebuild the order but internal dissent was rife, and by 1466 the knights were left with much smaller territories under the overlordship of Poland. By 1561 the order was confined to Germany alone.

The French Revolution saw it stripped of its principal remaining estates; in 1801 the territories to the west of the Rhine were absorbed by France, and in 1809 the order was suppressed and its land divided between the various secular provinces. In 1840, however, the order was revived in Austria as a semi-religious knighthood, under the patronage of the emperor, its grand masters being drawn from the ranks of the Hapsburg arch-dukes. When that dynasty fell, the order was, in 1929, reconstituted as the 'Brothers of the German Order of St Mary's of Jerusalem', a clerical organization under the patronage of the Vatican, with headquarters in Vienna.   JC-K

Textiles Textiles of many materials and designs may be found in stately homes, public buildings and churches.

Most significant of these are tapestries used as wall

hangings and draught excluders, many of which were commissioned for specific locations in a house, and often included coats of arms and other devices either within the over-all design or, more likely, in the border. However, not all have remained at their intended location: at Hardwick Hall, Derbyshire, there are tapestries bought by Bess of Hardwicke from the family of Sir Christopher Hatton. The Hatton arms were overpainted with her own but are now visible once again. There are fine fifteenth-century tapestries at Haddon Hall, Derbyshire, one of which incorporates the royal arms five times, and at Montacute House, Somerset, is the famous *millefleurs* tapestry depicting a mounted knight holding a guidon charged with an alphyn and gold cyphers. This was probably commissioned by the town of Tournai in 1477-79 as a gift to the Governor of Dauphiné, Jean de Daillon, whose arms are woven in the top left-hand corner.

Small items such as bed hangings, cushion covers, table carpets, etc., were often embroidered by the ladies of a household to occupy their time. Mary Queen of Scots embroidered several during her captivity. These invariably incorporated heraldic devices, especially personal badges and cyphers, though it is often difficult to distinguish them from the purely decorative. Many examples have survived from the sixteenth and seventeenth centuries, as have the embroidered fire screens, foot-stools and other furnishings of later periods. Embroidery was both a favourite occupation and a necessary skill of countless generations of ladies from the Dark Ages to the Great War. Indeed, it remains a singularly popular pastime today, and one which is enjoying a revival in the field of heraldic design.

Textiles of various kinds are to be found in most churches, but many are easily overlooked. The altar cloth, frontal and curtains are the most common and mostly date from the nineteenth and twentieth centuries. Few of these feature heraldry, though some armorial frontals are to be found, at the chapel of Haddon Hall, for example. During the present century there has been a movement away from symbolic representation in church furnishings to abstract and often complex designs. However, vernacular heraldry abounds in colourful, embroidered kneelers, cushions and chair backs. Favourite subjects include the arms of lords of the manor and past patrons of the living, attributed arms of saints, diocesan arms and Christian symbols, often depicted on shields. At Wells Cathedral in Somerset the cushions of the prebendal stalls are embroidered with the arms of past bishops.

In the Middle Ages ecclesiastical vestments, copes, chasubles, maniples, etc., as well as altar frontals and other furnishings, were often embroidered with heraldry. The few surviving examples are generally to be found in museums.

Carpets and rugs often incorporate armorial devices,

The *millefleurs* tapestry at Montacute House, Somerset. Woven at Tournai in France as part of a set commissioned by the town as a gift for the Governor of Dauphiné, whose arms are depicted in the top left corner. The unidentified knight carries a guidon charged with an alphyn, and the horse caparison is decorated with I-E cyphers.

though rarely complete coats of arms. At Berkeley Castle in Gloucestershire there is a superb heraldic carpet in red and white (the Berkeley colours), charged with silver mitres (the Berkeley crest) and crosses paty from the family arms. Clearly the expense of 'custom-made' carpets restricts ownership, but there is no reason why corporations and commercial organizations should not use devices from their arms when commissioning large lengths of carpeting for their premises.

See also BAYEUX TAPESTRY

Further reading

English Heraldic Embroidery and Textiles at the Victoria and Albert Museum London, 1976. A select list with introduction by C. Lamb, R.M. Collins and C.J. Holyoake.

Theow *or* **Thos** It would seem that this imaginary animal is a muddled version of a natural one, perhaps a wolf, a fox or a jackal. It is spoken of by Pliny and recorded in medieval bestiaries, where it is called a 'Thea'. It is described as being a kind of wolf, with a thick mane of many colours. It was thought to be able to fly as well as run on the ground. During winter its hair was thick, but in summer it was naked. Its nature was such that it would never attack a man, and it was said to live in Ethiopia, this being given as the place of origin for any animal whose native land was not known. The heraldic animal has acquired cloven feet, although in other ways it has remained wolf-like.   MY

Thistle, The Most Ancient and Most Noble Order of the The Order of the Thistle was 'revived' by King James VII of Scotland (James II of England) on 29 May 1687, the king stressing that the order had been founded by King Achaius *c.* 800 AD. It was King James' intention that the order should comprise the sovereign and twelve knights 'in allusion to the Saviour and His Twelve Apostles'. For his new order the king designed the most sumptuous mantle ever worn by a British order: green velvet powdered with over 250 embroidered gold thistles. The king appointed only eight

knights before fleeing the country in 1688, and the order fell into desuetude. On 31 December 1703, Queen Anne truly revived the order, the number of knights remaining at eight until 1827, when it was increased to twelve.

Today the Thistle comprises sixteen Knights Companion (Abbr. KT), plus the sovereign and foreign royalty. The officers of the order are the Chancellor, the Dean, Lord Lyon King of Arms and Secretary, and the Gentleman Usher of the Green Rod.

The chapel of the Order of the Thistle is located within St Giles Kirk in Edinburgh. It was opened and dedicated in 1911 in the presence of King George V. The chancery of the order is at the Court of Lord Lyon. The ceremonies take place in the chapel and the annual service is held there on St Andrew's Day (30 November) or on the Sunday immediately following. The Sword of State is brought from Edinburgh Castle for the occasion. The Thistle is the premier Scottish order and is normally awarded to Scotsmen of distinction.

The Mantle of the order is of green velvet lined with taffeta and tied with cords and tassels of green and gold. On the left side is the figure of St Andrew bearing the saltire in silver embroidery on green within a circlet of gold inscribed with the words 'Nemo Me Impune Lacessit', the lower edge charged with a thistle. The Star of the order consists of a St Andrew's cross (a saltire) of silver embroidery with rays emitting from between the points of the cross. In the centre is a thistle of green and gold upon a gold field and within a circlet of green bearing the motto of the order in gold letters. The badge or jewel is worn pendent from a collar or from a dark green sash worn over the left shoulder. It consists of the figure of St Andrew in gold enamel, his gown green and surcoat purple, bearing before him the saltire enamelled in white, the whole surrounded by rays of gold. The Collar is of gold and consists of sixteen sprigs of thistle and rue (*Andrew*) enamelled in their proper colours with the badge pendent therefrom.

Further reading

Lawrence-Archer, J.H. *Orders of Chivalry* 1887.
Summers, A. *The Buke of Thrissel Knichts* Dover, 1987.

Throughout An armorial term meaning to cover entirely the surface of a shield or armorial flag. Also applied to an armorial charge, the extremities of which would not normally touch the outer edge of a shield or armorial flag, but do so when so blazoned.

Thunderbolt A twisted column of flame with wings and jagged darts of lightning issuing saltirewise.

Tierced *or* **Triparted** Divided into three.

Tierced in Pairle Divided into three. A clumsy substitute for the more simple per pall. *See also* FIELD, PARTED

Tiles, Heraldic *see* **Floor Tiles**

Tilting Helm A fourteenth and fifteenth-century closed helm, usually of steel, and specially designed and strengthened to absorb the impact of a lance on the vulnerable left-hand side which faced across the barrier at the joust. To facilitate vision in the jousting position (with the head and torso leaning forward) the protruding edges of the eye-slit overlapped, the lower edge projecting beyond the upper. This must have made vision impossible when standing in the normal upright position. Correctly termed a 'helm', this type of HELMET is that which is commonly used for armorial purposes, as in the arms of English gentlemen and esquires.

Timbre The crest or crested helm, wreath or crest coronet, mantling and other objects such as crowns and mitres, placed above the shield in an achievement of arms.

Tincture Convention The single most important convention in armory: **metal shall not lie on metal, nor colour on colour**. The convention appears to have been universally accepted from the earliest times and its purpose is clear. Ownership of territory, and the rights and authority which accompanied it, had to be recognizable. On the battlefield and without the walls of a castle or fortified town, accurate identification of an armed man and his retinue was essential — mistaken identity could prove fatal. The flag was widely used for these purposes, and the devices it carried had to be recognizable from a considerable distance. Whereas a fluttering blue lion on a black field would be impossible to identify with any certainty from more than a few yards, there could be no mistaking the *Gules a Lion rampant Argent* banner of Mowbray.

Of course, there are exceptions to the rule. Usually these take the form of AUGMENTATIONS OF HONOUR,

Thunderbolt

such as the *Fess embattled counter-embattled Sable fretty Gules* in the arms of Sir John Codrington, banner bearer to Henry V at Agincourt, granted for his services to the House of Lancaster. However, this type of augmentation would not affect recognition in the field, the original arms being unchanged except in detail.

There are many circumstances in which contravention is unavoidable: charges placed over all on parted or varied fields; the claws, tongue, etc., of animals and monsters; sub-ordinaries used as augmentations, for cadency, etc.; charges enfiling other charges and so on.

FURS are not subject to the tincture convention, neither are charges blazoned proper, but in practice it is most unlikely that the kings of arms would allow certain combinations of fur and metal or colour, e.g. a pean eagle on a sable field.

Tinctures The metals, colours and furs used in armory.

Metals

Or (Or)	gold
Argent (Ar. or Arg.)	silver

Colours

Gules (Gu.)	red
Azure (Az. or B.)	blue
Sable (Sa.)	black
Vert (Vt.)	green (Fr. = sinople)

Three further colours are uncommon:

Purpure (Purp.)	purple
Bleu-céleste (Bl.C.)	sky-blue
Murrey (Mu.)	mulberry

See individual entries under metal or colour name.

The so-called 'stains' are rare:

Sanguine	blood-red
Tenné	tawny

See STAINS

Furs

Ermine (Erm.)	white with black 'tails'
Vair (Vair)	white and blue 'pelts'

each of which is possessed of numerous variations.
Plumeté of feathers
Papelloné of scales
are here classified as furs.
See FURS

When a charge is depicted in its natural colour it is termed 'proper' (Ppr). The PETRA SANCTA system of hatching to represent tinctures in uncoloured illustrations is used where appropriate throughout this book.

In 1583, Richard Robinson, a citizen of London and aspirant armorist and man of letters, produced a book of fifty-eight blazons in verse, each relating to a member of King Arthur's court. Based on *La Devise des Armes de Chevaliers de la Table Ronde*, published in Paris in about 1546, it contains also a series of 'significations' of the tinctures, here presented in modern English for the reader's pleasure. (An original copy of Richard Robinson's book may be seen at the Bodleian Library, Oxford.)

Gold (Or) Signifies the four virtues of nobleness, goodwill, vigour and magnanimity. Of stones, it signified the carbuncle. Of planets, the Sun. Of the four elements, fire. Of temperaments, the sanguine person. And of the days of the week, Sunday.

Silver (Argent) Signifies the five virtues of humility, beauty, purity, clarity and innocence. Of precious stones, the pearl. Of planets, the Moon. Of the elements, water. Of temperaments, the phlegmatic. Of the days of the week, Monday. Of the twelve signs, Cancer, Leo, Scorpio and Pisces.

Red (Gules) Signifies valiance. Of precious stones, the ruby. Of elements, fire. Of temperaments, the choleric. Of days of the week, Saturday. Of the twelve signs, Aries, Leo and Sagittarius. Of metals, copper.

Blue (Azure) Signifies renown and beauty. Of stones, the sapphire. Of planets, Venus. Of the elements, air. Of temperaments, sanguinity. Of days of the week, Friday. Of the twelve signs, Gemini, Libra and Aquarius. Of metals, silver.

Black (Sable) Signifies mourning and sorrow. Of precious stones, the diamond. Of planets, Mars. Of the elements, earth. Of temperaments, the melancholic. Of days of the week, Tuesday. Of the twelve signs, Taurus, Virgo and Capricorn. Of metals, iron.

Green (Sinople) Signifies honour, love and courtesy. Of precious stones, the emerald. Of planets, Mercury. Of the days of the week, Wednesday. Of metals, mercury. And it signifies all plants, trees, herbs and 'all green thinges that groweth uppon the earth'.

Purple (Purpure) Signifies moderation and has three virtues: liberality, abundance and richness. Of precious stones, the amethyst. Of planets, Jupiter. Of days of the week, Thursday. Of metals, tin.

During the fifteenth and sixteenth centuries, a curious system of blazoning arms in terms of precious stones became popular. Fortunately the practice did not survive — except in one, entirely appropriate circumstance: that of the grant of arms to the Gemmological Association of Great Britain in 1967, *Pearl [Argent] on a Cross formy quadrate throughout Ruby [Gules] and Sapphire [Azure] a closed Book bound and clasped Topaz [Or] the cover set with an Emerald environed of Pearls between two Sapphires in pale and two Rubies in fess between in chief within an Annulet Topaz [Or] a rose-cut*

Diamond proper in fess two Lozenges Pearl [Argent] each charged with a fillet Cross Diamond [Sable] and in base a Ring Topaz [Or] gemmed Pearl [Argent].
See also ART WORK AND MATERIALS; PRONUNCIATION; TINCTURE CONVENTION; TRICK

Tines *see* **Deer**

Toison d'Or, La *see* **Armorial Equestre** *and* **Golden Fleece, Order of**

Tomb Chest The term 'tomb chest' is a misleading one, in that the chest does not contain the coffin and is simply a form of MONUMENT. They first appeared in the early thirteenth century and were probably inspired by the shrines of saints whose bodies were enclosed in a chest-like structure above ground level. Early tomb chests were surmounted by a coped top, but soon either two or three-dimensional figures were adopted for commemorative purposes.

Many tomb chests were designed to be free standing and could be viewed from all four sides. Over the centuries some have been moved to a side wall and the surviving decoration and carving may still be seen to continue to what is now the back of the chest. Where monuments were intended to be against a wall they were usually set back in a low arch with the wall itself providing a canopy above. Occasionally the tomb may have been placed under an existing arch. Alternatively the tomb chest, its canopy, pillars and arch may be combined to form a screen between two parts of the church, e.g. the chancel and a chapel.

The top of the chest will normally bear a figure of the deceased, either as a three-dimensional EFFIGY, a two-dimensional BRASS, or an INCISED SLAB. This may then be surmounted by a canopy. Visitors to churches will find tomb chests without canopies and/or effigies, but in some cases close examination will reveal that the original monument is far from complete.

The sides and ends of tomb chests are often decorated. In the thirteenth and fourteenth centuries this reflected current domestic style. One form of decoration was to create panels containing quatrefoils (more rarely trefoils, hexafoils and octofoils). These quatrefoils from mid-thirteenth century would contain shields. The other form was a series of panels, typically six or more, between columns and surmounted by arches. Again from the later part of the thirteenth century these arched panels were decorated with shields. On the tomb of John Drokensford (d. 1329) in Wells Cathedral, Somerset, the arcading is hollow and shields are displayed on either flank (spandrel) of each arch. The arches became more and more recessed, and miniature figures representing family and, occasionally, friends of the deceased were introduced into these niches. Shields for each of these 'weepers' are often displayed below them, as on the

Tomb chest and brasses to Roger Wake (d.1504) and his wife Elizabeth Catesby at Blisworth, Northamptonshire. The irregular quatrefoil panels on the sides of the tomb contain the arms of Wake (*Or two Bars Gules in chief three Torteaux*), together with various impalements. These panels alternate with beautifully carved badges of the Wake Knot. It is possible that this tomb chest has been moved from its original, freestanding, position.

tombs of Thomas Beauchamp (d. 1369) at Warwick, King Edward III (d. 1377) at Westminster Abbey, and Richard Beauchamp (d. 1439, tomb erected later) again at Warwick. In the latter cases the shields are within quatrefoils.

During the fifteenth century a number of variations are to be found: weepers may be replaced by angels or alternate with shields, and some or all of the weepers may carry shields. At Ewelme, Oxfordshire, there is a contrast between the two tomb chests of Thomas Chaucer (d. 1475) and his daughter, Alice, Duchess of Suffolk (d. 1475). In the latter, angels bear shields for members of her family; on her father's tomb there are no figures but in each panel are mounted two shields, one above the other. The tomb of Guy de Brien (d. 1390) at Tewkesbury shows one further style. The side of the tomb contains three square panels, each containing a shield. The ornament around the shield is a very shallow octofoil outlined in stone cord. The over-all effect is very similar to that of later monuments of the sixteenth century. (Excavation has revealed that De Brien was not buried beneath his tomb chest at Tewkesbury, but at Slapton in Devon.)

The Renaissance brought about a change in style. The first monuments from this period in England are those of Henry VII (d. 1509, monument completed 1513) and his mother Margaret Beaufort (d. 1509). At the end of Henry's tomb in Westminster Abbey is a crowned shield of his arms impaling those of his queen, Elizabeth of York, supported by two cherubs. Above are the royal arms within the Garter flanked by two angels dressed in classical style. The tomb chest of Lady Margaret Beaufort is decorated with shields enclosed in wreaths.

The change to the Renaissance style was gradual,

with some parts of England retaining 'traditional' motifs, and occasionally the styles became mixed. The Renaissance at first affected only the design of the surface decoration. The sides of the chests were divided into panels using balusters, pilasters and later colonettes. The use of figures bearing shields lapsed and the shield became a principal form of decoration, often with one or two on the ends of the tomb chest, and two or three on the side or sides. The use of wreaths as an ornamental surround to shields was gradually replaced by strapwork or ribbonwork as the sixteenth century came to a close. Splendid heraldic displays were achieved in this period by combining the tomb chest with an heraldic canopy.

The next development occurred at the end of the sixteenth century, when the tomb chest was constructed on two levels, each with an effigy upon it or, in some instances, a central higher level with two lower flanks to accommodate three effigies. Heraldic treatment was very similar to that before, with the use of cartouches to display arms.

From the mid-seventeenth century the tomb chest was superseded by the hanging WALL MONUMENT, and it was not until the gothic revival in the nineteenth century that tomb chests reappeared, and as in the Middle Ages shields once again were used in arched panels or quatrefoils. JET

Torse *see* **Wreath**

Torteau A red roundel. Derived from the Latin *torta*, a round loaf of bread or tart. In French blazon, all coloured roundels are termed *torteau*, spherical ones being *boules*.

Tournament The tournament began as a form of training for battle, later becoming largely recreational and ultimately an event for entertainment and ceremonial. Although opposed by the church on moral grounds, and by some monarchs who were fearful of armed assemblies other than those of their own summons, tournaments continued from Norman times through the Renaissance period and into the 1600s.

The word 'tournament' itself is compounded of several Latin roots, *tourneo, turnio,* etc., and *mentum,* meaning a joust or skirmish to which there was a specific result with winners and losers. Perhaps the best early contemporary definition of the event itself is that by·Roger de Hoveden, who described a tournament as a 'military exercise carried out, not in the spirit of hostility, but solely for practice and the display of prowess.' The tournament appears to have been the invention of a French baron, Geoffroi de Pruelli, who was himself killed in such an event in 1066, and for centuries it was referred to in England as *conflictus gallius.*

In the twelfth century the 'apeing of the feats of war' consisted, in Smithfield (London) at any rate, of noble, young mounted men, divided into 'teams' rushing all over the place trying to unhorse one another. By the next century, however, the tournament had become more organized, an occasion for pageantry and feasting, and professional jousters travelled Western countries seeking and offering challenges. Some, like the legendary William the Marshal (later Regent of England), became very rich.

But many an early knight was killed in combat. At one tournament the Earl of Salisbury died of his wounds and his grandson was killed by his own father. The great William Longespée was so battered that he never recovered his former strength. Around 1292 a 'Statute of Arms for Tournaments' laid down that swords must be blunted, and that maces and clubs were not to be used. There were 'Jousts of Peace' with silvered swords of whalebone and even parchment. Despite this and other attempts at emasculation, the tournaments remained popular, and in 1344 prior to the jousts at Windsor on St George's Day the heralds went through France, Scotland, Flanders, Brabant, Hainault, and Burgundy, publicizing the lists and guaranteeing their king's safe conduct to the competitors.

By the fourteenth century, however, considerations of safety and good sense began to prevail. Coronal (crown-shaped) heads were fitted to lances in place of points, and special harnesses developed which facilitated both stability and manoeuvrability. However, the most significant innovation was undoubtedly the tilt, a stout wooden barrier which separated opponents.

The early mêlée or free-for-all mixed-weapons fight evolved into a more stylized form known as the

The Tournament of Love from the Chronicles of Jean Froissart (*c.*1337-1400).

tourney, in which two parties of knights fought on horseback according to agreed conventions and rules. Individual knights, locked in harness with reinforced grand-guards, heavily helmed and carrying blunted lances, would attempt to unseat one another whilst charging along the barrier in what was, by then, known as tilting. Knights would also fight on foot, with sword or pike, across the wooden barrier in a form of joust known as the barriers. All these activities, and the ceremonial and pageantry which accompanied them, were marshalled by the heralds, who also kept the scores on JOUSTING CHEQUES.

The cost, both of providing the necessary horse and equipment and of participating in the attendant festivities and pageantry (which often went on for several days), effectively restricted entry to the nobility, particularly in the late fifteenth and sixteenth centuries when the joust 'became increasingly the ceremonial shattering of fragile, deeply grooved lances, and the literary and pageant elements already dominant in its history gained almost complete ascendancy' (R.C. Strong). The practice of wearing flamboyant crests was, therefore, associated with those of 'tournament rank' — those who possessed the requisite number of noble ancestors *and* were able to meet the enormous expense. No wonder the gentry of the sixteenth century scrambled to record newly acquired crests at the visitations for they had become symbols of what we now call 'upward mobility' par excellence.

The death of Henri II of France in 1559 (who was killed by the splintered lance of Gabriel de Montgomerie) failed to abate the enthusiasm for tournaments amongst the nobility and (increasingly) the gentry, though by the end of the sixteenth century they had become bloodless spectacles, arranged for the delight of ladies as well as gentlemen. There were parades of squires carrying the elaborately crested helms of the participants (reminiscent of the medieval HELMSCHAU), displays of shields with prizes for the most original design, side shows (such as the harrying of a deer with greyhounds) and processions of ladies dressed as Greek goddesses, all watched by members of the privileged classes gathered in the terraced stands surrounding the arena, which also included pavilions for the contestants and enclosures for the common people.

Perhaps the best known, and certainly the most spectacular, of these pageants was the FIELD OF THE CLOTH OF GOLD in 1520 which, marked by vainglorious vulgarity, was far removed from the simple and honourable war-games of earlier centuries.

In 1839 the Earl of Eglington attempted to revive the spectacle of the fifteenth-century tournament at his castle in Ayrshire, Scotland. There were a 'king' and 'queen' of love and beauty, fifteen caparisoned knights entered the lists, there were tilting and barriers, and many noblemen including the future Napoleon III participated. The event was considered to be a success by many despite the inclement weather, but it was not repeated.

Further reading

Anglo, S. (Ed.) *Great Tournament Roll of Westminster* London, 1968.

Young, A. *Tudor and Jacobean Tournaments* London, 1987.

Tournament Rank *see* Helmschau

Tower and the Sword, The (Ordem Militar da Torre e Espada) This Portuguese order was originally founded in 1459, the present statutes dating from 1963. The order has a Grand Collar and five classes: Grand Cross, Grand Officer, Commander, Officer and Knight. The badge is a five-pointed white enamelled star crowned by a tower, the obverse bearing a sword. The star is pentagonal in gold (or silver) with faceted rays. The collar of the order is of gold with longitudinal and lateral laurel-garlanded towers and swords.   JC-K

Towered *see* Attributes

Tractatus de Armis *see* Treatises

Tracts The barry field of a Scottish livery flag may be blazoned, e.g. *of five tracts of these liveries Argent and Vert.* Scottish regulation of livery flags (guidons, standards, etc.) is strict. The number of tracts indicates the armiger's rank, and the livery colours on which badges should be displayed are specified. In England, the standard has degenerated into a convenient and decorative means of depicting badges on a patent of arms. It is neither granted nor blazoned on the patent, and the choice of tinctures for the field and its composition is entirely arbitrary.

Trade Marks and Service Marks A trade mark is a device used by a trader to identify the goods he is

supplying. A service mark is similarly a device used by the purveyor of a service for which he receives payment.

Today, a trade mark or service mark may be linguistic or non-linguistic or a combination of the two. The former is normally a word or name which can be spoken and the latter a logotype which is visually unique and easily identified. A good example of the combined type is the Ford Motor Company's distinctive lettering which is protected both as a linguistic trade mark and a symbol.

In Britain, the Trademarks Act of 1938 and further legislation in 1986 (applicable to service marks) provide for the registration of devices by which the owner has a legal monopoly when his mark is applied to the goods or services specified in the registration. For the purposes of classification trade marks are arranged into thirty-four different classes and service marks into eight, all of which are recognized internationally. Registration is obtained by applying to the Trade Marks Registry at the Patent Office (*see* ADDRESSES), and it is advisable to obtain the services of a specialist adviser, preferably a patent or trade mark agent.

It is interesting to note that devices borne on shields, sometimes accompanied by wreath, crest and mantling and even supporters, have been accepted for registration as trade marks. These are, by definition, armorial and by registering them it may be that the Trade Marks Registry is prejudicing the rights of the kings of arms and is, therefore, acting unlawfully. Further, it may be that an armorial trade mark has already been granted by the College of Arms or Lord Lyon as armorial bearings. If it is the armiger himself who is registering his own device as a trade mark, no harm is done, but if it is not then who, in law, is entitled to use the device, the armiger who bears it by the sovereign's authority or the trader who has registered his mark according to the law of the land? Clearly, it should be incumbent upon the Trade Marks Registry to forward all applications for armorial trade marks to the College of Arms or Lord Lyon for scrutiny before allowing them to proceed to registration. Under Section 11 of the Trade Marks Act of 1938, 'it shall not be lawful to register as a trade mark or part of a trade mark any matter the use of which would, by reason of its being likely to deceive or cause confusion or otherwise, be disentitled to protection in a court of justice, or would be contrary to law or morality or any scandalous design.' Clearly in England and Wales the armorial trade mark would, by this section, fall within the jurisdiction of the High Court of Chivalry, and in Scotland within that of the Court of Lord Lyon.

Trade Tokens Tradesmen's tokens were widely used during the seventeenth century in place of lawful coinage which, in the smaller values, was frequently in

short supply, or even non-existent. Trade tokens were, in consequence, an illegal but tolerated system of money-by-necessity, privately issued by merchants, particularly between the years 1648-79 when legally minted petty coinage was especially scarce. A very large group was that issued by taverners, it being estimated that in London alone nearly one third of the 3000 or so different tokens in circulation were of this type.

Almost every trade issued tokens: barbers, wool-merchants, apothecaries, fishmongers, tobacco sellers and so on. Much of this substitute money bore designs which were armorial in character, and these provide a fascinating subject of study for the armorist.

Further reading

Berry, G. *Taverns and Tokens of Pepys' London* London, 1978.

Boyne, W. *Tokens issued in the Seventeenth Century* 1858.

Williamson, G.C. *Trade Tokens issued in the Seventeenth Century* 1889-91 (reprinted in 3 vols., London 1967).

Tragopan An eagle with curved horns.

Traite sur le Blason des Armes *see* **Treatises**

Transfixed *see* **Attitude**

Transfluent *see* **Attitude**

Transposed To depict a charge in a position directly opposite its accustomed one, e.g. *a pile transposed* is depicted in base, not in its conventional position in chief.

Trapper Horse covering for protection and display, either of mail or material or of both. *See also* CAPARISON

Trappings A general term to describe the bridle, saddle, etc., of a horse.

Traversed *see* **Attitude**

Treatises Early manuscripts devoted wholly or in part to armory are difficult to categorize. Many ROLLS OF ARMS were later cut and bound into book form, and a number of well-known medieval treatises containing armorial material were essentially works on kindred subjects such as the arts of war, ceremonial, etc. The following treatises are in chronological order of compilation.

De Heraudie Anglo-Norman treatise of *c.* 1300. Author-ship unknown. Included in *St Alban's Formulary* of 1382. Significant in that it provides evidence of established armorial practice, conventions and grammar in the late twelfth century.

De Insigniis et Armis Latin treatise of *c.* 1355, possibly compiled by Bartolo de Sasso Ferrato.

L'Arbre de Batailles 'The Tree of Battles', a French treatise on the laws of art and war including chapters on armory. Written *c.* 1382-7 by Honoré Bonet. Two excellent manuscript copies in the British Museum.

Tractatus de Armis One of the most significant armorial treatises — entirely devoted to armory and written by John de Bado Aureo *c.* 1395. The author was possibly Bishop Siôn Trevor (see below). Compiled in Latin, many copies were made through to the sixteenth century. The treatise begins with the origin of arms and the tinctures, beasts, etc., and their significance, followed by crosses, ordinaries and a brief section on the royal arms of England. One of the most attractive manuscript copies, a late fifteenth-century translation into English, may be seen in the Bodleian Library, Oxford.

Llyfr Dysgread Arfau A Welsh treatise by Bishop Trevor written *c.* 1405-10. An almost verbatim translation of the *Tractatus de Armis* of *c.* 1395.

Le Livre des Faits d'Armes et de Chevalerie A French treatise on the laws and arts of war written by Christine de Pisan *c.* 1400. Only a small section of one of the four books deals with armory, and this appears to be taken directly from Honoré Bonet's *L'Arbre de Batailles*. Translated into English and printed by Caxton in 1490.

Le Blason des Couleurs A French heraldic treatise from *c.* 1416-36 by Jean Courtois of Hainault. He describes himself as Sicily Herald to Alphonso, King of Aragon, Sicily, Valence, Majorca, Corsica and Sardinia.

Mowbray's French Treatise An early fifteenth-century French treatise possibly compiled by a herald in northern France during the English occupation. The only known copy is in the library of the College of Arms. The only authority for several (otherwise unrecorded) chimerical creatures.

Banyster's French Treatise Early fifteenth-century French document possibly compiled by a herald in northern France during the English occupation. The only known copy is in the library of the College of Arms.

Prinsault's Treatise An early fifteenth-century French work, probably by Clément Prinsault. Five copies are in the Bibliothèque Nationale, Paris. A manuscript copy of the augmented version is in the British Museum and a further four in Paris. The so-called *Passion Version* may also be seen in the Bibliothèque Nationale, where there are four manuscript copies.

Normandy Treatise A fifteenth-century French docu-ment of unknown authorship dealing with miscellan-

Militari) A Latin treatise on the laws and practice of war, including armorial material, compiled by Nicholas Upton *c.* 1446. Many manuscript copies were made in the fifteenth and sixteenth centuries, two of which are in the British Museum (London) and the Bodleian Library (Oxford), the latter copy being an English translation by John Blount. *Baddesworth's Version* of 1458, again in Latin but extensively rearranged, is also in the British Museum. There is also a copy in the possession of the College of Arms.

Strangway's Book An English document comprising notes on armory compiled by Richard Strangways when a student at the Inner Temple, 1447-9. Only known copy is in the British Museum, London.

John's Treatise (John's Tretis on Armes) A mid-fifteenth century English compilation, possibly a grammar of armory used for teaching purposes at the Inns of Court. Many later treatises appear to have the same derivation. There are two known contemporary copies in the British Museum, London, and one in private ownership.

Heralds Tract An English work of *c.* 1460. The authorship is unknown but the tract is similar to *John's Treatise*. The only known copy is in the College of Arms.

Ashmolean Tract A mid-fifteenth century manuscript, authorship unknown but similar to *John's Treatise* and the *Heralds Tract*.

Patrick's Book An English treatise of *c.* 1465, authorship unknown but similar to *John's Treatise* and the *Heralds Tract*. It is now in the Plantin-Moretus Museum, Antwerp.

Sloane Tract An English document of *c.* 1470, though opening and closing sections are in Latin. The authorship is unknown but the work is similar to *John's Treatise* and the *Heralds Tract*. Now in the British Museum, London.

Pakenham Tract A Latin treatise of 1449, authorship unknown but based on *Tractatus de Armis* and other sources. Now in the British Museum, London.

Ashmole Tract A mid-fifteenth century French manuscript compiled from earlier works but with some new material. Now in the Bodleian Library, Oxford.

Les Drois d'Armes A French treatise of 1481 compiled by Gille, King of Arms to Emperor Maximilian of Austria and Count of Flanders. Material includes the conventions of tournaments, ceremonies, armory, etc. Now in the Bibliothèque Nationale, Paris.

Cottell's Book A late-fifteenth century work in English comprising notes from a variety of sources and periods including 'A Tretys of Armes' which is similar to *John's Treatise*. Now in the British Museum, London.

An unidentified English king of arms, crowned, holding a wand of office and wearing a tabard is approached by a knight and his squire: 'Sir King of Armys I you pray Tenduce me in armys to say.' The king of arms replies: 'Sone for that in armys diffuseness is I council you attend to this tretis.' The arms, *Or on a Cross quarter pierced Azure four Lions rampant of the field*, are also unidentified but may be those of Francis Foveis who is mentioned in the dedication. From *Tractatus de Armis c.*1395.

eous heraldic subjects. It is housed in the Bibliothèque Nationale, Paris.

Cordeboeuf's Treatise A mid-fifteenth century work by Merlin de Cordeboeuf, though similar in content to the *Normandy Treatise*. Bibliothèque Nationale, Paris.

L'Art Heraldique A French manuscript, written in *c.* 1441. Authorship unknown but similar to *Cordeboeuf's Treatise*. Bibliothèque Nationale, Paris.

Le Bouvier's Treatise Compiled in French *c.* 1450 by Gilles le Bouvier, Berry King of Arms. Bibliothèque Nationale, Paris.

Valera's Treatise A fifteenth-century Spanish document by Diego de Valera. British Museum, London.

De Officio Militari et Insigniis Armorum (De Studio

Blasons des Batailles A late-fifteenth century French manuscript comprising notes on the conduct of war, heralds' duties, etc., and similar to *L'Arbre de Batailles*. The armorial section may have been influenced by English treatises of the mid-fifteenth century.

Sequier's Book A late-fifteenth century work on armory with a general roll of arms. Poor quality illustration and badly compiled.

Franquevie Treatise A French treatise on armory, compiled by Franquevie, Herald of Valenciennes in 1485. British Museum, London.

The Boke of St Albans A famous English volume of 1486 attributed to Dame Juliana Berners by Wynken de Worde, who printed the book as 'The Treatyse perteyning to Hawkyng, Huntyng and Fyshyng with an Angle; and also a right noble Treatyse which specyfyeth of Blasybge of Armys.' The authorship cannot be verified, however.

Traite sur le Blason des Armes A French treatise on armory and blazon written by Jehan Pierre in 1489. British Museum, London.

Loutfut's Book A work on the duties of heralds and on armory, apparently intended as a guide to the Scottish heralds and compiled in c. 1494 by Adam Loutfut, Kintyre Pursuivant of Arms under the direction of Sir William Cumming of Inverlochy, Marchmont Herald and later Lord Lyon. British Museum, London.

Details of these, and other early manuscripts, may be found in Rodney Dennys' *The Heraldic Imagination* London, 1975. A list of medieval treatises from 1300 to 1500 includes information regarding the location of original manuscripts or copies with references, and of printed texts and commentaries. A further chapter deals with the most important of these treatises in greater detail.

Trefoil An armorial charge resembling a clover leaf.

Trellisé A variation of fretty in which the pieces are not interlaced, all those in bend being depicted as overlaying those in bend sinister. Sometimes also 'cloué', i.e. fastened with nails where they intersect.

Tressure *see* **Orle**

Trial of the Pyx *see* **Livery Companies of the City of London**

Trian aspect, in *see* **Attitude**

Trick A sketch of armorial bearings in which abbreviations and numbers or letters are substituted for TINCTURES and charges (verb = to trick). Most armorists develop their own system of abbreviations, the most common being:

	Abbr.	Trick
Or	Or	O
Argent	Ar(g)	A
Gules	Gu	G
Azure	Az	B
Sable	Sa	S
Vert	Vt	V
Purpure	Purp	P
Bleu-Céleste	BlC	BC
Murrey	Mu	M
Ermine	Erm	E
Vair	Vair	

Where charges are repeated, only one need be sketched and the tinctures noted, numbers (1-2-3, etc.) or letters (A-B-C, etc.) being substituted for other similar charges.

Tricorporate *see* **Attitude**

Trippant *see* **Attitude**

Triptych A set of three painted panels hinged together so that the outer two may fold over each other to cover the central one. Usually placed against a wall or free-standing. The triptych probably originated in the portable altars of the medieval nobility.

In England there are very few known triptychs of any antiquity. Those containing armorial devices are even more rare. The smallest is at the church of Besford, Worcestershire. It was made as a memorial for a member of the Harewell family c. 1594, and displays many shields of local families. A similar triptych is that of the Cornewall family (1588) at the church of Burford, Shropshire.

The finest is the St John triptych at Lydiard Tregoze church, Wiltshire. This was erected c. 1615 for Sir John St John (d. 1594) by his son, Sir John, Bart. The front displays a number of genealogical trees with arms in each generation. When the panels are opened they reveal paintings of the deceased and his wife kneeling on a sarcophagus and flanked by their daughters and their son, Sir John, and his wife.

A fourth triptych at Appleby Castle, Cumbria, was not painted as a memorial. It was made in 1640 at the instruction of Lady Anne Clifford. She was the daughter of George Clifford, 3rd Earl of Cumberland, and after his death was involved in a dispute with her uncle (and later her cousin) as to who was the rightful heir to her father's estates. She is depicted in a family group and there are two columns of shields showing the ancestry and alliances of the family.   JET
Further reading
Williamson, G.C. *Lady Anne Clifford* Kendal, 1922.

Triton The son of Poseidon and Amphitrite in mythology, he lives beneath the sea and is depicted as a man with a dolphin's tail and usually holding a coiled sea shell.

Trogodice A reindeer with long forward-curving horns.

Trotting *see* **Attitude**

Troubadour One of a class of lyric poets of chivalric love, who first appeared in Provence and flourished during the eleventh, twelfth and thirteenth centuries. *See also* MINNESANGERS; MINSTRELS

Trumpet Banner The use of the trumpet for communication purposes during a military campaign predates heraldry by several hundred years and is, of course, referred to in the stories of the Old Testament. Throughout history there has been a trumpeter at a commander's right hand, and the instrument was often used for the display of the commander's armorial bearings on a small banner, fringed with the livery or armorial colours. The modern trumpet banner has degenerated to a small ensign banner, used on ceremonial occasions, and fringed with the regimental colours.

Trussed *see* **Attitude**

Trussing *see* **Attitude**

Tufted *see* **Attributes**

Turkey A turkey may be blazoned 'in his pride' and, like the peacock, his tail is then displayed.

Tyger The tyger of heraldry is quite unlike the tiger of nature. He has a body like a wolf, with a thick mane and a lion's tail. He has massive, powerful jaws and a pointed snout. He is described in medieval bestiaries as being speckled, although in later times he was believed to be red, and this became his usual colour in heraldry. Hyrcania, a region in Persia, is quoted as being the principal home of the tyger. He was very ferocious and very speedy, and famed for his swiftness by the Persians, who called their arrows 'tygris', and in his turn he gave his name to the fast-flowing river Tigris. In addition to their swiftness the female tygers showed great care and devotion to their cubs. There is a story concerning this in Guillim's *Display of Heraldry*: 'Some report that those who rob the tygre of her young, use a policy to detainne their damme from following them by casting sundry looking-glasses in the way, whereat she useth to long to gaze, whether it be to behold her own beauty or, because she seeth one of her young ones; and so they escape the swiftness of her pursuit.' Because of this fable the tyger often appears in arms either holding, or looking into, a mirror. In modern times the natural tiger is also used as an heraldic charge, but is blazoned as a Bengal tiger proper to distinguish it from its mythological cousin.

MY

Heraldic tygers, ducally gorged, supporting the Digby arms at Sherborne Castle, Dorset.

U

Ulster Historical Foundation, The A foundation established in 1957 by Sir Basil Brooke, Bart., the then Prime Minister of Northern Ireland, as a non-profit-making genealogical research facility serving clients worldwide. The Foundation also publishes books of genealogical and historical interest. *See* ADDRESSES.

MCM

Ulster King of Arms *see* **Norroy and Ulster King of Arms**

Ulster Office and the Genealogical Office Although a series of titular IRELAND KINGS OF ARMS existed from the last decades of the fourteenth century until the accession of King Henry VII, none of these officers is known to have exercised any real jurisdiction over matters heraldic within their designated province. It was only with the creation by King Edward VI of Bartholomew Butler as Ulster King of Arms in February 1552 that an effective heraldic authority was created in Ireland. The title of Ulster given by Edward to Butler has puzzled armorists for several hundred years since he designated the new king of arms by the name of a province rather than by that of the whole island. Exactly why the name Ulster was chosen may never be known, but the most probable explanation is that Edward was merely alluding to the fact that he enjoyed the title of Earl of Ulster through his descent from the House of York. Certainly the Crown was very much aware of this inheritance, since King Henry VIII had refused to bestow this earldom on O'Neill, the indigenous Prince of Ulster, a decade earlier, stating that it was one of the greatest titles in Christendom.

From the very inception of the office it was regarded as playing an important role in speeding up the process of the Anglicization of Ireland by introducing 'the manners of civility' to the Irish. Heraldry was seen as a civilizing influence which would wean the native Irish away from the tanistic form of succession which was the main-stay of the clan structure. This perception is borne out, for example, in the writings of Lord Justice FitzWilliam who, in 1562, wrote to the English Privy Council complaining that the local Gaelic bards 'were discountenancing heraldry . . . and setting forth the beastliest and most odious of mens doings.'

Since Ulster Office was the creation of an English sovereign (albeit that he also claimed to be King of Ireland) and imposed from without, rather than being an indigenous development, it is hardly surprising that it almost completely mimicked the practices of the College of Arms. This tendency was reinforced by the fact that three of the first six Ulster kings of arms were trained in the College of Arms and had served there in various capacities. As a result Ulster Office remained, to a certain extent, an Irish annex of the College of Arms rather than an institution which reflected the different social, cultural and political conditions prevailing in Ireland. In this respect it totally differed from the court of the Lord Lyon King of Arms, which, as a creation of the Scottish Crown, implemented its heraldic jurisdiction with regard to the cultural differences prevailing in that kingdom. The Ulster kings of arms attempted to enforce their authority within Ireland in much the same manner as their English contemporaries did. They resorted to holding heraldic visitations and obliged the gentry to return funeral certificates to their Office. Registers of grantees of arms were not maintained but lists of these have been prepared from various documents surviving in the Office, including the *Drafts of Arms* notebooks. These lists are of great interest as they underline the fact that Ulster Office hardly impinged on the consciousness of Gaelic Ireland whatsoever. The first evidently Irish recipient of a grant of arms was one Moretagh Oge Cavanage in 1582 (thirty years after the creation of the Office), and in the first one-hundred years of the existence of Ulster Office only twenty Gaelic names appear on the list of grantees. The reason is simple. The native Irish believed nobility, or gentility, to be derived from Milesian descent and not from the grant of a coat of arms by a herald based in Dublin.

Ulster King of Arms played an important role in the Irish House of Lords insomuch as he was responsible for maintaining 'Ulster's Roll'. No peer was permitted to take his seat in the Upper House until his right of succession had been verified by Ulster. Furthermore, the Lords actually declared that Ulster King of Arms was 'a servant of [their] House and entitled to [its] protection' and, in the eighteenth century, he was granted an office and suite of apartments for his private residence in the Parliament Building.

As well as being a servant of the House of Lords, Ulster King of Arms was the only permanent member of the Vice-Regal Household. It was natural, from the very inception of the Office, that he should play the major part in organizing the ceremonies of the Vice-Regal Court, and because Ireland lacked the office of Earl Marshal, Ulster King of Arms obtained a position and authority far surpassing that occupied by Garter King of Arms in England. In 1717 it was decreed that he was to be placed 'next to the person of the Lord Lieutenant, and after Ulster the other official personages of the Court followed.' This place in the Precedence List was much higher than that enjoyed by Ulster's English contemporaries. This position was confirmed in 1724, by Lord Lieutenant Carteret, and again in 1835 by King William IV.

Because the office of Earl Marshal did not exist in

Ireland, nor any rival kings of arms, Ulster enjoyed the sole privilege of granting arms without any restraint. In this respect he enjoyed the same capacity as the Lord Lyon King of Arms, and was able to act 'of his own mere motion'. Such a privilege is not enjoyed by the kings of arms in England. Ulster also enjoyed a total independence in registering the pedigrees of gentry families, there being no Chapter of Heralds to gainsay his decisions. Gradually, following the collapse of the independent Gaelic principalities in the early seventeenth century, the authority of Ulster King of Arms was enforced throughout Ireland and not just in the area of the Pale (an area of about thirty square miles around Dublin). By the eighteenth century Ulster Office had become an accepted facet of Irish life and even became a 'popular' institution. This is reflected in the enormous increase in business transacted by his office in this period.

From 1552 until 1943 the Office of the Ulster kings of arms continued to function without interruption. Even Cromwell, who destroyed almost one-third of the population of Ireland, left the Office unscathed, merely changing Ulster's title, as befitted a Republican, to the less regal form of Principal Herald of Arms of the Dominion of Ireland. The declaration of the Irish Free State in 1922 also left the Ulster kings of arms firmly entrenched in Dublin Castle, since the Crown, who appointed him, was still recognized as head of state. Eventually, however, as it became clear that the Free State was destined to become a Republic, it was determined that the heraldic authority exercised by Ulster as a servant of the British Crown would necessarily have to be 'repatriated' to a herald appointed by the Irish Government. This finally occurred on 1 April 1943, when Mr de Valera, Prime Minister of Eire, authorized the creation of the Office of Chief Herald of Ireland. This decision was followed on 24 July 1943 by the appointment of Dr Edward MacLysaght to that position. It should be stressed that the Office of the Chief Herald has inherited the full extent of the heraldic jurisdiction exercised by the Ulster kings of arms and, like them, he continues to act 'of his own mere motion'.

The British Crown, regarding Ulster King of Arms as an appointment vested in its gift, has united it with the office of Norroy King of Arms. Thus a National Kingship of Arms has become united with an English Provincial Kingship to form the office of the Norroy and Ulster King of Arms. It must be stated, however, that this merger was within the rights of the British Crown which had, indeed, created the Office of Ulster in the first instant. Furthermore, Bartholomew Butler, after his appointment as Ulster King of Arms, was considered to be an extra-ordinary member of the College of Arms, London (although all his successors were totally independent thereof). Accordingly the merger of these two kingships had some justification,

Arms of Office of the Chief Herald of Ireland.

although it has been argued that on the creation of the Office of Chief Herald that of Ulster should have been removed to Northern Ireland, which remained part of Great Britain, rather than to England with which it had no real connection. The Genealogical Office (also known as the Office of Arms) is the name given to the Chief Herald of Ireland's Office. It is located at Number 2, Kildare Street, Dublin, to which site it was removed from Dublin Castle. The Office incorporates the State Heraldic Museum, which is perhaps the finest institution of this kind in the world. The Chief Herald has inherited all of the faculties of the Ulster kings of arms, both with respect to granting and confirming arms and registering pedigrees.   MCM

See also IRELAND, LAW OF ARMS

Further reading

Kennedy, P. *Kennedy's Book of Arms* 1816 (reprinted 1969).

Undy *see* **Lines, Varied**

Unguled *see* **Attributes**

Unicorn The mystery and magic of the unicorn has been known to all civilizations; the stories and fables concerning it are without number. In the world of heraldry it became known as an elegant and beautiful animal, like a horse but with cloven feet, a lion's tail and a goat's beard, and a delicate spiralling horn on its forehead. To earlier civilizations it had been known with a different appearance, the flamboyant *ki-lin* of China, and the *kirin* of Japan. In Arabia and Persia it was the *karkardanh*, sometimes a violent and bloodthirsty creature, sometimes more graceful. The mount which Alexander the Great tamed and called Bucephalus was said to be a *karkardanh*.

In medieval times the unicorn became the symbol of Christ because of its purity and virtue. Besides these qualities it was believed to possess medicinal powers. The horn was an antidote to poison and no animal would drink from a pool until the unicorn had stirred the water with its horn, thus rendering innocuous any poison that a dragon or serpent had deposited therein. Powdered unicorn horn was used as a cure for many ills, and cups made from it were invaluable against poisoning.

The unicorn appeared in many fine tapestries, such as 'The Hunt of the Unicorn' now in the Metropolitan Museum of Art in New York, and 'The Lady and the Unicorn' in the Cluny Museum in Paris, in which the arms of the de Viste family appear.

The unicorn does not appear to have been used in early heraldry, because it was considered too sacred, but from the fifteenth century has become increasingly popular. Appropriately the Society of Apothecaries in London has two golden unicorn supporters, and in Scotland unicorn supporters were adopted in the hope that their virtue and purity would be a strength to the country in her struggles against foes.   MY

Unicorn Pursuivant of Arms A Scottish pursuivant of arms. The title was created after 1381, and derived from the unicorn. Unicorns are used as supporters for the royal arms of Scotland, and as a royal badge. The badge of office is *A Unicorn couchant Argent gorged of a Coronet of four Fleurs-de-lis and four Crosses paty proper.*   CJB

Union Flag A rectangular flag charged with the device of the United Kingdom of Great Britain and Northern Ireland. Commonly considered to be the 'national flag', though correctly a government and naval flag. It is blazoned *Azure a Saltire per saltire and quarterly Argent*

and Gules the latter fimbriated of the second surmounted by a Cross of the third fimbriated as the saltire. The St Andrew saltire and St George cross were first combined in a naval flag of 1606. At the union of England and Scotland in 1707 a new flag was recorded: the saltire of St Andrew on a blue field with the St George cross over all fimbriated argent. At the union with Ireland in 1801 the flag was altered once again and the FitzGerald saltire (spuriously described as the St Patrick cross) incorporated.

Both the silver saltire of Scotland and the red cross of England have been the military badges of the two countries since the Middle Ages, when they were placed in the hoist on military flags (standards and guidons) and were worn on the tunics of soldiery. It is as *badges* that they are incorporated in the Union Flag, which should therefore be regarded as a form of livery banner.

Such a complex design is open to a variety of blazons and differing interpretations of the same blazon. A particularly attractive variation is the square 'Great Union Flag', approved by the War Office in 1898 for regimental purposes.

The Union Flag should be hoisted so that at the corner nearest the head of the staff the broad white stripe is above the narrow one.

Union Jack A small version of the Union Flag flown from the jack staff at the bows of a Royal Navy ship.

United Kingdom, Military Insignia

Army uniforms and badges Vestiges of medieval armour and military liveries may be found in the ceremonial cuirasses of the Household Cavalry and the facing colours worn by members of individual regiments on collars, lapels, cuffs and the revers of coats. The East Kent Regiment, for example, is known as 'The Buffs' for this reason.

In Europe, the medieval chivalric tradition lingered on into the twentieth century and it was not until 1919 that the British Army finally abandoned the use of full dress uniform for all but ceremonial occasions.

A Royal Warrant of 1747 forbade the use of commanders' personal arms for military purposes, but from 1881, when regiments took territorial titles, traditional heraldic devices provided the inspiration for numerous regimental badges, though regrettably the conventions of armory were not always evident in their composition. These regimental badges are well worth further study.

With the introduction of khaki uniforms for all ranks during the First World War, a method of identification was required for divisions, formations and units: simple devices which could be stencilled quickly on vehicles, helmets and equipment and printed on felt to be sewn on uniforms. These were chosen by the individual units and were subject neither to approval nor control. Again, the absence of sound armorial practice is evident in many of the more obscure unit badges, but others were singularly successful and in the best heraldic tradition. Several were reintroduced in 1939.

Regimental flags and colours Flags have always been an important means of identification — the Bayeux Tapestry records at least thirty different command flags used in 1066 at the battle of Hastings. In the fourteenth and fifteenth centuries medieval retinues followed their commanders' standards and guidons into battle, and during the English civil wars of the mid-seventeenth century the companies comprising the Regiments of Foot each had its own flag or 'colour'. These were large, some 6 feet 6 inches (2 m) square, made of painted silk or taffeta, and within a regiment all flags were of the same basic colour and design, individual companies adding their own devices, often charges from the arms of the commanding officer.

After the Restoration, the army of the Commonwealth was disbanded, but several regiments were retained and some new ones formed. During the reigns of Charles II and James II, colonels virtually owned their regiments and it was again commonplace for devices from their personal arms to be used in regimental colours. A regulation issued in 1747 put a stop to this practice and introduced new rules governing colours, uniforms, drums, etc. The opening paragraph stated: 'No colonel to put his arms, crest, devices or livery on any part of the appointments of the regiment under his command.' The Royal Warrants of 1751 and 1768 defined the colours, standards and

The badge of the Prince of Wales' (North Staffordshire Regiment), once known as The Black Knots, formed in 1740 and now part of the Prince of Wales' Division. The well-known devices of the 'feathers' badge and the Staffords' knot are here combined.

guidons of the infantry and cavalry, and these definitions have remained to the present day. These new flags bore little resemblance to the medieval flags whose designations they assumed: they were no longer functional but were symbolic and ceremonial.

In infantry regiments the Union Flag is the basis of the First or Queen's Colour, bearing in the centre the title of the regiment surmounted by the Imperial Crown. The Second or Regimental Colour uses the facing colour as the field and has the title of the regiment in the centre, together with the badges, devices, mottoes, distinctions and battle honours as given in the Army List.

The Household Cavalry and the Dragoon Guards carry a rectangular standard, while a guidon is carried by Dragoons and Light Dragoons. This is rectangular in shape but slit in the fly with the upper and lower corners rounded. Hussars, Lancers and Rifle regiments, together with corps such as Royal Artillery, Royal Engineers, Royal Signals, Royal Corps of Transport, etc., do not carry standards, guidons or colours. The company colours of the Welsh Guards are of the same form and shape as medieval standards, but are only some 3 feet 6 inches (just over 1 m) long. There are fifteen companies, each having the same basic design and each differenced with the arms of one of the Royal or Noble Tribes of Wales (*see* WALES, ARMORY IN). The colours are symbolic of the regiment and are carried into battle in the centre of the line, where they are defended to the last man.

Drums and Trumpets The drum was prominent in the martial music of ancient civilizations, and used as a means of conveying orders during a military advance. Drake's drum, which accompanied him on his voyage of circumnavigation, was emblazoned with his arms, granted in 1581, a fact only revealed when the drum was restored and cleaned in 1910.

The shell of a modern drum offers a splendid surface for the display of heraldic and other devices. The background or field is normally the regiment's

NCO's armbadge in white metal of The Royal Gloucestershire Hussars, formed in 1830. Within a Garter ensigned by a ducal coronet is the portcullis crest of the dukes of Beaufort.

The Gordon crest and motto 'Bydand' (meaning 'vigilant') used as the badge of the Gordon Highlanders, formed in 1758 and now part of the Scottish division.

facing colour and on this is emblazoned the devices, distinctions, mottoes and battle honours of the regiment. The copper kettledrums of mounted regiments are draped with cloth banners, richly embroidered with insignia, battle honours, etc., in a fashion similar to that of infantry drums. Some regiments have silver kettledrums with the finest modelling and engraving on them, and in these cases the cloth banner is not always used. There are only two mounted bands remaining in the British army — the Life Guards and the Blues and Royals. The resplendent Drum Major wears a baldric or sash, again beautifully embroidered with regimental insignia, devices, battle honours, etc., together with the Royal Cypher and arms where appropriate. The base colour of the sash is again the regimental facing colour.

From medieval times heralds have employed trumpets to great effect when making proclamations, on ceremonial occasions and at tournaments. The herald did not play the trumpet himself but employed a musician, usually attired in a tabard bearing the arms of his master. Today this is the role of the State Trumpeters. Bugles and trumpets have always been used in time of war because of their potency in conveying orders over the noise of battle. They, too, are very suitable objects from which to hang banners decorated with armorial devices. The magnificent trumpet banners of the State Trumpeters of the Household Cavalry bear the royal arms embroidered in gold and silver wire and coloured silks on a crimson ground surrounded by a golden fringe, and are beautiful works of art in their own right.

Most branches of the armed services utilize fanfare trumpets, but the banners of the Royal Military School of Music (Kneller Hall) are truly armorial, and were designed in 1931 by the late George Kruger Gray, an heraldic artist of some eminence. The design includes

a crown and clarions, in allusion to the Royal School and its musical activities.

The pipe banners of the Scottish regiments are worthy of attention. They are similar in shape to the modern military guidon, but may be fishtailed, and their use can be dated to the seventeenth century. The display of insignia on pipe banners is largely a matter for regimental discretion, but usually the badges and insignia of the regiment are displayed on one side, while on the other side are the personal arms of the colonel of the regiment, the commanding officer or company commander.

The Royal Navy From the earliest times, when ships fought at close quarters, it was necessary for them to be identified easily. They flew banners and streamers, hung shields over the sides of the ship, painted designs on the sails or displayed large carved and painted figureheads. These were held in great esteem by the crews, but eventually the passing of sail and the changing design of iron warships made them obsolete. Highly decorated scroll work, incorporating the ship's name, sometimes with coats of arms, was popular for a time, but again passed into disuse.

After the disappearance of the figurehead, ships' crews often devised and used devices of their own, but in December 1918 official badges were introduced and the Ships Badges Committee established, together with an Admiralty Adviser on heraldry. Today, designs must be approved by the committee, and one of the officers of arms of the College of Arms is both a member and acts as adviser to the Navy Department on heraldic matters.

Early badges took their inspiration from several sources: some incorporated the design of the original figurehead, some a fanciful or obvious depiction of the ship's name while others, quite naturally, used devices from the arms, crest or supporters of the person or place after which the ship was named. One of the first decisions taken by the committee was to establish a uniform design of badge, but with a distinctive shape appropriate to the class of warship: circular for battleships, pentagonal for cruisers, shield-shaped for destroyers, and lozenge-shaped for aircraft carriers and ancillary vessels. The badge itself was carved in relief and coloured, and was surrounded by a gold border representing rope. This had, at the top, a panel for the ship's name, ensigned by a Naval Crown (i.e. a circlet on which are mounted alternately the sterns and sails of ships). The variation of shape to denote the different classes of ships has, since August 1942, been discontinued and all ships' badges are now circular, though shore establishments continue to use the lozenge, and vessels of the Royal Fleet Auxiliary Service use the pentagon.

Originally the badges were carved in yellow pine and then cast in brass in the foundry at Chatham

Dockyard. Today they are made of glass fibre and epoxy resin. Two sizes are made: large ships' badges for fixing to a prominent part of the ship, and smaller boats' badges, identical except for the omission of the Naval Crown and name of the ship. The badge was also cast on the brass gun tampions (plugs placed in the muzzle to protect the guns when not in use), but with the changing pattern of war at sea and naval armament, this practice is also disappearing.

Squadrons of the Fleet Air Arm have their own badges, as do helicopter units whose badges can be seen on the air crews' flying suits.

For many years the Royal Navy comprised three divisions: the Red (senior), White, and Blue (junior) Squadrons, each having its own ensign. This led to much confusion and in 1864 an Order in Council put an end to squadron colours and declared that the White Ensign 'be established and recognized as the colours of the Royal Naval Service.' The field of the ensign is white charged with the red cross of St George, with the Union Flag in the upper canton next to the mast. A Sovereign's Colour was authorized for use by the Royal Navy in 1925. This is a silk White Ensign with a superimposed Crown and Royal Cypher and no fringe.

The use of signal flags exemplifies the basic principles of armory — clear contrasting colours and simple shapes capable of identification over long distances. By 1901 an International Code of Signals had been established, and this has been modified and improved over the years. Despite the development of sophisticated electronic communications, these flags can still be seen in use by ships of the Royal Navy, in 'dressing ship' for special occasions when at anchor or in port.

The Royal Air Force Officers and other ranks of the Royal Air Force wear uniforms and devices to indicate rank, and membership of certain specialist categories such as medical officer, chaplain, RAF regiment and some 'trades'. All Royal Air Force squadrons, commands, stations and units have individual and distinguishing devices, though these are not worn on uniforms. They date from the formation of the Royal Air Force from the Royal Naval Air Service and the Royal Flying Corps, in April 1918, at which time crews painted a variety of unofficial emblems on their aircraft. The First World War saw the peak of this activity. The value of these symbols was recognized, and in 1935 the post of Inspector of RAF Badges was introduced to advise the Air Council on matters armorial and to control the design and issue of these devices. The first person to hold this post was Sir John Heaton-Armstrong MVO, the then Chester Herald of Arms, and he produced the basic pattern and format to be used for all future badges.

The unit badge is enclosed by a circular frame, coloured 'Royal Air Force Blue' and inscribed in gold lettering with the name and number of the squadron or unit, and the words 'Royal Air Force'. This in turn is encircled by a gold laurel wreath and the whole ensigned by a crown in proper colours. Below is a scroll with the unit's motto. The Tudor Crown was used prior to the accession of the present sovereign, when it was changed to the St Edward's Crown.

Since 1936 well over a thousand badges have been authorized, and many can be seen carved in slate and set into the floor of the Church of St Clement Danes in the Strand, London — the church of the Royal Air Force.

Perhaps the best known motif which identifies all British military aircraft is the roundel or target, red upon white upon blue. The official badge of the Royal Air Force has only been in existence since 1949 and is blazoned *In front of a Circle inscribed with the Motto 'Per Ardua Ad Astra' and ensigned by the Imperial Crown an Eagle volant and affronty Head lowered and to the sinister.* The motto may be translated as 'Through difficulties to the stars'. The ensign of the Royal Air Force is of 'RAF Blue'; in the canton is the Union Flag and in the fly the roundel of red, white and blue. In 1947 King George VI approved 'colours' for the RAF, and they now comprise the Queen's Colour of the RAF in the United Kingdom, the Queen's Colour of individual units, and standards for operational squadrons.

The Sovereign's or Queen's Colour of the RAF is of silk in RAF blue and is square in shape. Similar in appearance to the RAF Ensign, it also has the Crown and Royal Cypher in the centre. It has a fringe of light blue and silver, and was first presented on 26 May 1951. Squadron standards have a field of RAF blue, and within a border of roses, thistles, leeks and shamrocks is placed the squadron badge with not more than eight scrolls for battle honours.

Coats of arms have been granted to some RAF establishments, e.g. RAF College, Cranwell, granted in 1924, the crest is the winged god Daedalus of Greek mythology, commemorating the fact that Cranwell was a Royal Naval Air Service station (HMS Daedalus) prior to the formation of the RAF; RAF Staff College, Andover, the arms granted in 1970 incorporate *Three Pales Sable* from the arms of Viscount Trenchard, Marshal and 'Father' of the Royal Air Force; the College of Air Warfare, previously the RAF Flying College, with a crest of a pelican issuant from an Astral Crown with a Naval Crown round its neck, again a link between two services.   ENT

Further reading
Ascoli, D. *A Companion to the British Army 1660-1983* 1984.

Cole, H.N. *Heraldry in War, Formation Badges 1939-45.*

Cox, R.H.W. *Military Badges* London, 1982.

Edwards, T.J. *Standards, Guidons and Colours of the Commonwealth Forces* 1953.

Hollis, B.R. *Knights of the Sky, Heraldry of the Royal Air Force, Parts I and II* 1985.

Lawson, C.P. *History of the Uniforms of the British Army. Volumes I to V* 1949 (reprinted 1967).

Rosignoli, G. *Army Badges and Insignia of World War II* 1972.

— *Badges and Insignia of World War II, Air Force, Navy, Marine* 1980.

Smith, P.C. *Royal Navy Ships Badges* 1975.

— *Royal Air Force Squadron Badges* 1974.

Weightman, A.E. *Heraldry in the Royal Navy, Crests and Badges of HM Ships* 1957.

Wise, T. *Military Flags of the World 1618-1900* 1977.

United Kingdom, Royal Heraldry It was during the reign of Henry I (1100-35) that the first lion was seen in England, in the King's menagerie at Woodstock, and it is likely that a single lion was adopted by him as a device. All Henry's descendants through his illegitimate children bore lions, in various attitudes and with other charges. When in 1128 Henry knighted his son-in-law Geoffrey, Count of Anjou and father of Henry II, he gave him a shield charged with gold lions. From this may be traced the *Azure six Lions rampant Or three two and one* of Geoffrey's grandson, William Longespée, third Earl of Salisbury (d. 1226), which are evident today on his effigy at Salisbury Cathedral. The coat of *Gules two Lions passant guardant Or* is frequently attributed to the Norman kings, and the seal of Eleanor of Aquitaine, wife of the first Angevine king, Henry II (1154-89), shows three such lions, indicative perhaps of early marshalling, for Eleanor herself is known to have borne a single golden lion on red. A shield bearing the three lions later appears on the second great seal of Richard I (1195), and is used thereafter by succeeding monarchs until *c.* 1340 when Edward III adopted both the style and the arms of the kings of France, which he quartered with the lions of England. These arms, *Quarterly 1 and 4 Azure semy-de-lis Or 2 and 3 Gules three Lions passant guardant Or*, are known as *Quarterly France Ancient and England*. They were modified slightly during the reign of Henry IV when, in 1405, he followed the example of Charles V of France and reduced the number of fleurs-de-lis to three, the coat thereafter being known as France Modern. This shield of arms continued in use until James VI of Scotland succeeded Elizabeth I as James I of England, in 1603. At this time the arms of Scotland and Ireland were incorporated, and the arms of the Stuart monarchs became *Quarterly 1 and 4 Grand Quarterly i and iv France Modern ii and iii England 2 Or a Lion rampant within a double Tressure flory counter-flory Gules* (Scotland) *3 Azure a Harp Or stringed Argent* (Ireland). They were used by James I, Charles I, Charles II, James II and Anne. William of Orange and Mary II, for most of their joint and then individual reigns, used the Stuart arms with the arms of Nassau in

Edward I from the Memorandum Roll 1297/8 showing the royal arms of England *Gules three Lions passant guardant Or* **embroidered on his costume.**

pretence: *Azure billety a Lion rampant Or*. In 1707 the arms of Queen Anne were changed to *Quarterly 1 and 4 England impaling Scotland 2 France Modern 3 Ireland*. For almost a century, from 1714 to 1801, the Hanoverian kings, George I, George II and George III, placed the arms of Hanover in the fourth quarter, *Quarterly 1 England impaling Scotland 2 France Modern 3 Ireland 4 Hanover*. From 1801 the French quartering was at last omitted and other coats rearranged: *Quarterly 1 and 4*

England 2 Scotland 3 Ireland in pretence Hanover ensigned with the Electoral Bonnet. When Hanover became a kingdom in 1816 the Electoral Bonnet was replaced by the Royal Crown. In 1837, Salic Law precluded Victoria from becoming monarch of Hanover; the Hanoverian escutcheon of pretence was removed from the royal arms, which thus assumed their present form *Quarterly 1 and 4 England 2 Scotland 3 Ireland.*

Royal Labels Members of the Royal Family are granted arms, usually on a special occasion such as coming-of-age or marriage. They consist of the royal arms differenced by a label argent, of three points for children of the sovereign, and of five points for grandchildren or more distant relations.

The Prince of Wales bears a plain label of three points argent. The Duke of York bears a label of three points argent, the centre point charged with an anchor azure. The Princess Royal's three-pointed label bears a heart Gules between two crosses of St George. Princess Margaret bears three points, the centre with a thistle and the outer with Tudor Roses. The Duke of Gloucester has five points, the centre and outer points charged with St George's crosses and the inner with *Lions passant guardant Gules.* The Duke of Kent bears a five-point label, the centre and outer points charged with anchors azure. The late Duke of Windsor, after his abdication, bore a label of three points, the centre charged with the Imperial Crown.

Royal Crests From the reign of Edward III English monarchs have borne the crest of *a Lion statant guardant crowned Or.* Originally it was shown on a chapeau gules turned up ermine, but Edward IV encircled the cap with a coronet, and from Henry VIII's time the present form of the lion standing on a crown was adopted.

Royal Supporters Since 1603 the royal supporters have remained constant — the lion for England and the unicorn for Scotland. In Scotland their positions are reversed, but if the Scottish arms are used alone the supporters are two unicorns.

Before 1603 several of the ROYAL BEASTS had been used as supporters, the earliest probably being the two white harts of Richard II. Henry VI had two heraldic antelopes argent. Edward IV may have used two *Lions rampant guardant Argent*; others attributed to him include the black bull of Clarence, and the white boar. Richard III is associated with the white boar, which he used when Duke of Gloucester, but it is not certain that he retained boars as supporters when he became king.

Henry VII and Henry VIII both used the red dragon of Cadwallader and the white greyhound of Richmond, or two greyhounds; Henry VIII also used, for the first time, the *Lion imperially crowned Or* as the dexter supporter, with the red dragon as the sinister.

Mary I's arms, dimidiated by those of Philip of Spain, were supported by an *Imperial Eagle Sable crowned Or* for Spain, and the English lion of her father. Elizabeth I used the lion and dragon of her father, the dragon sometimes being shown with the underparts gold, and even gold all over.

Royal Liveries
Plantagenet: scarlet and white
Edward II: azure and gules
Edward III: azure and gules
Lancastrians: white and blue
Yorkists: blue and murrey
Tudors: argent and vert
Stuarts to the present day: gold and scarlet (undress livery: scarlet and blue)

Royal Badges
Henry II: Planta Genista (broom plant); a gold escarbuncle (Anjou?)
Richard I: Planta Genista; the sun and moon (a star and crescent); a mailed arm with the hand grasping a broken lance and the motto 'Christo Duce'; a sun above two anchors.
John: Planta Genista; star and crescent.
Henry III: Planta Genista; star and crescent; a red dragon (?).
Edward I: Planta Genista; a golden rose (Eleanor of Provence?).
Edward II: a gold castle (Castile).
Edward III: a sunburst; a tree stock (stump) eradicated (Woodstock); a falcon; a griffin; an ostrich feather; a fleur-de-lis; a sword; a sword enfiling three crowns and placed on a chapeau; a boar.
Richard II: a sunburst; a sun in splendour; an ostrich feather; a white hart lodged, ducally gorged and chained (from his mother, Joan of Kent); a tree stock eradicated gold; a white falcon; a broom plant with the pods empty; a clouded sun.
Henry IV: a monogram SS; a cresset; a fox's tail; a tree stock eradicated; a crowned eagle; an eagle displayed; a crowned panther; an ostrich feather environed by a circlet charged with the word *sovereygne*; a columbine flower; a sun in splendour; a red rose (Lancaster); a red rose en soleil; a white swan (De Bohun); a white antelope.
Henry V: a silver ostrich feather; an antelope chained and with the motto 'Dieu et mon Droyt'; a chained swan; a cresset; a tree stock eradicated; a red rose; a fox's tail.
Henry VI: a chained antelope; two ostrich feathers saltirewise, one silver and the other gold; a spotted panther.
Edward IV: a black bull (Clarence); a black dragon (Ulster); a white lion (Mortimer); a white hart; a falcon and fetterlock (York); a sun in splendour; a white rose; a white rose en soleil; a red rose en soleil; a red and white rose en soleil (for his marriage to the Lancastrian Elizabeth Woodville).

359

Edward V: a white rose; a falcon and fetterlock.

Richard III: a white rose; a sun in splendour, a white boar; a falcon with a maiden's face.

Henry VII: a gold portcullis (Beaufort), a portcullis ensigned with a crown and sometimes with the motto 'Altera Securitas'; a white greyhound; a red dragon; a dun cow (Warwick); a crowned hawthorn bush with the cypher HR; a crowned Tudor Rose; a crowned fleur-de-lis; a sunburst; a falcon on a fetterlock.

Henry VIII: a portcullis, a fleur-de-lis; a Tudor Rose (in a variety of forms); a white cockerel; a white greyhound.

Edward VI: a Tudor Rose; a sun in splendour.

Mary I: a pomegranate (Aragon); a pomegranate and rose conjoined; a Tudor Rose dimidiating a sheaf of arrows, the whole ensigned by a crown and surrounded by rays.

Elizabeth I: a crowned falcon with a sceptre (Boleyn); a crowned Tudor Rose with the motto 'Rosa sine spina'; a sieve; a phoenix; a gold harp, stringed argent and ensigned with a crown (Ireland).

James I: a Tudor Rose; a thistle (Scotland); conjoined red and white rose dimidiating a thistle and ensigned with the Royal Crown and with the motto 'Beati Pacifici'; a harp; a fleur-de-lis.

Charles I: as for James I, but the dimidiating rose and thistle without the motto.

Charles II: as above; also various devices (not strictly armorial badges) associated with his flight from Worcester, e.g. the oak wreath and crowned oak tree.

James II: as above.

Anne: a rose and thistle growing from a single stalk and ensigned with the Royal Crown.

Thereafter, successive monarchs made use of former royal badges, notably combinations of the rose, thistle and shamrock devices, and crowned cyphers.

Current royal badges: *The red and white Rose united slipped and leaved proper* (England); *a Thistle slipped and leaved proper* (Scotland); *a Shamrock Leaf slipped Vert* (Ireland); *a Harp Or stringed Argent* (Ireland); *the Rose Thistle and Shamrock engrafted on the same stem proper* (UK); *an Escutcheon charged as the Union Flag* (UK). All the above badges are ensigned with the Royal Crown. *Within a circular Riband Argent fimbriated Or charged with the Motto Y DDRAIG GOCH DDYRY CYCHWYN in letters Vert and ensigned with the Crown proper an Escutcheon per fess Argent and Vert thereon a Dragon passant Gules* (Wales 1953); *A Saltire Argent enfiling an open Crown Or* (for use in Scotland); *On a Mount Vert the Round Tower of Windsor Castle Argent masoned Sable flying thereon the Royal Banner the whole within two branches of Oak fructed Or and ensigned with the Imperial Crown* (House of Windsor 1938).   KH

See also IRELAND, ROYAL ARMS; SCOTLAND, ROYAL ARMS;

HANOVER, ROYAL ARMS; COMMONWEALTH, THE (1649-60); WALES, PRINCE OF; WALES, PRINCIPALITY OF

Further reading

Barker, B. *The Symbols of Sovereignty* 1979.

Brooke-Little, J.P. *Royal Heraldry* Derby, 1977.

— *The British Monarchy* Poole, 1976.

Fox-Davies, A.C. *Heraldic Badges* London, 1907.

Hasler, C. *The Royal Arms* 1980.

Montgomery-Massingberd, H. *Burke's Guide to the British Monarchy* 1977.

Petchey, W.J. *Armorial Bearings of the Sovereign of England* 1977. Standing Conference for Local History.

Pinches, J.H. and R.V. *The Royal Heraldry of England* Heraldry Today, 1974.

Williamson, D. *Debrett's Kings and Queens of Britain* 1986.

United States of America, Armorial Practice There is no official source of armorial bearings in the United States, the granting of hereditary honours being contrary to the Constitution. No American citizen is permitted to bear a title, though this does not preclude American women from becoming titled by right of marriage to a foreigner, and an American may be created a knight of an order of chivalry, though he is never addressed as 'Sir' and would be listed, for example, as Hon. KBE.

Armorial devices flourish in the United States, the majority obtained through the dubious services of firms who purvey 'family arms' in return for money. This practice is not peculiar to the United States, of course, and the 'bucket shops' are simply cashing in on a natural desire of many to record their European ancestry. However, many American students of armory have arrived at the subject through genuine genealogical research, and if a citizen of the United States can prove a right to arms from a British ancestor there is no need for him to apply to anyone in order to use them (though if his right to Scottish arms is through a younger son, he would be advised to matriculate them with Lord Lyon in the usual way). Those who are able to prove direct, legitimate, male-line descent from a British subject may also apply for HONORARY ARMORIAL BEARINGS, but such a grant would depend on the applicant recording incontestable genealogical proof in the records of the College of Arms, and would only have legal effect within the jurisdiction of the granting authority. So far as is known, a right to arms is not recognized by law in any state in the USA, but if an American citizen wishes to use arms within the jurisdiction of the British kings of arms, he would be required to comply with British law.

Since 1928 the heraldic Committee of the New England Heraldry and Historic Genealogical Society of Boston has issued rolls of arms in which have been entered the devices of those who have submitted claims to the committee. The introduction to the first roll observed: 'Taking into consideration the early history of coat armour there seems to be no reason in this country at least why anyone, provided he observes the simple rules of blazon and does not appropriate the arms of another, may not assume and use any coat he desires.' In the third roll of 1936 the committee stated that it was 'fully in agreement with the statements made by Oswald Barron, the foremost living authority on heraldry: "A coat is not held from the Crown, but it is a piece of personal property, the right to which depends simply upon user and the right as against others upon prior assumption".'

In 1966 a body calling itself the American College of Arms was established in Baltimore 'with co-operation from the City of Baltimore, the State of Maryland and the Federal Government'. This consisted of two divisions: the American College of Arms which registered personal arms, and the College of Arms of the United States which dealt with devices for corporate bodies, which it 'granted, matriculated and patented under the laws of trademark'. There were four officers: the Chief Herald, a Herald Marshal, a Herald Genealogist and a Herald Chancellor. Regrettably, all communications to the College's last known address have been returned without acknowledgement.

The American College of Heraldry was founded in 1972 and was subsequently chartered as a non-profit-making corporation by the State of Alabama. The College offers assistance to individuals, corporate bodies and towns in devising arms according to armorial conventions (*see* ADDRESSES). American corporations who obtain the consent of their state governor may apply to the College of Arms in London for a DEVISAL OF ARMS. The College has also recently established the COLLEGE OF ARMS FOUNDATION.

The official seals of the individual states were not necessarily adopted when a particular territory attained statehood, and consequently they display a considerable range of design styles, from the quasi-armorial device of Pennsylvania (1776 modified 1893) to that of Alabama (1939), which comprises a map of the state showing the main rivers, the whole surrounded by concentric circles within which is inscribed 'Alabama Great Seal'. These seals are affixed to such documents as patents, proclamations, commissions and papers of state in order that they may be recognized as authoritative. The Pennsylvania seal bears the state shield of arms and eagle crest, which are also emblazoned, together with black horse supporters and motto 'Virtue, Liberty and Independence' on the State Flag, a form of livery banner. The blazon of the shield of arms is *Per fess Azure and Vert on a Fess Or between in chief a three-masted Sailing Ship sails set proper and in base three Garbs Or a Plough also proper.* Typically,

the other 'Official Pennsylvanian Emblems' include the State Animal (Whitetail Deer), the State Bird (Ruffed Grouse or partridge), the State Dog (Great Dane), the State Flower (Mountain Laurel), and the State Tree (Hemlock).

American cities also have their seals. That of Philadelphia, Pennsylvania, is based on the arms of William Penn: *Argent on a Fess Sable three Bezants.* To the city 'arms' have been added a plough and a clipper ship below the fess. The supporters are two charming ladies, one holding a parchment, the other a cornucopia. The seal of the city of San Diego, California, officially recognized in 1914, bears witness to the city's early Spanish associations: 'Upon a gold shield is a blue wavy band with a Spanish caravel under full sail . . . in the lower part is an orange tree and two winged wheels.' The tree represents agriculture and the wheels commerce. The crest is a depiction of a Carmelite belfry and the supporters highly ornamented pillars of Hercules.

A quite different commemoration is that of the City Seal of Detroit, Michigan. It was adopted in 1827 and marks the great fire of 1805. The seal depicts two robed female figures and bears two defiant Latin mottoes: 'We hope for better things!' and 'It shall rise again from the ashes'. Surprisingly, there is no phoenix in the city's insignia.

Governmental insignia are, for the most part, in the best armorial tradition, the device of the National Security Agency, for example, being the American (or bald) eagle, wings inverted, grasping in its claws a key fesswise and charged on the breast with an escutcheon *Argent six Pallets Gules a Chief Azure*, the shield of the United States. It will be noted that this differs from the banner, which is *Gules six Barrulets Argent a Canton Azure charged with fifty Stars Argent in five rows of six and four rows of five*. The device of the United States is the American eagle, wings displayed and charged on the breast with the shield, holding in the dexter talon an olive branch proper, and in the sinister a bundle of thirteen arrows argent, and in its beak a ribbon on which is the motto 'E Pluribus Unum'. Above its head is a circle of cloud enclosing, on azure, thirteen stars arranged in the form of a six-pointed star. These, and the number of divisions on the shield, represent the original states. The blue canton represents Congress, the supreme governmental authority, and the olive branch and arrows declare the power of Congress to determine matters of peace and war. The proposition that the 'stars and stripes' originated in the arms of George Washington (*Argent two Bars and in chief three Mullets Gules*) is of doubtful validity, though they do appear in the flag of the District of Columbia. Perhaps the best known armorial banner is that of Maryland, which bears the arms of the Lords Baltimore, colonial proprietors prior to independence in 1776: *Quarterly 1 and 4 Paly of six Or and Sable a Bend counterchanged* (Calvert, Lord Baltimore) *2 and 3 Quarterly Argent and Gules a Cross botonny counterchanged* (Crosland of Crosland in Yorkshire, the heiress who married the first Lord Baltimore).

The leopard supporters of Baltimore's arms were replaced by a fisherman and ploughman for Maryland's arms.

Further reading
Filby, P.W. *American and British Genealogy and Heraldry* 1975 (selected bibliography).
Vermont, E. de V. (Ed.) *America Heraldica* 1886 (reprinted 1965).

United States of America, Military Insignia The authority responsible in the United States for matters of military armory is the Institute of Heraldry, United States Army, better known by its initials TIOH. This Institute is mainly concerned with authorizing military insignia for the various branches of the United States Armed Forces, and advises units on armorial practice. Before TIOH approval is sought, most units will have consulted their unit historian with regard to new insignia. TIOH imposes several constraints with regard to emblems, which should be in good taste and not include offensive words, should meet certain size specifications and be easily recognized. Of special interest to armorists are the United States Army Distinctive Unit Insignia (DIs). These are normally of metal and enamel and are worn in pairs on shoulder straps and certain types of headgear. Such insignia are more familiarly called unit 'crests'. At battalion and regimental level DIs often take the form of a coat of arms, those of colour-bearing units having crests. However, unit insignia may simply be a charge taken from the unit arms or an entirely different device. When the shield is used this is often accompanied by a unit motto.

Certain charges are used by TIOH to indicate war or peace-time service in various locations by a specific unit. Such devices often seen on unit arms and insignia include: a cactus plant (Mexican border duties); a fleur-de-lis (service during the First or Second World Wars in France); alerions (service in the Lorraine Province of France where alerions feature in the provincial arms); a golden sun (service in the Philippines); and a *teaguk* (a *Yin Yang* symbol indicative of service in the Korean War). Arms and insignia can become cluttered, but many examples are in the best traditions of medieval armory, such as the arms of the 32nd Armoured Regiment (32nd Armor) blazoned *Or a Bend raguly Gules*. These arms are described as 'cutting firepower' (the bend raguly) placed on a field symbolizing the regiment's cavalry traditions (each branch of the US army has its own colours, yellow being that of the cavalry). The crest of the 32nd Armor is more complex and represents the wartime service of the unit in Europe. A red lion, symbolizing Belgium, holds the uprooted firtree of the Ardennes Campaign, whilst in the other paw it holds the flailing mace of armoured firepower, coloured blue to represent the ribbon the US Presidential Unit Citation awarded to the regiment in recognition of its assault on the German Siegfried Line. The lion stands somewhat

Arms of the 32nd Armored Regiment.

precariously on a section of five 'dragon's teeth' — the anti-tank defences blunted by the regiment.

Should a unit be a regiment or battalion of the US Army National Guard (a reserve-type organization responsible in peace-time to a state governor), it would normally place above its arms the distinctive crest of the state National Guard, though this is not normally used in the DIs of such a unit. The DI of the former 2nd Scout Battalion of the Alaska Army National Guard consists of the unit shield *Azure two Wolf's Heads erased in bend Argent a Chief rayonné of the like*. Blue and white are the colours of the US infantry, the wolf's heads represent surveillance in the northern and western coastal regions of Alaska, ferocity, cunning, etc., and the chief rayonné represents the Northern Lights and icicles. Its motto is 'Upingsukut' (Eskimo for 'We are ready'), and its crest an heraldic representation of the Aurora Borealis behind a totem pole palewise bearing the figures of an eagle, bear and walrus.

The distinctive insignia of the 203rd Engineer Battalion, Missouri Army National Guard, taken from its coat of arms, is *A Houn' Dawg statant proper standing on a Gold Ribbon-Scroll bearing the motto 'Don't Kick Our Dog' in red*.

Regiments and separate battalions of the United States Army Reserve bear above their arms the crest of that organization: *On a Wreath of the Unit Colours a Statue of the Lexington Minute Man* (Captain John

Emblem of the 501st Tactical Missile Wing USAF

Parker) *proper*. This statue stands in Lexington, Massachusetts.

In recent years, when designing insignia, TIOH has applied not only armorial terminology and conventions, but also imagination. DENTAC (dental activity) units often have insignia including a maroon fess charged with *Nine Silver Squares four above and five below with corners conjoined*, which look like a set of human teeth.

During the Vietnam War many US military units, not authorized to wear their own distinctive insignia, had unofficial emblems, often in the form of metal badges made out of empty beer cans. Many of these are crude and non-armorial, but because of their scarcity they are greatly sought after in the United States, and are termed 'Beer Can DIs'.

US Naval and Marine Corps unit insignia are normally made of cloth and appear as shoulder patches. They do not have the same armorial interest as those of the Army, but sometimes bear the arms of naval heroes or state or municipal devices.

United States Air Force Regulation 900-3 specifically deals with Air Force insignia and flags. One section requires that USAF emblems at squadron level should show a pictorial device on a disc, whilst the emblems of flag-bearing units (those with a headquarters component) should be of an armorial nature with a device upon a shield. One example of the latter is the emblem of the 501st Tactical Missile Wing USAF, based at RAF Greenham Common in England, and currently equipped with the controversial Cruise missiles.

When a USAF unit wishes to have a new emblem, certain criteria have to be observed in the design. These include the requirement that the emblem should be of yellow and ultramarine blue, and that it should *not* depict specific types of aircraft, missile, etc. When the emblem is approved by the unit historian it is passed to the Airforce, who forward the application to the USAF Historical Research Center at Maxwell Air Force Base, Alabama, and finally the emblem is sent for approval to TIOH. Other procedures may be employed, but TIOH always has the final say in matters of US military heraldry. USAF emblems often appear in cloth patch form for use on uniform, or on transfers and decal.

Further information is available from the American Society of Military Insignia Collectors (*see* ADDRESSES).

SS

Urchin A hedgehog. Sometimes called a herisson or herizon in allusion to a name such as Harrison.

Urdy *see* **Lines, Varied**

Uriant *see* **Attitude**

Urinant *see* **Attitude**

V

Vair, Vair en Point *and* **Vair in Pale** *see* **Furs**

Vairy A variation of the fur vair, the tinctures of which have to be specified.

Vallary *see* **Lines, Varied** *and* **Crest Coronet**

Vambrace Armour for the forearm.

Vambraced *see* **Attributes**

Vane (weather vane) Col. R. Gayre devotes an entire chapter of his book *Heraldic Standards and other Ensigns* (1959) to the subject of heraldic vanes, and rightly so. They are a traditional and eminently suitable means of displaying armorial devices, though Col. Gayre's proposition that a vane's shape was dictated by its owner's rank requires further substantiation. The use of vanes, which probably originated in France, is evident in England from the thirteenth century, and it is likely that the word 'vane' is a corruption of *fane*, and therefore derived from *fannion*, a banner.

On churches, vanes are frequently in the form of a cockerel, symbolizing vigilance, or emblems of patron saints, such as the gridiron of St Lawrence on the churches of St Lawrence, Jewry in the City of London, Ramsgate in Kent, and Tidmarsh in Berkshire. At St Mary-le-Bow, Cheapside in the City of London, is a 9 foot dragon vane weighing 2 cwt, and similar monsters may be seen at Ottery St Mary in Devon, Sittingbourne in Kent, and Upton in Norfolk.

Truly armorial vanes are, however, an entirely different breed and are generally found gracing the gables and pinnacles of major domestic buildings, particularly those of the Tudor period. Two excellent examples are the banner-shaped vanes of the Lucy family at Charlecote in Warwickshire, and the swallow-tailed pennon-type vanes at Lambeth Palace. Both sets are charged with the arms, the borders, decorative fleurs-de-lis and 'tails' being gilded to catch the sun.

The term may also be applied to a small masthead pennant (*see* FLAGS), and to the early rigid 'flag', modelled or cut in the form of a creature and borne on a pole, as in the Bayeux Tapestry.

A weather vane as an armorial charge may be encountered, but this rarely resembles the real thing. One of the very few examples is blazoned *a weather-cock* in the arms of Fitz-Alwyn, the first Mayor of London.

Variation of Line *see* **Lines, Varied**

Varied Field *see* **Field, Varied**

Vaulting *see* **Ceiling**

Vavasour The principal vassal of a baron.

Veiled *see* **Attributes**

Veneration, in *see* **Attitude**

Vert (Abbr. Vt.) The armorial tincture green (French = sinople). Pronounced to rhyme with 'skirt'.

Vervelled *see* **Attributes**

Vested *see* **Attributes**

Vexillology The study of flags (from Latin *vexillum* = flag).

Vicomte *see* **Viscount**

Victoria and Albert, Royal Order of Instituted in 1862 as a purely courtly distinction for ladies. It is no longer bestowed.

Vigilance, in its *see* **Attitude**

Viroled *see* **Attributes**

Viscount The fourth rank in the British peerage, the first creation being in 1440. The title itself is considerably older: in the days of the Carolingian empire the *vice-comites* were the deputies of the counts and gradually assumed hereditary rights. The creation of 1440 appears to have been made so that the 'Viscount' Beaumont would have precedence over all the barons.

The robes of a viscount are similar to those of a DUKE, with the exceptions that his coronation robe has two and a half rows of ermine, and his parliamentary robe two guards of plain white fur. The coronet of a viscount has, on the circle, sixteen silver balls. The armorial privileges of a viscount are as those of a duke. The wife of a viscount is called a countess, or viscountess.   JC-K

Viscountess The wife of a viscount, or a lady who holds a viscountcy in her own right.

The robe of a viscountess is similar to that of a DUCHESS, except that it is trimmed with two and a half rows of ermine, the edging being 2 inches broad and the train 1¼ yards on the ground. The coronet of a viscountess is also like that of a duchess, except that it is circled by sixteen silver balls (representing pearls) not raised on points. The arms of a viscountess in her own right are similar to those of a duchess, but surmounted by the coronet of her own degree.   JC-K

Visitations in England By the fifteenth century, the use and abuse of arms was becoming widespread. One of the duties of the kings of arms, conferred on Sir William Bruges, the first Garter King of Arms (1415-50), was to survey and record the bearings and pedigrees of those using arms and to correct irregularities. There is some evidence that occasionally in the fifteenth century the heralds made tours of various parts of the country, to enquire into matters armorial, but it was not until the sixteenth century that this was done on a widespread and regular basis.

The beginnings of the systematic heraldic visitations may be found in the warrant of Henry VIII, dated 6 April 1530, to Thomas Benolt, Clarenceux King of Arms (1511-34), who was commissioned to travel throughout his province and given authority to enter all dwellings and churches, etc., to survey and record whatever arms he might find and 'to put down or otherwise deface at his discretion . . . in plate, jewels, paper, parchment, windows, gravestones and monuments or elsewhere wheresoever they may be set or placed' those arms used unlawfully. He was also to enquire into all those using the title of honour or dignity such as Knight, Esquire or Gentleman, and if such a style or arms had been falsely usurped was to denounce the offender by proclamation.

This writ of Henry VIII, repeated in 1555 and also in 1558, marked a new stage by compelling the county sheriffs and their officers to assist the heralds in their survey. The king of arms or his deputy would visit an area and, by displaying the Royal Commission to the High Sheriff, would set the visitation in motion. The High Sheriff then collected from the bailiff of each hundred within his county a list of all such persons using titles or arms, who were then summoned to appear before the herald or his deputy at a stated time and place. By this means, none escaped the enquiry, for the bailiff was certain to know all who were important enough to make use of arms. Each person so summoned was to bring with him the arms he was using and the authority under which he bore them. This might consist of a pedigree signifying ancient usage or a grant of arms, or a confirmation. The herald would then record the pedigree and sketch the achievement with sufficient detail to enable the information accurately to be transferred at a later date to manuscript volumes kept at the College of Arms. These volumes now form the Library of Visitation Books, which is the authoritative record of all the arms recognized and issued by the College during that period.

If the arms and pedigree were found to be in order, perhaps by comparison against earlier visitations, then they were confirmed. If the arms were legally held but defective, corrections to them were made, and if the herald could find no justification for the use of the arms then the usurper was to renounce any right to them and sign a disclaimer. His name was added to the list, subsequently published, of those whose claims had been refused.

Not everyone answered the summons. It is recorded that Daniel Wyborne, Yeoman of Northbourne, ignored the herald's summons at the Visitation of Kent in 1665 because 'the plague was hott at Norborne'. Such persons were warned to appear before the Earl Marshal under penalty of £10. Those who stubbornly refused to withdraw their claim to bogus arms were dealt with by the Court of the Earl Marshal. The major visitations of the whole country took place around 1580, 1620 and 1666. At other times minor journeys were made, and the practice was finally discontinued when the political climate created by William of Orange made it inadvisable to have attention drawn to those who remained loyal to the old system.

The original notebooks used by the heralds during the visitations were not retained by the College and have been used as the basis for other manuscript copies, most of which have now been published. It should be emphasized that the manuscript volumes in the College which are not generally accessible have not hitherto been printed and are the only definitive record. The published visitations are a very useful source of early pedigrees, especially for the period for which parish registers are now less complete through losses or neglect, and are substantially accurate, but it must be borne in mind that they may contain unauthorized additions and alterations which may not be immediately apparent. Many of these volumes have been published by the Harleian Society, and some others by county record societies. A number have been privately printed. It will be found that in some of the visitation books there is much additional later detail on armigerous families, often bringing the record to the nineteenth century. This can provide a valuable short cut to tracing family ancestors. As with every other printed record, nothing should be assumed to be absolutely accurate unless it can be checked against other documents. A good many of the manuscripts on which the printed versions are based are now in the British Library in London.

There are other good collections of printed records of visitations at the Guildhall Library, London, at the Society of Genealogists and at the Institute of Heraldic and Genealogical Studies (*see* ADDRESSES). County record offices and reference libraries (local studies) usually have copies of publications relating to their areas.

In the following list, manuscripts are shown in italics. Those marked (a) are in the library of Queen's College, Oxford; those marked (b) are in the Bodleian Library, Oxford, and those marked (c) are in the Manuscript Department of the British Library, London. The College of Arms has almost all the visitation records, but since their library is not open to the public it is included in the table (d) only if this is the only source of the manuscript.

Almost all the printed books are likely to be in the British Library, London, though in practice the Guildhall Library, also in London, is of easier and quicker access. Printed books which are not available at the Guildhall Library, but are available elsewhere, are marked (e).

Printed and Manuscript Records of Visitations

Bedfordshire	1566	1582	*1586a*	1634	1669	
Berkshire	1532	1566	*1597ab*	1623	1665/6	
Bucks	1566	*1574c*	1634			
Cambs	1575	*1590c*	1619			
Cheshire	1533	1566	*1569d*	1580	1591 (fragment)	
	1613	1663				
Cornwall	1530	1573	1620			
Cumberland	1530e	1615	1666			
Derbyshire	1530e	*1569c*	*1611c*	1615e	*1634d*	*1662c*
Devon	1531	1564	*1572b*	1620		
Dorset	1531e	*1565e*	1623	1677		
Durham	1575	1615	1666			
Essex	1552	1558	1570	1612	1634	1664/8
Gloucs	*1530d*	1569	1582/3	1623	1682/3	
Hampshire	1530	*1552c*	1575	1622	1634	1686e
Herefordshire	1569	*1586c*	*1634e*	1683e		
Hertfordshire	1572	*1615a*	1634			
Hunts	*1564c*	*1566d*	1613			
Kent	1530/1	1574	1592	1619/21	*1623c*	1663/8
Lancashire	1533	1567	1613	1664/5		
Leics	*1563e*	1619	1683e			
Lincolnshire	1562/4	1592	1634	1666		
London	1568e	*1633/4e*	1664e	1687e		
Middlesex	*1572d*	*1634e*	1663			
Norfolk	1563	1589	1613	1664		
Northants	1564	1618/9e	1681			
Northumb.	*1575ac*	1615	1666			
Notts	1530e	1569	*1575d*	1614	1662/4	
Oxfordshire	*1530d*	1566	1574/5	1634	1668e	
Rutland	1618/9	1681/2				
Shropshire	*1569d*	*1584c*	1623	1663e		
Somerset	1531	1573	1591	1623	*1672d*	
Staffordshire	*1563c*	1583	1614	1663/4		
Suffolk	1561	1577	1612	1664/8		
Surrey	1530	*1552c*	1572	1623	1662/8	
Sussex	1530	*1570e*	*1574c*	1633/4	1662	
Warwickshire	*1656c*	1619	1682/3			
Westmorland	1615	1664/6				
Wiltshire	*1530d*	*1565e*	1623	1628	1677e	
Worcs	*1533e*	1569	1634	1682/3		
Yorkshire	1530e	*1552d*	1563/4	*1574c*	1584/5	1612
	1665/6					
Wales and the Marches	*1530d*	1586-1613				

Further reading

Sims, R. *Index to the Pedigrees and Arms contained in the Heralds' Visitations and other genealogical manuscripts in the British Museum* 1849 (reprinted 1970).

Squibb, G.D. *Visitation Pedigrees and the Genealogist* 1978.

Visitations and Funeral Certificates in Ireland

Since the practices of Ulster Office so closely followed those of the English College of Arms it is hardly surprising that the Ulster kings of arms undertook heraldic visitations within their province, and also recorded the arms and pedigrees of the deceased gentry of the kingdom. In both cases the purpose behind the compilation of such records was two-fold: to prevent the assumption of arms by persons unqualified to bear them, and to record the arms of gentry families unknown to Ulster Office. The social upheavals which followed on several plantation schemes of the sixteenth and seventeenth centuries, produced considerable social changes in Ireland, including a substantial influx of English and Scottish families, many of whom claimed the right to bear arms. The Ulster kings of arms attempted, through the Visitation and Funeral Certificate series, to update their records and to prevent the abuse of armory within their province.

The first visitation was held in 1568 by Nicholas Narbon, the second Ulster, within sixteen years of the foundation of the office. According to the terms of the Royal Warrant he was authorized to reform any practices in armory which were 'contrary to the laudable usage of the realm of England.' He conducted six visitations, all of which survive: Dublin City and County (with random entries for Louth) 1568-73; Drogheda and Ardee 1570; Dublin City 1572; Swords 1572; Cork Town 1574; Limerick Town 1574. His immediate successor, Christopher Ussher, did not continue the series but in 1603 Daniel Molyneux, who succeeded Ussher, obtained a renewed warrant to hold visitations. Under the terms of this authorization he was commanded to take note 'of the arms of the Irish chieftains in their countries' but unfortunately this injunction was not obeyed. The following visitations undertaken by Molyneux survive: Dublin City 1607; Dublin County 1610; Wexford County 1618; Wexford Town 1618. There is evidence to suggest that a visitation of Kildare was undertaken, but that the manuscript had been lost by the 1650s. The Narbon visitations only survive in the form of a transcript compiled by Molyneux *c.* 1607, by which date the originals were in a state of decay. Unfortunately, whilst Molyneux carefully transcribed the narrative pedigrees, he failed to complete the copy by including tricks, or any details, of the arms used by the families concerned. Fortunately his own visitations included many of these families and their arms are painted in full colour.

Although the visitation of Wexford Town, 1618, was the last proper example of this genre, two other 'visitations' should be noted. In 1647 Doctor Roberts, Ulster King of Arms, made a 'Military Visitation' of the officers of the regiment under the command of Colonel Castle, which the English parliament had sent into Ireland to fight the forces of the Catholic Confederation of Kilkenny. This manuscript contains twelve folios of narrative pedigrees with full blazons of the arms of each officer. In 1649 Albon Leveret,

Athlone Pursuivant, made a similar visitation of the officers of Colonel Tothill's regiment. The total number of entries of the combined Irish visitations 1568-1649 is quite small and certainly less than three hundred.

One of the reasons why so few visitations were conducted in Ireland was that the disturbed state of the country was such that the Ulster kings of arms preferred to remain within the comparative safety of Dublin. Furthermore, they developed a system whereby death, which visited every home, acted as a deputy on their behalf. In 1627 Daniel Molyneux, Ulster King of Arms, obtained an Order in Council from the Lord Lieutenant of Ireland, compelling the heirs or executors of deceased armigers to return a certificate to Ulster Office listing their arms and pedigrees. This order, which was supported by the Privy Council, was enforced through a system of provincial deputies, licensed heraldic painters, and fines for failure to comply with its provisions. Although the Funeral Certificate series only covers the period *c.* 1560s-1690s, it contains over 3000 separate entries, many of which include long narrative pedigrees as well as tricks or paintings of arms. This is an invaluable source for Irish genealogists and armorists alike, but unfortunately is much neglected by both.

The original Visitation and Funeral Certificate manuscripts are in the custody of the Chief Herald of Ireland. Copies of both series are also on deposit in the College of Arms, London. MCM

Visitations in Scotland The 1672 Act of Parliament gave the Lord Lyon authority to visit any part of Scotland in pursuit of his statutory duties as head of the heraldic executive. Such visits have been made in the past, and the Lord Lyon and his officers of arms continue the practice down to the present time. However, these visits are not organized information-gathering exercises covering specific areas. Heraldic control in Scotland is such that it has never been necessary to have a periodic inspection to check the legality of arms being used. Thus Scottish visitations are quite different from those that have been undertaken in England and Ireland. CJB

Visor *or* **Vizor** Face guard affixed to the helmet with slits for the eyes (sights) and mouth (breathes), and usually holed for ventilation.

Voided see **Attributes**

Vol a see **Attitude**

Volant see **Attitude**

Voluted see **Attributes**

Vorant see **Attitude**

Vulned see **Attributes**

Vulning see **Attitude**

W

Wales, Armory in

Bearers of Arms The armorial families of Wales consist of three distinct groups, namely the advenae, the aristocracy of Welsh blood, and the non-tribal Welshmen. The advenae, Norman and English, were of two kinds: the most famous were the feudal lords whose conquering swords brought under their sway wide lands in the Welsh marches; they are sometimes called 'Adventurers' in Welsh manuscripts. In their wake came retainers, officials and traders, burgesses of the towns and garrisons of the castles, an immigration that has continued to modern times. One of the earliest known bearers of arms, the De Clare family, was connected with Wales from an early date, and it is not unlikely that the first heraldic banners to wave over Welsh soil bore the golden chevronels of that baronial house. The second class, consisting of the royal, noble and gentle families, forms the backbone of Welsh armory. In all, there were some twenty-three royal or quasi-royal dynasties; beneath them came the territorial lords who owned sovereignty within their boundaries; and, finally, a vast network of warrior-farmers with an intense pride in their *limpieza de sangre* and a strongly marked local patriotism. Thus, the majority of the nation consisted of a pedigreed population, a distinct caste, whose concept of blood descent has had a direct bearing on the development of Welsh armory. The proudest claim was descent from the princes and the great medieval chieftains, over 150 of whom were Heraldic Ancestors, whose significance we shall observe presently. The third class consists of Welsh families whose origins were outside the charmed circle of blood aristocracy, but whose aptitudes and abilities enabled them to become part of the ruling elite; generally speaking, the armory of these families is comparatively free from the complexities associated with that of the preceding group.

Medieval armory Welshmen were brought into contact with Anglo-Norman advenae in early times, and their medieval armory developed along lines similar to that of England. Evidence during the period 1150-1300 is scanty, but sufficient has survived, mainly from seals, to show that arms were used by the more important people, while the lesser folk used personal seals, some of which developed at a later date into armorial bearings. The earlier Welsh princes and nobles used equestrian seals. Among these, the equestrian seals of Prince Gwenwynwyn of Powys (1200, 1206) and Llewelyn the Great (*c.* 1222), and of nobles like Elisse ap Madog and Morgan ap Caradog of Afan (both sealed in 1183), Howel ap Howel (1198), Madoc ap Owen (1215), and Madoc ap Caswallon (1231), are notable examples. Armorial seals were not unknown. The seal of Prince David (1246), son of Llewelyn the Great, showed a lion rampant, and Madoc ap Griffith (great-great-grandson of Bleddyn ap Cynfyn) sealed with a similar charge in 1225; John ap John of Grosmont, in 1249, sealed with a lion rampant in a border charged with six escallops. About 1295, David ap Cynwric and Howel ap Meredydd, two nobles from North Wales, sealed, respectively, with a lion rampant, and with paly of six on a fess three mullets. About 1300, Ithel ap Bleddyn bore two lions rampant addorsed, their tails inter-twined, with a coronetted maiden's head as crest — an early example of the use of a crest by a Welsh family.

From 1300 to 1500 a great deal of evidence has survived, showing that arms had become general and, in some cases, hereditary. Thus, Owen ap Gruffydd (grandson of the above Gwenwynwyn) bore a lion rampant which his daughter carried into the achievement of the house of Cherleton, while another member of the Powysian line, Gruffydd de la Pole, sealed in 1310 and 1321 with a similar charge. We find Leison de Afan (great grandson of that Morgan who had used an equestrian seal in 1183) affixing to a deed about 1300 a seal bearing three chevronels, while his son employed the same device in 1330 with the addition of a Paschal lamb which may be interpreted either as a crest or a conventional decoration — in any case it became the heraldic crest of his descendants. In 1302, Sir John Wogan (descendant of Bleddyn ap Maenarch) sealed with an eagle displayed bearing on its breast a shield charged with three birds on a chief, arms which were borne by his descendants, who converted the eagle into a cockatrice crest. Effigies and tomb-slabs, often bearing the names of the deceased on the borders of armorial shields, also indicate the degree of general usage. Poems by fourteenth and fifteenth-century bards, valuable genealogical and heraldic records, contain many allusions to the arms of the 'native-born', and one of them refers to the painting of shields on walls, a practice that lingered long, so that in the seventeenth century we still find coats of arms being painted on the interior walls of Welsh country houses.

The theory of Welsh gentility In Wales there was no such being as 'the armigerous gentleman'. The theory was that a man was gentle by virtue of his genealogy. Gentility followed the blood. This conception of biological aristocracy had deep roots, and it continued

to be asserted even as late as the nineteenth century. It is of particular importance to note that the English heralds in Tudor and later times recognized this evaluation of gentility in relation to Welsh armorial claims.

The Heraldic Ancestor Although the Welsh had been acquainted with armory throughout the Middle Ages, it was not until the early part of the Tudor period that they reduced it to a system. The method employed was ingenious. The bards decreed that all the royal and tribal ancestors should be given coats of arms. But what arms were they to be given? Where a family bore arms, the bards stated that, in reality, these had been inherited from a tribal ancestor, and accordingly assigned them to that ancestor. Thus the golden eagles of the House of Gwydir winged their way back from Tudor days until they perched upon the princely shoulders of Owen Gwynedd, who had ruled in the twelfth century. The arms of the House of Talbot, descendants in the female line from the Princes of South Wales, had already, in earlier times, been identified with the southern dynasty; the lions that crouched with their tails curled between their legs on the shields of the fifteenth-century Imperial Princes of Wales were alleged to have been derived from one of the coats of Rhodri Mawr, who had been king of Wales in the ninth century. All ancestors were to have arms, and coats of many colours were bestowed upon Howel Dda who had lived in the tenth century, to Cadwaladr who had lived in the seventh, to Cunedda who had lived in the fifth, and to Beli Mawr who probably had never lived at all. It was asserted that since a Welshman derived his gentility from ancestors, he was entitled also to derive from them his arms, real or assigned. As large numbers of the ancient stocks had survived and had shown a remarkable degree of stability, these tribal arms assumed a topographical distribution. The ninety-eight families descended from Urien Rheged, all in Carmarthenshire, bore in their entirety, or differenced, the assigned arms of the said Urien. The hundreds of families descended from Hwfa ap Cynddelw, Cilmin of the Black Foot, Llewelyn of the Golden Torque, Cadwgan Whetter of the Battle Axe, Morgan of the Hound's Lair, and Rhirid the Wolf, and many other chieftains, all bore the devices that had been assigned posthumously to those worthies. Thus, at one stroke, the bards brought within the heraldic fold droves of wild hidalgoes of the western hills — shepherds, farmers, nobles, landowners, tinkers, tailors, blacksmiths, lawyers, parsons, even paupers, and invested them with a dignity that had hitherto inhered only in their blood. And so was born the idea of the 'tribal' arms. A Welshman displayed arms because they proclaimed him to be the descendant of some particular ancestor — that was what really mattered. Accordingly, Welsh armory acquired a dual purpose. In England a coat of arms was often entirely divorced from ancestry; in Wales it was the result of ancestry. The Welsh coat of arms is not merely a mark of gentility — it is the portrait of an ancestor, as vivid as the canvas of a Goya, or Vandyke, or Graham Sutherland.

But what of families who had borne no arms at all? Lack of imagination is a charge that can be levelled at no Welshman, and none was better qualified in the exercise of that talent than the bard. In such cases arms were invented and described as being the true and undoubted ensigns of ancient chiefs, some of whom had lived in days when woad was the only fashionable blazon.

Furthermore, probably to distinguish between the different branches of a parent stock, we find the emergence of secondary heraldic ancestors. A noted descendant of a primary heraldic ancestor would be granted his own particular coat, sometimes based on the earlier coat, sometimes entirely different. This practice may have been inspired by the fact that the different branches already bore these different arms when the systematization took place in the sixteenth century. So long as we appreciate the ploy that went on in Tudor Wales we shall be able to understand the principle that governed the acceptance of these coats. They cannot be called fictitious because they were actually borne by Welsh families, but they were most certainly not inherited from the heraldic ancestors. It was a present fact converted into a retrospective fiction.

Control The theory that heraldry followed the blood, allied to the rampant individualism of the Celtic temperament, might suggest that an impatient attitude towards control might have resulted. Indeed, it has been observed that Welsh families have shown hostility towards legally constituted heraldic authority. Such, however, is not the case. There is abundant evidence that large numbers of Welshmen flocked to the Herald's College, especially during the sixteenth and seventeenth centuries, in order to have their arms exemplified, confirmed, or allowed and, sometimes, to be granted *de novo*. It is pleasant to be able to say that the College met their claims with sympathy and understanding. An interesting example of Welsh attitude and English practice is provided by the case of Walter Jones of Worcester, a descendant of the princes of South Wales. As his arms were not recorded, he applied in 1603 to Dethick for exemplification, and enclosed his pedigree as his sufficient warrant. The action of Dethick is instructive. The great family of Talbot (Earls of Shrewsbury) also bore these arms. Dethick knew this, and he knew also that the Talbot coat was recorded in the College. He was also aware of the Welsh theory of armorial gentility. So he consulted the earl, showed him the pedigree, and asked him

whether he had any objection to the arms being exemplified to the applicant. Blood, especially Welsh royal blood, being thicker than water, the earl signified his assent, and thereupon Dethick exemplified the arms to the delighted Walter. The College recognized the special character of Welsh armory by appointing local men as deputy heralds, such as Gruffydd Hiraethog and Lewis Dwnn in the sixteenth century, and David Edwardes, Griffith Hughes and Hugh Thomas in the seventeenth.

There were, of course, some who proved leisurely enough about coming to terms with heraldic law. About 1550, the fourth son of Eyton of Eyton established a cadet house, and differentiated in an interesting and effective manner the arms of his heraldic ancestor, Tudor Trevor. Subsequent invitations to meet heralds for a discussion on the matter fell on deaf ears. Finally his descendant, William Eyton of Hope Owen, over a hundred years later, on Friday, 22 July 1670, between the hours of 9 and 12 in the forenoon, accompanied by Thomas Harris, a grim bailiff of the Hundred of Mold, presented himself at the Black Lion Inn, Mold, where he found waiting for him two deputies of William Dugdale, Norroy. The business was concluded satisfactorily, and the deputies, Robert Chaloner (Lancaster Herald) and Francis Sandford (Rouge Dragon) were pleased to confirm to him those differenced arms. Nicholas Parry of Grays Inn, member of an old Flintshire stock, proved to be a heraldic die-hard of similar calibre. He married Anne, the comely daughter of Thomas Segar, Bluemantle Pursuivant, son of Sir William Segar, a former Garter King of Arms. After a time, Bluemantle began to hint that it might be a sound proposition if the Parry arms were put on a legal footing, particularly in view of his relationship. Despite Bluemantle's prods, nudges and growls, Nicholas airily declined to apply for official recognition, although doubtless the subject of heraldry as an 'in-law' problem must have given him food for thought. It was not until two centuries had passed, in 1889, that those arms, slightly differenced, were exemplified to Nicholas Parry's descendant, who thereby purged the 'offence' of the ancestor who had been prepared to accept a herald's daughter but not his jurisdiction.

It is true that some families neglected to regularize their coat-armour in accordance with law, an omission that has resulted in difficulties in more modern times. This seems a pity since it is the authority of the Earl Marshal alone that can give a definitive quality to armorial bearings nowadays, and it is surely no disparagium for an ancient coat, hallowed by user, to be brought 'within the legal estate'.

Nomenclature and Arms Welsh surnames can often be will-o'the-wisps that lead the unwary into the quagmires of no return. Numbers of the advenae became absorbed so that they abandoned their English or Norman names for the Welsh nomenclature. A tenant farmer who lived among the Breconshire hills in 1701, bearing the pronounced Welsh name of Meredith Evans, was, in fact, a descendant in the male line from the Norman family of Surdwall whose arms he proudly exhibited over the lintel of his farmhouse door. When David Lewis, first Principal of Jesus College, Oxford, the possessor of a typical Welsh name, went to the Heralds' College in 1553, he received an exemplification of the arms of the well-known medieval family of Wallis. The pedigree that he produced to support his claim showed him to be the son of Lewis ap John ap Gwilym ap Robert Wallis, whose knightly ancestors had been settled in Monmouthshire from early times. There are families bearing names like Llewelyn, Rhys, Davies, Griffith and Howel, whose agnatic descents go back to names like Herbert, Clifford, Brown, Cantington, Stanley and Webb. Similarly, native families adopted English and Norman permanent surnames, among them being Almor, Bromfield, Chaloner, Goodrich, Herle, Myddelton, Purcell, Rosendale, Trafford, Wever, White and Young, whose agnatic trees trace to purely Welsh ancestors whose arms they bear. In these cases the coats of arms are a surer guide to family origins. Although it is generally true to say this, a caveat must be entered. Often, and the evidence is sufficient to show that it was not exceptional, families discarded their paternal arms and adopted those belonging to an ancestress. Over a dozen branches of the house of Herbert used, in lieu of their paternal arms, those of Welsh chieftains which they acquired through *ancestresses*. A sound knowledge of the genealogy of both the advenae and native families is essential to the study of Welsh armory.

The following example illustrates the possibilities of identification when heraldry is applied to Welsh nomenclature. On the wall of the Glamorganshire church of Michaelston-super-Ely is a curious tablet inscribed in Welsh and Latin to the memory of one Shon (d. 12 Feb. 1630/31, aged 107), and his son Risiart (d. 21 April 1658, aged 77). There are no surnames or place-names — but there is one vital clue, for the tablet shows a coat of arms, namely Jestyn ap Gwrgant impaling Bassett. Now, Risiart son of Shon would be described in English records as Richard Jones, and with this and the coat of arms in our minds we enter the portals of the Public Record Office to consult the invaluable Golden Grove manuscript. There, in the section of tribal pedigrees, under Jestyn ap Gwrgant, we find the descent of Richard Jones. His wife was Jane Bassett; his father, the centenarian Shon, appears as John ap George who had also married a Bassett; we read that Richard had a son called Doctor Bassett Jones; we find the will of Richard Jones of Michaelston-super-Ely, dated 16 April 1658 and

proved on the 20 August following, in which he refers to 'my wife Jane' and 'my son Bassett Jones'. Bassett Jones is recorded in the *Alumni Oxoniensis*; he became a doctor, and published a book in 1648 called *Lappis Chymicus*. We extend our pilgrimage to the British Museum where we are shown this rare work, and there, on the title page, below the author's name, we find his engraved coat of arms, which proclaims his descent from the princely Jestyn of Glamorgan's royal line. We have reached our journey's end. For a plain Mr Jones, I fear that there can be nothing more than the still shadows of perpetual anonymity. But for an *armigerous* Mr Jones there is hope.

Nature of the evidence Progress towards the production of a definitive work on Welsh armory has been retarded by the popularity of what might be termed copyist armory. Dozens of armorials exist in manuscript form, mainly copies of copies. This constant duplication and reduplication has been responsible for preserving useful material that might otherwise have been lost. But we have advanced far since the days of Simwnt Vychan and Robert Vaughan, and modern scholarship demands something more than the faithful transcripts of dedicated drudges. The first, and vital, task is to sift the historical from the 'paper' armory. Evidence of user, taken from contemporary material, effigies, monuments, brasses, seals, architectural remains, portraits, plate, bardic poetry, books of visitations, records of the College of Arms, etc., will serve to establish the existence of historical armory and so isolate the 'paper' armory. That accomplished, the medieval material must be analysed and edited, since it is this that forms the basis of all armory: then separate analysis will have to be made of the armory of the advenae and of the native-born, and this may require treatment on a genealogical and topographical basis, as well as a purely historical one. The bulk of these evidences must be looked for within Wales, among the muniments of surviving families, in local and national libraries and museums.

There is one extremely valuable source outside Wales which I should mention, namely the visitation pedigrees of the English counties. From 1485 onwards considerable numbers of Welshmen settled in England, and as I have shown above were meticulous about their genealogical and armorial pretensions. These have been recorded during visitations, and in many cases are the earliest references we possess of the armory of such families. The 'Welshman abroad' was touchy about his gentility and took pains to perpetuate its visual representation. Thomas Jones, a descendant of an ancient mid-Wales family, obtained a minor post at Court, and settled at Taplow, Buckinghamshire. When Harvey (Clarenceux) 'visited' that county in 1566, Thomas Jones answered the summons with alacrity, and his pedigree together with his arms and

| **Llywarch ap Brân** | **Gweirydd ap Rhys Goch** | **Collwyn ap Tangno** | **Nefydd Hardd** |

crest were duly recorded. Neither did he overlook his ancestral trappings when he received that summons which is the lot of all sinners, armigerous and otherwise. In his will, proved in 1583, we read that he desired to be buried in Taplow church, where 'a stone is to be laid shewing date of departure out of the world, and that I served King Henry VIII, King Edward VI, Queen Mary, Queen Elizabeth, and hope to serve the King of all kings, my arms to be engraven in copper and annexed to the said gravestone.' His wishes were carried out in respect of his armory, and the curious may still gaze upon his quartered coat proclaiming his descent from four chieftains who had once lorded it over remote commotes to the west of Severn.

It has been my object to show the attitude and approach of Welshmen towards heraldry. The lion of Mr Powell, the wyvern of Mr Pryse, the raven of Mr Rees, the scaling ladders of Mr Lloyd, and the fiery staff of Mr Meyrick, tell us of their roots rather than of their gentility. Welsh armory is an assertion of genealogy. FJ

The Royal Families of Wales

Gruffydd ap Cynan, King of Gwynedd
  Gules three Lions passant Argent
Rhys ap Tewdwr, King of Deheubarth
  Gules a Lion rampant within a Bordure engrailed Or
Bleddyn ap Cynfyn, King of Powys
  Or a Lion rampant Gules
Elystan Glodrudd, King of Rhyng Gwy ag Hafren
(between Severn and Wye)
  Gules a Lion rampant reguardant Or

Iestyn ap Gwrgant, King of Morgannwg
  Gules three Chevronels Argent
Ynyr, King of Gwent
  Per pale Azure and Sable three Fleurs-de-lis Or

The Noble Families

The 'Noble Tribes' are here listed in order.
Hwfa ap Cynddelw of Anglesey
  Gules a Chevron between three Lions rampant Or
Llywarch ap Brân of Anglesey
  Argent a Chevron between three Crows each holding in the beak an Ermine Spot Sable
Gweirydd ap Rhys Goch of Anglesey
  Argent on a Bend Sable three Leopard's faces of the field
Cilmin Troed-ddu of Caernarfonshire
  Quarterly 1 and 4 Argent a double-headed Eagle displayed Sable 2 and 3 Argent three Fiery Brands Sable enflamed proper on an escutcheon of pretence Argent a Man's Leg couped at the thigh Sable
Collwyn ap Tangno of Harlech
  Sable a Chevron between three Fleurs-de-lis Argent
Nefydd Hardd of Caernarfonshire
  Argent a Chevron between three Spearheads Sable the points embrued proper
Maeloc Crwm of Caernarfonshire
  Argent on a Chevron Sable three Angels in veneration Or
Marchudd ap Cynan of Caernarfonshire and Denbighshire
  Gules a Saracen's Head erased at the neck proper wreathed about the temples Argent and Sable

| **Maeloc Crwm** | **Hedd Molwynog** | **Edwin of Tegaingl** | **Ednywain Bendew** |

Hedd Molwynog of Denbighshire
  Sable a Hart passant Argent attired Or
Braint Hir of Denbighshire
  Vert a Cross flory Or
Marchweithian of Denbighshire
  Gules a Lion rampant Argent
Edwin of Tegaingl (Flintshire)
  Argent a Cross flory engrailed Sable between four Crows
  proper beaked and membered Gules
Ednywain Bendew of Flintshire
  Argent A Chevron between three Boar's Heads couped
  Sable
Eunydd of Gwerngwy in Denbighshire
  Azure a Lion rampant Or
Ednywain ap Bradwen of Merioneth
  Gules three Snakes nowed and interlaced Argent
Tudor Trefor of Flintshire (The Tribe of March)
  Per bend sinister Ermine and Ermines a Lion rampant
  Or

Wales Herald of Arms Extraordinary There was a
Wales Herald in the late fourteenth century, but the
office was shortlived. It was re-established in 1963 as
an officer of arms extraordinary. The badge dates from
1967 and depicts a treasured medieval Welsh possession, the *Croes Naid* — a cross heavily gilded and
jewelled and said to contain a fragment of the true
cross: *Issuant from an open Royal Crown of the 13th*
century Gold a representation of a Croes Naid also Gold
jewelled proper.

Wales, Prince of The first to be accorded the title of
Prince of Wales was Llewelyn the Great (d. 1240),
Prince of Gwynedd, who was so recognized by Henry
III of England following the nominal unification of the
Welsh kingdoms in the early thirteenth century.
Llewelyn's grandson, Llewelyn ap Gruffydd, was also
recognized as Prince of Wales by Edward I, but refused
to acknowledge Edward's overlordship and was
defeated in 1282 when the English king overran
Gwynedd. The arms attributed to the native princes of
Wales are now the arms of the Principality: *Quarterly*
Or and Gules four Lions passant guardant counterchanged.

The first English Prince of Wales was Edward, son of
Edward I and Queen Eleanor, who was so created in
1301. Legend has it that the Prince was born at
Caernarfon and presented to 'his people', though this
remains a matter for conjecture. From a political
viewpoint the story is a persuasive one, as is the notion
that the traditional motto of the Prince of Wales, 'Ich
Dien' (I serve), is not German but a corruption of the
old Welsh *Eich Dyn*, meaning 'Your man'. Subsequently,
most (but not all) heirs apparent to the English throne
have become princes of Wales, though not all have
been ceremonially invested. Edward of Caernarfon,
later Edward II, bore the arms of England (then simply
Gules three Lions passant guardant Or) with a white label
of three points. His father, Edward I, had been created
Earl of Chester in 1245 on the failure of the heirs of the
last earl, and since that time (with the exception of a
short period when the earldom was held by Simon de
Montfort) the dignity has been held by the heirs
apparent to the Crown. The arms borne by the Prince
of Wales as Earl of Chester are *Azure three Garbs Or*. The
badge of the Prince of Wales is *y ddraig goch*, the red
dragon, upon a green mount and with a white label of
three points about its neck. The so-called 'Prince of
Wales' Feathers' badge, which comprises three white
ostrich feathers enfiling a gold coronet of alternating
crosses paty and fleurs-de-lis and, on a blue scroll, the
motto 'Ich Dien', is the badge of the heir apparent to
the English throne. It is likely that the ostrich feather
badge was first used by Edward, the Black Prince, who
inherited it through his mother, Philippa of Hainault.
Since that time it has been the personal badge of the
heir apparent and may be used only by him or by his
specific authority.

The titles currently borne by the Prince of Wales are:
Prince of Wales and Earl of Chester, Duke of Cornwall
in the Peerage of England, Duke of Rothesay, Earl of
Carrick and Baron of Renfrew in the Peerage of
Scotland, Lord of the Isles and Great Steward of
Scotland. Prince Charles was created Prince of Wales
in 1958 and invested at Castell Caernarfon in 1969.

The Prince of Wales bears the arms of the sovereign
differenced by a label of three points argent on shield,
crest and supporters. His crown is similar to that of the
Queen but without the arch from front to back. On his
shield of arms he bears the arms of the Principality on
an inescutcheon ensigned by his crown. His achievement may include the shield of arms of the Duchy of
Cornwall *Sable fifteen Bezants*, and this is usually placed
below the principal shield of arms and ensigned by the
crown. In 1968 supporters were assigned to the
Duchy, *On either side a Cornish Chough supporting an*
Ostrich Feather Argent penned Or, and beneath the shield
is the motto 'Houmont' meaning 'high spirited'. This
was once a motto of the Black Prince. In Wales, the
Prince uses a personal banner of the arms of the
Principality, *Over all an Inescutcheon Vert charged with the*

Achievement of HRH the Prince of Wales painted by Gerald Cobb. The shield of arms, contained within a Garter, bears an inescutcheon of the arms of Llewelyn ap Gruffydd (d.1282), one of the last native princes of Wales. Below are the feathers badge of the Heir Apparent to the English throne, the arms of the Duchy of Cornwall and the royal badge of the Red Dragon.

Coronet of the Prince of Wales. In Scotland he uses a banner quarterly of the arms of the Great Steward of Scotland *1 and 4 Or a Fess chequy Azure and Argent*, and the Lord of the Isles *2 and 3 Argent a Lymphad Sable flagged Gules*, and over all, for the Duke of Rothesay, an inescutcheon *Or a Lion rampant Gules armed and langued Azure within a Royal Tressure Gules at honour point a Label of three points Azure.* This banner was matriculated by Lord Lyon in 1974.

Wales, Principality of The arms of the Principality have never been included in the royal arms, just as Wales is not represented in the Union Flag. However, during this century they have been borne on an inescutcheon in the arms of the Prince of Wales. The arms *Quarterly Or and Gules four Lions passant guardant counterchanged* are those of the old princes of Gwynedd, including Llewelyn ap Gruffydd, the grandson of Llewelyn the Great, and his brother David, the last

prince who was executed at Shrewsbury, in 1283. In the fifteenth century the arms were adopted by Owain Glyn Dŵr, who claimed descent from Llewelyn.

Y ddraig goch, the red dragon, is the royal badge for Wales and is properly depicted on a grassy mount or on a shield *per fess Argent and Vert* within a riband ensigned with the Royal Crown and bearing the motto 'Y Ddraig Goch Ddyry Cychwyn' (The red dragon gives the lead). The dragon appears in the arms or as the badge of several old Welsh families, notably the Tudors who, when they ascended the English throne through Henry VII, restored the red dragon to its ancient status as a royal device, together with the white and green liveries worn by Welsh archers who served under the Black Prince in the previous century.

The dragon is believed to have entered British armory through the standards of the Roman cohorts and to have been adopted by the shadowy Celtic warriors of post-Roman Britain, Arthur and Cadwallader among them. Another emblem which tradition ascribes to that period is the leek, which Cadwallader, at the suggestion of St David, is said to have ordered his men to wear in their battle caps. Shakespeare, on the other hand, believed it to have originated at Poitiers (1356): 'the Welshmen did good service in a garden where leeks did grow, wearing leeks in their Monmouth caps; which, your majesty know, to this hour is an honourable badge of service . . . .' (*Henry V*). However, it is more likely that it is the daffodil, also called St Peter's Leek, which is the true device of Wales.

It should here be noted that the so-called 'Prince of Wales' Feathers' device is in fact the badge of the heir apparent to the English throne and, as such, has no place in Welsh armory.

Wall Monument The wall monument was a late sixteenth-century development of the canopied TOMB CHEST set against a wall. Effectively the tomb chest was discarded and a canopied base was secured to the wall. Usually such monuments were positioned clear of the floor (hanging wall monument), but some were supported at ground level (standing wall monument). The style and decoration followed that of the canopied tomb chest, and the figures are often shown kneeling or as demi-effigies. The heraldic treatment of such designs was usually concentrated in the CANOPY during the sixteenth and seventeenth centuries. In the eighteenth century the canopy was abandoned, or at least reduced to an ornamental form rather than an architectural structure. A popular design was to show the figure of the deceased in front of a two-dimensional pyramid with an achievement of arms at the top of the pyramid.

More modest versions of the hanging wall monument are often called wall tablets. A central plaque contained the inscription and was made of stone. If a brass plaque was used then arms were often engraved on it. The plaque was usually set in a frame, which in the seventeenth century was often decorated with shields as well as being surmounted by the arms. A good example is the wall tablet of William Gilberd at Holy Trinity, Colchester in Essex, which has thirteen such shields for members of his family.

During the eighteenth century architectural styles were to change several times, and wall monuments ranged from the baroque through to the Greek Revival types of the early nineteenth century. Throughout these changing styles heraldry was treated very similarly, with a shield or cartouche at the top or in the base of the design. Apart from the use of coloured marbles the heraldry was normally the only colour in the design. The shield was small compared to the rest of the composition, and where the deceased had enjoyed a military career (and particularly if he had been killed in action) or had been a prominent ecclesiastic, it may also be flanked by guns, flags, a crosier or other appropriate devices.

Towards the end of the eighteenth century and in the early part of the nineteenth century there was a tendency to display no shield at all, or perhaps just the family crest, even though the family was armigerous. This tendency to minimize the heraldic display on monuments coincides with an increasing popularity of HATCHMENTS. Was it felt that a hatchment hanging in the church was sufficient display? Or was it the converse; did the fashion for showing minimal heraldry on the monument act as an incentive to provide a hatchment? At Pangbourne, Berkshire, there are hatchments to seven members of the Breedon family, but none of their monumental inscriptions (and each is recorded) includes an armorial display.

The late nineteenth and twentieth centuries have produced small wall tablets with simple carved and painted achievements. JET

Wall Painting Surviving wall paintings in churches are few, although from time to time new items are discovered under existing paint or plaster. Most painting is of allegorical and religious themes, but some surviving evidence shows that heraldry also featured. At Chalgrave church near Toddington, Bedfordshire, there are fifteen shields (some incomplete) painted in red on the walls. These may be connected with Sir Nele Loryng, a founder Knight of the Garter, whose tomb is also in the church. Even more unusual are two thirteenth-century scratchings of coats of arms, at Trumpington, Cambridgeshire.

Four seventeenth-century genealogical trees with shields painted on them have been revealed at Sandon church, Staffordshire. They are for four families who were ancestors of Samson Erdeswick, the county historian and antiquary. Another example of this practice is at Great Hampden, Buckinghamshire.

The coat of arms most frequently found painted on walls is that of the sovereign. These are usually above the chancel arch or at the back of the church. JET

Wands, Staffs and Rods of Office Wands and rod-like objects have, for thousands of years, been symbols of rank, power and significance in civilized countries. The regalia of Egyptian Pharaohs and Roman Emperors may be cited, and these latter rulers frequently gave such emblems to legates who represented them on Imperial business. It is, therefore, only to be expected that in countries where the Holy Roman Empire held sway, actually or symbolically, such devices continued to be used as indicators of rank or authority.

To appreciate the range of medieval offices in which wands and other such items played a part we need look no further than the names based on the Latin word *verga*, meaning 'reed' or 'shaft', given to such objects. Among these were *v. episcopalus* and *v. pastoralis* for wands of ecclesiastical office and other posts of jurisdiction; *v. aurea* for ducal emblems, and *v. tippata* for tipstaff. We may also note that the very word for 'wandbearer' (*vergiferarius*) has survived in our modern term 'verger' for the official who carries a staff before bishops and university chancellors.

Medieval bailiffs carried wands as accepted insignia of duty and these staves were sometimes put to actual use, a person tapped on the body by the 'tipstaff' being deemed to be under arrest. By the early thirteenth century serjeants of the City of London bore staffs of office, and this practice, like many others, spread to other cities and towns in the kingdom.

Throughout the centuries many civil and domestic officers of greater or lesser importance have carried staves or wands of authority. At one level there was in the sixteenth/seventeenth centuries the white rod of the household bailiff, and today the staff of the wardens of parish churches; at another the gold-staff officers attendant at the coronations of British sovereigns. Perhaps the most famous of all is the Gentleman Usher of the Black Rod, an official of the House of Lords whose duties date from the year 1350, and who is appointed by royal letters patent. His title is allusive to his staff of office: a black rod surmounted with a gold lion. He is a personal attendant of the monarch in the House of Lords, and usher of the Order of the Garter, being doorkeeper at meetings of the knights' chapter. A further well-known staff of high office is that employed by the Lord Great Chamberlain of England (also at the Palace of Westminster). This staff was formerly made of ivory, but is now of wood, but embellished.

In the military sphere a short baton or warder has from earliest civilized times been the symbol of the senior commander. This, from being a quite plain and simple object, gradually became richly ornamented. The holder of the premier dukedom and earldom of

England (the Duke of Norfolk) is hereditary Earl Marshal and displays behind his shield of arms *two Gold Batons saltirewise enamelled at the ends Sable* as a mark of his ancient and high office, the insignia of which were granted to the holder in the fifteenth century. A similar practice was adopted in European countries, notably Spain and France in the days of the Empire. In the former case the batons of *capitáns general* were similarly depicted saltirewise behind the shield, in the latter the batons of the Marshals of the Empire were likewise displayed. An outstanding case was that of Michel Ney, Duc d'Elchingen (1808), Prince of Moscow (1812).

William Bruges, who became the first Garter King of Arms in 1415, appears to have been granted a long white rod surmounted with a little banner of the arms of St George, and it seems likely that heralds carried rods (possibly unadorned) before that date. A painting dated 1475 shows Walter Bellengier, King of Arms of Ireland, carrying a long white rod, and a brass dated 1536 shows a later king with such a staff. There is also a painting of 1522 depicting an officer carrying a short silver rod with a rectangular 'tablet' at the top, bearing an enamelled representation of St George's cross impaling the royal arms.

Other documents indicate the use of white or silver rods topped with a martinet in blue and gold. Early in the twentieth century short black batons with gilded ends and each topped with an appropriate badge of office were given to all officers of arms except Garter. In 1953 these batons were replaced by white staves with gilt metal handles, and topped by a blue dove within a gold coronet, the crest of the College of Arms. Garter's sceptre has remained essentially that described above as being in use in 1522, except that in the mid-eighteenth century the silver staff, gilded at the ends only, was changed to a gold one.   SS

Further reading
Wagner, A. *Heralds of England* HMSO, 1967 (reissued 1985).

Ward A minor under the control of a guardian. In medieval times a wardship involved the guardianship of an infant heir, and the management of his estates, until he attained his majority. On occasion his marriage was arranged for him.   JC-K
See also WARDS, COURT OF

Warden A guardian. In earlier centuries, a regent appointed to rule a country or province on behalf of the king. A commander of a fortress on the border of a territory was sometimes called a Warden of the Marches. The term gradually widened to include many officers holding positions of trust: Wardens of the Cinque Ports, the Mint, the Stanneries and the Standards. Governors of prisons and elected lay

officers of the Church of England are also called wardens.   JC-K

Warder The baton of a constable or marshal. Sir Thomas Erpingham of Norfolk, Constable at Agincourt, was said to have thrown his warder into the air to mark the commencement of battle.

Wards, Court of An institution founded by King Henry VIII (and abolished in 1660) for the trial of cases relating to wards. The court was presided over by the Master of the Wards.
See also WARD

Warrant A document issued by the sovereign, the Earl Marshall or other official, or administrative body, authorizing a certain course of action to be taken. Often required in matters relating to heraldry and to the administration of the law.   SA

Warrener An officer (similar to a forester) appointed to watch over the game in a park or preserve.

Watermark A distinguishing mark in sheets of paper, visible when the paper is held to the light. Watermarks are created by wire which has been formed into the desired shape, and which is employed during the manufacturing process.

At first the devices found on both European and English paper were in the form of simple shapes: a ram's head on a Bordeaux paper of 1330, a sword in 1351. Bows and arrows appeared, a pomegranate leaved and stalked, the letter R surmounted by a cross. In the fifteenth century designs include a wyvern, balance-scales, a unicorn and a hunting horn. Some rather fine Italian paper carried watermarks depicting a vase and flowers, and a pine cone.

Armorial watermarks began to appear around the end of the fifteenth century. An escutcheon charged with a vat, or large tub, was employed in Munich around 1490, and a shield with a fess and the letters HS surmounted by a coronet in 1581. The quartered arms of Württemberg were used by a papermaker in that city in 1662.

In the seventeenth and eighteenth centuries, watermarks were used to denote paper quality and sheet sizes, and were often armorial in character, indicative of royal, noble or civic patronage. Eventually they were regulated by means of warrants and letters patent. More recently manufacturers began to employ logotypes, cyphers and trade marks to identify their own brands of paper, though grades of paper used exclusively by sovereigns and departments of governments have been marked with cyphers and badges for centuries. Another indication of patronage was the ream label which was attached to each ream of paper as an indication both of quality and of origin. Armorial ream labels are particularly rare.

Further reading

Hunter, D. *Papermaking Through Eighteen Centuries* New York, 1930.

Wattled *see* **Attributes**

Wavy *see* **Lines, Varied**

Westminster, Doorkeepers of the Palace of The doorkeepers of the Palace of Westminster are responsible for a range of duties, including attending to visitors to both the House of Lords and the House of Commons. Each doorkeeper wears formal tail-coated dress and a gilt chain collar bearing a badge of office, the main feature of which is a representation of the royal arms in gilt, beneath which is suspended a roundel charged with the Cross of St George. From this depends a further device: that for the doorkeepers of the House of Lords is a circlet bearing the motto of the Order of the Garter and the knot of the Garter collar ensigned with a crown, charged over all with a black rod; and that for the doorkeepers of the House of Commons is a flying figure of Mercury.   SS

White Lion Society, The Founded in 1986 by Ronald P. Gadd MBE, with the purpose of presenting to the Chapter of the College of Arms an annual gift of something or some service which Chapter would not normally acquire. Chapter nominates one member of the Council of the Society and three kings of arms sit on the council *ex officio* as vice-presidents. The Earl Marshal is the president. Membership is open to all. The Society is named after the White Lion supporters of the arms of the College and was originally the inspiration of the late Wilfrid Scott-Giles OBE, Fitzalan Pursuivant of Arms. *See* ADDRESSES.   JB-L

White Rod The office of 'Principal Usher of the King of Scotland at Parliaments, General Councils and Feasts' was bestowed upon Sir Alexander Cockburn of Langton and his heirs in 1373 and remained in his family until 1758, when it was sold. The title 'Usher of the White Rod' arose because it was the custom for the officer to carry such a rod when before the king in ceremonial procession. Prior to the abolition of the Scottish Parliament in 1707 White Rod was also responsible for the general custody of parliamentary premises. Subsequent to 1707 White Rod continued to draw a salary and to be granted fees from newly created peers, baronets and knights.

After its disposal by the Cockburn family in 1758, the office of White Rod was eventually bought by Sir Patrick Walker, and following his death in 1837 it passed to the Walker Trust which continues to receive the fees of office to the benefit of the Episcopal Church in Scotland, the salary having been commuted in 1897. The Walker Trustees are permitted to display insignia of office: *Two Batons saltirewise each ensigned with a Unicorn salient supporting a Shield Argent the Unicorn horned Or and gorged with an Antique Crown*, to which is affixed a chain passing between the forelegs and reflexed over the back.

White Rose of Finland, Order of Founded in May 1919, the order is in five classes. It is bestowed as an order of merit to Finnish citizens and distinguished foreigners.

Widow A widow continues to use the arms of her late husband with her own arms either impaled or in pretence, as appropriate. They are borne on a lozenge without helm or crest, but if she is the widow of a peer she may continue to use supporters and the appropriate coronet of rank. If a widow remarries she no longer uses the arms of her first husband.

See also MARSHALLING

Widower A widower ceases to use the arms of his late wife except on memorials and funeral hatchments. If he remarries he may impale the arms of *both* wives in the sinister half of his shield, either per fess (with the first wife's arms in chief and the second wife in base) or per pale with the first wife's arms to the dexter. Such a practice is rarely met with today and has always been confined to memorials, hatchments and memorial glass.

See also MARSHALLING

Wife *see* **Women Bearing Arms**

Window Glass *see* **Glass**

Window Marks Windows both in churches and domestic buildings are often 'autographed' by the painter, designer or workshop. These window marks are often of an armorial nature, cyphers and rebuses being particularly popular. Others are in the style of masons' marks or are themselves small panels within the over-all design.   JET

Windsor Beasts *see* **Beasts**

Windsor Herald of Arms in Ordinary It has been suggested that the office was instituted specifically for the Order of the Garter (1348), or that it predates the Order and was in use as early as 1338. However, it is more likely that it dates from 1364 when a pursuivant of Edward III, on bringing the king news of victory at Auray, was rewarded by promotion to the rank of herald with the title Windsor. Thereafter there is little mention of the office before 1418/19, when Windsor Herald was sent to the Duke of Brittany. Since that

time the office has been maintained. The badge of office is the sunburst badge of Edward III (Edward of Windsor) royally crowned.

Winged *see* **Attributes**

Wodehouse A wild man of the woods, covered in green hair except where the flesh is visible in the face, elbows, knees, hands and feet.

Women Bearing Arms Women may bear their father's arms on a lozenge with a motto but without helmet or crest. The contortions required of ordinaries, charges and (especially) beasts in order that they may fit artistically into the grotesque lozenge make it a very

A superbly carved wodehouse or wild man at the feet of the fifteenth-century effigy of Sir Robert Whittingham at Aldbury, Hertfordshire.

unsatisfactory substitute for the male shield. Quarterings and impaled arms look quite ridiculous and the armorist should be alert to the possibility of deliberate mis-marshalling of quarters for artistic purposes. Considerable artistic licence is needed to make the best of a bad job, and lozenges may come in a variety of shapes and sizes. When she marries, a woman simply impales her arms with those of her husband or, if she is an heraldic heiress, places them on a small shield (an escutcheon of pretence) at the centre of his. This practice is both clumsy and frequently confusing. A woman may display insignia and supporters if she is entitled to them, but not English marks of cadency. These days many more women are armigerous in their own right, and as such they may transmit their arms as a quartering to descendants, impaled with their husband's arms and both within an appropriate bordure. Significant advances in sexual equality of the past decades have naturally resulted in demands for a corresponding evaluation of women's status in matters armorial. Perhaps the days of the lozenge are numbered?
Further reading
Franklin C. *The Bearing of Coat Armour by Ladies* 1923.

Wood Carving Armorial devices carved in wood may be found embellishing the fabric and furnishings of many churches and domestic buildings. However,

Carved panelling at Haddon Hall, Derbyshire depicted the arms of Henry VII or, possibly, Henry VIII. When Edmund Tudor (d.1456), half-brother to Henry VI, was created Earl of Richmond, the king granted him the Lancastrian greyhound badge as a supporter. The red dragon was adopted as a badge by Owen Tudor (d.1461) who claimed descent from Cadwalader.

care should be exercised on occasions when the purely decorative or figurative may appear to possess armorial characteristics.

Wooden CEILINGS, church PULPITS, SCREENS, STAIR-CASES and the surrounds of FIREPLACES are all potential sources of heraldry, but it is often the mundane and the vernacular which are most likely to reveal unexpected heraldic treasures.

Misericords are a constant source of delight, and for the armorist there is always the possibility that the carvings may be armorial. For example, those at Ludlow parish church, Shropshire (dating from the period 1420-51), include no fewer than ten heraldic badges.

Miniature blind arcading lends itself to the insertion of shields of arms above the intersections of arches, particularly in otherwise unadorned wooden panels. The sides and front of pews and stalls provide convenient surfaces for wood carving, and the armorial shield or device is a popular motif. Such decoration may be restricted to a small number of pews at the front of the nave. Personal arms are usually those of the local nobility and gentry, the lord of the manor or patron who may have paid for the con-struction of a private pew or refurbished the church in some way. Many shields, particularly more recent ones, bear Christian symbols or the attributed arms of saints. Others bear the arms of the diocese in which a church is located. There are fine examples of pews embellished with armorial shields at North Cadbury, Somerset, and Weare Gifford, Devon (Fortescue family 1510). At Taunton, Somerset, there is an

Caption: Carved panelling at Haddon Hall, Derbyshire depicted the arms of Henry VII or, possibly, Henry VIII. When Edmund Tudor (d.1456), half-brother to Henry VI, was created Earl of Richmond, the king granted him the Lancastrian greyhound badge as a supporter. The red dragon was adopted as a badge by Owen Tudor (d.1461) who claimed descent from Cadwalader.

interesting collection of Gothic carvings dated 1847, and at Alwington, Devon, arms are carved on the fronts of several of the pews.

Wooden panelling is to be found in many older houses and in those of the Gothic Revival period. Arms, together with badges and crests, carved into the woodwork of panelling are common features of the Tudor period, and during the Gothic Revival small shields were often affixed to the frieze at the top of wall panelling.

Further reading

Bond, F. *Wood Carving in English Churches* Oxford, 1910 (4 vols.).

Howard, F.E. and F.H. Crossley *English Church Wood-work* London, 1927.

Smith, J.C.D. *A Guide to Church Wood Carving* Newton Abbot, 1974.

Wool Pack In armory, a charge with the appearance of a cushion tied with cords at the corners.

Wreath *or* **Torse** (i) A band of twisted strands of material worn about the helmet as decoration, or to conceal the base of the crest where it was laced or bolted to the tournament helm. In a coat of arms the wreath is conventionally depicted as having six visible twists. Normally only two or three different coloured strands are used (there are examples of four) and these are always depicted in sequence beginning (to the dexter) with that of the principal metal (i.e. gold or silver).

The term torse is preferable, wreath being also an armorial charge, but current terminology favours the latter and for this reason alone it is used throughout this book.

It is suggested that the origin of the wreath was from the practice of wearing a lady's favour in the form of a scarf (*contoise*) or sleeve upon the helmet at tournaments. This may certainly have been a practice, but the origin of the wreath is more likely to be found in the ceremonial torse of the Dark Age rulers of Western Europe and the colourful diadem of the Saracen (*see* CROWN). There can be little doubt that the crusading knight was attracted to the notion of wearing such an embellishment to restrain the mantling or lambrequin of his helm, and continued to do so on his return from the Holy Land, thereby advertising his participation in the Crusade. However, it is not without significance that in armory the mantling was universally adopted throughout Europe, but not so the wreath. It could be, therefore, that the wreath was simply the mantling, rolled up to form a convenient fillet and tied at the back of the helmet. If this were so it would explain the parallel development of the BANDEROLLE, with which the wreath is often confused. It would also call into question the not uncommon practice (which has existed from the mid-fourteenth century when the conventional wreath first entered British armory) of depicting the wreath in one set of tinctures and the mantling in another.

Many examples exist of European helms surmounted by crest and mantling (the two often artistically combined) but with no wreath or circlet of any kind. Conversely, the wreath (or crest coronet) is a characteristic of British armory and is considered to be an integral part of the crest. All grants of arms and crest now specify a wreath and/or crest coronet.

As has already been noted, from the mid-fourteenth century to the Tudor period the tinctures of wreaths *appear* to be arbitrary, but there are many examples of such wreaths, composed of tinctures which have no apparent relationship with either arms or crest, being adopted by succeeding generations of armigerous families. It may be that they represented the livery colours of the armiger or of a magnate by whom he was retained.

From the end of the sixteenth century to the mid-twentieth century it was usual to blazon the crest *upon a Wreath of the Colours*, that is the principal metal and colour of the shield of arms and those first mentioned in the blazon. This remains so in Scotland, where the term *on a Wreath of the Liveries* has the same meaning, and where wreaths of more than two tinctures or of tinctures other than those of the arms are rare. The English kings of arms now require the tinctures of the wreath to be specified in the patent of arms, and wreaths of three tinctures are currently popular, often reflecting the composition of the arms. However, this is not always so and many wreaths are granted without any apparent rationale for the selection of tinctures. Occasionally, genuine livery colours are used, but aesthetically the selection of tinctures which are not related to other elements of the arms can be most disconcerting. An altogether more satisfactory practice would be for the wreath and mantling to be considered as a single element and treated as such.

The blazon *on a Wreath* is inaccurate: early heralds used such expressions as 'set within a Wreath' and it seems sensible that 'within a Wreath' or 'out of a Wreath' should now be used. Even more misleading are the phrases 'on a Wreath of the Colours' (which colours?) and 'on a Wreath of the Liveries'. Such a blazon can only be acceptable when the tinctures used are indeed the livery colours (as is usually the case in Scotland) but even then they need to be specified.

The wreath should always be depicted as fitting securely to the helm. The notorious 'barber's pole' wreaths of the eighteenth and nineteenth centuries which floated above the helm resulted from a misunderstanding of the function of the wreath by armigers and engravers alike, and from the practice of detaching crests from their helms and using them in lieu of badges (which were then not available to newly armigerous families), the wreath performing the function of a platform upon which the crest was depicted (e.g. the black horse device of Lloyd's Bank). Crests and wreaths are still used in this way, even by those who possess armorial badges. Fortunately, the current enthusiasm for the medieval armorial style has restored the wreath to its former significance, and an inaccurate representation is a certain sign of bogus heraldry or amateur artistry.

(ii) An armorial charge consisting of a ring of twisted strands of material, the colours of which are specified. Occasionally used to describe a circlet of leaves or stylized foliage which has an opening in the perimeter, unlike the chaplet (also garland), which does not.

(iii) As a verb, the term wreath is used to describe an armorial charge which is adorned with a wreath of material or foliage.

Wreathed *see* **Attributes**

Wrythe Heraldic Trust, The A charitable trust founded in 1978 by John Brooke-Little, Norroy and Ulster King of Arms (then Richmond Herald), Rodney Dennys, Arundel (then Somerset) Herald, and Roland Rowe. The principal object of the trust is to encourage the development of heraldic art and design in all its forms. It has made donations to exhibitions of heraldic art and assisted students in this discipline. Enquiries should be made c/o the Heraldry Society (*see* ADDRESSES). JB-L

Württemberg, Royal Arms of Quarterly 1 *Or three Lions passant in pale Sable the dexter paws Gules* (Swabia) 2 *Paly bendy sinister Sable and Or* (Teck) 3 *Azure the Imperial Banner bendwise proper* (Standard Bearer of the Holy Roman Empire) 4 *Gules two Barbels hauriant addorsed Or* (Montebeliard) over all an escutcheon of pretence *Or three Stag's attires fesswise in pale points to the sinister Sable* (Württemberg). The shield ensigned with the Royal Crown of Württemberg.

Wyvern and Dragon The wyvern is a large scaly monster with wings and two legs. The dragon is essentially a four-legged development of the wyvern, unknown as such before the late Middle Ages.

The wyvern probably entered British armory as the standard of the Roman cohort and remained in the symbolism of the post-Roman era and in the 'burning dragon' of Cadwallader from which the red dragon of Wales is derived. It is also associated with the ancient kingdom of Wessex and appears in the Bayeux Tapestry as the personal device of King Harold. In more recent times, a number of dragons and wyverns have been granted to Welsh and English west-country civil authorities, including *a double-headed wyvern displayed* as a crest in the arms of Sherborne, Dorset in 1986.

'The voice of the dragon is thunder, the trembling of earthquakes his footfall, forest and heath fires are the heat of his breath. He is enormous, and has a scaly body, leathery wings and a forked tongue and tail.' The dragon is a mythical creature of great antiquity and is known equally well in the East as in the West. But in China and Japan, although it is similar in form, it is less forbidding and has very different characteristics. The Eastern dragon is benevolent and full of strength and goodness. It is associated with rain and water; in the evening it devours the sun and releases it in the morning. It takes treasure into its safe keeping from those who desire it from avarice. The Western dragon, however, is a malevolent and destructive power, and hoards gold and treasure for its own selfish purposes. There is an association with water in a legend of a water dragon in the River Seine, which ravaged Rouen in the seventh century. It was called Gargouille and has given its name in corrupted form to water spouts on churches.

The dragon was a symbol of sovereignty among the Celts. *Dragon* was the name for a chief and he who slew a chief slew a dragon, so the title became confused with the fabulous monster. This is a link with Arthurian legend and Arthur's father Uther Pendragon, also with the Welsh dragon of armory.

The dragon, in spite of its more unfortunate characteristics, symbolizes invincibility and the power to inspire terror in the foe, which makes it a suitable armorial emblem. Dragons are the supporters in the arms of the City of London, as a dragon was said to have lived in the River Thames as guardian of the City.

The wyvern still has a place of its own in modern armory. In addition to the attributes of the dragon it became the symbol of pestilence and plagues, and appears in the arms of the London Apothecaries' Society, beneath the feet of Apollo, the god of medicine. It typifies viciousness and envy, but it is used in armory as a symbol for overthrowing the tyranny of a demonic enemy. MY

Wyvern and dragon

Y

Yale The first recorded description of the yale was by Pliny, and it is thought that he had in mind the antelope Gnu. A number of natural animals are quoted as being the possible origin of the yale, but the most important feature of the mythical beast is that it can swivel its horns in any direction. In a twelfth century bestiary it is described as being the size of a horse and having the tusks of a boar. It had extremely long horns which were not fixed but could be moved according to necessity in fights. If the first one got broken, the second could still be brought into use. But in a very fierce battle, both horns could be used at once to meet aggression from any direction.

The yale of armory has retained the swivelling horns and the tusks of a boar, but has become more like an antelope than a horse. It was used as a supporter by John, Duke of Bedford, third son of Henry IV and so became one of the Royal Beasts of England. It was represented as a dainty creature with very long, thin horns. Later, members of the Beaufort family adopted it as supporters, although in appearance it became a much heavier, goat-like animal, and its horns, instead of being straight, were curved and serrated. The two yale supporters of Margaret Beaufort, mother of Henry VII, are well known, as her arms are carved above the gateways of Christ's College and St John's College, Cambridge.   MY

Yeoman Originally a 'young man', an attendant in a royal or noble household; in late medieval times a yeoman was an attendant on an official. The word came to be used in minor titles: yeomen of the robes, cellar, revels, wardrobe, and so on, and, most notably, for the members of the sovereign's bodyguard — the Yeomen of the Guard. The word was also used to describe a freeholder below the rank of gentleman. In the navies of Britain and the USA, 'yeoman' is the term applied to minor officers in charge of stores.   JC-K

Yeomen of the Guard A royal bodyguard founded by Henry VII in 1485 from his 'private guard of faithful fellowes' of the rank just below esquire. It is one of three such institutions, the others being the GENTLEMEN AT ARMS and the ROYAL COMPANY OF ARCHERS. Until the creation of a Standing Army by Charles II in 1661 the Yeomen and the Gentlemen were England's only permanent military forces. It was their duty to follow the king in war and to guard his person and throne in time of peace.

Today members of the Yeomen of the Guard are retired and distinguished members of the armed forces who serve for token payments only. The officers are a Captain (who is always a peer, and Government Deputy Chief Whip in the House of Lords), a Lieutenant, a Clerk of the Cheque plus three others. In all the force totals 87. Its duties are now wholly ceremonial and are performed at occasions such as coronations, Garter installations, State Openings of Parliament, and investitures.

The uniform of the Yeomen of the Guard (who are not the same as the YEOMEN WARDERS) has not changed, except for certain embroidered emblems, since Tudor times. It consists of a royal-red tunic with purple facings and stripes, and ornaments of gold lace. The emblems on the front and back of the tunic are the Tudor Crown with, below it, the Tudor Rose. The Stuarts added the motto 'Dieu Et Mon Droit'. Queen Anne added the Thistle in 1709, the Shamrock being added in 1801. A gold embroidered cross belt is worn over the left shoulder. Red kneebreeches and red stockings are worn, together with a brimmed flat hat ornamented with red, white and blue rosettes. The black shoes are similarly adorned. The ruff was added by Queen Elizabeth, but in Stuart times this was replaced by fancy lace, and a plumed hat was also adopted. Queen Anne discarded both, the ruff being again introduced in Georgian times. In 1830 William IV gave the officers a field dress similar to that of officers in the Peninsular War — a swallow-tail coat and a plumed cocked hat.

The weapons of the yeomen are gilded-steel halberds, each with a tassel of red and gold, and an ornamental sword.

It is the Yeomen of the Guard who are nicknamed 'Beefeaters' from a remark by Cosimo, Grand Duke of Tuscany, who, on seeing their magnificent stature in 1669, said, 'They are great eaters of beef, of which a very large ration is given them daily at the court, and they might be called "Beefeaters".'   JC-K

Yeomen Warders The name given to the men who have custody of the Tower of London. The present body dates from 1485, immediately after the victory of Henry VII over Richard III at Bosworth, although there had been full-time warders long before that date.

Warders today are former senior NCOs from the armed forces who have been awarded both the Long Service and the Good Conduct medals. The senior

Yeomen Warders

officer is the Chief Yeoman Warder, who on prescribed occasions carries the Silver Mace — a staff surmounted by a model of the White Tower — and the next most senior is the Yeoman Gaoler who has custody of the ceremonial Axe.

The uniform of the Warders dates from Tudor times. In all but one respect it is identical to that of the Yeomen of the Guard, the single difference being that the Yeomen Warders do not wear the over-the-shoulder cross belt.   JC-K

York Herald of Arms in Ordinary The first York Herald is believed to have been an officer to Edmund, Duke of York, *c.* 1385, but the first wholly reliable reference to such a herald is in February 1483/4, when he was granted certain fees by Richard III. The badge of office is the white rose of York en soleil ensigned by the Royal Crown.

Ypotryll A rare beast, and fortunately so for it has a boar's face with tusks, a camel's body with two hairy humps, and the legs, hooves and mane of an ox.

Yugoslavia, Armorial Practice The Kingdom of the Serbs, Croats and Slovenes was proclaimed in December 1918 after the union of Serbia, Montenegro and the southern Slav territories of Austria-Hungary. In 1929 it changed its name to the Kingdom of Yugoslavia and in 1945 was translated into a socialist federal republic, Federativna Narodna Republika Jugoslavija. Armorial practice in the pre-1945 kingdom and its constituent territories has not been well documented, but it is apparent from surviving sixteenth and seventeenth-century manuscripts that it was similar to Austria and Hungary, immediately to the north.

Yugoslavia, Royal Arms of *Gules an Eagle displayed Argent beaked and membered Or charged with an escutcheon tierced in pairle reversed 1 Gules a Cross Argent between four Furisons [steels] addorsed Or* (Serbia) *2 Chequy Gules and Argent* (Croatia) *3 Azure a Crescent Argent surmounted by three Stars one and two Or* (Slovenia).

York badge

Z

Zodiac The astronomical signs of the zodiac may be found as armorial charges.

Zule A stylized column with a shortened shaft and bifurcated capital and base, from Dutch *zuil* and Flemish *zoul*. Frequently confused with a chess rook.

Zule

382

Bohun

Mowbray

And yet time hath its revolution: there must be a period and an end to all temporal things. Finis rerum, an end of names and dignities, and whatsoever is terrene. Where is Bohun, where's Mowbray, where's Mortimer? Nay, which is more and most of all, where is Plantagenet? They are all entombed in the urns and sepulchres of mortality.

Sir Ranulph Crew
1·6·2·5

Mortimer

Plantagenet

Picture Credits

The editor and publishers would like to thank all those who have helped with illustrations in this book. Those listed by page numbers below are drawn, reproduced or loaned by courtesy of the individuals and organizations named. Abbreviations: t: top, b: bottom, l: left, r: right.

Photo John Adnams 129l, 239, 282; the Vicar and Wardens, Aldermaston Church, photo John Titterton 136tr; John Allen, painting by John Bainbridge 127rb; Alphabet & Image 23, 68b courtesy The Dorset Natural History & Archaeological Society, Dorset County Museum, Dorchester, 136tl by kind permission of Lady Cooke, 152, 153 courtesy The Dorset Natural History & Archaeological Society, Dorset County Museum, Dorchester, 154b, 169, 178 courtesy The Dorset Natural History & Archaeological Society, Dorset County Museum, Dorchester, 203, 225, 232, 233 courtesy The Swan Gallery, Sherborne, 247, 329b, 351; illustration supplied courtesy the Bank of New Zealand 295; Bibliotheque de l'Arsenal, Paris 48, 101; Blue Circle Industries, Aldermaston Court, photo John Titterton 136bl; Bodleian Library, Oxford (MS Ashmole 604.1 item) 284, (MS Laud.Misc. 733,f.1) 349; British Caledonian 14r; John Campbell-Kease 250; the Trustees of the British Museum 98; Dean and Chapter of the Cathedral Church of the Advent, Birmingham, Alabama 126; D.H.B. Chesshyre, Chester Herald, and Peter Spurrier, Portcullis Pursuivant 337; Christie's 102; the Chapter of the College of Arms (MS Shakespeare grant No. 1) 313; © Crown Copyright, reproduced with the permission of the Controller of Her Majesty's Stationery Office 57, © Crown Copyright 306, 307; by kind permission of the Master of the Worshipful Company of Engineers 249; John Ferguson 9, 50, 51, 80, 111, 117, 119, 121, 122, 123, 143, 145, 159, 179, 184, 211r, 212l, 216, 217, 259, 268, 274l, 311, 315, 331; Derek Forss 52; John Hamilton Gaylor 237; the Worshipful Company of Goldsmiths 319; Peter Greenhill 329t; Anthony Griffiths 177; the Master and Wardens of the Gunmakers' Company of London 251b; Robert Harrison 327; from *The Colour of Heraldry* (the Heraldry Society 1958) 21; by gracious permission of Her Majesty Queen Elizabeth II 142; Michael Holford 54; L.J. Keen and the Dorset Natural History and Archaeological Society 190; photo Jim Kershaw 49; The Mac Carthy Mor 255bl; John Mennell 146, 204; The National Trust 341; Peter B. Oughtred 301; The Police Federation 273; © The Post Office 326; Kenneth S. Pundyke 251t; The Royal Society 229r; the Dean and Chapter of Salisbury Cathedral 25; Scottish Tourist Board 328; Dr Conrad Swan CVO 52b; Swiss National Museum 316l; Tabard Publications Ltd 371, 373; The Tallow Chandlers Company 183; Brian Tilzey 88; Vienna Kunsthistorisches Museum 323; *Geschichte der Pareussischen Münzen und Siegel* by F.A. Vosberg (1842) 339, 340; West Dorset District Council 63r; G. Wheeler 3, 41, 42, 63bl, 70, 82, 100, 133, 156 (photo W. Menderson), 161, 167, 168, 173l, 195, 229tl, 245, 278bl, 286r, 309, 325, 335 by kind permission the Chapter of the College of Arms, 345, 377b; J.L. Wilson 65, 66; Anthony Wood 1, 77, 115, 136br, 193, 252, 302, 304, 336 (photo Edward Piper); Margaret Wood 304 (calligraphy); John Wright Photography Ltd, Warwick 243.

All other line drawings are by Andrew Jamieson.